Service Management in
Health & Wellness
Services

Jay Kandampully, Ph.D.

Kendall Hunt
publishing company

CONTENTS

1 SERVICE MANAGEMENT A NEW PARADIGM IN HEALTH AND WELLNESS SERVICES   1

    Jay Kandampully, The Ohio State University, Columbus, Ohio, United States

2 QUALITY AND VALUE OF HEALTH SERVICES   7

    Joris van de Klundert; Institute of Health Policy & Management, Erasmus University Rotterdam, The Netherlands

3 SERVICE CULTURE AS A MEANS FOR CREATING A COMPETITIVE ADVANTAGE: THE CASE OF PUBLIC HOSPITALS   23

    Victoria Bellou; University of Thessaly, Greece

    Aristea Bellou MD, Papageorgiou Hospital, Thessaloniki, Greece

4 IMPROVING PATIENT SATISFACTION: A SERVICE MANAGEMENT APPROACH   37

    Ravi Behara; College of Business, Florida Atlantic University, Boca Raton, Florida, United States

    Fabio Potenti; Cleveland Clinic Florida, Weston, Florida & Florida Atlantic University, Boca Raton, Florida, United States

5 MANAGING CUSTOMER RELATIONSHIP QUALITY IN HOSPITALS   57

    Miguel A. Moliner; Universitat Jaume I of Castellón, Castellón, Spain

    Miguel A. López; Universitat Jaume I of Castellón, Castellón, Spain

6 THE EFFECT OF SERVICESCAPES ON CONSUMER'S WELLNESS EXPERIENCE   77

    Hye Yoon Choi, Department of Consumer Sciences, The Ohio State University, Columbus, Ohio, United States

    Kathryn Stafford, Department of Consumer Sciences, The Ohio State University, Columbus, Ohio, United States

7 TOWARD IMPROVING PERFORMANCE MANAGEMENT IN A HEALTHCARE OPERATIONAL ENVIRONMENT: A CUSTOMER-ORIENTATION APPROACH 99

> Carlos F. Gomes, School of Economics, University of Coimbra, Coimbra, Portugal
>
> Mahmoud M. Yasin, Department of Management & Marketing, East Tennessee State University, Johnson City, United States
>
> Phillip E. Miller, Department of Management & Marketing, East Tennessee State University, Johnson City, United States

8 AN OPEN-SYSTEMS PERSPECTIVE OF MENTAL HEALTH SERVICES 121

> Mark Anderson; Faculty of Business, Government & Law, University of Canberra, Australia
>
> Byron Keating; Faculty of Business, Government & Law, University of Canberra, Australia
>
> Anton Kriz; Newcastle Business School, University of Newcastle, Callaghan, Australia

9 LEAN HOSPITALS: FIVE TOOLS THAT POSITION HEALTHCARE ORGANIZATIONS FOR SUCCESS 137

> Kenneth K. Boyer; Fisher College, The Ohio State University, Columbus, Ohio, United States
>
> Luv Sharma; Fisher College, The Ohio State University, Columbus, Ohio, United States

10 THE EMERGING HEALTHCARE SERVICE PLATFORM 153

> Ravi S. Behara; College of Business, Florida Atlantic University, Boca Raton, Florida, United States
>
> C. Derrick Huang; College of Business, Florida Atlantic University, Boca Raton, Florida, United States
>
> Jahyun Goo; College of Business, Florida Atlantic University, Boca Raton, Florida, United States

11 FROM HEALTHCARE TO e-HEALTHCARE: ARE PEOPLE READY? 171

> Tor W. Andreassen; BI Norwegian Business School, Oslo, Norway.
>
> Even J. Lanseng; BI Norwegian Business School, Oslo, Norway.

12 Service Focus through Technology for Health Promotion: A Review of Multidimensional Market   201

Carolin Durst, Institute of Information Systems,
University Erlangen-Nuremberg, Nuremberg, Germany

Andreas Hamper, Institute of Information Systems,
University Erlangen-Nuremberg, Nuremberg, Germany

Tino Mueller, Institute of Information Systems,
University Erlangen-Nuremberg, Nuremberg, Germany

13 The Role of E-Health Information in Customer Empowerment   233

Johanna Gummerus, Department of Marketing, HANKEN School of Economics,
Helsinki, Finland

Veronica Liljander; Department of Marketing, HANKEN School of Economics,
Helsinki, Finland

Catharina von Koskull; Department of Marketing, HANKEN School of
Economics, Helsinki, Finland

14 Telemedicine, Remote Monitoring, in-home Health and Medical Technology Services for Elderly Patients   257

Catherine Berry, Consumer Sciences, The Ohio State University,
Columbus, Ohio, United States

15 Do Seniors Accept Technology-Based Service Innovations? A Qualitative Approach   275

Jens Hogreve, Catholic University of Eichstaett-Ingolstadt, Ingolstadt, Germany

Nicola Bilstein, Catholic University of Eichstaett-Ingolstadt,
Ingolstadt, Germany

16 Creating New Paradigms of Health Service for Older People: A Management Opportunity   289

Liz Gill, Sydney Medical School, The University of Sydney, Sydney, Australia

17 COLLABORATIVE CARE FOR PATIENTS WITH PARKINSON'S DISEASE: COMBINING AN OFFLINE PROFESSIONAL NETWORK WITH AN ONLINE HEALTH COMMUNITY FOR THE SUSTAINABLE PROVISION OF CARE   311

A.C.R. van Riel, Institute for Management Research, Radboud University Nijmegen, Nijmegen, The Netherlands

L.M. Visser, Institute for Management Research, Radboud University Nijmegen, Nijmegen, The Netherlands.

M. van der Eijk, Radboud University Nijmegen Medical Centre, Nijmegen, The Netherlands.

M.J. Faber, Radboud University Nijmegen Medical Centre, Nijmegen, The Netherlands.

M. Munneke, Radboud University Nijmegen Medical Centre, Nijmegen, The Netherlands.

B.R. Bloem, Radboud University Nijmegen Medical Centre, Nijmegen, The Netherlands.

18 PRACTICAL EXAMPLES OF SERVICE DEVELOPMENT AND INNOVATIONS IN THE NORDIC WELLBEING INDUSTRY   325

Anja Tuohino, Centre for Tourism Studies, University of Eastern Finland, Savonlinna, Finland

Henna Konu, Centre for Tourism Studies, University of Eastern Finland, Savonlinna, Finland

Anne-Mette Hjalager, Danish Centre for Rural Research, University of Southern Denmark, Esbjerg, Denmark

Edward Huijbens, Icelandic Tourism Research Centre, University of Akureyri, Akureyri, Iceland

19 CROSS-CULTURAL ISSUES IN HEALTH AND WELLNESS SERVICES IN ESTONIA   347

Heli Tooman, University of Tartu, Pärnu College, Pärnu, Estonia.

Kai Tomasberg, University of Tartu, Pärnu College, Pärnu, Estonia.

Melanie Smith, Budapest Business School, Budapest, Hungary

20 AYURVEDA   363

Anupama Kothari; Robert H. Smith School of Business, University of Maryland, College Park, United States

21 TRADITIONAL CHINESE MEDICINE 369

Tingting (Christina) Zhang, Hospitality Institute, Beijing International Studies University, Beijing, China

22 PARADIGM SHIFTERS IN HEALTH AND WELLNESS SERVICES (CASES) 381

1 ARAVIND EYE CARE SYSTEM (INDIA) 381

Anupama Kothari; Robert H. Smith School of Business, University of Maryland, College Park, United States

2 APOLLO HOSPITALS (INDIA) 385

Anupama Kothari, Robert H. Smith School of Business, University of Maryland, College Park, United States

3 THE SCHWARZ ***** ALPINE SPA & RESORT (AUSTRIA) 388

Anita Zehrer, MCI, University of Applied Sciences, Innsbruck, Austria

Hubert Siller, MCI, University of Applied Sciences, Innsbruck, Austria

4 GRAND PARK HOTEL BAD HOFGASTEIN (AUSTRIA) 391

Maria Wiesinger, Hospitality Schools Salzburg, Bad Hofgastein, Austria

Silvia Listberger, Hospitality Schools Salzburg, Bad Hofgastein, Austria

Claudia Wachter, Grand Park Hotel, Bad Hofgastein, Austria

5 SAMADHI SPA & WELLNESS RETREAT (AUSTRALIA) 394

Haywantee Ramkissoon, Faculty of Business & Economics, Monash University, Australia

6 CONSTANCE LE PRINCE MAURICE HOTEL AND SPA (MAURITIUS) 398

Roubina T. D. Juwaheer, Faculty of Law & Management, University of Mauritius, Reduit, Mauritius

7 CARDINAL HEALTH (UNITED STATES) 402

Jichul Jang, Consumer Sciences, The Ohio State University, Columbus, Ohio, United States

8   CLEVELAND CLINIC EXPERIENCE (UNITED STATES)   406

Soyeon Kim; Consumer Sciences, The Ohio State University, Columbus, Ohio, United States

9   CLIFTON SPRINGS HOSPITAL AND CLINIC (UNITED STATES)   410

Hye Yoon (Rebecca) Choi, Department of Consumer Sciences, The Ohio State University, Columbus, Ohio, United States

10   WEXNER MEDICAL CENTER, OSU (UNITED STATES)   412

Anupama Sukhu; Consumer Sciences, The Ohio State University, Columbus, Ohio, United States

Hyejin Park; Consumer Sciences, The Ohio State University, Columbus, Ohio, United States

Service Management:
A New Paradigm in Health
and Wellness Services

Jay Kandampully

LEARNING OBJECTIVES

Upon completing this chapter, you should be able to do the following:

1. Understand the importance of service in the context of the changing focus of health service.

2. Explicate the interrelationships of health and wellness services.

3. Define the consumption experiences of health service customers.

4. Investigate the growing customer focus and service orientation in health services.

KEYWORDS

Health service, wellness generation, cycle of health, customer focus, customer driven, service alchemy, service paradigm, service orientation, service experience, service management, service continuum, service blueprint, value co-creation, stages of consumption, pre-consumption, consumption, post-consumption, technical attribute, functional attribute, baby boomers, Mayo Clinic

Today more than ever, people want to look and feel better, to slow the effects of aging, to manage stress, and to prevent age-related illnesses. This growing social phenomenon takes the name *wellness generation*. Including wellness goals within health service provision marks a notable difference from traditional concepts of health services, which focused on the service provider and treatment, with limited input from patients. To incorporate this new dimension of wellness, health care practitioners must change their approach and way of thinking. Modern consumers of health services increasingly assume decision-making roles and thus control over the service. This paradigm shift in the composition of health services, accompanied by changes in the needs and expectations of health care consumers, is transforming health care into a largely consumer-driven service sector. In such an environment, service management approaches represent effective tools for managing health services, providing customers with the superior service and value they demand.

WELLNESS GENERATION

As affluent consumers in developed nations age (i.e., the Baby Boomers), they seek ways to maintain their youth and vitality. These multidimensional approaches to regain youth and vitality incorporate all aspects of the person: wellness of mind, body, and spirit, exemplified by quality of life and a sense of well-being. Wellness entails proactive, natural steps to extend the years people can maintain their strength and vitality. Unlike traditional health services, which tend to be reactive in nature and undertaken only after the onset of illness, wellness is proactive and voluntary, practiced to enrich good health or prevent poor health. Traditional health services were directed by the knowledge and beliefs of the physician; wellness is a customer-driven service requirement. Therefore, as the consumer population orients itself toward wellness, it will demand higher levels of service and satisfaction. From a service management perspective, health care organizations need to commit to becoming customer focused and service oriented.

Interest in wellness and its growing significance in the health care sector further require that health care managers expand both the range of care and services they offer and the paradigm through which they provide this care. What was primarily a focus on the management of illness and treatment must be superseded by the management of wellness and illness (see Figure 1), according to their prominence in the various stages of a person's life span. Therefore, within health services, care and service must coexist; the expectations of the experience, as perceived by customers, differ markedly from the past. Despite increasing interest in quality and patient/customer satisfaction among health service managers, the concept of managing customer experience, as a means to gain a competitive advantage, is a relatively new and growing area within the sector. The general comparability of expertise and facilities among health service providers therefore means that the differentiating factor, from customers' perspective, must be their experience.

People live longer than ever before, but they hope not only to extend their longevity but to improve the quality of their healthier lives (Gustavo, 2010). Most people hope to remain active as they age, as well as to look younger, if possible, such that there is considerable demand for wellness-related activities and services. At the same time, modern lifestyles representing limited physical activity at home and in the workplace have reduced the need for physical exercise associated with most professions. The resulting lack of physical activities has given rise to many types of chronic illnesses, including heart disease, diabetes, and depression (Ciarrochi et al., 2002; Frese, 1985).

These conflicting desires and trends reflect the growing social phenomenon of the so-called wellness generation. With their higher living standards and less physical engagement in the workplace, people need other ways to maintain their wellness (Joppe, 2010). In this context, wellness refers to the promotion of health and prevention of illness by pursuing a healthy, natural lifestyle, engaging in varied activities to enrich daily live (Kannan, Gaydos, Atherly, & Druss, 2010; Mueller and Kaufmann, 2000).

Wellness can be defined as a way of life that the individual pursues to achieve his or her highest potential for well-being, involving the actions that he or she is able to control, such as exercise, diet, stress management, and environmental influences. Most researchers agree that optimum wellness derives from a balance of wellness in the body, mind, and spirit (Kelly, 2010). Thus, the idea of wellness within a health service scheme comprises two components: a preventative phase initiated and managed by customers, and a treatment phase, often managed by medical caregivers, that follows from a disease or injury.

Customers, whether young or old, are more proactive in general, particularly with regard to health, and they take the initiative to participate in decision making. The difference between traditional health care customers and wellness customers is that the former mainly adopt a reactive philosophy, such that they consider health care only when they were unwell. In contrast, the latter includes people who are well and choose to proactively engage in activities that they believe will help them sustain this state of wellness.

As illustrated in Figure 1, when customers' needs change from a health focus to a wellness focus, their expectations also shift, from treatment-oriented needs to wellness-oriented demands. They thus incorporate experience-oriented needs, representing their preferences and choices. Health care managers must understand their customers' changing needs for service and experience, focused on improving their health and progress through recovery to wellness. Thus, it is imperative to manage the various services and service interactions in an effort to provide positive experiences at different stages of a customer's interactions with a health care facility.

SERVICE EXPERIENCE

Although a relatively recent addition to business/service management literature, the concept of experience holds great interest for both academics and practitioners. Experience proposes various concepts that might influence and enhance customers' perception of value. The expectation, of course, is that delivering a positive experience will provide firms with a competitive advantage. Whereas Pine and Gilmore (1999) discuss experience in terms of an economic offering, service researchers recognize it as an

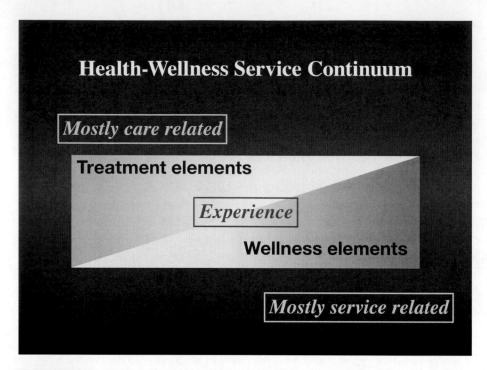

Figure 1.1 HEALTH AND WELLNESS SERVICE CONTINUUM

inherent component of value co-creation for both products and services (Vargo and Lush, 2004). Value in the context of health services is co-created by the customer and service provider. Managing service co-creations through extensive cycles of health services thus is imperative to ensure a positive service experience, which should be the result of customers' multiple service interactions across various areas of the health service organization. The health and wellness sector is one such field, for which the formation of a positive experience is complex, due to the multiple and diverse points of encounter. As the number of interactions between the service provider and the customer increases, the experience aspect of the service becomes more critical (Gentile, Spiller, & Noci, 2007). Medical care remains the core of health services, but the wellness component of the health service has the ability to signal the superiority of the service and experience to customers (see Figure 1.2) throughout all stages of health service consumption.

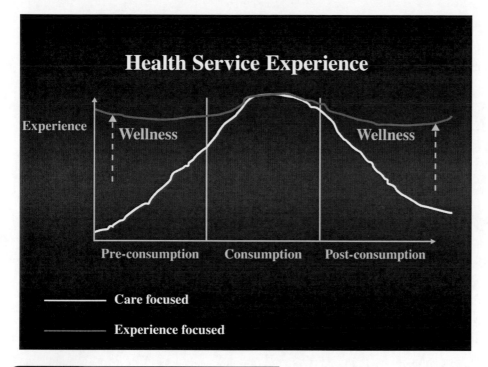

Figure 1.2 HEALTH SERVICE EXPERIENCE

DISCUSSION QUESTIONS

1. What changes have customers initiated in how health service organizations operate?

2. Why is wellness more important today than before?

3. What role do customers play today, as opposed to in the past?

4. What benefit does organizations' focus on service provide?

5. Why are alchemic or dramatic changes are needed in some service organizations?

REFERENCES

Ciarrochi, J., Dean, F. P., & Anderson, S. (2002). Emotional intelligence moderates the relationship between stress and mental health. *Personality & Individual Differences, 32*(2), 197–209.

Frese, M. (1985). Stress at work and psychosomatic complaints: A causal interpretation. *Journal of Applied Psychology, 70*, 314–328.

Gentile, C., Spiller, N., & Noci, G. (2007). How to sustain the customer experience: An overview of experience components that co-create value with the customer. *European Management Journal, 25*(5), 395–410.

Gustavo, N. S. (2010). A 21st-century approach to health tourism spas: The case of Portugal. *Journal of Hospitality & Tourism Management, 17*, 127–135.

Joppe, M. (2010). One country's transformation to spa destination: The case of Canada [special section]. *Journal of Hospitality & Tourism Management, 17*, 117–126.

Kannan, V. D., Gaydos, L. M., Atherly, A. J., & Druss, B. G. (2010). Medical utilization among wellness consumers. *Medical Care Research and Review, 67*(6), 722–736.

Kelly, C. (2010). Analysing wellness tourism provision: A retreat operators' study. Journal of *Hospitality and Tourism Management, 17*, 108–116.

Mueller, H. & Kaufmann, E. L. (2000). Wellness tourism: Market analysis of a special health tourism segment and implications for the hotel industry. *Journal of Vacation Marketing, 7*(1), 5–17.

Pine, B., & Gilmore, J. (1999). *The experience economy: Work is theatre and every business a state*. Cambridge, MA: Harvard Business School Press.

Vargo, S. L., & Lush, R. F. (2004) Evolving to a new dominant logic for marketing. *Journal of Marketing, 68*(1), 1–17.

Chapter 2

Quality and Value of Health Services

Joris van de Klundert

LEARNING OBJECTIVES

Upon completing this chapter, you should be able to do the following:

1. Place various paradigms regarding quality and value of services in a historical perspective.

2. Understand the concepts of quality and value in the health services research community.

3. Interrelate the various quality and value concepts and understand their differences and commonalities.

4. Choose appropriate definitions for practical and scientific problems at hand and understand the strengths and weaknesses of the choices made.

KEYWORDS

health services, service quality, value of health services

ABSTRACT

The health services research community on the one hand and the service marketing and service operations research communities on the other hand have progressed with limited exchange of concept and theory. As a result their contributions to the development of research and practice of health services have not always reinforced one another. This holds particularly true for the two constructs *quality of health services* and *value of health services*, which presently top political and research agendas around the globe. This paper presents a historical perspective on quality of health services and value of health services and discusses the interrelationships between the paradigms developed in the aforementioned communities.

In the Beginning

As humankind developed itself and acquired the skills to grow out of the hard lives of hunters and gatherers, the first communities, villages, and eventually, cities emerged. Such developments took place in the Americas, in Eastern Asia, and in India. In the Middle East these developments first took place in Mesopotamia, in present-day Iraq. Mesopotamia is therefore often considered to be the cradle of Western civilization. Urban societies started around 5000 B.C.E. and progressed over the following millennia, developing many concepts and practices still in use today. Mesopotamia is one of the regions in the world where writing developed. Mesopotamia is also the region where more complex agricultural societies developed, relying on systems of irrigation, which needed regulation and governance. The famous Code of Hammurabi, dating from around 1780 B.C.E., is considered among the oldest writings of significant length; it stipulates regulations for the Babylonian society. It addresses several topics, among which are health services (Johns, 1904, p 68):

> *215. If a surgeon has operated with the bronze lancet on a patrician for a serious injury, and has cured him, or has removed with a bronze lancet a cataract for a patrician, and has cured his eye, he shall take ten shekels of silver.*

> *216. If it be a plebeian, he shall take five shekels of silver.*

> *217. If it be a man's slave, the owner of the slave shall give two shekels of silver to the surgeon.*

This fragment teaches us that surgeons existed in Babylon, and that Babylonian surgeons provided cataract surgery. At present, almost 4000 years later, cataract surgery is among the most performed surgeries globally and its number grows as the prevalence of cataracts increases due to global aging. The number of performed cataract surgeries is estimated to be 14 million in the year 2004 (WHO, 2005). Although curable, cataracts are still the cause of 51 percent of the world's blindness, accounting for approximately 20 million blind people (Pascolini & Mariotti, 2012).

In addition, we may learn from the aforementioned laws that Hammurabi attached different values to cataract service for different patients, depending on their social status. Practical as it is, the Code of Hammurabi therefore appears to be the first text to touch on the complex topic of value in relation to health services.

The succeeding laws in Hammurabi's Code address the value of health services when the results do not meet the expectations. The Code of Hammurabi can therefore also be considered the first text that addressed the quality of health services:

> *218. If a surgeon has operated with the bronze lancet on a patrician for a serious injury, and has caused his death, or has removed a cataract for a patrician, with the bronze lancet, and has made him lose his eye, his hands shall be cut off.*

219. If the surgeon has treated a serious injury of a plebeian's slave, with the bronze lancet, and has caused his death, he shall render slave for slave.

220. If he has removed a cataract with the bronze lancet, and made the slave loose his eye, he shall pay half his value. (John, 1904, p 68)

Here we notice that although the value still depends on social status, the quality requirements are equitable, and quality of care is, indeed, enforced by law.

Before taking a more theoretical perspective, let us move to the Indian subcontinent, where civilization also developed early, to study contemporary health services for cataracts. In 1976 Dr. Govindappa Venkataswamy started an 11-bed hospital by the name of Aravind Eye Hospital (see Case Study: Aravind Eye Care System). His mission was to prevent avoidable blindness in India (Aravind, 2012). In 2010 the five hospitals of Aravind Eye Care System together performed more than 2.5 million surgeries per year (not all of them for cataracts), and have treated more than 20 million patients since 1976 (Pahls, Pons, & Díaz, 2010). Thus Aravind Eye Care System (to be called Aravind hereafter) presently has a significant impact on the prevalence of avoidable blindness in India; nevertheless, around 8 million people are blind due to cataracts (Murthy, Gupta, John, & Vashist, 2008). The absolute number of people developing cataracts is growing rapidly in India because of the rapidly growing population of people aged 50 years or older (Murthy et al., 2008).

As was the case in Babylon, the price of health service varies at Aravid and is value-based. Initially, 5 of the 11 beds were intended to treat patients without charge, and the other 6 beds were intended for paying customers. In 2010, of 3,649 beds, 2,850 are for patients who are serviced free of charge. The rates for the paying customers vary per room and treatment. For cataracts the maximum rate has been reported to be 8,700 INR in 2003 (Manikutty & Vohra, 2004), which in 2003 was approximately equivalent to 187 USD.

Aravind is held by the private GOVER foundation, started by Dr. Venkataswamy, and—as opposed to Hammurabi's Babylon—relies very much on positive incentives and intrinsic motivation to provide high-quality care. Quality is explicit in Aravind's mission statement: To eradicate needless blindness by providing appropriate, compassionate and high quality eye care for all. Dr. Venkataswamy phrases his ambitions as follows (Aravind, 2012):

Intelligence and capability are not enough. There must also be the joy of doing something beautiful. Being of service to God and humanity means going well beyond the sophistication of the best technology, to the humble demonstration of courtesy and compassion to each patient.

Table 2.1 illustrates the quality of cararact surgery services by Aravind from a medical perspective, benchmarking data from two of Aravind's hospitals (Prahalad, 2009) with the UK's National Health Service and the American Academy of Ophthalomology Preferred Practice Pattern (Royal Society of Ophthalmologists, 2010) in terms of adverse events. Let it be noted that the reported data are not corrected for differences in the populations taken into consideration.

Table 2.1	Benchmarking Aravind's adverse event outcomes against UK and U.S. averages (in percentages)				
	Aravind Coimbatore 2004	Aravind Madurai 2003	UK NHS 1999	UK NHS 2009	USA AAO 2006
Endophthalmitis	0.05	0.09	0.03		0.14
Wound gape/iris prolapse	0.3		0.25	0.16	0.6
Anterior chamber hemorrhage	0.3		0.5	0.05	0.5
Hypopyon	0.04	0.09	0.02		0.2
Iris trauma	0.3		0.7	0.55	1.3
Capsule rupture and vitreous loss	2	≥1.06	4.4		3.9
Uveitis	5		5.6	3.29	1.8

Quality and Value

The first written text that addresses *quality of health service* is the dialogue *Theaetetus by Plato*, the ancient Greek philosopher and founder of the first institute on higher education in Western civilization. Sower and Fair (2005) and Sower (2011) provide excellent discussions of the history of quality of health care and point out with Barfield (1926, p 19.) that Plato "invented the new word *poiotes*, what-ness, as we might say, or of-what-kindness, and Cicero translated it by the Latin *qualitas*, from *qualis*." Initially, quality referred primarily to defining features or properties. It has subsequently been considered and debated much in philosophical and other sciences, where Plato and Aristoteles already considered that the assessment of [qualities of] an object also requires a subject. In present-day use of the word *quality*, we see the subjectivity of the concept of quality reflected in the perhaps disappointing initial wording of the definition of quality by the American Society for Quality: "A subjective term for which each person or sector has its own definition (American Society for Quality, 2012).

The subjectivity of the quality of an object, or—perhaps even more precise—of the distinguishable qualities of an object (tangible or intangible) plays a dominant role in today's views on service quality in general and health service quality in particular. Further, the current definition of quality not only assumes a subjective perspective, but typically also a normative perspective. Historically this normative perspective—which regards the qualities appreciated or highly valued by the subject—appears to have been introduced centuries after Cicero's writings (see, e.g., Mauthner, 1923, Barfield, 1926). Plato devoted much effort to exploring the concept of value, and he related intrinsic value to *fine* or *good*: κάλον. In fact, through Socrates, he considered "a general explanation of what feature any object, action, person, or accomplishment of any kind has to have in order correctly to be characterized as highly valued or worth valuing in this broad way" (this broad way refers to κάλον (Woodruff, 1997, p 899))." Dr. Venkataswamy, founder of Aravind, addresses features of highly valued health services in the aforementioned quote when stating that intelligence and capability are not enough. There must also be the joy of doing something beautiful.

During the centuries to follow, *value* has been reconsidered by many scientists. For the purpose of this chapter, it is important to note that Plato's view is not empirical. Throughout his work, Plato places the fine, the good, far away from our everyday life. In more recent times, by contrast, value has often been considered in empirical terms, where it does not address the intrinsic qualities of an object, action, person, or accomplishment, but rather, what is perceived by a subject when externally evaluating it. In present-day use, *quality* thus often implicitly refers to qualities that are required to be "highly valued." For instance, this is reflected in the definition proposed by the American Society for Quality about the technical use of *quality*, which consists of two parts. The first part appears to refer to intrinsic qualities, but the second part clearly is more normative: "In technical usage, quality can have two meanings: 1. the characteristics of a product or service that bear on its ability to satisfy stated or implied needs; 2. a product or service free of deficiencies" American Society for Quality, 2012).

The latter normative definition, *free of deficiencies* is also the quality that Hammurabi aimed to enforce by law for the health service cataract surgery and is empirically analyzed in the benchmark in Table 1. Hippocrates refers to this quality in the second part of the following sentence which is central in his oath for the medical profession: "*I will use treatment to help the sick according to my ability and judgment, but I will never use it to injure or wrong them*" (Jones, 1924, pp 11-12).

Obviously, Aravind aims beyond treating and not injuring or wronging the sick when it seeks to eradicate needless blindness by providing appropriate, compassionate, and high quality eye care for all, as mentioned above. (Notice the use of the descriptor high quality). Aravind aims to provide the value of sight to all. This value goes beyond ability to see. Blindness has many consequences, such as loss of earning capacity, inability to perform the activities of daily living, or take care of others. The value of these consequences may be highest for those who can least afford the service.

Quality and Value of Health Services

We have learned already from the American Society for Qualiy that each individual or sector has its own definition of *quality*. We therefore first present the definition of *health services quality* proposed by the Institute of Medicine (IoM, 1990. p 21): "The degree to which health services for individuals and populations increase the likelihood of desired health outcomes and are consistent with current professional knowledge."

This definition is empirically oriented, as the likelihood of desired health outcomes is typically assessed empirically by observation (and not derived theoretically). The definition is normative as it considers the degree to which health services *increase* the likelihood of desired health outcomes, thus implying that increasing this likelihood increases the value of the health services. The definition is subjective as it considers *desired* health outcomes, and such desires can be subjectively defined. Like Aravind's mission statement, however, the definition not only addresses quality for individual subjects, but also addresses quality at the level of populations. Rather than measuring the quality through evaluation of individual patients, it considers likelihoods of outcomes at the population level. As such, the definition "recognizes a stochastic attribute of outcome" (IoM, 1990, p 21) , and hence, the quality sought is to increase the likelihood of desired health outcomes.

The definition of *health services quality* above leaves unspecified who desires the outcome, whether it is the health service user, the medical professionals, and/or other stakeholders. In 2001 the IoM judged it necessary that the patient's norms and values take a central place. The Institute selected six "dimensions" of health service provisioning for which, in its opinion, the American health care system "functions at far lower levels than it can and should" (IoM, 2001, p 5). The Institute of Medicine identified six qualities that show that the current health services are not of high value (in the words of Plato) and proposed them as six specific aims for improvement (Institute of Medicine 2001, p 39-40) "

> Safe—avoiding injuries to patients from the care that is intended to help them.

> Effective—providing services based on scientific knowledge to all who could benefit and refraining from providing services to those not likely to benefit (avoiding underuse and overuse, respectively).

> Patient-centered—providing care that is respectful of and responsive to individual patient preferences, needs, and values and ensuring that patient values guide all clinical decisions.

Timely—reducing waits and sometimes harmful delays for both those who receive and those who give care.

Efficient—avoiding waste, including waste of equipment, supplies, ideas, and energy.

Equitable—providing care that does not vary in quality because of personal characteristics such as gender, ethnicity, geographic location, and socioeconomic status."

Note that the first dimensions refers to the Hippocratic Oath: will never injure or wrong them (that is, the sick). Patient safety is selected as a first quality dimension because the IoM reported stunning statistics on safety in the USA: "as many as 98.000 die in any given year from medical errors that occur in hospitals" (Kohn, Corrigan, & Donaldson, 1999, p 1).

Interestingly, changes that improve health service performance of one of the six dimensions may worsen performance of another dimension. Timeliness, for example, which is often seen to be a quality problem for emergency rooms (Green 2008), may be improved by enlarging capacity. However, enlarging capacity reduces efficiency. Likewise patient-centeredness may conflict with effectiveness. Hence it is is an ambiguous task to even determine whether any change made to the health service provisioning is an improvement.

Health economists approach the question of valuing health services from the viewpoint of cost effectiveness, which relates effectiveness (health outcomes) to efficiency (not wasting monetary resources) at the population level. Cost effectiveness analysis refers to a broad class of methods in which a health service is evaluated by the ratio of the effect on health outcomes and the cost. Costs are typically expressed in monetary terms. Outcomes can be calculated using a variety of measures.

Cost utility analysis refers to the special case where outcomes are measured using an assessment of the quality of life of the health service user. In quality of life, quality has an empirical, normative interpretation; for instance, a utility score between 0 and 1, where 1 refers to perfect health and 0 to death. The *quality adjusted life year* (Qaly) is a measure that multiplies the utility by the time period over which it occurs (expressed in years). Thus 1 Qaly is the value of 1 life year in perfect health. The utility of a health service can subsequently be determined as the sum over a number of years of the (discounted) improvement in quality of life in the corresponding years as it results from the intervention. For example, for cataract surgery as performed in eye camps in India, the utility is estimated at 0.92 when considered over a period of 12 years (Agarwal & Kumar, 2011). Considering that the costs of cataract surgery can be as low as 1000 Rupees (US$20) in India, US$20 then delivers the equivalent value of 0.92 life years in perfect health.

Cost effectiveness and cost utility analysis are mature fields of science (see, e.g., Levin & McEwan, [2000] for further reading), which we do not explore in depth in this chapter. Instead, we shift our attention to drawing an analogy with the health value chain paradigm of Porter and Olmsted Teisberg (2006). They address at length the problems of the American health care system, which they show to have high costs without providing better outcomes when compared to other countries. When compared to the United States, for example, Aravind provides eye care that is comparable in terms of effectiveness (see Table 1) at less than 2 percent of the cost. Hence these authors claim that the health-per-dollar, and hence, essentially the cost effectiveness, are the measure by which to value the performance of health service provisioning. Moreover, they point out that the health service, or the health service provider, is not the appropriate unit of analysis, as meeting the health service needs of health service users may require the joint efforts of multiple providers, refered to as the health service value chain. An important aspect of health service value chains is that the costs and effects of the various service providers involved are interrelated, and therefore, the cost reduction of one provider may result in cost increases elsewhere, or reduced effectiveness elsewhere. Hence they propose the health service value chain to be the appropriate unit of analysis, and to consider the cost effectiveness of the health service value chain.

For cataract surgery, the value chain comes into play when the surgical procedure removes the clouded lens using intracapsular cataract extraction and glasses are needed to restore sight (as opposed to extracapsular cataract extraction, where a new lens is implanted). This surgical procedure is relatively inexpensive and, hence, reduces costs for the surgery provider. Baltussen et al. (2004) however report that effectiveness is often reduced because health service users do not wear their glasses, do not have glasses, or glasses are broken, scratched, etc. In rural India for instance, seemingly minor problems with glasses may be difficult to solve due to distance or cost. Naturally such difficulties with glasses reduce the effectiveness of the chain, and Baltussen et al. (2004) conclude based on the existing evidence that the initially more expensive extracapsular cataract extraction is more cost effective.

Obviously, costs and health outcomes of a particular health service vary by country, and indeed, by health service value chain. The same holds true for the valuation of the outcome. For a same outcome, average valuations may differ by country or over populations. The Code of Hammurabi already valued cataract surgery differently for different populations, when it sets the price at respectively 10, 5, and 2 shekels. Moreover, the valuation depends on individual characteristics of the health service user. Hence the IoM's plea for patient-centered health services in which the norms and values of the patients guide the decision making.

In health services research, various related models have been developed that address individual, or subjective, service valuation processes by service users. Interestingly, these empirically developed valuation models do not explicitly find that outcomes are consistent with professional knowledge, as does the IoM's definition. Instead health services research typically operationalizes quality in terms of the normative quality perceptions of the health service users. Indeed, it emphasizes the "patient centeredness," which differs from the professional perspective or the population perspective.

It was originally proposed that the assessment of the service users must be considered in relation to their expectations (Parasuraman et al., 1985, Zeithaml, 1988). For instance, this is echoed in the common phrase: 'quality is meeting or exceeding customer expectations'. Indeed, the classic conceptual model of service quality proposed by Parasuraman, Zeithaml, and Berry, (1985) posits that satisfaction follows if, and only if, perceived quality is not below the expected quality. Cronin and Taylor (1992), however, find that, for services in general, expectations are not significant predictors of satisfaction. They derive the same conclusion for health services. Likewise, Babakus and Mangold (1992) and Bowers, Swan, and Koehler (1994) show empirically that health outcomes are not a significant predictor of satisfaction for health services. Subsequent research however (see, e.g. Cronin & Taylor, 1994) has provided mixed results regarding the relationship between expectations and satisfaction.

On the one hand, the ambiguous results suggest that the construct of health service quality may not yet be well operationalized. Perhaps the features of health services that play a role in the perceptions of quality are not yet well understood. On the other hand, the ambiguity regarding the relationship between satisfaction and quality may also be due to the fact that satisfaction not only depends on the perceptions of the service qualities, but also on the perceived sacrifices. This brings us to the construct of health service value, which Zeithaml (1988) models to depend on the value of the service qualities and on the value of the sacrifices (monetary or otherwise) made to use the service. In this definition, service value is stretched beyond the valuation of the service quality. In fact, the proposed definition is general in that it specifies the service value as a function of the value of the service quality and the value of the sacrifices. For instance, when service quality is valued as perceived quality of life and sacrifices are valued in terms of cost, then this definition encompasses traditional cost utility. The definition is general enough to include "health per dollar" as a special case. However, the definition does not impose generally applicable evaluation functions for quality and sacrifices and their interrelationship, as they are, for instance, made explicit and applied at the population level when valuing health services using the QALYs-per-dollar ratio. Indeed, the definition leaves room for service valuation to vary among health service users and not to depend only on outcomes and/or consistency with professional standards. This broader perspective may help, in turn, for health services to become more patient centered, a quality dimension in need of improvement according to the IoM (2001).

As also becomes clear through the Aravind Eye Care System case study, the design and improvements of the cataract services provided by Aravind appear to fit well with

Zeithaml's (1988) value paradigm. Notice first of all how the sacrifice of payment relates to the capacity to pay, thus preventing the sacrifice from being too high. Naturally, this is only possible because of the very low cost of the health service provisioning; otherwise the paying customers might seek service elsewhere. Likewise, Aravind organizes diagnosis and screening camps, thus allowing the rural blind to avoid the difficult travel to the hospital. In addition, Aravind provides transportation to and from the hospital for those diagnosed as needing treatment. Other patients who come to the hospital simply queue up and are served the same day, so the trip is simple and affordable for them and the caregivers. Nevertheless, if patients and caregivers must remain overnight, they can do so free of charge (Viassa Monteiro & Janeiro Dias, 2006).

MEASURING HEALTH SERVICE QUALITY

Before concluding the paper, we briefly address how the scientific work on modelling service quality and value, as discussed above, is presently applied in health service practice. Independent of the services marketing research community, which has embraced the SERVQUAL (and SERVPERF) measurement instruments stemming from Parasuraman, Zeithaml, and Berry (1988), health services researchers have investigated quality perceptions and health service user satisfaction. This has resulted in a variety of interrelated methods to develop standardized and validated service quality measurement instruments for specific health services (e.g., cataract care, elderly homes, etc.). In the United States, the Agency for Healthcare Research & Quality provides the CAHPS 'surveys and tools to advance patient-centered care' (CAHPS, 2012). In The Netherlands for instance, health service quality and satisfaction are systematically measured through the Customer Quality Index. The resulting service quality and satisfaction reports play an increasingly important role in contracting and reimbursement of care by insurers and commissioners in many countries. In The Netherlands, for instance, the health insurers founded Miletus, an organization that measures health service user experiences (miletus.nl). Miletus reports for cataract care that health service users rated the doctors, nurses, and hospitals with 9.0, 8.9, and 8.9, respectively, on a 1 (lowest) to 10 (highest) scale (Stichting Miletus, 2011). The article by Muralikrishnan and Sivakumar (2002) contains an example of the customer experience and satisfaction questionnaires employed by Aravind.

CONCLUDING REMARKS

As we have demonstrated in this chapter, the value of health, and consequently, of health services, has received attention since the earliest civilizations. The examples and references above show that even for a relatively simple procedure such as cataract surgery, which is performed millions of times yearly around the globe, quality and valuation issues continue to receive attention. In the Code of Hammurabi, the quality and value of care are addressed through inspection of the medical outcomes of care.

This practice is still in place, and as it was the case in Mesopotamia, hospitals may still lose their license, temporarily or permanently, if they provide unsafe care. Not injuring or wronging the sick remains of prime importance.

Fitzsimmons and Fitzsimmons (2006), however, point out that inspection is a primitive quality management instrument, as further illustrated by the observation of W. Edwards Deming that "you cannot inspect quality into a product (Deming, 1992, p 227)." Deming argues how inspection is too late. Quality management has advanced also in health services, and now seeks continuous feedback from health service users through validated measurement instruments to increase health service quality.

These instruments, however, mostly address experiences, as opposed to outcomes. Grönroos (1990) defines a service as "an activity or series of activities of more or less intangible nature that normally, but not necessarily, take place in interaction between customer and service employees and/or physical resources or goods and/or systems of the service provider, which are provided as solutions to customer problems." In terms of this service definition, experiences and experience based quality definitions relate to the interaction between the customer and the service system during the series of activities of more or less intangible nature. This contrasts for example with the Code of Hammurabi that in terms of Grönroos' definition addresses the solution to the customer problem—the outcome. As observed above, the IoM's definition of health service quality also focuses on outcomes. Where the definition does address the activities, it doesn't consider patient experiences, but consistency with professional standards. The latter might be explained by the assumption that consistency with professional standards leads to outcomes of higher value. Interestingly, Bowers et al. (1994) have found that outcomes are not a predictor of satisfaction. This leads to the question how outcomes are a determinant of perceived value.

From the above, we may derive partial answers to this question. First of all, quality and value of health services cannot be objectively assessed and understood at the population level. Subjective perceptions and individual evaluations determine the qualities and values attached to health services by individual health service users. This is all the more important for health services for chronic and progressive conditions, which form an important and growing part of the total burden of disease for today's populations (Yach et al. 2004). Experience and satisfaction can be considered to be less important for a patient receiving a one-day cataract procedure than it might be for a dementia patient who resides in an elderly home for two years until death. Likewise, when an effective treatment is not known, outcomes cannot be influenced, and hence, appear to be inappropriate to value the quality of care. Thus, unless health service user experiences are considered as an outcome of care, defining value and quality of care in terms of outcomes and professional standards does not recognize the full essence of quality and value. As Plato would put it, this definition falls short of recognizing some of the features health services must have to be highly valued.

Another partial answer to the question above can be derived from Bowers et al. (1994). If experiences and outcomes are unrelated, then obviously, the experience can be improved without negatively affecting the outcomes, and conversely, improving outcomes does not have to impact the experience. There is no a priori trade-off between these features. Aravind serves as prime example of an organization with highly valued outcomes and highly valued service experiences as well.

Nevertheless, many health service users choose to visit a health service provider because of a desired health outcome; the service experience is not a primary reason for the visit. This is a crucial distinction with many other services. It is, however, difficult to assess the service quality in relation to the outcomes. Many health service users lack the information and knowledge to assess whether poor outcomes are caused by initial health conditions or by poor service provision. This may hold true in particular for the actual outcomes in their own case, as opposed to the likelihood of outcomes for populations as they are provided in Table 1. This might explain why the SERVQUAL quality dimension assurance is commonly found to be significant as a determinant of quality by researchers.

Naturally, this does not lead to the conclusion that outcomes and quality of life are not of highest importance. They form the prime reasons for health-seeking behavior. But service users' subjective perceptions of service provision only partly relate to these outcomes, and the service provision sometimes has limited effect on the outcomes. Hence, quality and value of health services go well beyond likelihood of outcomes at the population level and consistency with professional standards. Along these lines, Dr. Venkataswamy argued that the value of health service provisioning goes well beyond the sophistication of the best technology to the humble demonstration of courtesy to and compassion for each patient.

REVIEW QUESTIONS

1. Why are the definitions of *health service quality* and *health service value* normative and empirical?

2. What qualities and sacrifices are involved when evaluating cataract surgery?

3. How can the Institute of Medicine's definition of *health service quality* be extended to include health service user experiences and perceptions?

4. Give an example of cataract care showing that there may be a trade-off between the quality dimensions equity and efficiency of the IoM definition.

5. The Code of Hammurabi provides regulations that penalize providing unsafe care. Propose positively framed regulations for providing safe care. Are such positive incentives regulations valuable?

REFERENCES

Agarwal, A., & Kumar, D.A. (2011). The cost effectiveness of cataract surgery. *Current Opinion in Ophthalmology, 22*(1), 15–18.

Agency for Healthcare Research and Quality. (2012). CAHPS surveys and tools to advance patient-centered care. Retrieved from cahps.ahrq.gov

American Society for Quality. (2012). *Quality glossary.* Retrieved from www.asq.org

Aravind, 2012. Retrieved from aravind.org. Babakus, E., & Mangold, W. G. (1992, February). Adapting the SERVQUAL scale to hospital services: An empirical investigation. *Health Services Research, 26*(6), 767–786. Baltussen R., Sylla, M., Mariotti, S.P., (2004), Cost-effectiveness analysis of cataract surgery: a global and regional analysis, Bull World Health Organ vol.82 n.5 Genebra May. 2004

Barfield, O., (1926). *History in English words.* London: Methuen & Co.

Bowers, M. R., Swan, J. E., & Koehler, W. F. (1994). What attributes determine quality and satisfaction with health care delivery? *Health Care Management Review, 19*(4), 49–55.

Cronin, J. J., & Taylor, S. A. (1992, July). Measuring service quality: A reexamination and extension. *Journal of Marketing, 56*(3), 55–68.

Cronin, J. J., & Taylor, S. A. (1994, January). SERVPERF versus SERVQUAL: Reconciling performance-based and perceptions-minus-expectations measurement of service quality. *Journal of Marketing, 58*(1), 125–131.

Deming, J.E., (1992), Out of the Crisis, MIT Press, Cambridge, Massachusetts, USA.

Fitzsimmons, J., & Fitzsimmons, M. (2006). *Service management: Operations, strategy, and information technology.* Homewood, IL: Mc Graw-Hill.

Green, L., (2008), Using Operations Research to Reduce Delays for Healthcare, in Tutorials in Operations Research, Institute for Operations Research and the Management Sciences, Hanover, MD, USA.

Grönroos, C. (1990). Relationship approach to marketing in service contexts: The marketing and organizational behavior interface. *Journal of Business Research, 20*(1), 3–11.

Institute of Medicine, (1990), *Medicare: A Strategy for Quality Assurance.* Vol.1. Washington, DC: National Academy Press, USA.

Institute of Medcine, (2001), Crossing the quality chasm, A new health system for the 21st century, Committee on quality of healthcare in America, National Academic Press, USA.

Johns, C. W. H. (1904). *Babylonian and Assyrian laws, contracts and letters.* New York: Scribner.

Jones, W.H.S., (1924) The Doctor's Oath, Cambridge University Press, Cambridge, UK.

Kohn. L. T., Corrigan, J. M. & Donaldson, M. S. (Eds.). (1999). To err is human: Building a safer health system. Washington, DC: Institute of Medicine, National Academies Press.

Levin, H. M., & McEwan, P. J. (2000). *Cost effectiveness analysis*. Thousand Oaks, CA: SAGE Publications.

Mauthner, F. (1923). *Wörterbuch der philosophie*, Leipzig.

Manikurry, S., Vohra, N., (2004) Indian Institute of Management, Achmedabad, India.

Muralikrishnan, R., & Sivakumar, A. K. (2002). Patients'perspective: An important factor in assessing patient satisfaction. *Journal of Community Eye Health, 15*(41), 1–6.

Murthy, G., Gupta, S. K., John, N., & Vashist, P. (2008). Current status of cataract blindness and vision 2020: The right to sight initiative in India. *Indian Journal of Ophthalmology, 56*, pp. 489–494.

Pahls, S., Pons, J., & Díaz, A. (2010). Aravind: The McDonald's of health organizations.

Parasuraman, A., Zeithaml, V. A., & Berry, L. L. (1985). A conceptual model of service quality and its implications for future research. *Journal of Marketing, 49*(4), 41–50.

Parasuraman, A., Zeithaml, V. A., & Berry, L. L. (1988). SERVQUAL: A multiple-item scale for measuring consumer perceptions of service quality. *Journal of Retailing, 64*(1), 12–40.

Pascolini, D., & Mariotti, S. P. (December, December 1). Global estimates of visual impairment: 2010. *British Journal of Ophthalmology, 96*, 614–618. doi:10.1136/bjophthalmol-2011-300539

Prahalad, C. K. (2009). The fortune at the bottom of the pyramid: Eradicating poverty through profits (2nd ed.). Philadelphia: Wharton School Publishing.

Porter, M. E., & Olmsted Teisberg, E. (2006). *Redefining health care: Creating value-based competition on results*. Boston: Harvard Business School Press.

Royal College of Ophthalmologists. (2010, September). *Cataract surgery guidelines*. London: Scientific Department, The Royal College of Ophthalmologists.

Sower, V. E. (2011). Essentials of quality with cases and experiential exercises. Hoboken, NJ: John Wiley & Sonns.

Sower, V. E., & Fair, F. (2005). There is more to quality than continuous improvement: Listening to Plato. *Quality Management Journal, 12*(1), 8–20.

Stichting Miletus. (2011). Retrieved from www.stichtingmiletus.nl

Viassa Monteiro. E., & Janeiro Dias, A. (2006). *Aravind Eye Care System case study of AESE research center*. Portugal.

Woodruff, P., (1997), *Greater Hippias*, in Cooper, J.M., Hutchinson, D.S., Plato, *Complete Works*, Hackett Publishing Company Incorporated, Indianapolis, Indiana, USA.

World Health Organization (WHO) International Agency for the Prevention of Blindness. (2005). State of the world's sight, vision 2020: The right to sight 1999–2005. Retrieved from www.visions 2020.org

Yach, D., Hawkes, C. Gould, C.,L., Hofman, K.J., (2004), The Global Burden of Chronic
    Diseases: Overcoming Impediments to Prevention and Control *Journal of the American
    Medical Association, 291*(21), 2616-2622. Zeithaml, V. A. (1988). Consumer perceptions
    of price, quality and value: A means-end model and synthesis of evidence. *Journal of
    Marketing*, (3), 2–22.

Service Culture as a Means for Creating a Competitive Advantage: The Case of Public Hospitals

Victoria Bellou
Aristea-Lia Bellou

LEARNING OBJECTIVES

Upon completing this chapter, you should be able to:

1. Recognize the challenges that public hospitals currently face.

2. Realize the importance of quality in the health care industry as a means for enhancing patient satisfaction.

3. Explain the importance of building an employer brand to achieve premium service quality and patient satisfaction.

4. Recognize the key organizational values for introducing a service culture and creating a strong employer brand.

5. Suggest appropriate human resource management policies and practices for competitive health organizations.

KEYWORDS

Service quality, public hospitals, competitive advantage, service culture, service climate, employer brand, organizational values, patient satisfaction, employee attitudes, health care, human resource management

THE CHALLENGING CONTEXT FOR PUBLIC HEALTH ORGANIZATIONS

Traditionally, public health care institutions were characterized by monopolist thinking, due mainly to the nature of services offered and the protective context in which they operated. Over the last several years, significant changes have taken place. The constant pressures for cost reduction and the extensive public scrutiny on behalf of governments and citizens, along with increased patient expectations have made public health care another market-sensitive industry. Globalization has posed another challenge, especially for health organizations in developing countries, as an increasing number of individuals are willing to pay for or even travel abroad to get the best possible health care. Moreover, health care organizations are constantly faced with rapid changes in medicines, medical tests, and approaches, which stress the need for mechanisms that gather and disseminate information as well as promote and apply new knowledge if they are to survive, let alone remain competitive in the long run. Thus, it appears that health organizations need to find ways to become more competitive. Still, other than the battle to attract new patients, organizations also need to win the fight to attract talented employees.

To successfully manage all these challenges, health organizations around the world have been taking several change initiatives, including product line management, cost accounting systems, business process reengineering, and patient-focused care. These initiatives are of great importance when trying to build more efficient organizations; however, redesigning or restructuring internal processes and procedures alone can neither improve the experience of medical care received by patients nor enhance the attractiveness of the organization, unless it is supported by the appropriate organizational culture.

ORGANIZATIONAL AND SERVICE CULTURE

The term *culture* was initially introduced by social anthropologists to describe and understand "primitive" societies. Gradually, it was incorporated into the organizational context to explain the superiority of Japanese organizations over the American ones, as the former were considered to employ highly motivated individuals, who shared core values, beliefs, and assumptions. Hofstede (1980) went a step farther and argued that culture within the national context can explain the economic supremacy of certain countries over the others, while Schein (1980) insisted that culture at the organizational level could explain differences between organizations, regardless of the national context in which they operate, and defined *culture* as "a pattern of basic assumptions that a group has invented, discovered or developed in learning to cope with its problems of external adaptation and internal integration, and that have worked well enough to be considered valid, and therefore, to be taught to new members as the correct way to perceive, think, and feel in relation to those problems" (p. 111).

Generally, *culture* is an organizational phenomenon, comprised of a set of values and assumptions that are common to its members, partially changeable and, thus, amenable to managerial intervention (Bellou, 2008). Organizational values determine employee perception and interpretation of the organizational reality and formulate a common way to think and act, thus influencing employee priorities, attitudes, and behaviors (Deshpandé & Webster, 1989). To the extent that the organization emphasizes values that support and enhance the production and offer of outcomes of premium quality, the organization is characterized by a service culture. According to Gummesson (1991) and Hartline and Jones (1996) frontline employees in service organizations are responsible to a great extent for the customer experience. Consequently, convincing employees that the focal points of care are service quality and customer satisfaction is important for turning values into behaviors. In turn, employee attitudes and behavior are linked with the outcomes and the performance of the organization (James & Jones, 1980).

ORGANIZATIONAL AND SERVICE CLIMATE

Tagiuri and Litwin (1968) defined *organizational climate* as "the relatively enduring quality of the total environment that (a) is experienced by its members, (b) influences their behavior, and (c) can be described in terms of the values of a particular set of characteristics (or attributes) of the organization" (p. 25). Generally, *organizational climate* refers to the work atmosphere, ways, methods, and rules that organizational members are expected to operate within. *Service climate* in particular has been conceptualized as "employee perceptions of the practices, procedures, and behaviors that get rewarded, supported and expected with regard to customer service and customer service quality" (Schneider, White, & Paul, 1998, p. 151). For organizations, the importance of service climate has been proved by, among others, Schneider and his colleagues. For instance, Schneider et al. (1980) found a strong correlation between employees' view of the extent to which their organization emphasized specific aspects of a service climate and customers' perceptions toward these aspects, along with perceptions of the service quality offered. Recently, Holcombe Ehrhart, Witt, Schneider, and Perry (2011) revealed that the extent to which internal services are of high quality predicts the extent to which the service climate can actually ensure high-quality services to external customers. As is apparent, creating a service climate is important in convincing customers that their satisfaction is the organization's top priority.

Organizational culture and organizational climate are often used interchangeably and are easy to confuse, as they are both used to explain how employees experience their organizations. As Patterson et al. (2005) conclude, however, organizational climate is behaviorally oriented and can be understood as "a surface of manifestation of culture" (p. 381). To delineate the terms within the health care context, *service climate* reflects the expected behaviors for offering high-quality medical care to patients, whereas *service culture* relates to the inherent organizational values that guide employees toward these expected behaviors. Consequently, building a service culture is the basis for a service climate. In the present chapter, emphasis is given to organizational culture, as it is the starting point for ensuring quality of health care and patient satisfaction.

QUALITY IN THE HEALTH CARE INDUSTRY AND PATIENT SATISFACTION

Since most health care providers offer similar services, service quality is essential in the eyes of patients. The quality of medical care, however, is a complex issue, as the service context of health care is multifaceted. As with all services, the production and consumption phases are inseparable, making quality control hard to design and implement. Furthermore, patients can be either more or less active participants in their medical care. This fact means not only that the medical service quality depends on patients, but that health care organizations find great difficulty in assuring consistency and reliability over time. A service cannot be tested before it is sold; it cannot be stored, returned, or exchanged. Also, medical care is based on several interrelated subsystems, such as technology, facilities, and interpersonal interactions with health professionals and administrative staff.

Nevertheless, given that patients cannot adequately assess all interacting elements of the service, they tend to focus on interpersonal interactions. Besides, their inability to evaluate the medical service itself means that they rely to a great extent on attitudes toward caregivers when assessing their medical experience. Subsequently, patients' perceptions of their care experience and their interpretation of it are what matter most.

Customer satisfaction is currently considered to be "the new standard by which customers are measuring business performance" (Nagel & Cilliers, 1990, p. 4). Within the health care industry, Pascoe (1983, p. 189) defined patient satisfaction as the "patients' emotional reaction to salient aspects of the context, process and result of their experience." Yet, satisfying patients has multiple benefits for the health organization. As with every product or service, a satisfied patient is likely to display patronage behavior and, thus, repeat his or her health service purchase when needed and recommend the service to other consumers. Under the circumstances, health care organizations not only increase their sales but also reduce their advertising and promotion costs, increasing their chances to be or become profitable and create an increased market base. On the other hand, patient dissatisfaction may be followed by underutilization, limited use, or use only as a last option, replacement with another hospital, or legal action.

KEY VALUES TO ACHIEVE PREMIUM SERVICE QUALITY AND PATIENT SATISFACTION

According to Porter (1985), organizations hold a competitive advantage when they maintain an edge over their rivals in retaining customers and positioning themselves to take advantage of environmental changes. To manage this dual challenge, health care organizations need first to build on their ability to adapt to the external environment by collecting and disseminating market information, and then developing, sharing, and using that new knowledge (Bellou, 2010). Then, internal processes must be redesigned to produce superior value for patients.

The organizational values that are vital in this case are learning orientation and customer orientation. *Learning orientation* refers to the "organization-wide activity of creating and using knowledge to enhance competitiveness" (Calantone, Cavusgil, & Zhao, 2002, p. 516) and depicts the organization's commitment to challenge fundamental knowledge, beliefs, and practices systematically. An organization with a learning orientation will consider responsiveness to changes and challenges as critical for its survival. Hence it is expected to be committed to learning, create a shared vision, and be open-minded (Sinkula, Baker, & Noordewier, 1997).

Learning-oriented organizations tend to emphasize learning from previous errors, thus refining their operation to enhance knowledge sharing among their members and achieve improvement in performance, gather and disseminate patient, competition, and market related information, promoting hence new approaches for fulfilling the needs and expectations of their patients.

Deshpandé, Farley, & Webster (1993, p. 27) conceptualized *customer orientation* as "the set of beliefs that put the customer's interest first, while not excluding those of other stakeholders such as owners, managers and employees, in order to develop a long-term profitable enterprise." Customer orientation focuses primarily on realizing customers' interests and needs and delivering appropriate solutions. When it comes to health care organizations, customer orientation refers to adjusting the organizational operation in a way that best reflects patients' expectations, priorities, needs, interests, and wants, and makes their fulfillment a top priority.

Although being patient-focused is essential and expected, effective patient orientation presupposes that the needs of internal customers are also identified and satisfied. The importance of internal customers is emphasized by the theory of Internal Marketing (IM), which recognizes all employees as internal customers and suggests that if employees are to be willing to do their best to satisfy the needs of patients, they first need to believe that fair and appropriate internal exchanges at their level have taken place, too (George, 1990). Evidence from IM research implies that satisfying internal customers enables them to perform their tasks better, thus creating effective networks, and enhances their pride in their job, thus making them more likely to do their best to serve customers. As a result, unless a health organization focuses on its internal operational excellence, its internal customers (health professional and administrative staff) will be unwilling, unready, and uninterested in serving patients. The absence of focus on internal customers, however, puts performance and profitability in danger.

Starting with the adaptation to its external environment, a learning-oriented health care organization will aim at constantly gathering patient- and market-related information, in addition to any piece of information that could help it improve its operation and outcomes in the present and/or the future. By the same token, if the organization is oriented toward servicing patients, it focuses on recognizing their changing needs, desires, priorities, and expectations and ascertaining the best alternatives to fulfill them.

When it comes to improving its internal operation, a learning orientation will grant the health care organization shared mental models, organizational vision, and open-minded approaches in organizational policies, practices, and procedures. Through internal customer orientation the organization will realize and recognize the contribution of every organizational member (not only frontline employees) in producing and offering medical care of supreme quality.

EMPLOYER BRAND

Public hospitals operate in a hostile environment where one misstep may have multiple and irreversible negative consequences. This is why hospitals must be constantly alert if they are to secure themselves against competition. Securing their position, however, is twofold. Other than attracting and keeping patients, which can be supported by customer and learning orientations, health care organizations must also attract and keep skilled employees, who will work to attract and keep patients. This second objective can be achieved through acquiring an employer brand (EB). According to the American Marketing Association, a *brand* is "a name, term, sign, symbol, or design, or combination of them which is intended to identify the goods and services of one seller or group of sellers and to differentiate them from those of competitors." An *employer brand* refers to "the package of functional, economic and psychological benefits provided by employment, and identified with the employing company" (Ambler & Barrow, 1996, p. 182) and reflects the employer's unique characteristics make preferable over its competitors to existing and potential employees. This means the organization presents its brand image to its employees and prospective employees and inspires them to embrace it. The systematic attempt and process of organizations in building a strong EB is called *Employer Branding* (EBing).

Through EBing, employees grasp the brand image that the company wishes to deliver and they advocate for the brand. In addition, comprehension of what the organization stands for and what its goals are is likely not only to enhance person-organization fit (as people tend to be attracted by organizations they regard as similar), but also increase employee willingness to remain with an organization whose values they respect. It appears hence that an organization can gain a dual advantage over competition through EBing.

Embracing the key organizational values boosts trust in the organization and its representatives, to the extent that all parties are in agreement. In such a case, current employees are more likely to become attached to their jobs and improve their performance levels. Prospective employees are more likely to be attracted to employers whose profile is discernible and desirable.

Employee realization and acceptance of a strong brand image has been linked to several positive results both in terms of employees and in terms of customers. In particular, with regard to employees, an EB has been linked to reduced turnover, greater performance and satisfaction of current employees, along with the attraction of more skillful prospective employees (Backhaus & Tikoo, 2004). Concerning customers, EB supports an organization's attempt to build a strong and respected position of itself and its offerings in customer minds, as well as to build customer satisfaction, trust, and loyalty. In the case of customers, a brand's success depends greatly on employees, as they are considered the ones who breed a brand's values in consumer's minds, especially in the case of services (Aaker, 1996). As Bendapudi and Bendapudi (2005) indicate, employees are the living brand of the organization, and investing in them is vital for the brand's success. Within health care organizations, satisfied employees are more likely to have a greater appreciation of the organization and to pass this on to patients, influencing the way the latter perceive the corporate brand. Moreover, when considering current and prospective employees, they must also be seen as consumers who buy, recommend, or reject certain brands. Therefore, a strong EB among current and prospective employees is necessary to remain or become competitive.

KEY VALUES TO SUPPORT A STRONG EMPLOYER BRAND

To create a strong EB and secure it over the competition, a health care organization must be brand oriented, demonstrating both its ability and willingness to be the market leader. Convincing applicants and insiders accordingly necessitates the adoption and infusion of several key values. First of all, team orientation and supportiveness are critical for health organizations. To produce medical care, it is imperative that doctors, nurses, and administrative staff cooperate effectively, as no single professional can offer the service alone to a premium level. The cooperation must go beyond what is obvious or significant for any professional involved and cooperation must seek to maximize quality of care and patient satisfaction.

Attention to detail is necessary to convince employees that it is quality and not quantity that matters the most. Additionally, the organization must stress the importance of doing the job right the first time, as a second chance may not be an option. Even the smallest piece of information overlooked may hinder a correct diagnosis, harming the patient's quality of life if not the life itself. Attention to detail must be coupled with decisiveness. As time may be critical in terms of patient survival, it cannot be wasted; however, doctors must have sufficient time to make decisions. It is a fact that pushing medical professionals to serve as many patients as possible is financially beneficial in the short term. Yet, if that is followed by a reduction in service quality and a failure to address patients' individual needs, that imperils the organization's survival in the long run.

In line with being customer oriented and learning oriented, health organizations need to become aggressive toward competitors and they must become innovative, stressing the need to recognize those services and processes that will produce medical care of superior quality and ensure patient satisfaction. In all cases, it is vital to discourage all competition among organizational members. In an era of extreme outside pressures and uncertainty, a ruthless working environment only makes employees feel insecure and threatened.

One must always remember that employee attitude and behavior are designated by the reciprocity norm and the equity theory. Reciprocity norm refers to how positive actions bring about more positive actions while negative actions bring about more negative actions (Gouldner, 1960). Equity theory suggests that individuals tend to compare their job inputs and outcomes with those of others inside and outside the organization; should any inequities arise, the individual will try to eliminate them (Adams, 1963). For this reason, it is vital to create a clear connection between employee rewards—regardless of job position—and the quality of medical care delivered and patient satisfaction achieved. In addition, fair organizational processes and evaluations enhance employee trust toward the organization and increase job satisfaction and loyalty. Under the circumstances, employees are more likely to build their future within their organization, to the extent that opportunities to grow and develop are provided for them.

Introducing and Presenting the Service Culture

Processes

As mentioned earlier, becoming competitive and successful in the health care industry is a challenging task for organizational agents. They must convince patients that they offer the best possible medical care, preferably in a cost-effective manner, and they must convince current and prospective talented employees that this organization is the employer of choice. To achieve this, the organizational agent should start with culture reformation by introducing a service culture.

Changing cultures is neither easy nor simple; yet it is a must. Before an organization introduces any change, it should ensure that it has fully decoded the key elements of the operating culture in order to identify divergences between the desired state and the actual state. The extent to which patients and employees are valued should be incorporated in the organization's vision and mission and communicated to all employees, regardless of whether they hold a frontline position or not, a managerial job position or not.[1] Knowing what the organization seeks to achieve is essential for planning and decision making (Bendapudi & Bendapudi, 2005).

Systemic changes regarding internal operations and customer service cannot be neglected. Policies and practices should aim at assessing processes and procedures, then adjusting processes and procedures followed so they adhere to certain quality standards. The first step is to create work flows that depict the internal supply-customer chain. The creation of quality improvement steering councils, task forces, and committees would also offer the health organizations an opportunity to reexamine the appropriateness of existing routines and replacing them with new, more effective and efficient routines to serve internal and external customers.

Adoption of information systems that will allow information diffusion and knowledge exchange among organizational members will support the organizations' learning as well as its team orientation. Forming ad hoc work groups would also help move the organization in this direction, enabling employees to handle patients' needs and requests more effectively and efficiently.

Additionally, the organization should promote itself as the preferred employer. The health organization should start by creating and transmitting a clear picture of itself. Today's employees demand more of the company they wish to work for and may be fully informed about the company before they get in touch with it. Being attractive as an employer necessitates that the organization emphasize its vision and mission, present its key values and image, and ultimately form a brand that differentiates itself from competitors. Convincing potential employees that the organization is a great place to work will stem from applicants' knowledge of the advantages they will enjoy as employees. The role of current employees is critical, as they must be the first to be happy with their employer; the EB must be promoted among insiders through effective communication and training. Concerning prospective employees, the organization may use some marketing tools, such as advertising and public relations, to make its values widely known. Clearly communicating what the organization can offer with regard to benefits and working environment should be included in job advertisements and on the organization's Web pages. Moreover, publicizing successful management of difficult incidents, adoption of new technology, use of new techniques, and engaging famous professionals strengthens the public's recognition and appreciation of the corporate brand and enhances satisfaction among patients and employees (current and prospective). A well-known "product" is more likely to be sold, especially when it brings pride to those involved. In turn, this attracts more applicants whose skills complement the

---

[1] At this point, it is worth noting that organizational culture is not uniform. Therefore, recognizing that subcultures are inherent in the main culture is necessary for gaining an overall understanding of culture components. Different subcultures may be observed among medical professionals and administrative staff, between doctors and nurses, between individuals holding managerial and those in nonmanagerial job positions, as well as between men and women, older and younger, permanent employees and contractors (Bellou, 2008).

organization. Having more and better options from which to choose means the organization will select the best qualified and of those fitting. Additionally, current employees will develop greater pride in their organization, while patients will gain greater trust in the quality of service on offer.

All these recommendations should take place in organizations that adopt facilitative leadership styles and use decentralized decision-making styles, which are necessary for ensuring flexibility and leadership by those who are committed to the new culture and supportive of the employees. Facilitative leadership requires the adoption of truthful two-way communication, based on which decision making is made on a democratic basis (Sosik et al, 1997).

THE SUPPORTING HRM POLICIES AND PRACTICES

It is obvious that a change of culture necessitates exposing all organizational members to the new values, not merely by disseminating information, but through extensive two-way communication and the appropriate formation of human resource management (HRM) policies and practices. As Schneider and Bowen (1985) have argued, effective HRM practices are necessary in service organizations when trying to infuse a service climate, expecting employees to devote themselves to serving customers. With regard to HRM, everything should start with job analyses, namely current and comprehensive job descriptions and job specifications that reflect the key values of the organization.

After that, the organization should upgrade its recruitment strategy appropriately, adopting methods that match the organization's profile and ensuring that it offers the applicants the opportunity to learn all the critical information relating to the organization as an employer and as a health provider.

To achieve person-organization and person-job fit, the organization must use multiple selection methods, in multiple stages, performed by multiple organizational agents. In particular, the organization should link the outcome of interviews with personality tests to assess applicant suitability. Conducting multiple interviews will also uncover any contradictions between the desired and the actual profile of the applicant. This way, confident conclusions can be drawn as to whether the applicant is able to perform the required tasks to the desired level of quality and that he or she can also become an active supporter of organizational choices.

Hospitals that wish to offer their patients better-quality services in a cost-effective manner must mold employees' values, priorities, attitudes, and behaviors through truthful two-way communication and infuse those same values in newcomers through the socialization process. A straightforward communication of expectations to employees will limit future psychological contract breaches and will solidify employee trust in management.

Employee training should identify key organizational characteristics and clearly communicate what employees are expected to adopt and implement. To create a strong corporate brand that enables the organization to convince current and prospective employees and patients that it is the best choice, the organization needs to promote positive thinking about the organization itself and about its services. Such a communication program should go far beyond training frontline employees to recognize patients' needs. Such communication is about acquainting everyone with the company's policies and true values. The use of key words and short statements that reflect the essence of the desired organizational culture is imperative, as a successful service company must first sell the job to its employees before it can sell services to its customers. Concerning employee development, hospitals should encourage their employees toward lifelong learning and pursuit of educational degrees, in any subject, as this enhances their confidence and critical thinking (Bendapudi & Bendapudi, 2005).

In terms of evaluating employee performance, the introduction of 360° performance appraisals would take into consideration both internal customers' and patients' views of the service experience, helping employees to realize the importance of service quality for achieving individual and organizational goals. In addition, Management by Objectives would make the organizations more patient oriented and learning oriented, by relating goals to extra role behaviors that outreach the specifications of the job description and are based on employee willingness.

Having attracted talented employees and ensuring they embrace the new organizational culture necessitates that they feel valued by the organization. The rewards scheme adopted should reflect the extent to which individuals and teams enhance organizational adaptability, internal and external customer satisfaction, and brand equity. To achieve this, organizations should adopt reward plans that link organizational success with individual and team rewards. Pay-for-performance on an individual basis is not a good option as medical care both individualized, leaving room for standard approaches, and based on cooperation, necessitating the adoption of team-based rewards. Finally, recognition of significant achievements, both within the organization and outside of it, can act as motivators of employee performance.

CONCLUSIONS

In the current changing and challenging business context, public health organizations strive to survive. To achieve that, they need to be patient oriented to fulfill patient needs and expectations; be learning oriented to increase their adaptability and efficiency; and be brand-oriented to attract and retain talented employees. Infusing employees with such priorities necessitates making appropriate adjustments to the organizational values and aligning HRM policies and practices. The rationale is simple. The best possible professionals can ensure the best possible quality of medical care, to the extent that they embrace the organization's initiative to form its operation around serving patients well and leading the market.

The mostly challenged health organizations are those operating in developing countries, where their managers are expected to make greater steps to reach this goal. Private hospitals seem to have already started working on both orientations. The clock is ticking for public health organizations.

REVIEW QUESTIONS

1. List potential underlying values of a service organization. Identify as many values as possible.
2. Identify the difference between service culture and service climate.
3. Discuss the importance of service quality for patient satisfaction.
4. Describe the challenges that health organizations must manage successfully to survive today
5. Evaluate the role of health organization employees in the effort to create a competitive advantage.

REFERENCES

Aaker, D. (1996). *Building strong brands.* New York: The Free Press.

Adams, J. (1963). Toward an understanding of inequity. *Journal of Abnormal and Social Psychology, 67,* 422-436.

Ambler, T., & Barrow, S. (1996). The employer brand, *The Journal of Brand Management, 4*(3), 185–206.

Backhaus, K., & Tikoo, S. (2004). Conceptualizing and researching employer branding. *Career Development International, 9*(5), 501–517.

Bellou, V. (2008). Identifying organizational culture and subcultures within Greek public hospitals, *Journal of Health Organization and Management, 22*(5), 496–509.

Bellou, V. (2010). The role of learning and customer orientation for health care quality: Some evidence from Greece. *Journal of Health Organization and Management, 24*(4), 383–395.

Bendapudi, N., & Bendapudi, V. (2005). Creating the living brand, *Harvard Business Review, May*, 1–6.

Calantone, R. J., Cavusgil, S. T., & Zhao, Y. (2002). Learning orientation, firm innovation capability, and firm performance. *Industrial Marketing Management, 31*(6), 515–524.

Deshpandé, R., Farley, J. U., & Webster, F. E. (1993). Corporate culture, customer orientation, and innovativeness in Japanese firms: A quadrad analysis. *Journal of Marketing, 57*(1), 23–27.

Deshpandé, R., & Webster, F. E. (1989). Organizational culture and marketing: Defining the research agenda. *Journal of Marketing, 53*(1), 3–15.

Hartline, M. D., & Jones, K. (1996). Employee performance cues in a hotel service environment: Influence on perceived service quality, value, and word-of-mouth intentions. *Journal of Business Research, 35*(3), 207-215.

Hofstede, G. (1980). *Culture's consequences: International differences in work-related values.* Beverly Hills, CA: SAGE Publications.

Holcombe Ehrhart, K., Witt, L. A., Schneider, B., & Perry, S. J. (2011). Service employees give as they get: Internal service as a moderator of the service climate-service outcomes link. *Journal of Applied Psychology, 96*(2), 423–431.

George, W. R. (1990). Internal marketing and organizational behaviour: A partnership in developing customer-conscious employees at every level, *Journal of Business Research, 20*(1), 63–70.

Gouldner, A. W. (1960). The Norm of Reciprocity: A Preliminary Statement. *American Sociological Review 25*, 165-170.

Gummesson, E. (1991). Truths and Myths in Service Quality, *International Journal of Service Industry Management, 2*(3), 7 – 16.

James, L. R., & Jones, A. P. (1980). Perceived job characteristics and job satisfaction: An examination of reciprocal causation. *Personnel Psychology, 33*, 97-1 35.

Kotler, P. (1997). *Marketing Management*, 7th ed. Englewood Cliffs, NJ: Prentice Hall.

Nagel, P., & Cilliers, W. (1990). Customer satisfaction: A comprehensive approach. *International Journal of Physical Distribution and Logistics, 20*(6), 2-46.

Pascoe, G. C. (1983). Patient satisfaction in primary health care: A literature review and analysis. *Evaluation and Program Planning, 6*(3–4), 185–210.

Patterson, M. G., West, M. A., Shackleton, V. J., Dausin, J. F., Laythom, R., Maitlis, S., Robinson, D. L., and Wallace, A. M. (2005). Validating the organizational climate measure: Links to managerial practices, productivity and innovation. *Journal of Organizational Behavior, 26*(4), 379–408.

Porter, M. E. (1985). *Competitive advantage.* New York: The Free Press.

Schein E. H. (1980). *Organizational psychology* (3rd ed.). Englewood Cliffs, NJ: Prentice-Hall.

Schneider, B., Parkington, J. J., & Buxton, V. M. (1980). Employee and customer perceptions of service in banks. *Administrative Science Quarterly, 25*, 252-267.

Schneider, B., & Bowen, D. E. (1985). Employee and customer perceptions of service in banks: Replication and extension. *Journal of Applied Psychology, 70*(3), 423–433.

Schneider, B., White, S. S., & Paul, M. C. (1998). Linking service climate and customer perceptions of service quality in banks: Test of a causal model. *Journal of Applied Psychology, 83*(2), 150–163.

Sinkula, J. M., Baker, W. E., & Noordewier, T. (1997). A framework for market-based organizational learning: Linking values, knowledge and behavior. *Journal of Academy of Marketing Science, 25*(4), 305–318.

Sosik, J. J., Avolio, B. J, & Surinder, K. S. (1997). Effects of leadership style and anonymity on group potency and effectiveness in a group decision support system environment. *Journal of Applied Psychology, 82*(1), 89-103.

Tagiuri, R., & Litwin, G. H. (1968). *Organizational climate: Explorations of a concept.* Boston: Division of Research, Graduate School of Business Administration, Harvard University.

Chapter 4

Improving Patient Satisfaction: A Service Management Approach

Ravi Behara
Fabio Potenti

LEARNING OBJECTIVES

Upon completing this chapter, you should be able to do the following:
1. Recognize the need for a paradigmatic foundation in service research.
2. Understand health care quality improvement efforts from multiple perspectives.
3. Understand the development of an emergent framework for improving patient satisfaction based on unstructured (text) data analysis of patient comments.
4. Identify various patient satisfaction issues that need further research.

INTRODUCTION

There are many compelling reasons behind the significant increase in academic and industry interest in health care. These include the increasing cost burden of health care on individuals and the economy at large, the aging population creating an increasing demand, the U.S. federal government involvement through financial incentives and penalties, and the opportunity to improve a complex and significant sector of the economy. Involvement at a personal level is also appealing. First, the problems are multifaceted, so they can be approached from the perspective of many areas of specialization, such as medical, economic, policy, and technology, so experts from a variety of fields can make positive contributions. The other reason for personal involvement is that contributing to this field gives individuals a greater sense of purpose because it ultimately deals with the human condition. In this context, we present the following discussion, which takes a service management approach to improving patient satisfaction in health care services.

Service management has traditionally addressed managerial challenges in the field by addressing the intangibility, heterogeneity, inseparability, and perishability characteristics of service. Other approaches have evolved, including the customer cocreation of the value approach and the systems approach to service as advocated by service science. But Tronvoll, Brown, Gremler & Edvardsson (2011) suggest a paradigmatic framework that could be used to provide "different paradigmatic points of departure" to help develop new understanding and frameworks to meet the managerial challenges in services. We begin by identifying our research paradigm.

Tronvoll et al. (2011) suggest four paradigms using the two dimensions of the origins of concepts and problems (a priori vs. emergent) and the nature of relationships (static vs. dynamic). The paradigms are: Positivistic (a priori static), Monologic (a priori dynamic), Hermeneutic (emergent static), and Dialogic (emergent dynamic). They also found that much of service management research comes from the positivistic paradigm, reiterating the need for varying paradigms to address service issues. The study discussed in this chapter addresses patient satisfaction from an emergent perspective. Since it is based on patient comments on a single experience, it may be considered hermeneutic, but it must be remembered that in health care even an "episode" of hospitalization and the following recovery is really a dynamic situation. In addition, Tronvoll et al. (2011) state that adopting a hermeneutic paradigm requires analyzing subjective data from individual actors to capture complex patterns involved in the service, and such an analysis would require advanced computer programs to analyze narratives. This study operationalized the hermeneutic paradigm by using advanced text-analysis software to analyze individual patient narratives about their recent (specific) hospitalization experience. Further, the fact that one of the authors is a physician closely involved in the patient care issues discussed (pain management of perioperative care) ensures that the researchers are sensitive to the participants' perceptions as required by the paradigm.

From a practical perspective, Ostrom et al. (2010) provide research priorities that address a variety of emerging challenges in services. Taken from this practical perspective, this study is located at the intersection of patient well-being and the health care services. This study specifically falls under the research priority of "improving well-being through transformative services," and specifically under the subpriority of "enhancing access, quality, and productivity in health care and education." (Ostrom et al., 2010, p.6) However, while they call for macro-level studies on transformation, we believe a better understanding of well-being of individuals in health care has the potential to impact care at the community level. Our discussion begins by reviewing various ongoing efforts to improve health care quality. Our aim is to introduce the reader to the many professional perspectives that have been adopted in addressing health care quality. The role of the patient is then explored from a process or transactional perspective and from a transformational perspective. The case study involving an analysis of patients' perioperative satisfaction comments is then presented. Our focus is on patient dissatisfaction as a basis for improvement efforts. The emergent framework for service management to improve patient satisfaction in this context is then discussed, and implications for health care managers and care providers are explored. Finally, future directions in patient satisfaction research are discussed.

HEALTH CARE QUALITY

Delivering safe and high-quality care while controlling costs is the holy grail of health care services in the United States today. Delivering on this promise is challenging since these issues are interdependent. The presence of multiple participants (patients, providers, payers, and the government) and their varying objectives adds to the complexity of the health care service system. Further, health care quality itself comprises clinical care quality and patients' experiences with health care services. In addition, health care customers are usually unable to align the quality they receive with the price, and hence, they are unable to discern the value of the service they purchase. This is especially the case in situations when the payment is partly or completely covered by insurance or government program payers. Also, patients are generally unaware of quality and safety issues, unless they experience failures. Studies indicate that most health care consumers are either unaware of available health care quality information or do not use it effectively (Dolan, 2008; Kaiser Family Foundation, 2004). Nor do consumers use the information provided because they find it difficult to understand (Hibbard & Peters, 2003). Thus, care experiences and health outcomes, especially those of relatives, friends, and even acquaintances, generally tend to influence patients' evaluation and selection of health care services (Peters, Dieckmann et al., 2007a Peters, Hibbard et al., 2007b). In addition, when patients have limited past experiences, as is the case with most patients, they typically make health care services decisions based on advice from their trusted primary care doctors, word of mouth, and in response to direct patient marketing.

ONGOING EFFORTS IN HEALTH CARE QUALITY

Various federal agencies and professional nonprofit organizations have been focusing on quality of U.S. health care for many years. These include the Agency for Healthcare Research and Quality (AHRQ), Centers for Medicare & Medicaid Services (CMS), Department of Veterans Affairs, Hospital Quality Alliance (HQA), The American Customer Satisfaction Index, National Institute of Standards and Technology's Malcolm Baldrige National Quality Award, The Joint Commission (JCAHO), and the American Medical Association.

Most efforts to improve U.S. health care quality are spearheaded by federal agencies. The mission of AHRQ is to improve the quality, safety, efficiency, and effectiveness of health care for all Americans. One of the agencies in the Department of Health and Human Services (DHHS), AHRQ supports research that helps people make more informed health care decisions and improves the quality of health care services (www. ahrq.gov).

Since 1996, AHRQ has been conducting the Medical Expenditure Panel Survey (MEPS), which is a set of large-scale surveys of families and individuals, their medical providers (doctors, hospitals, pharmacies, etc.), and employers across the United States. In addition to collecting data on specific health care services, frequency of use, cost, payment methods, and insurance, MEPS collects data on patient care experiences in all care delivery contexts (acute/non-acute). For instance, the key measures of patient experience for 2009 (the most recent data available) are shown in Table 4.1. Even at this basic level of reporting, it is obvious that patient satisfaction still has a significant opportunity for improvement. It is also interesting to see that the evaluation is significantly higher for patients below 18 years of age. Thus, it would be useful to study what other health care providers can learn from pediatric care providers. Majzun (2011) makes this point in the context of hospital-based care by identifying strategies that adult care hospitals can learning from pediatric hospitals and then adopt.

Table 4.1 AHRQ (MEPS) Household Responses		
MEPS Measures 2009	Adults age 18 and over who reported going to a doctor's office or clinic in the last 12 months (n=155,909,000)	Children under age 18 who had a doctor's office or clinic visit in the last 12 months (n=57,543)
Respond "always" for how often their health providers listened carefully to them/their parents	60.5%	76.6%
Respond "always" for how often their health providers explained things clearly	59.3%	76.6%
Respond "always" for how often their health providers showed respect for what they/their parents had to say	64.2%	78.9%
Respond "always" for how often their health providers spent enough time with them/their parents	51.5%	72.6%
Respond by giving a 9–10 overall rating for health care received (1–10 scale, max =10)	50.1%	70.1%

CMS, another federal agency within DHHS, along with the HQA, has developed Hospital Compare (http://www.hospitalcompare.hhs.gov) to better inform health care consumers about the quality of care being provided at U.S. hospitals. CMS also provides comparison data for physicians, nursing homes, and home care and dialysis facility services.

The American Customer Satisfaction Index (ACSI) is a national index that is updated quarterly, while the ACSI index for the various sectors is reported monthly throughout the year. It collects and reports customer satisfaction scores on a scale of 0–100 at the national level and produces indexes for 10 economic sectors, 47 industries, more than 225 companies, and over 100 federal or local government services. The measured companies, industries, and sectors are broadly representative of the U.S. economy serving American households. Specifically, in the health care sector, customer satisfaction with hospital services has been measured since 1995, with health insurance since 2001, and ambulatory care since 2008. Figure 4.1 shows the national ACSI as well as averages for specific service industries. It shows the ambulatory care industry significantly above the national average, while the health insurance sector is below it, and the hospital sector customer satisfaction index fluctuates near the national average.

The ACSI collects customer satisfaction data at the individual level. Scores for a company's customers are aggregated to produce the company-level results, while industry scores are the weighted (by revenue) average of the component companies. Sector scores consist of industry scores, weighted by industry revenues. Finally, the national ACSI comprises sector scores weighted by each sector's contribution to the GDP.

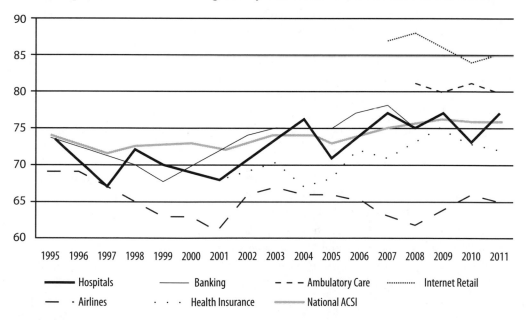

Figure 4.1 The American Customer Satisfaction Index 1995–2011.

At this writing, customer satisfaction in the health care and social assistance sector was last reported in April 2011 (www.theacsi.org). This sector consists of private-sector hospitals and ambulatory care. As is evident in Figure 1, customer satisfaction with private-sector hospitals increased to an ACSI score of 77. Customer satisfaction with ambulatory care services, which includes visits to doctors, dentists, and optometrists, was down slightly to 80, but these services continue to provide significantly higher levels of patient satisfaction compared with hospital services. It was also reported that among hospital services, patient satisfaction was highest for outpatient visits and procedures, with an ACSI score of 80; inpatient satisfaction followed at an ACSI score of 79; emergency room services had the lowest score, at 72. The hospital industry's recent focus on patient satisfaction, efforts to reduce ER wait times, availability of after-hours urgent care clinic services, and shorter inpatient stays has contributed to the overall improvement in patient satisfaction.

Over the past few years, efforts are ongoing to better inform U.S. consumers of health care services (patients/potential patients) about quality and safety of care so that they can make more informed decisions. For instance, the Leapfrog Group, founded in 2000, is a national not-for-profit organization driven by the largest employers and purchasers of health care benefits in the United States. It is a voluntary program that leverages its purchasing power to recognize and reward health care providers who deliver on health care safety, quality, and customer value (www.leapfroggroup.org). The Leapfrog Group's primary focus is hospital-based safety of care, and assessments are conducted through self-reported surveys by participating hospitals. The quality of care centers on clinical quality and improved safety is achieved by avoiding preventable errors.

There is a growing emphasis on understanding, measuring, and improving the patient experience. To empower U.S. consumers to make informed health care decisions, the CMS requires hospitals to report performance measures, also known as core measures, for specific clinical issues. However, since these medical outcome measures alone provide insufficient information, patient satisfaction has become an important additional metric.

Further, to provide evidentiary basis of patient satisfaction, the CMS and the AHRQ have designed the Hospital Consumer Assessment of Health Care Providers and Systems (HCAHPS; pronounced H-caps) survey. This is a national, standardized survey instrument that captures the patient's perspective on hospital care. Survey results are reported on the Internet and updated each quarter. This public exposure creates incentives for hospitals to improve quality outcomes and enhance accountability through transparency. Currently, CMS mandates a pay-per-reporting policy by retaining 2 percent of payments. Starting in 2013, the failure to meet a set percentile of HCAHPS scores results in financial losses. This Hospital Value-Based Purchasing Program will apply from the beginning of applies beginning in FY 2013 to payments for discharges that occurred on or after October 1, 2012. Under this program, CMS will make value-based incentive payments to acute-care hospitals based either on how well the hospitals perform on certain quality measures (including HCAHPS scores) or how much the hospitals' performance improves on certain quality measures from their performance during a baseline period. Higher payments are made to hospitals with higher performance or greater improvements from their baselines. Thus, we see patient satisfaction with hospital services directly tied to financial performance. In a tightening fiscal environment, this issue more than anything else has heightened management focus on improving patient satisfaction.

The eight critical aspects of care covered in the HCAHPS survey include: overall hospital rating and recommendation, communication with doctors, communication with nurses, communication about medicine, responsiveness of hospital staff, cleanliness and quietness of hospital environment, pain management, and discharge information. Patient satisfaction is also being evaluated in other areas of the health care system, from primary care physician clinics to elder care facilities.

This chapter examines the dimensions of patient satisfaction with health care services, and discusses how health care service providers are addressing the challenges in measurement and improvement.

UNDERSTANDING PATIENTS' ROLE

Customer satisfaction research has a decades-long tradition in marketing in the context of goods and services. Efforts to understand patient satisfaction also have been underway for many years. As expected, patient satisfaction research has been strongly influenced by the literature on customer satisfaction, but there are differences. We can start at the beginning by examining the word (noun) *patient*, which we take for granted in health care to mean "one who receives medical attention, care, or treatment." But it also means someone "acted upon or who undergoes an action." In addition, the word (adjective) also means to endure pain and difficulty with calmness and to be understanding and capable of waiting calmly (see Table 4.2). The semantics of the word imply of an individual who calmly endures difficulty while being the target of another's actions. Thus, the term *patient satisfaction* is an oxymoron, for how can an individual be "satisfied" (pleased, contented, gratified) to be a "passive target" for another person's action?

Table 4.2	The Meanings of *Patient* (Source: www.thefreedictionary.com).

pa·tient (pā' shənt)

adj.

1. Bearing or enduring pain, difficulty, provocation, or annoyance with calmness

2. Marked by or exhibiting calm endurance of pain, difficulty, provocation, or annoyance

3. Tolerant; understanding (*an unfailingly patient leader and guide*)

4. Persevering; constant (*With patient industry, she revived the failing business and made it thrive.*)

5. Capable of calmly awaiting an outcome or result; not hasty or impulsive

6. Capable of bearing or enduring pain, difficulty, provocation, or annoyance (*"My uncle Toby was a man patient of injuries"; Laurence Sterne*)

n.

1. One who receives medical attention, care, or treatment

2. *Linguistics* A noun or noun phrase identifying one that is acted upon or undergoes an action. Also called *goal*

3. *Archaic* One who suffers

Middle English pacient, from Old French, from Latin patiᵉns, patient-, present participle of patⁱ, *to endure*; see pᵉ(i)- in Indo-European roots

So to be able to understand patient satisfaction, we need to first get a better understanding of "the patient." We identify four characteristics of patients in health care services that make them different from customers of other services.

1. **Patient as service-provider:** Patients are "cocreators" of the service. At an observable level, most patients participate in their own care through compliance with the physician's (and other health care providers') instructions. In the case of pediatric (very young) and geriatric (very old) patients, the involvement of a family/other caregiver creates an additional actor in the service-provider role who is not the patient.

2. **Patient as service-product:** The patient is the "product" that is "transformed" through the service. The service is performed "on" the patient, not on something that "belongs" to the patient.

3. **Patient as service-outcome:** The outcome of a service in health care also depends on the "initial condition" of the patient. The fact that the human body is dynamic introduces a degree of uncertainty in how a patient will respond to treatment. This is not simply the state of the patient's health immediately prior to needing service; it involves his or her genetic makeup (e.g., family history) and environmental

conditions (e.g., physical, economic, social) that influence responses to treatment (both preventative or acute/chronic treatment).

4. **Patient as service-value:** There is probably nothing as valuable to a patient as his or her own life and well-being. As such, since health care services have a direct impact on one's life and well-being, the value of the service is manifested in patients themselves.

Patient as service-provider, -product and -outcome follow a process view of service. While this certainly has operational use in effecting improvement, patient as service-value is the transformative perspective (Ostrom et al., 2010). The purpose of quality health care is to improve the well-being and lives of individuals, their immediate families, and the larger community. So we propose that, while practitioners and researchers adopt any of the above perspectives of a patient, the transformative definition of *patient as service-value* should be the underpinning of all service efforts. The well-being of the individual and the community is the only sustainable common ground between clinical health care providers and managers of health care services.

UNDERSTANDING PATIENT (DIS)SATISFACTION: A CASE STUDY

Tversky and Kahneman (1974) found that consumers usually revert to using simple heuristics when faced with having to work to select among alternatives and when this effort involves evaluating complex data. Further, the vividness with which the information is described is more persuasive than plain information (Rook, 1986, 1987). Taken together, we can understand why health care consumers give more credence to anecdotal information from friends, relatives, and even casual acquaintances than to quantitative data analyzed and presented by experts (Schwartz, 2004). Huppertz and Carlson (2010) conducted an experiment on intentions to choose a hospital for elective surgery. Consumers were provided with HCAHPS quantitative ratings and a relative's narrative email. The researchers found that the impact of the HCAHPS ratings was reduced by an anecdotal narrative that provided conflicting information from the relative.

However, little work has been done to trace the origins of these "vivid heuristics" (Huppertz and Carlson, 2010, p.1603) that are provided by a consumer's social network. Taken to its logical next step, one can assume that many of the sources of these anecdotes were themselves patients who based their comments on personal experience, thereby making them vivid and personal. Thus, it is imperative that we listen to patients and not evaluate only their survey responses quantitatively on scale-based questions. A case study following this reasoning to its logical next step follows. Patient comments expressed in the HCAHPS survey responses related to perioperative care were analyzed using SPSS Text Analysis for Surveys 3.0 software. The unstructured data included 2,954 comments (verbatims) collected from patients discharged over a one-year period. The comments were taken from 1,526 unique patient surveys, with patients making multiple comments in each survey, commenting on one or more of the HCAHPS categories. A text analysis of patient satisfaction responses was conducted, focusing on pain management of perioperative care. While the patient comments were predominantly positive, as stated earlier, the focus of this discussion is only on the negative comments to facilitate improvements by better understanding the underlying dimensions of patient dis-satisfaction. The negative comments fell primarily in two areas: negative patient sentiment and medication related. The authors, one of whom is a surgeon, reviewed the patient comments in both categories. Based on our combined expertise in service operations and clinical care, the comments were classified into the following mutually exclusive patient comment categories:

- Negative sentiment: Communication (physician, nurse, administration/ staff), treatment protocol, personnel (nurse, staff), and care process (patient waiting time)
- Medication: Communication (physician, nurse, administration/staff), treatment protocol, personnel (nurse), and care process (transition of patient care)

PATIENT RESPONSE TO PAIN MANAGEMENT: NEGATIVE SENTIMENT

We have identified four categories related to negative sentiment associated with pain control in the perioperative phase of hospital care. Some examples are presented in Table 4.3. The first category is *communication with physician, nurse, administration, or staff.* Communication between patient and health care personnel plays an important role in satisfaction scores. We have grouped all the caregivers together because patients often cannot recognize one from the other, all dressed in hospital attire and all apparently attending to similar tasks. Particularly in the perioperative phase, when patients have been treated with benzodiazepines or other anesthetics, anything rather than a very clear communication can be misinterpreted. Health care professionals must focus on the two main components of communication: listening and delivering information. Often, we forget to listen and we miss opportunities to learn from the patient regarding the type of treatment has worked best for him or her in the past. As an example, the comment "I was in pain and nobody noticed" exemplifies the patient's feeling of lack of control and power as he or she attempts to communicate the pain, which translates into a low level of satisfaction with the entire hospitalization.

Patients also frequently comment that they did not receive adequate advice or education during their hospitalization. In the era of knowledge availability and ease of connectivity to the Internet, health care professionals must step up from what is considered "lay terminology." Patients may seek advice in real time from friends or by searching the Internet, challenging the philosophy that "the doctor knows best."

Table 4.3	Patient Response to Pain Management: Negative Sentiment
Patient Comment Categories	**Patient Comments**
Communication (Physician, Nurse, Administration, Staff)	• I learned more about my procedure when I called my friend—a veterinary technician—she gave me advice to help the pain which the doctor did not. • I was in pain, nobody notice. • When I complained of pain in neck to chest, nurse asked me if she should call the doctor, I said yes. Nothing was done until the doctor pulled the IV in my neck during rounds that morning.
Treatment Protocol	• I had pain during my entire stay. One of the nurses suggested a change in medication and once the medication was changed I had no pain—this was done right before discharge. • The pain was the only negative issue but I understand one can only be given so much Morphine • IV pain medications made me sick; I felt that pain was better than throwing up. Once I was able to take oral pain medications I got more relief. I feel that intramuscular shot should be used sometimes.
Personnel (Nurse, Staff)	• I was in pain and it took some time before I was admitted. I asked if I was in the right place but was not given a clear answer if it was Admittance Dept. or not. No signs! • I had one unfriendly nurse and one that caused me unnecessary pain. Otherwise superb care • Several times I asked for a bed pan, until I was begging because I was in pain & about to wet the bed!
Care Process (wait)	• There was an occasion where I was in tremendous pain. I was considering jumping from the window to my death. I begged the nurses for pain medication. It took 4 hours before I finally received medication that put me to sleep. No one should suffer like that. • I spent 1½ hr. waiting period on ER and acute pain (appendicitis). After that, it was very good. • Long time to answer call button at times. Do not like how they wait until a number of regular meds are due to address acute pain, nausea etc., I feel they are trying to decreases the number of trips into the room.

The second category relates to *treatment protocols*. The treatments available are rarely unable to control surgical pain. Often by critically reading patients' comments, we can identify that the negative sentiment is attributable to poor communication or poor service rather than to ineffective pharmaceutical treatment. In one example, a patient had a reaction from IV pain medication, developing nausea and vomiting. This is a case in which anti-emetics or a different delivery modality for the medication should have been employed. In another example, a patient complained of pain during the entire hospitalization. A nurse apparently was able to communicate that a change of medication might help; unfortunately, the patient's medication was not altered until immediately before discharge. This example can be interpreted in two ways: 1) a change in therapy leading to improvement or 2) the normal course of surgical pain naturally disappearing as the patient improves, which happens at the time of discharge.

The third is a *personnel category*; it demonstrates negative sentiment elicited by perception of poor service from nurses and ancillary staff. Patients' expectations of service vary significantly based on cultural, educational, social, and financial status. It is difficult for the patient in the perioperative phase to differentiate between service and clinical quality; for example, when a noisy alarm goes off signaling an emergency or when immediate attention is not given to pain, the patient translates the event as poor care. In one example, a patient perceived failure of the nurse or ancillary staff to immediately attend to his bathroom needs. The patient interpreted the event as causing unnecessary pain. In another example, the patient believed the nurses delivered pain treatment on a schedule that was convenient for their workflow rather than the patient's needs. In another case, a patient complained that the lack of signs describing his exact location in the hospital upset him, causing him to focus on his pain.

The fourth category relates to the *process of care* focusing mainly on the waiting period. When a patient is in pain, the subjective experience of time slows. What a nurse perceives as a few minutes, the patient may perceive as an eternity. In one comment, a patient complained of having to wait 1½ hours for appendicitis surgery. While the patient perceived an excessively long wait, this is, in fact, a short time to adequately prepare a patient for surgery for acute appendicitis. Patients may report waiting for hours for pain medications to be delivered. If this is found to be true in a particular institution, it indicates a clear opportunity for improvement of treatment protocols, services, and care processes. By analyzing verbatim data and comparing them with nursing clinical charts, we can discern those instances where the delay is a subjective perception.

PATIENT RESPONSE TO PAIN MANAGEMENT: MEDICATION

Comments related to the use of pain medications during the perioperative phase of hospitalization can be also divided into four categories: communication with physicians, nurses and administration and staff; treatment protocol; service by nurses; and transition of care process. Sample comments are given in Table 4.4 *Poor communication* appears to be the underlying issue in most categories. We identified examples that offered clear opportunities for improvement of communication between caregiver and patient. One comment involved two surgeons giving different instructions about diet, time of discharge, and pain medications. This case illustrates the complexity of communication during inpatient hospital care. The presence of multiple consultants, nurses, and ancillary services creates a conversation grid with multiple inputs and outputs. Coordination of all voices is necessary to avoid conflicting messages.

Once again we can identify a feeling of helplessness in patients commenting that their concerns were unheard or disregarded. One patient commented that he had his own pain medication, which he was given by his primary care doctor, but that the hospital nurse would not let him use it. Usually, hospitals will not accept medications that patients bring in, especially narcotic medications. Drugs that have been in the unmonitored possession of third parties pose a liability such as expired medications, poor storage, and contamination. However, in this case, it appears that the patient did not receive a clear explanation about *why* his own medications could be not administered by the hospital nurse.

Treatment protocols related to the use of pain medications show an exceptional paucity of negative comments. This is due to the documented effectiveness of many available therapies developed over the course of the past decade to treat surgical pain. The side effects of pain therapy, including nausea and vomiting, skin rash and allergic reactions, are at the center of most complaints relating to medications.

Comments relating to *personnel* identify a problem with a possible stigma associated with requesting narcotics. One patient commented that when he asked for pain medication, the nurse responded, "You must have a low tolerance." This response is judgmental and may be perceived as a label of drug addiction. Nurses should be educated that the comment "I can't give you any more meds yet" should be followed by offering alternative solutions. The nurse can say, "We can ask the doctor for alternative medications or other options for pain relief, such a warm compress, an ice pack, or even a massage." By offering these suggestions, the caregiver communicates eagerness to help.

Table 4.4	Patient Response to Pain Management: Medication
Patient Comment Categories	**Patient Comments**
Communication (Physician, Nurse, Administration, Staff)	• I had 2 surgeons giving 2 different status as to diet and discharge time & pain relief • Pain management the 1st night was poor, my concerns were disregarded until the following morning • I had poor pain control immediately post-op, despite the fact that I repeatedly told the nurses that I had my pain meds (prescribed by my doctor of 8½ yrs.) with me. I was in severe pain for a day and a ½.
Treatment Protocol	• I kept throwing up pain medication and was not able to control my pain. • Two different nurses tried to give me a pain med I was allergic too. • I was given a pain shot which made me feel lousy.

Personnel (Nurse)	• During my stay I had to call many times for pain killers. I begged but no-one came until 12 p.m. midnight. The nurses kept leaving my door open. • When I asked the nurse for more pain meds he said "Oh, you must have a low pain tolerance, I can't give you any more meds yet." • The only bad experience I had was when trying to get my pain medication administered.
Care Process (transition)	• I felt that I was sent home w/improper pain management medications. • Was sent home w/weak pain meds (4 day supply). I was still in bad pain 8 days later. • I was discharged from hospital without a prescription for pain or any other medication. I was told that the doctor who was to sign the prescription was in surgery.

The *transition of care* is the critical point when a patient is transferred to another hospital, a rehabilitation facility, or home with the help of visiting nurses or the patient's family and friends. This critical milestone is especially important for elderly or high-risk patients with multiple medical problems. Postsurgical patients clearly fall into the latter category. A focus on the type, frequency, and supply of medication is essential in the transition of care process. Once the patient is discharged, patient and family are responsible for following physicians' orders for pain management. In an environment where hospital length of stay is becoming shorter, patients are sent home in the immediate postoperative phase and with a residual amount of pain. By reviewing patients' comments, we can identify an underlying problem with supply of medications. We can also identify an opportunity for improvement in the process of discharge. Consider, for example, a patient who commented that he was sent home without a prescription because the doctor was unavailable at the time of discharge. Even though this is an impossible occurrence in a hospital staffed 24 hours a day, it appears this perception was created by poor communication, which can be avoided by the adoption of a checklist confirming patients' understanding of discharge instructions; we should accept only 100 percent compliance.

In summary, the emergent framework from this study for improved pain management for perioperative care has four dimensions: *communication, treatment protocol, personnel, and care process.* But on further examining the patient comments from a clinical perspective, we recognize that the core is the need for more effective communication. This communication is both between patient and care provider as well as among the providers themselves.

Implications for Care Providers and Managers

Better listening and a greater awareness of the patients' perspective are central to better communication. It is imperative that care providers (physicians, nurses, staff) are always cognizant of the vulnerability and lack of control that most patients experience when they are in the hospital. In addition, the patients' lack of medical expertise is only compounded by their anecdotal evidence and Internet-based research. So a central part of any strategy to improve patient satisfaction would have to be a comprehensive and sustained communications effort with, and about, the patient. This has to be designed in such a way as to ensure two specific goals: that every care provider communicate effectively with the patient, and that care providers communicate among themselves in the hospital.

It is also interesting to note that in the HCAHPS survey, pain management is considered a different category than others related to communication. But the emergent framework in this study that adopted a hermeneutic paradigm clearly shows the limitations of an a priori method that is embedded in the standardized HCAHPS survey. The central role of communication is reiterated by our framework. Managers should develop a comprehensive plan for design, training, and delivery of consistent communications across all patient care needs.

Many strategies are being adopted to deliver on this all-pervasive communications requirement in patient care. These include the use of health IT solutions, scheduled rounding by nurses (nurses visiting with patients on a schedule), understanding patient expectations, and educating patients. However, these are usually not identified as communication strategies, but would help managers and care providers by being recognized as such. It would give greater coherence to the often seemingly disparate efforts in patient satisfaction improvement efforts.

MOVING FORWARD: RESEARCH IN PATIENT SATISFACTION

Beyond the specifics of the framework developed in this study, current literature and research directions in patient satisfaction indicate a variety of research interests. These varied interests are classified below and provide service management researchers with a patient satisfaction research agenda. It would be useful if they were approached by researchers from an emergent perspective, because of the unexpected and interesting outcomes that could result as in the case of this study.

ANTECEDENTS OF PATIENT SATISFACTION

Health Care Information Technology and Patient Satisfaction: One of the major initiatives in U.S. health care today is the implementation of health information technology (HIT) across the industry. Technology use in health care affects the way patients receive care and how they perceive it. Whitten, Mylod, Gavran, and Sypher, (2008) reported that patients in the most wired hospitals were more satisfied. This suggests that HIT is an important antecedent for patient satisfaction. Many aspects remain to be further understood, including the relative impact of different technologies on satisfaction and the variability of satisfaction due to HIT relative to patient demographics.

Drivers of Patient Satisfaction: Further research continues into other antecedents for patient satisfaction. For instance, Blakely, Koth, and Gregson, (2011) found that a nurse rounding program designed to frequently anticipate and address patient needs had an immediate impact on overall patient satisfaction. Investigating drivers of patient safety in hospital and nonhospital settings is an area of research to be pursued as there is an increased business need for improvements in satisfaction.

CONSEQUENCES OF PATIENT SATISFACTION

Patient Satisfaction and Loyalty: Reichheld and Sasser (1990) introduced the concept of satisfaction as a key driver to loyalty. But recently, Kessler and Mylod (2011) showed for the first time that patient satisfaction affected hospital choices. While this study involved large, nonprofit teaching hospitals in competitive markets, the relationship between satisfaction and loyalty in various care settings is still generally unexplored.

Cost of Satisfaction: Customer satisfaction at any cost is certainly an inappropriate approach, especially in a budget-constrained service environment. Increasingly, we face such an environment in health care costs, which are exacerbated by a growing federal budget deficit, an ageing population, and increasingly expensive treatment options. Research suggests that the link between patient satisfaction and health care quality and outcomes is tenuous at best (Sequist et al., 2008). Higher patient satisfaction is also associated with physicians providing discretionary services, at the request of the patient, that have little or no medical benefit (Kravitz et al., 2005). Fenton, Jerant, Bertakis, and Frank, (2012), in studying a large, nationally representative sample over multiple years, found that higher patient satisfaction was associated with greater inpatient use of services, higher overall health care and prescription drug costs, and increased mortality. Higher patient satisfaction appears to be expensive but clinically ineffective in the long run. These studies indicate that instead of studying the traditional cost of quality, it would be more worthwhile to address the question, "Patient satisfaction—at what cost?" The current focus of hospital-based health care is one of improving patient satisfaction under the threat of reduced reimbursement from Medicare and Medicaid for lower satisfaction scores. So it would be worthwhile to further study the cost-benefit relationship of improving patient satisfaction.

ROLE OF PATIENTS

Patient Expectation: While the role of customer expectation has been researched extensively in the consumer and service literature, only recently (Rozenblum et al., 2011) has this been explicitly explored in health care. This study addressed the clinicians' awareness, attitudes, competence, and performance with respect to patient expectations in four hospitals in Denmark, Israel, the UK, and the U.S. While physicians and nurses mostly believed it was important to ask patients about expectations, most did not actually ask their patients. Further, few felt they were adequately trained to handle patient expectations. Many dimensions of patient expectations can be researched, such as understanding patient expectations in various care settings; variations in patient expectations based on cultural, regional, and socioeconomic differences; and how patients have different expectations for different service providers (physicians, nurses, technicians, etc.).

Patient Responsibilities: Patients today have greater access to information about their specific medical conditions as well as the types and effectiveness of available services. There is also a greater emphasis on patient cocreation of health care services, aided by technology. This is especially true when patients are dealing with non-acute (preventative or chronic) conditions at home or in other nonhospital settings. Patient satisfaction in these situations is invariably affected by how responsible patients are in attending to their own care; this should be further explored.

PATIENT CONTEXTS

Patient Satisfaction in Non-Hospital Settings: The current literature is dominated by patient satisfaction in the hospital-based context, driven primarily by the HCAHPS data and satisfaction-based reimbursement policies that are being implemented. Other settings also need to be investigated. For instance, with increasing chronically ill and elderly populations, it would be useful to study dialysis centers and nursing homes. In addition, the growing trend of home-based care highlights the need to focus on patient satisfaction in this setting. Some preliminary data are available at data.medicare.gov.

In conclusion, we find that the challenges in designing and delivering services that result in higher patient satisfaction provide a fertile area for service researchers. But understanding and adopting an emergent research paradigm is essential because of the complexity of the service and the significant involvement of the non-expert, vulnerable patient. Service researchers must collaborate with clinical care providers (physicians or nurses) so as to truly understand the patient context. We believe the case study presented here is a useful example of such an effort. Through such efforts we will invariably impact and improve patient satisfaction, for the individual and the larger community, thereby delivering on the transformative promise of service management.

DISCUSSION QUESTIONS

1. Discuss the paradigmatic foundation of any one of your current research projects.

2. What are the similarities and differences between customer satisfaction and patient satisfaction?

3. Discuss the central role of communication in patient care. What strategies would you adopt to improve communication in hospital-based patient care?

4. Discuss the dimensions of patient satisfaction from a service research perspective.

REFERENCES

Blakely, D., Koth, M., & Gregson, J. (2011, November-December). The impact of nurse rounding on patient satisfaction in a medical-surgical hospital unit. *Medical-Surgical Nursing*, 20(6), 327–332.

Dolan, P. L. (2008). Patients rarely use online ratings to pick physicians, *American Medical News, 51*, 24.

Fenton, J. J., Jerant, A. F., Bertakis, K. D., & Frank, P. (2012, February 13). The cost of satisfaction: A national study of patient satisfaction, healthcare utilization, expenditures, and mortality. *Archives of Internal Medicine*, E1–E7. Retrieved from www.archinternmed.com

Hibbard, J. H., & Peters, E. (2003). Supporting informed consumer healthcare decisions: Data presentation approaches that facilitate the use of information in choice. *Annual Review of Public Health, 24*, 413–433.

Huppertz, J. W., & Carlson, J. P. (2010, December). Consumers' use of HCAHPS ratings and word-of-mouth in hospital choice, Part 1. *Health Services Research, 45*(6), 1602–1613.

Kaiser Family Foundation. (2004). *National survey of consumers' experiences with patient safety and quality information*. Retrieved from http://www.kff.org/kaiserpolls/upload/ National-Survey-on-Consumers-Experiences-With-Patient-Safety-and-Quality-Information-Survey-Summary-and-Chartpack.pdf

Kessler, D. P., & Mylod, D. (2011). Does patient satisfaction affect patient loyalty? *International Journal of Healthcare Quality Assurance, 24*(4), 266–273.

Kravitz, R. L., Epstein, R. M., Feldman, M. D., Franz, C. E., Azari, R., Wilkes, M. S., Hinton, L. et al. (2005). Influence of patients' requests for direct-to-consumer advertised antidepressants: A randomized controlled trial. *Journal of the American Medical Academy, 293*(16), 1995–2002.

Majzun, R. (2011). Sometimes children are the best teachers, *Healthcare Executive, March/April*, 60–63.

Ostrom, A. L., Bitner, M. J., Brown, S. W., Burkhard, K. A., Goul, M., Smith-Daniels, V., Demirkan, H. et al. (2010). Moving forward and making a difference: Research priorities for the science of service. *Journal of Service Research, 13*(1), 4–36.

Peters, E., Dieckmann, N., Dixon, A., Hibbard, J. H., & Mertz, C. K. (2007a). Less is more in presenting quality information to consumers. *Medical Care Research and Review, 64*(2), 169–190.

Peters, E., Hibbard, J. H., Slovic, P., & Dieckmann, N. (2007b). Numeracy skills and the communication, comprehension, and use of risk-benefit information. *Health Affairs, 26*(1), 741–748.

Reichheld, F. F., & Sasser, W. E. (1990). Zero defections: Quality comes to services. *Harvard Business Review, September-October*, 105–111.

Rook, K. S. (1986). Encouraging preventative behavior for distant and proximal health threats: Effects of vivid versus abstract information. *Journal of Gerontology, 41*(4), 526–534.

Rook, K. S. (1987). Effects of case history versus abstract information on health attitudes and behaviors. *Journal of Applied Social Psychology, 17*(2), 533–553.

Rozenblum, R., Lisby, M., Hockey PM, Levtizion-Korach O, Salzberg CA, Lipsitz S, & Bates DW.(2011), Uncovering the blind spot of patient satisfaction: an international survey, *British Medical Journal (BMJ) Quality and Safety, 20*, 959-965.

Schwartz B. (2004), *The paradox of choice: Why more is less*, New York: Harper-Collins.

Sequist TD, Schneider EC, Anastario M, et al. (2008), Quality monitoring of physician: linking patients' experiences of care to clinical quality and outcomes, *Journal of General Internal Medicine, 23*(11), 1784-1790.

Tronvoll, B., Brown SW, Gremler DD & Edvardsson B. (2011),Paradigms in service research, *Journal of Service Management, 22*(5), 560 - 585

Tversky A, &Kahneman D. (1974), Judgment under uncertainty: Heuristics and biases, *Science, 185*(1457), 1124-1131.

Whitten, P, Mylod, D, Gavran, G, & Sypher, H. (2008), "Most wired hospitals: Rate patient satisfaction, *Communications of the ACM, 51* (4), 96-102.

Chapter 5

Managing Customer Relationship Quality in Hospitals

Miguel A. Moliner
Miguel A. López

LEARNING OBJECTIVES

Upon completing this chapter, you should be able to do the following:

1. To highlight the importance of customer orientation in hospital management.

2. To establish a hospital management model based on customer orientation.

3. To understand the concept of customer relationship quality and its components.

4. To identify the tools hospital managers have available for managing customer relationship quality.

KEYWORDS

customer orientation, relationship quality, satisfaction, trust, loyalty, perceived value, facilities, professionalism, service quality, price, non-monetary costs, emotional value, social value.

INTRODUCTION

The health system is one of the sectors with the greatest impact on developed societies. Its importance lies not only in the overwhelming social significance involved in managing such a critical service for human life but also the financial resources it manages and the number of employees it employs. For example, the World Health Organization (WHO) calculates that world health expenditure in 2005 was $4.4 trillion. This huge quantity of resources is managed by diverse organizations whose mission is taking care of health. The national health systems are organized differently, but at global level, it can be said that the health service is a public one. According to the WHO, the resources devoted to general government and social insurance account for 59 percent of total world spending, compared to 37 percent on private insurance and out-of-pocket expenses.

In practically all countries, public systems coexist with private systems, although there are considerable differences between nations. In Brazil, Egypt, India, Mexico, South Africa and USA, the private system accounts for more than 50 percent of total spending, while in France, Great Britain, Japan and Germany the private system accounts for less than 25 percent of the total in 2009 (Table 5.1).

Table 5.1	Private Expenditure on Health as % of Total Expenditure on Health (2009)						
Albania	58.8%	Cuba	7.3%	Kenya	56.7%	Saudi Arabia	37.6%
Argentina	37.6%	Democratic Republic Congo	55.3%	Luxembourg	16.0%	South Africa	56.2%
Australia	32.0%	Egypt	60.5%	Malaysia	44.3%	Spain	26.4%
Bangladesh	67.0%	France	22.1%	Mexico	51.6%	Sudan	72.5%
Bolivia	35.4%	Germany	23.1%	Namibia	45.0%	Sweden	18.5%
Brazil	56.4%	Guinea	91.8%	Nicaragua	45.2%	Turkey	24.9%
Burkina Faso	50.3%	Haiti	78.2%	Pakistan	65.2%	Ukraine	45.0%
Canada	29.4%	Honduras	33.7%	Paraguay	61.0%	United Kingdom	15.9%
Central African Republic	65.8%	India	69.7%	Poland	27.7%	USA	52.3%
China	47.5%	Italy	22.1%	Republic of Korea	41.8%	Zambia	41.4%
Colombia	28.9%	Japan	17.7%	Russian Federation	36.6%		

Source: Author's Presentation from WHO (2012)

Other data show the differences between countries: spending per capita on health services in the developed countries is more than $1,000, with per capita figures above $5,000 in the United States and Norway and less than $200 in China and most African countries (Table 5.2).

A significant characteristic of the health services sector is its importance at a macroeconomic level. The management of these resources is an important aspect that affects not only the basic good that is people's lives but also the management efficiency of a large quantity of economic and human resources.

Table 5.2	Total Health Expenditure per Capita 2009 (US$)							
Equatorial Guinea	804	USA	7960	Luxembourg	8262	Australia	3945
Botswana	581	Canada	4519	Norway	7533	Japan	3754
South Africa	521	Bahamas	1714	Switzerland	7185	New Zealand	2702
Namibia	297	Chile	802	France	4840	Republic of Korea	1184
Algeria	181	Argentina	734	Germany	4723	China	191
Congo	67	Brazil	734	United Kingdom	3440	India	44
Nigeria	67	Cuba	672	Italy	3323		
Central African Republic	18	Paraguay	147	Spain	3032		
Madagascar	18	Honduras	134	Turkey	575		
Democratic Republic Congo	17	Nicaragua	104	Russian Federation	476		
Ethiopia	16	Bolivia	90	Ukraina	200		
Eritrea	11	Haiti	40	Armenia	129		

Source: Author's Presentation from WHO (2012)

From a microeconomic point of view, concerning the management of an organization that runs health services, the first issue to bear in mind is the coexistence of public services with private services and the management implications of this. The main difference between public and private services lies in the fact that, while the former does not seek to make financial profits, the latter must be accountable to shareholders who demand a return on their investments. However, the most widespread trend at the moment considers that this different nature does not justify different management.

A second aspect to bear in mind is that the health service network usually has two levels of care. First there is a primary care service, which is more generalist, dealing with the most common diseases and making a preliminary diagnosis of more complex diseases. Second there is a specialized care service that can be offered by an independent network of health professionals who are specialists in a particular branch of health or that can be grouped in complex organizations offering an integrated specialized service. These multiservice organizations are hospitals. In the case of public hospitals, user satisfaction is part of the organizational mission, and in the case of private health services, income and profits are important but they, too, require a satisfactory customer relationship.

In this chapter we focus on hospitals. Complex hospitals are a key element in national health systems. The main objective of this chapter is to show how important it is for hospitals to maintain quality relationships with their clients and to identify the available tools for hospital managers to deliver value and improve customer relationship quality.

This chapter highlights the importance of hospitals' customer orientation. It highlights the importance of managing the quality of relationships as a condition of customer-oriented strategy, defining the three key elements to be monitored on a balanced score-board: commitment, trust, and satisfaction. It also describes the tools the hospital manager must employ to provide appropriate value to the patient that has a positive impact on relationship quality. In this sense, hospital managers should establish specific programs and actions related to facilities, professionalism of health personnel, perceived quality, monetary cost and nonmonetary costs, and emotional and social values.

THE IMPORTANCE OF HOSPITALS' CUSTOMER ORIENTATION

The importance of patient relationship quality in hospital management lies in the fact that it forms part of the essence of any health organization's mission, and also in the influence customer management exerts over outcomes. To achieve the objectives of any organization, it is necessary to care for customers and maintain customer orientation. Bigné, Moliner, and Sánchez (2005) demonstrated the existence of a causal relationship between market orientation and business results measured through profitability, sales growth, and marketing effectiveness. In the case of a hospital, this customer orientation has more important implications than it does for any other type of organization, as the customer's health has an incalculable value. It is impossible to imagine a hospital without users, or one that patients could not go to. Because of all this and regardless of their public or private nature, hospitals must put the user first in their priorities.

To help in understanding the relationship between customer management and financial results, Kaplan and Norton (2009) provided a good operational diagram when they established their balanced scoreboard proposal. This model identifies four groups of indicators any organization should establish to control the implementation of its strategy: financial, customer, internal business, and learning and growth. If a hospital invests in developing people and learning, its staff will be better able to carry out its internal processes, allowing it to achieve loyal and satisfied customers, leading to good financial outcomes. This sequence is clear for the case of a private hospital, where the financial results take the form of a growth in income or in profits. In the case of a public hospital, the financial results do not take the form of profit figures, but rather the achievement of financial sufficiency. None of this affects a hospital as it fulfils its mission to achieve loyal and satisfied customers.

Hospital customer orientation is therefore profitable. For hospitals, the concept of customer must be defined more precisely than for other multiservice organizations. Patients undoubtedly make up the principal public for a hospital, as they directly receive the diagnosis and treatment. But as the customers evaluate the services offered by a hospital, the people who accompany the customer exert a direct influence on the customer/patient. Those companions, either entirely or partially, have the same experience as the patient, and they also assess the service provision. The level of involvement of both stakeholders is high, and their perceptions feed off each other's evaluations. To appreciate the importance of the patient's companion, we can use two extreme examples. The first example is the case of a child, whose experience of hospital services is low, and the parent accompanying the child takes the initiative in the service. In another example, a patient with a serious illness cannot get out of bed. In this case, their companion assesses the services existing beyond the four walls of the room. This broad concept of a hospital customer is important when it comes to identifying the stakeholders, strategy, and specific action programs.

After making the broad definition of a hospital customer, we take a look at how to manage relationships between a hospital and its users. Figure 5.1 illustrates the causal relationship guiding the management logic of these relationships. Following Kaplan and Norton (2009), it is clear there is a direct relationship among customer management, financial results, and the hospital's mission. This chapter suggests that, to achieve the hospital's mission and financial outcomes, the hospital must achieve a high-quality relationship with its customers. Hospital relationship quality is measured through three variables: customer loyalty, customer trust, and customer satisfaction. These three variables should be incorporated into the hospitals' Balanced Scoreboards.

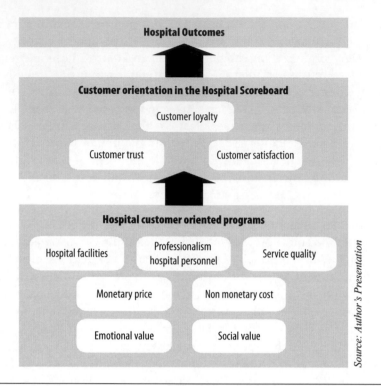

Figure 5.1 HOSPITAL CUSTOMER RELATIONSHIP QUALITY AND ITS ANTECEDENTS.

But, at a second level, it is necessary to establish programmes making it possible to affect these three indicators. The literature on perceived value makes an important contribution in this respect. Moliner (2009) compares the existence of causal relationships between the value perceived by a hospital customer and relationship quality. This means that, from a customer point of view, a hospital should be oriented towards setting up programmes that provide value for its customers. More specifically it is suggested that it should establish programmes taking seven aspects into account: hospital facilities, personnel professionalism, service quality, monetary cost, non-monetary costs, emotional value and social value. In the following pages, we will describe the details of this customer management model.

CUSTOMER RELATIONSHIP QUALITY IN THE HOSPITAL SCOREBOARD: OLD WORDS, NEW PARADIGM

The relationship established between two parties may take different forms, for example, a contract. This formula is widespread at the level of relationships in the hospital context where public and private insurance is taken out. Independent of the formal aspects that regulate a relationship, each participant in the exchange evaluates it him- or herself.

This evaluation is decisive for the continuity of the relationship; hospitals must be familiar with the key mechanisms that guide customer behavior. The concept of customer relationship quality is a reflection of customer's evaluation of the hospital's actions.

Relationship quality can be seen as a construct of other key components that reflect the nature of a relationship between hospitals and customers (Hennig-Thurau, Gwinner & Gremler, 2002). Gummeson (1987) considers *relationship quality* to be the quality of the interaction between a customer and a hospital, and it can be interpreted in terms of accumulated value.

The most recent literature agrees in identifying the components of relationship quality. For the case of a hospital, Moliner (2009) talks about customer satisfaction with the hospital, customer trust in the hospital, and customer loyalty to the hospital.

CUSTOMER SATISFACTION WITH THE HOSPITAL

According to the disconfirmation paradigm, *satisfaction* is a comparison of performance to expectations (Oliver, 1981). But, according to Oliver (1999), this is a definition based on what the customer does, and not on the psychological meaning of satisfaction. He therefore proposes that "satisfaction is defined as pleasurable fulfilment" (Oliver, 1999). That is, the customer senses that consumption fulfils some need, desire, or goal, and that this fulfilment is pleasurable. Thus, satisfaction is the patient's sense that hospital service provides outcomes against a standard of pleasure versus displeasure. This view of satisfaction reflects, on the one hand, its cognitive nature (comparing expectations against performance) and, on the other, its affective nature (associated feeling of pleasure). The level of satisfaction achieved by the customer is therefore a signal of the relationship's health (relationship quality).

Satisfaction's impact on hospital choice is particularly important (Kessler & Mylod, 2011). Hospitals with higher patient satisfaction scores have lower mortality rates and better process measures (Edlund, Young, Kung, Sherbourne, & Wells, 2003; Gesell, Clark, Mylod, Wolosin, & Drain, 2005; Jaipaul & Rosenthal, 2003). Satisfied patients are more likely to adhere to recommended treatment (Finkelstein, Harper, & Rosenthal, 1999) and less likely to sue for malpractice (Stelfox, Gandhi, Orav, & Gustafson, 2005). With respect to loyalty, patients say they would consider changing hospitals in response to satisfaction information (Boshoff & Gray, 2004; Sofaer, Crofton, Goldstein, Hoy, & Crabb, 2005), and probably would return to the hospital for treatment if they were satisfied (Garman, Garcia, & Hargreaves, 2004). Kessler and Mylod (2011) found a statistically significant link between patient satisfaction with the hospital and patient loyalty to the hospital.

Patient satisfaction is generated by their own experience with the hospital's service, but it is also influenced by their companion's satisfaction. While patients received a medical service that was important to them, their companions based their evaluations on more peripheral, but no less relevant, aspects. It is clear that the main reason for patient satisfaction is that their expectations of a cure for their disease have been fulfilled. In addition, an important emotional component depends not only on the patient's feelings but also on the feelings and evaluations of their companion. Companions often perceive details that patients do not consciously observe due to their concern for the technical aspects of the medical service.

In this sense, hospital managers must remember how important it is to measure the level of patient and companion satisfaction and to study their expectations. Mittal and Baldasare (1996) found that private hospitals that fail to meet patient expectations lose market share. These analyses undoubtedly enable hospitals to better adapt their services to customers' requirements. A final element that the hospital manager should bear in mind is the level of service at his or her hospital compared to other hospitals. The customer makes an evaluation based on comparisons with the similar experiences of others. The patient may make that comparison based on their own or a companion's personal experience or a third party may have told the patient of their experiences with another hospital. In this sense, it seems appropriate to compare the service level of one hospital against other, similar hospitals.

Patient's Loyalty to the Hospital

Customer loyalty is one of the elements most studied by organizations. Normally in consumer markets, customer loyalty is understood as repeat purchase behavior. Translating this concept to the hospital sphere is inappropriate, as customers do not go to a hospital of their own free will, but rather, because a need for medical service arises. We consider that, in this context, loyalty means the patient has a more or less favorable predisposition toward the hospital. This predisposition can take the form of choice of hospital at the time when the illness arises, positive comments that patients and companions share with third parties, and complaint behaviour and a willingness to forgive mistakes.

In the case of a private hospital, where there is freedom of choice and a direct payment is made for each visit, the hospital manager has a clear interest in developing loyal patients who choose the hospital when they need it, disseminate positive messages about it, and show understanding about mistakes (Anbori, Ghandi, Yadav, Daher, & Su, 2010). In the case of a public hospital, where the patient does not have freedom of choice and where hospital incomes derives from taxes, loyalty takes the form of positive messages and understanding when there are mistakes.

Ultimately, the hospital manager must understand customer loyalty as the patient or companion's level of commitment to the hospital. Morgan and Hunt (1994) consider that the commitment-trust pairing is the indivisible axis that leads to the efficiency, productivity, and effectiveness of relationships. The basis for maintaining relationships is the keeping of promises, such that if a promise is unfulfilled, the patient will not return to the hospital and the patient-hospital relationship will end (Moliner & Callarisa, 1997).

Some authors consider commitment to be the highest level of relational bond (Dwyer, Schürr, & Oh, 1987). The literature has established two dimensions of commitment: affective commitment and calculated or cognitive commitment (Geyskens, Steenkamp, Scheer, & Kumar, 1996; Wetzels, de Ruyter, & Van Birgelen, 1998). The former captures the emotional elements of commitment; the latter refers to a more rational analysis.

A patient's (and companion's) affective commitment is based on emotions, such as the feeling of belonging and respect for the hospital (Geyskens & Steenkamp, 1995). Numerous studies have shown that individuals remain in a relationship because positive feelings emerge that associate feelings of belonging with a high degree of respect for the other party (Geyskens & Steenkamp, 1995; Geyskens et al., 1996; Morgan & Hunt, 1994).

Patient's (and companion's) cognitive commitment is an exercise of economic calculation, and two types can be distinguished: negative and positive. A patient's cognitive commitment is negative when the relationship is maintained due to the costs and penalties associated with abandoning it (Young & Denize, 1997). As soon as alternatives appear, relationships based on negative commitment dissolve (Rusbult, 1980, 1983). A patient's commitment is positive if the motive for remaining in the relationship is the possibility of obtaining benefits. This commitment is said to be based on cognitive value (Rusbult, 1980).

PATIENT'S TRUST IN THE HOSPITAL

In addition to commitment, trust is the other key element the hospital must establish to maintain a long-term relationship (Morgan & Hunt, 1994). The patient must feel trust in the hospital, according to Morgan and Hunt (1994), as this is the basic element that permits the promises and relationships to be established and maintained. The patient's (and companion's) trust implies that the customer does not question the hospital and personnel's good intentions, that the promises made do not generate uncertainties in the patient, and that the communication between the parties is honest, open, and frequent (Czepiel, 1990).

At a general level, the patient's trust comprises two major dimensions: honesty (belief that the hospital will keep its word and has the capacity to do so, the staff are trustworthy and honest, and they have integrity and a good reputation) and benevolence (belief that the hospital and its personnel are interested in the patient's well-being) (Garbarino and Johnson, 1999; Morgan & Hunt, 1994). In this sense, patient trust is an affective construct because it is based on two dimensions with a strong emotional component.

MANAGING CUSTOMER RELATIONSHIP QUALITY THROUGH CUSTOMER VALUE PROGRAMS

Customer satisfaction, customer loyalty, and customer trust are three indicators the hospital manager must monitor, as a negative change in any of them could have a direct impact on the organization's results. In the case of a private hospital, financial outcomes can suffer immediately, because there are few costs associated with change. In the case of a public hospital, a negative change in an indicator can lead to a reduction in the hospital's subsidy in the medium and the long term. Neither of the two organizations would be aligned with the health organization's mission.

The question is: What tools does the hospital manager have to manage customer relationship quality? The literature establishes the necessity of managing the organization's value chain and, more specifically, establishing programs that provide value to patients and their companions.

Perceived value is the essential result of marketing activities and is a first-order element in relationship marketing (Oh, 2003; Ravald & Grönroos, 1996). Perceived value is understood as a construct configured by two parts, one of benefits received by the patient (economic, physical, social, and relationship) and another of sacrifices made (price, time, effort, risk, and convenience) (Bigné, Moliner and Callarisa, 2000; Cronin, Brady, Brand, Hightower, & Shemwell, 1997; Cronin, Brady, & Hult, 2000; Oh, 2003).

Regarding the elements that must be considered in perceived value management, by general consensus the functional factors include quality and price; the affective factors include feelings and social impact (Sánchez, Callarisa, Rodríguez, & Moliner, 2006; Sheth, Newman, & Gross, 1991a, 1991b). Starting from there, important efforts to test this theoretical proposal were made by Sweeney and Soutar (2001), who designed a measurement of perceived value (PERVAL).

On the basis of Sheth et al. (1991a, 1991b) and the PERVAL scale by Sweeney and Soutar (2001), Sánchez et al. (2006) developed the GLOVAL model, which identifies the perceived value elements. Based on this proposal, Moliner (2006, 2009) established the dimensions for hospital perceived value: hospital facilities, hospital personnel professionalism, service quality, monetary cost, non monetary costs, emotional value, and social value. Moliner (2009) found that the establishment of programmes to improve these dimensions has a direct impact on customer satisfaction, customer loyalty, customer trust, and therefore, on outcomes.

HOSPITAL FACILITIES

Facilities are an important element at several levels. On one hand, possessing technological medical equipment determines the possibilities of treating some diseases. Although most patients and their companions are incapable of assessing the technical value of the medical equipment, this does not prevent them making a subjective evaluation of it, either directly or indirectly, influenced by third parties. On the other hand, the facilities and the comfort they provide are another aspect assessed by both the patient and the companion. In this sense, it is appropriate to take care over elements related to hospital accommodation services, including everything from the cleanliness and comfort of the rooms to the catering service. Moliner (2009) points out the special care needed so that the facilities promote the consultation privacy; that are well organized and tidy; that are spacious, modern, and clean; and that are easy to find and to access with good transport links.

In Moliner's (2009) study, focused on Spanish hospitals, facilities were found to significantly influence customer relationship quality. In Spain, a large public hospital system coexists with a small private network of hospitals. In the case of public hospitals, Moliner (2009) noted that facilities significantly influenced patient satisfaction. In the case of private hospitals, the facilities not only influenced patient satisfaction, they also affected trust in the hospital. This suggests that well-maintained facilities makes a positive impression on the customer, which translates into greater trust, apart from the fact that the level of comfort generates satisfaction in the patient.

These findings indicate that designing modern and comfortable facilities and establishing internal processes that enables staff to keep them clean and well organized are important. Given the importance of clean facilities, the hospital is well advised to institute communication programs that allow the best use of hospital facilities, as they generate trust in potential patients and their companions.

PROFESSIONALISM OF HOSPITAL PERSONNEL

The doctor-patient relationship is technically known as an *agency relationship*; that is, there is asymmetry of information, as the doctor has some specialized knowledge that neither patients nor their companions have, so the latter are incapable of technically assessing the service received. The diagnosis and treatment of a disease are beyond the reach of the patient or companion, and they must trust in the doctor's competence and await the result of the treatment delivered.

Patients and their companions assess whether the medical staff and their assistants know their job well, are up-to-date in their knowledge, whether the advice provided by the staff has been very valuable, and whether the staff know about all the services offered by the hospital. This means the patients and companions indirectly assess the technical capability of the health staff and whether the diagnosis and treatment are appropriate.

In Moliner's (2009) study, the health staff's professionalism has a considerable effect on patient satisfaction regardless of the public or private nature of the hospital. The essence of the health service is understandably at the center of customer's evaluations. In the case of a private hospital, the health staff's professionalism directly influences patient trust. As with facilities, patients and their companions need indications that the hospital deserves their trust and that they have made the correct choice. Because of this, the hospital needs to carry out external communications with patients and their companions affecting the technical training of health staff.

Tortosa, Moliner, and Sánchez (2009) show that the employment satisfaction of health staff has a positive influence on the quality of the result (an appropriate diagnosis and treatment), which is the main indicator of patient satisfaction. The aim of this study was to analyze the importance of a hospital's internal market orientation, understood as internal communication management. The most important recommendation for hospital managers lies in the necessity to establish internal communication programs aimed at health staff, because communicating the organization's objectives and strategies generates job satisfaction.

Service Quality

The content of the health service is associated with the technical aspect and the diagnosis and treatment of the disease. Another aspect is how the service is offered, which is associated with empathy (the way the patient is treated), the hospital organization's capacity to respond, and the patient care processes and protocols. A hospital must identify the different moments of truth—the moments when a patient comes into contact with the organization by email or telephone or through personal attention. Diagnoses and treatments require patients to consult various specialized hospital services. The synchronization between patients and hospital becomes a key aspect for customer perceived quality. Thus, hospital management needs to study whether the services are well organized, whether quality is maintained throughout customer and companion relationships, whether the level of quality is acceptable compared to other hospitals, whether the staff are always kind and friendly, and whether the medical team provides an accurate diagnosis and treatment.

Moliner's (2009) study determined that, although service quality affects patient satisfaction, it fundamentally affects user trust. In light of this, hospital managers should set up programs to foster empathy for patients and deal with them in a friendly way. Managers should also design a process map that allows a continuous coordination among the specialized services. These actions are necessary because the health staff are the main agents in service quality management. Along these lines, Tortosa, Moliner, and Sánchez (2009) highlighted the fact that, when internal communication programs are established, they generate greater job satisfaction among hospital (not only health) staff, which results in a higher quality of patient/companion interaction. The importance of the interpersonal component of private hospital service quality was confirmed in other studies (Anbori et al., 2010).

Monetary Cost

Monetary cost is one aspect that affects patient's evaluation of a service. Obviously, price has an economic component, involving the money payment the patient must make for the health service received. In the case of a public hospital, payment is made indirectly through taxes or with public insurance. In the case of a private hospital, payment is made via private insurance or directly to the hospital. But cost also has a psychological component. In the case of a complex product or service that is difficult for the customer to value, the monetary cost becomes an indicator of service quality: the customer usually associates a high price with high quality. The price issue is not exclusively the issue of the hospital as, to make a more accurate analysis, private or public insurance should be considered.

Patients and their companions also assess such aspects as whether the money spent is fully justified, whether the service is worth the cost, and whether the financial cost is high or not.

Moliner (2009) found that, for private hospitals, monetary cost is a particularly important evaluation criterion in patient satisfaction. In the case of public hospitals financed through taxation or public insurance systems, the user's perception of the monetary cost is that it is a free service. Because of this, private (and private insurance) hospitals could establish loyalty programs with discounts for patients who repeatedly choose the hospital when they need a health service. In the case of a public hospital financed through taxation or public insurance, discount programs make no sense.

Nonmonetary Costs

The literature on services has identified a series of nonmonetary costs that affect service evaluation and that, in the case of hospitals, appear frequently. These nonmonetary costs involve expenditures of time and effort as well as psychological costs. Most nonmonetary costs are associated with waiting lists to access a medical professional. Not only is there a time cost, a psychological state of anxiety is generated in patients and their companions when the wait is considered too long (Liu et al., 2010).

It is not easy to manage waiting patients because it is almost impossible to forecast demand. A hospital can move from a quiet state to overcrowded in a few minutes, and these crises are difficult to manage without requiring less urgent cases to wait. The only solution is to have an excessively large staff available to deal with any eventuality, but this is not a viable solution. The hospital manager must design adaptable and flexible processes while studying the points in time when demand historically rises or falls. This does not guarantee a reduction in waiting lists, but it can mitigate them to some degree.

The literature on queue (waiting list) management stresses the importance of offering patients and their companions information to reduce their anxiety and the negative feelings generated by uncertainty (Liu et al., 2010).

Emotional Value

The feelings of patients and their companions are present in any evaluation of the hospital and the services received. Emotional involvement is high because what is at stake is so important. This high level of emotional involvement leads to the emergence of positive and negative feelings that greatly affect the perception of the value and quality of the relationship. The generation of positive feelings by hospital staff (relaxation, understanding) or negative feelings (hassle, dislike, powerlessness) has a great deal to do with the staff's verbal and nonverbal communication, as well as the details of the different moments of truth (encounters between patients and staff) (ibid., 2010). This can be summed up in one question: did the patient and the companion like the hospital experience?

Emotional value entirely affects relationship quality, as it leads to satisfaction, trust and commitment from patients and their companions. The positive or negative feelings generated during the hospital service experience have a high level of influence on patient loyalty. Even, the effect of satisfaction with hospitalization experience to patient's loyalty would be larger than overall satisfaction's effect (Kessler & Mylod, 2011).

There are no programs for managing emotional value beyond staff incentive systems and training programs, as patient and companion feelings are the result of all the hospital programs. This does not mean that hospital managers must not take user's emotions into account. It is essential that the generation of user's emotional value is present in all hospital programmes, particularly those aimed at managing moments of truth.

Social Value

Fishbein and Ajzen (1975) consider that people's behavior is determined by two fundamental factors: a personal or attitude factor and a social or normative factor. The *social factor*, which we call social value, refers to the influence of the social environment on behavior. Social value is the perception of what the companion and other people important to the patient think about what the patient should or should not do with respect to the hospital service (Dick & Basu, 1994). When a person feels unwell for a while, family members or friends often pressure that person to visit a specialist or a hospital. Some people consult acquaintances about an ailment they have shared. In these conversations, comments and suggestions are made about the best specialist or best hospital for treating the disease. Human beings are social and much of their behavior is guided by the family and friends environment.

The choice of a hospital and the evaluation of the service received are usually mentioned by people close to the patient, who make positive or negative evaluations of the health experience. Individuals or reference groups important to the patient may like or dislike some aspects of the hospital service, which can lead to psychological rewards or penalties for family and friends. The patient's personality moderates the importance of the social factor and reference groups, as some people are more sensitive to others' comments and evaluations and other people are immune to others' opinions.

Hospital managers can try to influence the social environment, for example, through a marketing plan that views community and former patients as among the hospital's important stakeholders. Just as important is establishing a specific policy concerning companions, with a strategy especially designed for them while they are at the hospital, and carrying out post-service follow-up with companions. Finally, in relation to the impact on community, branding helps to generate reputable brands that usually achieve a good social evaluation and, therefore, a positive image and social opinion.

CONCLUSIONS

Throughout this chapter we have tried to demonstrate the need for hospital managers to incorporate customer relationship quality indicators into the hospital Balanced Scoreboard. High levels of satisfaction, trust, and loyalty from patients and their companions are translated into good financial outcomes. That means a hospital must adopt a customer orientation, analyzing the expectations and perceptions of patients and their companions and making decisions based on this information. High levels of satisfaction means that patients, with all their emotional and social needs, must become the focus of hospital strategy, regardless of whether the hospital is public or private.

For the customer relationship management model presented, it is proposed that management undertake specific programs to provide patients and their companions with value. Several specific programs have been proposed that should form part of an integrated strategy.

One program should be based on the constant care and maintenance of facilities, which not only influence customer satisfaction but also generate trust.

A second program should be to design internal processes that enabling management to coordinate the hospital's services and specialities so that all moments of truth (contact between customer and staff) are satisfactory and require minimum costs in terms of the patient's time.

A third program should focus on staff, promoting continuous professional training and individual customer orientation (empathy, likeability). Along these lines, health staff selection should focus on professional training as well as on emotional intelligence and customer orientation.

A fourth program should focus on marketing, integrating an internal communication plan and an external communication plan. The former should translate the hospital's objectives and strategies to all staff, to align them with institutional objectives and promote greater job satisfaction. With the latter (external) communication, the idea should be to generate a positive social image of the hospital. This should be integrated into a branding strategy based on the most important attributes of the hospital, which will generate social reputation.

Programs should not focus exclusively on functional elements, but should also pay special attention to affective factors. The feelings generated in the patient during the service experience are caused fundamentally by relationships with the hospital and the contact personnel. It is therefore necessary, not only to care for the intangible aspects of the hospital services, but also to ensure that contact personnel show empathy.

REVIEW QUESTIONS

1. Insurance organizations are the third pillar of the health system. They control the care team and collect insurance premiums from users. How do the insurance companies affect the quality/price relationship perceived by patients?

2. A hospital's hiring practices vary among countries. In some cases, the staff are public employees and in others they are hired based on goals. How do you think this labour contract affects the health staff in terms of their professionalism and the quality of service they offer users?

3. Quality measurement and perceived value are essential to properly managing the relationship quality. In the case of a hospital, with multiple services, how do you think customer relationship quality could be measured? What about customer perceived value?

4. Patients' companions play an important role in evaluating the hospital experience. However, their expectations are not normally studied. Suggest a methodology for studying companions' expectations.

REFERENCES

Anbori, A., Ghandi, S. N., Yadav, H., Daher, A. M., & Su, T. T. (2010). Patient satisfaction and loyalty to the private hospitals in Sana'a, Yemen. *International Journal for Quality in Health Care, 22*(4), 310–315.

Bigné, J. E., Moliner, M. A., & Callarisa, L. J. (2000). El valor y la fidelización de clientes: una propuesta de modelo dinámico de comportamiento. *Revista Europea de Dirección y Economía de la Empresa, 9*(3), 65–78.

Bigné, J. E., Moliner, M. A., & Sánchez, J. (2005). El enfoque cultural de la orientación al mercado y los resultados empresariales. El efecto moderador del entorno. *Cuadernos de Economía y Dirección de Empresas, 23*, 139–164.

Boshoff, C., & Gray, B. (2004). The relationships between service quality, customer satisfaction, and buying intentions in the private hospital industry. *South African Journal of Business Management, 35*(4), 27–37.

Cronin, J., Jr, Brady, M., Brand, R. R., Hightower, R., Jr. & Shemwell, D. J. (1997). A cross-sectional test of the effect and conceptualization of service value. *Journal of Services Marketing, 11*(6), 375–393.

Cronin J., Jr., Brady, M., & Hult, T. (2000). Assessing the effects of quality, value, and customer satisfaction on consumer behavioral intentions in service environments. *Journal of Retailing, 76*(2), 193–218.

Czepiel, J. A. (1990). Service encounters and service relationships: Implications for research. *Journal of Business Research, 20*(1), 13–21.

Dick, A & Basu, K. (1994). Customer Loyalty: Toward an Integrated Conceptual Framework. *Journal of Academy of Marketing Science, 22* (2), 99-113.

Dwyer, F. R., Schürr, P. H., & Oh, S. (1987). Developing buyer-seller relationship. *Journal of Marketing, 51*(April), 11–27.

Edlund, M. J., Young, A. S., Kung, F. Y., Sherbourne, C. D., & Wells, K. B. (2003). Does satisfaction reflect the technical quality of mental health care? *Health Services Research, 38*(2), 631–645.

Finkelstein, B. S., Harper, D. L., & Rosenthal, G. E. (1999). Patient assessments of hospital maternity care: A useful tool for consumers? *Health Services Research, 34*(2), 623–640.

Fishbein, M., & Ajzen, I. (1975). *Belief, attitude, intention, and behavior: An introduction to theory and research*. Reading, MA: Addison-Wesley.

Garbarino, E., & Johnson, M. K. (1999). The different roles of satisfaction, trust and commitment in customer relationships. *Journal of Marketing, 63*(April), 70–87.

Garman, A. N., Garcia, J., & Hargreaves, M. (2004). Patient satisfaction as a predictor of return-to-provider behavior: Analysis and assessment of financial implications. *Quality Management in Health Care, 13*(1), 75–80.

Gesell, S. B., Clark, P. A., Mylod, D. E., Wolosin, R. J., & Drain, M. (2005). Hospital level correlation between clinical and service quality performance for heart failure treatment. *Journal for Healthcare Quality, 27*(6), 33–44.

Geyskens, I. & Steenkamp, J. B. (1995). An investigation into the joint effects of trust and interdependence on relationship commitment. *24th Annual EMAC Conference Proceedings*, Paris, 351–371.

Geyskens, I., Steenkamp, J. B., Scheer, L., & Kumar, N. A (1996). Effects of trust and interdependence on relationship commitment. *International Journal of Research in Marketing, 51*, 303–318.

Hennig-Thurau, Th., Gwinner, K. P., & Gremler, D. D. (2002). An integration of relational benefits and relationship quality. *Journal of Service Research, 4*(3), 230–247.

Jaipaul, C. K., & Rosenthal, G. E. (2003). Do hospitals with lower mortality have higher patient satisfaction? A regional analysis of patients with medical diagnoses. *American Journal of Medical Quality, 18*(2), 59–65.

Kaplan, R. S., & Norton, D. P. (2009). *El cuadro de mando integral* (3rd ed.). Barcelona: Ed. Gestión, Barcelona (Spain)

Kessler, D. P. & Mylod, D. (2011). Does patient satisfaction affect patient loyalty? *International Journal of Health Care Quality Assurance, 24*(4), 266–273.

Liu, S. S., Franz, D., Allen, M., Chang, E. C., Janowiak, D., Mayne, P. & White, R. (2010). ED services: The impact of caring behaviors on patient loyalty. *Journal of Emergency Nursing, 36*(5), 404–414.

Mittal, V., & Baldasare, P. M. (1996). Eliminate the negative. Managers should optimize rather than maximize performance to enhance patient satisfaction. *Journal of Health Care Marketing, 16*, 24–31.

Moliner, M. A. (2006). Hospital perceived value. *Health Care Management Review, 31*(4), 1–9.

Moliner, M. A. (2009). Loyalty, perceived value, relationship quality & agency theory. *Journal of Service Management, 20*(1), 76–97.

Moliner M. A.. & Callarisa, L. J. (1997). El marketing relacional o la superación del paradigma transaccional. *Revista Europea de Dirección y Economía de la Empresa, 6*(2), 67–80.

Morgan, R. M., & Hunt, S. D. (1994). The commitment-trust theory of relationship marketing. *Journal of Marketing, 58*(July), 20–38.

Oh, H. (2003). Price fairness and its assymmetric effects on overall price, quality, and value judgements: The case of an upscale hotel. *Tourism Management, 24*, 241–249.

Oliver, R. (1999). Whence consumer loyalty? Journal of Marketing, 63, 33–45.

Oliver, R. L. (1981). Measurement and evaluation of satisfaction processes in retail setting. *Journal of Retailing, 57*, 25–48.

Ravald, A., & Grönroos, C. (1996). The value concept and relationship marketing. European *Journal of Marketing, 30*(2), 19–30.

Rusbult, C. E. (1980). Commitment and satisfaction in romantic associations: A test of the investiment model. *Journal of Experimental Social Psychology, 16*, 172–186.

Rusbult, C. E. (1983). A longitudinal test of the investment model: The development (and deterioration) of satisfaction and commitment in heterosexual involvements. *Journal of Personality and Social Psychology, 45*(1), 101–117.

Sánchez, J., Callarisa, L., Rodríguez, R. M., & Moliner, M. A. (2006). Perceived value of the purchase of a tourism product. *Tourism Management, 27*(3), 394–409.

Sheth, J. N., Newman, B. I., & Gross, L. G. (1991a). *Consumption values and market choice.* Cincinnati: South Western Publishing.

Sheth, J. N., Newman, B. I., & Gross, B. L. (1991b). Why we buy what we buy: A theory of consumption values. *Journal of Business Research, 22*, 159–170.

Sofaer, S., Crofton, C., Goldstein, E., Hoy, E., & Crabb, J. (2005). What do consumers want to know about the quality of care in hospitals. *Health Services Research, 40* 6(Part II), 2019–2036.

Stelfox, H., Gandhi, T., Orav, E., & Gustafson, M. (2005). The relationship of patient satisfaction with complaints against physicians and malpractice lawsuits. *American Journal of Medicine, 118*(10), 1126–1133.

Sweeney, J. C., & Soutar, G. (2001). Consumer perceived value: The development of multiple item scale. *Journal of Retailing, 77*(2), 203–220.

Tortosa, V., Moliner, M. A., & Sánchez, J. (2009). Internal market orientation and its influence on the organisational result. *European Journal of Marketing, 43*(11/12), 1435–1456.

Wetzels, M., de Ruyter, K., & Van Birgelen, M. (1998). Marketing service relationships: The role of commitment. *Journal of Business & Industrial Marketing, 13*(4/5), 406–423.

WHO (2012), *World Health Statistics 2012*, World Health Organization Press, Geneve (Switzeland)

Young, L., & Denize, S. (1997). *Towards measuring commitment in business service relationships.* (Working Paper). Sydney: School of Marketing, University of Technology.

Chapter 6

The Effect of Servicescape on Customers' Wellness Experience

Hyeyoon Choi
Kathryn Stafford

LEARNING OBJECTIVES

Upon completing this chapter, you should be able to do the following:

1. Compare and contrast similarities and differences between traditional health care and wellness health care.

2. Explain the meaning of the term *servicescape* and its importance within a health and wellness care setting.

3. Explain why customer experience is important in the health and wellness industry.

4. Explain why service orientation and customer focus have become central to the health and wellness industry.

KEYWORDS

servicescape, health and wellness experience, health and wellness care, service orientation, customer focus, physical evidence

INTERDEPENDENCY OF HEALTH AND WELLNESS

The burden of risk factors of having a disease is becoming so great that it is now being referred to as a health "crisis." Society bombards citizens with health-related warnings about lives full of stress and high tension, people gaining too much weight with high cholesterol, and not enough sleep and exercise (Joppe, 2010). For example, stress has been estimated as the cause for 50–70 percent of all types of illnesses, such as heart disease, diabetes or depression, to name a few (Ciarrochi, Dean, & Anderson, 2002;

Frese, 1985). At the same time, people are living in a polluted society where there is always a risk to clean water and air, and with an abundance of sugar-, salt-, and fat-laden foods (Joppe, 2010). All these factors have made Americans anxious, if not paranoid, about potential health risks (ibid., 2010).

This is where the concept of "worried well" comes in. People who are worried well are especially concerned about their health, and are always seeking reassurance (Lipsitt, 1982). In other words, this term refers to those who are healthy, yet are worried about becoming ill, so they engage in every possible action to be healthy, even when being cautious is unnecessary. One reason for the rise of this particular concept is the realization that the current health care system focuses more on elimination and management of particular illnesses than the promotion of overall health.

In a postmodern world, people increase their demand for longevity and healthy lifestyles (Gustavo, 2010). In response, the health care industry is innovatively changing its service delivery (Lee, 2011). According to the World Health Organization, health is now defined as a preventive way of life that reduces, and even eliminates, the need for a cure (Joppe, 2010). A new preventive health market has emerged that offers new health and wellness services (Gustavo, 2010).

The concept of wellness was coined by the American doctor Halbert Dunn in 1959 (Mueller & Kaufmann, 2000). So far, compared to the term *health*, the term *wellness* has been too broad. It has been noted that the term wellness is generally used without adequate clarification or clear articulation (Cameron, Mathers, & Parry, 2006).While the term wellness lacks an exact definition due to diverse opinions and interpretations, regardless, almost invariably the term wellness has its core value embedded in the holistic approach to health as a means to cure various illnesses (Erfurt-Cooper & Cooper, 2009). More specifically, the term wellness closely relates to health promotion and primary prevention by striving for a healthy and natural lifestyle by engaging in a variety of activities (Schuster, Dobson, Jauregui, & Blanks, 2004). These active health seekers have shown interests in holistic approach to informed health promotion, education and nutrition. One thing about which researchers agree is that the optimum level of wellness is derived from a balance of wellness in the body, the mind, and the spirit (Kelly, 2010). Wellness care is now regarded as a sub-category of health care.

However, it should be noted that incorporation of wellness within health care substantially changes the traditional concept of health care. In the past, health care service providers have been only concerned with curing the illness occurred with limited input from customers (Joppe, 2010). The term *customer* is used in this chapter to refer to patients and their families. Now, however, customers are taking control of their own well-being and preventing occurrence of the disease in the first place by living a healthier life (ibid., 2010). In other words, the main difference between traditional health customers and wellness customers is that while the former deals with sick people, the latter generally refers to healthy ones, who still seek therapies to maintain this state of wellbeing.

The concept of wellness emphasizes the personal responsibility for managing one's own quality of life (ibid., 2010). The growing public concern about the quality of health care is also contributing to this phenomenon (Mahon, 1996). The role of customers is changing from passive recipients of health and wellness care to active health and wellness customers (Laschinger et al. 2005; Tzeng & Katefian, 2002). Today's customers of health and wellness services are better educated and have more knowledge than the past customers (Andaleeb, 1998). The abundance of wellness-related marketing information and other published literature through the mass media, books, and magazines has reflected this (Erfurt-Cooper & Cooper, 2009). These ever-increasing health and wellness information supplies have made health seekers even more conscious of the long-term benefits of maintaining personal health. These customers know more clearly what they need and want than in the past. According to Kurz and Wolinsky (1985), customers are relying less on doctors when deciding on a hospital. This phenomenon has led customers to be more involved in the decision-making process, thus creating more customer-driven service. Accordingly, this shift in the composition of health care customers and changing customer behavior will require health and wellness organizations to expand their service offerings to meet the diverse needs and expectations of wellness customers.

The changing composition of health care customers is already reflected in the growth of holistic medicine. Many health professionals view health from a holistic perspective and take an approach that incorporates traditional and alternative medicine (Synovitz & Larson, 2013). As an alternative venue to optimize health and wellness, many American adults venture away from standard biomedicine, employing outside biomedical therapies, referred to as complementary and alternative medicine (CAM) (D'Crus & Wilkinson, 2005; Schuster, Dobson, Jauregui, & Blanks, 2004). While the term *alternative medicine* refers to treatments that work as a substitute for conventional therapies, *complementary medicine* implies that the two are used in conjunction (Druss & Rosenheck, 1999).

Interest in unconventional therapies in both the scientific literature and the press has increased exponentially during the past few decades (Jonas, 1998). CAM customers are considered as active health care participants who are wellness oriented (Vincent & Furnham, 1996). Not only does CAM help to alleviate symptoms with minimal side effects, but more important, the fact that the doctors in the traditional health care setting only spend no more than 8–12 minutes per patient brought a rise in the complementary therapies. Customers want to feel cared for, listened to, and supported, and complementary therapies have been the perfect solution to address these needs. When the traditional treatment is compared to 20 minutes or more of a hands-on CAM therapy, it is more likely that customers will feel truly cared for with CAM treatments. It is becoming more evident that wellness customers would rather spend money on modalities that give one-on-one attention and caring.

For example, Europe has long been a popular health and wellness destination. Among European countries, Germany is especially renowned. In Germany, it is mandatory for the medical doctors to undergo a specialized post-medical education that combines the discipline of balneology, climatology, and natural therapies (Frost, 2004). This is to promote the use of natural therapies before relying on medical drugs (ibid., 2004). In addition, the role of European insurance companies paying for cure-related spa vacation stays since the 1960s has shown noticeable results. The benefits show a 60 percent drop in sick days, 66 percent decrease in prescription drug consumption, in addition to long-term mental, physical, emotional, and spiritual improvements that cannot be overlooked (ibid., 2004).

Relative to the long-term successful wellness intervention in European countries, the United States, on the other hand, is still in the beginning stage. Despite the advantage of rich natural resources and a variety of climates in the United States (Kovacs, 1945), it is only recently that much attempt has been made to demonstrate the curative features of wellness treatments (McNeil & Ragins, 2005). In the United States, one example is Clifton Springs Hospital and Clinic in New York City. Clifton Springs Hospital and Clinic is a local hospital that incorporates CAM into conventional medicine.

Traditionally, health care services had their emphasis mainly on the functional delivery of the service. Now, as can be evidenced in CAM treatments, the emphasis has shifted toward creating health and wellness service environments that are psychologically supportive. In this sense, service orientation and customer focus are especially important in a health and wellness care environment because customers are part of the service production process. The degree of customers' engagement in the health and wellness care facility and service providers can affect the service outcome. The more engaged the customers are, the more likely the organization is to meet customers' needs, leading to the beneficial outcome of health and wellness service (Bitner, Faranda, Hubbert, & Zeithaml, 1997). Therefore, the health care firms should focus on service orientation and customer focus techniques to satisfy their customers (Bowen, Siehl, & Schneider, 1989).

A customer focus means putting customers at the heart of an organization's service (Nwankwo, 1995). Being service-oriented organizations, the health and wellness industry cannot neglect customers' perceptions of service relative to provider performance, service quality, and service environment (Brady & Cronin, 2001). After all, it is the service that attracts customers to these health and wellness organizations and, therefore, customer focus is a crucial aspect of business profitability (Diamantopoulos & Hart, 1993). It is vital for health and wellness organizations to adopt a customer focus to become more committed to quality service, ease of service delivery, and an efficiently designed work environment (Dienhart, Gregoire, Downey, & Knight, 1992).

Not only this, health and wellness organizations are realizing the importance of service orientation. In a health and wellness care setting, total customer care is a combination of technical and nontechnical (social) skills (Hogan, Hogan, & Busch, 1984). Service orientation is a nontechnical aspect, referring to set of attitudes and behaviors that influence the quality of the interaction between health and wellness care service providers and customers (ibid., 1984). The experience may depend on the quality of customer engagement during the whole process (Prahalad, 2004). To be service oriented generally refers to those employees who are pleasant, attentive, and responsive to customer's needs as a way to achieve better customer service (Dienhart et al., 1992). All these aspects of service orientation relate to overall customer care quality as the degree of service orientation highly impacts customers' perceptions of service (ibid., 1992).

The goal of health and wellness organizations should be to make customers feel that they are getting appropriate care from service-oriented providers. Health and wellness organizations implementing this perspective bring about greater customer satisfaction (Bowen et al., 1989). The presence of these techniques when delivering service helps customers believe that the service they receive is accountable, efficient, and more important, a value for their money (Smith, 2003). Not only can service orientation and customer focus create a competitive advantage, but can be carefully implemented as a business strategy (Albrecht & Zemke, 1984). Day and Wensley (1988) contend that these are not optional, but compulsory. To remain competitive, health and wellness service providers must continuously strive to differentiate their offerings to provide a unique overall experience for their customers (Berry, Carbone, & Haeckel, 2002; Morrison, Gan, Dubelaar, & Oppewal, 2011).

GROWING AWARENESS OF HEALTH AND WELLNESS EXPERIENCE

Marketing professionals are now studying the concept of "experience." In fact, creating an optimal experience for customers seems to be one of the most important marketing strategies in today's service environment (Verhoef et al., 2009). When customers purchase products or services, the customers have an experience, whether it is good, bad, or indifferent (Berry et al., 2002). *Customer experience* refers to the outcomes of relationships among organizations, systems, service employees, and customers (Bitner et al., 1997). These experiences are strictly personal and dependent on customers' involvement at different levels (Gentile, Spiller, & Noci, 2007).

Health and wellness organizations recognize the relevance of customer experience in creating value for their customers (Berry et al., 2002). The role of the health and wellness service providers is to meet customers' needs and to understand what customers expect and experience in providers' facilities. More so than other health customers, wellness customers no longer want mere products or services; rather, they seek an optimal experience (Trauer, 2004). As the number of interactions between the service provider and the customer increases, the more important the experience aspect of the service becomes (Gentile et al., 2007). For example, a customer who considers interpersonal elements important visits a health care organization repeatedly for allergies or weight gain. Yet during the visit, a busy health care service provider may only take the time to focus on the appropriate treatment of the symptoms, neglecting the personal interaction. Such an experience can influence the customer's purchase decisions, as well as their preferences (ibid., 2007).

The key lies in the organization's effectiveness in managing the experience. Indeed, the focus on "customer experience" evolved over time. In the past, research practitioners in various disciplines such as retailing, marketing, and service management had never previously regarded customer experience as a distinct construct (Verhoef et al., 2009). However, since the plateau of marketing core products in terms of tangible differentiation in the 1970s, the focus shifted to services and, later, to relationships. It was not until the late 1980s that the concept of experience evolved, acting as a differentiator when relationships ceased to be a competitive market edge. In what is referred to as the "progression of economic value", "experience" emerged as the next step after commodities, goods, and services (Gentile et al., 2007).

Today, health and wellness service delivery is increasingly competitive and is reflected by proliferating of health and wellness care services (Gustavo, 2010). It is important for health and wellness organizations to understand what contributes to customers' experiences when they receive care, because these experiences and perceptions of care have a significant impact on managing and healing an illness (Institute of Medicine, 2001). Customer experience is widely used as a measure of evaluating the performance of health and wellness organizations. Customers judge their total experience by comparing their experiences with their expectations. Influential factors consist of interpersonal care, technical quality of care, convenient access, competence, finances, physical environment, availability of providers and resources, and desirable outcomes (Mahon, 1996).

However, note that health and wellness organizations do not sell the actual experience. Rather, their role is to provide the appropriate environment and setting so the optimal customer experiences can emerge. Then, it is up to the customers to cocreate their individual experiences with the organization. An increasing number of health and wellness organizations, such as Kaiser Permanente and Mayo Clinic, have demonstrated the practice of providing service in a way that enhances the value of the customer experience (Brown, 2008).

The health and wellness industry is considered as one of those service industries that provides a multidimensional experience (Gentile et al., 2007). A wellness experience is an outcome shaped by numerous interactions between the firm and the customer, referred to as *service encounter* (Bitner, Booms, & Tetreault, 1990). A good experience does not only come from one point of encounter. The health and wellness industry is one of those domains where the experience formation is complex due to multifactorial points of encounter. These include relationships with health and wellness service providers, the physical environment, and the healthcare organization itself (Johansson, Oleni, & Fridlund, 2002). Not only this, health and wellness service is constantly altered and shaped by different aspects of service, such as admission, nurse-patient encounters, physician-patient encounters, housekeeping, food service, technical services (e.g., x-rays), and discharge. These, in turn, influence overall customer satisfaction.

The success or failure of a health and wellness organization will be based upon how customers evaluate health and wellness service such as patient satisfaction and patient outcomes (Mahon, 1996). Customers want validation of their experiences, emotional support, and care. During the many points of encounter a customer experiences, it is not surprising that customer satisfaction is multidimensional. For example, customers might be satisfied with the treatment itself, but not with the environment in which the treatment was provided. Therefore, the overall hospital experience plays an essential role in customer satisfaction. To actively respond to this issue, companies must understand the customer's entire process, from their initial expectations to the end of the experience when they make their assessment (Berry et al., 2002).

Two main components comprise the customer experience (ibid., 2002). First is the actual consumption of goods or services. The second deals with emotions, and includes sounds, aromas, tastes, sights, and touches of the product or service, as well as the surrounding environment. Emotions encompass subjective characteristics, such as cheerfulness. Therefore, emotional cues are crucial to the customer experience and work in conjunction with functional cues (ibid., 2002). It is only when all points of encounter meet the customer's expectations that the experience is satisfactory (ibid., 2002). Not only is the relationship between service providers and customers important, but the environment also plays a major role in enhancing the experience (Turley & Chebat, 2002). Providing a pleasant atmosphere is one way to customize the environment (Baker, Levy, & Grewal, 1992). In fact, some health and wellness organizations' satisfaction surveys show that the environment plays a crucial role in the total health care experience (Fottler, Ford, Roberts, Ford, & Spears, 2000). The environment is the first impression customers receive, even before the service experience, providing the first impression (ibid., 2000).

In other words, everything perceived or sensed in the environment contributes to each experience cue (Berry et al., 2002). The product and service offered provide one set of cues, and the physical environment provides another. For example, a clean, safe, and user-friendly environment significantly adds to the quality of a healthcare experience (Fottler, et al., 2000). The environment is also known to influence the customer's mood. Therefore, it is when all the cues are combined that they make up the customer's total experience (Berry et al., 2002).

Then, what specific role does the environment play in terms of deriving an optimal health care experience? The recent interest and concern of the health and wellness organizations to enhance customers' experiences have led to putting more emphasis on designing on environment to promote the healing process (Devlin, 2003). Bitner, Booms, & Mohr (1992) refers to the built environment as the servicescape, the physical environment in which services take place. The role of the servicescape is more than being aesthetically appealing; it accounts for the level of comfort as well (Wakefield & Blodgett, 1994). This customer-focused health and wellness care has become a driving force for health and wellness organizations' servicescape design (Lee, 2011). Consequently, understanding physical environmental stimuli in health and wellness care would lead health and wellness care facilities to create a better environment that positively affects the healing and well-being of customers; thereby creating for customers the optimal experience of the health and wellness service organization.

THE ROLE OF SERVICESCAPES IN FORMING CUSTOMERS' HEALTH CARE EXPERIENCES

Evidence from previous literature shows that customers expect more than mere quality of health and wellness service. A relationship exists between a customer outcome and what a customer wants in an environment (Ulrich, 2001). Indeed, due to the simultaneous occurrence of production and consumption, the supporting role of the environment becomes part of the service itself (Fottler, et al., 2000). The environment in which the customer experiences the service is one of the key components that plays a crucial role in forming the service experience (Bitner, et al., 1992). Because the place where the service is provided is open to customers, the place counts as one aspect of their entire experience, making a strong impact on the customer's overall perception (ibid., 1992; Parish, Berry, & Lam, 2008). Value is provided not only in terms of products and services, but also by creating a pleasant atmosphere (Dawson, Bloch, & Ridgway, 1990). This can be done by manipulating the environment (Turley & Chebat, 2002).

The physical environment's influence on the health and wellness experience is not a new phenomenon. Florence Nightingale began her nursing career in 1845. In her seminal book, *Notes on Nursing*, she mentioned the importance of health care environmental issues, such as windows, light, plants, music, furnishings, walls, and color (Nightingale, 1859/1969). Despite this early recognition, the health and wellness industry has only recently begun to emphasize this issue.

Due to the intangible nature of service, customers often depend on physical evidence when evaluating service (Zeithaml & Bitner, 1996). Physical evidence is composed of an organization's physical facility and the other tangible aspects (ibid., 1996). Physical evidence is also referred to as the servicescape (ibid., 1996). Specifically, the servicescape comprises exterior attributes such as parking, signage, and landscape, and interior attributes such as layout, design, décor, and equipment. However, these examples indicate that the servicescape needs to work synergistically with functional cues to produce a good customer experience (Berry et al., 2002).

Among service industries, especially health and wellness service communicates heavily through physical evidence. For example, a hospital building has many floors, consisting of rooms and various equipment. The design of the health and wellness care setting is an important component of the healing experience (Fottler, et al., 2000). Complex functions are performed within the physical facility every day (Bitner, et al., 1992). Most customers come to health and wellness care organizations distressed, concerned, and anxious (Lee, 2011). Among the constant complaints about health and wellness organizations were the lack of privacy, noise, lack of nice view outside a window, and confusing way-finding cues (Ulrich, 1992). These problems can be remediated by carefully designing the physical environment and creating the servicescape (Edvardsson, Enquist, & Johnston, 2005). While a superior healing-promoting environment reinforces positive feelings regarding the health and wellness service quality, an unfamiliar environment only worsens negative feelings (Fottler, et al., 2000). Due to this characteristic, whether the physical environment of the health and wellness care industry has an encouraging or discouraging effect on behaviors and emotions needs to be investigated closely. Such servicescapes, as complicated as health care settings can be, are termed "elaborate" environment by Bitner, et al., (1992).

Environmental factors such as sound, music, color, aroma, and lighting are known to affect the sensory impressions that bring out positive experiences (Pine & Gilmore, 1998). The importance of sensory experiences can outweigh the customer's consideration of value (Berry et al., 2002). Previous evidence shows that environmental factors such as the comfort of resting areas, overall cleanliness, and décor positively impact not only patients' satisfaction (Hall & Dornan, 1988), but also healing (Stichler, 2001). In response, Ohio State University's Richard M. Ross Heart Hospital has been implementing an innovative customer-focused care effort to create the best possible healing environment and outcome for their customers. They have a "universal room," a spacious hospital room equipped with portable diagnostic and therapeutic equipment, to allow customers to receive care in private rooms. This customer-driven, personalized care and customer satisfaction have made the Ross Heart Hospital stand out. It is currently ranked 29th leader in cardiology and heart surgery among nearly 5,000 U.S. heart hospitals, according to the 2012-13 survey by U.S. News & World Report (U.S. News & World Report, 2013). As can be evidenced from this example, the service environment can actually make up most of what constitutes a customer's health care experience (Fottler, et al., 2000). Regardless of its importance, management of servicescape is something that many in the health and wellness industry neglect and often consider as less important than other aspects of management (Parish et al., 2008). Therefore, providing a relevant and effective "atmospheric environment", also referred to as a "healing environment", should be a primary goal for health and wellness service providers to become and retain competitive.

In addition to the servicescape's influence on customer behavior, it also affects the nature and quality of interactions between customers and employees (Bitner, et al., 1992). Bitner et al., (1992) categorized servicescapes into three segments: self-service, remote service, and interpersonal service. Among these categories, health and wellness organizations are included in the interpersonal services category (Zeithaml & Bitner, 1996). Interpersonal services are located in an environment in which both the customer and the employee must be present (ibid., 1996). Because wellness services are generally purchased and consumed at the same time, health care providers and customers engage together in the servicescape. How the servicescape is designed influences customer expectations, choices, satisfaction, and other behaviors (ibid., 1996). The servicescape must be managed in a way that it attracts, satisfies, and promotes the activities for both parties.

Health and wellness facilities are manifested by servicescape factors (ibid., 1996). Sensory information of health and wellness care atmospherics influence both cognitive and affective states, which in turn affect purchasing behavior (Grossbart, Hampton, Rammohan, & Lapidus, 1990). The physical environment of health and wellness organizations even influence how fast the customer recovers from or adapts to their health conditions (Stichler, 2001). Customers who go through treatments often feel anxious in expectation of uncomfortable and unfamiliar events (Mok & Wong, 2003). In addition, hospitals are equipped with many rooms, a variety of sophisticated equipment, and a range of functions performed (Zeithaml & Bitner, 1996). When the servicescape is appropriately designed, the integration of senses such as smell, décor, music, and the layout makes a stronger perception of the environment (Calvert, Brammer, & Iversen, 1998). The servicescape can work as a tool to calm preoperative anxiety by providing a nonthreatening and noninvasive environment. For example, a treatment room can be designed to enhance customers' comfort and satisfaction while simultaneously facilitating health service providers' productivity (Zeithaml & Bitner, 1996). Take, for example, a spa treatment in a natural spring. The integration of the feeling of the hot water on the skin, the sound of water flowing, as well as the smell of nature enhances the entire wellness spa experience. To fully manage the customers' total experience, organizations must put just as much emphasis on the emotional component of experience as the product and service (Berry et al., 2002). Understanding the effects of servicescape stimuli in health and wellness facilities would lead to the provision of environments that derive a positive outcome for both healing process and the customers' well-being (Dijkstra, Pieterse, & Pruyn, 2006).

In daily life, events integrate our several senses. Various environmental cues send input to customers' sensory systems, which then transform them into a set of impressions (Lin, 2004). Similarly in the health and wellness service setting, customers do not evaluate a specific servicescape feature based on only one environmental stimulus (ibid., 2004). The physical environment includes objective physical aspects that the health and wellness organization can control to enhance or constrain the customer's experience; there is an endless set of possibilities—lighting, color, layout, wall décor, music, aroma, and so on (Zeithaml & Bitner, 1996). It is only when the physical stimuli combine harmoniously that these can speed and enhance the perception of the environment (Calvert et al., 1998). Therefore, each stimuli should be added and mixed with all others based on customer behavior as customers tend to respond to their environment holistically prior to making specific judgments (Lin, 2004).

1. Auditory Cues (Music)

There has been a remarkable increase in music usage in the health and wellness care field (Kneafsey, 1997). Music is often used as a tool to minimize the negative consequence of waiting time before receiving service (Hui, Dube, & Chebat, 1997). Music is also known to evoke psychological and physiological responses (Kneafsey, 1997). In fact, the multidimensional nature of music arouses physical, psychological, spiritual, and social levels of consciousness (ibid., 1997). Listening to music produces change in the autonomic nervous system that is associated with emotional states. There is evidence of the effectiveness of listening to music during the treatment (Augustin & Hains, 1996). Customers who have to undergo treatments often experience anxiety, even for a minor procedure (Mok & Wong, 2003). Music creates significant mood changes, reduces situational anxiety, improves mobility, and facilitates communication (Kneafsey, 1997). Calm music sounds have been shown to have therapeutic effects (Lin, 2004).

In addition, music makes the body synchronize its rhythms with the rhythms of the flowing music (Marwick, 1996). Music acts as a catalyst by releasing emotions and even leading to more openness (Kneafsey, 1997). During a treatment, slow music slows the heartbeat of anxious customers who may have a racing heart, synchronizing the heart to the music and relaxing the patient (ibids., 1997). Playing music that evokes pleasant memories has a soothing effect. Another study found that music in combination with relaxation reduces postoperative pain during both ambulation and rest (Good et al., 2001). Music is also known to have beneficial effects by mitigating unwanted sounds and improving the interaction between the customer and health and wellness service provider (Devlin & Arneill, 2003).

2. Olfactory Cues (Aroma)

Aromas can be detected in our daily functions and play an important role in our lives. Olfaction is not only integral in eating food in terms of flavor, but it also significantly influences detection of threats such as fire, spoiled food, or toxic fumes. On the other hand, fragrances have a positive effect, improving the quality of life such as the pleasant fragrance of flowers and perfumes (Kurtz, Emko, White, Belknap, & Kurtz, 1995).

Human behavior can even be manipulated in numerous ways with aromas (Field et al., 2005). Although other types of stimuli can also relax humans, aromas are especially adept at promoting calm and elevating mood, because the primary olfactory parts of the brain connect directly to the limbic system (Eichenbaum, 1996) and aromas activate the autonomic nervous system (Van Toller & Kendal-Reed, 1989). Aroma's physiological effects of humans relate to emotions and memory, which modulate both physical and mental health (Moss, Cook, Wesnes, & Duckett, 2003). Aroma can cause physiological changes in the body, such as blood pressure, muscle tension, skin temperature, heart rate, and sleep and arousal states (Kuroda et al., 2005). Because aroma influences the unconscious level of awareness, it is used to affect the psychoneuro-immune function to promote healing (ibid., 2003). Pleasant odors positively influence health. When pleasant, ambient aromas are a part of the environment, people feel happier, and anxiety and stress are reduced (Knasko, 1992).

Aromatherapy is an effective method for prevention and treatment of emotional distress. Aromatherapy can be ingested, applied, or inhaled; the most effective way to decrease anxiety is through inhalation (Butje, Repede, & Shattell, 2008). The medical use of aromatic oils has a long history going back to Egyptian and Chinese cultures (Lis-Balchin, 2006), it was mainly from 1980 that aromatherapy began to get attention as a serious discipline (Robins, 1999). The primary reason of this increased interest on aromatherapy is due to mind-body healing and emerging research on the use of aromatherapy to alleviate emotional and mental stress (d'Angelo, 2002).

Aromatherapy is usually applied in conjunction with other wellness treatments such as massage and reflexology (Buckle, 2007); however, it can also function as a stand-alone therapy (Butje et al., 2008). While some aromas, such as lavender and rose, increase relaxation, other aromas, such as jasmine and citrus, have a stimulating and antidepressant effect (Yagyu, 1994). Each distinct aroma links closely to daily functions such as alertness, relaxation, attention, performance, and healing (Field et al., 2005). Aromatherapy is often not prescribed by U.S. medical practitioners; however, its use has increased among CAM and nursing practitioners (d'Angelo, 2002).

3. VISUAL CUES (COLOR, LAYOUT AND FUNCTION, LIGHTING)

Among servicescape dimensions, the visual cues to the environment include color, space and function, lighting, plants, artifacts, and layout (Bitner, et al., 1992). The room layout and the wall colors play a role in creating a welcoming environment, having a significant impact on the customer's health and wellness experience (Fottler et al., 2000). These settings influence customers' feeling of comfort, competence, and security (ibid., 2000). The challenge is to create this environment while incorporating the technology necessary for the health and wellness care setting (Devlin & Arneill, 2003). Different functional areas may be differentiated by changing color, layout of furnishings, or lighting.

Color, one of the most discernible visual cues, is used in the formation of interior settings for health and wellness facilities (Lin, 2004). Altering the atmosphere of an environment with color is easy (Dijkstra, Pieterse, & Pruyn, 2008), and different colors are known to evoke diverse moods and emotions (Lin, 2004). While warm colors give people a feeling of arousal and excitement, cool colors engender reactions of calmness, peacefulness, and pleasantness (Bellizzi & Hite, 1992). In addition, the appropriate-ness of the color varies according to the room's function (Slatter & Whitfield, 1977). Health and wellness organizations commonly use color as a navigation system, which minimizes customer disorientation (Devlin & Arneill, 2003). Some atmospheric stud-ies have shown color's ability to attract customers as well as imbue them with pleasant feelings (Bellizzi, Crowley, & Hasty, 1983).

Layout refers to how objects are arranged within the health and wellness care setting. Depending on how these spaces are designed, they can make the customer's wait time before the service seem either long and tedious or short and beneficial (Fottler et al., 2000). The service design has been shown to influence customer's responses to the quality of care (Arneill & Devlin, 2002). The layout helps customers create a mental picture prior to their affective response to and judgment of a health and wellness ser-vice environment (Lin, 2004). How these layouts are designed directly impacts the customers' perception of quality, pleasure, and excitement, while having an indirect impact on the desire to return (Wakefield & Blodgett, 1994). The hospital layout can impact the ease of navigation as well as the speed at which one can reach various loca-tions (Carpman & Grant, 1993). For example, single or nondormitory patient rooms suggest a feeling of privacy and intimacy, leading to better participation in treatment activities (Karlin & Zeiss, 2006). In addition, high ceilings are associated with feelings of spaciousness, while low ceilings convey intimacy and coziness (Ching, 1996).

Windows affect the quality of the customer's experience. Several research findings provide evidence of customers' preference for rooms with windows, especially those with a nature-view (Verderber, 1986). Environments with views of nature are found to reduce the customer's psychological distress and recovery time. Whether the environ-ment has a window also influences the attachment a customer has towards the health and wellness organizations (Baird & Bell, 1995). Overall, the past research findings suggest that windows may have healing and stress alleviating influences on customers (Devlin & Arneill, 2003). The rationale for this influence might relate to customers linking windows and views perceptually and cognitively to the external environment, bringing in a positive therapeutic effect (Verderber & Reuman, 1987).

Lighting impacts the customer's perceptions of the health and wellness care environ-ment, and the customer derives value, not only aesthetically but also psychologically (Benya, 1989; Ching, 1996). However, the health and wellness industry is still in its infancy stage in terms of lighting. Some of the lighting issues are related to the sources of light, reduction of glare, more daylight, less institutional lighting, and softer lighting (Benya, 1989). In health care settings, soft, indirect, full-spectrum lighting is found to be preferable to spotlight-type, recessed lighting as customers do not like lights to focus directly on them (Karlin & Zeiss, 2006). Moreover, sunlight in health and wellness care facilities is known to promote recovery for depressed customers (ibid., 2006). Lighting can also influence interpersonal communication, comfort, and arousal (Lin, 2004).

CONCLUSION

Each customer perceives environmental cues differently, so one reaction to the servicescape probably differs from that of the next customer. Nonetheless, these environmental aspects create unique mood states for customers and employees. These mood states, in turn, create the customer's internal responses and behaviors, contributing to the evaluation of the overall health care experience.

Customer satisfaction is viewed as a customer's reaction to their individual health service experience (Pascoe, 1983). As customer satisfaction can serve as a critical factor in evaluating the quality of the service provided, it is now a widely used criterion for evaluating the performance of health and wellness organizations (Meterko, Mohr, Young, 2004). Many health and wellness organizations use customer satisfaction data for internal evaluation of their performance (Young, Meterko, & Desai, 2000). Given the importance of health and wellness services to the customer, health and wellness organizations should make the most use of their healing environment to achieve the desired outcomes of patient satisfaction and overall experience.

Organizations will have the competitive edge when they combine both functional and emotional benefits in their service offerings. Only those health services that conceptualize and manage the health care offering as essentially a "service" offering will gain an advantage in the understanding of and ability to deliver service excellence. Once the emotional bonds between health and wellness organizations and customers are formed, it is difficult for competitors to break them, because the holistic nature of experiential service delivery makes it hard for competitors to copy (Berry et al., 2002). Therefore, through managing the servicescape aspect, health and wellness organizations can obtain the maximum opportunities to personalize service.

If and only if the health and wellness care industry can meet and exceed what customers consider their optimal experience would it bring lots of benefits to company. Customers not only respond better to treatment, but staff morale improves, the facility becomes the facility of choice in any particular location, and the finances of the institution improve. To be competitive in this health and wellness service market, a growing number of organizations are strategically applying the tools and principles of customer-experience management as a way to offer the optimal customer experience (ibid., 2002).

REVIEW QUESTIONS

1. Give some examples of health-and wellness-related activities.

2. Discuss why the health and wellness industry is booming.

3. List some measures health and wellness service managers can take to differentiate their offerings and provide a unique "total experience."

4. Discuss why wellness customers are no longer satisfied with mere products or services, but rather why they seek an optimal experience.

5. Describe how customers can cocreate their unique experience in conjunction with the health and wellness care industry professionals.

6. Give some examples that illustrate the interrelatedness of multidimensional experience factors in health and wellness services.

7. In what ways can the servicescape impact a customer's overall health and wellness experience?

8. Discuss why customers often rely on physical evidence to evaluate health and wellness services.

REFERENCES

Albrecht, K., & Zemke, R. (1984). *Service America: Doing business in the new economy.* Homewood, IL: Dow Jones-Irwin.

Andaleeb, S. S. (1998). Determinants of customer satisfaction with hospitals: A managerial model. *International Journal of Health Care Quality Assurance, 11*(6), 181–187.

Arneill, A., & Devlin, A. (2002). Perceived quality of care: The influence of the waiting room environment. *Journal of Environmental Psychology, 22*(4), 345–360.

Augustin, P., & Hains, A. (1996). Effects of music on ambulatory surgery patients' preoperative anxiety. *Association of Perioperative Registered Nurses Journal, 63*, 750–758.

Baker, J., Levy, M., & Grewal, D. (1992). An experimental approach to making retail store environmental decisions. *Journal of Retailing, 68*, 445–461.

Baird, C. L., & Bell, P. A. (1995). Place attachment, isolation, and the power of a window in a hospital environment: A case study. *Psychological Reports, 76*, 847–850.

Bellizzi, J. A., Crowley, A.E., & Hasty, R. W. (1983). The effects of color on store design. *Journal of Retailing, 68*(4), 21–45.

Bellizzi, J. A., & Hite, R. E. (1992). Environmental Color, Consumer Feelings, and Purchase Likelihood. *Psychology and Marketing, 9*(5), 347–363.

Benya, J. (1989). Lighting for healing. *Journal of Health Care Interior Design, 1*, 55–58.

Berry, L., Carbone, L., & Haeckel, S. (2002). Managing the total customer experience, *MIT Sloan Management, 43*(3), 85–89.

Bitner, M. J., Booms, B. H., & Tetreault, M.S. (1990). The service encounter: Diagnosing favorable and unfavorable incidents, *Journal of Marketing, 54*, 71–84.

Bitner, M, J., Booms, B. H., & Mohr, L. A. (1992). Servicescapes: The impact of physical surroundings on customers and employees. *Journal of Marketing, 56*, 57–71.

Bitner, M. J., Faranda, W. T., Hubbert, A. R., & Zeithaml, V. A. (1997). Customer contributions and roles in service delivery. *International Journal of Service Industry Management, 8*(3), 193–205.

Bowen, D.F., Siehl, G., & Schneider, B. (1989). A framework for analyzing customer service orientation in manufacturing. *Academy of Management Review, 14*(1), 75–95.

Brady, M.K., & Cronin, J., Jr. (2001). Customer orientation: Effects on customer service perceptions and outcome behaviors. *Journal of Service Research, 3*(3), 241–251.

Brown, T. (2008). Design thinking. *Harvard Business Review, 86*(6), 84–92.

Buckle, J. (2007). Literature review: Should nursing take aromatherapy more seriously? *British Journal of Nursing, 16*, 116–120.

Butje, A., Repede, E., & Shattell, M. (2008). Healing scents: An overview of clinical aromatherapy for emotional distress. *Journal of Psychosocial Nursing and Mental Health Services, 46*(10), 46–52.

Calvert, G.A., Brammer, M.J. & Iversen, S.D. (1998) Cross-modal identification. *Trends in Cognitive Sciences, 2*(7), 247–253.

Cameron, E., Mathers, J., & Parry, J. (2006). 'Health and well-being': Questioning the use of health concepts in public health policy and practice. *Critical Public Health, 16*, 347–354.

Carpman, R. J., & Grant, M. A. (1993). *Design that cares: Planning health facilities for patients and visitors* (2nd ed.). Chicago: American Hospital Publishing.

Ching, F. (1996). *Architecture: Form, Space, and Order.* New York Van Nostrand.

Ciarrochi, J., Dean, F. P., & Anderson, S. (2002). Emotional intelligence moderates the relationship between stress and mental health. *Personality & Individual Differences, 32*(2), 197–209.

d'Angelo, R. (2002). Aromatherapy. In S. Shannon (Ed.), *Handbook of complementary and alternative therapies in mental health* (pp. 71–92). San Diego: Academic Press.

Dawson, S., Bloch, P.H., & Ridgway, N. (1990). Shopping motives, emotional states, and retail outcomes. *Journal of Retailing, 66*(4), 408–28.

Day, G.S., & Wensley, R. (1988). Assessing advantage: a framework for diagnosing competitive superiority, *Journal of Marketing, 52*, 1–20.

D'Crus, A., & Wilkinson, J. M. (2005). Reasons for choosing and complying with complementary health care: An in-house study on a South Australian clinic. *The journal of Alternative and Complementary Medicine, 11*(6), 1107–1112.

Devlin, A. S., & Arneill, A. B. (2003). Health care environments and patient outcomes: A review of literature. *Environment & Behavior, 35*(5), 665–694.

Diamantopoulos, A., & Hart, S. (1993). Linking market orientation and company performance: Preliminary evidence of Kohli and Jaworski's framework. *Journal of Strategic Marketing, 1*, 93–121.

Dienhart, J.R., Gregoire, M.B., Downey, R.G., & Knight, P.K. (1992). Service orientation of restaurant employees. *International Journal of Hospitality Management, 11*(4), 331–346.

Dijkstra, K., Pieterse, M., & Pruyn, A. (2006). Physical environmental stimuli that turn healthcare facilities into healing environments through psychologically mediated effects: Systematic review. *Journal of Advanced Nursing, 56*(2), 166–181.

Dijkstra, K. D., Pieterse, M. E., & Pruyn, A. T. (2008). Individual differences in reactions towards color in simulated healthcare environments: The role of stimulus screening ability. *Journal of Environmental Psychology, 28*, 268–277.

Druss, B., & Rosenheck, R. A. (1999). Associations between use of unconventional therapies and conventional medical services. *Journal of the American Medical Association, 282*, 651–656.

Dube, L., Chebat, J.C., & Morin, S. (1995). The effects of background music on consumers' desire to affiliate in buyer–seller interactions. *Psychology and Marketing, 12*, 305–319.

Edvardsson, B., Enquist, B., & Johnston, R. (2005). Cocreating customer value through hyperreality in the prepurchase service experience. *Journal of Service Research, 8*(2), 149–161.

Eichenbaum, H. (1996). Olfactory perception and memory. In R. R. Llinas & P. S. Churchlan (Eds.), *The mind-brain continuum: Sensory processes.* Cambridge, MA.: The MIT Press.

Erfurt-Cooper, P., & Cooper, M. (2009). *Health and wellness tourism. Spas and Hot Springs.* Ontario: Channel View.

Field, T., Diego, M., Hernandez-Reif, M., Cisneros, W., Feijo, L., Vera, Y., & Gil, L. (2005). Lavender fragrance cleansing gel effects on relaxation. *International Journal of Neuroscience, 115*, 207–222.

Fottler, M. D., Ford, R. C., Roberts, V., Ford, E. W., & Spears, J. D. (2000). Creating a healing environment: The importance of the service setting in the new customer oriented health system. *Journal of Healthcare Management, 45*(2), 91–106.

Frese, M. (1985). Stress at work and psychosomatic complaints: A causal interpretation. *Journal of Applied Psychology, 70*, 314–328.

Frost, G. J. (2004). The spa as a model of an optimal healing environment. *The Journal of Alternative and Complementary Medicine, 10*(1), 85–92.

Gaberson, K. B. (1995). The effect of humorous and musical distraction on preoperative anxiety. *Association of Perioperative Registered Nurses Journal, 62*, 784–791.

Gentile, C., Spiller, N., & Noci, G. (2007). How to sustain the customer experience: An overview of experience components that co-create value with the customer. *European Management Journal, 25*(5), 395–410.

Good, M., Stanton-Hicks, M. S., Grass, J. A., Anderson, G. C., Lai, H. L., Roykulcharoen, V., & Adler, P. (2001). Relaxation and music to reduce postsurgical pain. *Journal of Advanced Nursing, 33*, 208–215.

Grossbart, S., Hampton, R., Rammohan, B., & Lapidus, R. (1990). Environmental dispositions and customer response to store atmospherics. *Journal of Business Research, 21*(3),225–241.

Gustavo, N. S. (2010). A 21st-century approach to health tourism spas: The case of Portugal. *Journal of Hospitality & Tourism Management, 17*, 127–135.

Hall, J., & Dornan, M. (1988). What patients like about their medical care. *Social Science and Medicine, 27*(4), 935–939.

Hogan, J., Hogan, R., & Busch, C. M. (1984). How to measure service orientation. *Journal of Applied Psychology, 69*(1), 167–173.

Hui, M.K., Dube, L., & Chebat, J. (1997). The impact of music on consumers' reactions to waiting for services. *Journal of Retailing, 73*(1), 87–104.

Institute of Medicine. (2001). *Crossing the quality chasm: A new health system for the 21st century.* Washington, DC: The National Academy of Sciences.

Jonas, W. B. (1998). Alternative medicine—Learning from the past, examining the present, advancing to the future. *Journal of the American Medical Association, 280*, 1616–1618.

Johansson, P., Oleni, M., & Fridlund, B. (2002). Patient satisfaction with nursing care in the context of health care: A literature study, *Scandinavian Journal of Caring Sciences, 16*(4), 337–344.

Joppe, M. (2010). One country's transformation to spa destination: The case of Canada [special section]. *Journal of Hospitality & Tourism Management, 17*, 117–126.

Karlin, B. E., & Zeiss, R. A. (2006). Environmental and therapeutic issues in psychiatric hospital design: Toward best practices. *Pyschiatric Services, 57*(10), 1376–1379.

Kelly, C. (2010). Analysing wellness tourism provision: A retreat operators' study. *Journal of Hospitality & Tourism Management, 17*, 108–116.

Knasko, S. C. (1992). Ambient odor's effect on creativity, mood, and perceived health. *Chemical Senses, 17*(1), 27–35.

Kneafsey, R. (1997). The therapeutic use of music in a care of the elderly setting: A literature review. *Journal of Clinical Nursing, 6*, 341–346.

Kovacs, R. (1945). American health resorts: The problem of the American spas. *Journal of the American Medical Association. 127*(15), 977–981.

Kuroda, K., Inoue, N., Ito, Y., Kubato, K., Sugimoo, A., Kakuda, T., et al. (2005). Sedative effects of the jasmine tea odor and (R)-(-)-linalool, one of its major odor components, on autonomic nerve activity and mood status. *European Journal of Applied Physiology, 95*, 107–114.

Kurtz, T., Emko, P., White, T., Belknap, E., & Kurtz, D. (1995). The rose less sweet [letter]. *The Journal of Family Practice, 41*(5), 433.

Kurz, R. S., & Wolinsky, F. D. (1985). Who picks the hospital: practitioner or patient? *Hospital & Health Services Administration, 30*(2), 95–106.

Laschinger H.S., Hall L.M., Pedersen C. & Almost J. (2005). A psychometric analysis of the patient satisfaction with nursing care quality questionnaire: An actionable approach to measuring patient satisfaction. *Journal of Nursing Care Quality, 20*(3), 220–230.

Lee, S. (2011). Evaluating serviceability of healthcare servicescapes: Service design perspective. *International Journal of Design, 5*(2), 61–71.

Lin, I. Y. (2004). Evaluating a servicescape: The effect of cognition and emotion. *Hospitality Management, 23*, 163–178.

Lipsitt, D. R. (1982). Who are the 'worried well'? *General Hospital Psychiatry, 4*(2), 93–94.

Lis-Balchin, M. (2006). *Aromatherapy science: A guide for healthcare professionals*. London: Pharmaceutical Press.

Mahon, N. (1996). New York inmates' HIV risk behaviors: The implications for prevention policy and programs. *American Journal of Public Health, 86*(9), 1211–1215.

Marwick. C. (1996). Leaving concert hall for clinic, therapists now test music's charms. *Journal of American Medical Association, 275*(4), 267– 268.

McNeil, K. R., & Ragins, E. J. (2005). Staying in the spa marketing game: Trends, challenges, strategies, and techniques. *Journal of Vacation Marketing, 11*(1), 31–29.

Meterko, M., Mohr, D. C., & Young, G. J. (2004). Teamwork culture and patient satisfaction in hospitals, *Medical Care, 42*(5), 492–498.

Mok. E., & Wong, K. (2003). Effects of music on patient anxiety. *Association of Perioperative Registered Nurses Journal, 77*(2),96–410.

Morrison, M., Gan, S., Dubelaar, C., & Oppewal, H. (2011). In-store music and aroma influences on shopper behavior and satisfaction. *Journal of Business Research, 64*, 558–564.

Moss, M., Cook, J., Wesnes, K., & Duckett, P. (2003). Aromas of rosemary and lavender essential oils differentially affect cognition and mood in healthy adults. *International Journal of Neuroscience, 113*, 15–38.

Mueller, H., & Kaufmann, E. L. (2000). Wellness tourism: Market analysis of a special health tourism segment and implications for the hotel industry. *Journal of Vacation Marketing, 7*(1), 5–17.

Nightingale, F. (1969). *Notes on nursing: What it is, and what it is not*. New York: Dover. Originally published 1859.

Nwankwo, S. (1995). Developing a customer orientation. *Journal of Customer Marketing, 12*(5), 5–15.

Parasuraman, A., Zeithaml, V. A., & Berry, L. L. (1985). A conceptual model of service quality and its implications for future research. *Journal of Marketing, 49*(4), 41–50.

Parish, J. T., Berry, L. L., & Lam, S. Y. (2008). The effect of the servicescape on service workers. *Journal of Service Research, 10*(3), 220–238.

Pascoe, G. C. (1983). Patient satisfaction in primary health care: A literature review and analysis, *Evaluation and Program Planning, 6*(3), 185–210.

Pine, J., & Gilmore, J. (1998). Welcome to the experience economy. *Harvard Business Review, 76*, 86–91.

Prahalad, C. K. (2004). The blinders of dominant logic, *Long Range Planning, 37*(2), 171–179.

Robins, J.L. (1999). The science and art of aromatherapy. *Journal of Holistic Nursing, 17*, 5–17.

Schuster, T. L., Dobson, M., Jauregui, M., & Blanks, R. H. I. (2004). Wellness lifestyles I: A theoretical framework linking wellness, health lifestyles, and complementary and alternative medicine. *Journal of Alternative and Complementary Medicine, 10*, 349–356.

Slatter, P. E., & Whitfield, T. W. (1977). Room function and appropriateness judgments of Color. *Perceptual and Motor Skills, 45*(3), 1068–1070.

Smith, E. H. (2003). Customer focus and marketing in archive service delivery: Theory and practice. *Journal of the Society of Archivists, 24*(1), 35–53.

Stichler J. F. (2001). Creating healing environments in critical care units. *Critical Care Nursing Quarterly, 24*(3), 1–20.

Synovitz, L., & Larson, K. (2013). *Complementary and alternative medicine for health professionals: A holistic approach to consu¬mer health*. Brulington, MA: Jones & Bartlett Learning

Trauer, B. (2004). Conceptualizing special interest tourism: Frameworks for analysis. *Tourism Management, 27*, 183–200.

Turley, L., & Chebat, J.C. (2002). Linking retail strategy, atmospheric design and shopping behaviour. *Journal of Marketing Management, 18* (1/2), 125–144.

Tzeng H.M., & Katefian S. (2002). The relationship between nurses' job satisfaction and inpatient satisfaction: An exploratory study in a Taiwan teaching hospital. *Journal of Nursing Care Quality, 16*, 39–49.

Ulrich R.S. (1991). Effects of health facility interior design on wellness: Theory and scientific research. *Journal of Health Care Design, 3*, 97–109.

Ulrich, R. S. (1992). How design impacts wellness. *Healthcare Forum Journal, 35*, 20–25.

U.S. News & World Report. (2013). Top-ranked hospitals for cardiology & heart surgery. Retrieved from http://health.usnews.com/best-hospitals/rankings/cardiology-and-heart-surgery

Van Toller, S., & Kendal-Reed, M. (1989). Brain electrical activity topographical maps produced in response to olfactory and chemosensory stimulation. *Psychiatry Research, 29,* 429–430.

Verderber, S. (1986). Dimensions of person-window transactions in the hospital environment. *Environment and Behavior, 18*, 450–466.

Verderber, S., & Reuman, D. (1987).Windows, views, and health status in hospital therapeutic environments. *Journal of Architectural and Planning Research, 4*, 120–133.

Verhoef, P. C., Lemon, K. N., Parasuraman, A., Roggeveen, A., Tsiros, M., & Schlesinger, L. A. (2009). Customer experience creation: Determinants, dynamics and management strategies. *Journal of Retailing, 85*, 31–41.

Vincent, C., & Furnham, A. (1996). Why do patients turn to complementary medicine? An empirical study. *British Journal of Clinical Psychology, 35*, 37–48.

Wakefield, K. L., & Blodgett, J. G. (1994). The importance of servicescapes in leisure service settings. *Journal of Service Marketing, 8*(3), 66–76.

Yagyu, T. (1994). Neurophysiological findings on the effects of fragrance: Lavender and Jasmine. *Integrative Psychiatry, 10,* 62–67.

Young, G. J., Meterko, M., & Desai, K. R. (2000). Patient satisfaction with hospital care: Effects of demographic and institutional characteristics. *Medical Care, 38*(3), 325–334.

Zeithaml , V. A. & Bitner, M. J. (1996). *Service marketing.* New York: The McGraw-Hill Companies.

Toward Improving Performance Management in a Healthcare Operational Environment: A Customer-Orientation Approach

Carlos F. Gomes
Mahmoud M. Yasin
Phillip E. Miller

LEARNING OBJECTIVES

Upon completing this chapter, you should be able to do the following:

1. Understand the emerging forces in the healthcare competitive environment.

2. Understand the role of performance management in health care organizations.

3. Highlight the role of operational modifications on organizational performance improvements.

4. Understand the role of customer-orientation in a health care environment.

5. Understand the impact of operational tools and philosophies on improving the patients' orientation.

6. Understand the role of the patient's orientation in shaping the strategic performance of first-class health care organizations.

7. Understand the role of people and operational technologies in serving the patient.

8. Understand that the business of health care is still about people serving people.

INTRODUCTION

Health care organizations are unique operational systems. These systems are being challenged by an increasingly competitive environment where patients, the government, and other stakeholders are demanding improved and efficient medical services. Health care organizations in both the for-profit and not-for-profit sectors are paying closer attention to the different facets of their organizational performance. In this context, these organizations must shift their performance cultures from a mere medical outcome-based culture to a blend of a broader operational and strategic performance, customer-oriented culture. This cultural performance shift represents a drastic departure from a health care perspective of "we know what is good for patient" to an emerging perspective of "we need to know what the patient wants and values." Therefore, the patient is becoming the cornerstone of the performance measurement system of health care organizations. In this context, measuring, tracking, monitoring, and improving health care performance from a patient perspective requires a systematic approach. This systematic approach must use a broader orientation where operational and strategic aspects of performance should be integrated to make the health care organization more patient focused. Such focus must be managed effectively in pursuit of a competitive strategic advantage. At the heart of this performance management approach should be a well-designed performance measurement system. Such a system must be supported by a health care culture that is motivated by a patient' orientation. The patient' orientation not only makes good business sense, but also improves the bottom line. In this context, the Mayo and Cleveland clinics are cases in point.

Under this performance approach, performance improvement tools and philosophies must be deployed and used effectively to foster a continuous performance improvements health care operational and strategic culture. This culture should be guided and motivated by operational gains that have strategic significance. The aim of this chapter is to explore the facets of this performance measurement and improvement approach. The conceptual framework in Figure 7.1 is used to guide the coverage.

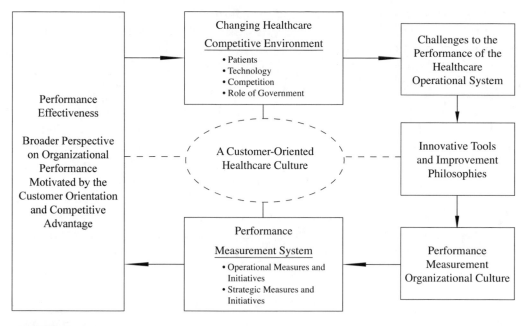

Figure 7.1 **Figure 7.1** IMPROVING THE HEALTH CARE OPERATIONAL SYSTEM PERFORMANCE THROUGH CUSTOMER ORIENTATION.

THE HEALTH CARE COMPETITIVE ENVIRONMENT

Health care was, until a few years ago, considered a social service, exclusively provided by most western governments. Due to recent environmental changes, the health care industry has been transformed into for-profit, nonprofit, and government-owned organizations. These organizations, for the most part, compete for the same patients (Goldstein, Ward, Leong, & Butler, 2002).

The health care industry has been under strong pressure to reduce costs and improve patient' satisfaction. In this context, the health care industry is not unique, as other service and manufacturing industries have encountered similar pressures to shift toward a customer-orientation business model. There is no doubt that the health care system tends to have unique operational realities and constraints. This operational uniqueness has been, at times, exaggerated to justify the apparent reluctance of health care policy makers and hospital' administrators to modify health care operational practices and systems (Ferreira, Gomes, & Yasin, 2011). The fact is that, despite its uniqueness, the health care operational system remains a system of people serving people.

Health care organizations have been facing increasing pressures due to drastic environmental changes that redefined markets, patients, customers, and even operational technologies. Due to rapid changes in medical technology and population structure, most health care service delivery systems have been under increased pressure to adopt modern corporate management practices (Alexander, Weiner, & Griffith, 2006). This has required health care organizations to change their organizational cultures from a seller orientation to a customer orientation (Eiriz, Barbosa, & Figueiredo, 2010; Kunst & Lemmink, 2000).

In recent years, changing disease patterns have led to advances in medical knowledge and technology. This, among other factors, has resulted in a steady increase in the costs of providing health care services (Kumar & Shim, 2005). The growing public awareness of new medical possibilities, coupled with an aging population, has increased health care costs (Myllykangas et al., 2003; Roland, Martinelly, Riane, & Pochet, 2009). Therefore, efforts to contain the increasing health care costs through better use of the scarce health care resources have been viewed as critical. Also, due to increasing levels of competition in the health care industry, organizations in this industry are becoming more aware of the need to customize services and improve service performance (Raju & Lonial, 2002).

Responding to Competitive Changes

Today's organizations in both the manufacturing and service sectors are attempting to deploy innovative competitive methods and tools to respond to a rapidly changing marketplace. Some innovative competitive methods and tools tend to emphasis operational efficiency, quality, and the customer orientation. Tools such as Total Quality Management (TQM), Continuous Improvement (CI), Just-In-Time (JIT), Business Process Reengineering (BPR), and Benchmarking (BM), among others, have been employed effectively in manufacturing and in hospital service operational settings (Kilo et al., 2000a; Kilo et al., 2000b; McAulay, 2001; Persona et al., 2008; Rad, 2006; Smith & Offodile, 2008). Other competitive methods used tend to emphasize the broader aspects of competitiveness, such as innovative marketing techniques, competitive pricing, customer service, and effective use of the workforce, among others (Yasin, Gomes, & Miller, 2011).

Hospitals, regardless of type, size, and operational characteristics, are being forced to reconsider their operations, strategies, and relationships to patients in favor of better alignment with new demands of the competitive environment. In the process, hospitals are re-examining the strategic competitive profiles, competitive methods used, and operational and strategic performance. In an attempt to improve strategic competitive standing and the different aspects of operational effectiveness, some hospitals are deploying quality improvement tools and initiatives. The effectiveness of this effort has strong implications for the strategic competitiveness of the hospital and its operational effectiveness. The aim of innovative strategic orientations and operational tactics should target improving the customer orientation of the hospital. Therefore, hospital' administrators and policy makers must integrate customer orientation into their organizational cultures and performance systems.

A strategic emphasis on patient' satisfaction as a strategic goal appears to be universal among these health care organizations. While these organizations appear to be using different competitive and operational tactics, they seem to realize the importance of patient' satisfaction as a strategic goal. Some seem to be making more effort to train and develop personnel. This perhaps is responsible for better clinical effectiveness.

Not-for-profit, general medical surgical organizations appear to emphasize only traditional competitive methods. They appear to be less innovative relative to their counterparts; however, they tend to be similar to their for-profit counterparts in terms of the emphasis placed on competitive methods, quality improvement deployment, and outcomes.

Patient satisfaction appears to drive customer service in all the strategic groupings. To have the best customer service, hospitals need a highly trained, experienced, and knowledgeable workforce. A combination of improved customer service and increased workforce performance will enhance any hospital's reputation in the industry.

It seems that hospitals are attempting to deploy certain competitive methods in response to the new demands of the health care environment. However, some of these hospitals appear to be approaching the competitive challenge from an operational perspective. While these hospitals appear to understand the importance of patient' service and satisfaction, they are not communicating this emphasis to potential patients through effective advertising. The integration of operational and marketing initiatives might lead to a better overall strategic effectiveness for hospitals. Therefore, well-designed and implemented operational and marketing initiatives may lead to improved performance in these two key areas, which, in turn, may contribute to strategic performance.

PERFORMANCE MEASUREMENT AND MEASURES

Despite the difficulties associated with measuring certain aspects of service performance, managers of service organizations are becoming increasingly aware of the need to capture, monitor, and improve their organizational performance to create or sustain a competitive strategic advantage (Forslund, 2007; Tiernan, Rhoades, & Waguespack, 2008; Urban, 2009). However, due to their intense interaction with customers, the main concerns of organization managers in service industries have been focused on measuring customer satisfaction and service quality (Chen, 2009; Deng, 2008).

Although customer satisfaction and service quality are considered critical aspects of performance, other aspects of service performance, such as operations efficiency, competitive environment, and human resources utilization, among others, should not be overlooked. While studies of these performance-related concerns in manufacturing operational settings have been forthcoming (Gomes, Yasin, & Lisboa, 2004, 2011; Pun & White, 2005; Shepherd & Gunter, 2006), this has not been the case in most service operational settings (Jusoh & Parnell, 2008).

A *performance measurement system* (PMS) can be defined as a set of metrics used to quantify the efficiency and effectiveness of actions (Neely, Gregory, & Platts, 2005). It also can be viewed as a balanced, dynamic system that supports the decision-making process by monitoring, gathering, and analyzing performance-related information (Bititci & Turner, 2000; Garengo & Bititci, 2007). This system includes a set of performance measures that provide service managers with useful information, which helps to plan, manage, control, and effectively improve the many facets of organizational competitiveness.

Some authors emphasize the managerial and management aspects of performance measurement. These authors advocate a balanced, systematic performance management organizational approach, rather than a narrowly defined performance measurement perspective (Dey, Hariharan, & Despic, 2008; Greiling, 2005). Such an systematic, integrated approach requires the support of integrated organizational information systems.

The PMS-managed information must be accurate, relevant, timely, and accessible. These informational capabilities and characteristics must be incorporated into the PMS design (Cavalluzzo & Ittner, 2004; Franco & Bourne, 2003; Garengo, Nudurupati, & Bititci, 2007; Nudurupati & Bititci, 2005). Furthermore, performance measures must also be carefully designed to reflect the most important factors influencing the productivity of the processes found in the organization (Tangen, 2005).

A well-designed performance measurement system is vital for ensuring that an organization delivers cost-effective and high-quality services that are capable of meeting and exceeding the evolving needs and wants of customers (Moullin, 2004a). In this context, performance measures and measurement are viewed as important drivers of increased efficiency and improved service delivery quality (Greiling, 2005). Therefore, the performance measurement system and related processes and activities are critical to the effectiveness of the service operational system (De Bruijn, 2002).

There are several difficulties associated with performance measurement efforts in any organization; however, these difficulties are even more pronounced in service operational environments. Health care and public services are cases in point (Gomes & Yasin, 2010; Gomes, Yasin, & Lisboa, 2008). In most cases, these difficulties are attributed, in part, to the diverse interests of the stakeholders (De Bruijn, 2002; Moullin, 2007). These stakeholders may have different and sometimes conflicting agendas and performance expectations (Wisniewski & Ólafsson, 2004).

These stakeholders tend to have diverging perspectives on organizational performance. In such operational environments, it is difficult to set targets or to make decisions solely based on measured results. Therefore, when designing and implementing a performance measurement system, the conflicting views and needs of the stakeholders must somehow be reconciled (Lawton, McKevitt, & Millar, 2000; Mettnen, 2005).

Performance measurement systems and related processes must be designed carefully to incorporate these differing perspectives on organizational performance. This is critical to the success of the performance management effort in manufacturing operational environments (Neely, Adams, & Crowe, 2001) as well as service operational environments (Dey et al., 2008).

Perhaps the focus on assessing service organization performance by emphasizing customer service quality may have led to overlooking other important aspects of service performance, such as the environmental- and supplier related aspects (Yasin & Gomes, 2010).

Due to recent changes in the competitive environment, service managers are facing increased pressure to improve all aspects of organizational performance (Agus, Barker, & Kandampully, 2007; Beamon & Balcik, 2008; Jaaskelainen & Lonnkvist, 2009). On the other hand, the literature reviewed underscores the overemphasis placed on selective performance dimensions, such as the financial and customer satisfaction.

Service organizations should pay closer attention to service innovations and incorporate performance measures related to these innovations into their performance measurement approach. As the service sector becomes more competitive, service innovation has the potential to differentiate the services delivered to the customer. This innovation, in turn, adds value to the service encounters with customers and, in the process, creates more customer/market opportunities for the organization.

Service organizations are also advised to devote more effort to tracking performance aspects related to their operational environments. This may improve the linkages between service organizations and their environments, thus making them truly open operational systems. The performance of such systems should be measured, monitored, and managed effectively to facilitate improvement of the various aspects of the performance of these open systems.

Since service organization executives value and use such measures, despite lack of information, service organizations' information systems need to be modified to ensure the availability of information on these measures. This requires a joint organizational effort among information systems specialists and those managers concerned about the facets of the performance management process. A joint organizational effort is also needed among the financial department and those in charge of performance measurement to financially quantify some important aspects of service performance (C. F. Gomes & Yasin, 2012).

Therefore, the delicate balance between financial and nonfinancial performance measurement practices has not yet been reached by service organizations. In this context, certain nonfinancial measures of service performance are still being overlooked by service managers. The lack of information on such measures appears to be hindering their use despite their relevance to today's competitive service environment. Therefore, managers of service organizations are called on to invest and reengineer their organizational information systems to make the needed information on the nonfinancial performance measures more readily available.

In this context, service organizations must be willing to redesign their performance measurement systems and measurement practices. The motivation for the redesign of the performance measurement system should be guided by continuous performance improvement efforts and overall organizational competitiveness. While many approaches have been proposed to improve the performance measurement system, managers still struggle with the practical aspects of effective implementation.

THE PERFORMANCE MEASUREMENT PROCESS

Since the 1980's organizational changes aimed at improving performance in a changing environment have been a perennial management concern. Reflecting such concern, performance measurement and evaluation became the subject of practical research aimed at addressing management's operational concerns. Some organizations have responded to these operational concerns with radical re-engineering efforts. Others, however, belonging to more stable organizational environments have either resisted external pressures or adopted a slower pace to change.

Manufacturing organizations were the first to realize that focusing the performance measures only on financial aspects was not enough to maintain effective performance in global markets. This lead to an increasing emphasis on the nonfinancial aspects of organizational performance (Abdel-Maksoud, Dugdale, & Luther, 2005; Gomes et al., 2004). Some service organizations followed the lead of manufacturing organizations with regard to emphasizing the nonfinancial performance aspects. They began to employ similar performance measurement systems and approaches similar to those of their manufacturing counterparts (Brignall & Ballantine, 1996; Denton & White, 2000; Jones, 2004; Neely et al., 2002; Phillips & Louvieris, 2005). However, other, more service-specific performance measurement approaches were offered (Carr, 2007; Chow & Luk, 2005; Kang & Bradley, 2002; Parasuraman, 2004). Due to political pressures in the form of the New Public Management initiatives (Brignall & Modell, 2000), public sector organizations are slowly beginning adopt the performance measurement approaches used in the private sector (Chan, 2004; Johnsen, 2001; Wisniewski & Ólafsson, 2004).

The health care industry has been slow to accept the new performance measurement approaches that are customer-driven (Butler, Leong, & Everett, 1996). This is attributed to industry characteristics, as it has different segments such as the primary, secondary and tertiary health care services. In the last two levels, one finds for-profit, not-for-profit, and government-owned organizations competing with each other for the same patients (Goldstein et al., 2002). Despite these unique characteristics, some health care organizations are trying to complement their traditional output-related performance measures such as mortality rates, capacity, and accounting ratios with new, nontraditional performance dimensions. As such, some of the health care organizations are beginning to adopt innovative performance measures and measurement approaches similar to those found in other industries (Inamdar, 2002; Schmidt, Bateman, Reilly, & Smith, 2006; Stewart & Bestor, 2000; Urrutia & Eriksen, 2005). Others are attempting to adapt these measurement approaches to their specific organizational operational environments (Moullin, 2004b; Yap, 2005). However, some of these efforts have been hindered by the inability of health care organizations to implement the necessary changes dictated by the industry's unique characteristics. Some of these characteristics are:

- Differences among organizations due to their different roles in this industry. For example, this industry includes hospitals with clear boundaries where patients are admitted and discharged. It also includes primary health care organizations, which are open, community-based systems with unclear boundaries (Amado & Dyson, 2006). This makes performance measures and measurement subject to the organization's public role, and the constraints imposed on its operations.
- Differences among the health care services delivered and patient's expectations (health)(Amado & Dyson, 2006), thus, making it difficult to measure patient's satisfaction due to different service/patient contexts.
- The existence of different stakeholders with, sometimes, conflicting interests and expectations. These stakeholders include those who consume health care services (patients), those who ultimately pay for them (taxpayers or insured individuals), those who purchase them on the public's behalf (fund holdings), and those who provide them (health care delivery operational systems) (Ballantine et al., 1998). This presents difficulties and challenges in establishing performance-related strategies, objectives, and goals.
- The existence of differing perspectives on performance between managers on the business side of operations (administrators) and the managers on the clinical side of operations (physicians) (Butler et al., 1996). This in turn makes it difficult to define performance measures and measurement approaches.
- The primacy of legitimacy relative to profit in public health care organizations (Lemieux-Charles et al., 2003). This makes performance relative rather than absolute in nature.

- The complex and multidimensional nature of health care service quality, combined with the fact that many patients lack the clinical expertise to judge some key aspects of the health care service delivery systems, tends to complicate the performance measurement process (Silvestro, 2005).

Not unlike other industries, the health care industry has used specific performance measures, measurement models, and approaches to evaluate performance. For example, in the case of hospital services scheduling (Kim & Horowitz, 2002), hospital bed allocation (Kim et al., 2000), predicting waiting times for surgery services (Cipriano, Chesworth, Anderson, & Zaric, 2007), and master surgical schedule (Testi, Tanfani, & Torre, 2007) have been used. However, using these models and tools represents a stand-alone effort that lacks the systematic integration of information. In most cases there is no integrated performance measurement system responsible for the organizational performance measurement effort. In this context the performance measurement system must be viewed as a complete organizational system (Chenhall, 2005; Lohman et al., 2004).

As health care organizations attempt to use the innovative performance measurement approaches found in other industries, they will struggle with issues that these industries have already dealt with. Among these issues is the increasing emphasis on non-financial measures (Amado & Dyson, 2006) and the temptation to resort only to the well-known traditional financial measures.

The future of performance measurement systems will not only be judged on their aggregation or integration features, but also on their abilities to incorporate the dynamic relationships among efficiency-specific and effectiveness-oriented organizational measures (Gomes et al., 2004b). Thus, to avoid emphasizing one at the expense of the other, the performance measurement system should incorporate two types of organizational performance evaluation platforms. The first platform maintains a measure-specific perspective, defining the relationship between specific measures and the organizational units responsible for them. Under this performance evaluation platform, individual performance measures can be used to evaluate the reliability, availability, efficiency, and quality aspects of the operational system. To accomplish this goal, diverse individual measures should be used individually or as a small group of measures. These measures are critical to detecting and dealing with specific performance deviations. The key to improving performance, under this measure-specific platform, is training and developing employees to promote responsibility and accountability. Thus, investments on the part of health care organizations to promote operational efficiency and employee'' productivity should lead to performance improvements. However, such investments are only part of the organizational effort to improve overall performance of the operational system.

The second performance evaluation platform is motivated by an organization-wide or systemwide perspective. Thus it has a strategic organizational focus. This platform focuses on a few main performance measures that reflect critical organizational performance dimensions. The number of measures included in this platform should be consistent with the executives' individual cognitive capacities (Garg et al., 2003; Lipe & Salterio, 2000). This platform stresses an organizational effectiveness approach to organizational performance measures and measurement. Therefore, the measures of this platform should be consistent with strategic indicators designed to gauge the organization's competitiveness in the marketplace (Basu & Wright, 1997; Chenhall, 2005). The emphasis of this platform is on the effective flow and delivery of services throughout the organization. Thus, the involvement of the top management of health care organizations is critical to the success of the organizational performance measurement effort consistent with this platform.

OPERATIONAL PERFORMANCE IMPROVEMENTS

Recent environmental changes are forcing organizations to re-invent their operating models to improve resource usage and customer satisfaction. Public health care organizations are no exception because all the health services components face economic pressure to be maximally efficient, as well as political and commercial pressures to adopt a more positive customer orientation.

In many cases, the traditional business and operational models used by health care organizations have failed to satisfy the increasing demands from patients for higher service quality and less waiting time for surgical procedures. Therefore, these organizations are looking for more innovative operational practices that place the patient at the heart of the operational health care service system.

Recent literature has stressed the importance of effective health care information systems to improve health care service efficiency and patient satisfaction (Park et al., 2008). Information is viewed as a valuable organizational resource with the potential to play an important role in improving patient' satisfaction, operational efficiency, and clinical governance. Information from present activities can be used to model, simulate, and refine future activity.

This study presents an applied research effort aimed at using information to re-engineer certain operational aspects of a public hospital, to improve its efficiency and its patient orientation, specifically, to enhance resource use represented by operating rooms and surgical teams. In the process, the role of information systems in providing health care administrators with timely and relevant performance-related information is stressed.

In the short-term, hospitals' performance can be improved through relaxing binding system constraints. On the other hand, long-term performance can be improved through systemwide investments (Dorsch & Yasin, 1998; Yasin et al., 1996). For example, the ability of a hospital to handle the demand for surgery can be improved in the short term through better use of existing surgical resources. However, long term capacity improvements require that the hospital expand critical, binding surgical resources.

Hospitals' performance should be viewed from a broader, systemwide perspective. This is achieved by modifying existing operational practices. These modifications would relax the critical surgical capacity constraint by using patterns of existing resources. While relaxing the surgical capacity constraint is operational in nature, it has strategic significance as it increases the capacity of the hospital to serve more patients.

Implementation Issues

The conceptual framework in Figure 7.2 is designed to aid the management of health care organizations by approaching the performance improvement and management more systematically.

Phase I: Start

In this context this phase should be motivated by better patient service and satisfaction. The initiation process involves determining the initial values and establishing performance target benchmarks.

Phase II: Monitor

In this phase, it is critical to make available the relevant information needed to evaluate the patient-driven performance indicators. The role of organizational information systems in providing the required information is critical. Based on the evaluation, performance gaps are identified and plans to address them are formulated and implemented.

The monitoring is needed, not only to maintain high level of motivation for this approach, but also to identify improvement opportunities. If the implementation process is inefficient, or and takes too much time, this may encourage dysfunctional behaviors (Almgren, 1999).

Phase III: Plan

During this stage, carefully formulated plans and strategies are deployed. These plans and strategies should focus on operational and organizational dimensions, such as capacity, supplier relationships, processes and technology, operations activities, and service delivery.

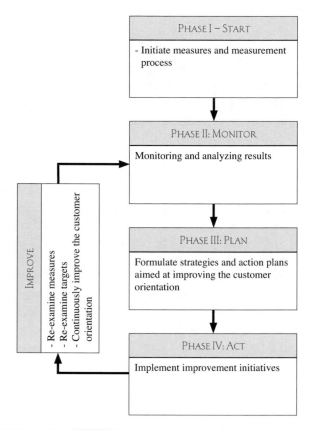

Figure 7.2 A CONCEPTUAL FRAMEWORK FOR THE IMPLEMENTATION OF CUS-
TOMER-ORIENTED HEALTH CARE PERFORMANCE IMPROVEMENTS.

PHASE IV: ACT

During this phase, needed procedural modifications can be made in ways consistent
with existing organizational practices or based on methodologies presented in the literature. Such methodologies may include statistical quality control procedures, theory of
constraints (Goldratt & Fox, 1986), and simulation. Upon the completion of this effort,
a continuous improvement cycle focusing on the performance aspects to be improved
is launched.

IMPROVEMENT CYCLE

A continuous improvement cycle should be used to facilitate the verification of progress
of the improvement efforts. In this context, it is critical for health care organizations
to be willing to commit the resources needed to foster improvement. The involvement of employees, management, and patients in this process is stressed. Therefore, the
improvement cycle must make the patient the cornerstone of a well-designed continuous improvement effort.

CONCLUSION

The dynamic, competitive health care environment is forcing health care organizations to re-engineer their organizational performance measurement cultures and performance measurement systems to become more patient orientated. In this context, these organizations are being challenged to broaden their perspective on organizational performance. This broader perspective must incorporate operational and strategic facets of organizational performance, which are motivated by the customer orientation. In many cases this leaves health care organization management with many questions and few answers. This chapter attempts to explore some of the relevant issues and management concerns of these organizations. In this context, organizational resources and goals must be focused on establishing a viable performance measurement system capable of promoting a patient orientation. Such a system must incorporate and integrate the operational and strategic facets of organizational performance. This broader perspective on performance must be complemented with innovative and proven tools and philosophies aimed at continuously improving organizational performance. Used effectively, operational performance improvements can and should be deployed strategically to improve the competitive strategic position of the health care organization. To facilitate these performance improvement objectives, health care organizations must be willing to invest in new information systems and technologies in order to capture, analyze, and use information related to operational and strategic performance.

In the final analysis, health care operational systems are systems of people serving people. Therefore, the patient should have the final say when it comes to service quality. In this context, the customer orientation must shape the future strategies and operations of first-class health care organizations.

REVIEW QUESTIONS

1. What are some of the fundamental competitive challenges facing today's health care organizations?

2. In the context of health care service, what do the terms *seller-market* and *buyer-market* mean?

3. What are the major activities of a performance measurement system?

4. How can operational performance improvements lead to a better customer orientation? Give examples.

5. What is meant by *customer orientation* in a health care operational environment?

REFERENCES

Abdel-Maksoud, A., Dugdale, D., & Luther, R. (2005). Non-financial performance measurement in manufacturing companies. *The British Accounting Review*, 37(3), 261–297. doi:10.1016/j.bar.2005.03.003

Agus, A., Barker, S., & Kandampully, J. (2007). An exploratory study of service quality in the Malaysian public service sector. *International Journal of Quality & Reliability Management*, 24(2), 177–190.

Alexander, J. A., Weiner, B. J., & Griffith, J. (2006). Quality improvement and hospital financial performance. *Journal of Organizational Behavior*, 27(7), 1003–1029. doi:10.1002/job.401

Almgren, H. (1999). Start-up of advanced manufacturing systems - A case study. Integrated Manufacturing Systems, 10(3), 126–136.

Amado, C. A. F., & Dyson, R. G. (2006). On comparing the performance of primary care providers. *European Journal of Operational Research*. doi:10.1016/j.ejor.2006.02.052

Ballantine, Joan, Brignall, Stan and Modell, Sven (1998). Performance measurement and management in public health services: A comparison of U.K. and Swedish practice. Management Accounting Research, 9(1), 71-94.

Basu, Ron and Wrigth, J. Nevan (1997). Total manufacturing solutions. Butterworth and Heinemann.

Beamon, B. M., & Balcik, B. (2008). Performance measurement in humanitarian relief chains. *International Journal of Public Sector Management*, 21(1), 4–25.

Bititci, U. S., & Turner, T. (2000). Dynamics of performance measurement systems. *International Journal of Operations & Production Management*, 20(6), 692–704.

Brignall, S., & Ballantine, J. (1996). Performance measurement in service business revisited, 7(1), 6–31.

Brignall, S., & Modell, S. (2000). An institutional perspective on performance measurement and management in the 'new public sector.' Management Accounting Research, 11(June 1999), 281–306. doi:10.1006/mare.2000.0136

Butler, T. W., Leong, G. K., & Everett, L. N. (1996). The operations management role in hospital strategic planning. *Journal of Operations Management*, 14, 137–156.

Carr, C. L. (2007). The FAIRSERV ` : Consumer reactions to services based on a multidimensiona evaluation of service fairness. Decision Sciences, 38(1), 107–130.

Cavalluzzo, K. S., & Ittner, C. D. (2004). Implementing performance measurement innovations : Evidence from government. Accounting, Organizations and Society, 29(3–4), 243–267.

Chan, Y.-C. L. (2004). Performance measurement and adoption of balanced scorecards. *International Journal of Public Sector Management*, 17(3), 204–221. doi:10.1108/09513550410530144

Chen, S.-H. (2009). Establishment of a performance-evaluation model for service quality in the banking industry. *The Service Industries Journal*, 29(2), 235–247.

Chenhall, Robert H. (2005). Integrative strategic performance measurement systems, strategic alignment of manufacturing, learning and strategic outcomes: An exploratory study. Accounting, Organizations and Society, 30(5), 395-422.

Chenhall, Robert H. (2005). Integrative strategic performance measurement systems, strategic alignment of manufacturing, learning and strategic outcomes: An exploratory study. Accounting, Organizations and Society, 30(5), 395-422

Chow, C. C., & Luk, P. (2005). A strategic service quality approach using analytic hierarchy process. *Managing Service Quality*, 15(3), 278–289. doi:10.1108/09604520510597827

Cipriano, L. E., Chesworth, B. M., Anderson, C. K., & Zaric, G. S. (2007). Predicting joint replacement waiting times. *Health Care Management Science*, 10, 195–215. doi:10.1007/s10729-007-9013-z

De Bruijn, H. (2002). Performance measurement in the public sector: Strategies to cope with the risks of performance measurement. *International Journal of Public Sector Management*, 15(7), 578–594.

Deng, W.-J. (2008). Fuzzy importance-performance analysis for determining critical service attributes. *International Journal of Service Industry Management*, 19(2), 252–270.

Denton, G. A., & White, B. (2000). Implementing a balanced-scorecard approach to managing hotel operation: The case of White Lodging Services. *Cornell Hotel and Restaurant Administration Quarterly*, March, 94–107.

Dey, P. K., Hariharan, S., & Despic, O. (2008). Managing health care performance in analytical framework. Benchmarking: *An International Journal*, 15(4), 44–468.

Dorsch, J, Yasin, M 1998. A framework for benchmarking in the public sector: A literature review and directions for future research. *International Journal of Public Sector Management*, 11(2), 91-115.

Eiriz, V., Barbosa, N., & Figueiredo, J. (2010). A conceptual framework to analyse hospital competitiveness. *The Service Industries Journal*, 30(3), 427–448. doi:10.1080/02642060802236137

Ferreira, J., Gomes, C., & Yasin, M. (2011). Improving patients' satisfaction through more effective utilization of operating rooms resources: An informational-based perspective. *Clinical Governance: An International Journal*, 16(4), 291–307. doi:10.1108/14777271111175341

Forslund, H. (2007). The impact of performance management on customers'' expected logistics performance. *International Journal of Operations & Production Management*, 27(8), 901–918.

Franco, M., & Bourne, M. (2003). Factors that play a role in managing through measures. Management Decision, 41(8), 698–710.

Garengo, P., & Bititci, U. S. (2007). Towards a contingency approach to performance measurement: An empirical study in Scottish SMEs. *International Journal of Operations & Production Management*, 27(8), 802–825.

Garengo, P., Nudurupati, S., & Bititci, U. S. (2007). Understanding the relationship between PMS and MIS in SMEs: An organizational life cycle perspective. Computers in Industry, 58, 677–686.

Garg, Vinay K., Walters, Bruce A. and Priem, Richard L. (2003). Chief executive scanning emphases, environmental dynamism, and manufacturing firm performance. *Strategic Management Journal*, 24(8), 725-744.

Goldratt, E. M., & Fox, R. E. (1986). The race. Croton-on-Hudson, New York: North River Press.

Goldstein, S. M., Ward, P. T., Leong, G. K., & Butler, T. W. (2002). The effect of location, strategy, and operations technology on hospital performance. *Journal of Operations Management*, 20(1), 63–75.

Gomes, C. F., & Yasin, M. M. (2010). Assessing operational effectiveness in health care organizations: A systematic approach. *International Journal of Health Care Quality Assurance*, 23(2), 127–140.

Gomes, C. F., & Yasin, M. M. (2012). An assessment of performance-related practices in service operational settings: Measures and utilization patterns. *The Service Industries Journal*, 32(16). doi:10.1080/02642069.2011.600441

Gomes, C. F., Yasin, M. M., & Lisboa, J. V. (2004). An examination of manufacturing organizations' performance evaluation: Analysis, implications and a framework for future research. *Journal of Operations & Production Management*, 24(5), 488–513.

Gomes, C. F., Yasin, M. M., & Lisboa, J. V. (2008). Project management in the context of organizational change: The case of the Portuguese public sector. *The International Journal of Public Sector Management*, 21(6), 573–85.

Gomes, C. F., Yasin, M. M., & Lisboa, J. V. (2011). Performance measurement practices in manufacturing firms revisited. *International Journal of Operations & Production Management*, 31(1), 5–30.

Gomes, Carlos F., Yasin, Mahmoud M. and Lisboa, João V. (2004b). A literature review of manufacturing performance measures and measurement in an organizational context: A framework and direction for future research. *Journal of Manufacturing Technology Management*, 15(6), 511-530.

Greiling, D. (2005). Performance measurement in the public sector: The German experience. *International Journal of Productivity and Performance Management*, 54(7), 551–567.

Inamdar, N. (2002). Applying the balanced scorecard in healthcare provider organizations. *Journal of Healthcare Management*, 47(3), 179–195.

Jaaskelainen, A., & Lonnkvist, A. (2009). Designing operative productivity measures in public services. Vine, 39(1), 55–67.

Johnsen, A. (2001). Balanced scorecard: Theoretical perspectives and public management implications. *Managerial Auditing Journal Auditing.* 16(6), 319 – 330.

Jones, C. R. (2004). A scorecard for service excellence. Measuring Business Excellence, 8(4), 45–54. doi:10.1108/13683040410569406

Jusoh, R., & Parnell, J. A. (2008). Competitive strategy and performance measurement in the Malaysian context: An exploratory study. Management Decision, 46(1), 5–31.

Kang, H., & Bradley, G. (2002). Measuring the performance of IT services: An assessment of SERVQUAL. *International Journal of Accounting Information Systems*, 3, 151–164.

Kilo, C. M., Horrigan, D, Godfrey, M. and Wasson, J. (2000a). Making quality and service pay: Part 1, The Internal Environment, Family Practice Management, available at http://www.aafp.org/fpm/20001000/48maki.html.

Kilo, C. M., Horrigan, D, Godfrey, M. and Wasson, J. (2000b). Making quality and service pay: Part 1, The External Environment, Family Practice Management, available at http://www.aafp.org/fpm/20001100/25maki.html.

Kim, Seung-Chul and Horowitz, Ira (2002). Scheduling hospital services: The efficacy of elective-surgery quotas. Omega, 30(5). 335-346.

Kim, Seung-Chul, Ira Horowitz, Karl K. Young and Thomas A. Buckley (2000). Flexible bed allocation and performance in the intensive care unit. Journal of Operations Management, 18(4), 427-443.

Kumar, A., & Shim, S. J. (2005). Using computer simulation for surgical care process reengineering in hospitals. INFOR, 43(4), 303–319.

Kunst, P., & Lemmink, J. (2000). Quality management and business performance in hospitals: A search for success parameters. Total Quality Management, 11(8), 1123–1134.

Lawton, A., McKevitt, D., & Millar, M. (2000). Coping with ambiguity: Reconciling external legitimacy and organizational implementation in performance measurement. Public Money & Management, 20(3), 13–19.

Lemieux-Charles, Louise, McGuire, Wendy, Champagne, François, Barnsley, Jan, Cole, Donald and Sicotte, Claude (2003).The use of multilevel performance indicators in managing performance in health care organizations. Management Decision, 41(8), 760-770.

Lipe, Marlys G. and Salterio, Steven E. (2000). The Balanced Scorecard: Judgmental effects of common and unique performance measures. The Accounting Review, 75(3), 283-298.

Lohman, Clemens, Fortuin, Leonard and Wouters, Marc (2004). Designing a performance measurement system: A case study. *European Journal of Operational Research*, 152(2), 267-286.

McAulay, B. (2001). Total quality practice management: Putting TQM to work in the chiropractic office, available at http://www.chiroweb.com/mpacms/dc/article.php?id=31664

Mettnen, P. (2005). Design and implementation of a performance measurement system for a research organization. Production Planning & Control, 16(2), 178–188.

Moullin, M. (2004a). Evaluating a health service taskforce. *International Journal of Health Care Quality Assurance*, 17(5), 248–257.

Moullin, M. (2004b). Eight essentials of performance measurement. *International Journal of Health Care Quality Assurance*, 17(2/3), 110–112.

Moullin, M. (2007). Performance measurement definitions: Linking performance measurement and organisational excellence. *International Journal of Health Care Quality Assurance*, 20(3), 181–183.

Myllykangas, M., Ryynanen, O.-P., Lammintakanen, J., Isomaki, V.-P., Kinnunen, J., & Halonen, P. (2003). Clinical management and prioritisation criteria: Finnish experiences. *Journal of Health Organization and Management*, 17(5), 338–348. doi:10.1108/14777260310505110

Neely, A., Adams, C., & Crowe, P. (2001). The performance prism in practice. Measuring Business Excellence, 5(2), 6–11.

Neely, A., Adams, C., & Kenerly, M. (2002). The Performance Prism- The scorecard for measuring and managing success, Pearson Education Limited, London.

Neely, A., Gregory, M. J., & Platts, K. W. (2005). Performance measurement system design: A literature review and research agenda. *International Journal of Operations & Production Management*, 25(12), 1228–1263.

Nudurupati, S. S., & Bititci, U. S. (2005). Implementation and impact of IT-supported performance measurement systems. Production Planning & Control, 16(2), 152–162.

Parasuraman, A. (2004). Assessing and improving service performance for maximum impact: Insights from a two-decade-long research journey. Performance Measurement and Metrics, 5(2), 45-52.

Parasuraman, A., Zeithaml, V. A., & Berry, L. L. (1988). SERVQUAL: A multiple-item scale for measuring consumer perceptions of service quality. *Journal of Retailing*, 64(1), 12–40.

Park, J, McAlaney, C and Connolly, M 2008. Improving patient care and clinical governance through the utilisation of a clinical information system. *Clinical Governance: An International Journal*, 13(4), 254-260.

Persona, A, Battini, D and Rafele, C (2008). Hospital efficiency management: Tthe just-in-time and Kanban technique. *International Journal of Healthcare Technology & Management*, 9(4), 373-391

Phillips, P. A., & Louvieris, P. (2005). Performance measurement systems in tourism, hospitality, and leisure small medium-sized enterprises: A balanced scorecard perspective. *Journal of Travel Research*, 44, 201–211. doi:10.1177/0047287505278992

Pun, K. F., & White, A. S. (2005). A performance measurement paradigm for integrating strategy formulation: A review of systems and frameworks. *International Journal of Management Reviews*, 7(1), 1131–1152.

Rad, A. M. M. (2006). The impact of organizational culture on the successful implementation of total quality management, The TQM Magazine, 18(6), 606-625.

Raju, P. S., & Lonial, S. C. (2002). The impact of service quality and marketing on financial performance in the hospital industry: An empirical examination. *Journal of Retailing and Consumer Services*, 9(6), 335–348.

Roland, B., Martinelly, C. D., Riane, F., & Pochet, Y. (2009). Scheduling an operating theatre under human resource constraints. *Computers & Industrial Engineering*, 58(2), 212–220.

Schmidt, S., Bateman, I., Reilly, J. B.-o, & Smith, P. (2006). A management approach that drives actions strategically health trust case study. *International Journal of Health Care Quality Assurance*, 19(2), 119–135. doi:10.1108/09526860610651663

Shepherd, C. D., & Gunter, H. (2006). Measuring supply chain performance: Current research and future directions. *International Journal of Productivity and Performance Management*, 55(4), 242–258.

Silvestro, R. (2005). Applying gap analysis in the health service to inform the service improvement agenda. *International Journal of Quality & Reliability Management*, 22(3), 215–233.

Smith, A. D. and Offodile, O. F. (2008). Data collection automation and total quality management: Case studies in the health-service industry. *Health Marketing Quarterly*, 25(3), 217-240

Stewart, L. J., & Bestor, W. E. (2000). Applying a balanced scorecard to health care organizations. *Journal of Corporate Accounting & Finance*, 11(3) 75–82.

Tangen, S. (2005). Improving the performance of a performance measure. Measuring Business Excellence, 9(2), 4–11.

Testi, A., Tanfani, E., & Torre, G. (2007). A three-phase approach for operating theatre schedules. Health Care Management Science, 10, 163–172. doi:10.1007/s10729-007-9011-1

Tiernan, S., Rhoades, J. A., & Waguespack, B., Jr. (2008). Airline service quality: Exploratory analysis of consumer perceptions and operational performance in the USA and EU. Managing Service Quality, 18(3), 212–224.

Urban, W. (2009). Organizational service orientation and its role in service performance formation: Evidence from Polish service industry. Measuring Business Excellence, 13(1), 72–81.

Urrutia, I., & Eriksen, S. D. (2005). Application of the balanced scorecard in Spanish private health-care management. Measuring Business Excellence, 9(4), 16–26.

Wisniewski, M., & Ólafsson, S. (2004). Developing balanced scorecards in local authorities: A comparison of experience. *International Journal of Productivity and Performance Management*, 53(7), 602–610.

Yap, C. (2005). A comparison of systemwide and hospital-specific performance measurement tools. *Journal of Healthcare Management*, 50(4), 251–262.

Yasin, M, Czuchry, A and Dorsch, J 1996. A framework for establishment of an optimal service quality level in a hospitality operational setting. *Journal of Hospitality and Leisure Marketing*, 4(2), 25-48.

Yasin, M. M., & Gomes, C. F. (2010). Performance management in service operational settings: A selective literature examination. *Benchmarking: An International Journal*, 17(2), 214–231.

Yasin, M. M., Gomes, C. F., & Miller, P. E. (2011). Competitive strategic grouping for hospitals: Operational and strategic perspectives on the effective implementation of quality improvement initiatives. *TQM Journal*, 23(2), 301–312.

Chapter 8

An Open-Systems Perspective of Mental Health Services

Mark Anderson
Byron Keating
Anton Kriz

ACKNOWLEDGMENTS

This research has been supported by a grant from the Australian Department of Families, Housing, Community Services, and Indigenous Affairs (FaHCSIA). We also acknowledge the valuable contribution of TeamHealth, the largest provider of nongovernment mental health services in the northern territory. The views expressed here are solely those of the authors, who have contributed equally to this paper and have been listed here in alphabetical order.

LEARNING OBJECTIVES

Upon completing this chapter, you should be able to do the following:

1. Understand the nature of mental health services, and how such services have evolved over time.

2. Appreciate the value of an open-systems perspective for understanding the interrelationships among the functions and processes that support mental health services.

3. Describe the unique elements of the mental health service package, the role of service operations manager within mental health services and the importance of service process interventions.

4. Understand the special role that evaluation plays in the mental health services context and the need for unique service outcome measures and approaches.

KEYWORDS

mental health services, open-systems perspective, service operations management, service systems.

Abstract

Mental health is a global issue, with governments investing billions of dollars annually to try to ameliorate this growing epidemic. Recognized as one of the more complex health services, psychosocial rehabilitation has many important service-related nuances that influence client recovery. This chapter draws on contemporary services literature to review the key characteristics of mental health services, before adopting an open-systems perspective to investigate the interactions among/between the elements of the mental health service system. An open-systems approach is a novel but timely contribution that responds to the complex nature of high-contact health services. By employing an open-systems view, this chapter highlights the important role that effective service management plays in improving mental health services and client outcomes, and provides a scope for a new stream of future research.

Introduction

Understanding recovery is a priority of governments internationally. Instances of mental health disorders have increased significantly over recent years, with a recent World Health Organization (WHO) report highlighting that an estimated 450 million people worldwide are suffering from mental illness. The WHO further asserts that at any given time 10 percent of the adult population is affected by mental illness, with 25 percent suffering from a mental health disorder during their lifetimes (WHO, 2009). Recent economic analysis suggests that mental health disorders now account for about 13 percent of the burden on national health systems; this number is expected to grow to 15 percent by 2030 (Mathers & Loncar, 2006). These factors resulted in a revised resolution by the WHO urging member nations of the 65th World Health Assembly to develop "comprehensive policies and strategies that address the promotion of mental health, prevention of mental disorders, and early identification, care, support, treatment and recovery of persons with mental disorders" (2012, p. 3).

The emergence of the mental health epidemic has attracted significant government investment around the globe and, accordingly, has resulted in considerable research attention. However, to date, much of the focus of the mental health literature has been, understandably, on learning how particular interventions facilitate client recovery. While there is an implicit recognition that the quality of the services delivered by caseworkers and the service environment that encompasses the delivery of mental health services influence mental health outcomes (Anthony, W., Cohen, M., & Farkas, M., 1990), little research attention has been given to understanding what aspects of the service system contribute to or hinder the recovery process. A better appreciation of the service system is critical to improving the efficiency and quality of mental health services. To this end, Berry and Bendapudi (2007) assert that while effective management of health services has the greatest impact on quality of life, it also carries the largest number of challenges and consumes the most resources.

This research investigates mental health services from an open-systems perspective. This approach embraces the complexity of mental health services, recognizing the difficulty of standardizing service delivery in high-contact human services and the inherent barriers to productivity and efficiency that constrain this and many of the allied health disciplines. An *open-systems approach* provides a lens for understanding how the various functions and processes of the service system interact to achieve improved recovery outcomes for individuals suffering from mental illness. The role of the service operations manager within an open-systems view of mental health services is critical to achieving these outcomes.

Our work is among the first to use open-systems theory to investigate mental health services. In doing so, we develop a model that shows the interrelationships among the different functions and processes that support mental health services. Interestingly, this broader systems perspective is consistent with the progressive shift away from psychiatric-based models of mental health that emphasize outcomes toward a psychosocial rehabilitation approach that emphasizes the recovery process. This model will aid practitioners in understanding how service processes (interventions) are influenced by and related to other elements of the service system.

Seeing mental health interventions as a series of service processes is relatively new for the industry. Historically, mental illness sufferers were institutionalized. The introduction of psychosocial rehabilitation has seen a shift in terminology away from patients (more outcome focused) to clients or consumers (process focused). Psychosocial rehabilitation is now viewed as more than treating symptoms. More emphasis is placed on both understanding and addressing individual client needs, leading to the development of customized service interactions (Anthony 1993). Viewing psychosocial rehabilitation as an open system is, therefore, an important move forward in this evolution. The open-systems approach also implicitly recognizes heterogeneity among consumers of mental health services. Clients have different illnesses, different personal circumstances, different resources and support requirements, and ultimately, engage with the service system in different ways, requiring different service delivery approaches and service interventions. Our open-systems model for mental health services responds to this complex reality.

To advance the aims of this chapter, we begin with a background discussion of mental health services. This discussion will include an exposition of the characteristics of mental health services vis-à-vis other service contexts. The chapter then focuses on the nature of open systems and how such systems can be adopted to understand the delivery of mental health services. This includes an identification of the key service functions and processes, and an articulation of the importance of the service operations manager. Interventions and the special role of evaluations are also discussed before the chapter concludes.

THE MENTAL HEALTH SERVICES CONTEXT

Over the past two decades, recovery has become the dominant ideology among consumers and others who advocate for people with mental illness. Though different definitions of *recovery* exist, most people who use the term agree that it represents a process that encourages people diagnosed as having mental illness to feel hope, healing, empowerment, and connection (Jacobson & Greenley, 2001), giving them a sense of control over their lives and moving them toward the goal of maximizing their ability to function in the world (Ranz & Mancini, 2008). This view of recovery draws on self-determination theory, where recovery is less concerned about whether the person achieves some kind of symptom- and disability-free endpoint, and more about whether he or she can achieve meaning in life and personal comfort (Campbell & Schraiber, 1989; Ralph, 2000).

In this sense, recovery is as viewed less than an outcome and more as a process of psychosocial rehabilitation. The role of mental health service providers is to facilitate recovery through the development and delivery of psychosocial interventions. These interventions vary greatly depending on the specific nature of the mental illness being treated, but should ultimately contribute positively to a client's movement along the recovery continuum (more information on specific interventions are provided later in the chapter). The recovery continuum is dynamic, with some clients experiencing improvements and setbacks during their treatments, thus making the process of recovery nonlinear (Anthony, 1993). Within this context, the service operations manager works with service personnel (caseworkers) to ensure that the most appropriate mix of interventions (service process) is available to the client. The manager also manages the physical resources (service package) and is responsible for balancing the supply of resources against demand (service delivery).

An interesting complication is that mental health services are often delivered by third-party, nonprofit providers contracted by governments to reduce demand on public health systems. This embeds the providers within a complex network of private and public responsibilities. For instance, their clients can be outpatients of public psychiatric facilities, persons recovering from substance dependencies, or those transitioning from criminal incarceration. Clients can also be private citizens who are seeking support or have been referred by general medical practitioners.

In many cases, the services provided are either met or subsidized by governments. This brings an added challenge, as governments often desire to see people move along the recovery continuum as quickly as possible with a view to reducing the drain on public resources by returning them to productive employment. Burgess, Pirkis, Coombs, & Rosen, (2010) assert that there must also be a recognition of the factors outside mental health services that foster or impede an individual's recovery. To this end, they highlight that governmental and nongovernmental agencies from other sectors affecy how people with mental illness can maximize their quality of life, including sectors such as employment, education, and housing. They also highlight that communities have an important role to play—the support provided by social networks and the collective community attitudes toward people with mental illness influence the extent to which an individual's recovery goals can be realized.

While considerable attention has been afforded to the clinical nature of psychosocial interventions, there has been comparatively less research exploring the role that the service context plays on such intervention efficacy. This is evident through an examination of the different recovery measures that have emerged to evaluate mental health services, where much of this research tends to view psychosocial rehabilitation as special type of psychological treatment, rather than a program of service-related interventions (see for example, Burgess et al., 2010; Campbell-Orde, Chamberlin, Carpenter, & Leff, 2005). Anthony (1993) argues that these service-related interventions (or triggers) are integral to a recovery-focused service system. The remaining sections of this chapter seek to address this gap, first through a discussion of the characteristics of mental health services, and then through a presentation and discussion of an open-systems model for mental health services.

CHARACTERISTICS OF MENTAL HEALTH SERVICES

Mental health services share many characteristics with other types of services. Schmenner (1986) asserts that such services are characterized by relatively high levels of labor intensity, client interaction, and customization. In this sense, mental health services are similar to other professional services, such as those offered by physicians, lawyers, accountants, and architects.

Berry and Bendapudi (2007), however, point out the unique aspects of health service delivery that set this sector apart from other service-based industries:

- Many of the service interactions are initiated on a "needs" basis, rather than on a "wants" basis.
- Services received are intangible. Clients must pay for a service, and no physical product results.
- Clients must be physically interacting or present with their service provider.
- Clients receiving the service are actually sick, and factors such as illness, pain, uncertainty, and fear may result in initial resistance to the treatments.

Lovelock (1983) provides a useful and popular framework for classifying services based on the (1) nature of the service act, (2) relationship between customers and service provider, (3) required level of customization and judgment, (4) nature of demand and capacity, and (5) method of service delivery. A summary of the characteristics of mental health services is provided in Table 8.1.

Table 8.1	Classification of Mental Health Services.		
	Defining characteristics	Special considerations	Examples of similar services
Nature of service act	Directed at people rather than property, tend to be more intangible than tangible.	While the majority of services are intangible, there are some exceptions. For instance, mental health service providers sometimes provide transition accommodation and physical equipment if they support a client's progress toward recovery.	Education, broadcasting, information services, theaters, museums.
Relationship with clients	Relationships tend to be formal and discrete.	While the service interventions provided may be discrete, the relationship of the client with a service provider can often extend over years. The formality of the relationship may change over time as the client moves out of a mandated program, and he or she may re-engage at a later point based on self-assessment.	Theater season tickets, airline frequent flyer, wholesale buying club.
Customization and judgment	Require high degree of customization and judgment by service personnel.	Heterogeneity in client needs and intervention options provides a significant barrier for new entrants to the mental health service sector, and makes it difficult to recruit and train prospective caseworkers. While formal training is important, judgment is largely subjective and based on experience and tacit knowledge.	Surgery, taxi service, gourmet restaurant.
Nature of demand	Wide fluctuations in demand, which exceeds capacity at peak times.	The absence of clear indicators for mental health services demand makes it difficult to schedule supply. A particular challenge relates to the provision of crisis interventions that can't be delayed, and the tendency of governments to only engage a limited number of service providers within particular jurisdictions.	Passenger transportation, hotels, emergency medical services.
Method of service delivery	Service is provided at a limited number of sites and requires customers to travel to service firm.	Depends largely on the mental health service provider and the type of service intervention. Can be a walk-in service, a hostel with 24-hour support, or home visit. The method of service delivery often depends on demand and available government funding.	Theater, barbershop, hospital.

From this model we see that the role of service operations managers is central to the management and control of service delivery. They must manage human and physical resources in order to meet demand and realize the service delivery goals. We will now spend some time elaborating on the various processes and functions depicted in the model as they apply to the mental health services setting.

ELEMENTS OF THE SERVICE PACKAGE

Fitzsimmons and Fitzsimmons (2011, p. 22) define the service package as the "bundle of goods and services with information that is provided in some environment." They describe this bundle in terms of five features: (1) supporting facilities, (2) facilitating goods, (3) information, (4) explicit services, and (5) implicit services. The quality of the service experience is viewed as the outcome of the interaction between these features, where the relevance and importance of any given consideration vary depending on the unique service setting and the specific needs of the customer.

The supporting facilities relate to the physical resources that must be in place before a service can be offered. In the case of mental health services, these facilities usually relate to a suitably appointed treatment center equipped with training and counseling rooms. Likewise, facilitating goods relates to the material purchased or consumed by the customer during the service act. This varies in mental health services depending on the specific psychosocial intervention. For example, prior to a client's placement within a treatment program, a caseworker completes a rehabilitation readiness assessment using a predetermined assessment protocol. This assessment requires both client and caseworker to complete a range of paper-based forms.

Information represents the sharing of data and knowledge during the service encounter to facilitate an efficient and effective service experience. This may relate to the provision of a prior medical history in the mental health context, as well as the explanation of the intention and purpose of an intervention program. Mental health services also often employ group-based therapy in which information is shared among users to facilitate self-development. It is noteworthy that the recovery-based approach to mental health treatment employs far less asymmetrical psychiatric models of treatment that use limited disclosure.

Explicit services relate to the benefits and outcomes usually associated with consumption of a service offering and are readily observable by the senses. Conversely, implicit services relate to the psychological benefits that the customer may sense only vaguely. For example, in the case of mental health services, an explicit service could relate to the provision of supported housing, whereas a counseling session would be an example of an implicit service.

ROLE OF THE SERVICE OPERATIONS MANAGER

From the open-systems perspective, service operations managers are central to the service system. They manage the production function to ensure quality in service delivery, the operations function to control human and physical resource allocation, and the marketing function to ensure that there is sufficient demand for available service capacity. While the exact title of this role may vary across mental health service providers, the nature of the functions performed is universal.

A key responsibility of the service operations manager is to smooth out fluctuations in consumer demand. In the mental health service context, this means anticipating demand for the different intervention programs from formal and informal sources of referral. By formal sources, we mean referrals from institutional sources such as hospitals, medical practitioners, and other government programs, including corrective services. In some cases, these referrals originate from other mental health service providers seeking to respond to oversupply. Informal sources relate to self-referral from former clients or from persons who recognize that they need some support dealing with a particular mental illness.

In responding to demand, service operations managers must balance the needs of the particular client against the capacity and potential impact on other clients. For example, in resource-intensive service interventions, such as supported accommodation, there are obvious resource constraints relating to available beds and rooms. However, the service operations manager must also consider the potential emotional impact that adding a client may have on the well-being of other clients within the facility. Other considerations of note relate to the availability of alternative services and the priorities of government (and other) funding bodies. Together, these considerations typically result in excess demand for available supply.

One way to increase supply is by recruiting additional service personnel. However, attracting employees with the appropriate mix of skills and attitude is not easy, particularly when incentives and remuneration in the sector are typically lower than in other allied health services. The service operations manager must also consider the capacity of personnel. The diverse range, specialized nature, and legal requirements of mental health services require sophisticated human resource management systems that support the selection, training, and empowerment of service personnel. Beyond human resources management, the service operations manager must also manage supply. Implicit within this task is an ability to forecast demand, schedule staffing, and maximize the yield of available service personnel without sacrificing service quality.

The service operations manager also manages the composition of the service package. The key challenge here is to manage the physical resources (in addition to the human resources) to meet anticipated and realized demand. As such, the service package has a direct influence on decisions regarding staffing and demand management, where the recruitment of certain skills and experience often offsets resource limitations. In this regard, it is important to acknowledge that some elements of the service package are difficult to change in the short term (e.g., physical location and facilities). One strategy used by mental health service providers to overcome location constraints is to provide services in the client's home. However, this is not an option for service interventions that require specialized equipment or for clients suffering from more extreme types of mental illness (e.g., psychotic illnesses such as schizophrenia).

INTERVENTIONS AS SERVICE PROCESSES

Within the context of mental services, the service process is represented by interventions. An open-systems view posits that an intervention has the purpose of converting the client from an input to an output, where the actual conversion requires the active engagement of the client and results in the co-creation of value for both the service provider and the consumer. Though these interventions can take many forms, they share certain characteristics depending on their intended purpose. Drawing on the work of Anthony (1993), Table 8.2 provides an overview of the broad types of mental health interventions available and their associated outcomes.

Table 8.2   Types and Focus of Mental Health Interventions.

Intervention type	Description	Nature of Mental Illness				Client outcome	Examples of specific interventions
		Impairment: disorder in thought, feelings, and behavior	Dysfunction: task-performance limited	Disability: role-performance limited	Disadvantage: Opportunity restriction		
Treatment	Alleviating symptoms and distress	Yes	No	No	No	Symptom relief	Pharmacology
Crisis intervention	Controlling and resolving critical or dangerous problems	Yes	No	No	No	Personal safety assured	Critical incident debriefing
Case management	Obtaining the services the client needs and wants	Yes	Yes	Yes	Yes	Services accessed	Individual recovery plans
Rehabilitation	Developing clients' skills and supports related to clients' goals	No	Yes	Yes	Yes	Role functioning	Individual/group counseling
Enrichment	Engaging clients in fulfilling and satisfying activities	No	Yes	Yes	Yes	Self-development	Personal development programs
Rights protection	Advocating to uphold client rights	No	No	No	Yes	Equal opportunity	Community outreach programs
Basic support	Providing the people, places, and things a client needs to survive	No	No	No	Yes	Personal survival assured	Supported housing
Self-help	Exercising a voice and choice in one's life	No	No	Yes	Yes	Empowerment	Online interventions for depression

From Table 8.2, we can see that there are different consumer-provider interfaces depending on the type of intervention being delivered and the nature of the mental illness being treated. Drawing on the work of Gadrey and Gallouj (1998), we see that interfaces within professional services can be defined in terms of two dimensions, the "mode of interaction" and the "degree of implementation." While their work focused on business-to-business services, the characteristics of the interfaces in mental health services are not entirely dissimilar. In terms of interaction mode, we tend to differentiate between discrete forms of interaction and more continuous forms of interaction undertaken over time. The degree of implementation distinguishes between whether the service provider acts as a catalyst for change (i.e., provides information only) or an agent of change (i.e., gets involved in creating change).

This framework is useful in understanding and describing the mental health service interventions presented in Table 8.2. For instance, treatments and crisis interventions tend to be discrete in nature and require active involvement by service provider. Likewise, case management and rehabilitation require active involvement, but are more continuous in nature and tend to be delivered over an extended time. Rights protection and self-help also tend to be continuous in nature; however, they require little direct engagement with the client. The final intervention category, basic support, varies significantly depending on the specific type of intervention. Some interventions (e.g., providing a meal) are discrete, whereas others (e.g., support housing) involve long periods of support. Likewise, some basic support interventions involve active involvement by service providers (e.g., training), while others are delivered by third parties (e.g., health care).

Other considerations that impact on nature and efficacy of certain mental service interventions are related to the heterogeneity of demand and the embeddedness of mental health services within a broader support structure. The heterogeneity of demand captures the reality that mental health service interventions require high levels of customization, as clients present with different needs. Likewise, clients enjoy different support structures. Prior research has found strong links between the quality of the support provided by friends and family and the speed and quality of recovery.

SPECIAL ROLE OF EVALUATION

The role of evaluation in a traditional service context is the domain of the consumer. However, in a mental health service setting there are multiple layers of evaluation that can have far-reaching impacts. While there is still a need for mental health service professionals to understand how clients perceive the quality of the services delivered, there is a much stronger focus on understanding whether a particular service interventions has had a favorable (or unfavorable) impact on clients' perceptions of their recovery progress and the tangible evidence of clients' movement along the recovery continuum.

Services systems need to account for various stages of the recovery process, knowing that occasionally clients return to seek help. Ironically, repeat visitation in mental health services, unlike in other service settings, is not necessarily a good thing. Lifetime customer value has a whole new meaning in this context. Care is aimed at moving people toward independence, where repeat or continued use of mental health services can sometimes mean a failure of the system rather than success.

Within the open-systems model of mental health services, evaluation provides valuable feedback to the service operations manager to assist in the continuous improvement of operations or it can result in a feedback loop in which a client may repeat an intervention until specific recovery goals are met or be referred to another intervention better suited to his or her particular needs. This frames mental health services in a different light than other services, in that the duration of service consumption is longer than traditional service encounters (even in many other allied health fields), and the post-service evaluation can often be delayed or contaminated by the feedback loop. This provides challenges for the service operations manager in monitoring service quality.

There is also a clinical role to consider within the evaluation process. Where access to mental health services is mandated, client eligibility can sometimes be contingent on a favorable psychiatric assessment. These assessments can also be used at times to move clients out of mental health service programs and into other government-supported programs (e.g., employment participation programs) or to motivate a return to institutionalized psychiatric care where appropriate.

CONCLUSION

This chapter has used an open-systems perspective as a framework for understanding how a better comprehension of the service-related aspects can lead to better mental health services. To achieve this objective, the chapter presented a synopsis of recovery as an emergent ideology for mental illness treatment. This was followed by an explication of the service characteristics of mental health services, and then a presentation and discussion of the open-systems model for mental health services.

Despite its intuitive value as a theoretical lens for understanding the complex interactions that take place among the competing functions and processes that comprise the mental health system, we believe this is the first attempt to use open-systems theory to illuminate the important role of services in the support and delivery of mental health services. It is hoped that this contribution will motivate a new stream of research that better articulates the contribution of services-thinking to the conceptualization, design, and delivery of health services.

This also has important implications for management and policymakers. The model presented here will aid service operations managers in monitoring a client's recovery journey using an open-systems perspective, taking into account the role of service operations as a tool for managing supply and demand, and aiding the efficient use of human and physical resources. Systems such as these are also necessary to assist caseworkers to make meaningful judgments, and to recognize needs for interventions and opportunities to provide additional support.

DIRECTIONS FOR FUTURE RESEARCH

Future research should seek to empirically test the premises of the open-systems perspective presented in this chapter through rigorous empirical research. As the mental health sector becomes further deinstitutionalized and clients are given more autonomy and a louder voice in terms of their treatment, research must now shift to investigating program satisfaction and service quality in an effort to better understand the holistic role that services play in contributing to a client's recovery progress.

There is also a need to ground this research in a "real" mental health service setting. The nature of service delivery in this setting is constrained by convoluted reporting mechanisms, changing government priorities, and a fluid regulatory and compliance environment. Research is needed to understand the implications of shifting the focus for mental health services from outcomes to process, and accordingly, from clinical evaluation to service evaluation. Operationally, this change of thinking will, at the very least, carry a burden for mental health service providers to ensure staff members are adequately trained to interpret such measures, and that management is able to take action on the insights likely to emerge.

REVIEW QUESTIONS

1. Mental health services have shifted focus from psychiatric to psychosocial rehabilitation. What are the characteristics of modern mental health services?

2. Mental health services are complex, interpersonal services that are highly customized with fluctuating demand. Why are such services ill suited to closed-systems approaches?

3. The service operations manager is at the heart of the open-systems perspective. Describe the role that the service operations manager plays in coordinating mental health service provision.

4. Explain the special role that evaluation plays in the mental health services context, and the need for unique service outcome measures and approaches?

5. Evaluation is traditionally the domain of the consumer. How and why is this different in a mental health service setting?

REFERENCES

Anthony, W. (1993). Recovery from mental illness: The guiding vision of the mental health service systems in the 1990s, *Psychosocial Rehabilitation Journal*, 16(4), 11–23.

Anthony, W., Cohen, M., & Farkas, M. (1990). *Psychiatric rehabilitation*. Boston: Boston University, Center for Psychiatric Rehabilitation.

Berry, L., & Bendapudi, N. (2007). Health care: A fertile field for service research. *Journal of Service Research, 10*(2), 111–122.

Burgess, P., Pirkis, J., Coombs, T., & Rosen, A. (2010). *Review of recovery measures* (Version 1.01) Canberra, Australia: Australian Mental Health Outcomes and Classification Network.

Campbell, J., & Schraiber, R. (1989). *The well-being project: Mental health clients speak for themselves* Sacramento: California Department of Health.

Campbell-Orde, T., Chamberlin, J., Carpenter, J., & Leff, H. (2005). *Measuring the promise: A compendium of recovery measures*. Cambridge, MA: Human Services Research Institute.

Chase, R. (1978, November-December). Where does the customer fit in a service operation? *Harvard Business Review, 56*(6), 137–142.

Chase, R. (1983). The customer contact model for organization design. *Management Science*, 29(9), 1037–1050.

Cohen, M., Cohen, B., Nemec, P., Farkas, M., & Forbess, R. (1988). *Psychiatric rehabilitation training technology: Case management* (trainer package). Boston: Boston University, Center for Psychiatric Rehabilitation.

Fitzsimmons, J., & Fitzsimmons, M. (2011). *Service management: operations, strategy and information technology* (7th ed.). New York: McGraw-Hill Irwin.

Gadrey, J., & Gallouj, F. (1998). The provider-customer interface in business and professional services. *Service Industries Journal*, 18(2), 1–15.

Jacobson, N., & Greenley, D. (2001). What is recovery? A conceptual model and explication. *Psychiatric Services*, 52, 482–485.

Lovelock, C. (1983). Classifying services to gain strategic marketing insights. *Journal of Marketing, 47*(3), 9–20.

Mathers, C., & Loncar, D. (2006). Projections of global mortality and burden of disease from 2002 to 2030. *PLOS Medicine, 3*, 2011–2030.

Ralph, R. (2000). Recovery. *American Journal of Psychiatric Rehabilitation, 4*(3), 480–517.

Ranz, J., & Mancini, A. (2008). Public psychiatrists' report of their own recovery-oriented practices. *Psychiatric Services, 59*, 100–104.

Schmenner, R. (1986). How can service businesses survive and prosper? *Sloan Management Review, 27*(3), 21–32.

Thompson, J. (1967). Organizations in action: *Social science bases of administration theory.* New York: McGraw-Hill.

World Health Organization (WHO). (2009). *Improving health systems and services for mental health.* Geneva: World Health Organization.

World Health Organization (WHO). (2012). Global burden of mental disorders and the need for a comprehensive, coordinated response from health and social sectors at the country level. *65th World Health Assembly, Agenda item 6.2* (EB130.R8). Retrieved from http://www.who.int/mental_health/mh_draft_resolution_EB130_R8_en.pdf

Chapter 9

Lean Hospitals: Five Tools that Position Healthcare Organizations for Success

Kenneth K. Boyer
Luv Sharma

LEARNING OBJECTIVES

Upon completing this chapter, you should be able to do the following:

1. Provide a framework for effective process improvement initiatives at hospitals.

2. Know the tools needed to obtain management involvement and buy-in for improvement initiatives.

3. Understand the foundational tools to acquire staff involved in identifying and improving processes.

4. Discuss the benefits of using process improvement and the proposed framework in health care settings.

KEYWORDS

process improvement, lean, business reviews, dashboards, process mapping, 5S, standard work

Health care spending in the United States reached a staggering $2.3 trillion in 2008. This number is approximately 16.5 percent of the U.S. GDP and is expected to increase to 20 percent by 2017. Many believe that the current state of the U.S. health care system is unsustainable. The American Recovery and Reinvestment Act (ARRA) is designed to control health care costs and make it affordable for everyone. The ARRA calls for a number of initiatives, including patient-centered care, accountable care organizations, and enormous incentives (up to $19 billion) for investments in health care information technology. Many of these initiatives have been effectively applied in a broad range of private-sector industries and companies. Thus, there is room for optimism regarding the potential to substantially reduce U.S. health care costs and alter the ever-rising trajectory. However, there are also enormous challenges and barriers. With approximately 5,700 hospitals in the United States, each needs to cut an average of $2.6 million annually for the next 10 years to meet the targets set by the proposed health care reforms. This is a challenging task for hospitals, considering their minimal exposure to continuous improvement tools and the fact that more than half the hospitals lose money, thus putting serious constraints on their ability to support cost-cutting initiatives. Recognizing this, the ARRA has allotted $147 billion to be disbursed over the next 10 years on initiatives directed to lowering health care costs by reducing waste and improving efficiency.

The motivation to reduce costs combined with the availability of funds to support these initiatives has led a number of hospitals to pursue the continuous improvement route. Despite an emerging awareness of the benefits of continuous improvement and financial/legislative support for programs, the lack of experience with continuous improvement tools is causing a number of these initiatives to fail or to underdeliver. In this chapter we examine five tools that will lay a strong foundation for continuous improvement initiatives and can be successfully applied.

Hospitals are complex systems with multiple departments and levels of decision making and power. Poor communication and information flow within and outside the hospital system can lead to increased uncertainty, causing inferior performance. According to the Information Processing Theory (Galbraith, 1973), this increased task complexity and uncertainty can be mitigated by increasing coordination among involved parties, formalization of procedures, and division of work (Daft & Lengel, 1986). Process integration and standardization across departments within the hospital and between the hospital and its outside vendors can lead to improved performance. Process improvement initiatives achieve this goal by encouraging innovation in the workplace and by providing on-the-job training and promoting skill development for employees (Deming, 1982). These projects result in improved communication across departments, improved utilization of services, and increased efficiency.

Three factors have been identified as important for the longterm success of any continuous improvement initiative. They are (1) leadership support, (2) company culture, and (3) technological expertise in the tools.

Leadership support from the top levels of the company/organization is critical since this sets the direction for movement and aligns incentive structures while providing resources to support of these initiatives. Second, developing a company culture centered on a continuous improvement philosophy promotes problem identification and solution at the source. The literature clearly supports the need for a company culture that continuously reinforces the need to work for improvements and to challenge the status quo on a daily basis. Finally, technological expertise provides the necessary tools to frontline staff so they can develop solutions to identified problems. The essence of continuous improvement is having all levels of the organization involved and actively participating. Thus, it is critical that the majority of individuals in the organization develop at least a familiarity with the essential tools and their application.

This chapter provides an overview of five key tools, which, if applied in sequence, will help build leadership commitment, followed by a transformation of the corporate culture. Differentiated customer focus in health care is imperative, considering the growing demand of customers for higher quality and service standards. These tools drive customer-oriented operations and provide customers with higher levels of service and a uniform service experience. The first two tools are designed to promote leadership and management involvement in the continuous improvement initiatives, while the other three are tools needed to ensure success at the ground level. A brief description of these tools is provided below, with a more detailed examination to follow:

1. **Business Reviews:**[1] These are monthly or quarterly meetings of the management of a department, unit, or the entire hospital to review operational metrics and to design projects to improve them. These meetings provide management with insight and support projects, while helping to address issues of resource availability, communication, and accountability through higher visibility. These meetings also drive projects to increase customer focus in hospital operations.

2. **Dashboards:** These are boards displaying metrics, current projects, and success stories for individual areas within the organization. The metrics from individual dashboards roll up to the metrics at higher levels for evaluation during Business Reviews. These dashboards are prepared and managed by employees within the area. The purpose of dashboards is to involve employees in the problem-solving process by allowing them to select metrics to track progress on key measures and to design and run projects to improve them (Womack & Jones, 2003).

3. **Process Mapping:** Every improvement initiative starts with an understanding of the current process. This provides a benchmark for improvement, identification of stakeholders, and problems at different stages of the current process. Some of the techniques used for process mapping are flowcharts, spaghetti diagrams, and value stream maps (George, Maxey, Rowlands, & Price, 2005).

4. **5S:** This is one of the first tools implemented in an area to prepare it for other continuous improvement tools. 5S focuses on having visual order, organization, cleanliness and standardization and results in improved efficiency and safety (ibid.).

5. **Standard Work:** Standardized work defines the sequence, description, time and outcome of every activity within a process. It is one of the most powerful Continuous Improvement tools and forms the baseline for future improvement. Improving standardized work is a never-ending process (ibid.).

---

[1] For an example, see Balanced Scorecard - Continuous Improvements in Overall Patient Care: http://www.clevelandclinicmeded.com/live/courses/2011/quality11/abstracts/10-Quality-Summit-Abstract.pdf

BUSINESS REVIEWS

The business review process should be the foundation that provides a framework for all process improvement initiatives. A *business review* is a monthly or quarterly meeting of hospital management to evaluate performance based on pre-identified metrics and to assign improvement projects. A sample business review scorecard appears in Figure 9.1. The frequency of meetings varies depending on the level at which the business review is conducted. For example, business review meetings at the hospital level are more infrequent compared to the meetings at the department level.

	Actual	Target
■ Company Performance		●
□ Financial Performance		●
□ Increase Revenue		●
□ Maintain Overall Margins		▲
Net Profit	10.00%	▲
Net Profit Margin %	6.00%	◆
YOY Revenue Growth	22.00%	●
New Product Revenue	$2,463,887	●
□ Control Spend		▲
Expense as % of Revenue	85.00%	◆
Expense Variance %	3.00%	●
□ Customer Satisfaction		▲
Count of Complaints	127	◆
Market Share	22.00%	●
Unique Repeat Customer Count	785	▲
Avg Customer Survey Rating	7	●
⊞ Acquire New Customers		●
⊞ Operational Excellence		●
⊞ People Commitment	5	●

Note: Adapted by Authors

Figure 9.1 A SAMPLE BUSINESS REVIEW SCORECARD.

Note: Adapted by authors from http://nickbarclay.blogspot.com/2008_05_01_archive.html

The mechanism by which the business review process works in providing a framework for process improvement initiatives is shown in Figure 9.2. The business review process at the hospital level sets the agenda and scope for process improvement initiatives. Each project is owned by a member of the business review committee and progress on it is tracked at every meeting. This provides the necessary leadership support and buy-in for the projects vital for their success. The projects initiated by the hospital level business review are transferred to the individual departments that are closest to it. These projects and finer metrics to evaluate it are then tracked at the business reviews for the department. The rolled-up metrics for projects at the department level and other performance data like sales, financials, operational, and quality metrics, etc., are used to populate the business review scorecards for the hospital-level business review scorecard. The actual project implementation is done using cross-functional units within each department. These projects use tools such as process mapping, 5S, and standard work and feed metrics for the project to the department business review.

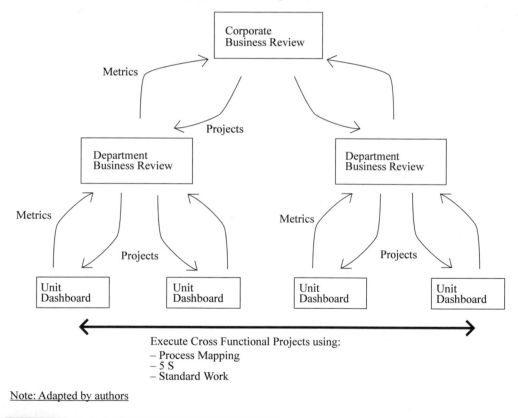

Note: Adapted by authors

Figure 9.2 THE BUSINESS REVIEW PROCESS.

Thus, we can see that a business review at multiple levels in the hospital provides an effective framework to initiate, execute, and monitor process improvement projects.

CASE STUDY: CLEVELAND CLINIC[2]

Business reviews are used at different levels of the organization that follow the continuous improvement cycle consisting of four iterative steps: 1) Set goals, 2) Measure/review performance, 3) Improve and 4) Reward/Recognize top performing staff. The stakeholders involved in the business review at a given level brainstorm and decide on which metrics to track in four categories: Quality, Service, Financials, and Employee Engagement. Targets are selected and set for each metrics. The metrics selected under each heading are then assigned an owner who is responsible for populating and tracking them regularly. Once the business review scorecard has been designed, successes and failures are discussed at monthly meetings and projects are designed to address any gaps in performance. The business review process has led to significant improvements in not only organizational performance but has also led to higher standards of quality and patient experience.

DASHBOARDS

Business reviews are conducted at the management level. However, to get the whole organization involved and empowered, dashboards are a critical tool at the individual process level. *Dashboards* are a form of visual process controls that tie individual efforts to organizational goals. Dashboards communicate metrics, provide feedback, and engage employees in the continuous improvement process. Metrics and status are displayed for all employees to review progress and improve response time to issues. Visual progress quickly highlights issues and priorities leading to improved performance results for both the department and organization.

Dashboards can also be used to track ongoing projects and progress that feed into the department-level business review scorecards. A dashboard is generally divided into four to six sections, with each section tracking different quality measures important for the process at hand. These sections also list current projects, previous successful projects, and information about employees involved in projects. A sample visual board template is shown in Figure 9.3. The sections in a dashboard vary depending on the area implementing them and topics important to them.

---

[2]This section is drawn from the following source and informed by one of the author's personal experiences while working as a lean black belt: http://www.clevelandclinicmeded.com/live/courses/2011/quality11/abstracts/10-Quality-Summit-Abstract.pdf

Department: Unit:		Owner: Date Updated:
Metric-1	Metric-2	Metric-3
Metric-4	Projects	Employee of the Month

Note: Adapted by authors

Figure 9.3 A SAMPLE DASHBOARD.

CASE STUDY: EAST TENNESEE CHILDREN'S HOSPITAL[3]

A continuous improvement dashboard was created to involve employees in improvement initiatives. The dashboard owner updated the metrics and other content on the dashboard. Weekly 15-minute meetings are conducted to go over the dashboard and brainstorm improvement projects. Employees attend these meetings, working in the given area as well as the hospital management. The dashboard for this specific case is given in a weblink.It has four sections, some of which are different from the basic template shown in Figure 9.3. The Front Line Walks section is a sign-off sheet for the managers who attended the weekly meeting. The "Problems to Solve" section lists projects that are under different stages of implementation (from ideas to completed projects). The A3 section describes each of the ongoing projects on an A3-sized paper. The description may contain the problem statement, project goals, current status, proposed solutions, etc. The Kaizen Wall of Fame reports success stories, showcases

---

[3] Adapted from http://www.hckaizen.com/east-tennessee-childrens-hospital-ci-board/

improvement projects, and acknowledges team members for their efforts. Figure 4 shows a more generic version of a continuous improvement dashboard from a hospital different from East Tennessee Children's Hospital.

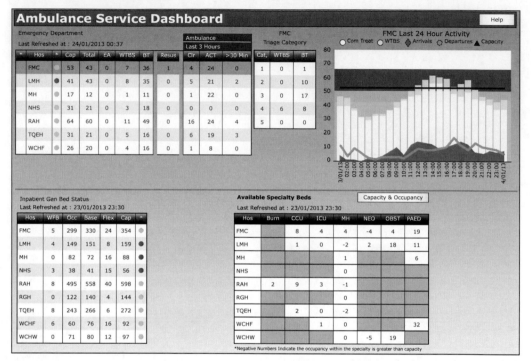

A specific example from East Tennessee Children's Hospital is available at: http://www.hckaizen.com/east-tennessee-childrens-hospital-ci-board/

Figure 9.4 A TYPE OF CONTINUOUS IMPROVEMENT DASHBOARD.

PROCESS MAPPING

Every process improvement project should start with a good understanding of the process under consideration. *Process mapping* is a tool that allows individuals to develop an understanding of the steps, stakeholders, times, and interdependencies among process steps. A number of process mapping tools are available that capture the types and volume of information and, thus, are used at different stages of the improvement project. A flowchart is the simplest form of process mapping; it shows the steps and decision points in a process. A sample flowchart is shown in Figure 5. A swim lane diagram is a more advanced version of a flowchart and shows process transitions among stakeholders. A study of these transitions is important because most of the information loss and errors are introduced at these transitions. Further, swim lane diagrams show segregation of responsibilities that facilitate an increase in project accountability. Figure 6 shows a sample swim lane diagram. A more advanced tool used for process mapping is a value stream map. A value stream map [7] collects many details about individual tasks like task times, number of operators, delays between processes, inventory levels, etc. A value stream map as shown in Figure 7 is a tool that helps identify areas of waste, imbalance or other areas of opportunity in a visual manner. This tool identifies bottlenecks in the process and specific areas of problems to design kaizan events (often half day or day long work groups focused on a specific process to identify improvements) around it.

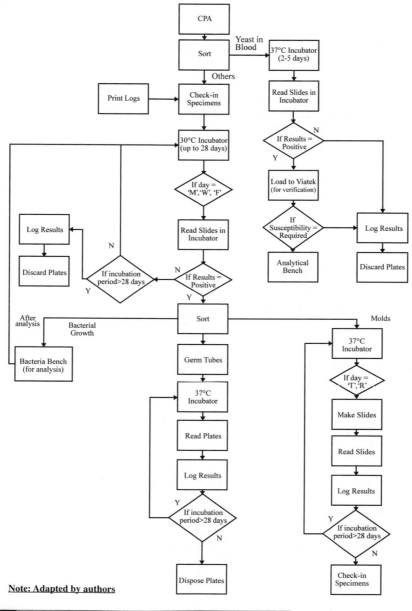

Note: Adapted by authors

Figure 9.5 FLOWCHART OF A HOSPITAL LAB PROCESS

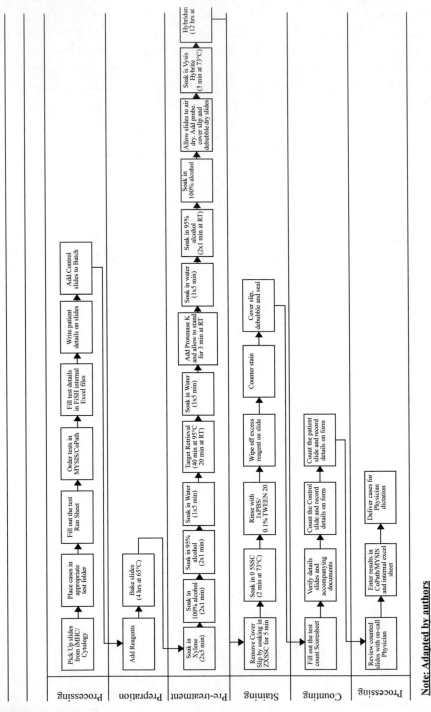

Figure 9.6 A SWIM LANE DIAGRAM.

Note: **Adapted by authors**

Case Study: Cleveland Clinic[4]

The microbiology lab forecasted an increase in influenza cases and wanted to plan in advance by providing appropriate resources for the influenza test. The process for testing was semi-automatic, i.e., had both manual and automated steps. To solve the problematic delays in processing test that could result from the increased volume the process improvement team created a value stream map for the entire process. Creation of the value stream map required collection of the cycle times at each process step, the type of step (automatic or manual), the batch size, etc. The value stream map appears in Figure 9.7 and shows the cycle times and usage for each step. The step with the highest use is the bottleneck and needs to be addressed first. It can be seen from the map that an automated step (Rotogene) is the bottleneck step with a utilization of 77.4 percent. Thus, a new Rotogene machine must be purchased, or an alternative, such as working longer hours with this machine, must be implemented, if the volume increase in tests pushes utilization close to 100 percent capacity.

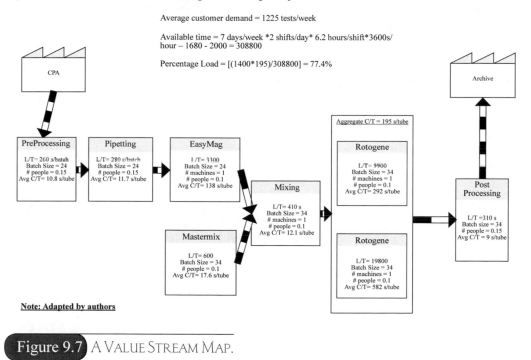

Figure 9.7 A Value Stream Map.

[4] This data are drawn from the author's personal experience. Numbers have been disguised to preserve confidential information.

5S TOOL

5S is a quick improvement tool that creates and maintains an organized, clean, safe, and high-performance work area. It is useful at the beginning of projects to prepare the process area for continuous improvement and engage team members with immediate results. This simple, effective tool leads to improvements in quality, efficiency, productivity, and safety in a health care setting. 5S was developed on the automobile manufacturing floors in Japan. The process has five stages: Sort (Seiri), Simplify (Seitan), Shine/Sweep (Seiso), Standardize (Seiketsu), and Sustain (Shitsuke). They are described in the following sections.

SORT: IDENTIFY AND REMOVE UNNECESSARY ITEMS

The goal of Sort is to identify and eliminate unnecessary items from the area. The first step is to identify the items not needed to complete the job task. Defective, outdated, and excess items that have accumulated are tagged for removal from the area. After unnecessary items are identified, the team evaluates and determines the disposition of the items. The key is to leave only the bare essentials necessary to do the job.

SET IN ORDER/SIMPLIFY: ORGANIZE THE GOODS

The next step is to simplify the area by arranging items to maximize workflow. The items needed to complete the job should be arranged and labeled so anyone new to the area can perform the job. Process mapping is useful in this step to determine an optimal location based on the workflow. After the location is determined, label items and keep only necessary inventory levels.

SHINE/SWEEP: KEEP IT CLEAN

The sweep step determines the program for keeping the area clean and organized. Maintaining the 5S area is a daily activity. Housekeeping schedules are useful visual tools to assign tasks and hold employees accountable for keeping the area clean.

STANDARDIZE: MAINTAIN THE FIRST 3S STEPS

Consistent and standardized procedures help to maintain sort, simplify, and sweep in daily activities. All employees working in the area should know the procedures and responsibilities for their daily tasks. Standard Operating Procedures document the process steps to complete tasks. Visual Process Controls including labels ensure items are placed in the correct location and in the correct quantity. Checklists hold people accountable for daily, weekly, and monthly tasks.

SUSTAIN/SELF DISCIPLINE: SUSTAIN 5S

Long-term sustainability requires periodic checks to ensure compliance. A strong control system is needed to prevent the area from returning to its original state. Audit systems are a great way to measure compliance, identify gaps, and improvement opportunities.

CASE STUDY: BETH ISRAEL DEACONESS HOSPITAL[5]

Figure 8 shows the results of the 5S initiative in a neonatal intensive care unit (NICU). The initiative followed the 5S process in the sequence specified above. The effort took six weeks of pre-work and two days of 5S effort to complete. It resulted in reduced inventory levels and a well-organized and clean work area.

Note: Adapted by authors

Figure 9.8 NICU 5S EFFORT AT A LEADING HOSPITAL IN BOSTON.

STANDARD WORK

Standardized work is a living document that defines the sequence, description, frequency, and result of process activities. Standardizing procedures reduces the variation among people completing the same task. Documentating each process step helps to train new employees, reset expectations for existing employees, and identify areas for process improvement. The document should be reviewed with all employees and

Note: Adapted by authors from http://runningahospital.blogspot.com/2009/11/nicu-goes-lean.html

[5] The NICU goes Lean: http://runningahospital.blogspot.com/2009/11/nicu-goes-lean.html

updated a periodically. It should be easy to understand and easily accessible to employees in the work area.

A standard work template is shown in Figure 9.9. The table on the top left half of the template is used to document the sequence, description, frequency, and results of individual tasks in a process. The blank area at the bottom of the table is used to draw a flow diagram depicting the location and interactions among the activities.

Process Owner Overview		**Date:**		**Time:**		
	Major Steps	**Work Time**	**Wait time**	**Process Observations**	**Diagram, Work Flow, Picture, Time Grid**	
1					☺ ◆ ◎ ▽ Critical ✚ Team	
2					Tip Tollgate WIP step Safety	
3						
4						
5						
6						
7						

Note: Adapted by Authors

Figure 9.9 STANDARD WORK TEMPLATE.

CONCLUSION

This chapter provides a framework and an overview of some tools and techniques that hospitals new to process improvement can adopt. The framework proposes the adoption of five tools in a specific sequence to increase the effectiveness of process improvement initiatives at hospitals. The first two tools (Business Reviews and Dashboards) are designed to promote leadership and management involvement in the continuous improvement initiatives. These tools are also instrumental in involving employees at all levels in process improvement initiatives and empowering them to make a difference in the workplace. The last three (5S, Process Mapping, and Standard Work) are

Note: Adapted by authors from http://www.hospitalmedicine.org/AM/BOOST/PDFs/Thedacare-Completing_ Initial_Assessment.pdf

important tools needed to ensure success at the ground level. These tools provide the foundation for process improvement initiatives and identify and define problems as well as standardize current processes. Using the proposed framework helps lay a strong foundation for process improvement initiatives and adds more advanced tools at a later stage. A strong Process Improvement foundation helps hospitals achieve a cost-competitive position while increasing their level of customer focus and service orientation. This overview is meant as an introduction. There are many resources and publications, several cited here, that can help ground and educate health care professionals interested in applying process improvement.

REVIEW QUESTIONS

1. What are the critical factors affecting the success of process improvement initiatives.

2. Do you think process improvement tools can be effective in health care settings? Why or why not?

3. Hospitals have a decentralized structure in which physicians play a dominant role in decision making and project success. How should implementation of process improvement initiatives be designed in such an environment?

4. Which process improvement tools are important for ensuring management buy-in and changing company culture?

5. Which are the basic process improvement tools that lay the framework for more advanced tools? How do these tools work? Is there a sequence in which they should be implemented

REFERENCES

Daft, R. L., & Lengel, R. H. (1986). Organizational information requirements, media richness and structural design. *Management Science*, 32(5), 554–571.

Deming, E. W. (1982). Improvement of quality and productivity through action by management. *National Productivity Review*, 1(1), 12–22.

Galbraith, J. R. (1973). *Designing complex organizations*. Reading, MA, Addison-Wesley.

George, M., Maxey, J., Rowlands, D., & Price, M. (2005). The lean Six Sigma pocket toolbook: A quick reference guide to 100 tools for improving quality and speed. New York: McGraw Hill.

Womack, J. P., & Jones, D. T. (2003). Lean thinking: Banish waste and create wealth in your corporation (rev ed.). London: Simon & Schuster.

Chapter 10

The Emerging U.S. Health Care Service Platform

Ravi S. Behara
C. Derrick Huang
Jahyun Goo

LEARNING OBJECTIVES

Upon completing this chapter, you should be able to do the following:

1. Understand health care service from a systems perspective.

2. Understand the aspects of HIT including EHRs, HIEs, privacy and security, and clinical decision support.

3. Recognize some of the emerging innovations in health care services such as ACOs

4. Understand the emergence of a health care service platform.

INTRODUCTION

The U.S. health care spending in April 2012 was at a seasonally adjusted annual rate (SAAR) of $2.79 trillion, which represents nearly 18 percent of GDP (Altarum, 2012). The size and rate of growth of this cost became a major national concern. The costs are increasing for many reasons, including a greater use of expensive and innovative methods of care, demographic changes where a larger number of elderly require service, litigation against service providers and associated insurance costs, and an inefficient delivery system. The discovery, development, and use of advanced medical technologies to provide high-quality care have always been a hallmark of U.S. health care leadership in the world. Such technologies include advanced clinical solutions driven by the latest pharmaceutical- (biochemical) and biotechnology- (genetic, biologic) based treatments that are leading to us toward the emerging reality of personalized medicine, advanced medical diagnostic equipment and instrumentation, and medical device technologies for individual patients. But the use of information technology (IT) to facilitate efficient and effective care delivery has been conspicuously slow in development and deployment in the U.S. health care industry, trailing many other leading economies in the world.

The advanced economies that lead the United States in IT use in health care have significantly smaller populations and have national health care systems. But the U.S. health care system not only has to deliver care to a larger population, it must do so in a more complex and a combined public/private sector context. So the role of the federal government in setting the context is important. The philosophy underlying the current surge in IT use in U.S. health care is well captured in the following quote:

> We are not your mother's HHS, we are committed to fueling the emerging "Open health data" ecosystem with data and through work as a facilitator and catalyst which create value for consumers, providers, employers, governments, helping them make better decisions and get better outcomes. (Anonymous, 2010. p.8)

What we are currently experiencing is not merely IT adoption but a more far-reaching structural innovation in health care services. The extant academic literature in service highlights the limited work in implemention of service technologies (Roth & Menor, 2003) and innovation in technology-based services (Menor, Tatikonda, & Sampson, 2002). In addition, Essen (2009) discusses how existing research on IT in services is largely limited to addressing specific customer needs with certain technology-based services. She identifies a significant gap in the related literature and the need to explicitly address the inherent complexity involved in IT-based services and the innovation that invariably emerges from technology adoption. Essen (2009) develops such a framework in the context of remote health monitoring and home-care services for the elderly, where service innovation is attained through (nonlinear) emergence triggered by the injection of energy (new technology) into the system. This is also influenced by individual and institutional constraints and stabilizing mechanisms (regulations, culture, and values) and positive and negative feedback from personnel using the technologies. It highlights the need to take a more comprehensive view of the problem context, and refrain from looking at technology in services from narrow perspectives such as customer needs or interactions. This is especially the case in complex services such as health care, where the both the individual and the context have to be equally understood to develop a comprehensive understanding of IT use. Such a formulation of IT applications in health services is indispensable because the ultimate purpose of these services is our own well-being.

This chapter begins with a brief look at the regulatory origin for the current push toward wide-scale Electronic Health Records (EHRs) adoption across the United States. It is increasingly being acknowledged that this is primarily being driven by the financial incentives provided by federal government. The health IT incentive program has jump-started EHR adoption among U.S. health care service providers. Before we continue the discussion on health care IT, we step back to truly understand health care from a systems perspective. We believe this is an important first step, so as to understand the complexity inherent in this service. We review some emerging ideas in service management related to service platforms. Our own interpretation of a service platform is then presented. It is in the context of this framework that we then discuss the key elements of health care IT and its adoption, and the emergence of health care service innovations based on this technology. We then discuss the emergence of a health care service platform, the coordination that provides the foundation for patient-centered care on this platform, and some of the opportunities it presents for service management researchers.

REGULATORY DRIVERS

The American Recovery and Reinvestment Act of 2009 (ARRA) became law in February 2009, and it was a significant effort to jumpstart a stalled U.S. economy. One of its objectives was to modernize the nation's infrastructure, including the health care information infrastructure by promoting and expanding the adoption of health information technology (HIT). This was addressed by the Health Information Technology for Economic and Clinical Health Act (HITECH Act) of 2009. It authorizes the Centers for Medicare & Medicaid Services (CMS) to provide a reimbursement incentive for physicians and hospital providers for the "meaningful use" of "certified" EHR technology. This reimbursement, together with other related investments, totals $25.9 billion for HIT-related expenditures within ARRA. It represents the biggest federal technology initiative since the Manhattan Project for the creation of the atomic bomb during the Second World War. This HIT initiative is just as strategic for the United States, because of the combined cost escalation of health care impacting competitiveness of the country as well as the aging demographic profile of the country. But in many ways, this technology initiative may be viewed as being far more difficult than the Manhattan Project because it is a "distributed problem," with individual physician practices, hospitals, and other service providers all having to make a transition to integrated and secure EHR systems.

Further, the HITECH Act also provided the Department of Health & Human Services with the authority to disseminate regulations and guidance to support the development of an interoperable, private, and secure nationwide health information technology infrastructure through the newly formed Office of the National Coordinator for Health Information Technology. This has unleashed a major IT overhaul of the entire health care sector in the United States. Electronic medical records (EMRs) systems, electronic health records (EHRs) systems (an EMR with interoperability), and the Health Information Exchange (HIE) infrastructure are the core IT systems that facilitate the implementation of the HITECH Act.

The EHR implementation has been driven primarily by a combination of initial incentives for adoption, followed by future penalties for non-adopters. Incentive payments began in 2011 and will gradually phase out in 2016 for Medicare EHR, while Medicaid EHR incentive payments end in 2021. Starting in 2015, providers are expected to have adopted and be actively using an EHR in compliance with the "meaningful use" definition or they will be subject to financial penalties under Medicare (and later under Medicaid) reimbursement rules.

Let's take a look at the incentives paid to date to get a sense of the scope of EHR implementation. The EHR incentive program reported that starting in 2011 and as of March 2012, $4.48 billion was paid out in incentives. This included over $792 million to 44,014 Medicare-eligible professionals, over $628 million to 29,931 Medicaid-eligible professionals (physicians, dentists, nurse practitioners, etc.), and $3.06 billion to 2,667 eligible hospitals that serve both Medicare and Medicaid recipients. While we typically look at such payments as a "government program," it must be recognized that the CMS is a customer of the private for-profit and not-for-profit physician practices and hospitals, and is the largest payer to the health care service providers. In fact, what we are seeing is a large, concerned, and motivated customer paying the service providers to improve their service delivery using technology paid for by the customer. This is because the customer (CMS) believes that this EHR technology implementation will result in improved quality, better safety, and ultimately, a lower cost of health care service. In addition, this will positively impact the customers of other for-profit payers (insurance companies), thereby improving health care service to all citizens.

Beyond the individual use of EHRs, the need to coordinate patient care across varied providers has resulted in the need to develop and provide Health Information Exchange (HIE) services. Most HIEs are formed to share information among health care providers and organizations within a specific geographic area. However, others are designed for unique purposes, such as to collect and share information about participants involved in a state Medicaid program. HIEs are being established by state governments, by private organizations, or by public-private partnerships, or collaborations among providers. This effectively creates a complex network that handles the supply chain of patient information in health care today to facilitate coordination as a way to improve quality, safety, and efficiency of patient care. So regulatory mandates as well as financial incentives and penalties are driving the implementation of EHR and HIE technologies. But, while there is significant focus on IT implementation, we recognize that it is a means toward a larger goal. What we are being witness to is not simply a large-scale build-out of the health care service infrastructure to improve quality, safety, and cost. It is the beginning of the development of an entirely new service platform in health care services.

Health Care Service: A Systems Perspective

There is sometimes a tendency to view the "the system" in health care service as the "delivery system," leading to a limited perspective. A *system* is typically defined as an entity of component parts that individually establish relationships with each other and that interact with their environment both as individuals and as a group. According to Checkland (1987), at a conceptual level, *system* is a name for an abstract intellectual construct that an observer may choose when analyzing a problem situation. Four types of systems may be identified based on an intuitive attempt to describe the external world. Checkland (1984) refers to these as natural systems, physical designed systems, designed abstract systems, and human activity systems. Human activity systems encompass all types of human activities and include organizations. Such systems perpetuate their own existence through a number of important functions: adaptation, regulation, renewal, communication, and transformation. Four broad categories of systems perspectives are Living Systems Theory, Socio-Technical Systems, Systems Dynamics, and the Non-linear Systems Paradigm. Since systems approaches could provide health care services researchers with appropriate frameworks in which to develop studies related to health care IT, an elaboration of one of these approaches (Socio-Technical Systems) is worth undertaking.

The Socio-Technical Systems (STS) approach is a guide to ensure that the social system and its individual members are an integral part of the organizational improvement efforts in order to facilitate a smooth transition of people and technology to a new state. The STS concept is simple: It states that a change in structure and technology must necessarily consider the impact on human efforts. The difficulty is that reactions of personal frustration and tensions could surface at unexpected parts of the social system.

Systems theory provides appropriate integrative models with which to understand service organizations and the change initiatives they are implementing. The STS perspective was developed to explain the critical relationships that exist between people and technology. It calls for a joint-optimization of the social and technical subsystems in an organization (Emery, 1959). Joint-optimization "regards man as complementary to the machine and values his unique capabilities for appreciative and valuating judgment. He is a resource to be developed for his own sake" (Trist, 1981, p. 42). Joint-optimization considers that the most effective arrangement of human organizations is that which integrates the demand of both technical and social aspects of interactions. As the complexity in organizations, industries, and the overall economy continues to increase, simplistic analyses of interactions that exclude technical or social systems cannot provide answers for improvement. An STS approach provides an alternative framework for analysis of health care services.

Ashby's Law of Requisite Variety (Waelchli, 1989) proposes that only variety can control variety. This law suggests that the complexity of a system can be reduced only when the means used for reduction are at least as complex as the system itself. Since health care services are multifaceted, the processes and organizations that deliver and manage these services should necessarily be multidimensional and complex. Therefore, an effective understanding of health care services is likely only when they are viewed from a number of possible perspectives. Consequently, a more comprehensive and integrated representation of health care services is required to understand them.

A socio-technical systems perspective provides an initial step in understanding health care systems. Such systems exhibit other characteristics. System characteristics of nonlinearity and complexity are present. Some of the features possessed by complex nonlinear systems are (adapted from Reason, 1990; Perrow, 1984):

- The system has many components whose failure can have multiple effects downstream.
- Due to a high degree of specialization there is little interchangeability of personnel, equipment, or supplies.
- There are many control parameters that could potentially interact.
- Certain information about the state of the system must be obtained indirectly or inferred.
- There is only a limited understanding of some transformation processes.
- Unfamiliar and unintended feedback loops exist.

System components can be linked to each other, or coupled, either tightly or loosely. While the overall health care system may be considered to be loosely coupled, there exist some tightly coupled subsystems in health care, e.g., operating theaters. Some of the characteristics are compared below (adapted from Reason, 1990; Perrow, 1984):

Tightly Coupled Systems	Loosely Coupled Systems
• E.g., operating theaters	• E.g., care at physician's office
• Production sequences are relatively unchangeable	• Production sequences can be changed
• Few ways to achieve a particular goal	• Many ways to achieve a particular goal
• Buffers and redundancies deliberately designed into the system	• Buffers and redundancies not deliberately designed into the system
• Processing delays are unacceptable	• Processing delays are acceptable

In loosely coupled systems, efforts to tighten the coupling between components is attempted to improve system efficiency, while tight coupling between system components is loosened to reduce system vulnerability. Health care services are also human activity systems; i.e., the purpose of the system is advanced through human action.

One of the characteristic features of humans is the ability to adapt to a changing and complex environment. The very evolution and resilience of the species is testimony to this fact. This adaptive nature of the key component of health care systems (human actors) must be given due consideration when studying such systems. Hence health care services may be considered adaptive, complex, nonlinear, and loosely coupled socio-technical systems. It is from this perspective we review the ongoing efforts in health care IT infrastructure transformation.

SERVICE PLATFORMS

The increased implementation of technology is not limited to health care services, but is impacting all services. This is driven by both a need to improve operational performance and to leverage new technologies for innovation. Ostrom et al. (2010) identify and articulate 10 research priority areas in the science of service. While the first nine initiatives involve service strategy, development and execution are all driven by the "pervasive force" of technology; the 10th initiative on "leveraging technology to advance service" directly addresses the use of technology in services. Specifically, this theme includes building business models for new technologies, accelerating adoption of new technology, supporting real-time decision making, enabling mobile solutions, enhancing information privacy and security, using the service system paradigm to drive innovation, and enabling agility and integration. The discussion also highlights the emerging "freedom economy" in which customers are at the center of "boundary less relationships and low-friction transactions, exchanges, and business operations," in which "capabilities come to the customer" and not the other way around (Ostrom et al. 2010, p.29-30). Further, the idea of technology as a service is not fully integrated with traditional service concepts. This is evident in the emerging service science efforts, where the technology-oriented thought leaders are simply wrapping technology issues in a service packaging. While this is a start, Ostrom et al. (2010) call for an increased insight into "service platforms" as a way to integrate the technology service perspectives with mainstream service management ideas.

We find such a situation in health care services. The current dominant effort at IT adoption (EHR, HIE, etc.) in health care seems to drive much of the current debate, but a larger systemic perspective is needed to define a "health care service platform" that is emerging. We attempt to define such a platform in this discussion (Figure 10.1).

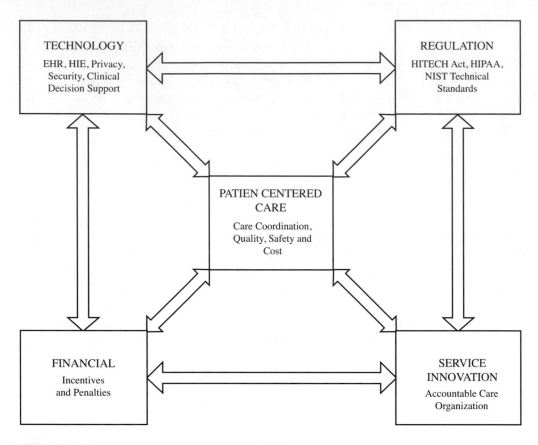

Figure 10.1   STANDARD WORK TEMPLATE.

The key elements of the health care "service platform" are the technology component that makes for improved operational efficiency and effectiveness, measured by the improved quality, safety, and reduced cost of the service. But, as technology adoption crosses a threshold, it also allows for the possibility of innovative business models to emerge. These service innovations are also being introduced in small pockets, with the intent that multiple successful efforts will eventually reach a tipping point and lead to broad-based adoption. So both technology and innovation adoption in health care appear to follow an approach of incentive-based adoption that is being pushed toward a broad-enough acceptance so as to become the "new normal." But there is a core philosophy that is emerging at the crossroads of health care IT and innovation adoption. That is the philosophy of patient-centered care. Each of these key elements of the emerging health care service platform: health care IT and service innovation, is discussed in the following sections.

HEALTH CARE IT

While EHR adoption is the headline for all current health care IT (HIT) efforts, we need to recognize that the key elements of HIT are:

- EHR implementation
- Interoperability and HIE implementation
- Health care information privacy and security
- Clinical decision support

EHR Implementation: As mentioned in the previous section, EHR implementation has been primarily driven by federal financial incentives. But these incentives are tied to the notion of "meaningful use" of EHR; that is, CMS has defined specific targets that must be attained so the health care providers can be eligible to receive incentive payments. As it currently stands, meaningful use will be evaluated in three distinct stages: Stages 1, 2, and 3. Providers should implement EHR technologies and attest that they have demonstrated meaningful use. Of the three stages of meaningful use (MU), currently only MU Stage 1 is fully defined and is the current target for providers to accomplish. Some of the main elements of MU Stage 1 are for providers (professionals and hospitals) to use Computerized Physician Order Entry (CPOE); generate and transmit permissible prescriptions electronically (eRx); incorporate clinical lab test results into certified EHR technology as structured data; record and chart changes in vital signs; maintain active medication, allergy, and diagnoses list; provide patients with an electronic copy of their health information; perform medication reconciliation at relevant encounters and each transition of care; and send reminders to patients per patient preference for preventive/follow-up care. Implementing these practices using EHR technology is targeted at ensuring better coordination of care among providers, reduced errors, and improved involvement of the patient through information. Stage 2 MU that is to begin in 2013, and build on Stage 1 MU, is still under significant dispute.

Studies analyzing the impact of EHR implementation to date report both positive and negative outcomes. Buntin, Burke, Hoaglin, & Blumenthal, (2011) conduct a comprehensive analysis of 154 peer-reviewed studies over a three-year period and found largely positive effects of health IT on care delivery and on provider and patient satisfaction. They found that over 92 percent of the studies reached positive conclusions on the effects of the health IT implementation, and that these positive effects were present in both large health care systems as well as smaller practices. But they also found studies reporting shortcomings and highlighting the importance of the "human elements," such as strong leadership and staff support for the change when transitioning to health IT. At the other end of the spectrum, there are significant concerns about the design of the technologies themselves. The Agency for Healthcare Quality and Research (AHRQ) conducted a study that emphasized the need to promote standards in usability and information design in the development of EHRs (Armijo, McDonnell,

& Werner, 2009). Since usability and information design are highly correlated with successful implementation and effective use of computer systems, these disciplines should be promoted in the EHR market to ensure realization of the benefits expected from federal investments in HIT. The National Institute for Standards and Technology (NIST) has devised a technical document for technology vendors and users to evaluate the usability of EMRs. There are deeper issues in that not all EHRs have the same design effectiveness across multiple clinical disciplines. Consultants from Booz Allen Hamilton (Leslie, Doscher, & Toner, 2012) found in a study that there are deep-rooted problems in the technical design of EMRs beyond usability. These problems are:

- EHRs were originally designed for billing, coding, and documentation, so their developers had few incentives to maximize quality and efficiency. This initial focus is a major roadblock to EHR innovation.
- It is challenging for EHRs to facilitate clinical decision making while remaining user-friendly for physicians.
- There is a limited focus on information exchange since the majority of EHRs operate on closed networks that do not easily connect with other systems. This limits its usefulness in care coordination and delivery.

While it is still being debated whether the federal government or the private sector should spur EHR adoption and innovation, Leslie et al. (2012) identify four themes that are emerging on the future of EHRs in the next few years:

- Further integration with mobile technologies
- Greater affordability and personalization for providers
- More accessibility and interoperability with other systems
- Greater emphasis on patient centeredness to encourage patient engagement in care decisions and communication with providers

Other technical evolutions are taking place, for instance, a growing shift to cloud-based EHRs (Hirsch, 2012). Specifically, this Software as a Service (SaaS) approach appears to have the following four advantages:

1. EHR response time, such as the loading time between clicks
2. Customer support, such as frequent updating and enhancements
3. Product quality/usability
4. "Bang for the buck," i.e., attractive pricing

So we find that, while there is a growing adoption of existing EMRs with positive outcomes, there are also many deep-rooted technical and design issues that remain to be addressed. Some of these are being addressed through the use of new and emerging technologies, while others must be based on a fundamental rethinking of the way the EMR solutions are developed. There continues to be both optimism and opportunity to improve, making this space a dynamic area of continued development in HIT.

HIE Implementation: There have been many efforts in the past few decades to share health care information among service providers. For various reasons, including cost and implementation challenges, Health Information Exchange (HIE) implementation did not reach the threshold of success. HIE efforts are under the direction of the Office of the National Coordinator for Health IT (ONCHIT) that was formed under ARRA. The HITECH Act allocated $2 billion to support HIE activities, and the widespread use of EHRs integrated with HIEs is slated for Stage 3 MU. Specifically, the HITECH Act supports two main HIE initiatives. The first is a $560 million effort at the state level, where the State Health Information Exchange Cooperative Agreement Program is a state-federal program to facilitate and expand the secure electronic movement and use of health information among organizations within/between states in accordance with nationally recognized standards. The second $200 million initiative is a smaller, targeted community program to further enhance ongoing HIE efforts by organizations and agencies.

The need to coordinate patient care across varied providers has resulted in the need to develop and provide Health Information Exchange (HIE) services. Most HIEs are formed to share information among health care providers and organizations within a specific geographic area. However, others are designed for unique purposes, such as to collect and share information about participants involved in a state Medicaid program. HIEs are being established by state governments, by private organizations, or by public-private partnerships, or collaborations among providers. Some initial results are encouraging. For instance, Frisse et al. (2012) found that the sharing of electronic data among 12 Memphis-area emergency departments reduced hospital admissions and redundant imaging tests. The total annual savings of $1.9 million were largely attributable to avoidance of admissions. At a wider state level, the Washington State Health Care Authority started using an HIE in June 2012 to share patient information between its EDs and physicians, thereby reducing unnecessary emergency room visits. They expect a savings of $31 million (Bowman, 2012).

The long-term goal for HIE efforts is the development of a broad-based interoperability and a national network. In fact, there is a broader initiative under ONCHIT called the Nationwide Health Information Infrastructure (NwHIN). The NwHIN is a community of providers to create the standards and services that, within a policy framework, enable simple, directed, routed, scalable transport over the Internet to be used for secure and meaningful exchange between known participants in support of meaningful use. Here we begin to see the early markers of a health care service platform governed by appropriate policies and standards, and one that becomes the framework for future services.

But one of the key prerequisites for this to be successful is the assurance of privacy and security of health care information, both within EHRs and in interoperable HIEs. We discuss this issue in the next section.

Health care information privacy and security: The federal Health and Human Services (HHS) Office for Civil Rights (OCR) enforces the Health Insurance Portability and Accountability Act (HIPAA) Privacy and Security Rules. The HIPAA Privacy Rule applies to patient health information (PHI), including electronic, oral, and paper form. It provides federal protections for personal health information held by covered entities that cover health care providers, health plans, and a health care information clearinghouse. The Privacy Rule gives patients an array of rights with respect to that information. At the same time, the Privacy Rule permits the disclosure of personal health information needed for patient care and other important purposes. The HIPAA Security Rule applies to electronic patient health information (EPHI) and specifies a series of administrative, physical, and technical safeguards for covered entities to use to assure the confidentiality, integrity, and availability of patients' electronic protected health information.

But unlike the EHR and HIE initiatives, no specific financial incentives under ARRA exist to implement HIPAA privacy and security rules in the context of EPHI. On the contrary, the federal government issues penalties for violations. In fact, in May 2012 a federal appeals court upheld the conviction of a researcher at the UCLA Healthcare System for accessing the hospital's EHR system without authorization in violation of HIPAA. This was the first person to receive a (four-month) prison sentence for violating HIPAA privacy laws by merely snooping into medical records on individuals, even though there was no known personal gain. This highlights the increased enforcement of HIPAA laws, especially significant because of the low threshold for violation set by this ruling. Other violations, especially of security breaches however small, have received significant financial penalties.

As required by section 13402(e)(4) of the HITECH Act, the HHS Secretary must post a list of breaches of unsecured protected health information affecting 500 or more individuals. Since 2009, this has been publicly available at www.hhs.gov/ocr/privacy/hipaa/administrative/breachnotificationrule/breachtool.html. A quick review of this website shows that there have been many breaches since the beginning of public records, with 49 breaches reported in 2009 (September through December), 212 in 2010, 146 in 2011, and 28 in the first half of 2012. Each of these breaches involve anywhere from a few hundred (over 500) individual medical records to hundreds of thousands (even millions) of records being compromised in each event. A total of more than 20 million individuals were affected by these 435 security breaches. The data storage included paper, laptop, removable storage drives, and network servers. The common thread underlying all these breaches was a lack of security planning and protocols and the significant level of internal (employee) attacks. There is a growing realization that managing security and risk is an ongoing managerial responsibility, and one that must include building a risk management mindset, establish a security governance structure, define and implement a security management plan that includes risk assessment and access control, and finally, an ongoing review and audit of the effectiveness of the plans in use.

In addition to securing stand-alone EHR systems against potential breaches, the security problem has become more complex because of the variety of medical devices that contain electronic patient records. The burgeoning use of mobile devices significantly increases the data security problem. Further, the implementation of HIE and other efforts at system interoperability have essentially created a vulnerable network of systems and devices, thereby increasing many fold the likelihood of security breaches. These new security challenges have increased the need for effective planning and management, both in the technical and organizational contexts.

Clinical decision support: While Stage 1 MU of EMR implementation is considered to include some level of clinical decision support, it is expected to be largely implemented through Stage 2 MU. But that effort, which was to begin in 2013, has been stalled since mid-2012. The HIMSS (the professional society for health care information and management) defines *clinical decision* support as

> a process for enhancing health-related decisions and actions with pertinent, organized clinical knowledge and patient information to improve health and health care delivery. Information recipients can include patients, clinicians and others involved in patient care delivery; information delivered can include general clinical knowledge and guidance, intelligently processed patient data, or a mixture of both; and information delivery formats can be drawn from a rich palette of options that includes data and order entry facilitators, filtered data displays, reference information, alerts, and others. www.himss.org/asp/topics_clinicaldecision.asp

While clinical decision support efforts are in their early stages, it is a logical extension of the increased data collection that is integral to the widespread use of EMR technologies.

HEALTH CARE SERVICE INNOVATIONS

CMS has also initiated federal incentives for innovations. As in the case of technology adoption incentives, there is debate about government- vs. industry-led innovation, but it must be remembered that the federal government (through CMS) is the largest customer with every (cost and quality) incentive to demand better service from health care providers. So the government- vs. industry-led innovation may be considered a false dichotomy, a better approach is to consider it a customer-led innovation strategy. Innovations are under way by the CMS Innovation Center, which facilitates health care transformation by finding new ways to pay for and deliver care that improve quality and safety of care and while lowering costs. One such initiative is the creation of the Accountable Care Organizations (ACOs).

ACOs are groups of doctors, hospitals, and other health care providers, who come together voluntarily to give coordinated high quality care to the Medicare patients they serve. Coordinated care helps ensure that patients, especially the chronically ill, get the right care at the right time, with the goal of avoiding unnecessary duplication of services and preventing medical errors. When an ACO succeeds in both delivering high-quality care and spending health care dollars more wisely, it will share in the savings it achieves for the Medicare program. innovations.cms.gov/initiatives/ACO/index.html

ACO success requires transparency in policy and data analytics between payers and providers. This openness is a prerequisite to coordinated efforts at improving care and reducing waste, which is central to the ACO payment model. Other ACO efforts are implementing HIEs to allow physicians a complete view of patients' medical records, while at the same time allowing patients to interact with the system via mobile apps for appointment registration. The ACO initiative is also bringing together partners from different parts of the health care spectrum, such as insurers and hospitals, hospitals and specialty care providers, or simply a group of physicians. Since there is no preset model, an eventual ACO model(s) will have to emerge through experimentation.

DISCUSSION

The central thesis of this chapter is the emergence of a service platform (shown in Figure 1) primarily through the deployment of various IT initiatives in health care services. But we need to recognize that IT implementation is not only that of EHRs or "systems." An implementation of a true "system of technologies" is under way. We can see that in addition to the typical transactional hardware and software systems in EHRs, there is a significant communication element in the deployment of HIEs, cloud technologies, and mobile applications. But an often-ignored core of technology, the use of decision support tools, is gaining its rightful place at the center of the IT deployment effort. Finally, successful technological initiatives always have a basis in technical standards. In the case of health care, due to the larger public good involved, there is an associated need to address regulatory requirements. The HIPAA laws of privacy and security, as applied to electronic medical patient information, is a core element in the regulatory environment that contributes to the success of HIT.

We are also seeing true emergence at play: Initial IT deployment of stand-alone systems allow for the emergence of networked systems in HIEs; this then allows for the deployment of clinical decision support tools, which eventually allow us to rethink delivery business models, enabling us to experiment with ACOs. This hierarchical emergence of the service platform is the result of real-time experiments. While some experiments may not produce positive outcomes, the large number of experiments and the various ideas being unleashed will eventually transform the health care service platform from its current pay-for-service model to a new patient-centric coordinated care model. Such an emergent approach to change is the most effective way to deal with a complex, dynamic health care service system.

The central issue that needs consideration is that of coordination. There are many claims and counterclaims about the increased quality, improved safety, and lower cost that result from the various HIT efforts. But what is lost is the core advantage that is being sought: that of improved coordination of patient-centric care. Since, as was identified early in this discussion, health care services may be considered as adaptive, complex, nonlinear, and loosely coupled sociotechnical systems. The human at the center of the care effort is a dynamic being, and so the system that is designed to serve the patient should also be dynamic. This results in many "moving and changing parts" that need coordination. In addition, the loosely coupled nature of care in many instances means there are built-in delays between the various subsystems (e.g., labs, physicians' offices, etc.). These are not problematic, but an integral part of non-urgent or noncritical care. So the coordination of the specialized care processes should reflect the coordination of the "target human subsystems." In fact, the holy grail of coordinated care is to build sociotechnical health care service systems that reflect the coordination that is integral to the human subsystems in the body. The extent of coordination should be the same as what the human body uses to manage itself. That is why we find HIT use as a means of information coordination is the essence of all health care service platforms.

In summary, we find that it is both an opportunity and a challenge for service researchers that they engage in understanding not only the details of each element of HIT or regulatory compliance, but begin to focus on the holistic evolution of the service platform. We have a tremendous opportunity to be part of a generational shift in health care services, and it would be of significant value to practitioners and patients for service researchers to bring their expertise to understand and improve the entire system.

REVIEW QUESTIONS

1. Discuss health care services from a systems perspective.
2. What are the advantages and challenges involved in EHR use?
3. Discuss the central role of coordination in patient care. How does HIT facilitate this coordination?
4. Discuss the various dimensions of a health care service platform.

REFERENCES

Anonymous. (2010). DC to VC Summit outlines the future of health IT technology. *International Journal of Micrographics & Optical Technology, 28*(4/5), 8.

Altarum Institute. (2012, July 15). Health sector economic indicators briefs. (Spending Brief). Retrieved from http://www.altarum.org/research-initiatives-health-systems-health-care/altarum-center-for-studying-health-spending/health-indicator-reports

Armijo, D., McDonnell, C., & Werner, K. (2009, October). Electronic health record usability: Evaluation and use case framework. AHRQ Publication No. 09(10)-0091-1-EF. Rockville, MD: Agency for Healthcare Research and Quality, U.S. Department of Health and Human Services.

Bowman, D. (2012). HIEs aim to curb ED overuse. *FierceHealthIT.* Retrieved from http://www.fiercehealthit.com/story/hies-aim-curb-ed-overuse/2012-05-22

Buntin, B. M., Burke, M. F., Hoaglin, M. C., & Blumenthal, D. (2011, March). The benefits of health information technology: A review of the recent literature shows predominantly positive results. *Health Affairs, 30*(3), 464–471.

Checkland, P. B. (1984). *Systems thinking, systems practice.* Chichester, UK: John Wiley.

Checkland, P. B. (1987). A note on the use of systems thinking in the provision of health care. *Journal of Applied Systems Analysis, 14,* 129–130.

Emery, F. E. (1959). *Characteristics of socio-technical systems* (Document No. 527). London: Tavistock Institute of Human Relations.

Essen, A. (2009). The emergence of technology-based service systems: A case study of a telehealth project in Sweden. *Journal of Service Management, 20*(1), 98–121.

Frisse E. M., Johnson, K. B., Nian, H., Davison, C. L., Gadd, C. S., Unertl, K. M., Turri, P. A. et al. (2012, May/June), Focus on health information technology, electronic health records and their financial impact: The financial impact of health information exchange on emergency department care. *Journal of the American Medical Information Association, 19*(3), 328–333.

Hirsch, M. D. (2012, May 15). More docs gravitating to cloud-based EHRs. *FierceEMR.* Retrieved from http://www.fierceemr.com/story/more-docs-gravitating-cloud-based-ehrs/2012-05-15

Leslie, T., Doscher, M., & Toner, B. (2012, March 19). 5 reasons EHR functionality hasn't changed since 1982., *Government Health IT*, Retrieved from http://www.govhealthit.com/news/5-reasons-ehr-functionality-hasnt-changed-1982

Menor, L. J., Tatikonda, M. C., & Sampson, S. E. (2002). New service development: Areas for exploitation and exploration. *Journal of Operations Management, 20,* 135–157.

Ostrom, A. L., Bitner, M. J., Brown, S. W., Burkhard, K. A., Goul, M., Smitth-Daniels, V., Demirkan, H. et al. (2010). Moving forward and making a difference: Research priorities for the science of service. *Journal of Service Research, 13*(1), 4–36.

Perrow, C. (1984). *Normal accidents: Living with high-risk technologies.* New York: Basic Books.

Reason, J. (1990). *Human error.* Cambridge: Cambridge University Press.

Roth, A. V., & Menor, L. J. (2003). Insights into service operations management: A research agenda. *Production and Operations Management, 12*(2), 145–164.

Trist, E. (1981). *The evolution of socio-technical systems: A conceptual framework and an action research program.* Ontario Ministry of Labor, Toronto, Canada.

Waelchli, F. (1989). The VSM and Ashby's Law as illuminants of historical management thought. In R. Espejo & R. Harnded (Eds.), *The viable system model* (pp. 51–75). Chichester, UK: John Wiley.

Chapter 11

From Healthcare to e-Healthcare: Are People Ready?

Even Johan Lanseng
Tor Wallin Andreassen

"We are about to see a fundamental transformation in the way [medical] care is delivered and the way patients are engaged with that care."

Professor Frank Moss, Ph.D.
Head of the New Media Medicine Group
at the M.I.T. Media Lab

LEARNING OBJECTIVES

Upon completing this chapter, you will understand and be able to argue that:
1. Healthcare services are different from ordinary services.
2. E-health care can improve service quality, customer satisfaction, and service productivity.
3. Citizens' technology readiness defines how fast technical solutions used for health care services can be implemented or how advanced they can be.
4. If the content and logic of a self-diagnosis decision support application is provided by a trustworthy source, customers are willing to adopt it.

KEYWORDS

healthcare costs, e-health care, technology acceptance model, technology readiness

INTRODUCTION

Imagine the following happens to you. It is a Sunday morning and you wake up suffering from a fever and a heavy, itching red rash. You are worried and want to get in touch with a doctor to receive a diagnosis and treatment. You have two options: You may visit a public emergency room or log onto the Internet and use the emergency room's self-diagnosis application. What would you do? Would you use the online application, see a doctor, or both?

Many customers, i.e. patients, would often prefer to avoid the hassle of seeking medical help or a consultation when they are in need. For a number of reasons, people are concerned about personal health issues, and in fact, in most countries the demand for medical health care services far exceeds the supply. Low fees (in some European countries health care is free), growing population, and people living longer are some of the main reasons for the increased demand, though this is not new. It has been like this for many centuries now, but has been accentuated with the increased importance of services in the private sector. Customers of private service organizations are often showered with services and attention, and when it comes to government services, they expect the same. Data from both the Norwegian Customer Satisfaction Barometer (NCSB) and the American Customer Satisfaction Index (ACSI) document that government services receive the lowest satisfaction scores. One reason for this low score is the lack of customer segmentation and the adaptation of government services to segments, while other reasons relate to insufficient funding, lack of availability of services, and variable quality.

Beyond these issues, governments around the world are working hard to improve the situation, as "more health care per dollar invested" is not an uncommon phrase to hear around the world. However, we have come to a tipping point, in which both policymakers and citizens realize that we need to look outside the box for a solution to this global problem. In this respect, electronic health care services (e-health care) have emerged as a promising area. *E-health care* is defined as "the application of the Internet and other related technologies in the health care industry to improve the access, efficiency, effectiveness and quality of clinical and business processes utilized by health care organizations, practitioners, patients, and consumers in an effort to improve the health status of patients" (Marconi, 2002). In short, e-health care is health care supported by technology and the Internet, and because we are in dire need of e-health care, a lot is happening in this field.

In an April 11, 2012 article entitled "Vital Signs by Phone, Then, With a Click, a Doctor's Appointment,"[1] the *New York Times* claim that the American health care industry is ready for change. Despite spending close to USD 8,000 a year per person on health

---

[1]www.nytimes.com/2012/04/12/business/smallbusiness/start-ups-use-technology-in-patient-doctor-interaction.html?_r=1

care, 50 percent of the adult population lives with a chronic disease with close to three weeks waiting time to see a doctor. Entrepreneurs have responded to the situation by establishing health care technology companies that are changing the way patients interact with the health care system.

In the same article, the several examples of newly established health care companies are mentioned, including:

- **AirStrip:** This company's technology connects a hospital's various bedside devices, e.g., an EKG machine, a ventilator, and a fetal heart monitor, to its server and then transmits the data to a smartphone or tablet.
- **Avado:** A doctor subscribes to Avado and gets an array of tools that enables the easy creation of a website in which patients can fill out intake forms, schedule appointments, ask for weekly medication reminders, and track symptoms for chronic conditions.
- **ClickCare:** Doctors and nurses post a photo of and information about a patient's problem on ClickCare's secure website. A link is then sent to a consulting physician who logs in, looks at the data and photos, and responds.
- **ZocDoc:** On ZocDoc's site, consumers can see a doctor's qualifications, read patient reviews, check the insurance plans the doctor accepts, and look at photos of the doctor's office.
- **Telcare:** Their first product is an FDA-approved glucose meter that transmits each reading to a cloud, where it can be read by a group of people preselected by the patient, with feedback being sent back to the patient's meter from a diabetes educator, pharmacist, nurse, or parent.

From the examples above, we learn that a patient's role in and contribution to the service production and delivery differs from that of the traditional doctor/hospital-patient relationship. Nevertheless, the question remains, Will they adopt and use the new technology? This chapter reports on a study on citizens' willingness to use an e-health care self-diagnosis application as a function of the application's user friendliness and the provider's credibility with regard to informational content. But first, let's take one step back. How does the future look for health care as an industry?

THE FUTURE OF HEALTHCARE

According to recent statistics from the U.S. Bureau of Labor Statistics (BLS), industries and occupations related to health care, personal care, and social assistance are projected to have the fastest job growth between 2010 and 2020. Specifically, the BLS projects that the health care and social assistance industry will create about 28 percent of all new jobs in the U.S. economy. This industry—which includes public and private hospitals, nursing and residential care facilities, as well as individual and family services—is expected to grow by a staggering 33 percent, or close to 6 million new jobs. An aging population and longer life expectancies, in addition to new treatments and technologies, are the key drivers of the employment growth. In sum, health care is expected to be a booming industry, although the paradox is that from a service marketing perspective, we know little about these unique services. Trust us, they are different!

HEALTH CARE SERVICES ARE DIFFERENT

For a number of reasons, health care services are radically different from ordinary services. First, the demand for many types of health services are negative; even though they are in need of them, people are not likely to look forward to vaccinations, vasectomies, gall bladder surgery, etc. (Kotler, 1973), as patients and their families typically demand health care services under considerable stress (Berry, Parker Coile, Hamilton, O'Neil, and Sadler 2004). Second, since the service is targeted at the receiver's mind or body, patients are the coproducers of medical services (Berry and Bendapudi, 2003). In this respect, health care services are prime examples of customers working together with the provider in cocreating value (Vargo & Lusch, 2004). Third, health care services are high in credence properties: services (for example medical and legal) that are difficult to evaluate even after consumption (Darby & Karni, 1973), as the provider knows much more than the receiver who has to trust the provider with his or her life, and any incidence of service failure puts the confidence of patients (or family members) at risk (Berry & Leighton, 2004). For all the aforementioned reasons, we need to develop a deeper understanding of health care services.

WHY ARE E-HEALTH CARE SERVICES IMPORTANT TO STUDY?

There are at least two important factors that make consumers' readiness and attitudes toward accepting and adopting self-service technology in the area of health care relevant. First, in most countries, health care is an expensive service, as spending on health care in most OECD[2] countries has increased dramatically over the past several years, outpacing economic growth by 1.7 times. Today, the average health care spending in OECD countries accounts for 9 percent of gross domestic product (OECD, 2005), while in the United States that number is in double digits. Second, there is a growing concern in most countries that current health care finance models are unsustainable in future years, when an aging population will only further increase the demand for health care services (The Economist, 2005).

---

[2] Organisation for Economic Co-operation and Development

Triggered by these two issues, Alvin and Heidi Toffler asked the rhetorical question: "How far can that [health care] number grow before the bankruptcy lawyers arrive?" (Toffler & Toffler, 2006, p. 162). For countries with a finite budget, particularly European countries with huge government debt, this development should call for a search for new, more efficient and effective ways to provide health care services. Thus, the question guiding our thinking can be expressed as:

> If the introduction of self-service technology is to contribute to increased capacity, improved quality, and cost reduction in the private sector, what are citizens' readiness and attitudes toward adopting such technology in the health care area? Furthermore, will they use e-health care applications?

Answering these two questions will have practical value for governments, public policy makers, (hospital) managers, and health care service managers, alike. As we progress through the chapter, we learn that despite the fact that previous research on the Technology Acceptance Model (TAM) has mainly been conducted in workplace settings, it also works well in the health care sector. In this unique context, people's attitudes, intentions, behaviors, and interrelationships are likely to be shaped by formal authority and directives, although the theoretical underpinnings of the model (i.e., Theory of Recent Action) assume that these factors are formed under an individual's volitional control. In this regard, employing the TAM framework in a context in which attitudes are formed on the basis of one's motivation and learning contributes to assessing the TAM-framework's validity.

Next, the health care setting is one in which the credence, coproduction, and cocreation of value are key components. As previous settings (outside the workplace environment) have consisted of relatively uncomplicated services such as in fast-food restaurants (Dabholkar, 1996; Dabholkar & Bagozzi, 2002), employing TAM in a health care context will extend its applicability.

The rest of this chapter is organized as follows: We begin by first discussing service quality and productivity pertaining to health care. Second, we describe the technology's readiness framework and present the findings from a representative sample of the inhabitants of a county in Norway. We then move on to develop and empirically test a theoretical model of attitudes, using a self-diagnosis application. We conclude with a discussion of the findings, with managerial implications, limitations, and suggestions for future research.

SERVICE QUALITY AND PRODUCTIVITY IN HEALTH CARE

Hospital quality has been widely debated in public policy circles. One challenge when debating hospital quality is that it means different things to different stakeholders, which is elegantly summarized in the following quote:

To a surveyor for the Joint Commission, quality means conformity to a text of accreditation goals and standards. To a hospital CEO, quality can mean an absence of adverse publicity, a larger market share than competitors, and an established quality program. To a health plan purchaser or insurer, quality may be equated with cost efficiency and resource utilization as measured by some standard, such as Health Plan Employer Data and Information set. To physicians and professional organizations such as the American Medical Association, quality is best measured by peer review organizations. To clinicians, quality is tied to medical outcomes. For many marketers, quality is best measured by patient satisfaction. (Turner & Pol, 1995, pp. 45–49)

There are a number of ways to enhance the perceived service quality of public medical services, e.g., by upgrading and redesigning physical facilities, by providing patients with more information, and by improving the organizational culture. In a recent article, University of Miami professor A. Parasuraman (2002) suggests that higher levels of service quality can be obtained not only through more consistent quality over time, but also by reducing customer inputs (time, effort, emotional energy) and increasing company input (labor, technology, equipment, etc.). Because health care services are coproduced, service quality will influence outputs from both a company and customer perspective. Parasuraman defines *customer output* as service performance and satisfaction, and *company output* as sales, profits, and market share. However, since profit motivation is of lesser relevance in the public sector, we define *company output* as the liberation of scarce resources and the number of patients treated as a satisfactory goal. Finally, customer satisfaction should increase (while alternatively, customer dissatisfaction should decrease) with an increase in perceived service quality.

Because of an ill person's reduced health condition, we assume that he or she spends more physical and mental energy relative to a healthy person when in need of medical care. Reducing a sick person's input through the use of an Internet-based self-diagnosis system (e.g., performing it at your convenience and tempo, with no travel to or waiting time at the health care provider) may improve patients' perceived service quality and satisfaction, while simultaneously reducing providers' costs at the same time. From a welfare perspective, injecting self-service technology (SST) into health care may prove to have a huge potential for both the user (e.g., increased satisfaction) and provider (e.g., reduced costs or improved capacity).

Independent of how promising SST may seem in theory, merely introducing e-health care is not a guarantee of success. Obviously, the use of SST is likely to differ on the basis of individual psychographic characteristics such as the readiness of technology. The Technology Readiness Index (TRI), a concept developed by Parasuraman, refers to people's propensity to embrace and use new technologies for accomplishing goals in life and at work. Whereas targeting different segments on the basis of different characteristics is normal in the private sector, customer differentiation is difficult with government services in relation to focusing on equality in service provision to citizens. Hence, governments must take into account the consumer technology readiness to predict the perception and behaviors of consumers with regard to adopting a new e-health care system.

In addition, it is necessary to determine relevant factors that consumers use to evaluate the service quality of an e-health care system. A core model in this respect is TAM, which specifies the determinants of acceptance and the use of new technology. TAM has received massive empirical support in explaining and predicting the acceptance and use of technology in various settings, including that of SST (see for example Dabholkar, 1996; Dabholkar & Bagozzi, 2002).

In addition to TAM, the value of measuring TRI relates to the novelty of e-health care. When you invite people to state their beliefs and express their attitudes and usage intention concerning a service with which they have virtually no experience, their responses might give little guidance as to what will be their actual behavior. In particular, when people respond to attitude and intention questions (such as in TAM), but lack any knowledge on which to base their responses, they are instead likely to use whatever response they gave to previous items in the survey (such as belief questions about the technology) as a basis (Feldman & Lynch, 1988). Therefore, attitude and intention are only restatement of beliefs, rather than valid predictors of e-health care adoption. Since TRI measures a population's propensity to embrace and use a new technology, high scores suggest that the general public has reached a certain level of comfort with a given technology through its usage in other areas. This is then an indication that responses in TAM are based to a certain extent on experience and knowledge, which results in more valid predictions of actual e-health care adoption.

In the next section, we elaborate on a study that explores a defined population's readiness to adopt technology in general. We then test the same population's attitudes and behavioral intentions with regard to adopting an electronic self-diagnosis application. As mentioned earlier, we believe that the adoption and, thus, the gains of a technology-based application are, to a large degree, a function of the population's technology readiness, which exerts an impact on adoption rate and speed.

STUDY # 1: PEOPLES' TECHNOLOGY READINESS

The notion of technology readiness refers to people's tendency to embrace and adopt technology-based products and services for everyday use, both at home and at work (Parasuraman, 2000). A population's technology readiness forms a foundation for adoption, thereby underpinning the main objective of this study: examining drivers for the acceptance of a Web-based, self-diagnosis application. Often the challenge with SST is not the capability or sophistication of the technology, but getting customers to use the it, as well as making sure that it is reliable and available (Bitner, Ostrom, & Meuter,

2002). Because users can choose between using SST or an interpersonal alternative, they need to perceive an advantage for using the technology and feel comfortable with it to select that option (Meuter, Ostrom, Bitner, & Roundtree, 2002). According to Bitner et al. (2002), effective and successful self-service technologies have customer satisfaction as their primary goal in the design and implementation, and from the first stage onward, have customers' motivations and expectations in mind. In other words, successful SSTs are designed with a customer focus and based on technology that is relevant for the task.

A survey on Norwegian consumers' use of online health services (Andreassen, Sandaune, Gammon, & Hjortdahl, 2002) showed that approximately one third of the Norwegian population had used the Internet for health purposes such as requesting a physician appointment, ordering medicine, checking on a waiting list, contacting others with the same health problems, making inquiries to physicians, and reading information pages, which represented a 12 percent increase from the previous year. Thirteen percent of this segment expressed anxiety regarding information found on the Internet, while 48 percent were calmed. These results support the assumption that there is an emerging market for a self-diagnosis application provided by, for example, public medical emergency rooms.

Data Collection and Sample Statistics

The population for this study is limited to people between the ages of 18 and 65. Whereas the lower age limit reflects the defined legal age in Norway, the upper age limit was selected due to cohort effects that will occur as a self-diagnosis application will most certainly take years to develop.

A translated version of the Technology Readiness Index (TRI) assesses Norwegians' receptivity to and use of technology-based services. TRI has four subdimensions measured on 36 items (Optimism = 10 items; Innovativeness = 7 items; Discomfort = 10 items; Insecurity = 9 items). Each item was accompanied by a five-point strongly disagree/strongly agree scale. A pre-test confirmed that the questions were understandable.

Survey respondents comprised 160 randomly selected individuals (74 women and 86 men) from a county located outside the capital of Norway. Respondents were given three options: filling out a paper version of the questionnaire, having it verbally communicated to each, or completing it online. Twenty-eight completed the survey online and 132 responded by manually completing the questionnaire. The responses did not differ between these two survey modes. The sample was diverse and the demographic differences were well covered so as to obtain a realistic picture of the inhabitants (see Table 11.1 for more sample details).

Table 11.1	Respondents' Demographics, Technology Readiness Study.				
Age	# of respondents	Education	# of respondents	Occupation	# of respondents
18–30	22	Elementary and secondary school	3	Student	27
31–50	78	High school	41	Working	122
51–65	60	Bachelor.	58	Homemaker	4
Not reported	0	Graduate, 4+ years	55	Retired	2
		Other	3	Other	5
Total	160	Total	160	Total	160

RESULTS

The scores from the TRI survey are in keeping with the recommendations provided by Rockbridge Associates, Inc. (www.rockresearch.com), a marketing consulting firm administering the TRI in the United States. The mean score on the TRI for the population studied here was 107.4, which is significantly higher than the U.S. average of 100 (107.4 − 100 = 7.4, t-value = 6.214) and has been virtually unchanged from 1999 to 2004 (Rockbridge, 2005). According to Rockbridge, respondents with a score of 104–122 are labeled Pioneers. These people are "…mostly young and middle class, who believe in technology, but are not as comfortable in stickhandling it compared to Explorers. They are optimistic and somewhat innovative, and even impulsive and success oriented. Yet they are still hampered despite their motivation. Willing to tinker and try new things, in fact heavy technology users, they still have more problems than Explorers in making technology work for them" (http://www.technoreadymarketing .com/tech-segments.php).

Explorers have a TRI score of above 123 and are further defined as "…typically young, upscale males, who are extremely innovative and uninhibited when it comes to technology. They are also optimistic, comfortable and secure with technology. Explorers are curious about the world, which also explains why these heavy users of technology are the first on the block with the latest gadgets - the ones who can turn on the computer and never look back" (http://www.technoreadymarketing.com/tech-segments.php).

In summary we claim that inhabitants of the county studied would be (highly) receptive to the introduction of technology-based public services, which indicates that a self-diagnosis technology has the potential to diffuse in the population to which it is introduced. In the next section, we develop a conceptual model for attitudes toward adopting a self-diagnosis service technology.

STUDY # 2: ATTITUDES TOWARD E-HEALTH

The research model in this study is an extended and adjusted version of the technology acceptance model (TAM) (Davis, 1986). At the heart of TAM, we find the theory of reasoned action (Ajzen & Fishbein, 1980), but attuned to explain information technology adoption and use. In essence, TAM specifies that the actual use of information technology is determined by usage or behavioral intentions and attitudes, which in turn is determined by two key constructs, namely that of perceived usefulness and perceived ease of use. Our model extends the TAM by adding trust as another determinant of attitude, and adjusts it by substituting the variable "usefulness" with "convenience." The model results in seven hypotheses (see Figure 1), and we elaborate next the basis for these hypotheses.

THE CONCEPTUAL MODEL

USEFULNESS (CONVENIENCE) AND EASE OF USE

The original TAM model suggests that when users are presented with a new technology, two notable factors influence their attitudes toward using the application, i.e., perceived usefulness and perceived ease of use. *Perceived usefulness* refers to the degree to which a person believes that using a particular system will enhance his or her job performance. *Perceived ease of use* refers to the degree to which a person believes that using a particular system would be free from effort (Davis, 1989). A number of studies have provided empirical support for the determinant roles of usefulness and ease of use in TAM (see Davis, 1989 and Davis, Bagozzi, & Warshaw, 1989, 1992 for overviews).

Since perceived usefulness in Davis' model refers to "enhanced job performance," it fails to capture the essential value of self-service technology and must be adapted to better reflect a self-service context. Consumers value self-service because it reduces the cost (e.g., monetary, time, energy, or psychological costs) that they expect to incur in evaluating, obtaining, and consuming a particular service offering. In the context of workplace technology, employees are unlikely to value the cost savings in the same way. First, employees are only users or consumers of technology, not evaluators or purchasers. In this respect, consumer psychology suggests that the decision making involved in consumption differs systematically from those of evaluation and purchase. Second, potential savings in the workplace are unrelated to personal goals, rather to organizational goals. The literature on goal commitment and goal acceptance suggests that these two types of goals are likely to differ (Hollenbeck & Klein, 1987). Reflecting the fundamental differences of consumer and employee roles, we adopt the notion of service convenience (Berry, Seiders, & Grewal, 2002), which is conceptualized in terms of consumers' perceptions of time and effort in relation to purchasing or using a service that reflects consumers' interest in saving time and effort. In particular, convenience is part of customer-delivered value. Time and effort are opportunity costs that prevent customers from participating in other activities, hence reducing the customers' perception of a service's value. In this respect, the concept of convenience reflects the underlying reason for using self-service—a reduction in time, effort, and money. From the discussion above, we define convenience as the degree to which an individual believes that a self-diagnosis computer application will reduce the amount of physical and mental energy spent when in need of medical help or advice. Consequently, a health care manager should ask:

QUESTION #1: WILL EXPECTED CONVENIENCE HAVE A DIRECT, POSITIVE EFFECT ON ATTITUDES TOWARD USING A SELF-DIAGNOSIS APPLICATION?

Expected convenience is likely to affect behavioral intention. In addition to affecting intention indirectly by evoking positive or negative feelings (attitude) toward adopting the application (discussed below), convenience has a more cognitively based influence. Adopting a new technology may be instrumental in providing consumers with more service value (by reducing monetary and energy costs), with the intentions involved in such instrumental considerations theorized to be influenced by cognitive factors, including beliefs about convenience (Bagozzi, 1982; Davis et al., 1989). That is, if the consumer believes that a certain technology is instrumental in improving the outcome of his or her behavior, that technology is seriously considered as an intended purchase regardless of the influence of the effect (i.e., attitude) associated with the outcome of adopting it. For this reason, a health care manager should ask:

QUESTION #2: WILL EXPECTED USEFULNESS HAVE A DIRECT, POSITIVE EFFECT ON THE INTENTION TO USE A SELF-DIAGNOSIS APPLICATION?

The second determinant, ease of use, is more directly applicable to the context of a self-service health diagnosis. Although a particular SST is convenient because it reduces costs in certain respects (e.g., the time and energy needed to obtain a diagnosis), it may not be easy or effortless to use because it demands costs in other ways (e.g., learning efforts, frustration). Ease of use has been found to strongly influence attitudes and technology acceptance in another (e.g., fast-food restaurant) self-service setting (Dabholkar, 1996; Dabholkar & Bagozzi, 2002). If people who feel sick are to accept a service delivery option in which they are required to function as their own "doctor," the application used must be simple, understandable, and easy to handle. Otherwise, they may as well spend this learning cost (i.e., the time and energy used in learning to operate the system) on physically visiting a doctor. Furthermore, since a self-diagnosis application will be a public service and targeted to all inhabitants, ease of use is particularly important, as technology skills and knowledge are likely to vary substantially within a given population. As a result, a health care manager should ask:

QUESTION #3: WILL THE EXPECTED EASE OF USE HAVE A DIRECT, POSITIVE EFFECT ON ATTITUDES TOWARD USING A SELF-DIAGNOSIS APPLICATION?

In Figure 11.1, we illustrate and summarize all key management questions.

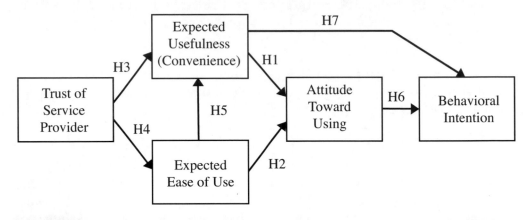

Figure 11.1 THE CONCEPTUAL MODEL WITH HYPOTHESIZED RELATIONSHIPS.

We have argued that consumers perceive a service such as a health care SST to be convenient to the extent that it will reduce the amount of time and effort spent when in need of medical services and/or advice. Since we have also argued that ease of use concerns consumers' perception that the same service can be used relatively free of effort, a positive relationship between these two constructs can be expected. More precisely, the less effort needed to use the application, the less extra time and effort will be needed (to learn how to use it) and the better the chances that such energy might be reduced (i.e., usefulness). Therefore, the fourth question a health care manager should ask is:

QUESTION #4: WILL EASE OF USE HAVE A DIRECT, POSITIVE EFFECT ON USEFULNESS?

TRUST IN THE SERVICE PROVIDER

In a health service context, not only will the usefulness and ease of use of the e-health application count, but also the beliefs about the entity providing the technology. Generally speaking, health services are rich in credence properties (properties that normally cannot be verified or evaluated, even after the consumption of a service) such as the diagnosis given by a physician. Because these properties are difficult to verify for the consumer, they must rely on an assessment made by experts or other external capacities (Darby & Karni, 1973; Zeithaml, 1981). Based on a large case study of a hospital, Berry and Bendapudi (2003) concluded that assessing the quality of a health care service is difficult: "You can't try it on, you can't return it if you don't like it, and you need an advanced degree to understand it—yet it's vitally important" (p. 100). Moreover, consumers are likely to look for information cues by which they can assess the quality of the external sources, such as the formal training of a physician or specific certifications. Services high in credence properties are associated with higher levels of perceived risk among consumers (Ostrom & Iacobucci, 1995), which is exaggerated when the health service is provided online. It is more difficult to derive quality cues concerning a health care provider when the consumer and service provider are separated, both spatially and temporarily.

The credence quality of a health service and the absence of information cues to assess the quality of the provider in an online setting make trust in the provider a crucial factor in determining the acceptance of self-serviced health care. Conceptually, trust consists of two dimensions: credibility and benevolence (Doney & Cannon, 1997; Ganesan, 1994; Mayer, Davis, & Schoorman, 1995). *Credibility* refers to the extent to which one partner believes that the other has the required expertise to perform effectively and reliably, whereas *benevolence* is the extent to which one partner believes that the other has beneficial intentions and motives and will not take advantages of any vulnerabilities (Ganesan, 1994). We incorporate a trust in the service provider as being consistent with that of Pavlou (2003). Trust is a determinant of usefulness (convenience) in an online setting because part of the guarantee that the consumer will gain from the expected usefulness depends on the provider of the online application. If the provider cannot be trusted, there is no reason why the consumer should expect to gain from using it (Pavlou, 2003, p. 110). In the context of e-health care, if users trust the provider to fulfill his or her promises (including observing privacy and safety regulations), then the consumer is more likely to view the technology as something he or she can safely benefit from. Trust makes it more likely that the application is designed according to the patients' own best interests, rather than being made to reduce the provider's costs. Consequently, a health care manager should ask:

QUESTION #5: WILL TRUST IN THE SERVICE PROVIDER HAVE A DIRECT, POSITIVE IMPACT ON THE EXPECTED USEFULNESS (CONVENIENCE) OF A SELF-DIAGNOSIS APPLICATION?

Trust influences ease of use since trust reduces the need for consumers to understand, monitor, and control the situation, thereby making it more effortless to use (Pavlou, 2003, p. 111). In a health care context, the consumer trusts the provider of an online application and does not have to search for information cues to assess its quality. Hence, trust eases the burden of learning and heightens appreciation of an application associated with a high degree of credence quality. Thus, a health care manager should ask:

Question #6: Will trust of the service provider have a direct, positive impact on the expected ease of use of a self-diagnosis application?

In addition to attitudes, the TAM includes the consumers' behavioral intention as a dependent variable, which is typically used because it is easy to measure and because of the practical difficulties associated with measuring actual behavior (e.g., Mathieson, 1991). The assumption that intention is a reliable predictor of behavior has been supported in both attitudinal research and research on technology adoption (e.g., Ajzen, 1991; Sheppard, Hartwick, & Warshaw, 1988; Venkatesh & Speier, 1999). The link between attitudes and intention is fundamental in attitudinal research and has received support in various settings, including research on TAM (Ajzen & Fishbein, 1977; Bagozzi, 1981, Dabholkar & Bagozzi, 2002; Davis, 1989; Shepard et al., 1988). Consequently, a health care manager should ask:

Question #7: Will attitudes toward using a self-diagnosis application have a direct, positive effect on the intention to use a self-diagnosis application?

We answer the management questions one through seven above by examining the path between attitude and intention. In the following section, we elaborate on the methodology for the second study.

Methodology

To test the model, we conducted a survey with an Internet-based medical self-diagnosis application as the focal technology. We felt this technology represented a strong test of consumers' acceptance of new technology in a service sector, one that puts the consumer increasingly in charge of the service product's performance. Despite the patient and provider cocreating value, patients themselves are relatively passive receptors of medical diagnoses (i.e., they provide information about themselves), while expert physicians perform all elements in this service.

Stimuli

A scenario was chosen for the stimulus. First, since a self-diagnosis application does not yet exist in the targeted region, a scenario was deemed appropriate to explain its functioning. Second, a written scenario allows the respondent to answer the questionnaire anywhere and at any time to help ensure thoughtful answers. Compared to laboratory research, the validity of the results from the scenario method has been well documented when it comes to the similarity of results (Bem, 1967).

The scenario method has been proven to be most successful when the subjects must play themselves, i.e. they become part of the scenario (Erogul, 1987). The scenario (see Appendix 2) described a situation in which the consumer felt ill and could receive medical advice by either using an Internet-based, self-diagnosis application or physically visit the medical emergency room. To make the scenario as realistic as possible, it was reviewed by a panel of doctors and modified according to their advice.

DATA COLLECTION AND SAMPLE STATISTICS

To ensure that the survey questionnaire was clear and understandable, a pilot study was conducted on 30 respondents of varying backgrounds. Respondents were asked to provide comments on the relevance and wording of the questionnaire items, the length of the survey, and the time needed to complete it. Based on their comments, items with the same meanings were merged and the wording of some of the questions was changed.

To obtain a demographically wide-ranging sample, respondents were reached at different places and by the use of multiple approaches. More specifically, we asked people in the street, as well as professional employees in offices and shops around the municipality, to participate. Questionnaires from the latter groups were collected at an arranged time to avoid hasty and ill-considered answers. More than 1,000 flyers with an invitation to participate in the survey over the Internet were distributed to household mailboxes. In addition, some people were encouraged to participate at a stand set up in the town center on a busy Saturday, offering all participants a piece of a cake and an opportunity to take part in a drawing for a gift card as incentives to respond. To make it more comfortable for the respondents, we provided chairs to facilitate completion of the questionnaire. Approximately 35 percent of the participants answered the questionnaire at their workplace, 35 percent responded on the Internet, 20 percent responded on the street, and about 10 percent at the cake stand. The sample consisted of 470 inhabitants (192 men and 278 women) of an affluent Oslo suburb, and was consistent with the demographic distribution of the population of the area (see Table 11.2 for more sample details).

Table 11.2	Frequency Distributions for Respondents' Demographics; Technology Acceptance.		
Age	# of respondents	Education	# of respondents
18–30	169	Elementary and secondary school	14
31–50	209	High school	99
51–65	91	Bachelor, 1–3 years	142
Not reported	1	Graduate, 4+ years	200
		Other	15
Total	470	Total	470
Occupation	# of respondents	# of persons in household	# of respondents
Student	78	1	69
Working	371	2	154
Homemaker	6	More than 2	244
Retired	5	Not reported	3
Other	10		
Total	470	Total	470

MEASURES

Since our study addressed SSTs outside an organizational context, the measures offered by Davis et al. (1989) had to be adjusted.

Expected usefulness (convenience) was measured on six items accompanied by seven-point strongly disagree/strongly agree scales. Four items were adopted from a study applying the usefulness construct in an e-commerce setting conducted by McCloskey (2003/2004). Item statements were: "Self-diagnosing over the Internet will be useful because it will save me time," "Diagnosing yourself by using the self-diagnosis service over the Internet will be more convenient than visiting the medical emergency ward," "Self-diagnosing over the Internet will be useful because medical advice can be easily found" and "Diagnosing yourself by using the self-diagnosis service over the Internet will be easier than visiting the medical emergency room to be diagnosed." To fully cover this construct, two additional items were added: "Self-diagnosis over the Internet will be useful because it will save me effort" and "Self-diagnosis over the Internet will make the emergency room more available."

Expected ease of use was measured using five items from a study on the acceptance of non-existing SST (Dabholkar, 1994). The participants were instructed to rate their agreement on seven-point strongly disagree/strongly agree scales in relation to whether a self-diagnosis application over the Internet will be "confusing to use," "time consuming," "take a lot of effort to use," "be complicated to use," or "require little work to use."

Trust of service provider was hypothesized to impact users' expected reliability and accuracy of the outcome, as well as expected security. Once again, seven-point strongly disagree/strongly agree scales were used, and two items were adapted from Pavlou (2003) to measure the construct, but were modified to this study. Statements accompanying the two scales were: "The municipality will be a reliable provider of a self-diagnosis application over the Internet" and "I will feel safe that the self-diagnosis application over the Internet is developed to keep my best interests in mind if the municipality administers its development."

Attitudes toward using a self-diagnosis application were measured using a four-item scale, and the participants were asked to describe their feelings toward using the self-diagnosis application/service over the Internet in terms of goodness (very good = 7/very bad = 1), pleasantness (very pleasant = 7/very unpleasant = 1), harmfulness (very harmful = 7/very beneficial = 1) and favorability (very favorable = 7/very unfavorable = 1). All of these were adopted from Dabholkar and Bagozzi (2002), only modified to suit this study.

Intention to use was measured by asking the participants to rate their intention to use a self-diagnosis application over the Internet based on the described scenario, with the responses captured on a seven-point most likely/most unlikely scale.

To ensure that respondents had properly understood the scenario, realism checks were conducted using a two-item, seven-point scale. The statements in these items were taken from Dabholkar (1996) and were: "The situation described in the scenario was realistic" and "I had no difficulties in imaging myself in the situation described in the scenario."

INTERNAL CONSISTENCY

All scales representing the constructs had a Cronbach's alpha above the standard guideline of 0.70–0.80 (Nunnally, 1978), with the overall measures being reported in Table 11.3. Being a directly measured predictor, the reliability of intention to use could not be empirically assessed, as this is impossible for such measures. Following Hair,

Anderson, Tatham, & Black's (1992) suggestion for specifying the reliabilities of single-measured items and common practice in research, the reliability of intention to use was set to 1.0, even though the absence of a measurement error in almost all instances is seen as erroneous.

Table 11.3	Internal Consistency, Cronbach's Alphas.
Construct	Cronbach's alpha
Convenience	0.927
Ease of Use	0.842
Trust	0.828
Attitude	0.886
Intention	1 (fixed)
Total	160

RESULTS

To test the hypotheses, structural equation modelling using LISREL was performed. The results are shown in Figure 11.2, and the overall fit of the model was good. The chi-square statistic was found to be significant ($X^2 = 353.75$, df $= 129$), although this statistic is often considered inappropriate because it depends on the number of observations. The RMSEA displayed an acceptable fit (RMSEA $= 0.062$), and the remaining goodness of fit measures passed the less-conservative recommended values (see Table 11.4). The results show that the path diagram for the proposed research model is adequate.

Table 11.4	Fit statistics

Overall model fit index	Value	Recommended value (Hair et al., 1998, pp. 654–659)
χ^2	353.75	
p-value	0.000	
Degrees of freedom	129	
RMSEA	0.062	≤ 0.05 good model ≤ 0.08 acceptable model
CN	225.43	≥ 200
AGFI	0.89	> 0.90 (0.80 = lower recommended value)
GFI	0.92	> 0.95 (0.80 = lower recommended value)
CFI	0.99	> 0.90

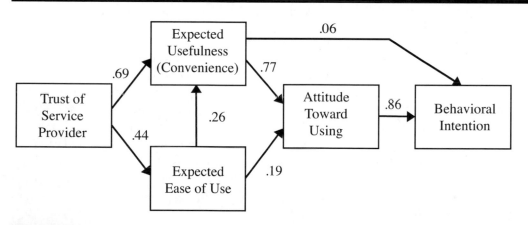

Figure 11.2 PATH COEFFICIENTS OF TAM/TRUST MODEL.

Hypothesis 1, stating that there is a positive relationship from Expected Usefulness to Attitude Toward Using is fully supported (Figure 11.2 , b = 0.77, p < 0.001). However, Hypothesis 2, which states that behavioral intention is influenced by expected useful-ness (b = 0.06, p < 0.1), is not supported in our model. Hypothesis 3, which claims that Expected Ease of Use positively influenced Attitude is supported (b = 0.19, p < 0.001), with the model accounting for 80 percent of the variation in Attitude Toward Using.

Expected Usefulness is positively influenced by expected Ease of Use (b = 0.26, p < 0.001), which lends support to Hypothesis 4. There are also statistically significant and positive relationships between Trust in Service Provider and Expected Usefulness (b = 0.69, p < 0.001) and Expected Ease of Use (b = 0.44, p < 0.001). These relationships support Hypotheses 5 and 6. The model accounts for 71 percent of the variation in Expected Usefulness and 19 percent of the variation in Expected Ease of Use. These findings imply that people's trust in the application provider is fundamental to their perceived usefulness and ease of use, while trust indirectly impacts attitude and subsequently behavioral intention.

As hypothesized in Hypothesis 7, behavioral intention is positively influenced by attitude (b = 0.86, p < 0.001), with the model accounting for 83 percent of the variation in behavioral intention. To assess our model, we used the two-step approach proposed by Anderson and Gerbing (1988), in which five nested models (i.e., parameters in one model are a subset of the parameters in a second model, and the parameters in the second model are a subset of parameters in a third model, and so on).

DISCUSSION

In the context of increased health care spending and possibly unsustainable health care funding models, the current research investigated people's readiness and attitudes toward performing self-diagnosis, which may offer a patient-centered access (Berry, Seiders, & Wilder, 2003) to health services.

Results from two studies—a survey measuring people's Technology Readiness and a survey testing the Technology Acceptance Model in the context of a medical self-diagnosis—suggest the introduction of SST is likely to diffuse within the population, and that the expected convenience and ease of use of the self-diagnosis service application at the individual consumer level will assist in contributing to this diffusion. Following the Technology Readiness Index's typology, people in the studied population are labeled technology "Pioneers": a group who has a more positive attitude toward SST in health care. Based on the data sampled and analyzed, we claim for this group that the more they perceive the convenience and ease of use for the proposed e-health solution, the more likely they are to actually adopt it.

MANAGERIAL AND POLICY IMPLICATIONS

For policymakers, these findings suggest that they should focus on three issues: 1) information material must focus on the expected usefulness and convenience of performing a self-diagnosis, 2) when developing the application, policymakers must instruct the developers to focus on ease of use, thereby reflecting the population's technology readiness. Populations with a lower/higher technology readiness index require more/less user friendly applications, 3) whereas Trust of Service Provider was found to have a high impact on Expected Usefulness and Expected Ease of Use, the latter also directly and indirectly impacts Attitude toward Using through Expected Usefulness. Thus, by promoting usefulness and ease of use, trust in the provider will influence people's judgment of the outcome as being reliable and accurate—a key driver for adoption and usage. However, while usefulness can be communicated and ease of use can be designed into the system, trust is earned. Trust in the provider is a function of people's general perception of competence within the sector, which is formed through, for example, word of mouth or self-experiences. More specifically, if the institution responsible for the development of the self-diagnosis system has a good reputation, this may strengthen people's trust in the technology, a prerequisite for later adoption.

A self-diagnosis application should be pre-tested thoroughly and sufficiently across a wide range of users to see whether it has actually been designed to be easy to use by the average consumer, and that the outcome is actually reliable and accurate. With a failure to do so, implementation may prove unsuccessful, and more resources will have been spent than saved. As previously pointed out, if only part of the population adopts the self-diagnosis system and the majority of them have a positive experience, using the application adoption by the remaining parts of society will be a function of word of mouth and access to the Internet. Hence, the potential savings to society could be significant.

THEORETICAL IMPLICATIONS

This research has empirically supported TAM in a consumer context in which respondents are free to form their own beliefs, attitudes, and intentions. Because much of previous TAM research has been conducted in settings where these variables, as well as their interrelationships, have been co-shaped by organizational authority and directives, this support contributes to the general validity of the model. In particular, finding that ease of use and usefulness help explain attitudes and use in a setting in which the respondents have real choices between alternatives (e.g., diagnosis based on face-to-face consultancy vs. online) suggest that these constructs are valid predictors of attitudes and usage intentions toward new technology. Moreover, our findings lend support to TAM's theoretical foundation, the Theory of Reasoned Action, which assumes that beliefs, attitudes, and intentions are formed under the individual's volitional control.

TAM was also supported in a health care setting in which credence, coproduction, and cocreation of value are key components. Since previous settings (outside the workplace environment) have consisted of relatively uncomplicated services such as in fast-food restaurants (Dabholkar, 1996; Dabholkar & Bagozzi, 2002), this support extends its generality and applicability, which are further corroborated by the finding that the included concept of trust in the service provider did not improve the model. One might expect that including trust would improve the overall fit of the model in a context characterized by complexity and uncertainty. One explanation for this could be that the sample on which the model was tested is drawn from a consumer population characterized by having a high degree of technology readiness. For these consumers, beliefs about usefulness and expected ease of use are most likely sufficient for explaining the development of attitudes and usage intentions toward a service technology such as medical self-diagnosis.

Based on this result, we suggest that in the context of high technology readiness among consumers, their beliefs about usefulness and expected ease of use are sufficient for explaining the development of attitudes and usage intentions toward medical self-diagnosis. From these findings researchers can learn that for use as a framework for analyzing the adoption of SST in a credence coproduced-based service context, TAM is most appropriate. We therefore take this as evidence of the strength of the underlying theory.

Our findings also emphasize the role of technology in services that are high in credence properties and perceived risk, as the quality of a service such as a medical diagnosis is nearly impossible for the consumer to assess or evaluate even after it is performed (i.e., a credence service). As a result, one normally has to trust the skills and knowledge of the performing physician making expert knowledge and the cocreation of value a crucial quality component. However, if available technology is convenient and easy to use, consumers appear to be willing to forgo a face-to-face consultation, instead trusting their own skills with assistance from technology. One possible reason for this is that the technology component makes the service more tangible, thus, easier to evaluate (Zeithaml, 1981).

LIMITATIONS

The study reported in this chapter is (among) the first to be conducted on the acceptance of SST in health services. As it is in its infancy in terms of research, it is not surprising that there exist many limitations in this study. First, we recommend a re-test based on a real pilot self-diagnosis application, rather than using a written scenario.

Second, despite the scenario approach being a commonly used research method, the findings in this study may be less applicable to the real world. First of all, the situation described in the scenario could have created bias in relation to user acceptance, since if you have a rash, you may be more inclined to go online than appear in public. Furthermore, compared to former studies of technology acceptance in which the scenario approach has been used, our scenario was longer and contained more details. In combination with a long questionnaire, possible difficulties in going back and rereading the scenario may have caused some bias in the answers. In contrast, this way of completing the survey may have decreased the possibility of a "self-generated validity", i.e. the act of measuring beliefs, attitudes, intentions, and behaviors affects observed among them, that commonly occurs in studies using paper-and pencil measures (Feldman & Lynch, 1988).

Third, the data-collection method used may represent a weakness, as the flyers used required Internet access. Consequently, this method excluded many who received the flyer from participating, thereby violating the criteria for random sampling.

Fourth, most of the questions were adopted from former research and only modified for this setting. The items used should, therefore, be reviewed and improved for later research, whereas the results in this study must be viewed with a critical eye. Finally, we have only tested our model in one geographical area described as "Pioneers." Populations described otherwise may generate different findings.

REVIEW QUESTIONS

1. How do health care services differ from other types of services?
2. What role(s) can SST play in health care?
3. Why is information about peoples' technology readiness valuable when studying attitudes toward SST in health care?
4. What factors determine people's attitude toward using a self-diagnosing application?
5. What should policy makers focus on when considering introducing SST to health care?

APPENDIX 2: SCENARIO

It is a Sunday morning and you wake up suffering from a fever and an itching red rash. You are worried and want to get in touch with a medical doctor to receive a diagnosis and treatment. You have two options: You may visit the public emergency room or log onto the Internet and use the emergency room's self-diagnosis application.

The self-diagnosis application is built on intelligent software, which in turn is based on medical science and questions that doctors use to make a diagnosis. You log onto the Internet service using your social security number and your personal pin code/log-in code that you have been given from the municipality, which allows you to save general personal information (such as your name, allergies, etc.) so that you will not have retype this at a later use of the service. You will also be given the opportunity to take a guided tour through the process to receive a diagnosis and advice.

The self-diagnosis program asks a series of questions that you must respond to by clicking on the response alternative you find most suitable to your condition. You also have the opportunity to add supplementary information if necessary. The questions asked enable the self-diagnosis program to obtain an overall picture of your problem and to confirm/disconfirm any possible diagnoses. To start with, the questions are general (such as where on the body the rash is, if you have a case history, if you are on medications and if so, which, etc.). As you progress, the questions are more specific as information is added (such as: is the rash running, does it sting, does it lie on a line or is it clustered, what did you eat yesterday, etc.).

Additionally, you are asked to perform simple self-examinations (such as checking your temperature and pulse, turning your head up and down, etc.). You will have the opportunity to correct your responses if you make a wrong click.

Both the doctor at the emergency room and the self-diagnosis application over the Internet will make it possible to receive a diagnosis and provide advice as to what to do next (e.g., you can have chicken pox and be ordered to rest, or you can have an allergy and be advised to buy antihistamines). Advice from the self-diagnosis option is given automatically by the decision-support algorithms built into the software and developed by medical experts. Finally, the self-diagnosis application/service may advise you to contact the emergency room.

APPENDIX I: INTERVIEW GUIDE TO TECHNOLOGY ACCEPTANCE

I expect the emergency room's self-diagnosis application over the Internet …

CONVENIENCE $\alpha = 0.927$

1. Self-diagnosing over the Internet will be useful because it will save me time.
2. Diagnosing yourself by using the self-diagnosis service over the Internet will be easier than visiting the medical emergency room to be diagnosed.
3. Diagnosing yourself by using the self-diagnosis service over the Internet will be more convenient than visiting the medical emergency room.
4. Self-diagnosing over the Internet will be useful because medical advice can be easily found.
5. Self-diagnosis over the Internet will be useful because it will save me effort.
6. Self-diagnosis over the Internet will make the emergency room more available.

EASE OF USE $\alpha = 0.842$

1. Will be confusing to use
2. Will be time consuming to use

3. Will take a lot of effort to use
4. Will be complicated to use
5. Will require little work to use

* Items were rescored in the analyses.

TRUST $\alpha = 0.828$

1. The municipality will be a reliable provider of a self-diagnosis application over the Internet.
2. I will feel safe that the self-diagnosis application over the Internet is developed to keep my best interests in mind if the municipality administers its development.

ATTITUDE $\alpha = 0.886$

In the situation/scenario described above, how would you describe your feelings toward using the self-diagnosis application/service over the Internet?

Endpoints:

1. Very good (7) – Very bad (1)
2. Very pleasant (7) – Very unpleasant (1)
3. Very harmful (7) – Very beneficial (1)
4. Very favorable (7) – Very unfavorable (1)

* Items were rescored in the analyses.

INTENTION TO USE

Based on the scenario described, would you use the self-diagnosis application over the Internet?

Most likely (7) – Most unlikely (1)

REALISM CHECKS

1. Was the situation described in the scenario realistic/understandable?
2. I had no difficulties imagining myself in the situation (described in the scenario).

DEMOGRAPHICAL MEASURES

1. Gender

2. Age: younger than 18, 19–30, 31–50, 51–65, older than 65

3. Number of persons in household: 1, 2, more than 2

4. Occupation: student, working, homemaker, retired, other

5. Education: elementary and secondary school, high school, bachelor, 1–3 years graduate education, 4+ years, other

REFERENCES

Ajzen, I. (1991). The theory of planned behavior. *Organizational Behavior and Human Decision Processes, 50*(March), 179–211.

Ajzen, I., & Fishbein, M. (1980). *Understanding Attitudes and Predicting Social Behavior.* Englewood Cliffs: Prentice-Hall.

Ajzen, I., & Fishbein, M. (1977). Attitude-behavior relations: A theoretical analysis and review of empirical research. *Psychological Bulletin, 84*(5), 888–918.

Anderson, J. C., & Gerbing, D. W. (1988). Structural equation modeling in practice: A review and recommended two-step approach. *Psychological Bulletin, 103*(3), 411–423.

Andreassen, H., Sandaune, A. G., Gammon, D., & Hjortdahl, P. (2002). Norwegians use of Online Healthcare Offers. *Tidsskriftet for den Norske Lægeforrening*, 17, 1640–1644.

Bagozzi, R. P. (1981). Attitudes, intentions, and behavior: A test of some key hypotheses. *Journal of Personality and Social Psychology, 31*(October), 607–626.

Bagozzi, R. P. (1982). A field investigation of causal relations among cognitions, affect, intentions, and behavior. *Journal of Marketing Research, 19*(4), 562–583.

Bem, D. J. (1967). Self perception: An alternative interpretation of cognitive phenomena. *Psychological Review, 74*(May), 183–200.

Berry, L. L., & Leighton, J. A. (2004). Restoring customer confidence. *Marketing Health Services* (Spring), 15–19.

Berry, L. L., & Bendapudi, N. (2003). Clueing in customers. *Harvard Business Review, 81* (February), 100–106.

Berry, L. L., Parker, D., Jr., Coile, R. C., Hamilton, D. K., O'Neil, D. D., & Sadler, B. L. (2004). Can better buildings improve care and increase your financial returns? *Frontiers of Health Services Management, 21*(1), 3–24.

Berry, L. L., Seiders, K., & Grewal, D. (2002). Understanding service convenience. *Journal of Marketing, 66*(3), 1–17.

Berry, L. L., Seiders, K., & Wilder, S. S. (2003). Innovations in access to care: A patient-centered approach. *Annals of Internal Medicine, 139*(7), 568–574.

Bitner, M. J., Ostrom, A. L., & Meuter, M. L. (2002). Implementing successful self-service technologies. *Academy of Management Executive, 16*(4), 96–109.

Dabholkar, P. A. (1994). Incorporating choice into an attitudinal framework: Analyzing models of mental comparison processes. *Journal of Consumer Research, 21*(June), 100–118.

Dabholkar, P. A. (1996). Consumer evaluations in new technology-based self-service options: An investigation of alternative models of service quality. *International Journal of Research in Marketing, 13*(1), 29–51.

Dabholkar, P. A., & Bagozzi, R. P. (2002). An attitudinal model of technology-based self-service: Moderating effects of consumer traits and situational factors. *Journal of the Academy of Marketing Science, 30*(3), 184–202.

Darby, M. R., & Karni, E. (1973). Free competition and the optimal amount of fraud. *Journal of Law and Economics, 16*(April), 67–88.

Davis, F. D. (1986). A technology acceptance model for empirically testing new end-user information systems: Theory and results (Ph.D. Dissssertation, Massachusetts Institute of Technology).

Davis, F. D. (1989). Perceived usefulness, perceived ease of use, and user acceptance of information technology. *MIS Quarterly, 13*, 319–339.

Davis, F. D., Bagozzi, R. P., & Warshaw, P. R. (1989). User acceptance of computer technology: A comparison of two theoretical models. *Management Science, 35*, 982–1003.

Davis, F. D., Bagozzi, R. P., & Warshaw, P. R. (1992). Extrinsic and intrinsic motivation to use computers in the workplace. *Journal of Applied Social Psychology, 22*(14), 109–1130.

Doney, P. M., & Cannon, J. P. (1997). An examination of the nature of trust in buyer-seller relationships. *Journal of Marketing, 61*(April), 35–51.

The Economist. (2005). Financing health care: Searching for a miracle solution. August 20, pp. 23–24.

Erogul, S. A. (1987). The scenario method: A theoretical, not theatrical, approach. In S. P. Douglas et al. (Eds.), *AMA Summer Educator Conference*, Chicago: American Marketing Association, 220.

Feldman, J. M., & Lynch, J. G. (1988). Self-generated validity and other effects of measurement on belief, attitude, intention and behavior. *Journal of Applied Psychology, 73*(August), 421–435.

Fishbein, M., & Ajzen, I. (1975). *Belief, attitude, intention and behavior: An introduction to theory and research.* Reading, MA: Addison-Wesley.

Ganesan, S. (1994). Determinants of long-term orientation in buyer-seller relationships. *Journal of Marketing, 58*(April), 1–19.

Hair, J. F., Anderson, R. E., Tatham, R. L., & Black, W. (1992). *Multivariate data analysis: With readings* (3rd ed.). New York: Macmillan Publishing Company.

Hollenbeck, J. R., & Klein, H. J. (1987). Goal commitment and the goal-setting process: Problems, prospects, and proposals for future research. *Journal of Applied Psychology, 72*(2), 212–220.

Kotler, P. (1973). The major tasks of marketing management. *Journal of Marketing, 37*(4), 42–49.

Marconi, J. (2002). *E-health: Navigating the Internet for health information healthcare.* (Advocacy White Paper). Healthcare Information and Management Systems Society, Chicago (http://www.himss.org/content/files/whitepapers/e-health.pdf).

Mathieson, K. (1991). Predicting user intentions: Comparing the technology acceptance model with the theory of planned behavior. *Information Systems Research, 1*(3), 173–191.

Mayer, R. C., Davis, J. H., & Schoorman, F. D. (1995). An integrative model of organizational trust. *Academy of Management Review, 20*(3), 709–734.

McCloskey, D. (2003/2004). Evaluating electronic commerce acceptance with the technology acceptance model. *Journal of Computer Information Systems* 44 (2), 49-57.

Meuter, M. L., Ostrom, A. L., Bitner, M. J., & Roundtree, R. (2002). The influence of technology anxiety on consumer use and experiences with self-service technologies. *Journal of Business Research, 56*, 899–906.

Nunnally, J. C. (1978). *Psychometric theory* (2nd ed.). New York: McGraw-Hill.

OECD (2005). OECD health data 2005: Statistics and indicators for 30 countries, *OECD*, Paris.

Oliver, R. L. (1980). A cognitive model of the antecedence and consequences of satisfaction decisions. *Journal of Marketing Research, 17*(September), 46–49.

Ostrom, A., & Iacobucci, D. (1995). Consumer trade-offs and the evaluation of services. *Journal of Marketing, 59*(January), 17–28.

Parasuraman, A. (2000). Technology readiness index: A multiple-item scale to measure readiness to embrace new technologies. *Journal of Service Research, 2*(4), 307–320.

Parasuraman, A. (2002). Service quality and productivity: A synergistic perspective. *Managing Service Quality, 12*(1), 6–9.

Pavlou, P. A. (2003). Consumer acceptance of electronic commerce: Integrating trust and risk with the technology acceptance model. *International Journal of Electronic Commerce, 7*(3), 101–134.

Rockbridge Associates Inc. (2005, February 3). *2004 National Technology Readiness Survey* (Summary Report). Retrieved from www.technoreadymarketing.com/research3.html

Sheppard, B. H., Hartwick, J., & Warshaw, P. R. (1988). The theory of reasoned action: A meta-analysis of past research with recommendations for modifications and future research. *Journal of Consumer Research, 15*(December), 325 343.

Toffler, A., & Toffler, H. (2006). *Revolutionary wealth.* New York: A. A. Knopf.

Turner, P. D., & Pol, L. G. (1995, Fall). Beyond patient satisfaction. *Journal of Health Care Marketing, 15*(3), 45–49.

Vargo, S. L., & Lusch, R. F. (2004). Evolving to a new dominant logic for marketing. *Journal of Marketing, 68*(January), 1–17.

Venkatesh, V., & Speier, C. (1999). Computer technology training in the workplace: A longitudinal investigation of the effect of mood. *Organizational Behavior and Human Decision Processes, 79*(1), 1–28.

Zeithaml, V. A. (1981). How consumer evaluation processes differ between goods and services. In J. Donnelly & W. George (Eds.), *Marketing of services* (pp. 186–190). Chicago: American Marketing Association.

ACKNOWLEDGMENTS

The empirical study reported in this chapter has benefited greatly from the help and assistance offered by Nanna Reis and Karine Sveli.

Service Focus Through Persuasive Technology for Health Promotion: A Multidimensional Market Analysis

Carolin Durst
Andreas Hamper
Tino Mueller

LEARNING OBJECTIVES

Upon completing this chapter, you should be able to do the following:

1. State the importance of disease prevention and relevant preventive measures.

2. Describe the process of behavior change toward a healthier lifestyle.

3. Explain how smartphone technology can support preventive behavior.

4. Understand how persuasive technologies can support service management for the patient, the practitioner, and other health care stakeholders.

5. Analyze existing mobile applications that address preventive measures.

6. Derive recommendations for future development of health care applications.

KEYWORDS

mobile health care, personal health, prevention, health-relevant behavior, smartphones, mobile technology, mobile features, persuasive technology, health behavior change, transtheoretical model, ubiquitous computing

PREVENTION IN HEALTH CARE

To support public health, health care systems should address all stages of diseases. This comprises medical approaches to treat acute diseases as well as approaches to avoid or prevent diseases in the first place. While the technological progress in diagnostic methods and therapy was the key to a vastly improved service of health care providers in the last decades, many diseases rely on the participation of the health care customer to be treated successfully. Such lifestyle diseases like adiposity, postural deformities, and diseases caused by irresponsible use of luxury food and addictive drugs can be avoided by changing personal behavior and habits. Although technology is extensively used in professional health care and also available on the customers' side, personal actions for healthy living are mostly not backed by technology.

Today, smartphones are ubiquitous companions. App stores provide easy access to a vast number of apps related to illness prevention and health care in general. Generally, these apps are not released by the player of the health care systems, for example, insurance companies or hospitals. The apps address amateur athletes, support physical activities with location-based services, or coach people who want to stop smoking.

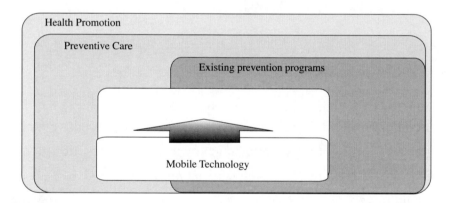

Figure 12.1   MANAGING MOBILE TECHNOLOGY FOR PREVENTIVE CARE

These observations lead to the question: What mobile technology exists to support goals of primary prevention? Analyzing these applications helps answer the question: What mechanisms can be used to increase motivation and support a healthier behavior?

Understanding the mechanisms of mobile health care applications can put health care professionals and service providers in the place where they can manage consumer health care technology.

During the 1990s a long-term study examined the causes of deaths in the United States. The authors found out that approximately one half of all deaths occurred in the year 2000, and those deaths can be attributed to a limited number of largely preventable behaviors and exposures. The top three causes of death were tobacco use, poor diet and physical inactivity, as well as alcohol consumption.

Mokdad, Marks, Stroup and Gerberding (2004) emphasize the need to establish a comprehensive preventive orientation in health care.

Today, the focus of public health insurance is primarily on medical cures, therapy, rehabilitation, and nursing. Less than 5 percent of the total budget is spent on preventive interventions (Hurrelmann, Klotz, & Haisch, 2004).

Cohen et al. (2007) reveal that just a 5 percent reduction in preventable diseases could reduce health care costs significantly. A 5% decrease of heart diseases can lead to $974,078,000 annual savings, 5% decrease of tobacco-caused illnesses leads to $386,650,000 annual savings, 5% Diabetes (Type II) decrease to $79,102,320 annual savings. These savings only include the costs of medical treatments. The cost of lost productivity is not incorporated (Cohen et al., 2007).

All the above-mentioned diseases are preventable to a great extent. In its literal sense, *prevention* means "to keep something from happening." (Hurrelmann, Klotz, & Haisch, 2004) This includes interventions such as the promotion of a healthy lifestyle, immunization campaigns, preventive examinations, and general education on diseases, as well as the suppression of harmful environmental factors, for example, in the air or water (Bürger, 2003).

The basic assumption of preventive interventions is that diseases occur due to different risk factors (Hurrelmann et al., 2004). According to Hurrelmann et al. (2004), risk factors can be divided into three groups:

1. Genetic, physiological, and psychological dispositions
2. Regional environment-related dispositions
3. Behavioral dispositions

Genetic, physiological, and psychological dispositions include, for instance, narrowing of the blood vessels and mental stress. Regional environment-related dispositions might include an increased level of ozone concentration or an increased danger of radiation in areas of uranium mining; however, in this work, the emphasis is on behavioral dispositions, for instance tobacco smoking, unhealthy diet, insufficient physical activity, or unsafe sex. These behaviors are identified as causes of various chronic diseases (Hurrelmann et al., 2004).

Caplan (1964) proposed a three layered classification of prevention that is commonly used in medicine. He divided prevention into categories arranged along a timeline (Caplan, 1964):

1. Primary prevention
2. Secondary prevention
3. Tertiary prevention

Primary prevention includes all actions that prevent the first occurrence of a disease. Therefore, measures address healthy people or people without manifested symptoms (Leppin, 2007). The goal of primary prevention is to reduce the incidence of a disease through education, motivational encouragement, social support, laws and policies, and physical environmental changes (Gullotta, Bloom, & Connecticut, 2003).

Secondary prevention refers to the early detection of a disease. At that time, individuals still have no recognizable symptoms, although the pathogenic process has already started (Leppin, 2007). Interventions in secondary prevention aim at averting or weakening the progression of a disease. Here, the goal is to reduce the duration of the cure or healing process through early recognition, identification, and intervention (e.g., cancer screenings) (Gullotta et al., 2003).

Tertiary prevention addresses individuals whose disease is obvious and manifest. Measures in this category are targeted at softening the consequences of the disease and mitigating potential complications (Leppin, 2007). Hence, it is about reducing the recurrence of the disease (Gullotta et al., 2003).

Referring to the three main causes of death shown in Figure 12.2, this chapter focuses solely on the use of technology in primary prevention.

In the 1980s McQueen introduced the so-called "holy four" health-relevant behaviors, such as smoking, poor nutrition, low level of exercise, and alcohol misuse (see Figure 12.2), which can lead to different diseases like lung cancer, diabetes or adiposity (Lengerke, 2007).

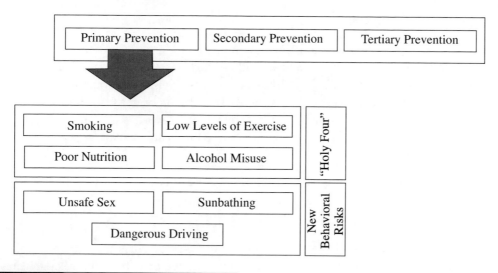

Figure 12.2 Health-Relevant Behaviors

Similar and newer behavioral threats are linked to unsafe sex (AIDS), sunbathing (skin cancer), and dangerous driving (death in traffic accident) (Lengerke, 2007).

Primary preventive interventions always aim to eliminate the cause(s) of a disease by reducing risk factors (GKV-Spitzenverband, 2010). To achieve preventive measures, three techniques or methods can be used:

1. Educational techniques
2. Normative-regulatory techniques
3. Economic incentive or punishment systems

Educational techniques primarily refer to health education, consultation, and self-assessment training. The measures focus on motivation and self-judgment. Normative-regulatory techniques are enforced by regulations and laws (e.g., mandatory seatbelt wearing, smoking bans, or the drunk-driving alcohol limits). The third method enforces behavior change with economic incentives or punishment. Well-known examples are the constant increase on cigarette on cigarettes or the possibility of discounts on health insurance for being physically active (e.g., through lower insurance charges) (Leppin, 2007).

The change of an individual's behavior is the key to successful primary prevention. The next section of this chapter deals with behavior change theory and the factors that influence an individual's behavior.

BEHAVIOR CHANGE THEORY

Behavior change, in general, is a difficult, complex, and long-term process. Many factors determine how individuals behave and perform certain actions. Behaviors are integrated deeply into people's daily lives. A tiny change in daily routines may have a great impact on an individual's decision to restructure his or her priorities. Especially when individuals try to adapt new, fragile habits, many factors can lead to relapse and setbacks (Klasnja, Consolvo, & Pratt, 2011), such as internal, social, logistical or environmental factors.

To achieve long-term sustainability when adapting to new habits, it is important to integrate strategies that reinforce motivation—intrinsically and extrinsically (Bielik, Tomlein, & Barla, 2012).

In psychology the Transtheoretical Model of Behavior Change is used to describe, explain, and evaluate the mechanisms of behavioral change, particularly for health-related behaviors, like physical activity, nutrition, tobacco smoking, and alcohol consumption (Ahtinen et al., 2009; Consolvo, McDonald, & Landay, 2009; Mattila et al., 2010).

STAGES OF CHANGE

The Transtheoretical Model of Behavior Change was developed by James O. Prochaska (Prochaska, Redding, & Evers, 2008). He used this model to analyze the behavior of self-changers and individuals with professional treatment for smoking cessation (Prochaska et al., 2008). Originally people thought of behavior change as a discrete event, where individuals stopped smoking or unhealthy eating at a certain point in their lives, Whereas in Prochaska's theory, behavioral change is described as a process over time (Prochaska, 2007). Individuals pass through five stages of the behavior change process: precontemplation, contemplation, preparation, action, and maintenance (Prochaska, DiClemente, & Norcross, 1992)

In the *precontemplation* stage an individual has no intention of changing his or her behavior in the near future. The main characteristics of this stage are:

- Timeframe of about six months
- Uninformed individual, not aware of the consequences
- Discouraged (already tried and failed)
- Not motivated to change his or her behavior
- Underestimating the advantages of behavioral change
- Overestimating the disadvantages of behavioral change (Prochaska, 2007)

In general, the individual has no idea that there is a problem (unawareness), the individual knows that the behavior needs to be changed but does not perceive the problem as urgent (low involvement), and the individual considers the positive and negative consequences of the behavior change (undecided) (Elder, Ayala, & Harris, 1999). Most of the persons trying to change a behavior are stuck at this stage (Prochaska, 2007).

In the *contemplation* stage, individuals intend to change their behavior within the next six months. They have a better understanding of the advantages of a behavior change, compared to the precontemplation stage, but they take no action. In a study about self-changers in smoking cessation Prochaska discovered that people can remain in this stage for long time (Prochaska et al., 1992). This phenomenon is often known as *chronic contemplation* or *behavioral procrastination*, where people are unready for action-oriented programs (Prochaska et al., 2008). They know about their problem, but, for some reason, cannot change.

The *preparation* stage is characterized by individuals who intend to take action within the next month. They are ready to change and preparing themselves to take action. The action plan is developed and some have already tried some small changes, like smoking five cigarettes less or delaying the first cigarette (Prochaska et al., 1992). Action plans include, for instance, joining a health education class, consulting a counselor, talking with a physician, buying a self-help book, or relying on a self-change approach (Prochaska, 2007).

The *action* stage is characterized by individuals who modified their behavior and took visible action to change their lifestyle. In this stage it is necessary to define a criterion or goal to measure progress and reach the next stage of behavior change (e.g., exercising three times a week over a specific period to leave the action stage and move to the next stage).

Maintenance is the stage in which individuals have already modified their behavior and tried to avoid a relapse. The behavior change has been introduced successfully into their daily life and the risk of a relapse is lower than in the previous (action) phase. The main characteristics of the maintenance stage are (Prochaska et al., 1992):

- Timeframe of six months to five years
- Stabilization of behavioral change
- Relapse avoidance

The theory postulates that in the first 2 stages, the individual perceives the disadvantages more strongly than the advantages of a behavior change. While progressing through the stages, advantages for adopting a new behavior become more obvious.

Strategies of Change

In each stage, specific strategies are suggested to support the individuals in achieving the transition to more advanced stages. According to empirical research, nine strategies—divided along two dimensions: cognitive-affective and behavioral procedures—are identified as important for intervention programs (Prochaska et al., 2008).

Cognitive-affective strategies are mainly applied in the early stages of behavior change to increase awareness. The individual must realize the impact of the negative behavior and the relevance of the positive behavior.

- Consciousness raising: Finding and learning new facts, ideas, and tips that support the healthy behavior change (Increasing awareness)
- Dramatic relief: Experiencing the negative emotions (fear, anxiety, worry) that go along with unhealthy behavioral risks (Emotional arousal)
- Environmental reevaluation: Realizing the negative impact of the unhealthy behavior or the positive impact of the healthy behavior on one's proximal social and/or physical environment *(Social reappraisal)*
- Self-reevaluation: Realizing that the behavior change is an important part of one's identity as a person *(Self reappraisal)* (Cancer Prevention, n.d.; Prochaska et al., 2008)

On the other hand, behavioral strategies focus on the later stages of the behavior change process: preparation, action, and maintenance stage.

- Self-liberation: Making a firm commitment to change *(Committing)*
- Counterconditioning: Substitution of healthier alternative behaviors and cognitions for the unhealthy behavior *(Substituting)*
- Helping relationships: Seeking and using social support for the healthy behavior change *(Supporting)*
- Reinforcement management: Increasing the rewards for the positive behavior change and decreasing the rewards of the unhealthy behavior *(Rewarding)*
- Stimulus control: Removing reminders or cues to engage in the unhealthy behavior and adding cues or reminders to engage in the healthy behavior *(Re-engineering)* (Cancer Prevention, n.d.; Prochaska et al., 2008).

It is important to understand that the strategies mentioned must be linked into the appropriate stages of change. For instance, consciousness raising and dramatic relief can support individuals in the precontemplation or contemplation stage, whereas these strategies might not be helpful for people in the action or maintenance stage

(Pro-Change, 2012). Table 12.5 shows the allocation of the strategies to the appropriate stages, proposed by Prochaska et al. (2008).

Table 12.1	Applicable Strategies of Change During Each Stage of Change			
Precontemplation	Contemplation	Preparation	Action	Maintenance
Consciousness raising				
Dramatic relief				
Environmental reevaluation				
	Self-reevaluation			
		Self-liberation		
			Counterconditioning	
			Helping relationships	
			Reinforcement management	
			Stimulus control	

Motivation and persuasion play a crucial role in behavior change. Traditionally, those concepts are established by human-to-human communication. Today, new technologies enable different ways of communicating via the Internet, mobile devices, and other ambient technologies, which may also be persuasive or foster motivation (Oinas-Kukkonen & Harjumaa, 2009). Consequently, it might be possible to use software systems to direct an individual's behavior toward a healthier lifestyle. The next section introduces persuasive services, referring to applications and technology designed to change people's attitudes or behaviors (Fogg, 2003).

PERSUASIVE SERVICES

Persuasion is defined as the influence of beliefs, attitudes, intentions, motivations, or behaviors (Wood, 2000). No matter what individuals are doing—shopping, watching television, or talking with friends—persuasion and its influence are all around. Technology can be used to influence individuals by sending persuasive messages to motivate them to purchase, donate, vote, or act (Ijsselsteijn, Kort, Midden, & Eggen, 2006). Those technologies—although they are persuasive in nature—provide numerous services that are valuable to individuals.

The Internet, in combination with mobile technologies, offers new services based on persuasive technologies that enable innovative ways to interact with individuals (Oinas-Kukkonen, 2010a). Especially powerful mobile devices, like smartphones, facilitate an easy and fast way to communicate (Oulasvirta, Rattenbury, Ma, & Raita, 2011) by creating, accessing, and sharing information (Oinas-Kukkonen, 2010b). In the health care context, services connect individuals with similar interests, for example, via online communities. Providing social support (Hwang et al., 2010) and informational support, online health communities allow people to seek information, communicate with others with the same or similar diseases, share health guidance, and compare treatment and medication strategies. Ubiquitous accessibility for everywhere at any time, the anonymity of the medium, as well as the access to greater expertise are regarded as the main benefits of online health communities (Maloney-Krichmar & Preece, 2002).

Traditionally *persuasion* is defined as "human communication designed to influence the autonomous judgments and actions of others" (Simons, Morreale, & Gronbeck, 2001, p. 7). Persuasive technology pursues the same objective but uses either computer-human persuasion or computer-mediated persuasion, for example, persuasion through discussion forums, emails, instant messages, blogs, or social network (Oinas-Kukkonen & Harjumaa, 2008).

B. J. Fogg, a pioneer in persuasive systems design, defines *persuasive technology* as "a computing system, device, or application intentionally designed to change a person's attitudes or behavior in a predetermined way" (Fogg, 1999, p. 27). A similar but more precise definition was proposed by H. Oinas-Kukkonnen. According to him, persuasive technology (or a *behavior change support system* [BCSS]), is defined as "an information system designed to form, alter, or reinforce attitudes or behaviors or both without using coercion or deception" (Oinas-Kukkonen, 2010a, p. 2).

Fogg describes six distinct advantages of modern technology over human persuaders: Technology

1. is more persistent than humans,
2. enables anonymity,
3. accesses and manages huge amounts of data,
4. uses many modalities to influence,
5. scales easily, and
6. is ubiquitous (2003, p. 7).

According to the definitions, persuasive technology is described as any computing system or device intentionally designed to change a person's attitudes or behavior. Consequently persuasive technology comprises a wide range of devices, whereas this chapter focuses on powerful handheld personal computers, so-called smartphones.

Smartphones represent the recent step in the evolution of portable information and communication devices (Oulasvirta et al., 2011). A *smartphone* is defined as "a device that combines a cell phone with a hand-held computer, typically offering Internet access, data storage, e-mail capability, etc." (Dictionary.com, 2011). These devices provide the following advantages compared to traditional personal computers:

- High penetration (Klasnja et al., 2011)
- High availability (Mattila et al., 2010)
- High technological abilities (Holzinger, Dorner, & Födinger, 2010)

Due to growing computing functionalities and reasonable costs, the penetration rate of smartphones continues to rise (Klasnja et al., 2011). According to Gartner (2012), approximately 1.774 million mobile devices (including smartphones) were sold in 2011. Smartphone sales account for 31 percent, or 472 million, of mobile communication device sales. These numbers state plainly that the smartphone market is booming.

Smartphones are personal and pervasive devices (Arteaga, Kudeki, Street, & Woodworth, 2010). Due to persistent network connectivity, smartphones are called always-on devices (Mattila et al., 2010). They offer the possibility of interacting with the user anywhere and at any time (Arteaga et al., 2010). Using communication technology, appropriate services (e.g., social networking services) can build connections among individuals with similar interests, fostering information exchange and social support (Ahtinen et al., 2009).

Moreover, smartphones provide additional technological features. They run powerful operating systems (Abroms, Padmanabhan, Thaweethai, & Phillips, 2011)—comparable to personal computers—and have the ability to install third-party applications. Smartphones come with built-in sensors (e.g., GPS, camera, microphone, compass, etc.) that allow the device to track the user's position or send messages to the user, for instance. Furthermore, modern smartphones are able to integrate external sensor technologies (Arteaga et al., 2010), like heart rate sensors or GPS tracking devices (WahooFitness, 2012; Zephyr Technology, 2012).

According to several investigations and studies, smartphones are suggested as promising platforms for health promotion and disease prevention. Recent studies focus on:

- Physical activity (Ahtinen, Huuskonen, & Häkkilä, 2010; Arteaga et al., 2010; Buttussi, Chittaro, & Nadalutti, 2006; Chuah & Sample, 2011)
- Nutrition (Breton, Fuemmeler, & Abroms, 2011; Grimes, Kantroo, & Grinter, 2010; Kim et al., 2010; Pollak et al., 2010)
- Addiction (Abroms et al., 2011; Backinger & Augustson, 2011)

In 2003 Fogg conducted the study "Mobile Health Applications" looking at the features of 72 health care applications for PDAs (personal digital assistants), mobile phones, and pagers. All identified applications are intended to change individuals' health-related behavior. Looking at the applications from a behavior change perspective, the features do not support behavior change strategies sufficiently. Features are mainly used to track certain behaviors and to calculate data, such as calories or indices like the body mass index. The applications provide further information, including articles, charts, and definitions. Fogg (2003) concluded that there is a major opportunity for health applications in the future enabled by technological development of mobile devices.

Smartphones combine and enhance the features of PDAs, mobile phones, and pagers. We assume that today more behavior change strategies can be supported by new features. Trends like social sharing or gamification provide room for more innovative, more motivating, and more persuasive applications. Smartphones offer a broad set of features and are suited to provide persuasive services to the user.

Today, many persuasive services focus on education (Consolvo et al., 2009) by providing health-related information, hints, instructions, or recommendations. Some services offer data analytics, tracking, or even virtual coaching to provide feedback to the user concerning a certain kind of behavior. Powerful features relate to social interaction, including social communication or social sharing, which are of special interest in the action and maintenance stage. Games encourage the user in playful ways to use techniques like levels, badges, or scores.

The framework in the next section links preventive health care, behavior change theory, and persuasive technologies. These technologies, provided in a suitable environment of preventive health care measures, can provide persuasive services to the users that enable them to change personal behavior permanently.

FRAMEWORK

The Transtheoretical Model proposes different strategies for each stage of change to progress successfully toward advanced stages. These strategies can be supported by smartphones features and help individuals throughout the whole process of change. For instance, a smoking cessation application contains features that focus on education by providing health-related information, tips, and recommendations. Thus, these features support the strategy of consciousness raising, which belongs to the precontemplation stage of behavior change (Consolvo et al., 2009). Figure 5 describes the relationship among application features, strategies of change, stages of change, and preventive measures.

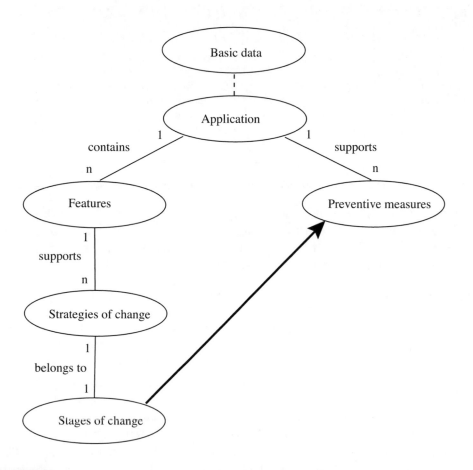

Figure 12.3   RELATIONSHIP AMONG APPLICATION FEATURES, STRATEGIES OF CHANGE, STAGES OF CHANGE, AND PREVENTIVE MEASURES

Applications can be described by their *basic data*, for example, the name or developer, price, version, size, etc. Each application supports one or more *preventive measures*. Hence, our study distinguishes between four main categories of preventive measures: physical activity, nutrition, addictions, and other health-related behaviors (see Table 6).

Table 12.2	Categorization of Preventive Interventions.		
Physical activity	Nutrition	Addictions	Others
• Aerobic or cardiovascular exercise • Strength or resistance exercise • Stretching or flexibility exercise	• Weight management • Nutritional information • Nutrition diary • Nutrition advice	• Alcohol consumption • Tobacco use • Illicit drug use	• Stress reduction • Healthy sleep • Immunization • Dental hygiene • Sex education

A health care application can be composed of different features, like tracking, social sharing, or rewards. Those features are linked to strategies of change. Table 7 shows the four categories of education, feedback, social interaction, and gamification with their corresponding features, each allocated to the strategies of change.

Educational features provide information about health-relevant behaviors to increase awareness for the need of behavior change. Three types of features can be distinguished. Namely, educational features can be categorized as general health information, personalized risk illustration and instructions to lower the risks. General health information can be retrieved from the Internet and displayed in applications like wikis or mobile browsers to foster learning and consciousness raising. Personalized information services can increase risk awareness by providing such things as risk calculators or threat meters that are based on the user's personal profile. According to Prochaska et al. (2008), these features support the strategy of dramatic relief. Dramatic relief helps to increase the awareness for a problematic behavior. It happens before an action is taken and aims at a change of mind. Instructions offered by mobile applications provide personalized training schedules or training tutorials. Individuals are ready to take action and seek further information on how to proceed with their behavior change; this referred strategy is called *self-liberation* (Prochaska et al., 2008).

Table 12.3	Application Features Linked to Strategies of Change	
Category	Feature	Strategy of change
Education	Information	Consciousness raising
	Risk	Dramatic relief
	Instructions	Self-liberation
Feedback	Tracking	Self-liberation
	Analysis	Self-liberation
	Coaching	Self-reevaluation Self-liberation
	Reminder	Stimulus control
Social interaction	Communication	Helping relationships
	Sharing	Helping relationships
Gamification	Competition	Self-liberation
	Goal setting	Self-liberation Counterconditioning Reinforcement management
	Rewards	Reinforcement management

Autonomous feedback is possible by using the computing capabilities of smartphones. Smartphone sensors can measure an individual's activities. Based on the generated data, an application can provide context-based services. Tracking user data is essential for feedback features, whichcan be done manually or automatically with integrated sensors. Analysis and visualization of collected data provide the user with visual feedback. Additional coaching features suggest and adjust personalized training schedules. Each feature (tracking, analysis, and coaching) facilitate the strategy of self-liberation. Coaching supports the strategy of self-reevaluation. Reminders detect reduced commitment and notify the user going backward in the behavior change process. The strategy stimulus control can use reminders to prevent a relapse.

Social interaction addresses the friendships within virtual communities. Features can be divided into communication features to exchange messages (i.e. personal messages, forums, etc.) and sharing features where users share their progress and achievements with a group of friends. Prochaska et al. (2008) suggests that social interaction support and encourage and individual's health-related behavior in a positive way.

Gamification describes the use of game elements in nongame environments. This can be implemented through competition. Users compete with other users in virtual contests, like running competitions, without the restriction of having to be in the same location at the same time. Healthy Competition with others fosters the commitment to change and relates to the strategy of self-liberation. Self-liberation is the development of the belief that one can change habits and behavior (Prochaska et al., 2008). Goal setting is also motivating when the individual defines goals to achieve personal progress. According to Prochaska et al.(2008), goal setting supports the strategies self-liberation, counterconditioning like learning healthier behaviors, and reinforcement management like increasing the personal rewards for healthy behavior. Achievements or rewards are also used to motivate individuals in a playful way. Rewards can either be monetary goods from participating companies or virtual, like reputation and virtual points. Prochaska et al. (2008) proposes that the importance of positive rewards is their ability to prevent setbacks. The corresponding strategy where positive rewards are used is called reinforcement management.

In future studies, emerging application features can be added to those already listed in Table 7. The continuous development of smartphone apps will expand the elements in the mobile application field.

According to Prochaska et al (2008) all change strategies can be assigned to the *stages of change*. The allocation is mutually exclusive, as each strategy corresponds to only one stage of change. Keep in mind that applications can support different behavior change strategies. Table 8 shows the four stages of change (precontemplation, contemplation, preparation, action) with the corresponding application features and the behavior change strategies. For instance, the application feature Goal Setting supports the strategies of self-liberation, counterconditioning, and reinforcement management; therefore, it belongs to the Preparation and Action stages. As Goal Setting is part of the Gamification category, you can also say that Gamification belongs to the Preparation and Action stages.

Table 12.4	Application Features Linked to 4 Stages of Change			
	Four Stages of Change			
Category	Precontemplation	Contemplation	Preparation	Action
Education	Information		Instructions	
	Risks			
Feedback		Coaching	Tracking	Reminder
			Analysis	
Social interaction				Communication
				Sharing
Gamification			Competition	Competition
			Goal setting	Goal setting
				Rewards

The developed mapping framework draws a link between application features and the stages of change. Based on this framework we conduct a market analysis of mobile health care applications. As strategies of change are are applied in certain stages of change, features of mobile applications can be mapped to certain stages. Keep in mind that these features are not used exclusively in the corresponding stage but are most effective in a certain stage.

MARKET ANALYSIS

A sample of 100 applications, available for download at the Apple App Store and Google Android Market, is the basis for our market analysis. From each platform we collected 50 applications, choosing from the most popular application list (paid and free) within the category "Health and Fitness." Applications that included a basic (free) and pro (paid) version were counted as separate applications, as they might differ in the range of functions. Applications available on both platforms are counted as separate applications. Each application is reviewed by the information available on the store's online Web page (e.g., general description with a list of features, user reviews, and screenshots). If the information provided is insufficient, the application developer's Web page is examined for more details.

In the first step, we reviewed the collected applications (apps) to determine which preventive measures are primarily addressed (see Figure 5). An app can be designed to support one or more preventive measures. Most of the apps focused either on encouraging more physical activity (n = 50) or better nutrition (n = 39). Physical-activity apps often provided features to support cardiovascular and strength exercises, whereas, nutrition-related apps focused on weight management, nutritional information, and journaling the user's food consumption. Six apps covered reducing or discouraging addictions, which focuse primarily on ending tobacco use. Twelve apps addressed other health-related behaviors, focusing either on stress reduction or promotion of healthy sleep habits. The promotion of immunization, sexual education, dental hygiene, sunbathing, and road safety were not addressed in any of the investigated apps.

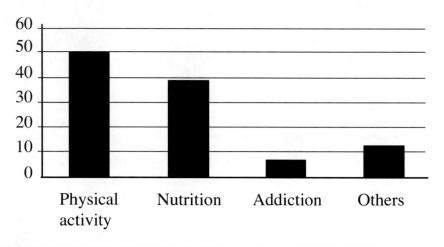

Figure 12.4 PREVENTIVE MEASURES ADDRESSED BY MOBILE APPS

Most of the investigated apps used educational features (n = 66) and feedback features (n = 76), whereas, social interaction features (n = 31) and gamification (n = 35) are underrepresented.

Figure 7 shows each prevention category and its features.

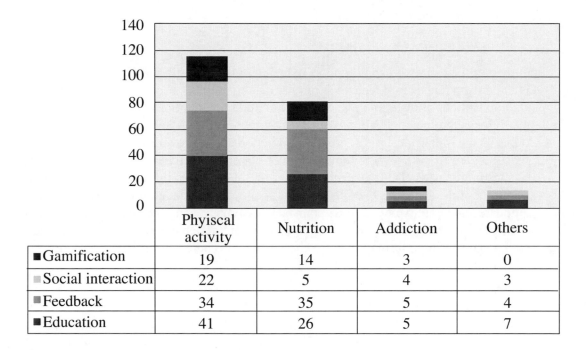

	Phyiscal activity	Nutrition	Addiction	Others
■Gamification	19	14	3	0
▨Social interaction	22	5	4	3
▨Feedback	34	35	5	4
■Education	41	26	5	7

Figure 12.5 APPLICATION ANALYSIS REGARDING FEATURES AND
PREVENTIVE MEASURES

Physical activity (n = 39)

Promoting physical activity is the most commonly addressed preventive intervention in the examined sample. Most of the apps in this group motivate through education (n = 41; 82% of physical activity applications) by providing fitness plans or instructions on how to perform various exercises. Many apps focus on encouragement through tracking and analysis of exercise-related parameters (n = 34; 66% of physical activity applications). Fewer apps included social interaction features (n = 22; 44% of physical activity applications) and gamification features (n = 19; 38% of physical activity applications).

Nutrition (n = 39)

Nearly all apps that focus on nutrition give some form of feedback by providing tools for weight tracking, food journaling, or BMI (body mass index) calculations and interpretations (n = 35; 87.2% of nutrition applications). Twenty-six apps (66.7% of nutrition applications) include educational material, such as diet plans or general nutritional information. Gamification is used in 35.9 percent (n = 14 of nutrition applications) of the nutrition apps. Interestingly, only 5 of 39 applications provide social interaction features (12.8% of nutrition applications).

Addictions (n = 6)

Only 6 of the examined apps support reducing or discouraging addictions. Addictions is the only category in which each motivational method is used in at least half of the six applications (Education: n = 5; 83.3% of addiction applications; Feedback: n = 5; 83.3% of addiction applications; Social Interaction: n = 3; 50% of addiction applications; Game Mechanics: n = 4; 66.7% of addiction applications). However, these results must be viewed critically, as they might not be representative due to the low number of apps in this category.Apps primarily incorporate features for increasing health consciousness and depicting benefits, such as money saved since quitting (based on the quit date and quantity of cigarettes smoked per day) or raising the awareness of general risks of tobacco use. Many also integrate social interaction components for communicating and sharing information with others. Four apps apply gamification features, like achievements, badges, or leaderboards.

Others (n = 12)

The category of other health-related behaviors includes apps focusing on stress reduction and promotion of healthy sleep habits. Most of the investigated apps in this category address alternative medicine and provide hypnosis techniques, relaxing melodies, or audio relaxation instructions. Some apps provide features to track sleeping behavior. Most apps have only a few features and show a low level of interactivity. Only seven apps provide educational material, like hypnosis techniques or instructions for relaxation. Four apps provide feedback using tracking features of sleep behavior. Social interaction apps are barely represented (n = 3), and gamification features are not addressed at all.

In total, 348 features were identified in 100 examined applications. Most apps incorporated more than one feature and complementary sets of features were often used together. For instance, the analysis of training data was often combined with features to share the individual training results with friends in social networks. Figure 8 shows the identified features.

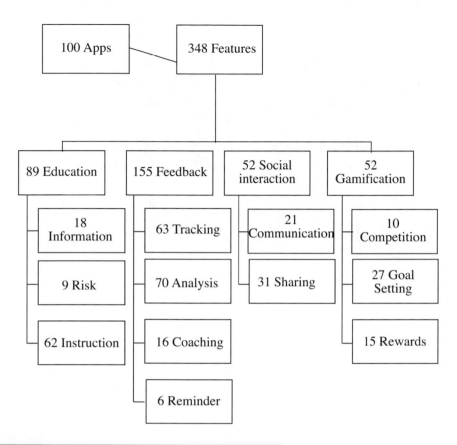

Figure 12.6 IDENTIFIED APPLICATION FEATURES

As described in the framework, the identified features can be mapped to the corresponding stages via the strategies of change. In Figure 9 the example set of applications is divided into preventive measure (Z axis) and the stages of change (X axis). The Y axis shows the number of apps that implement features to support the corresponding stage of change.

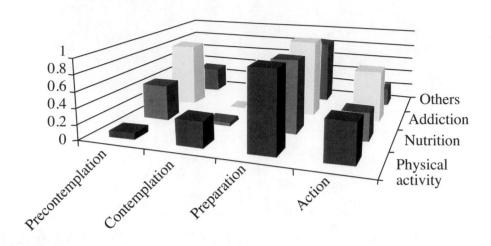

Figure 12.7 DISTRIBUTION OF FEATURES IN MEASURES AND STAGES

Most applications across all preventive measures provide features to support the preparation stage (physical activity: 100%; nutrition: 92.3%; addiction: 100%), whereas the contemplation stage is supported by only a few features (physical activity: 32%; nutrition: 5.1%). A clear shift toward support in later stages of behavioral change can be seen throughout all preventive measures because later-stage features mostly implement an action or behavior such as measuring data or sharing results, whereas features for early-stage behavior change focus on a change of mind with, for example, educational features.

Examining the apps by the number of supported stages, only one app supports all the stages of behavior change. Of the apps, 22 support three stages, 37 support two stages, and 37 facilitate one stage. Three apps in the example do are not support any stage. They refer to marketing activities without any impact on preventive care.

With regard to each preventive measure, it is of particular interest which features support which stages of behavior change. Apps for physical activity (PA in Figure 10) rarely inherit features applicable to the precontemplation stage. Apps supporting the preparation stage and action stage use features from the feedback and education categories. The results show that newer features, like social communication and gamification, are still underrepresented (see Figure 10).

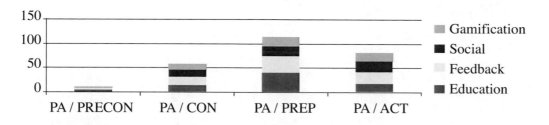

Figure 12.8 OPEN-SYSTEMS MODEL OF MENTAL HEALTH SERVICES.

In the precontemplation stage, apps allocated to nutrition (N in Figure 11) focus on feedback and educational features. In contrast to physical activity, almost no apps support the contemplation stage. The underrepresentation of gamification features is similar to physical activity and the number of social features is even fewer than physical activity. The small number of social features might be explained by the personal and intimate nature of weight management.

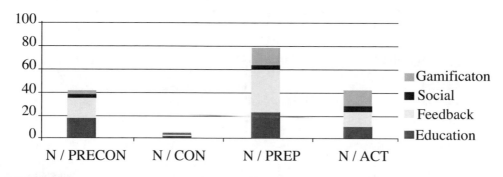

Figure 12.9 DISTRIBUTION OF APPLICATIONS FOR NUTRITION

Applications related to addictions (A in Figure 12) often implement features to support the precontemplation stage. Many apps fostering smoking cessation provide educational material, smoking diaries, and goal-setting features to reduce the number of cigarettes per day. This is a typical feature set of addiction apps. Therefore, the distribution of features is concentrated on the stages precontemplation, preparation, and action.

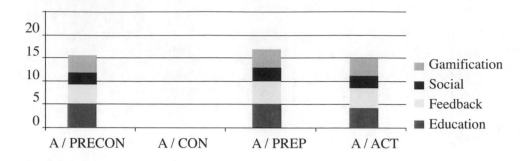

Figure 12.10 DISTRIBUTION OF APPLICATIONS FOR ADDICTIONS.

BEST PRACTICE: NOOM - WEIGHT LOSS COACH

Noom—Weight Loss Coach is a mobile app, available on the Google Android Market, that focuses on encouraging and supporting individuals who want to lose weight. The app provides several features that assist the user during the change process, primarily by giving specific weight loss instructions. Table 9 gives an overview of the app's features.

Table 12.5	Motivation Methods in Noom - Weight Loss Coach		
Education	Feedback	Social Interaction	Gamification
• Information on healthy, un-healthy food • Personalized instructions	• Recording of meals, exercise, weight loss • Graphs, charts to track progress • Coaching • Reminders	• Community forum • Progress sharing on Twitter and Facebook	• Scores for completed tasks • Worldwide high scores

Of 100 examined apps, Noom—Weight Loss Coach is the only one to include features that address all stages of change. This does not imply that all features are well implemented, but it illustrates that each stage of change is addressed by the application features. For instance, the Coach seems to be useless to the following user: "New update allows me to now log workouts :) i like the calorie counter but the coach is still useless[1]".

---

[1] Forum statement from 2012: https://play.google.com/store/apps/details?id=com.wsl.noom&hl=de.

Figure 12 shows screenshots of the smartphone app. Users are able to record their daily food consumption (screenshot 1). They can track their body weight manually or automatically via an externally connected weight scale. They can also review their progress toward predefined goals (screenshot 2). Moreover, it is possible to record physical activity with integrated smartphone sensors (screenshot 3). The combination of meal tracking and exercise tracking is especially helpful as it requires an integrated user context (e.g., daily calorie consumption vs. burned calories) and leads to more precise coaching instructions. The community forum offers members the option to discuss topics related to weight management within the weight loss community, whereas the social sharing option allows users to promote the positive effects of behavior change on Facebook or Twitter. Gamification features, like scores for completed tasks or worldwide high scores, motivate users to maintain their new lifestyle (screenshot 4).

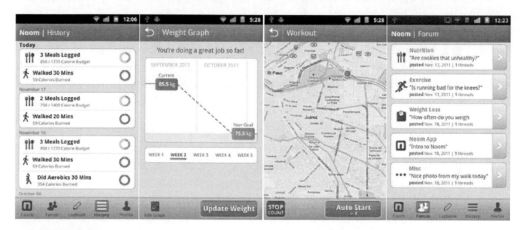

Figure 12.11 NOOM - WEIGHT LOSS COACH SCREENSHOTS 1–4.

We cannot offer reliable results concerning the app's track record, but looking at the evaluations in the Google Android Market, 18,478 users rated Noom an average of 4.3 0out of 5 points. Many users seem get sufficient support. For example, some users in 2012 posted: "This totally helps me a lot. This encourages me to go to gym!!!! ;-)[2]" or "This app keeps me on track so I never forget anything. Fantastic[3]."

---

[2]Forum statement from 2012: https://play.google.com/store/apps/details?id=com.wsl.noom&hl=de.
[3]Forum statement from 2012: https://play.google.com/store/apps/details?id=com.wsl.noom&hl=de.

SUMMARY, DISCUSSION, AND MANAGEMENT IMPLICATIONS

According to recent literature, persuasive technologies are used to support behavior change. Some of the distinctive features of smartphone, like built-in sensors or Internet connections, offer new ways to motivate and persuade users toward a health care behavior change. Using a framework that links application features, strategies for change, stages of change, and preventive measures, we conducted a market analysis to get a better understanding of the state of the art of preventive health care, using smartphones.

The process of change comprises five stages: precontemplation, contemplation, preparation, action, maintenance (Prochaska et al., 1992). Our study results reveal that persuasive smartphone features support the behavior change processes in health care, especially encouraging features such as encouraging physical activity, better nutrition and coping with addictions —but this support does not cover all stages of this process. Of the 100 apps examined, only 74 supported up to two stages of behavior change. Only one application, Noom—Weight Loss Coach, supported all stages and is described as our best practice case. Social interaction and gamification features supporting the preparation and action stages are still underrepresented compared to education and feedback features.

Future application development should focus on complementary features that support all five stages of behavior change. Oftentimes social support is crucial for individuals to maintain a healthy life style. Today, those features are integrated in physical activity applications and implemented by simple sharing functionalities for Facebook and Twitter. Only 3 of 39 nutrition applications incorporated platforms for an confidential information exchange among users. Closed communities would work better for weight management applications due to the personal and intimate nature of weight issues, hence, social features must be enhanced and incorporated into other application for preventive measures.

Feedback features are based on data analysis. The usability of these features would be enhanced if the data collection process were done automatically. Still, many applications ask the user to ennter data manually. Here we need to consider external sensor technology, such as heart rate sensors, which enable automatic data acquisition.

With regard to the developers of the apps that we investigated, we found that the majority of the apps were provided by companies for their own marketing purposes. Sports companies, like Nike, adidas, or Puma, provide running applications to boost their market position instead of promoting a healthy lifestyle. A few applications are offered by health insurance companies. Health applications could extend existing prevention programs with technical features or enable insurance companies to track the process of behavior change. The same idea could be applied to hospitals or general practitioners to monitor a patient's healing progress.

Based on these findings, the authors conclude that health promotion with persuasive technologies offers significant opportunities for preventive health care and should be developed.

REVIEW QUESTIONS

1. Do certain features (e.g., social, inbuilt sensors) have an impact on the acceptance of a technology?

2. What are the target groups for persuasive technology and which IT-affinity is needed for them to be successful?

3. What are the implications of an increased use of smartphones?

4. How do existing approaches for prevention align with the possibilities of mobile technologies?

REFERENCES

Abroms, L. C., Padmanabhan, N., Thaweethai, L., & Phillips, T. (2011). iPhone apps for smoking cessation: A content analysis. *American Journal of Preventive Medicine*, 40(3), 279–285. doi:10.1016/j.amepre.2010.10.032

Ahtinen, A., Huuskonen, P., & Häkkilä, J. (2010). Let's all get up and walk to the North Pole: Design and evaluation of a mobile wellness application. *Proceedings of the 6ᵗʰ Nordic Conference on Human-Computer Interaction* (pp. 3–12). Reykjavik.

Ahtinen, A., Mattila, E., Vaatanen, A., Hynninen, L., Salminen, J., Koskinen, E., & Laine, K. (2009). User experiences of mobile wellness applications in health promotion. *Proceedings of the 3ʳᵈ International Conference on Pervasive Computing Technologies for Health care* (pp. 1–8). London.

Arteaga, S. M., Kudeki, M., Street, W. I., & Woodworth, A. (2010). Mobile system to motivate teenagers' physical activity. *Proceedings of the 9ᵗʰ International Conference on Interaction Design and Children* (pp. 1–11). Barcelona: ACM.

Backinger, C. L., & Augustson, E. M. (2011). Where there's an app, there's a way? *American Journal of Preventive Medicine*, *40*(3), 390–391. doi:10.1016/j.amepre.2010.11.014

Bielik, P., Tomlein, M., & Barla, M. (2012). Move2Play: An innovative approach to encouraging people to be more physically active. *Proceedings of the 2ⁿᵈ ACM SIGHIT International Health Informatics Symposium* (pp. 61–70). Miami.

Breton, E. R., Fuemmeler, B. F., & Abroms, L. C. (2011, September 13). Weight loss—There is an app for that! But does it adhere to evidence-informed practices? *Translational Behavioral Medicine*, 1, 1–7. doi:10.1007/s13142-011-0076-5

Buttussi, F., Chittaro, L., & Nadalutti, D. (2006). Bringing mobile guides and fitness activities together: A solution based on an embodied virtual trainer. *Proceedings of the 8th International Conference on Human-Computer Interaction with Mobile Devices and Services.* Helsinki.

Bürger, C. (2003). *Patientenorientierte information und kommunikation im gesundheitswesen* (p. 415). DUV. Retrieved from http://books.google.com/books?id=JLAxNkdj5zoC&pgis=1

Cancer Prevention Research Center. (n.d.). Detailed overview of the transtheoretical model. Retrieved from http://www.uri.edu/research/cprc/TTM/detailedoverview.htm

Caplan, G. (1964). *Principles of preventive psychiatry* (p. 304). New York: Basic Books.

Chuah, M., & Sample, S. (2011). Fitness tour: A mobile application for combating obesity. *Proceedings of the Mobile Health 2011 Conference.* Paris: ACM Press.

Cohen, L., Davis, R., Cantor, J., Srikantharajah, J., Bazell, N., Mikkelsen, L., Masters, B. et al. (2007). Reducing health care costs through prevention (Working paper).

Consolvo, S., McDonald, D. W., & Landay, J. A. (2009). Theory-driven design strategies for technologies that support behavior change in everyday life. *Proceedings of the 27th International Conference on Human Factors in Computing Systems* (pp. 405–414). Boston: ACM Press. doi:10.1145/1518701.1518766

Dictionary.com. (2011). smartphone. Retrieved from http://dictionary.reference.com/browse/smartphone

Elder, J. P., Ayala, G. X., & Harris, S. (1999). Theories and intervention approaches to health-behavior change in primary care. *American Journal of Preventive Medicine, 17*(4), 275–284. Retrieved from http://www.ncbi.nlm.nih.gov/pubmed/10606196

Fogg, B. J. (1999). Persuasive technologies. *Communications of the ACM, 42*(5), 26–29.

Fogg, B. J. (2003). *Persuasive technology: Using computers to change what we think and do* (p. 283). San Francisco: Morgan Kaufmann. Retrieved from http://books.google.com/books?hl=de&lr=&id=9nZHbxULMwgC&pgis=1

GKV-Spitzenverband. (2010). *Leitfaden prävention* (pp. 1–92). Berlin.

Gartner. (2012). Gartner says worldwide smartphone sales soared in fourth quarter of 2011 with 47 percent growth. Retrieved from http://www.gartner.com/it/page.jsp?id=1924314

Grimes, A., Kantroo, V., & Grinter, R. E. (2010). Let's play!: Mobile health games for adults. *Proceedings of the 12th ACM International Conference on Ubiquitous Computing* (pp. 241–250). Copenhagen.

Gullotta, T. P., Bloom, M., Connecticut, C., & F. A. of S. (2003). *Encyclopedia of primary prevention and health promotion* (p. 1179). Berlin: Springer. Retrieved from http://books.google.com/books?id=Elx37xzO0bsC&pgis=1

Holzinger, A., Dorner, S., & Födinger, M. (2010). Chances of increasing youth health aware-ness through mobile wellness applications. *Proceedings of the 6th Symposium of the WG HCI&UE of the Austrian Computer Society* (pp. 71–81). Graz.

Hurrelmann, K., Klotz, T., & Haisch, J. (2004). Einführung: Krankheitsprävention und gesundheitsförderung. *Lehrbuch Prävention und Gesundheitsförderung* (pp. 13–23). Bern: Verlag Hans Huber.

Hwang, K. O., Ottenbacher, A. J., Green, A. P., Cannon-Diehl, M. R., Richardson, O., Bernstam, E. V., & Thomas, E. J. (2010). Social support in an Internet weight loss community. *International Journal of Medical Informatics, 79*(1), 5–13. doi:10.1016/j.ijmedinf.2009.10.003.Social

Ijsselsteijn, W., Kort, Y. D., Midden, C., & Eggen, B. (2006). Persuasive technology for human well-being: Setting the scene. *Proceedings of the 1st International Conference on Persuasive Technology* (pp. 1–5). Eindhoven.

Kim, S., Schap, T., Bosch, M., Maciejewski, R., Delp, E. J., Ebert, D. S., & Boushey, C. J. (2010). Development of a mobile user interface for image-based dietary assessment. *Proceedings of the 9th International Conference on Mobile and Ubiquitous Multimedia* (pp. 1–7). Limassol, Cyprus.

Klasnja, P., Consolvo, S., & Pratt, W. (2011). How to evaluate technologies for health behavior change in HCI research. *Proceedings of the 29th International Confer-ence on Human Factors in Computing Systems* (pp. 3063–3072). Vancouver: ACM. doi:10.1145/1978942.1979396

Lazenbatt, A. (2002). *The evaluation handbook for health professionals* (p. 275). London: Routledge. Retrieved from http://books.google.com/books?id=DXmu8R9T_iIC&pgis=1

Lengerke, T. von. (2007). *Public health-psychologie: Individuum und bevölkerung zwischen verhältnissen und verhalten* (p. 260). Bern: Juventa. Retrieved from http://books.google.com/books?id=9VU4DM9zxG4C&pgis=1

Leppin, A. (2007). Konzepte und strategien der Krankheitsprävention. *Lehrbuch Prävention und Gesundheitsförderung* (pp. 31–40). Bern: Verlag Hans Huber

Maloney-Krichmar, D., & Preece, J. (2002). The meaning of an online health community in the lives of its members: Roles, relationships and group dynamics. *2002 International Symposium on Technology and Society ISTAS'02* (pp. 20–27). Raleigh.

Mattila, E., Korhonen, I., Salminen, J. H., Ahtinen, A., Koskinen, E., Särelä, A., Pärkkä, J. et al. (2010). Empowering citizens for well-being and chronic disease management with wellness diary. *IEEE Transactions on Information Technology in Biomedicine: A Publication of the IEEE Engineering in Medicine and Biology Society, 14*(2), 456–463. doi:10.1109/TITB.2009.2037751

Mokdad, A. H., Marks, J. S., Stroup, D. F., & Gerberding, J. L. (2004). Actual causes of death in the United States, 2000. *Journal of the American Medical Association, 291*(10), 1238–1245. doi:10.1001/jama.291.10.1238

Mrazek, P. J., & Haggerty, R. J. (1994). *Reducing risks for mental disorders: Frontiers for preventive intervention research.* Retrieved from http://books.google.com/books?hl=de&lr=&id=5V66-WRcGL8C&pgis=1

Oinas-Kukkonen, H. (2010a). Behavior change support systems: The next frontier for web science. *Proceedings of the Second International Web Science Conference.* Raleigh, NC.

Oinas-Kukkonen, H. (2010b). Behavior change support systems: A research model and agenda. In T. Ploug, P. Hasle, & H. Oinas-Kukkonen (Eds.), *Proceedings of the 5th International Conference on Persuasive Technology* (pp. 4–14). Copenhagen: Springer-Verlag. doi:10.1007/978-3-642-13226-1_3

Oinas-Kukkonen, H., & Harjumaa, M. (2008). Towards deeper understanding of persuasion in software and information systems. *Proceedings of the 1st International Conference on Advances in Computer-Human Interaction* (pp. 200–205). Sainte Luce . IEEE. doi:10.1109/ACHI.2008.31

Oinas-Kukkonen, H., & Harjumaa, M. (2009). Persuasive systems design: Key issues, process model, and system features. *Communications of the Association for Information Systems*, *24*(28), 485–500.

Oulasvirta, A., Rattenbury, T., Ma, L., & Raita, E. (2011). Habits make smartphone use more pervasive. *Personal and Ubiquitous Computing.* doi:10.1007/s00779-011-0412-2

Pollak, J., Gay, G., Byrne, S., Wagner, E., Retelny, D., & Humphreys, L. (2010, July). It's time to eat! Using mobile games to promote healthy eating. *IEEE Pervasive Computing*, *9*(3), 21–27. doi:10.1109/MPRV.2010.41

Pro-Change Behavior Systems Inc. (2012). Transtheoretical model. Retrieved from http://www.prochange.com/ttm

Prochaska, J. O. (2007). Stages of change: Phasen der verhaltensänderung, bereitschaft und motivation. In J. Kerr (Ed.), *ABC der verhaltensänderung: Der leitfaden für erfolgreiche prävention und gesundheitsförderung* (p. 368). München: Elsevier,Urban&FischerVerlag. Retrieved from http://books.google.com/books?id=MsKVeSInlN8C&pgis=1

Prochaska, J. O., DiClemente, C. C., & Norcross, J. C. (1992). In search of how people change: Applications to addictive behaviors. *The American Psychologist*, *47*(9), 1102–1114. Retrieved from http://www.ncbi.nlm.nih.gov/pubmed/1329589

Prochaska, J. O., Redding, C. A., & Evers, K. E. (2008). The transtheoretical model and stages of change. In K. Glanz, B. K. Rimer, & K. V. Viswanath (Eds.), *Health behavior and health education: Theory, research, and practice* (Vol. 4, pp. 1–552). San Francisco: Jossey-Bass.

Simons, H. W., Morreale, J., & Gronbeck, B. E. (2001). *Persuasion in society* (p. 440). Thousand Oaks. SAGE Publications, Inc. Retrieved from http://books.google.com/books?hl=de&lr=&id=3t55RAZOPVMC&pgis=1

WahooFitness. (2012). Fitness sensors. Retrieved from http://www.wahoofitness.com/Products/Products.asp

Wood, W. (2000). Attitude change: Persuasion and social influence. *Annual Review of Psychology, 51,* 539–570. doi:10.1146/annurev.psych.51.1.539

Zephyr Technology. (2012). Consumer HxM. Retrieved from http://www.zephyr-technology.com/consumer-hxm

Chapter 13

The Role of E-Health Information in Customer Empowerment

Johanna Gummerus,
Veronica Liljander,
Catharina von Koskull

LEARNING OBJECTIVES

Upon completing this chapter, you should be able to do the following:

1. Understand how service technology supports consumers in resolving health-related questions, both within and outside of the official health care system.

2. Understand the differences among consumers in their opportunities, motivations, and abilities to use e-health for their benefit.

3. Discuss the role of the patient/customer in the realization of health service outcomes.

4. Critically analyze the positive and negative consequences of e-health use.

KEYWORDS

e-health, e-health information, health service, service technology, self-service, customer empowerment, customer behavior

ABSTRACT

This paper investigates the influence of e-health on health care management. In particular, it discusses the role of electronic health-related information in augmenting consumers' motivations, opportunities, and abilities to handle potentially stressful health-related issues and to make decisions regarding health, thus, becoming more empowered. This chapter draws on the service marketing literature to discuss how e-health services offer information that benefits consumers. A case study of an e-health site sheds light on some reasons why consumers continue to use e-health services and illustrates the positive influences that e-health can have in terms of increased motivation, opportunity, and ability. Managerial implications are provided.

INTRODUCTION

The health care industry is increasingly deploying information and communication technologies, also called e-health or health information technology (HIT). Consumer[1] adoption of technology-based health care services is strongly advocated, as they can improve customer health and the efficiency of the health care system (Blumenthal, 2009). Reported benefits include improvements in health quality, enhanced disease monitoring, and fewer medication errors (Chaudhry et al., 2006). Technology deployment in health care is driven by the need to cut costs, technology advancements that enable more efficient information flows (Blumenthal, 2009), and the increasing numbers of citizens worldwide who use the Internet and who are willing to adopt new technological solutions.

Electronic health care, or *e-health*, can be defined as "health services and information delivered or enhanced through the Internet and related technologies" (Eysenbach, 2001). The technology-based services may target health care professionals (medical professionals, technicians, paramedics, clinical staff, administrative staff) or patients and the general public (e.g., preventive health care). Several technological innovations purposively help professionals to provide care, e.g., electronic health records, which enable storage and sharing of data, and video conferencing, which is used to identify medical conditions and diagnose patients (LeRouge, Hevner, & Webb Collins, 2007). Likewise, several services for patients exist such as websites that offer information and interactive services (Gummerus, Liljander, Pura, & van Riel, 2004), kiosks that are used for educational purposes (Lober & Flowers, 2011), tele-homecare that enables in-home monitoring of elderly patients (Essén & Conrick, 2008), and self-monitoring devices that track health-related behaviors (Liljander, Gummerus, Pihlström, & Kiehelä, 2012).

Technology-based services are developing hand-in-hand with two major changes in how the health care industry views the patient's role. First, patients today are the starting point for health care providers offering health care, as outlined in patient-centered care (Lambert et al., 1997). As noted by Sepucha et al. (2008), according to the Institute of Medicine, patient-centered care implies that the practitioner-patient relationship is based on partnership and that the health services management decisions need to "reflect patients' wants, needs and preferences" (p. 504). The second change involves the role of the patient, who has shifted from a passive subject to an active participant (see Lober & Flowers, 2011). These trends can be discerned in service marketing as well, where a customer orientation (Lengnick-Hall, 1996) and customer participation

---

[1] In this chapter, we use the terms customer, consumer, and patient interchangeably. Notably, customer/consumer has a broader meaning, encompassing either the patient or the patient's family.

in the service process are highlighted as prerequisites for high-quality service provision (Bitner, Faranda, Hubbert, & Zeithaml, 1997; Ouschan, Sweeney, & Johnson, 2006; Solomon, Surprenant, Czepiel, & Gutman, 1985).

For health care providers (e.g., physicians) and for other service employees, customer inputs are crucial in terms of information, needs, wishes, and expectations (Bitner et al., 1997; Bitner, Brown, & Meuter, 2000; Edvardsson, 1997; Zeithaml, Parasuraman, & Berry, 1990). Consequently, the better informed the customer is and the better the customer communicates his or her expectations to the service provider, the better the outcomes of the health care service are expected to be. This means that information, that is, "data that has been organized or given structure—and thus endowed with meaning" (Glazer, 1991, p. 2), has an important role in the realization of health service outcomes. Customers' use of e-health (information and services)—in particular, collective knowledge built online—has been said to empower customers (Constantinides, 2008), that is, it helps to shift decision-making power from health care professionals to health care customers (Toofany, 2006).

Against this backdrop, we propose that health care professionals need to understand how the use of e-health influences the customers (patients and their families), and we suggest that this influence can be understood with the help of the motivation, opportunity, and ability (MOA) framework (MacInnis, Moorman, & Jaworski, 1991) and the customer/patient empowerment literature. We propose that technology-based services increase health care customers' motivation, opportunity, and ability to evaluate and use information for their own or others' benefit, either in traditional encounters with practitioners or online as self-service.

First, we start by discussing e-health and the information that it provides. Then we introduce our proposed framework. We continue by presenting the results of an empirical study of an e-health portal, which reveals consumers' reported reasons for continued use of the service. Such reasons are expected to reflect the positive outcomes customers receive from using an e-health service. We conclude with implications for managers and future research.

Electronic Health Care (E-Health)

Electronic health care, or *e-health*, entails the use of interactive technologies to enable health improvement and health care services (Ahern, Kreslake, & Phalen, 2006, p. 2). The predominant channel today is the Internet; in one U.S. study of adults, 49.4 percent reported health information seeking behaviors on the Internet. The reported behaviors covered illness-only (28.6 percent) and wellness-only (30.8 percent) information, as well as searching for both (40.6 percent) (Weaver et al., 2010). In another study, Schiavo (2008, p. 10) reported that 80 percent of U.S. Internet users search health-related information. European usage levels are approaching those of the United States. In a study of

European citizens' Internet use, Andreassen et al. (2007) found that 71 percent of the Internet users had employed it for health purposes (corresponding to 44 percent of the total sample). The respondents used the Internet before or after doctor's appointments and reported feeling reassured twice as often as feeling anxious after using the Internet. Based on these figures, it is clear that e-health has a prominent role in health care. However, further analyses of the U.S. data revealed that education is positively related to e-health use, with only one quarter of people with less than a high school education looking up online health information (Fox, 2011). Health literacy, cultural and motivational factors, as well as self-efficacy and empowerment, are some of the factors that affect consumer behavior toward health issues (Schiavo, 2008).

Figure 13.1 illustrates consumer uses of e-health. E-health is provided by health professionals, nonprofessionals (private consumers without professional health care education), and commercial stakeholders, who have an interest in promoting certain goods and services. Customers often demand health care services under considerable stress (Berry & Bendapudi, 2007). Since health services are high in credence properties (Darby & Karni, 1973), customers often face difficulties in evaluating the services, even after using them. These factors drive consumers to seek additional information online during different parts of the service process.

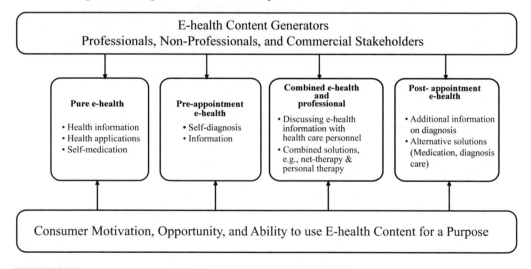

Figure 13.1 CONSUMER USES OF E-HEALTH WITH EXAMPLES

Consumers use e-health for a variety of private purposes, such as to learn about their own or a relative's illness or to monitor their own progress via online health applications (e.g., curves of daily calorie intake, calories burned through exercise, or pulse monitoring). They use e-health services to prepare for a meeting with a health professional or to gather more information after the meeting. For example, a recently introduced service provides video interviews with therapists to help consumers choose a licensed therapist who fulfills their needs and suits their personality (Winter, 2012). The service also helps the therapists in that they get more suitable patients. It is worth remembering that the Internet is likely to be used for health purposes parallel to other service channels, as electronic channels complement other channels rather than replace them entirely (Dutta-Bergman, 2004). Consequently, e-health applications are used increasingly as supporting services to make health care more efficient. For example, consumers are taught to perform simple tests at home (e.g., blood sugar and blood pressure monitoring) and to upload the results into online programs that are monitored by both the consumers and medical professionals. Well-developed e-health solutions can provide, in some instances, quicker care or provisional self-help as a complementary service to health professionals. This is the case, for example, with net-therapy, which is used for quick self-help and for obtaining further insights before, between, and after medical appointments. However, when not used with licensed professionals, the quality of the services offered are difficult for consumers to evaluate; for example, the quality of a therapy appointment between two avatars (the consumer and the therapist) in the virtual world Second Life. There are also reports of frustration among funders and purchasers of e-health services due to the difficulties of assessing consequences of e-health usage (or nonusage) and the difference between users liking the service and the actual effect that it has on their health (Ahern et al., 2006).

In general, consumers need to be able to trust online health information, something that is difficult without quality assurances. There are many websites sponsored by insurers, hospitals, medical companies, and other stakeholders with subjective interests in selling health-related goods and services (Ahern et al., 2006; Bodie & Dutta, 2008; Chandra, Sikula, & Paul, 2004). Unsurprisingly, health care researchers worry about the poor quality of some online information (Erdem & Harrison-Walker, 2006). Consumers may or may not be able to discern any underlying interest, and they find it difficult, if not impossible, to evaluate the credibility and trustworthiness of the information provided on e-health sites, blogs, online communities, and other social media. To sum up, it is clear that more research is needed to understand the consequences and challenges of using e-health services, particularly information.

CUSTOMER EMPOWERMENT

Empowerment has become a necessary ingredient in the shift from curing illnesses toward preventive health care, self-help, and consumer wellness (Ouschan et al., 2006) and in the need to reduce health care costs (Lenert, 2010). Consumers are encouraged to actively participate in making their own health decisions, and new technology provides the necessary tools. Electronic health care services and, particularly, informational services may increase customers' motivation, opportunity, and ability to take care of their own health, both taking preventive measures (e.g., weight control, smoking cessation, alcohol intake) and seeking remedies to sickness, i.e., acting on the information they have collected. This phenomenon is particularly emphasized as customers are largely left to themselves when it comes to interpreting e-health information. Their ability to perform this task will depend on skills learned through sources other than traditional interpersonal interactions with health care workers.

The framework adopted in this study proposes linkages among e-health service use, consumers' motivation, opportunity, ability (MOA), and empowerment. It builds on the MOA framework originally created to explore activities related to consumers' information processing (MacInnis et al., 1991). This framework was later employed for understanding customer-to-customer know-how exchange in e-communities (Gruen, Osmonkekov, & Czaplewski, 2005). Motivation and ability are used to frame consumers' behavior in service settings (Bowen, 1986) where these are expected to influence consumers' degree of participation and, thus, affect the actualized results of the health care service (Dellande, Gilly, & Graham, 2004). The proposed framework of the influence of e-health use on customer empowerment is depicted in Figure 13.2.

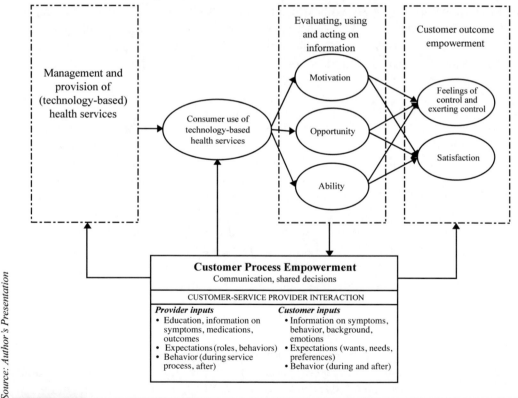

Source: Author's Presentation

Figure 13.2 THE INFLUENCE OF E-HEALTH USE ON CUSTOMER EMPOWERMENT.

In the service provider–customer interaction, the customer has a focal role in the realization of positive service outcomes. First, the customer acts as a *coproducer of the service*, meaning that the customer and the firm's front-end personnel interact and jointly produce the service (Bendapudi & Leone, 2003; Gill, White & Cameron, 2011). During this interaction, the customer shares information on symptoms, behavior, and background, as well as information on his or her emotions and expectations. Customers' inputs can further include their needs, wishes, and expectations, all of which are important indicators for service providers (Edvardsson, 1997). While customer needs are basic, such as the need to cure an illness, *wishes* refer to "the way in which the customer wants to satisfy a specific need" (Edvardsson, 1997, p. 32). Expectations, in turn, refer to a particular service. Customers' expectations are formed through planned communication, word-of-mouth, and the firm's image (Grönroos, 1984). During customer-provider interactions, customers can communicate their expectations and, thus, provide valuable information for the service provider (Parasuraman, Zeithaml, & Berry, 1985). Customers' expectations influence perceived service quality (Grönroos, 1984), and an important task for managers is to manage and understand these expectations and to close the gap between the expected and the perceived service (Zeithaml, Parasuraman, & Berry, 1990). Second, the customer defines the quality of the service interaction (Zeithaml et al., 1990), and the perceived quality influences the customer's satisfaction (e.g., Bloemer, de Ruyter, & Peeters, 1998). One particular challenge in health care provision is the provider's inability to always fulfill the customer's basic needs (curing an illness, for example). In such cases, the service provider must help the customer to try to come to terms with this fact.

We suggest that e-health service use is linked to motivation, opportunity, and ability in the following ways. First, we propose that the use of e-health services makes consumers more motivated to evaluate, use, and act on the information collected in offline and online service encounters because consumers can collect more information and compare their situation with those of their peers. Consumers are also potentially more "willing to allocate processing resources" (MacInnis et al., 1991, p. 34) to the information they have. Second, consumer ability, which refers to the set of knowledge and skills regarding health-related issues, may be enhanced because customers can exchange information and opinions with peers and seek information. When consumers exchange know-how online, "the interactions among individuals serve as an information source that enhances those individuals' competency and knowledge of the object or field of interest" (Gruen et al., 2005, p. 37). Third, e-health offers a large amount of information and a wide range of information sources, thereby increasing the opportunities to acquire and employ information, as the Internet is generally reported to increase consumers' reach to offerings (Grewal, Iyer, Krishnan, & Sharma, 2003). Taken together, we believe these aspects lead to consumer empowerment. Next, we separately discuss opportunity, motivation, and ability.

Opportunity

A prerequisite to gaining access to e-health information and, thus, the opportunity to gather, evaluate, and use information is having access to the Internet via computers, tablets, smartphones, or other suitable devices. Internet access varies widely around the world. According to one source (Internet Usage, 2012) the penetration of Internet usage for the world population in 2011 was 32.7 percent, varying among the continents as follows: Africa 13.5 percent, Asia 26.2 percent, Europe 61.3 percent, Middle East 35.6 percent, North America 78.6 percent, Latin America/Caribbean 39.5 percent, and Oceania/Australia 67.5 percent. Smartphone use is increasing rapidly, and many observers expect smartphones to be the main source for consumer information in the near future. Furthermore, consumers in developing economies will be more likely to own a smartphone than a computer. Worldwide, sales of all mobile phones increased from 19 percent in 2010 to 31 percent in 2011 (Brownlow, 2012). According to Nielsen statistics (NielsenWire, 2012), more than 46 percent of mobile phone owners in the United States had smartphones at the end of 2011, compared with 25 percent the year before. Of recent mobile phone buyers, 60 percent had chosen a smartphone. Within the European Union, smartphone ownership increased by 41 percent between 2009 to 2010[2]. According to another source,[3] 31 percent of mobile phone owners had adopted a smartphone by December 2010. The penetration rate of smartphones is highest in Singapore (90 percent), with Australia, the Nordic countries, and some European countries trailing behind at a little above 40 percent (Sterling, 2011).

Taken together, this means that e-health information is increasingly available to a larger population around the world. However, opportunity is only the starting point. Consumers need motivation to use the services and the ability to evaluate the accuracy of the available information.

Motivation

Customers' motivation to gather, evaluate, and use information about e-health services is expected to increase. One reason is that previous positive experiences with electronic services positively influence future use of technology-based services (Meuter, Bitner, Ostrom, & Brown, 2005). In addition, the Internet can be used in many ways: as an information source, as a communication tool, as a social system used to affiliate with others or to avoid human interactions, and as a source of consumption-related fulfillment (Maignan & Lukas, 1997). E-health can fulfill all these functions: it may provide information, help consumers communicate, support affiliation with peers and practitioners, and enable transactions.

An interesting question for medical professionals is: What sparks customers' use of e-health. Dabholkar (1996) suggested that consumers would turn to self-service options

---

[2] www.onlinemarketing-trends.com (2011).

[3] www.digital-stats.blogspot.com (2011).

(such as the Internet) when they did not trust the service provider's ability to handle their situation correctly. Thus, many health care customers may take greater control by gathering information to corroborate or question the physician's diagnosis and decisions. Physicians need to involve patients in the decision-making process to establish physician trust (Ouschan et al., 2006). In the end, to follow the suggested regimen, patients need to trust the correctness of the information and the options that physicians present to them. Still, newspapers, TV programs, and peers present people with numerous cases where physicians have made the wrong decision or not presented all the facts to their patients, and where patients through their own research and diligence have been able to correct the diagnosis or find alternative treatment that cured them, or prolonged their life. In addition, tales of malpractice and low-quality products (e.g., hip replacements, breast implants), cost-cutting practices, or revelations about unlicensed doctors and nurses decrease consumers' trust in the health care system.

Consumers may also be reluctant to admit that they do not understand all the physician says. They may even have difficulty understanding the medical terminology. Recently, a survey of health care customers in a small Finnish community showed that up to 60 percent of patients in some parts of the community did not understand the physician. The survey did not reveal whether this was due to language[4] or other communication problems. Such experiences cause stress to patients who do not have the option of seeking alternative opinions, and they will try to find the missing information online. Time restrictions on appointments and the lack of self-confidence may hinder patients from saying outright that they do not understand what the doctor is saying. Studies on the role of language in services have shown that language has an important impact on consumer-service perceptions and behavior (Holmqvist & Grönroos, 2012).

In addition, previous research has demonstrated that people may turn to self-services, such as e-health, because they want to avoid interaction with service employees such as physicians (Dabholkar, Bobbitt, & Lee, 2003). Patients may also be reluctant to take up health care workers' time to ask more questions, or patients may think of new questions once leaving the doctor's office. Powell, Inglis, Ronnie, & Large, (2011) found that consumers searched for information online because they wanted to avoid pestering their physician or they wanted a second opinion. Clients may look up symptoms online before deciding whether to make an appointment with a health care worker (Powell et al., 2011). For example, they may search for answers to the following questions: What flu symptoms require prescribed medicines and when is bed rest enough? What could cause a rash on one's child? Has anyone else experienced the same problem and what

---

[4]In Finland, it is more difficult to recruit health care personnel in rural areas than to city hospitals or health care centers. It is especially difficult to recruit fully licensed doctors who can communicate in both official languages, Finnish and Swedish. Doctors often lack Swedish speaking skills, although the majority of the population in the area may be Swedish speakers. In addition, increased recruitment from neighboring countries has led to deficiencies in Finnish speaking skills. Sometimes, nurses are called in to interpret what the doctor says to the patient and vice versa.
[5]www.pisa.oecd.org

are their experiences of a good remedy? Furthermore, self-service technology use is driven by motivations to save time, as well as the ease and quickness of the service process (Liljander, Gillberg, Gummerus, & Van Riel, 2006).

ABILITY

An underlying assumption in e-health is that consumers will be able to make rational decisions based on the information provided. Although many decisions may not have life-threatening implications (cf. Lenert, 2010), research shows that consumers face many obstacles in making optimal decisions. To use e-health information, consumers need to be e-health literate, that is, possess "the ability to seek, find, understand, and appraise health information from electronic sources and apply the knowledge gained to addressing or solving a health problem" (Norman & Skinner, 2006, p. 2). Many consumers lack the necessary skills and, thus, cannot use the available information. Norman and Skinner (2006) list six literacy skills that underlie consumers' e-health ability: traditional, informational, and media literacy (analytical skills) and computer, science, and health literacy (context-specific skills). Health literacy has been related to demographic factors, such as education, income, social status, culture, ethnicity, age, and gender (Bodie & Dutta, 2008; Shaw, Huebner, Armin, Orzech, & James, 2009; Yaşin & Özin, 2011). In 2009, the Organisation for Economic Co-operation & Development (OECD) sponsored the PISA study[5] (Programme for International Student Assessment), which focused specifically on students' reading skills. The results from 65 countries showed remarkable differences in reading skills, which likely will affect the ability to understand and evaluate e-health information, even considering that reading skills form only a part of consumer health literacy (Bodie & Dutta, 2008).

A study of middle school students in one U.S. school showed that the students distrusted the health information of commercial and brand sites and that e-health literacy increased the perceptions of the unreliability of these sites (Paek, Hove, & Isaacson, 2011). Another study among college students taking health professional courses showed that even educated consumers have difficulties evaluating the reliability and credibility of information on e-health websites (Ivanitskaya, O'Boyle, & Casey, 2006). The study corroborated past findings by showing that consumers have difficulty conducting advanced searches and evaluating the information's trustworthiness. Paradoxically, the students considered their own research skills to be very good or excellent. These studies demonstrate the precariousness of e-health. Consumers need exceptional skills to evaluate the available information, and little seems to be known about consumer e-health misconceptions and their consequences for both consumers and health professionals. In addition to direct health consequences, doctors may have to use a disproportionate part of the short appointment time convincing patients of why a drug or treatment suggested by the patient is unsuitable for the diagnosed problem. This is likely to lead to frustration, job stress, and dissatisfaction for the doctor (cf. Chan, Yim, & Lam, 2010).

CASE STUDY

In this section, we report on a study of consumers' motivations to continue using an e-health service. The e-health portal is one of the most popular health-related sites in Finland, with more than 16,000 visitors weekly. The service is not provided in conjunction with a health care center or a hospital, or used as a combined treatment option. It provides health-related content to support consumers' interest in information related to wellness and illness. The studied site is targeted toward a particular audience and contains category-specific, detailed information. It includes advice from professionals, as well as from nonprofessionals (in discussion forums).

There are four main services: discussion forums, articles, a fee-based personal medical advice service in the form of online doctors, and a database containing free medical advice. The health care database includes past questions that customers have posed, as well as the medical advice a doctor has given to them. The portal also offers low-calorie recipes, video clips, and health care index calculators. The discussion forum is the portal's most popular service, with more than 50 subareas covering, for example, pregnancy, childcare, and a variety of diseases.

The users' motivations were probed with an open-ended question: Why do you continue to use this e-health service? The data were gathered as part of a larger study of the site. Consumer ability (such as e-health literacy) was not measured in this study, although all who participated were using the service at the time of the study, and thus, manifested some degree of e-literacy.

So the site users could remain anonymous, an online survey was chosen as the data collection method. A pop-up window invited all visitors during an 8-day period to participate in the study. During this time, 698 users clicked on the pop-up window, resulting in a response rate of 44 percent of those who opened the survey, or 4.8 percent of those who were shown the invitation banner. This response rate is comparable to other pop-up window studies, which typically result in 5–15 percent response rates (Rapp, 2001). In all, 325 respondents reported their motivations for revising the site.

FINDINGS

The textual answers were of varying length (from one word to five sentences). The answers were saved in a text file that served as a database for subsequent analysis. A content analysis was undertaken with the aim of representing the qualitative data with quantified categories (Kasserjian, 1987, as cited in Hopkinson & Hogarth-Scott, 2001). The analysis was conducted in three partially overlapping stages—data reduction, display, and interpretation—as suggested by Miles and Huberman (1994). The answers were first sorted inductively, and a classification scheme was developed based on the emerging themes. This part of the process consisted of repeated, careful readings and sorting the answers into groups according to similarities within them. The process followed Bitner, Booms, & Tetreault's (1990) ideas of categorization. The purposes of the categories was to simplify the data, to give the reader a general picture of the emerging issues from the respondents' answers, and to serve as a basis for further analysis. The results are displayed in Table 13.1.

Table 13.1	Classification of Mental Health Services.	
Categories	**% (N)**	**Consumer Comments**
1. Participation in discussions	39 (128)	• The discussion is matter-of-fact and competent in the groups I use, and I have received lots of advice and encouragement and sympathy from the different groups. • I need discussions because it is easier to discuss some topics with strangers, and exchange experiences with those in a similar situation. • The friends I've gotten from the discussion groups • I like to follow the conversations.
2. Situation-related need	16 (53)	• When some medical problem starts to trouble my mind • Long-term illness
3. Content	12 (38)	• Diversity. Questions, answers, discussions, etc.
4. Service access	10 (33)	• I can find information easily. • A quick, concise information package • When I look for health-related information, it is easy to search on a familiar site.
5. Trustworthiness	8 (27)	• Interesting, relevant, matter-of-fact information; the doctors are specialists!
6. Superiority to alternatives	6 (19)	• The quick availability of new information, don't have to flick through a medical book, for instance, ours is quite old. • It helps in deciding what kind of treatment to seek or whether it is necessary at all. • Somehow I feel that here my questions are answered, whereas, for instance, at the health care centre the answers [I get] are vague.
7. Other	9 (27)	• I like to read doctoral columns in general. • Price-quality ratio
Total	100 (325)	

The results affirmed the importance of other (nonprofessional) consumers' experiences and support as a motivating factor for visiting the site. By having access to a network of individuals with similar interests and drawing on their experiences, consumers obtain answers to questions that they cannot or dare not ask friends and relatives or that they cannot obtain from face-to-face interactions with health care professionals. The largest group of answers (39 percent of all responses) related to **participation in discussions**. Respondents appreciated the social ties created among the discussion forum users, referring to the other discussants as "friends" or "acquaintances." Most respondents were interested in knowing how the other discussants were doing. They further emphasized the importance of personal interaction, characterized by receiving advice, empathy, and support, and, to a minor extent, the ability to help others: "The discussions touch my life in many ways, I get advice and encouragement." In addition, the discussants often shared a similar medical situation, which enabled efficient transmission of relevant information and advice based on the participants' experiences, giving access to invaluable resources: "Discussing with people who share my problems and have questions & answers similar to my own problems is a very fine and useful way of communicating." Fellow discussants were perceived as a reliable information source, and the quality of the discussions was, in general, deemed high. Responses also referred to the general atmosphere of the discussion groups. Terms included "friendly atmosphere," "nice spirit," and "community spirit," indicating a positive evaluation of the less tangible characteristics of the discussions. Although most answers reflected active participation, they also revealed the presence of lurkers, i.e., people who only read the discussions.

Another major reason for revisits was the **situation-related need for information** (16 percent). The need was either temporary or enduring. Situational needs were related to conditions in life, for instance, an illness could trigger the need to find services that provide access to relevant information. Other triggers mentioned included life transition, dieting, childlessness, or personal problems in general. Some referred to the recurring nature of health-related problems, as well as unfulfilled needs where the person was drawn back to the site in the hope that the site would have provided more information on the topic of interest.

Different kinds of **content** (12 percent) was mentioned as a reason for revisits, referring to diversity and selection, including finding information in the medical database and articles, as well as following new research in health care. In addition, health-related automatic calculators—which calculate individual indices such as weight, children's growth curves, or expected time of fertilization—that is, interactive, personalized content, were deemed valuable.

The fourth category, **service access**-related factors (10 percent) referred to the minimal effort required to use the services, as well as saving time due to quick access to the information. Some respondents also pointed out that familiarity makes the site easy to use because the customer knows what type of information is available and how to navigate the site.

The **trustworthiness** of the doctors, of the other discussants, or of the site was mentioned (8 percent), in addition to the **superiority of this service to alternatives** (6 percent). The respondents perceived the site as either clearly superior or as a valuable complement. The qualities that were mentioned that made the site better than alternatives such as medical books, journals, or library visits involved speed and ease of obtaining up-to-date information. **Other reasons** (9 percent) included general interest in health-related issues and wanting to learn about health issues.

Next, we discuss the results of the study on consumers' motivations to use the studied e-health service and then discuss the research implications.

DISCUSSION OF THE STUDY AND FUTURE RESEARCH DIRECTIONS

During the interpretation of the study respondents' answers to the open questions, two general themes were identified. First, customers seemed to use the service for emotional support, partially to decrease anxiety or uncertainty. Receiving support is an important reason for consumers to interact in social media, such as online communities and blogs (Chung & Kim, 2008; Nonnecke, Andrews, & Preece, 2006). Customers gain more control over health care–related issues that may involve high risk by obtaining more knowledge about illnesses and learning from others' experiences. Such knowledge may enhance the customer's ability to act in a more beneficial way, for example, obtain better treatments within the traditional health care sector. Earlier research has emphasized that patients with chronic illnesses face considerable challenges, arguing that "not only do they have to learn a lot about the disease and its treatment, they are also often told to integrate a number of new lifestyle- or treatment-related behaviors into their everyday life" (Aujoulat, d'Hoore, & Deccache, 2007, p. 13). Gathering information may act as a coping strategy that reduces uncertainty and makes people more knowledgeable about their condition (Lazarus & Launier, as cited in Arntson & Droge, 1987) and thus, enhances empowerment. The importance of peer-to-peer communication is in line with the findings of Harris and Baron (2004), who reported in their study of consumer-to-consumer conversations that customers seemed to supply each other with information that "employees would normally be expected to supply" (p. 299). Thus, e-health may complement traditional health services by adding an emotionally supportive dimension.

Secondly, the cognitive, rationale-based reasons for using the site relate to evaluations of the different aspects of the service portal. The portal's general positive qualities, e.g., quickness, clarity, matter-of-factness, usefulness, ease of use, and competence give the e-health portal an air of a valuable information source. Consumers perceive it as easier to find information online than in books or journals from libraries. Superiority of alternatives has also been recognized in earlier studies as an important factor behind the use of e-services, with Meuter et al. (2000) finding that superiority to alternatives was an important reason underlying customers' satisfaction. In addition to specific health care sites, easy-to-use search engines deliver an abundance of information, which can be skimmed due to the short format of on-screen presentations. Searching for the same information in books and journals in libraries takes more time and requires high level of literacy skills. Our findings align with those of Dabholkar et al. (2003), who found that the attributes of self-service technology influence willingness to use the service in the future.

Our results have some limitations. The study was limited to one national health care site that provides advice from qualified professionals, but also from nonprofessionals (discussions and blogs). Advertisements are the only openly commercial aspect of the site, although commercial interests cannot be ruled out from blogs and discussions. It could be described as a safe environment for e-health consumption. However, as previous research has shown, consumers possess different degrees of e-health literacy, which affects what information consumers perceive, how credible and trustworthy they perceive the information, and how they act on it. In any case, our findings reflect consumers' motivations to revisit a health site that does not require registration, but allows users to remain anonymous. Furthermore, the provider moderates the discussions to decrease the amount of inappropriate behavior, which may partially explain why the discussions were deemed so important.

GENERAL DISCUSSION AND MANAGERIAL IMPLICATIONS

E-health is changing the health care experience for both consumers and health care workers by adding new service channels and empowering consumers with a plethora of self-help knowledge that was previously beyond their reach or difficult to obtain. E-health raises the question of to what extent health care service providers are aware of consumers' e-health use and how it changes consumers' perceptions and expectations relating to health care services. Managers of e-health sites and applications need to develop the services to fit consumers' practices and expectations, taking into account their ability to understand and use the service, as well as their opportunities to access the service through different devices. Meanwhile, managers of physical health care facilities need to educate their employees in how to meet and communicate with customers who are highly motivated to search for e-health information before and after meeting health care workers. With the proliferation of smartphones, tablets, and pads, health care workers need to be prepared to help consumers, even during appointments, to find and bookmark appropriate e-health information on devices they bring to the appointment. As consumer practices develop, so should the health care system's support of such practices as long as it helps consumers live a healthier life. Customer orientation involves understanding consumers' changing expectations and incorporating customers into the service strategy. It is evident that an enlightened consumer increases the pressure on health care workers and on the communication between workers and patients.

Health care professionals should consider consumers' motivation, opportunity, and ability to deploy information (through e-health and other channels) as important factors in realizing consumers' empowerment and as necessary steps to increase consumers' cocreation in health services. E-health increases the consumers' power in a traditionally hierarchical relationship, where consumers trusted their health care professionals for want of alternative information sources. Today, it is not uncommon for consumers to have superior knowledge about an ailment by virtue of having gathered information online. A consumer orientation requires that health care professionals show a sincere interest in and respect for the information gathered by consumers. This adds a new task to the interactions between consumers and professionals, adding time pressure to the appointment while requiring tact and knowledge in handling the information. Professionals need to communicate with customers in a way that supports their e-health initiatives, while also facing the difficult task of handling customers who have misunderstood sources or who have placed their trust in suspect sources. Empowering customers through e-health may add to the stress of health care workers to meet customers' expectations. Conflicts may arise between e-health information found by customers and prevailing norms in health care. Neither ignoring customers' concerns nor trying to invoke a power balance ("I know better because I am an educated professional") is likely to be a viable option. Managers must be aware of the potential stress and find ways to relieve it, for example, by educating professionals in effective communication strategies, describing best practices, and providing peer support. To our knowledge, no studies exist that would provide detailed help for professionals in this new context. We suggest that studies of the e-health experiences of both customers and professionals are needed. To begin with, collecting negative and positive incidents from both parties could yield useful data for both conceptual and educational purposes.

The above points are also directly related to role clarity, i.e., the extent to which patients and health care professionals know how they are expected to behave, and the different roles that they may take. For example, Lengnick-Hall, Claycomb, and Inks (2003) proposed that customers may act as buyers, recipients, resources, and coproducers. The extent to which customers' perceptions of motivation, opportunity, and ability to use e-health differ across these roles may reveal relevant areas for improvement of e-health services. Restrictions are placed on health care workers' roles by employers, insurance companies, and other stakeholders. A medical worker may understand the patient's need for further treatment or for an alternative, more expensive treatment as described on an e-health site, but the restrictions of a company's rules or insurance standards prevent other treatment. To some extent, customers could be educated on role expectations, but it is easier to educate customers in how to make an appointment online than to educate them in critical evaluation of e-health use. Some general information on good practices might be given with easy-to-understand cartoon posters, for example, showing customers discussing e-health information that they found with their doctor. Health care professionals need to support customers' motivation and ability by steering them toward suitable sources, while also being able to provide them with suggestions on how to access the sources (opportunity) in the event the customer does not have direct access to personal devices. In the past, handing out brochures was more common than handing out Internet addresses.

Although e-health providers can influence the quality of the e-health that they recommend to customers, they have less, if any, control over the social activity among customers. However, providers can try to increase positive behavior by engaging in customer compatibility management (see Martin & Pranter, 1989), meaning that they connect homogeneous customers and manage customer-to-customer encounters to create positive service experiences. In the presented empirical case, the health portal offers a wide range of discussion topics that attract customers with similar interests and allow anonymous interaction.

It is important to maintain the consumer's trust in the health care system and in health care workers. Consumers need to feel that they can discuss e-health with health care professionals and obtain respectful and reliable answers. Health care workers are generally well educated and, therefore, respected. On e-health sites, the credentials of moderators and the underlying purpose of the given information are harder to monitor and to evaluate. As extreme examples, virtual worlds such as Second Life are known for a reluctance to interfere with how the reality is shaped and used by its members. How can consumers ascertain the qualifications of content providers or the quality of advice given by total strangers? The answer is most likely that they cannot. What can be done is to educate consumers in e-health literacy, with the goal of aiding their ability to critically evaluate the information provided. So far, governments have expressed and provided support mainly for consumer opportunities to use the Internet, for example, by promising the availability of fast broadband to all citizens. Consumers' motivation and ability have been given much less attention and have been left to individual companies to deal with.

A vast number of studies on external and internal motivations to adopt self-services provide insights into consumers' motivations. In specific cases, when consumers have a customer relationship with one company, the motivation can be supported with positive incentives, such as consumer education (showing how easy it is to use), price policies (cheaper online than phone service), or by force (removing all but online services). For simple online services (e.g., making an appointment), which are performed in co-operation with a health care company, consumer e-health literacy will likely not be a problem. In these cases, consumers are not required to understand and evaluate complex pieces of information on their own. However, when consumers are driven to search for e-health information without outside help, their ability to evaluate the information retrieved is essential. This ability is needed by all citizens and should, therefore, be part of the primary education. Recently, for example, Finnish teachers expressed their worry about students' information literacy, and pointed out the necessity to develop the final baccalaureate exams in the students' mother tongue. The teachers proposed examples such as writing a topic-based essay or writing an essay that requires the ability to evaluate the credibility of the informational content of various texts. However, since only some of the students continue their education toward a baccalaureate, information literacy needs to be included much earlier and included in all alternative education.

Another important aspect to be acknowledged involves the regional differences in how health care is organized. In Finland, where the case study was conducted, health care is organized centrally, and one of the largest concerns for professionals is making sure that information systems, rather than the customer, are integrated into the health care system (see Maass, Asikainen, Mäenpää, Wanne, & Suominen, 2008). Similar challenges were reported in a Dutch context, where primary- and secondary-care providers exchange patient information (Bal, Mastboom, Spiers, & Rutten, 2007). In the United States, where the patient is responsible him- or herself for communicating, organizing, and storing information across parties (insurance company and different clinics), the emphasis seems to be on personal health information management (Pratt, Unruh, Civan, & Skeels, 2006). In such cases, the customer's motivation, opportunity, and ability to evaluate, use, and act on the information is important because the customer may be the person in receipt of all the relevant facts.

To conclude, e-health is an efficient way for consumers to increase their knowledge of health issues, and e-health technologies and applications save both consumers' and health care workers' time, thereby reducing health care costs. Governments should be encouraged to actively support the development of consumers' opportunity, motivation, and ability to use e-health. E-health empowers consumers take more control of their health, but the interpretation of the e-health offerings and consequent actions depend largely on their e-health literacy. There are both positive and negative consequences for all parties, none of which should be ignored. More studies are needed to better understand the consequences of consumers' use of different types of e-health in the service process.

REVIEW QUESTIONS

1. Why do consumers use e-health, and what are the positive consequences?

2. What negative consequences could there be due to consumers' use of e-health?

3. Discuss consumer expectations of health care workers with regard to e-health use in the service process.

4. Discuss health care workers' expectations of consumers with regard to e-health use in the service process.

5. Discuss how consumer e-health use could be encouraged and supported by health service providers.

6. If there is a gap between consumers' and health care workers' expectations of each other with regard to e-health use, what should be done to minimize or close the gap?

References

Ahern, D. K., Kraslake, J. M., & Phalen, J. M. (2006). What is ehealth? Perspectives on the evolution of ehealth research. *Journal of Medical Internet Research, 8*(1), e4.

Andreassen, H. K, Bujnowska-Fedak, M. M., Chronaki, C. E., Pudule, I., Dumitru, R. C., Santana Silvina, I., Henning, V., & Wynn, R. (2007). European citizens' use of e-health services: A study of seven countries. *BMC Public Health, 7*(53).

Arntson, P., & Droge, D. (1987). Social support in self-help groups: The role of communication in enabling perceptions of control. In T. L. Albrecht & M. B. Adelman (Eds.), *Communicating social support* (pp. 148–171). Newbury Park, CA: SAGE Publications.

Aujoulat, I., d'Hoore, W., & Deccache, A. (2007). Patient empowerment in theory and practice: Polysemy or cacophony? *Patient Education and Counseling, 66*(1), 13–20.

Bal, R., Mastboom, F., Spiers, H. P., & Rutten, H. (2007). The product and process of referral: Optimizing general practitioner-medical specialist interaction through information technology. *International Journal of Medical Informatics, 76*, 28–34.

Bendapudi, N., & Leone, R. P. (2003). Psychological implications of customer participation in co-production. *Journal of Marketing, 67*, 14–28.

Berry, L. L., & Bendapudi, N. (2007). Health care: A fertile field for service research. *Journal of Service Research, 10*, 111–122.

Bitner, M. J., Booms, B. H., & Tetreault, M. S. (1990). The service encounter: Diagnosing favorable and unfavorable incidents. *Journal of Marketing, 54*(1), 71–84.

Bitner, M. J., Brown, S. W., & Meuter, M. (2000). Technology infusion in service encounters. *Journal of the Academy of Marketing Science, 28*(1), 138–149.

Bitner, M. J., Faranda, W. T., Hubbert, A. R., & Zeithaml, V. A. (1997). Customer contributions and roles in service delivery. *International Journal of Service Industry Management, 8*(3), 193–205.

Bloemer, J., de Ruyter, K., & Peeters, P. (1998). Investigating drivers of bank loyalty: The complex relationship between image, service quality and satisfaction. *International Journal of Bank Marketing, 16*(7), 276–286.

Blumenthal, D. (2009). Stimulating the adoption of health information technology. *The New England Journal of Medicine, 360*, 1477–1479. Retrieved from http://www.nejm.org/doi/pdf/10.1056/NEJMp0901592

Bodie, G. D., & Dutta, M. J. (2008). Understanding health literacy for strategic health marketing: E-health literacy, health disparities and digital divide. *Health Marketing Quarterly, 25*(1–2), 175–203.

Bowen, D. E. (1986). Managing customers as human resources in service organizations. *Human Resources Management, 25*, 371–383.

Brownlow, M. (2012). Smartphone statistics and market share. Retrieved from http://www.email-marketing-reports.com/wireless-mobile/smartphone-statistics.htm#smartphones

Chan, K. W., Yim, C. K. & Lam, S. S. K. (2010). Is customer participation in value creation a double-edged sword? Evidence from professional financial services. *Journal of Marketing, 74*(3), 48–64.

Chandra, A., Sikula, A., Sr., & Paul, D. P., III (2004). Ethical considerations in the marketing of e-health products. *International Journal of Medical Marketing, 4*(2), 110–118.

Chaudhry, B., Want, J., Wu, S., Maglione, M., Mojica, W., Roth, E., Morton, S. C., & Shekelle, P. G. (2006). Systematic review: Impact of health information technology on quality, efficiency, and costs of medical care. *Annals of Internal Medicine, 144*(10), 742–752.

Chung, D. S., & Kim, S. (2008). Blogging activity among cancer patients and their companions: Uses, gratifications, and predictors of outcomes. *Journal of the American Society for Information Science and Technology, 59*, 297–306.

Constantinides, E. (2008). The empowered customer and the digital myopia. *Business Strategy Series, 9*(5), 215–223.

Dabholkar, P. A. (1996). Consumer evaluations of new technology-based self-service options: An investigation of alternative models of service quality. *International Journal of Research in Marketing, 13*, 29–51.

Dabholkar, P. A., Bobbitt, L. M., & Lee, E-J. (2003). Understanding consumer motivation and behavior related to self-scanning in retailing: Implications for strategy and research on technology-based self-service. *International Journal of Service Industry Management, 14*(1), 59–95.

Darby, M. R., & Karni, E. (1973). Free competition and the optimal amount of fraud. *Journal of Law & Economics, 16*, 67–88.

Dellande, S., Gilly, M. C., & Graham, J. L. (2004). Gaining compliance and losing weight: The role of the service provider in health care services. *Journal of Marketing, 68*, 78–91.

Dutta-Bergman, M. J. (2004). Complementarity in consumption of news types across traditional and new media. Journal of *Broadcasting & Electronic Media, 48*(1), 41–60.

Edvardsson, B. (1997). Quality in new service development: Key concepts and a frame of reference. *International Journal of Production Economics, 52*, 31–46.

Erdem, S. A. & Harrison-Walker, L. J. (2006). The role of the Internet in physician–patient relationships: The issue of trust. *Business Horizons, 49*(5), 387–393.

Essén, A., & Conrick, M. (2008). New e-service development in the homecare sector: Beyond implementing a radical technology. *International Journal of Medical Informatics, 77,* 679–688.

Eysenbach, G. (2001). What is e-health? *Journal of Medical Internet Research, 3*(2). Available at http://www.jmir.org/2001/2/e20/

Fox, S. (2011). Who doesn't gather health information online. Retrieved from http://www.pewinternet.org/Commentary/2011/October/Who-Doesnt-Gather-Health-Information-Online.aspx

Gill, L., White, L., & Cameron, I. D. (2011). Service co-creation in community-based aged healthcare. *Managing Service Quality, 21*(2), 152–177.

Glazer, R. (1991). Marketing in an information-intensive environment: Strategic implications of knowledge as an asset. *Journal of Marketing, 55,* 1–19.

Grewal, D., Iyer, G. R., Krishnan, R., & Sharma, A. (2003). The Internet and the price-value-loyalty chain. *Journal of Business Research, 56,* 391–398.

Gruen, T. W., Osmonkekov, T., & Czaplewski, A. J. (2005). How e-communities extend the concept of exchange in marketing: An application of the motivation, opportunity, ability (MOA) theory. *Marketing Theory, 5*(1), 33–49.

Grönroos, C. (1984). A service quality model and its marketing implications. *European Journal of Marketing, 18*(4), 36–44.

Gummerus, J., Liljander, V., Pura, M. & van Riel, A. (2004). Customer loyalty to content-based Web sites: The case of an online health-care service. *Journal of Services Marketing, 18*(3), 175–186.

Harris, K., & Baron, S. (2004), Consumer-to-consumer conversations in service settings. *Journal of Service Research, 6*(3), 287–303.

Holmqvist, J., & Grönroos, C. (2012). How does language matter for services? Challenges and propositions for service research. *Journal of Service Research, 15*(4), 430–442.

Hopkinson, G. C., & Hogarth-Scott, S. (2001).What happened was ... broadening the agenda for storied research. *Journal of Marketing Management, 17*(1), 27–48.

Internet World Stats. (2012). *Internet usage statistics, The Internet big picture, World Internet users and population stats.* Retrieved from http://www.internetworldstats.com/stats.htm

Ivanitskaya, I., O'Boyle, I., & Casey A. M. (2006). Health information literacy and competencies of information age students: Results from the interactive online research readiness self-assessment (RRSA). *Journal of Medical Internet Research, 8*(2), e6.

Lambert, B. L., Street, R. L., Cegala, D. J., Smith, D. H., Kurtz, S., & Schofield, T. (1997). Provider-patient communication, patient-centered care, and the mangle of practice. *Health Communication, 9*(1), 27–43.

Lenert, L. (2010). Transforming healthcare through patient empowerment. *Information Knowledge Systems Management, 8*(1–4), 159–175.

Lengnick-Hall, C. (1996). Customer contributions to quality: A different view of the customer oriented firm. *Academy of Management Review, 21*(3), 791–824.

Lengnick-Hall, C., Claycomb, V., & Inks, L. W. (2003). From recipient to contributor: Examining customer roles and experienced outcomes. *European Journal of Marketing, 34*(3–4), 359–383.

LeRouge, C., Hevner, A. R., & Webb Collins, R. (2007). It's more than just use: An exploration of telemedicine use quality. *Decision Support Systems, 43*, 1287–1304.

Liljander, V., Gillberg, F., Gummerus, J., & Van Riel, A. C. R. (2006). Technology readiness and the evaluation and adoption of self-service technologies. *Journal of Retailing and Consumer Services, 14*(3), 1–15.

Liljander, V., Gummerus, J., Pihlström, M., & Kiehelä, H. (2012). Mobile services as resources for consumer integration of value in a multi-channel environment. In I. Lee (Ed.), *Strategy, adoption and competitive advantage of mobiles services in the global economy.* IGI Global.

Lober, W. B., & Flowers, J. L. (2011). Consumer empowerment in health care amid the Internet and social media. *Seminars in Oncology Nursing, 27*(3), 169–182.

Maass, M. C., Asikainen, P., Mäenpää, T., Wanne, O., & Suominen, T. (2008). Usefulness of a regional health care information system in primary care: A case study. *Computer Methods and Programs in Biomedicine, 91*, 175–181.

MacInnis, D. J., Moorman, C., & Jaworski, B. J. (1991). Enhancing and measuring consumers' motivation, opportunity, and ability to process brand information from ads. *Journal of Marketing, 55*, 32–53.

Maignan, I., & Lukas, B. A. (1997). The nature and social uses of the Internet: A qualitative investigation. *Journal of Consumer Affairs, 31*(2), 346–371.

Martin, C. L., & Pranter, C. A. (1989). Compatibility management: Customer-to-customer relationships in service environments. *Journal of Services Marketing, 3*(3), 5–15.

Meuter, M. L., Bitner, M. J., Ostrom, A. L., & Brown, S. W. (2005). Choosing among alternative service delivery modes: An investigation of customer trial of self-service technologies. *Journal of Marketing, 69*, 61–83.

Meuter, M. L., Ostrom, A. L., Roundtree, R. and Bitner M. J. (2000). Self-service technologies: Understanding customer satisfaction with technology-based service encounters. *Journal of Marketing, 64*, 50-64.

Miles, M. M., & Huberman, A. M. (1994). *Qualitative data analysis: An expanded sourcebook* (2nd ed.): Thousand Oaks, CA: SAGE Publications.

NielsenWire. (2012). More US consumers choosing smartphones as Apple closes the gap on Android. Retrieved from http://blog.nielsen.com/nielsenwire/consumer/more-us-consumers-choosing-smartphones-as-apple-closes-the-gap-on-android/

Nonnecke, B., Andrews, D., & Preece, J. (2006). Non-public and public online community participation: Needs, attitudes and behavior. *Electronic Commerce Research, 6*, 7–20.

Norman, C. D., & H. A. Skinner. (2006). Ehealth literacy: Essential skills for consumer health in a networked world. *Journal of Medical Internet Research, 8*(2), e9.

Ouschan, R., Sweeney, J., & Johnson, L. (2006). Customer empowerment and relationship outcomes in healthcare consultations. *European Journal of Marketing, 40*(9/10), 1068–1086.

Paek, H.-J., Hove, T., & Isaacson, T. (2011). Adolescent ehealth literacy and trust in commercial websites: Implications for advertisers' socially responsible practices. In: Edwards, S. M. (Ed.), *Proceedings of the 2011 American Academy of Advertising Conference, Mesa, Arizona*, (pp. 76–77).

Parasuraman, A., Zeithaml, V. A., & Berry, L. L. (1985). A conceptual model of service quality and its implications for future research. *Journal of Marketing, 49*, 41–50.

Powell, J., Inglis, N., Ronnie, J., & Large, S. (2011). The characteristics and motivations of online health information seekers: Cross-sectional survey and qualitative interview study. *Journal of Medical Internet Research, 13*(1). Retrieved from http://www.jmir.org/2011/1/e20/

Pratt, W., Unruh, K., Civan, A., & Skeels, M. (2006). Personal health information management. *Communications of the ACM, 49*(1), 51–55.

Rapp, E. (2001). The catch-22 of online survey research. Available at http://www.researchsig.com/sig_article_catch22.htm

Schiavo, R. (2008). The rise of e-health: Current trends and topics on online health communications. *Journal of Medical Marketing, 8*(1), 9–18.

Shaw, S. J., Huebner, C., Armin, J., Orzech, K., & James, V. (2009). The role of culture in health literacy and chronic disease screening and management. *Journal of Immigrant and Minority Health, 11*(6), 460–467.

Sepucha, K. R., Levin, C. A., Uzogara, E. E., Barry, M. J., O'Connor, A. M., & Mulley, A. G. (2008). Developing instruments to measure the quality of decisions: Early results for a set of symptom-driven decisions. *Patient Education and Counseling, 73*, 504–510.

Solomon, M. R., Surprenant, C., Czepiel, J. A., & Gutman, E. G. (1985). A role theory perspective on dyadic interactions: The service encounter. *Journal of Marketing, 49*, 99–111.

Sterling, B. (2011). 42 major countries ranked by smartphone penetration rates, Retrieved from http://www.wired.com/beyond_the_beyond/2011/12/42-major-countries-ranked-by-smartphone-penetration-rates/

Toofany, S. (2006). Patient empowerment: Myth or reality? *Nursing Management, 13*(6), 18–22.

Weaver, J. B., III, Mays, D., Weavere Sargent, S., Hopkins, G. L., Eroğlu, D., & Bernhardt, J. M. (2010). Health information-seeking behaviors, health indicators, and health risks. *American Journal of Public Health, 100*(8), 1520–1525.

Winter, C. (2012). Lights … camera … therapy! *Business Week*, March 26, 24–26.

Yaşin, B., & Özen, H. (2009). Gender differences in the use of Internet for health information search. *EGE Academic Review, 11*(2), 229–240.

Zeithaml, V. A., Parasuraman, A., & Berry, L. L. (1990). *Delivering quality service: Balancing customer perceptions and expectations*. New York: Free Press.

Telemedicine, Remote Monitoring, and In-Home Health and Medical Technology Services for Elderly Patients

Catherine Berry

LEARNING OBJECTIVES

Upon completing this chapter, you should be able to do the following:

1. Describe why technology is important for the health and well-being of the aging population.

2. Detail the multiple dimensions that constitute successful aging.

3. Explain the popular trend of aging in place and how technology supports this trend.

TELEMEDICINE

Telemedicine refers to the use of health informatics, disease management, and home telehealth technologies to enhance and extend care and case management, as well as facilitates access to care and improves the health of designated individuals and populations, with the specific intent of providing the right care in the right place at the right time (Darkins et al., 2008). Traditional telemedicine programs provided care to people in remote areas, using existing communication technology, such as telephones or videoconferencing (McGowan, 2008). As an ever-expanding spectrum of communication technologies and their applications are more readily available, telemedicine has evolved into other areas, particularly with regard to the routine care of patients with chronic disease (Sood et al., 2007). Telemedicine applications can have profound effects on the health and welfare of aging populations, and they also offer important support for the rapidly growing trend that prioritizes *aging in place*.

THE SUCCESSFUL AGING MODEL

Rowe and Kahn (1997) describe the structure of successful aging according to an integration of three life elements: maintenance of high physical and mental functioning, disease avoidance, and social engagement (Figure 14.1). A growing body of disease prevention knowledge suggests a valid basis for strengthening preventive geriatrics efforts (Rowe, 1999); namely, that the major components of many age-associated declines reflect choices of life style, habits, diet, and other psychosocial factors, extrinsic to the aging process. In particular, it appears that diet, exercise, and nutrition have been underestimated as potential moderators of the aging process (Rowe and Kahn, 1987).

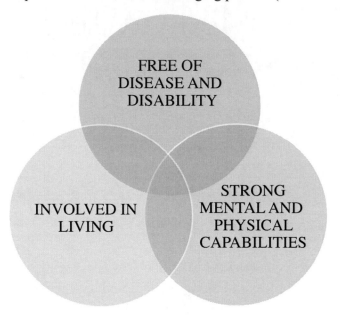

Figure 14.1 ADAPTATION OF ROWE AND KAHN'S (1997) MODEL OF SUCCESSFUL AGING

The National Center for Health Statistics at the Centers for Disease Control and Prevention tracks the leading causes of death in the United States; in 2009, the top of the list read as follows: (1) heart disease, (2) cancer, (3) chronic lower respiratory disease, (4) stroke, (5) unintentional injuries and accidents, (6) diabetes, and (7) Alzheimer's disease. Six of these causes of death are chronic ; that is, long-term illnesses that rarely can be cured. Although heart disease, stroke, cancer, and diabetes are among the most common and costly health conditions people face, they also are preventable or modifiable through behavioral interventions (Guarneri et al., 2010). Connected health care through the use of health informatics and home telemedicine technologies may provide an effective means to help people manage these chronic diseases, while also easing the strain that these conditions are likely to place on future health care systems. In this form of collaborative care, patients with chronic conditions work with health professionals, focused on self-management and self-care. Self-management, or the patient's ability to manage her or his own symptoms, treatment, lifestyle, and psychosocial changes related to the care of an ongoing medical condition (Green et al., 2008), offers an alternative to traditional health care models (Lorig and Holman, 2003). In an aging society, technological advances could help older adults live independently and alleviate pressures on their caregivers (Dishman, 2004).

AGING IN PLACE

Global society is entering a profound "age wave," leading to increased demand for health services and alternative living arrangements. In the United States, 75 million baby boomers born between 1946–1964 have retired, and between 2010–2030, the senior U.S. population, defined as those between 65–84 years of age, is likely to grow 80percent, while the elderly population (85 years and older) will grow 48 percent (U.S. Census Bureau, 2008). Aging populations around the world share a common goal: to age in place. The global movement to keep people in their own conventional housing, rather than moving them to institutional hospitals or nursing homes, relies on the use of better home care service systems, advanced communication technology, and monitoring equipment. Aging in place and care for older persons by communities is a more widely accepted social policy perspective today (Troise, 2007). For many people, it is important to maintain continuity with the past, connect with the familiar, and adapt their current situation to meet changing circumstances. This connection includes links to the physical environment and social connections, including friends, neighbors, and community institutions. A recent survey discovered that 90 percent of people aged 60 years and older preferred to stay at home rather than move to a group living situation. Yet this desirable and cost-efficient method of aging in place can be difficult, even in ideal conditions (Lawler, 2001).

REMOTE MONITORING AND MANAGING PATIENTS AGING IN PLACE

Several factors drive growth in the remote monitoring market, including the aging population, increasing healthcare costs, and dwindling healthcare resources that compel organizations to find new solutions to overcome staff shortages. Furthermore, the aging in place trend is well suited to the use of remote monitoring devices in care management programs for older adults (see Figure 14.2). Remote telemonitoring devices can transmit weight, blood pressure, and oxygen saturation levels to a healthcare professional (HCP) daily, if necessary. With touchscreen technology, patients can answer basic questions that alert HCPs of problems. Some devices being tested would stimulate brain activity to help improve attention spans, mental acuity, listening powers, and memory retention.

Telephone-based care by a live clinician and interactive voice response (IVR) systems allow patients to provide information for monitoring or assessment or receive health education or information. In particular, IVR is well suited to support administrative tasks, such as reminders of appointments, vaccine schedules, or medications.

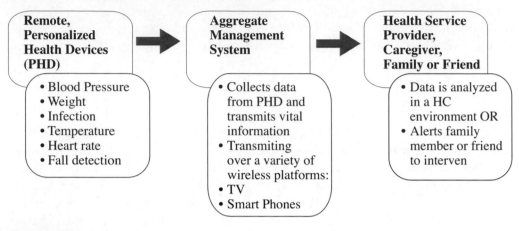

Remote, Personalized Health Devices (PHD)

- Blood Pressure
- Weight
- Infection
- Temperature
- Heart rate
- Fall detection

Aggregate Management System

- Collects data from PHD and transmits vital information
- Transmiting over a variety of wireless platforms:
- TV
- Smart Phones

Health Service Provider, Caregiver, Family or Friend

- Data is analyzed in a HC environment OR
- Alerts family member or friend to interven

Figure 14.2 FIGURE 14.2. BASIC WIRELESS HEALTH INFORMATION TRANSMISSION MODEL

REMOTE MONITORING AND HEART DISEASE

A good application example involves the management of heart failure (HF) episodes to reduce repeated hospital admissions (Kelsey, Silvestri, Gabutti, Regoli, & Auricchio, 2009). Such approaches include regularly scheduled, structured telephone contacts between patients and health care providers and electronic transfers of physiological data, using remote access technology with an external, wearable, or implantable electronic device. This device allows frequent or continuous assessment of some physiological parameters related to HF. Such technology-based monitoring supports not just early detection of HF episodes but also remote disease management. In a meta-analysis, Kelsey et al. (2009) reaffirm the benefits of remote patient monitoring for mortality and hospitalization rates. In a study of readmission rates among a Medicare Advantage population Graham et al. (2012) concluded that investing in automated monitoring systems may reduce hospital readmission rates among primary care case-managed patients. Evidence also demonstrates that the combination of telemonitoring and case management, compared with case management alone, can significantly reduce their readmissions.

REMOTE MONITORING AND DIABETES

A meta-analysis of 48 random clinical trials of computer-assisted diabetes care (Balas et al., 2004) showed that automated knowledge management interventions can improve care by (1) accelerating the clinical implementation of care recommendations, (2) empowering patients' self-management, and (3) supporting professional diabetes care over a distance. This evidence suggests the great benefits for people who face distance or other barriers to receiving just-in-time care to control their diabetes and avoid complications.

REMOTE MONITORING AND WEIGHT MANAGEMENT SYSTEMS

The cornerstone of healthy aging is the maintenance of normal body weight to prevent the development of diseases, yet many elderly people fail to consume a balanced diet that provides them adequate amounts of macro- and micronutrients. One of the greatest advantages of remote monitoring is patients' ready access to expert advice. A weight management system provides daily counseling to patients who have been losing or gaining weight. Such a system should combine four fundamental elements:

1. remote daily weight monitoring by the system and the health professional

2. daily feedback from the system and, when necessary, the health professional

3. customized information about dietary and activity needs and the desires of the particular patient

4. a proprietary algorithm to detect early signs of weight changes

In an investigation of several government initiatives and empirical studies, Gage (2011) determines that the most important attribute for preventing weight regain is access to a continuous third-party support system. Gage therefore suggests an Internet-powered weight management system, which in practice would include:

- A management program residing on a central server
- Interviews by clinical practitioners of clients, to collect data, such as personal metrics, history, and preferred communication style
- Data entry into the central server, creating a permanent client file
- Daily weigh-ins, or at least at reasonable intervals of the patient's choice
- Weight data capture by computer/personal digital assistants or other defined devices, sent automatically to the central server for analysis. The analysis then would be based on algorithms that include metrics, history, weight behavior (short- and long-term), social patterns (seasons, holidays) and overall health

TECHNOLOGY INTERFACING DEVICES WITH SENSORS

SMARTPHONES

Smartphones are essentially mini-computers, with memory and processing capabilities far exceeding early desktops. Medical apps are widely available for smartphones and can provide authorized clinical users with secure access to electronic health records (EHRs), clinic schedules, hospital patient lists, health summaries, test results, and medical notes, for example. Remote patient monitoring platforms provide a simple, easy, cost-effective channel for patient–doctor communication, especially compared with the hard-wired, proprietary telehealth systems of the past.

SMART PILLS

First introduced in 1992, a smart pill is any pill that delivers or controls the delivery of medicine without patient intervention beyond initial consumption. The most common application is controlled drug delivery in the gastrointestinal tract. Other apps include monitoring or electronic stimulation of the gastrointestinal tract to achieve the desired result, combined with a controlled pharmaceutical delivery. Variables that are monitored and measured include time, temperature, blood pressure, pH balance, and/or location in the intestinal tract. Another application aims at noncompliance, referring to patients not taking their medication. Tiny microchips can be embedded in pills, featuring a grain-of-sand-sized integrated circuit that is coated with essential minerals. When swallowed, those minerals generate a small amount of power, and this tiny voltage can be detected on the skin by a *smart bandage*. Then a message can be sent to a family member, friend, or care provider to confirm that the person being monitored has swallowed his or her pills.

SMART BANDAGES

This technology is cutting edge, but it builds on more than a decade of remote monitoring refinements, in which the earliest examples simply gave patients home diagnostic equipment connected to a network. As Figure 3 depicts, *smart bandages* can measure dozens of health indicators, then display the readings on a patient's mobile phone or the Internet. Furthermore, dressing a wound may stop the bleeding, but it cannot indicate whether the cut has become infected. Smart bandages change color to warn patients and doctors of an infection, as well as specify the bacteria present. These smart bandages feature a thin sensor, made of crystalline silicon and layers of porous silicon. The porous silicon is treated with a liquid that contains probe molecules engineered to bind to fat molecules on the surface of specific bacteria. When the bandage is applied over an infected area, bacteria from the wound move into the porous silicon and attach themselves to the probe molecules, altering the silicon's optical properties. Doctors illuminate the bandage with light from a handheld semiconductor laser device, and the bandage luminesces with colors to indicate the kind of bacteria present: red for *E. coli*, for example, or yellow for strep. With this immediate diagnosis of the culprit germs, doctors do not need to wait for the results of laboratory cultures.

SMART SLIPPERS

One of the most common and serious health problems facing older adults is the threat of falls (Evitt and Quigley, 2004). Fear of falling (FoF) is a disabling symptom of impaired mobility; estimates suggest that at least 30 percent of people age 65 years and 50 percent of those aged 80 years and older fall at least once annually (Tinetti,

Speechley, & Ginter, 1988). Furthermore, FoF itself has multiple consequences, including depression, functional limitations, and gait impairment (Chandler, Duncan, & Studenski, 1996), as well as activity restriction. This restriction then creates a vicious cycle of inactivity leading to muscle atrophy, deconditioning, and reduced health and physical functioning (Delbaere et al., 2006). Self-imposed restrictions affect the quality of life by limiting social contact and leisure activity. That is, decreased strength and mobility lead to greater risks of falling. Newly developing products, called smart slippers, contain pressure sensors in the soles, which transmit foot movement data over a wireless network. If something is amiss in an elderly patient's gait, the device alerts a doctor by e-mail or text message, perhaps preventing a fall and a costly trip to the emergency room.

TECHNOLOGY INTEGRATED SYSTEMS TO ENHANCE HEALTH SERVICE SUPPORT FOR THE ELDERLY

INTEGRATED SYSTEM RECOMMENDATIONS

The National Committee on Vital and Health Statistics (NCVHS) defines a national health information infrastructure (NHII) as "a set of technologies, standards, applications, systems, values, and laws that support all facets of individual health, health care, and public health" (NCVHS, 2002). The Institute of Medicine (IOM) Committee on Quality of Health Care in America has identified the critical role of information technology for designing health systems that produce care that is "safe, effective, patient-centered, timely, efficient, and equitable" (IOM, 2001). Some examples in practice include the following:

- *Specialist referral services*, which typically involve a specialist assisting a general practitioner to render a diagnosis. Thus the patient may "see" a specialist over a live, remote consult, or the specialist may simply review transmitted diagnostic images and/or video, along with patient data. Recent surveys indicate rapid increases in the number of specialty and subspecialty areas that successfully use telemedicine. Radiology continues to make the greatest use of telemedicine, such that thousands of images are "read" by remote providers each year.
- *Patient consultations* uses telecommunications (audio, still, or live images) to transmit medical data between a patient and a health professional for use in rendering a diagnosis and treatment plan. The communication might originate in a remote clinic and move to a physician's office using a direct transmission link or could include Internet-based channels.

- *Remote patient monitoring*, which uses devices to collect and send remote data to a monitoring station for interpretation. Such home tele-health applications might focus on a specific vital sign, such as blood glucose or heart ECG, or collect a variety of indicators for homebound patients. Such services can supplement the care of visiting nurses.
- *Networked programs* to link tertiary care hospitals and clinics with outlying clinics and community health centers in rural or suburban areas. The links might use dedicated high-speed lines or the Internet for telecommunication between sites.
- *Point-to-point connections* using private networks, as employed by hospitals and clinics to deliver services directly or contract out specialty services to independent medical service providers at ambulatory care sites. Radiology, mental health, and even intensive care services can be provided under contract, using telemedicine to deliver the services.
- *Primary or specialty care to the home connections*, which connects primary care providers, specialists, and home health nurses with patients over single-line, phone-video systems for interactive clinical consultations.
- *Home-to-monitoring center links*, do cardiac, pulmonary, or fetal monitoring, or home care and related services. Normal phone lines are sufficient to facilitate direct communications between the patient and the center, though some systems use the Internet.
- *Web-based e-health patient service sites*, provide direct consumer outreach and services over the Internet. In a telemedicine setting, these sites provide direct patient care.

IN-HOME HEALTH AND MEDICAL SERVICES MODELS

CARE COORDINATION/HOME TELEHEALTH (CCHT)

The U.S. Veterans Health Administration's national home telehealth program, Care Coordination/Home Telehealth (CCHT), as introduced in 2003, was created to remotely manage the care of older adults with chronic disease, to help them avoid long-term admission to hospitals or other care institutions (Darkins et al., 2008). The program monitors people with chronic conditions and intervenes if it detects any deterioration in disease control. Patients enrolled in the program must have a diagnosis of a chronic condition associated with significant health care resource use. Patients are assigned to Veterans Affairs Medical Center (VAMC) based on proximity and receive home tele-health equipment that reflects their underlying chronic condition.

The available equipment includes messaging devices (i.e., patients update information about their condition), videophones (to support audiovisual consultations between health professionals and patients), and biometric devices, such as home blood pressure (BP) monitoring equipment. Patient data are sent to an individual care coordinator, who monitors the status of up to 150 patients. In addition, on a daily basis, patients are stratified by risk threshold, following preset criteria, such as out-of-range BP. When a patient is identified as at risk and beyond a risk threshold, the care coordinator intervenes by contacting the patient. The main outcome measure of the CCHT program is patient usage of other services, such as hospital admission.

By 2007, the program had enrolled 43,430 patients. Those with the most common conditions—diabetes, chronic HF, and hypertension—reported large decreases in their hospitalization rates. The annual cost of the CCHT program per patient ($1600) is lower than that of other forms of home care, such as home-based primary care ($13,121 annually per patient) or nursing home admission ($77,745 annually per patient) (Darkins et al., 2008).

PATIENT-CENTERED MEDICAL HOME (PCMH)

Some integrative medicine leaders view the Patient Centered Medical Home (PCMH) as an optimal environment that reflects an integrative practice. In this model of practice, a team of health professionals, coordinated by a personal physician, works collaboratively to provide high levels of care, access and communication, care coordination and integration, and high quality and safety. In the PCMH, actions are organized around the patient, and communication is based on trust, respect, and shared decision making. Patients want convenient access to personal, practical information and coordinated, comprehensive primary care when they need it. A PCMH automates the business and clinical processes; uses e-prescribing, e-mail, and secure electronic messaging; relies on clinical decision support tools; connects patients with a health care team; captures and analyzes data; and uses these data to improve care. The U.S. Affordable Care Act includes specific language inviting PCMH operators to include chiropractors and licensed alternative and integrative practitioners as necessary. This team-based model of care is led by a personal physician, who provides continuous, coordinated care throughout a patient's lifetime, with the goal of maximizing health outcomes. The practice is responsible for providing for all of a patient's health care needs or appropriately arranging care with other qualified professionals, including the provision of preventive services, treatment of acute and chronic illness, and assistance with end-of-life issues.

PERCEIVED VALUE OF THE INTERNET

The use of IT, and especially the Internet, in healthcare settings has the potential to change the healthcare industry worldwide in terms of its infrastructure, costs, and service quality (Wickramasinghe & Goldberg, 2004; Wickramasinghe & Mirsa, 2004). In particular, the Internet offers a critical medium for marketers and healthcare providers to provide information and market a wide variety of healthcare services and products (Bodkin & Miaoulis, 2007). Perceived value also has a notable impact on the use of the Internet as a channel to seek and procure goods. In general, people seeking information related to health care act according to several motives (Williams et al., 2003): to find information as a health care professional, to establish a self- or other diagnosis as a consumer, to complement information received from a doctor as a patient, or to exchange information with peers or for general interest browsing for people in general. Consumers access online health information in three main ways: (1) searching directly for health information, (2) consulting with health professionals, and (3) participating in online support groups (Cline & Haynes, 2001). Goetzinger, Park, Lee, & Widdows (2007) assert that the Internet has revolutionized the way consumers search for information and completely changed consumers' decision-making processes, particularly in the healthcare industry.

Several studies confirm the usefulness of e-mail as a medium for patient–physician communication because it is efficient, convenient, and easily accessible, especially for purposes such as renewing prescriptions, communicating laboratory results, and making appointments (Sciamanna, Rogers, Shenassa, & Houston, 2007). Furthermore, older adults are the fastest growing segment of e-mail users (Quadagno, 2005). Finally, people often use the Internet to communicate with one another in support of special interest groups (Houston et al., 2004).

IMPROVING HEALTHCARE SPEED AND COSTS

Electronic medical records (EMRs) provide effective tools for assessing healthcare quality and may offer substantial advantages, especially over traditional forms of chart reviews. All patient data can be analyzed efficiently, because the data that are available in directly analyzable fields are standardized (McDonald, 1999). An electronic health record (EHR) provides an electronic version of a patient's medical history, maintained by the provider over time, which could include all key administrative or clinical data relevant to that person's care, including demographics, progress notes, problems, medications, vital signs, past medical history, immunizations, laboratory data, and radiology reports. By automating access to information, EHR have the potential to streamline clinicians' workflow while also supporting other care-related activities directly or indirectly, through various interfaces, including evidence-based decision support, quality management, and outcome reporting. In a sense, EHRs represent the next step in the continued progress of healthcare, in that they can strengthen the relationship between patients and clinicians. Data timeliness and availability enable providers to make better decisions and give better care. From the perspective of older adults, an EHR offers a permanent, sometimes extensive, ideally accurate record that might be difficult to remember in full. By providing a true summary, EHR can reduce medical errors and make health information readily available when needed. This access also could reduce duplicate tests and treatment delays, even as patients remain better informed and able to make better decisions.

HELPING ELDERLY PATIENTS AT HOME AND/OR IN RETIREMENT COMMUNITIES

Older people generally are oriented toward the present, and less concerned than the young with the far distant future (Fingerman & Perlmutier, 1995). Thus, for older adults,

> It becomes increasingly important to make the "right" choice, not to waste time on gradually diminishing future payoffs. Increasingly, emotionally meaningful goals are pursued. Activities that are unpleasant or simply devoid of meaning are not compelling under conditions in which time is perceived as limited. (Carstensen, Isaacowitz, & Charles, 1999, p.165)

Their present orientation often involves goals related to feeling states, including deriving emotional meaning and experiencing emotional satisfaction (Carstensen et al., 1999); because they are relieved of concerns about the future, older people's attention may shift to experiences in the moment. Brunstein, Schultheiss, and Grassman (1998) find that the achievement of goals congruent with motivational dispositions contributes to enhanced well-being; to encourage older people's participation in physical and social activity, it should be coupled with the experience of emotional satisfaction.

USING TECHNOLOGY TO AGE SUCCESSFULLY

As mentioned previously, Rowe and Kahn (1997) describe the structure of successful aging as an integration of three elements; maintaining high physical and mental functioning, avoiding disease, and engaging socially. Adapting their model to the development of a strategic program that employs technology to benefit the aging population, both physically and emotionally, this chapter proposes Figure 14.4, which includes the following *successful aging strategic initiatives*:

1. *Stay satisfied*. Exceed basic expectations of meeting daily living requirements (food, shelter, and companionship).

2. *Stay active*. Provide extraordinary amenities and programs for residents' participation.

3. *Stay well*. Proactively incorporate wellness attributes at all levels of the community: infrastructure, programs, staffing, and strategic partners.

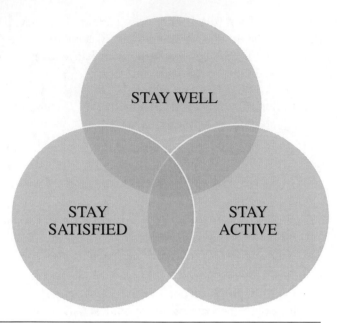

STAY WELL

STAY SATISFIED

STAY ACTIVE

Figure 14.3 MODEL ADAPTED FROM ROWE AND KAHN'S (1997) MODEL OF SUCCESSFUL AGING

NUTRIENT BIOMARKER PATTERNS

A growing body of evidence highlights the influence of nutritional factors on physical and cognitive health. Evidence relates nutrition to cognitive measures that assess cognitive change over time; for example, regarding the influence of blood markers of dietary intake (i.e., nutrient biomarkers) on brain health, a recent study has shown that specific dietary patterns help prevent cognitive declines in older people (Bowman, Silbert, & Howieson, 2012). That study works to define dietary patterns that promote cognitive health in the elderly, similar to how scientists have defined dietary patterns that promote cardiovascular health in other adults. The authors examined the blood concentrations of 30 nutrient biomarkers, in specific patterns, to determine their collective effect on cognitive functions; they determined that participants who had higher concentrations of vitamins (C, D, E, and specific B vitamins) scored higher on cognitive function tests and experienced less total brain shrinkage (measured by MRI) than those with lower concentrations. Likewise, participants with higher circulating omega-3 fatty acid concentrations achieved better executive function, whereas participants who exhibited higher plasma trans-fatty acids (as found in some margarines, commercial baked goods, and other foods made with or fried in partially hydrogenated oil) suffered worse cognitive function overall. These findings coincide with a recent proposal for improving health through nutrition:

Nutrition Rx (™): Eat Your Medicine. Include in patient electronic health records dietary "prescriptions" that address unique health issues identified using biomarker patterns. Co-brand with an institution of excellence in nutrition research to create dietary models that mimic pharmaceutical models for such conditions as controlling blood pressure, glucose and cholesterol levels, healthy bones, healthy hearts, and healthy brains.

TECHNOLOGY-BASED ACTIVITIES TO INCREASE PHYSICAL ACTIVITY AND SOCIAL/EMOTIONAL HEALTH

Of great importance to older adults, regular physical activity can help sustain their ability to live independently and age in place. Virtually all older adults benefit from regular physical activity. In particular, the mobility and functioning of frail and very old adults can be improved through regular physical activity, which can prevent chronic diseases and sustain active living. An active lifestyle is a key component of healthy and successful aging.

In older adults with chronic diseases, physical activity plays an important role in treatment. Physical activity effectively helps treat cardiovascular disease, high blood pressure, high cholesterol, chronic lung disease, diabetes, obesity, and osteoarthritis. Estimates have calculated that the direct medical costs attributable to inactivity and obesity account for nearly 10 percent of all U.S. health care expenditures (Colditz, 1999). Being inactive results in loss of muscle strength and balance, thus increasing the risk of falls. Every year, fall-related injuries among older people cost more than $20.2 billion; by 2020, the annual cost is projected to reach $32.4 billion (Stevens et al., 2006). Older persons thus benefit significantly from activities aimed to build or maintain their muscle strength and balance. A review of individually tailored programs for elderly people shows that programs to build muscle strength, improve balance, and promote walking significantly reduce falls (Gillespie, Gillespie, Robertson, Lamb, Cumming, Rowe, 2002).

Technology can help meet these activity demands, as well as the social, emotional, intellectual, and nutritional needs and wants of older adults and enable them to make healthy life choices. Health care and housing costs also can be reduced by incorporating technology in the home environment, leading to a better quality of life for society in general. Several possible applications of technology along these lines follow:

Talk While You Walk: A treadmill can be programmed to run at a very low pace and built with support armature. Rather than watching television on a treadmill, this program would incorporate social interaction scenarios to encourage the pursuit of emotional goals. For example, arranging two or more treadmills to put walkers face-to-face encourages conversation and socialization. Retirement community staff could make it a point to invite residents to join them on the treadmills for various reasons. Friends and family could be encouraged to spend part of the visit on treadmills with their loved ones.

Skype While You Bike: Taking a lesson from the *Treadmill Desk*, conceived of by Dr. James Levine of the Mayo Clinic, this proposal would make it easy for aging adults to visit with distant friends and relatives over the Internet and thus stay connected through Skype, though in this case, the treadmill might be replaced with a stationary bike. At the treadmill desk, people slowly walk while working at a desk that is built around the treadmill; Levine's research revealed that on average, workers burned 100 extra calories every hour while walking slowly (less than 1 mile per hour) at the Treadmill Desk. Stationary bicycles or tricycles might be adapted to enhance the stability and comfort of older adults. The speed and intensity of cycling would be up to the rider or perhaps a physical therapist.

Organized Wii™ Sport Events: Wii, from Nintendo, is a game machine but also a form of social and active entertainment that promises users it can "Power-up your family [or retirement community] game night" (Nintendo.com). Game offerings feature a broad range of interests, from bowling to baseball to ping pong to trivia contests. Participation must be specific unique to the abilities and desires of the individual, but the sports games get people in motion—a good thing all around.

REVIEW QUESTIONS

1. How does the demand for healthcare services differ among the aging population, compared with the general population?

2. What role can technology play to improve the delivery of healthcare services to older adults who hope to stay in their homes?

3. Is it better for the very elderly to age in place or enter some sort of retirement institution?

4. Do digital natives—the generations who have grown up with technology—have a better chance of aging successfully?

REFERENCES

Balas, E. A., Krishna, S., Kretschmer, R.A., Cheek, T.R., Lobach, D. F., & Boren, S. (2004). Computerized knowledge management in diabetes care. *Medical Care*, 42(6), 610–621.

Bodkin, C. and Mialous, G. (2007). EHealth information quality and ethics issues: An exploratory study of consumer perceptions. *International Journal of Pharmaceutical and Healthcare Marketing*, 1, (1), 27–42.

Bowman, G.L., Silbert, L.C., and Howieson, D. (2012). Nutrient biomarker patterns, cognitive function, and MRI measures of brain aging. *Neurology*, 78(4), 241–249.

Brunstein, J. C., Schultheiss, O. C., and Grassman, R. (1998). Personal goals and emotional well-being: The moderating role of motive dispositions. *Journal of Personality & Social Psychology*, 75, 494–508.

Carstensen, L. L., Isaacowitz, D. M., and Charles, S. T. (1999). Taking time seriously: A theory of socioemotional selectivity. *American Psychologist*, *54*, 165–181.

Chandler, J.M., Duncan, P.W., & Studenski, S. (1996). The fear of falling syndrome: Relationship to falls, physical performance and activities of daily living in frail older persons. *Top Geriatric Rehabilitation*, 11, 55–63.

Cline, R. J. W. and Haynes, K. M. (2001). Consumer health information seeking on the Internet: A state of the art. *Health Education Research*, 16, 6.

Colditz, G.A., (1999). Economic costs of obesity and inactivity. *Medicine and science in sports and exercise*, 31(11 Suppl.), S663.

Darkins, A., Ryan, P., Kobb, R., Foster, L., Edmonson, E., Wakefield, B., and Lancaster, A. E. (2008), Care coordination/home telehealth: The systematic implementation of health informatics, home telehealth, and disease management to support the care of veteran patients with chronic conditions. *Telemedicine and E-Health*, 14 (10), 1118–1126.

Delbaere, K., Van den Noortgate, N., Bourgois, J., Vanderstraeten, G. Tine, W., and Cambier, D. (2006). The physical performance test as a predictor of frequent falls: A prospective community-based cohort study. *Clinical Rehabilitation*, 20, 83-90.

Dishman, E. (March 16, 2004). As Chair, Center for Aging Services Technologies (CAST), A program of the American Association of Homes and Services for the Aging; Written testimony presented to the U.S. Senate Special Committee on Aging.

Evitt, C.P. and Quigley, P.A., (2004). Fear of falling in older adults. A guide to its prevalence, risk factors, and consequences. *Rehabilitation Nursing*, 29, 207–210.

Fingerman, K. and Perlmutter, M. (1995). Future time perspective and life events across adulthood. *Journal of General Psychology*, *122*, 95–111

Gage, D. (2011). Weight loss/maintenance as an effective tool for controlling type 2 diabetes: Novel methodology to sustain weight reduction. *Diabetes/Metabolism Research and Review*, 28, 214–218.

Gillespie, L.D., Gillespie, W.J., Robertson, M.C., Lamb, S.E., Cumming, R.G., Rowe, B.H. Interventions for preventing falls in elderly people. *Cochrane Database of Systematic Reviews* 2003, Issue 4. Art. No.: CD000340. DOI: 10.1002/14651858.CD000340.

Goetzinger, L., Park, J., Lee, J. P., and Widdows R. (2007). Value-driven consumer e-health information search behavior. *International Journal of pharmaceutical and Healthcare Marketing*, 1, (2), 128–142.

Graham, J., Tomcavage, J., Salek, D., Sciandra, J., Davis, D., and Stewart, W. F. (2012). Post-discharge monitoring using interactive voice response system reduces 30-day readmission rates in a case-managed Medicare population. *Medical Care*, 50(1), 50–57.

Green, B. B., Ralston, J. D., Fishman, P. A., Catz, S. L., Cook, A., Carlson, J., Tyll, L., Carrell, D., et al.. (2008). Electronic communications and home blood pressure monitoring (e-BP) study: Design, delivery, and evaluation framework. *Contemporary Clinical Trials, 29* (3), 376–395.

Guarneri, E., Horrigan, B.J., and Pechura, C.M., (2010). The efficacy and cost effectiveness of Integrative Medicine: A review of the medical and corporate literature. *Explore*, 6 (5), 308–312.

Houston, T. K., Sands, D. Z., Jenckes, M. W., and Ford D. E. (2004). Experiences of patients who were early adopters of electronic communication with their physician: Satisfaction, benefits and concerns. *American Journal of Managed Care*, 10 (9), 601–608.

Institute of Medicine. (2001). *Crossing the quality chasm: A new health system for the 21st century*. Retrieved from http://www.nap.edu/catalog/10027.html.

Kelsey, C., Silvestri, A., Gabutti, G., Regoli, F., & Auricchio, A. (2009). A meta-analysis of remote monitoring of heart failure patients. *Journal of the American College of Cardiology*, 54(18), 1683-1694.

Lawler, K., (2001). Aging in place: Coordinating housing and health care provision for America's growing elderly population. Working Paper W01-03. Cambridge, MA: Joint Center for Housing Studies of Harvard University Neighborhood Reinvestment Corporation.

Lorig, K. R. and Holman, H. (2003) Self-management education: History, definition, outcomes, and mechanisms. *Annals of Behavioral Medicine*, 26 (1), 1–7.

McDonald, C.J. (1999). Quality measures and electronic medical systems. *Journal of the American Medical Association*, 282(12), 1181–1182.

McGowan, J. J. (2008). The pervasiveness of telemedicine: adoption with or without a research base. *Journal of General Internal Medicine*, 23 (4), 505–507.

National Committee on Vital Health Statistics. (2002). *Information for Health: A strategy for building the national health information infrastructure*. Retrieved from http://aspe.hhs.gov.

Quadagno, J., (2005). *Aging and the Life Course* (3d ed.). New York: McGraw Hill.

Rowe, J.W. and Kahn, R. L. (1997), Successful Aging, *The Gerontologist*, 37 (4):433–440.

Rowe J.W., (1999). Geriatrics, prevention, and the remodeling of Medicare. *New England Journal of Medicine*, 340(9), 720-1

Rowe, J. W. and Kahn, R. L., (1987). Human aging: Usual and successful. *Science*, 237(4811), 143–149.

Sciamanna, C. N., Rogers, M. L., Shenassa, E. D., and Houston, T.K. (2007). Patient access to U.S. physicians who conduct Internet or e-mail consults. *Journal of Internal General Medicine*, 22 (4), 378–381.

Sood, S., Mbarika, V., Jugoo, S., Dookhy, R., Doarn, C. R., Prakash, N., and Merrell, R. C. (2007). What is telemedicine? A collection of 104 peer-reviewed perspectives and theoretical underpinnings. *Telemedicine and E-Health*, 13 (5), 573–590.

Stevens, J., Corso, P., Finkelstein, E., and Miller, T., (2006). The costs of fatal and non-fatal falls among older adults. *Injury Prevention*, 12, 290–295

Tinetti, M.E., Speechley, M., Ginter, SF. (1988). Risk factors for falls among elderly persons living in the community. *New England Journal of Medicine*, 319, 1701-7.

Troise, J., (July 7, 2007), Speech by the Director of the International Institute on Aging.

US Census Bureau, Current Population Survey, Annual Social & Economic Supplement, 2008.

Wickramasinghe, N., & Goldberg, S. (2004). How M = EC² in healthcare. *International Journal of Mobile Communications*, 2, 2.

Wickramasinghe, N. & Misra, S.K. (2004). A wireless trust model for healthcare. *International Journal of Electronic Healthcare*, 1(1), 60–77.

Williams, P., Nicholas, D. and Huntington, P., (2003). Health information on the Internet: A qualitative study of NHS direct online users. *Aslib Proceedings*, 55(5=6), 304–312.

Chapter 15

Do Seniors Accept Technology-Based Service Innovations? A Qualitative Approach

Jens Hogreve,
Nicola Bilstein

LEARNING OBJECTIVES

Upon completing this chapter, you should be able to do the following:

1. Understand technological services as a way to handle the demographic change.

2. Learn about seniors' general attitude toward technology.

3. Learn factors that boost or prevent seniors' acceptance of technological services.

4. Learn about the requirements in technological services design to increase the acceptance of technological service innovations.

5. Discover the importance of emphasizing the additional value of a technological service compared to the traditional service.

KEYWORDS

seniors, demographic change, health care, elder care, technological services, acceptance factors

---

[1]This chapter was written in the course of the joint research project "Micro-System Services Innovations for Seniors" ("Mikrosystemtechnische Dienstleistungs-Innovationen für Senioren," MIDIS, midis-kooperationsplatform.de). The project was sponsored by the German Ministry of Education and Research (Bundesministerium für Bildung und Forschung [BMBF]) under the registration numbers 01FC08033 to 01FC08040.

INTRODUCTION

Demographic change is the development of progressively increasing life expectancy in society along with steadily decreasing birth rates. Consequently, in the future, a growing elderly population stands in contrast with the diminishing younger part of society (Grougiou & Pettigrew, 2011; U.S. Census, 2012). This development is even more pronounced in the European Union, where fertility rates are below those in the United States (Kohler, Billari, & Ortega, 2006; U.S. Census, 2012). Predictions state that in the year 2050 the world's population of people 60 years or older will have tripled and reached 2 billion, which makes this age group the fastest growing demographic (WHO, 2011). Reasons for this are developing possibilities of individual medical care as well as improved working and living conditions (Hough, 2004). Both developments allow for the presumption that the changes to the population pyramid will continue (Hough, 2004).

The demographic change especially challenges personal services such as health or elder care, as in the future a decreasing segment of the population will be able to provide such services, while more and more seniors will need help, for example, taking care of basic needs (Gaul & Ziefle, 2009; Hough & Kobylanski, 2009; WHO, 2011). The desire of many seniors to live in their own homes as long as possible aggravates the problem. Thus, many seniors do not want to move into a nursing home, but prefer to become an outpatient taken care of by a mobile health or nursing service that comes to the seniors' home. Deploying technological services provides an alternative to keep pace with the growing demand for health or elder care. *Technological services* are combinations of services and novel technologies. These services can compensate for the lack of personal services, for example, by allowing for seniors to live autonomously longer (Sokoler & Svensson, 2007). For instance, they enable elderly citizens to carry out tests, etc., in their homes themselves that were formerly offered by medical providers in their offices (e.g., blood pressure measurements) or they help to monitor seniors (e.g., with fall detectors), in this way supporting seniors to remain in their homes. Seniors are, thus, less dependent on outside help, which corresponds to many seniors' desire for independence (Demiris, Hensel, Skubic, & Rantz, 2008).

However, seniors' acceptance of technological services is questionable. Even though technological services may be a way to provide health and elder care in times of demographic change and to increase seniors' independence by enabling them to live at home, elderly citizens are often judged as less ready to accept new technologies. For example, seniors are less likely to use personal computers or the Internet than other age groups (Hough & Kobylanski, 2009). This larger "distance" to technologies may be explained by the fact that they had less contact with new technologies during their (working) lives. Nevertheless, this barrier may not be the only reason influencing seniors' acceptance of technological innovations. Other factors are assumed to stimulate or decrease this acceptance as well (Gaul & Ziefle, 2009).

This study examines the factors that impact seniors' acceptance of technological service innovations. These factors are summarized in an acceptance model. As only a few empirical insights are available on this topic to date, we chose a qualitative approach to gain a better understanding of the topic. Our results shed light on how technological services need to be designed or which factors service providers should promote to increase acceptance of technological service innovations. Even though our results may be attributed to a variety of technological service innovations, they are of particular relevance for health and elder care providers. Thus, our results reveal under which circumstances technological health and elder care services may be accepted by senior citizens and how this acceptance may be encouraged.

This book chapter proceeds as follows. First we define the group *seniors* (section 2) and the meaning of *technological services* for health and elder care (section 3). After that, we briefly describe both the design of the qualitative study (subsection 4.1) and the sample we obtained (subsection 4.2). In subsection 4.3, we reveal the results of our qualitative study and summarize them in an acceptance model. We end by discussing our results and providing implications for service providers in section 5.

DEFINITION OF SENIORS

In literature, the term *senior* is defined mainly by age. According to Bartos (1980), individuals over the age of 50 belong to the group of seniors. In contrast, Kennet, Moschis, and Bellenger (1995) as well as Moschis, Curasi, and Bellenger (2004) characterize citizens over 55 years of age as seniors. Other studies set the threshold at 65 (Mattila, Karjaluoto, & Pento, 2003; Oumlil, Williams, & Oumlil, 2000). Leventhal (1997), however, emphasizes that the classification of seniors merely by age is problematic, as important differences concerning physical and mental capabilities exist (Temptest, Barnatt, & Coupland, 2002). Thus, an elderly's subjectively perceived age differs strongly from his or her chronological age (Lunsford & Burnett, 1992). Further, attitudes, needs, and values vary greatly and cannot be assigned to a certain age group. Developing innovations meant to fulfill the needs of as many senior residents as possible is therefore difficult. Even if the definition of seniors by age may have some drawbacks that should be borne in mind, we decided on a classification by age as the most feasible. To take into account the heterogeneity of the group referred to as seniors (Grougiou & Pettigrew, 2011), we chose a broad understanding of seniors by applying the approach "50 Plus."

TECHNOLOGICAL SERVICE AS THE NEXT FRONTIER IN HEALTH AND ELDER CARE

Technology has changed the way services are delivered (Meuter, Bitner, Ostrom, & Brown, 2005). On the one hand, technologies are used as substitutes for service employees. In this vein, customers coproduce a service by using technological devices or interfaces such as automated teller machines, self-service kiosks, or online platforms (Meuter, Ostrom, Roundtree, & Bitner, 2000). On the other hand, technology enables service providers to implement remote services. Encompassing those meanings of technology, we define *technological services* as combinations of services and novel technologies that allow delivery of a service by decreasing the required human resources.

Due to the possibility of serving the same or a larger number of people while reducing staff, technological services are especially important for health or elder care. Thus, an aging population goes along with an increase in chronic diseases, which stimulates the need for help in daily routines and medical care (Gaul & Ziefle, 2009; Storni, 2010). However, because of the demographic change toward an aging population, the increasing demands of this cohort stands in contrasts with a decreasing number of people who are able and willing to offer professional health or elder care services (Gaul & Ziefle, 2009; Hough & Kobylanski, 2009; Storni 2010). By empowering seniors to monitor themselves and carry out services that had previously been performed by outside providers, technological services are a means to satisfy this additional health and elder care demand.

Today, we already find examples of technological services in health or elder care. For example, aging-in-place equipment allows seniors as well as patients with chronic but easy-to-monitor diseases to live at home independently (Weintraub, 2009). Aging-in-place equipment is installed in the homes of patients and seniors to collect their vital signs and send them to the physicians' offices to be assessed. If the vital signs reveal abnormalities, the physician can directly talk with the senior/patient via an integrated videophone (Weintraub, 2009). Besides the use of technological services for monitoring purposes, technology may also be a way to increase security at seniors' homes. Sensor networks allow (remotely) controlling various home devices such as windows, ovens, or thermostats. Moreover, these sensors offer the possibility to automatically inform authorities or other persons about break-ins, fires, or water leaks (Viswanathan, Van Leeuwen, Liekens, Van Bogaert, & Acke, 2009). Fall detectors may also be included in such sensor networks. They notify relatives and authorities if a senior has fallen and is unable to stand up on his or her own. To sum up, all these technological services enable seniors and patients to extent the time they can live autonomously at home. Moreover, technological services allow professional health or elder care service providers to better allocate their time and abilities.

However, even if technological services represent a means of dealing with the challenges that accompany the demographic change, seniors' acceptance of technological services is questionable. Many seniors are unwilling to use those technological services in their homes or include them in their daily routines. In our qualitative study, we set out to learn more about those factors that stimulate seniors to or deter seniors from using technological services.

QUALITATIVE STUDY TO EXPLORE
ACCEPTANCE FACTORS OF TECHNOLOGICAL SERVICES

QUALITATIVE DESIGN

The aim of this qualitative study was to identify those factors that notably influence seniors' acceptance of technological products and services. The identified factors are then joined in an acceptance model. The qualitative study took place in three phases, using a different qualitative method in each. First, in problem-centered interviews, seniors were questioned about their needs and attitudes concerning the use of technological services. In the second phase, the seniors' assessments were complemented and then contrasted with statements of experts. Expert interviews made it possible to generate area-specific information on the basis of professional expertise and personal experience. Finally, group discussions allowed for a better generalization of the previous processes' findings. In the course of these discussions we were able to reassess whether the seniors' statements concerning the acceptance of technological services were unique evaluations or whether they were relevant to the majority of the target group. To direct the course of the conversations and to ensure that all central aspects would be discussed, an interview outline was developed beforehand for all three data acquisition instruments.

DESCRIPTION OF THE SAMPLE

In line with the definition, we used the approach "50 Plus" to identify suitable participants. To simultaneously account for the needs of future senior groups, the sample also included interviewees in the fourth decade of their lives (i.e., 40–49 yrs.). This inclusion of "future seniors" seemed appropriate, as several years are needed to develop technological services. This way, our findings should also be the basis for the development of sustainable future service concepts.

The data collection took place in Germany. All in all, 40 participants aged 40–89 were interviewed. We conducted eight interviews with seniors from each lifetime decade (e.g., 70–79 yrs.). For four members of the group of octogenarians (80–89 yrs.), lengthy personal interviews were not possible due to high age, so their caretakers' were interviewed instead. Even though qualitative research methods do not claim to be representative (Gummesson, 2005), we ensured that during the composition of the sample group, a sufficient heterogeneity of demographic and sociodemographic specifics of the participants was given. The number of men and women interrogated was roughly the same. Moreover, much attention was given to interviewing seniors with different marital statuses living in households of different sizes. In this way it was possible to avoid statements that would be too similar or one-sided.

Further, we interviewed 15 experts. The selected experts had either close private or professional contact with seniors and were well qualified as interviewees. As seniors need services in different areas of life, the areas most important in their daily lives were identified beforehand with the help of desk research. The following relevant areas resulted from this research: work, leisure activities, extension studies, social environment, health, fitness, mobility, living, and information and communication. According to these areas, occupational profiles were identified and corresponding experts were selected. In the area of mobility, for example, we interviewed a physiotherapist.

Finally, relevant results of the problem-centered and expert interviews were taken up in group discussions and, if possible, assigned to the nine previously identified areas of life. Based on this, those areas showing strong similarities concerning possible factors of acceptance were pooled and distributed to the different discussion groups. In all, three discussion groups were arranged with 18 seniors and three experts.

RESULTS OF THE QUALITATIVE STUDY

The qualitative data collected in the interviews and group discussions were processed following the analysis technique of the Grounded Theory (e.g., Strauss & Corbin, 1990). The study identifies eight essential factors that influence the acceptance of service innovations by seniors. These, in turn, can be assigned to two separate dimensions of acceptance: the user-specific dimension and the service-specific dimension.

User-Specific Factors of Acceptance

User-specific acceptance factors are those that are influenced by a person's personality, surroundings, or experience. In the course of the interviews, we were able to distill three major user-specific factors of acceptance: third-party assistance, affinity for technology, and fear of destroying or damaging the technological device.

The **third-party assistance** represents an important factor for increasing the acceptance of technological service innovations. This assistance can come from family members, friends, or a service provider. Seniors expect help to be effected promptly, competently, and priced reasonably. The importance of a constant contact person for problems, for example, was confirmed by a software instructor (expert in communication and information):

> And also when something is broken, even if it's only a small problem, when a toolbar disappeared or so, then they … also come to us and … we take care of it quickly and it's all good. Things like that … or also that people can call us really anytime … So being in good hands is really important to these folks.

A trusting relationship between the senior and the service provider is essential. Doris (age 83) described her experience of buying a television set:

And they know me, and then I always go to that store and then they set everything up for me. And when we'll get digital [TV] they'll come and take care of it!

Linda (age 68) also explained that, after purchasing a service, third-party assistance is important and especially so in the case of sudden problems:

> No, when I consider buying a new television set, for example, then I won't do that myself anymore, then I'll have someone come … . Recently it happened [that] the programs—the numbers of the programs—had partially changed. And first we did without those programs and then I said, "Nonsense! I'll have someone come and he or she shall set this back up for us." And that's what I did in the end.

Besides third-party assistance, **affinity for technology** is also a factor that increases seniors' acceptance of service innovations. Future seniors in their fifth decade (ages 40–49) are especially open minded when it comes to technological services. Here, the mere novelty of a service is sufficient to arouse interest.

> Yes, yes. I always want to know how … everything works. Even though I am no technician. But I am interested in it anyhow. (Bernd, age 47)

Many elderly, however, are skeptically about technological offerings, often **fearing to damage the devices**. This uncertainty becomes clear in this statement:

> They hide behind it, oh, modern technology, I don't need any of all that! In fact, they are only afraid they could break something. (press relations officer of an online community; expert in communication and information)

Many seniors know this fear of damaging something or doing something wrong. It often occurs in connection with Internet use. Anxious about purchasing, for example, something accidentally, many older individuals avoid modern technology:

> I am always afraid of the Internet. … I always think they'll send me a new washing machine, even though I didn't order one. … When you go and click on something and only want to have a look, "Oh, what's that?"; and all of a sudden, they'll send me a machine like that. (Edith, age 76)

> Oh, technology isn't my cup of tea. … I'm always afraid I'll break something. (Susanne, age 69)

Service-Specific Factors of Acceptance

Alongside the user-specific aspects, service-specific acceptance factors also determine service innovation acceptance. These factors are directly linked to the service itself: user-friendliness of the service, perceived additional value, financial risk as well as the risk of the technology's malfunctioning, and the time consumed by using the service.

Small keyboards, illegible displays, small writing, and user manuals written only in a foreign language hinder seniors from using new technology or service innovations.

Hence, **user friendliness** represents a critical acceptance factor. Simple handling without the need for help from outside is desirable here. Edith (age 76) emphasized this in her interview:

> Yes, with telephones. Also with the wireless ones. I have to use my fingernail like so and I need my glasses. … I would use a cell phone if the thing was this big. I don't want to shoot videos, I want none of that. I don't even want to save numbers in it. I just want to be able to hit the right buttons with my fingers. And that's how I want my telephone, too!

Jonathan (age 70) also sets value on simple usability of technological devices:

> Well, between TV, Internet and radio, to network all that, I'd think it's a practical thing, if it's user-friendly. I don't want another box, with which I'd own my seventh machine, and to push 33 buttons until I am where I want to go. I'd like it laid out clearly. … User friendliness should be such that the main functions that one uses, I mean recording, playing, saving and finding it all again, those are the most important things.

Problems that arise when using technological devices do not lead to seniors doubting their ability to handle them, but rather to the conclusion that the technological solution itself is faulty and, thus, to its rejection. The interview with the press relations officer of an online community explained the link this way:

> [The seniors] don't say, "I can't get it straight," but they say, "The product is bad." They do this well, and in fact, they are right. Maybe they are demotivated, but not because they are lacking self-confidence and say, "I can't get it straight." But because they say, "The product is bad. It's impossible to come to grips with this."

Perceived additional value of the service is another service-specific acceptance factor. The technological device is adopted when a considerable improvement in life circumstances can be derived by using the service. The degree of perceived additional value varies, depending on the individual's needs. These comprise, for example, economies of time or comfort and convenience. Willy (age 68) assesses the additional technological services that his car provides thusly:

> And then with all the electronics. And the question is, what good is it to me? Do I have to know… I always knew when I had a flat tire. I checked the air. Does the computer have to tell me that up in front? And then I knew how much gasoline I use. Does it always have to show me 9.2, 9.3, 9.6 [liters per 100km]?"

Furthermore, seniors fear risk (e.g., financial risk). Studies have shown that the perceived degree of risk when deciding to purchase increases with age. Compared to younger individuals, seniors act less spontaneously and weigh the possible advantages and disadvantages (Lunsford & Burnett 1992). When confronted with complex technological novelties, elderly citizens are often unable to cope with the evaluation of risks (John & Cole, 1986; Laukkanen, Sinkkonen, Kivijärvi, & Laukkanen, 2007; Lunsford & Burnett, 1992).

Perceived risk can be divided into financial risk, functional risk, and time risk. A **financial risk** exists when the price paid does not coincide with the satisfaction of a need. The customer judges the paid price as a loss, as he or she is disappointed by the service. Hence, financial risks constitute a reasonable reservation as seniors consider any innovation. Even though financial means aren't scarce, seniors think in a price-conscious way:

> For the simple reason, well, it is a waste of money in my opinion. And I ... don't have to think well of anything just because someone just invented it. It is like this: Let's suppose, this object here falls to the ground. Do I need a device that picks it up for me? It's the same for this as well. We discussed this ... earlier. The windows were opened automatically and so forth, you could control it all lying in bed. He, who needs this, is at the same time no longer mentally capable and ... he lies there, because he can't and he must receive help. The assistant could then open the windows for him. He doesn't need such a thing. So some problems are exaggerated. And that can also be found in prices. (Thomas, age 81)

To be sure the price of the technological service is reasonable and that the cost-performance ratio is acceptable, several service offers are compared with equivalent offers on the Internet. Doing this type of research is how Monika (age 45) minimizes her financial risk:

> "[W]hen you are looking for something and you take a look at the Internet, and you can find it there at a really cheap price, then you order a number of things through the Internet.

When seniors fear that a product will not perform as it should, this is called **functional risk** (Lunsford & Burnett, 1992). The following relationship applies: the higher the degree of product complexity, the higher the functional risk connected to it (Lunsford & Burnett, 1992). Many of the interviewees were afraid of malfunctioning and failure of the technology because they would no longer be able to control the situation. An increased degree of insecurity is caused by the thought of being overly dependent on technological devices in daily life. Marianne (age 51) stated that she did not trust new technologies in the area of "living," for example, automatic door and window locks on a car:

But I would always have concerns. You would then be very dependent on the technology functioning properly. If something doesn't work, that can very well turn into a problem.

A personal informational conversation can contribute to lessening the fear of functional risk. To gain the seniors' confidence and acceptance, the entire process of service delivery must be explained carefully and in a sufficiently detailed manner.

I myself don't trust myself with anything I am afraid of. Therefore, we are forced to check our medical instruments quite often and to credibly assure our residents: "This is a so-and-so and it works so-and-so. You don't need to be afraid when it'll lift you up and let you back down." (geriatric nurse, expert for health)

Finally, the **time consumed** figures in the service-specific acceptance factors. Frank (age 55) emphasized that he considers it too time consuming to get acquainted with new technologies:

At the moment, my time is too valuable to me to use my free time on this stuff.

Klaus (age 55) dislikes writing SMS as he considers it too inconvenient and not time efficient. Due to the long time required to become acquainted with it, he feels no motivation to deal with this technology.

The results of our qualitative study can be summarized in an acceptance model applicable to technological services (see Figure 1). As has been shown, both user- and service-specific factors influence seniors' acceptance of technological service innovations. While user-specific factors like the availability of third-party assistance or the seniors' affinity for technology may increase acceptance, the fear of damaging the technological device may decrease acceptance. However, not all the acceptance factors lie with the user, the service (design) also has a large impact on acceptance. In this vein, user friendliness or perceived additional value may stimulate senior's acceptance of technological service innovations, while perceived financial, functional, and time risk may lower acceptance.

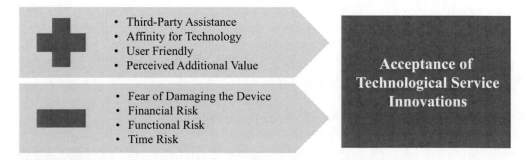

- Third-Party Assistance
- Affinity for Technology
- User Friendly
- Perceived Additional Value

- Fear of Damaging the Device
- Financial Risk
- Functional Risk
- Time Risk

Acceptance of Technological Service Innovations

Figure 15.1   Acceptance Model of Technological Service Innovations.

DISCUSSION AND IMPLICATIONS

As our results suggest, seniors do not show an outright refusal of technological services. Many of the interrogated seniors stated they would be willing to use technological services. However, many of them emphasized that to use a technological service; they needed to perceive an additional value from its use. They were unwilling to substitute a traditional service with a technological service just for the sake of technology. They needed to be convinced that the technological service innovation offered additional value. For example, services for monitoring one's own health state could increase a senior's independence and feeling of security. Due to the importance of the acceptance factor "perceived additional value," technological services providers should make sure they clearly communicate the benefits to their target groups. In this vein, it might be advisable to offer seniors the opportunity to use a service for a trial period. This would let them experience the benefits and additional value of a technological service.

"Affinity for technology," "third-party assistance," and "user friendliness" were identified as other factors that would stimulate seniors' acceptance of technological services. While affinity for technology is a factor that is deeply connected to a person's character, service providers could increase third-party assistance and user friendliness. To increase user friendliness, the technological services' design and development should begin in cooperation with some elderly citizens. Many of the seniors interviewed for the study said they preferred to use technical devices that provided only basic functions. For example, they wanted to use a mobile phone but not to text someone. Hence, it would be advisable for service providers to focus on the basic features that a technological service would offer to the elderly. For those seniors with a high affinity for technology, additional services could be offered; however, this should not be the service's default version. Moreover, service providers can boost user friendliness by improving the quality of the user manual. As our sample consisted of German seniors, many complained about manuals written only in English. This was especially true for many offerings connected to IT and personal computers.

Third-party assistance was identified as a further incentive to increase acceptance. Often the "third party" are friends and family of a senior. Thus, a service provider may only have limited possibilities to increase acceptance by stimulating third-party assistance. However, as our interviews showed, third-party assistance may also refer to the help of a salesperson or service provider. A senior often frequents the same salesperson or service provider, which leads to a bond of trust between the parties. Service providers can actively stimulate this kind of third-party assistance. Technological medical services providers could, for example, offer consultation hours to talk about problems and questions connected to a technological service.

In addition to acceptance factors that increase the acceptance of technological service innovations, we identified factors that decrease acceptance: fear of damaging the technical device and financial, functional, and time risks. All these factors have a basis in a lack of knowledge. The fear of damaging a device and the perception of functional risk may stem from inexperience with technology. To reduce these barriers, service providers must educate seniors. Providers must explain how a device works and how to handle it. Additionally, they need to make clear the extent to which the device can be relied on for care. This is especially important in health care, where technology can be supportive but cannot completely replace a human service provider. Therefore, seniors must know when the device is malfunctioning and when it is time to contact a doctor or nurse for medical assistance. This educational work may lower the perceived financial and time risks. With a better knowledge of the device and its limitations, elderly customers may be better able to assess the technological service's benefits and contrast that with the associated cost. Moreover, seniors would be able to better assess the time they need to spend using the technological service.

In sum, it can be stated that seniors' acceptance of technological services is not as questionable as often discussed in the literature. However, technological service providers must first design the service from the seniors' perspective and respect their needs. These study results offer major implications for the health and senior care sector. As these areas are experiencing a growing demand due to demographic changes, technological services may be a means of addressing this increased demand. To successfully implement those technological services, health and elder care providers must bear in mind the acceptance factors identified in this study.

REVIEW QUESTIONS

1. What are the opportunities and deterrents to using technological services as a way to handle the demographic changes?

2. Are there limitations to the use of technological services in health and elder care?

3. How do you judge the meaning of user-specific versus service-specific acceptance factors?

4. How can service providers overcome factors that decrease seniors' acceptance of technology?

REFERENCES

Bartos, R. (1980). Over 49: The invisible consumer market. *Harvard Business Review, 58*(1), 140–148.

Demiris, G., Hensel, B. K., Skubic, M., & Rantz, M. (2008). Senior residents' perceived need of and preferences for 'smart home' sensor technologies. *International Journal of Technology Assessment in Health Care, 24*(1), 120–124.

Gaul, S., & Ziefle, M. (2009). Smart home technologies: Insights into generation-specific acceptance motives. In A. Holzinger & K. Miesenberger (Eds.), USAB '09 Proceedings of the 5th Symposium of the Workgroup Human-Computer Interaction and Usability Engineering of the Austrian Computer Society on HCI and Usability for e-Inclusion (pp. 312–332). Berlin & Heidelberg: Springer. Retrieved from http://www.humtec.rwth-aachen.de/files/gaul_ziefle_smarthometechnologies.pdf

Grougiou, V., & Pettigrew, S. (2011). Senior customers' service encounter preferences. *Journal of Service Research, 14*(4), 475–488.

Gummesson, E. (2005). Qualitative research in marketing: Road-map for a wilderness of complexity and unpredictability. *European Journal of Marketing, 39*(3/4), 309–327.

Hough, M. G. (2004). Exploring elder consumers' interactions with information technology. *Journal of Business & Economic Research, 2*(6), 61–66.

Hough, M., & Kobylanski, A. (2009). Increasing elder consumer interactions with information technology. *Journal of Consumer Marketing, 26*(1), 39–48.

John, D. R., & Cole, C. A. (1986). Age differences in information processes: Understanding deficits in young and elderly consumers. *Journal of Consumer Research, 13*(3), 297–315.

Kennett, P. A., Moschis, G. P., & Bellenger, D. N. (1995). Marketing financial services to mature consumers. *Journal of Services Marketing, 9*(2), 62–72.

Kohler, H.-P., Billari, F. C., & Ortega, J. A. (2006). Low fertility in Europe: Causes, implications and policy options Retrieved from http://www.ssc.upenn.edu/~hpkohler/papers/Low-fertility-in-Europe-final.pdf

Laukkanen, T., Sinkkonen, S., Kivijärvi, M., & Laukkanen, P. (2007). Innovation resistance among mature consumers. *Journal of Consumer Marketing, 24*(7), 419–427.

Leventhal, R. C. (1997). Aging consumers and their effects on the marketplace. *Journal of Consumer Marketing, 14*(4), 276–281.

Lunsford, D. A., & Burnett, M. S. (1992). Marketing product innovations to the elderly: Understanding the barriers to adoption. *Journal of Consumer Marketing, 9*(4), 53–62.

Mattila, M., Karjaluoto, H., & Pento, T. (2003). Internet banking adoption among mature consumers: Early majority or laggards? *Journal of Services Marketing, 17*(5), 514–528.

Meuter, M. L., Bitner, M. J., Ostrom, A. L., & Brown, S. W. (2005). Choosing among alternative service delivery modes: An investigation of customer trial of self-service technologies. *Journal of Marketing, 69*(2), 61–83.

Meuter, M. L., Ostrom, A. L., Roundtree, R. I., & Bitner, M. J. (2000). Self-service technologies: Understanding customer satisfaction with technology-based service encounters. *Journal of Marketing, 64*(3), 50–64.

Moschis, G. P., Curasi, C., & Bellenger, D. (2004). Patronage motives of mature consumers in the selection of food and grocery stores. *Journal of Consumer Marketing, 21*(2), 123–133.

Oumlil, A. B., Williams, A. J., & Oumlil, L. (2000). Consumer education programs for mature consumers. *Journal of Services Marketing, 14*(3), 232–243.

Storni, C. (2010). Multiple forms of appropriation in self-monitoring technology: Reflections on the role of evaluation in future self-care. *International Journal of Human-Computer Interaction, 26*(5), 537–561.

Strauss, A., & Corbin, J. (1990). *Basics of qualitative research: Grounded theory procedures and techniques.* London: SAGE Publications.

Sokoler, T., & Svensson, M. S. (2007). Embracing ambiguity in the design of non-stigmatizing digital technology for social interaction among senior citizens. *Behaviour & Information Technology, 26*(4), 297–307.

Temptest, S., Barnatt, C., & Coupland, C. (2002). Grey advantage. New strategies for the old. *Long Range Planning, 35*(5), 475–492.

U.S. Census Bureau, International Data Base. (2012). Retrieved from http://www.census.gov/population/international/data/idb/country.php

Viswanathan, H., Van Leeuwen, T., Liekens, W., Van Bogaert, B., & Acke, W. (2009). Network and service architecture for emerging services based on home sensor networks. *Bell Labs Technical Journal, 14*(2), 235–249.

Weintraub, A. (2009, November 16). Elder care by remote. *Business Week*, 88–90.

World Health Organization (WHO). (2011, September). 10 facts on ageing and the life course. Retrieved from http://www.who.int/features/factfiles/ageing/en/index.html and http://www.who.int/features/factfiles/ageing/ageing_facts/en/index.html

Creating New Paradigms of Health Service for Older People: A Management Opportunity

Liz Gill

A human being would certainly not grow to be seventy or eighty years old if this longevity had no meaning for the species. The afternoon of human life must also have a significance of its own and cannot be merely a pitiful appendage to life's morning.

Carl Jung (1875–1961)

KEYWORDS

health service, structure, older people, demographic changes, policy, best practice, chronic illness, personalized medicine, consumer behavior, consumer change, aging, service needs, service quality, satisfaction, service cocreation, interaction, service demand, resourcing, system challenges, age discrimination, ageism, change impetus, service reorientation, new approach, positive aging

LEARNING OBJECTIVES

Upon completing this chapter, you should be able to do the following:

1. Describe the background to and the structure and functioning of the existing mainstream health services market; appreciate its current limitations and the emerging issues it confronts.

2. Identify how this market is changing and the drivers of this change; and explain the impact the aging of the population will have on this market.

3. Discuss the application and challenges for assessing service quality in this market; and the role interaction plays in the service formation process.

4. Present the issues confronting managers and providers in this market and the impediments to market change.

5. Argue the need for market reorientation; and consumer-centric research in the area of the older consumer.

6. Pinpoint the origins of the key negative factors impacting this market segment; and make a case for why a service model based on a new aging paradigm is necessary.

INTRODUCTION

Traditional health services continue to be designed around specific diseases and, therefore, fail to create environments that support interaction between the various parts of the system. This illness-focused paradigm situates control for the system's operation with the service provider. Governments, health service organizations, and individuals are spending increasing amounts on health, for decreasing returns. Unsustainable cost increases combined with poor quality and inequalities now confront health services, and the solution will not be found in an approach that involves rationing and replication. Market change factors can be identified: increasing consumer demand for quality, the rise in consumer interest in illness prevention and the desire for self-management and self-determination, access to medical knowledge through the Internet, and the pressure from the large cohort of baby boomers with high service expectations, who wish to maintain their vitality and investing in their health and well-being. A market shift is evident, from a provider- to a recipient-driven market, with the significant growth in the demand for and use of preventive and alternative health services. Managing this shift in the market and its clients is essential, and is only achievable by an emphasis on the client as a key contributor to their service. The significant growth in the number of older people over the next two decades makes the need for change particularly crucial for mainstream health services for this market segment.

This chapter outlines the rationale for health services marketing to take a leading role in locating solutions to the increasing dysfunctionality of mainstream health services for older people. The existing service system and its challenges are described from the perspective of the older client; the resultant key service issues confronting service providers are identified; and the implications for service planning and management are outlined. The pervasiveness of the negative aspects of aging drives this market and, therefore, service design and provision. It is imperative that research, focused on health services for older people, be driven by a positive aging paradigm so that more appropriate and responsive service models are identified and developed.

HEALTH SYSTEM DYNAMICS

HISTORICAL TRADITIONS

Health systems are complex and multilayered, with different structural models that can be considered on the basis of the following broad operating functions: hospital inpatient and outpatient, which includes diagnostic imaging and rehabilitation; community services, which includes family medical or general practice; public health and health promotion; and long-term and palliative service. Within this context, in most industrialized countries and some developing countries both a private and a public sector operate. The latter component provides publicly funded health services, with some degree of universal coverage as its goal. The private system is most commonly financed through private health insurance. System changes related to improvements in service design, quality, and outcome have been curbed by the traditional model of health service relationships, which is based on three assumptions: (1) the professional is the expert; (2) the system is the gatekeeper for socially supported services; and (3) the ideal client is compliant and self-reliant (Thorne, Ternulf Nyhlin, & Paterson, 2000). The current promotion of a client-centered approach to service requires health organizations and professionals to rethink their roles, especially if they are to foster clients who take an active role in choosing treatment options, developing desired outcomes, and self-managing. Further, client use of the Internet has been found to contribute to subtle changes in the relationship between health professionals and their clients (Hart, Henwood, & Wyatt, 2004).

SYSTEM STRUCTURE AND OPERATIONAL LAYERS

Berry and Bendapudi (2007) argued that the health sector poses many challenges due to its effects on economies and quality of life, along with the issues the sector faces due to its increasing complexity and costs. As health service has grown more complex in its delivery, compartmentalization has resulted in the growth of speciality and subspeciality areas where many health professionals work within a narrow and highly specialized area (Plsek & Greenhalgh, 2001). Further, primary health service is multifaceted and characterized by nonlinear relationships, with networks of feedback loops and multiple groups affecting each others' performance both over time and in different ways (Gatrell, 2005). Because service financing and delivery is distributed across a variety of distinct and often competing entities, each with its own objectives, obligations, and capabilities, fragmented organizational structures have resulted (Strange, 2009). These fragmented structures have led to disrupted relationships, poor information flows, and misaligned incentives that combine to degrade service quality and effectively increase costs (Cebul, Rebitzer, Taylor, & Votruba, 2008).

Demographic Changes

As a result of education, infectious disease control, public health initiatives, and new surgical and rehabilitation techniques, life expectancy has increased, resulting in significant growth in the number of people aged 65 and older (United Nations, 2005). Declining fertility, and improved health and longevity, have expanded the older population dramatically and at an unprecedented rate. Population aging has emerged as a major demographic trend worldwide. A person born in 1900 would have expected to live 47.3 years; by 1930 life expectancy had risen to 59.7 years, rising again in 1960 to 69.7 years. Life expectancy has continued this trajectory, increasing 1.4 years from 76.5 in 1997 to 77.9 in 2007. In 1950, the world's population was about 2.5 billion. By the end of 1999 it had reached 6 billion. By 2020 it is projected to reach 7.5 billion, and 9 billion by 2050. For the first time in history, people aged 65 and over will soon outnumber children under the age of 5. By 2040, the global population is projected to number 1.3 billion older people, or 14 percent. In contrast, by 2050 the UN estimates that the proportion of the world's population aged 65 and over will more than double, from 7.6 percent today to 16.2 percent (UN, 2009). The rise in the oldest of the old has been even more dramatic, and is best exemplified by the increasing number of people reaching age 100. Whilst the population of developed countries is stable, the population of developing countries is growing and accounts for 84 percent of global population, 90 percent of the global disease burden, and 20 percent of global gross domestic product, but only 12 percent of global health spending (Mathers, Lopez, & Murray, 2006). Under the current health service model, generating funding to adequately address the health needs of these different populations has become increasingly difficult (Fogel, 2003).

Health Policy and Planning

Health service in most developed countries exists as a mix of public- and private-sector components, with public sectors in the last 30 years having adopted many of the management practices of the private sector (Bevir, Rhodes, & Weller, 2003) in an attempt to contain rising costs and service demand well in excess of supply (Ovretveit, 1992). Quality expectations of patients have increased, along with government pressure to contain service costs (Sewell, 1997). The patients' rights movement has fostered the emergence of the patient-as-consumer (Williams, 1994). These factors have led to the adoption of a different approach to health service management: with a focus on quality, efficiency, and economic management. Health policy at the macro level now centres on these issues, with service integration becoming an integral part of health policy reform. In turn, this has determined the priorities for services planning, with the development of safe and effective service models that improve access and equity of service provision through more cost-effective means. Adverse events, poor health outcomes, and client complaints occur in sufficient numbers to underpin a systems planning approach. Ensuring effective and coordinated service between a range of health and social services has become a well-established policy focus in most developed countries (Allen, Griffiths, & Lyne, 2004), especially with the growth in the older population.

EVIDENCE-BASED MEDICINE AND BEST PRACTICE

To address service failure, best practice and evidence-based medicine approaches have been implemented through the development of clinical frameworks, protocols, and guidelines (Hughes & Mackay, 2006). *Evidence-based medicine* (EBM) involves the explicit application of validated knowledge to decision making about services for individual clients. EBM requires the integration of individual clinical expertise with the best available external clinical evidence, derived from systematic research, in deciding whether and how it matches the client's clinical state, predicament, and preferences. EBM is based on five premises:

1. Clinical decisions should be based on the best available scientific evidence.

2. The clinical problem should direct the type of evidence considered.

3. Epidemiological and biostatistical approaches to thinking should inform the identification and critical appraisal of best evidence.

4. Medical practice involves the application of conclusions in managing clients or making health service decisions.

5. Performance should be constantly evaluated (Sackett, Rosenberg, Muir Gray, Haynes, & Richardson, 1996).

EBM therefore concentrates on the technical aspects of service with medical and clinical audits used as the means for service evaluation. EBM is based on areas that service providers define as important, rather than on the evidence of what matters to service users (Wong, 2002).

CHRONIC ILLNESS

Overwhelming evidence shows that aging is associated with increased susceptibility to biophysical disorders, leading to chronic illnesses that are a major factor in the continuous growth in health services demand and spending (Roehrig, Miller, Lake, & Bryant, 2009). Health services for people with chronic disease occur at multiple levels due to patients' diverse needs; consequently, health services are experienced as inadequate, uncoordinated, confusing, and overwhelming (Anderson & Knickman, 2001). Not surprisingly, fragmented service is identified as the greatest weakness of westernized health systems, as the fragmentation contributes to the poor outcomes experienced by people with chronic and complex health needs (Coleman, 2002). Most researchers are clear that service fragmentation must be resolved if the system is to achieve improved outcomes. The rise in chronic illness amongst older people has resulted in an increasing emphasis on client empowerment, specifically that patients manage their condition on a daily basis. Michie, Miles, and Weinman (2003) refer to this as the client taking control of their illness. However, the listings of chronic illness frequently fail to include dementia, which is predicted to overtake chronic disorders, such as cardiovascular disease and cancer, as the major challenge to health services and people's quality of life (Alzheimer's, 2009).

Personalized Medicine

With the development of DNA health technologies comes the potential for the future customization of health services, which will result in all decisions and practices being uniquely tailored to the individual client. It is envisaged that molecular information from tissue combined with an individual's personal medical history, family history, and data from imaging and other laboratory tests will be used to develop client-specific therapy (Nicholson, 2006). Client-specific therapy will allow the individual's condition to be targeted by stratifying disease status, selecting the best medication, and tailoring dosages to the client's specific needs and preferences, thereby resulting in more effective treatments. The individual's involvement would be required in developing and delivering their service; the literature indicates that much of aging-related illness and disability is attributable to modifiable lifestyle factors present in middle age (Britton, Brunner, Kivimaki, & Shipley, 2011).

Aged Health Consumer: Services Issues

Consumer Health Behavior

Medical service usage patterns among seniors reflect their poorer health status. They visit physicians and use hospital and nursing homes considerably more frequently than the younger population, with the use rates rising significantly for the very old (Rosenberg & James, 2000). Educated people are reported as being healthier and engaging in healthier behaviors, with many researchers having established a correlation between health and level of education (Cowell, 2006). Studies have also found that the gap in health between those with high and low educations attainment increases with age (Ross & Mirowski, 2010). Personal factors influencing an individual's health behavior have been identified as the individual's ability to understand their health choices and health behavior, to anticipate the outcomes of behavior, to learn by observing others, to have confidence in performing a behavior (including overcoming the problems in performing the behavior), to self-determine or self-regulate behavior, and to reflect on and analyse their experience (Bandura, 1997).

Changing Face of the Older Consumer

Millions of baby boomers have unprecedented good health, energy, and expectations for longevity. By 2030 these boomers will be aged 66–84 and in the United States alone will number 61 million people (Knickman & Snell, 2002). The challenge will be to meet their service expectations and demands, ensuring the availability of sufficient resources and the existence of an effective service system. Boomers will be a market with different characteristics than their parents (Choi & Park, 2011). The 2010 baby boomer survey by Del Webb (2010) found that boomers believed that the concept of "old age" is simply a state of mind and officially begins at age 80, and they consider themselves much younger due to their "mental attitude," with an increasing gap between real and perceived age. They are better educated, feel 15 years younger than they actually are, with more than 50 percent exercising regularly and 50 percent expecting to work at least part-time once they retire. Faber, Shinkle, Lynott, Fox-Grage, & Harrell, (2011) reported that with retirement, 9 of 10 retirees will remain in their own home, preferring to grow old there. But this requires services and products that not only provide continued enjoyment and stimulation, but also that support declining functional limitations and enhance quality of life. Boomers demand more of everything that is important to them. They are more self-reliant and self-indulgent than past generations and will demand and seek out services that accommodate their needs and allow them to remain in control of their lives (Lynch, 2011).

IMPACT OF COGNITIVE AND PHYSICAL CHANGE

With age, the individual changes both biologically and psychologically, yet this age-related change in physical and cognitive functions varies considerably across individuals and across physical and cognitive domains. Physiological aging may involve changes in structure and functioning of any one or a combination of the body's functional systems such as cardiovascular, respiratory, musculo-skeletal, gastro-intestinal and so on. In the cognitive domain, many older people have been found to outperform young people on some cognitive tasks but, in general, attention and memory functions appear more susceptible to the effects of aging (Glisky, 2007). Multiple pathologies become common with aging, healing is slower, many treatments are palliative rather than curative, and the likelihood of an additional illness or condition occurring increases with age. A literature review of the behavioral determinants of healthy aging (Hartman-Stein & Potkanowicz, 2003) concluded that performing regular physical exercise, engaging in cognitively stimulating activities, maintaining an optimistic mental outlook, and finding meaning in life in middle age had a positive impact on health and quality of life in the seventh and eighth decades. The largest source of projected health and aged services spending relates to dementia, which is predicted to quadruple by 2050 and become the number-one chronic illness. Despite dementia's rising prevalence, Hellstrom, Nolan, Nordenfelt and Lundh (2007) highlight that people with dementia are one group most often excluded from services research, and that their exclusion appears to contravene the principles of the Declaration of Helsinki (World, 2008). Hellstrom, Nolan, Nordenfelt and Lundh (2007) argue that the issue is not, should people with dementia be included in research, but how can they best be included? Increasing research evidence shows that the views of people with dementia can be accessed and that their views are essential to understanding the service experience (Wilkinson, 2002).

ADDRESSING THE COMPLEXITY OF CONSUMER SERVICE NEEDS

Health systems in developed countries have introduced community-delivered services aimed at assisting older people to be holistically supported in their own homes, thereby achieving a reduction in costly hospital and residential aged services admissions (Holland & Harris, 2007). The importance of service continuity and coordination for this group is well documented (McKeown, 2007), with initiatives such as transitional services that foster the adoption of a holistic approach to the provision of services (Andrews, Manthorpe, & Watson, 2004). Rosich and Hankin (2010) have stated that the older population is increasingly diverse in ethnicity, dependence, health, economic status, and education. They argued that services targeting older adults will need to be more flexible to meet their demands. Despite this, evidence suggests that many health professionals have negative and typecast attitudes toward older people, resulting in the older person's dignity and autonomy not being maintained during service delivery (Lothian & Philp, 2001). McKeown's (2007) research demonstrated the value of listening to older persons' voices as consumers of health and community services; the measurement of the older client's perception of their service is therefore vital, as it will reveal the person's assessment of the service (Brady & Cronin, 2001).

Approaches to Service Quality and Satisfaction

Quality in a health service and its measurement have become important topics, especially as the volume and complexity of service provision has increased. The literature shows significant cost reductions when a service improves, with the dynamics of poor service often involving wasted effort, repetition, and misuse of skilled employees (Kenagy, Berwick, & Shore, 1999). However, the definition and management of health service quality have been the responsibility of the service provider. Health services have been largely introspective in defining and assessing quality, focusing mainly on the provider components (Bell, 2004). Whilst some work has been done to develop tools that measure perceived health service quality, proactive client research has primarily involved measuring satisfaction, with numerous studies published in peer-reviewed journals. The need to measure satisfaction has been largely driven by the underlying politics of new public management (Hood, 1995) and the concomitant rise in the health consumer movement, with satisfaction being one of the articulated goals of health service delivery. Widespread agreement in the literature exists to the effect that "patient satisfaction" suffers from inadequate conceptualization of the construct, a situation largely unchanged since the 1970s (Carr-Hill, 1992; Crowe et al., 2002; Hawthorne, 2006; Locker & Dunt, 1978; Sitzia & Wood, 1997), and there is no agreed definition (Hawthorne, 2006). Further, due to its multidimensional nature, the construct of patient satisfaction is complicated (Heidegger, Saal, & Nuebling, 2006). Patient satisfaction has been extensively studied, and considerable effort has gone into developing survey instruments to measure it; however, most reviews have been critical of the use of patient satisfaction, with the result that patient satisfaction remains undefined and is part of a yet-to-be-determined complex model (Hawthorne, 2006). The construct has little standardization, low reliability, and uncertain validity (Hawthorne, 2006; Sitzia, 1999), and in the health sector it continues to be used interchangeably with and as a proxy for perceived service quality (Turris, 2005). Despite this, satisfaction is still used to measure health outcome quality, which also encompasses clinical results, economic measures, and health-related quality of life (Heidegger et al.,

2006). This focus on measuring satisfaction has, according to Brown (2007), turned the client into an ever-more-silent partner in the health system's assessment of quality, since the client's views of the service and its quality have largely been sidelined by the system's sustained practice of considering only the client's satisfaction. Further, whilst existing formal complaint mechanisms could act as potential primary sources of client information, they are not normally used in proactively to gauge perceptions of service quality. Additionally, this approach relies on the aggrieved service recipient taking the initiative and, therefore, it largely fails to address the unequal power balance in the relationship between client and service provider, and importantly, people who lodge a complaint are not representative of the general population. Understanding quality has, therefore, become a critical area for health services, as it is a means of achieving improved health outcomes (O'Connor, Shewchuk, & Carney, 1994).

SERVICE PARTICIPANT CONTRIBUTION

A health service requires significant input from the client, the service provider, and the service manager. Donabedian's (1980) inaugural quality assurance work identified the importance of the interpersonal process in service delivery. Donabedian (1980) argued that the interpersonal component was the vehicle by which the technical component was implemented and on which its success depended. A health service encounter is based on the interactive process that occurs between the client and the service provider (Grönroos, 2001), with a health service requiring high consumer involvement in the consumption process. Lengnick-Hall (1995) argued that the traditional health sector views of quality and satisfaction were inadequate to manage the complex relationship between the provider and the client. Health services fundamentally rely on interactions between people, and Kenagy et al. (1999) pointed out that interactions with clients have remarkably strong effects on clinical outcomes, functional status, and even psychological measures of health. A study by Kuzel et al. (2004), focusing on client perspectives of medical errors after an adverse event resulting in harm, found that breakdowns in access to and relationships with clinicians may be more prominent in determining the client's perception of their service and its quality than technical errors in diagnosis and treatment. Therefore, the actual process of service creation and delivery can potentially be a major contributing source of the variation in clinical outcomes for exactly the same protocol.

INTERACTION AND SERVICE COCREATION

Most recently, the depiction of perceived service quality as a multidimensional, hierarchical concept has gained support, with interaction confirmed as a primary dimension (Dagger, Sweeney, & Johnson, 2007). The emerging theory fundamental to Service-Dominant Logic (Lusch,Vargo, & O'Brien, 2007) highlights that it is the interaction of the service participants that reciprocally cocreates the service and its quality. Interaction and collaboration between a service's client, provider, and manager encompass two essential components, namely the cocreation of value (as value creation is interactional and can only be determined by the client in the consumption process) and the integration of resources by the network participants (Vargo & Lusch, 2008). Fyrberg and Jüriado (2009) have shown that it is the interaction quality between the actors of a service network that is fundamental to service cocreation. Understanding the influencers of the interactive process for members of a service network offers a way to comprehend how a service and, ultimately, its interactional quality are formed. Each position in the network has associated with it an identifiable role that has implicit meaning and that encompasses reciprocal behavior and social exchange (Solomon, Surprenant, Czepiel, & Gutman, 1985). Colton (1987) stated that role adoption relates to socially defined expectations of an individual's behavior in a given social position, with the individual learning their role through their cultural and socialization experiences. As such, each network participant has learnt a relatively standardized set of behaviors appropriate for the circumstances and these behaviours will increase the likelihood of success in their role and achieving their desired outcomes (Broderick, 1998). Further, the literature indicates that meaning is created and revised through an experientially driven translational process, the result of which influences the role that an individual will adopt (Flint, 2006). Meaning is, therefore, derived from an individual's social interactions and, as such, is located within the service exchange, which the individual uses to make sense of their social interactions. Edvardsson, Tronvoll, and Gruber (2010) have argued that communication is central to social interaction, as it is through communication that information is exchanged between the provider and the client. Edvardsson et al. (2010) have proposed that service exchange and value cocreation should be considered within the framework of social construction theories. They argued that service exchange and perceptions of value are influenced by the social systems that direct an individual's position and role.

DETERMINANTS OF INTERACTION

The active role of clients in determining the quality of the health service they receive has been confirmed by a number of researchers (Carman, 2000; Dagger et al., 2007), and the investigative work of Gill, White, and Cameron (2011a) offers an explanation as to how an intensive and ongoing service is created. This work focused on understanding the interactions of the service manager, service provider, and client, all of whom play a role in forming the service, due to their interdependencies. Through qualitative investigation and a subsequent literature review, they located four factors that influence service participants' interactions: client orientation, provider empowerment, client involvement, and client empowerment. Their literature review also indicated that these four factors had been studied independently of each other. Gill, White, and Cameron (2011b) undertook further investigations to identify the key themes shared by all service participants that underlay each of the four factors. They found that a service should be oriented to the client by specifically addressing the commitment, benefits, priorities, improvements, worth, and focus of the service from the client's perspective. The creation of a responsive service would be achieved by ensuring that the direct service provider was empowered with the requisite job-related knowledge and was able to take initiative and exercise choice in executing their role. Client involvement could be facilitated by paying specific attention to the processes of informing; building confidence, trust, and relationship; engagement, and gaining the client's active participation. Further, client empowerment occurs through sharing and exchanging service-related knowledge, combined with facilitating the client in taking initiative and making choices. Gill et al. (2011b) segregated the data for each participant group and undertook further analysis. They found that although the themes for each of the four factors were shared across the participant categories, the implied meaning for each theme differed and related directly to the participant's service chain position. Gill et al. highlighted that the meaning clients attached to each theme could be encapsulated by the direct exchange occurring between them and their personal interface with their provider. The meaning that providers applied to each theme reflected their need to meet the expectations placed on them, first, by their manager and, second, by their client. The meaning that managers applied to make sense of each theme was related to their overall service results perspective, which they viewed as being achieved through their staff's performance. They pointed out that, as a consequence, each participant category had a different perspective of the shared theme common to all three groups.

In a service chain, service participants have a designated place. As such, their role and view of the world are located in the perspective that their position dictates (Solomon et al., 1985). A health service manager sits at the top of the service chain and, therefore, views their world from an organizational and managerial viewpoint, as they are primarily responsible for implementing and monitoring the organization's policy, managing the resources under their control, and ensuring that operational standards are met. The provider, on the other hand, sits between the manager and the client and is, therefore, in the position of being a servant of two masters. Consequently, they have both an upward-looking and downward-looking perspective in the service chain and they derive their role in the service process from this unique position. Finally, the client is the one who requires the service but sits at the bottom of the service chain, which in the health services sector has historically been a disempowering position. The client's role as a service participant originates from this subservient position. To comprehend any given service participant's interaction in the service formation process, it is necessary to appreciate the positional lens through which a participant contextualizes their location within this social structure.

These positional differences can be considered in the context of role theory, which suggests that service participant interaction is determined by the respective roles each participant adopts (Broderick, 1998), and these roles explicitly reflect each participant's position in the service network which, in turn, influence the interactions and relationships that form between the service participants in the service cocreation process. Combining the findings of Gill et al. (2011b) on service participant interaction with the effect a participant's service chain position has on the role adopted by each participant in the service formation process, the following model is proposed in Figure 16.1

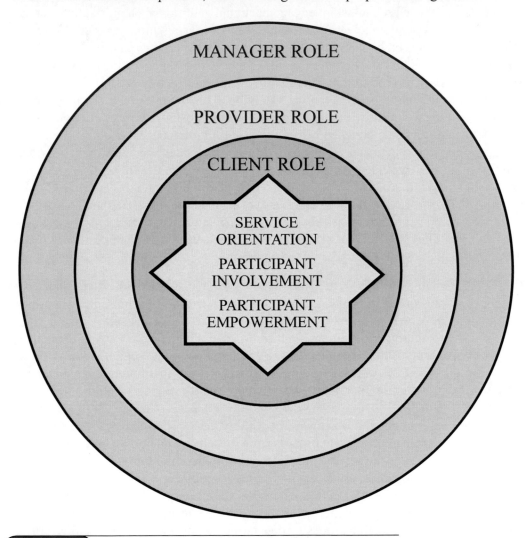

Figure 16.1 MODEL OF SERVICE PARTICIPANT INTERACTION AND ROLE HIERARCHY

MANAGER AND PROVIDER SERVICE ISSUES

DEMAND FOR SERVICES FOR OLDER PEOPLE

Health service organizations in developed countries are confronted with rising service demand due to the aging population and the increasing numbers of seniors with complex health problems requiring multiple service responses (Glendinning, 2003). At the same time, consumers are increasingly knowledgeable, discriminating, and demanding of health services (Ouschan, Sweeney, & Johnson, 2000; Singh, Cuttler, & Silvers, 2004), and Internet access has opened up the realm of consumer medical knowledge (Laing, Lewis, Foxall, & Hogg, 2002). These changes present challenges both for service planning and provision. There is now more pressure than ever for a shift in focus to coordinated and community-delivered services.

STAFFING AND RESOURCING

Community-delivered services are characterized by a number of features, including flexible delivery with adaptable, and highly personalized service plans. To achieve these goals, organizations must develop cultures that support interaction with and sensitivity to their clients and to train and develop staff to undertake new and expanding roles. These services most commonly receive funding from government health and social services budgets and in many countries are delivered by nongovernment, not-for-profit organizations. Most older clients want to continue living in their own homes for as long as possible. Many seniors live alone; they are often socially isolated, they refuse to live in a residential facility, and they wish to retain their independence; however, they need assistance and support to be able to do so. Many of these services go to the client's home, are responsive to the client's daily and changing needs, and are delivered on an increasingly frequent basis as the client's cognition and/or health deteriorates (Gill et al., 2011b).

SYSTEM LIMITERS

Eighty-eight percent of developed countries have some form of universal health coverage (Lemieux, 2008) and the changes necessary to reform services to meet the future needs of the aging population present many challenges. Despite the growing importance of publicly provided services for older people, the subject does not generate much political interest (Kane, 2005). Demand is already well in excess of supply; health is highly politicized, with ambitious politicians focused on progressing their careers; health professionals and their associations act to protect their powerbases and incomes; and bureaucratic regulations are awkward, expensive, and antimarket. The situation results in major inefficiencies and barriers to the provision of and access to service (Smith & Cherry, 2008; Walshe & Shortell, 2004).

Implications for Health Service Management and Planning

System Resistance

Old age is defined as a social phenomenon accompanied by prejudices, stereotypes, and negative images, with research studies demonstrating that perceptions of old age are erroneous, stereotypical, and negative (Ron, 2007). Many health professionals view services for older people as low status work and boring (Laurent, 1990), with attitudes toward aging and older people identified as culturally inherited and formed at an early age (Lovell, 2006). Consultations between doctors and older clients are dominated by a negative medical model where few health professionals are aware of the psychosocial aspects of aging; this, Bowling and Dieppe (2005) argued, created a focus on the burden of old age and the decline and failure of the body. They propose that successful aging needs to be viewed as a multidimensional ideal state existing on a continuum of achievement rather than subject to simplistic, normative assessments of success or failure. This has direct implications with regard to health professionals; it indicates that they should respect the values and attitudes of each person who asks for help, rather than imposing a medical model of services (Callahan, McHorney, & Mulrow, 2003).

Requirements for Change

System and political concerns about services have been largely driven by a need to control costs and the search for less expensive alternatives, with the result that the existing alternatives paradigm is simply a continuation of the same model in a less costly setting (Harrell, 1996). The failure of service managers to understand consumer priorities has therefore resulted in internally focused management plans and investment decisions (Berman, 1998), which in turn, has influenced the decisions of the service providers relating to the standards of what to provide and the place and means of service, which then lead to the quality experienced by the client (Walker, Johnson, & Leonard, 2006). Vaillant and Mukamal (2001) proposes that services that support successful aging should focus on disease and disability avoidance, maintenance of physical and cognitive function, and sustained engagement in social and productive activities. Research has found that the influence of client-related factors on various aspects of service continuity vary extensively (van Walraven et al., 2010). It has also found that people are interested in how a health service helps them accomplish what is important in their lives (Strange, 2009).

Necessity for Services Marketing Reorientation

In 1984, Cox highlighted that westernized society was becoming a "youth oriented society" in which the young individual received priority over the older person who was perceived as part of the past and a burden in the present. This change has had far-reaching consequences, particularly in the area of services so that, as a consequence, the predominant image of service for older people is underscored by ageist social attitudes (Ron, 2007). In the health sector, many services for older people have developed within a long-term service model, which is viewed as an essential social program that is unable to change the course of a person's life (Minichiello, Browne, & Kendig, 2000). Walker, Walker, and Ryan (1996) argued that ageist stereotypes underlie many of the existing services designed for older people, with the focus centered more on service and less on supporting the older person live to their full potential. In contrast, the literature indicates that many older people do not classify themselves as old and, therefore, seek ways to dissociate themselves from ageist stereotypes and behaviors. Minichiello et al. (2000) predict that with pressure from activist groups, a more accurate paradigm would evolve, making the concept of ageism unacceptable.

CONSUMER-CENTRIC RESEARCH

Existing services research has evolved against the background of the post-war baby boom, where consumer markets were dominated by the young and marketing practices by advertising and promotional activities (Thompson & Thompson, 2009), where age was not a "sexy" word. Advertising of products and services for the older consumer continues to be driven by a focus on youth, on making the consumer feel and look younger. The aging of this large consumer base requires a major shift away from this youth focus. Services research needs to place greater emphasis on the older consumer if it is to better understand the older consumer and develop customer-centric services models. Ron (2007) has found that a social process of positive change in attitudes and expectations of older people is underway and this process is impacting how seniors are perceived and how they perceive themselves. This change has significant implications for services and research. Szmigin and Carrigan (2001) argued the need to extend the study of consumption to our conceptualizations of consuming throughout life, and highlighted the need for more research into actual and desired consumption by the older consumer.

CONCLUSION AND MANAGEMENT IMPLICATIONS

Old age suffers from a bad reputation and has resulted in self-fulfilling prophesies, as existing ageism characterizes older people as unproductive, dependent, mentally diminished, and unimportant to society (Sousa & Figueiredo, 2002). This pessimistic, negative view of old age has impacted health policy frameworks, the development of services and products for older people, and the way many older people envisage their aging possibilities, and therefore, their choices, behaviors, and plans. It is time for the focus to move from depicting aging as a process of decline and degeneration. Based on the known characteristics of boomers, the next generation of older people is predicted to demand a change to this existing unconstructive aging paradigm. Many positives to aging can be identified, and it is time to concentrate on these, if services are to meet the needs of the older population and to attract and retain consumers. Research therefore must be based on positive images of aging and must include the phenomena of self discovery and making meaning of life combined with new vigour and roles (Bateson, 2010).

To effectively compete, health services organizations will need to create a service orientation that supports a positive older consumer-centric culture, especially as consumer pressure increases for the development of new ageism-free service models. This new vision will value and support seniors acting as thinkers and knowledge keepers, thereby facilitating their essential role in maintaining their own health as well as that of society's social fabric. Creating service models based on this scenario would bring dignity and meaning to the aging process, where seniors could make health service decisions based on what was important to them and their needs. Fostering an open organizational culture, which empowers older clients through valuing the knowledge they possess and encouraging them to make choices and take initiative in the development of services to meet their express needs and desires, is essential to organizational future success. To achieve this goal, administrators will need to develop position statements based on new service values and to recruit, select, and train management and frontline staff, thereby ensuring the older clients' participation and involvement in their service and ultimately assuring the organization's success. Organization-led research is urgently needed to identify what these new models could look like. That is now the challenge for health services marketing.

REVIEW QUESTIONS

1. How is the health services market changing, and why is the consumers' view of their health service now important to health services organizations?

2. In what ways do language and images impact on consumer perceptions of health service offerings and experience? How is this evidenced?

3. What would a new paradigm of positive aging look like, and how might that impact on the development of images and services in the health sector?

4. How could an organization providing health services for older people apply a positive aging model to developing future services?

5. What are the likely barriers and challenges to achieving a positive aging consumer perspective in the health services sector? How might these barriers and challenges be addressed?

REFERENCES

Allen, D., Griffiths, L., & Lyne, P. (2004). Understanding complex trajectories in health and social care provision. *Sociology of Health & Illness, S26*(7), 1008–1030.

Anderson, G., & Knickman, J. (2001). Changing the chronic care system to meet people's needs. *Health Affairs, 20*(6), 146–160.

Andrews, J., Manthorpe, J., & Watson, R. (2004). Involving older people in intermediate care. *Journal of Advanced Nursing, 46*(3), 303–310.

Alzheimer's Disease International. (2009). *World Alzheimers Report 2009*. London.

Bandura, A. (1997). *Self-efficacy: The exercise of control*. New York: W. H. Freeman.

Bateson, M. (2010). *Composing a further life: The age of active wisdom*. New York Knopf.

Bell, L. (2004). Developing service quality in mental health services. *International Journal of Health Care Quality Assurance, 17*(7), 401–406.

Berman, E. M. (1998). *Productivity in public and nonprofit organisations*. Thousand Oaks, CA: SAGE Publications.

Berry, L., & Bendapudi, N. (2007). Health care: A fertile field for service research. *Journal of Service Research, 10*(2), 111–122.

Bevir, M., Rhodes, R., & Weller, P. (2003). Traditions of governance: Interpreting the changing role of the public sector. *Public Administration, 81*(1), 1–17.

Bowling, A., & Dieppe, P. (2005). What is successful ageing and who should define it? *British Medical Journal, 331*(7531), 1548–1551.

Brady, M., & Cronin, J. (2001). Some new thoughts on conceptualizing perceived service quality: A hierarchical approach. *Journal of Marketing, 65*(3), 34–49.

Britton, A., Brunner, E., Kivimaki, M., & Shipley, M. (2011, October 29). Limitations to functioning and independent living after the onset of coronary heart disease: What is the role of lifestyle factors and obesity? *European Journal of Public Health*. doi:10.1093/eurpub/ckr150

Broderick, A. (1998). Role theory, role management, and service performance. *Journal of Services Marketing, 12*(5), 348–361.

Brown, C. (2007). Where are the patients in the quality of health care? *International Journal for Quality in Health Care, 19*(3), 125–126.

Callahan, C., McHorney, C., & Mulrow, C. (2003). Successful aging and the humility of perspective. *Annals Internal Medicine, 139*(5), 389–390.

Carman, J. (2000). Patient perceptions of service quality: Combining the dimensions. *Journal of Services Marketing, 14*(4/5), 337–352.

Carr-Hill, R. (1992). The measurement of patient satisfaction. *Journal of Public Health, 14*(3), 236–249.

Cebul, R., Rebitzer, J., Taylor, L., & Votruba, M. (2008). Organizational fragmentation and care quality in the U.S. health care system. *Journal of Economic Perspectives, 22*(4), 93–113.

Choi, J., & Park, S. (2011). What drives the baby-boomer athletes? An empirical study of the exercise motivation of senior athletes. *International Journal of Humanities and Social Science, 1*(17), 39–45.

Coleman, P. (2002). Improving oral health care for the frail elderly: A review of widespread problems and best practices. *Geriatric Medicine, 23*(4), 189–199.

Colton, C. (1987). Leisure, recreation, tourism: A symbolic interactionism view. *Annals of Tourism Research, 14*(3), 345–360.

Cowell, A. (2006). The relationship between education and health behavior: Some empirical evidence. *Health Economics, 15*(2), 125–146.

Cox, H. (1984). *Later life: The realities of aging.* Englewood Cliffs, NJ: Prentice Hall.

Crowe, R., Gage, H., Hampson, S., Hart, J., Kimber, A., Storey, L., & Thomas, H. (2002). The measurement of satisfaction with healthcare: Implications for practice from a systematic review of the literature. *Health Technology Assessment, 6*(32), 1–244.

Dagger, T., Sweeney, J., & Johnson, L. (2007). A hierarchical model of health service quality: Scale development and investigation of an integrated model. *Journal of Service Research, 10*(2), 123–142.

Del Webb. (2010). Baby boomer survey. Retrieved from dwboomersurvey.com

Donabedian, A. (1980). *Explorations in quality assessment and monitoring. Volume 1, The definition of quality and approaches to its assessment.* Ann Arbor, MI: Health Administration Press.

Edvardsson, B., Tronvoll, B., & Gruber, T. (2010). Expanding understanding of service exchange and value co-creation: A social construction approach *Journal of the Academy of Marketing Science, 39*(2), 327–339.

Faber, N., Shinkle, D., Lynott, J., Fox-Grage, W., & Harrell, R. (2011). Aging in place: A state survey of livability policies and practices. Retrieved from http://www.aarp.org/home-garden/livable-communities/info-11-2011/Aging-In-Place.html

Flint, D. (2006). Innovation, symbolic interaction and customer valuing: Thoughts stemming from a service-dominant logic of marketing. *Marketing Theory, 6*(3), 349–362.

Fogel, R. (2003). Forecasting the demand for health care in OECD nations and China. *Contemporary Economic Policy, 21*(1), 1–10.

Fyrberg, A., & Jüriado, R. (2009). What about interaction?: Networks and brands as integrators within service-dominant logic. *Journal of Service Management, 20*(4), 420–432.

Gatrell, A. (2005). Complexity theory and geography of health. *Social Science & Medicine, 60*(12), 2661–2671.

Gill, L., White, L., & Cameron, I. D. (2011a). Qualitative triadic study of the relational factors influencing the formation of quality in a community-based aged healthcare service network. *Health Marketing Quarterly, 28*(2), 155–173.

Gill, L., White, L., & Cameron, I. D. (2011b). Service co-creation in community-based aged healthcare. *Managing Service Quality, 21*(2), 152–177.

Glendinning, C. (2003). Breaking down barriers: Integrating health and care services for older people in England. *Health Policy, 65*(2), 139–151.

Glisky, E. (2007). Changes in cognitive function in human aging. In D. R. Riddle (Ed.), *Brain aging: Models, methods, and mechanisms.* Boca Raton, FL: CRC Press.

Grönroos, C. (2001). The perceived service quality concept—a mistake? *Managing Service Quality, 11*(3), 150–152.

Harrell, A. (1996). Evaluation strategies for human services programs: A guide for policy-makers and providers. Washington, DC: The Urban Institute Relationships.

Hart, A., Henwood, F., & Wyatt, S. (2004). The role of the Internet in patient-practitioner relationships: Findings from a qualitative research study. *Journal Medical Internet Research, 6*(3), e36.

Hartman-Stein, P., & Potkanowicz, E. (2003). Behavioral determinants of healthy aging: Good news for the baby boomer generation. *Online Journal of Issues in Nursing, 8*(2). Retrieved from www.nursingworld.org/MainMenuCategories/ANAMarketplace/ANAPeriodicals/OJIN/TableofContents/Volume82003/No2May2003/Behaviorand HealthyAging.aspx

Hawthorne, G. (2006). *Review of patient satisfaction measures*. Australian Government, Department of Health and Ageing.

Heidegger, T., Saal, D., & Nuebling, M. (2006). Patient satisfaction with anaesthesia care: What is patient satisfaction, how should it be measured, and what is the evidence for assuring high patient satisfaction? *Best Practice and Research Clinical Anaesthesiology, 20*(2), 331–346.

Hellstrom, I., Nolan, M., Nordenfelt, L., & Lundh, U. (2007). Ethical and methodological issues in interviewing persons with dementia. *Nursing Ethics, 14*(5), 608–619.

Holland, D., & Harris, M. (2007). Discharge planning, transitional care, coordination of care, and continuity of care: Clarifying concepts and terms from the hospital perspective. *Home Health Care Services Quarterly, 26*(4), 3–19.

Hood, C. (1995). The new public management in the 1980's: Variations on a theme. *Journal of Accounting, Organisations and Society, 20*(2/3), 93–109.

Hughes, C., & Mackay, P. (2006). Sea change: Public reporting and the safety and quality of the Australian health care system. *Medical Journal of Australia, 184*(10), S44–47.

Kane, R. (2005). Changing the face of long-term care. *Journal of Aging & Social Policy, 17*(4), 1–18.

Kenagy, J., Berwick, D., & Shore, M. (1999). Service quality in health care. *Journal of the American Medical Association, 281*(7), 661–665.

Knickman, J., & Snell, E. (2002). The 2030 problem: Caring for aging baby boomers. *Health Services Research, 37*(4), 849–884.

Kuzel, R., Woolf, S., Gilchrist, V., Engel, J., LaVeist, T., & Frankel, R. (2004). Patient reports of preventable problems and harms in primary health care. *Annals of Family Medicine, 2*(4), 333–339.

Laing, A., Lewis, B., Foxall, G., & Hogg, G. (2002). Predicting a diverse future: Directions and issues in the marketing of services. *European Journal of Marketing, 36*(4), 479–494.

Laurent, C. (1990). Time to listen. *Nursing Times, 86*(8), 20.

Lemieux, P. (2008). Public health insurance under a nonbenevolent state. *The Journal of Medicine and Philosophy, 33*(5), 416–426.

Lengnick-Hall, C. (1995). The patient as the pivot point for quality in health care delivery. *Hospital & Health Services Administration, 40*(1), 25–39.

Locker, D., & Dunt, D. (1978). Theoretical and methodological issues in sociological studies of consumer satisfaction with medical care. *Social Science & Medicine, 12*, 283–292.

Lothian, K., & Philp, I. (2001). Maintaining older people's dignity and autonomy in health-care settings. *British Medical Journal, 322*(7287), 688–670.

Lovell, M. (2006). Caring for the elderly: Changing perceptions and attitudes. *Journal of Vascular Nursing, 24*(1), 22–26.

Lusch, R., Vargo, S., & O'Brien, M. (2007). Competing through service: Insights from service-dominant logic. *Journal of Retailing, 83*(1), 5–18.

Lynch, F. (2011). One nation under AARP: The fight over Medicare, Social Security and America's future. ClaremontCA: University of California Press.

Mathers, C., Lopez, A., & Murray, C. (2006). The burden of disease and mortality by condition: Data, methods and results for 2001. In Lopez, Mathers, Ezzati, Murray, & Jamison (Eds.), *Global burden of disease and risk factors: Disease Control Priorities Project.* New York: Oxford University Press.

McKeown, F. (2007). The experiences of older people on discharge from hospital following assessment by the public health nurse. *Journal of Clinical Nursing, 16*(3), 469–476.

Michie, S., Miles, J., & Weinman, J. (2003). Patient-centredness in chronic illness: What is it and does it matter? *Patient Education and Counselling, 51*(3), 197–206.

Minichiello, V., Browne, J., & Kendig, H. (2000). Perceptions and consequences of ageism: Views of older people. *Ageing and Society, 20*(3), 253–278.

Nicholson, J., (2006). Global systems biology, personalized medicine and molecular epidemiology. *Molecular Systems Biology, 2*(10), 52–58.

O'Connor, S., Shewchuk, R., & Carney, L. (1994). The great gap. *Journal of Health Care Marketing, 14*(2), 32–39.

Ouschan, R., Sweeney, J., & Johnson, L. (2000). Dimensions of patient empowerment: Implications for professional services marketing. *Health Marketing Quarterly, 18*(1/2), 99–114.

Ovretveit, J. (1992). *Health service quality.* Oxford: Blackwell.

Plsek, P. & Greenhalgh, T. (2001). The challenge of complexity in health care. *British Medical Journal, 323*(7313), 625–628.

Roehrig, C., Miller, G., Lake, C., & Bryant, J. (2009). National health spending by medical condition, 1996–2005. *Health Affairs, 28*(2), 358–376.

Ron, P. (2007). Elderly people's attitudes and perceptions of aging and old age: The role of cognitive dissonance. *International Journal of Geriatric Psychiatry, 22*(7), 656–662.

Rosenberg, M. & James, A. (2000). Medical services utilisation patterns by seniors. *Canadian Journal on Aging, 17*(Suppl1), 125–142.

Rosich, K., & Hankin, J. (2010). Executive summary: What do we know? Key findings from 50 years of medical sociology. *Journal of Health and Social Behavior, 51*(1), S1–S9.

Ross, C., & Mirowsky, J. (2010). Gender and the health benefits of education. *The Sociological Quarterly, 51*(1), 1–19.

Sackett, D., Rosenberg, W., Muir Gray, J., Haynes, R., & Richardson, S. (1996). Evidence based medicine: What it is and what it isn't. *British Medical Journal, 312*(7023), 71–72.

Sewell, N. (1997). Continuous quality improvement in acute health care: Creating a holistic and integrated approach. *International Journal of Health Care Quality Assurance, 10*(1), 20–26.

Singh, J., Cuttler, L., & Silvers, J. (2004). Toward understanding consumers' role in medical decisions for emerging treatments: Issues, framework and hypotheses. *Journal of Business Research, 57*(9), 1054–1065.

Sitzia, J. (1999). How valid and reliable are patient satisfaction data? An analysis of 195 studies. *International Journal for Quality in Health Care, 11*(4), 319–328.

Sitzia, J., & Wood, N. (1997). Patient satisfaction: A review of issues and concepts. *Social Science & Medicine, 45*(12), 1829–1843.

Smith, A., & Cherry, M. (2008). First do no harm: Critical analyses of the roads to health care reform. *Journal of Medicine and Philosophy, 33*(5), 403–415.

Solomon, M., Surprenant, C., Czepiel, J., & Gutman, E. (1985). A role theory perspective on dyadic interactions: The service encounter. *Journal of Marketing, 49*(1), 99–111.

Sousa, L. & Figueiredo, D. (2002). Dependence and independence among old persons— Realities and myths. *Reviews in Clinical Gerontology, 12*(3), 269–273.

Strange, K. (2009). The problem of fragmentation and the need for integrative solutions. *Annals of Family Medicine, 7*(2), 100–103.

Szmigin, I. & Carrigan, M. (2001). Learning to love the older consumer. *Journal of Consumer Behaviour, 1*(1), 22–34.

Thompson, N., & Thompson, K. (2009). Can marketing practice keep up with Europe's ageing population? *European Journal of Marketing, 43*(11/12), 1281–1288.

Thorne, S., Ternulf Nyhlin, K., & Paterson, B. (2000). Attitudes toward patient expertise in chronic illness. *International Journal of Nursing Studies, 37*(4), 303–311.

Turris, S. (2005). Unpacking the concept of patient satisfaction: A feminist analysis. *Journal of Advanced Nursing, 50*(3), 293–298.

United Nations (UN). (2009). World population ageing 2009. Retrieved from http://www. un.org/esa/population/publications/WPA2009/WPA2009_WorkingPaper.pdf.

United Nations Dept. of Economic and Social Affairs, P. D. (2005). *World population prospects. The 2004 revision.* New York: United Nations.

Vaillant, G., & Mukamal, K. (2001). Successful aging. *American Journal of Psychiatry, 158*(6), 839–847.

van Walraven, C., Taljaard, M., Bell, C., Etchells, E., Stiell, I., Zarnke, K., & Forster, A. (2010). A prospective cohort study found that provider and information continuity was low after patient discharge from hospital. *Journal of Clinical Epidemiology, 63*(9), 1000–1010.

Vargo, S., & Lusch, R. (2008). Service-dominant logic: Continuing the evolution. *Journal of the Academy of Marketing Science, 36*(1), 1–10.

Walker, R., Johnson, L., & Leonard, S. (2006). Re-thinking the conceptualization of customer value and service quality within the service-profit chain. *Managing Service Quality, 16*(1), 23–36.

Walker, A., Walker, C., & Ryan, T. (1996). Older people with learning difficulties leaving institutional care: A case of double jeopardy. *Ageing and Society, 16*(2), 125–150.

Walshe, K., & Shortell, S. (2004). When things go wrong: How health care organizations deal with major failures. *Health Affairs, 23*(3), 103–111.

Wilkinson, H. (2002). Including people with dementia in research: Methods and motivations. In H. Wilkinson (Ed.), *The perspectives of people with dementia—Research methods and motivations* (pp. 9–24). London: Jessica Kingsley.

Williams, B. (1994). Patient satisfaction: A valid concept? *Social Science & Medicine, 38*(4), 509–516.

Wong, J. (2002). Service quality measurement in a medical imaging department. International *Journal of Health Care Quality Assurance, 15*(5), 206–212.

World Medical Association. (2008). The Declaration of Helsinki. Retrieved from http://www. wma.net/e/ethicsunit/helsinki.htm

ACKNOWLEDGMENTS

Liz Gill

Post-Doctoral Research Fellow

Rehabilitation Studies Unit, Northern Clinical School, Sydney Medical School,

The University of Sydney, Royal Rehabilitation Centre Sydney

PO Box 6, RYDE NSW Australia 1680

Tel. (+61) 2 9809 9036, Facsimile (+61) 2 9809 9037

Email: liz.gill@sydney.edu.au

Chapter 17

Collaborative Care for Patients with Parkinson's Disease

Allard C.R. van Riel
Laura M. Visser
Martijn van der Eijk
Marjan J. Faber
Marten Munneke
Bas R. Bloem

Combining an Offline Professional Network with an Online Health Community for the Sustainable Provision of Care

LEARNING OBJECTIVES

Upon completing this chapter, you should be able to do the following:

1. Understand the complexity of the service systems in health care.

2. Understand the concepts of multiple value creation and stakeholder integration in a health care setting.

3. Explore integrated care as a way to reduce the complexity of health care systems.

4. Understand the role of communication in integrating health care services.

5. Explore the role of online communities in patient-centered care.

KEYWORDS

integrated health care systems, multiple value creation, online health communities, patient-centered care

INTRODUCTION

In aging populations, as in most Western societies, increasing numbers of people are suffering from chronic neurodegenerative diseases such as Parkinson's, Alzheimer's, and Huntington's (Lees, Hardy, & Revesz, 2009). To treat this category of diseases, a complex, multidisciplinary mix of highly specialized care is required. Due to the necessary specialization of the care providers involved and the complexity of the treatments, an increased need for coordination among health care professionals can be observed. Health care providers must continuously improve the quality of care but are also under pressure from governments and insurance companies to reduce costs and improve efficiency. New ways to organize the treatment of patients with chronic neurodegenerative diseases must be found that increase quality and reduce total costs of care provision. For a number of years, the sector has been struggling to develop a more sustainable, high-quality health care system. A more integrated system of providing care appears to be a promising solution. From the perspective of integrated care, the various health care service providers are no longer considered independent operators; instead, they jointly contribute to the achievement of common objectives. The patient plays an integral role in this approach.

In this chapter, we present and discuss the Dutch ParkinsonNet. This organization implements a highly innovative, significantly integrated health care provision system. This system is intended to improve quality and lower the cost of care for Parkinson's patients by simultaneously facilitating the development of regional offline networks for health care professionals and online networks in which patients and health care professionals interact. We investigate whether and how the use of Web 2.0 principles and the partial virtual integration of several elements of this service system help health care providers address some of these challenges. We show how the innovative use of a Web-based communication system helps create sustainable value for all stakeholders involved (i.e., health care professionals, patients, and even insurance companies) by facilitating the integrated provision of care.

We use the idea of multiple value creation in a service value chain (or, more precisely, a service value network) as a conceptual framework. Especially in complex health care service systems, value is simultaneously created for and by many interdependent stakeholders. How efficiently value is created and how equitably the creation of value is distributed across the dimensions and stakeholders depend on the degree of the network's integration and coordination. The value created in the system can take many forms. Patients may value a cure for their disease, relief from their symptoms, or emotional support. Medical professionals may value being able to help more patients, being able to help patients get better in a shorter time, or having the opportunity to learn and improve their skills. Insurance companies, or society at large, may value obtaining better treatments for their money. The major stakeholders in the health care service system that may be able to take advantage of better system coordination and

Table 17.1	ParkinsonNet and Its Elements Explained.
ParkinsonNet	A network organization, aimed at improving care provision to patients with Parkinson's disease through a selection of specialized professionals who work according to evidence-based guidelines and who attract large volumes of patients.
Regional Networks	Networks of health care professionals located in the same region. These professionals interact regularly to discuss issues related to the treatment of Parkinson's disease.
MyCareNet (MijnZorgnet)	Organization that provides an online (Web-based) platform for health care communities that facilitates both professionals and patients who collaborate within ParkinsonNet.
Online Health Communities	Internet-based platform that facilitates online connections among people with a common interest at different levels: • Open communities for Parkinson patients and their families as well as for interested professionals, across the Netherlands • Closed community for health professionals working within the national ParkinsonNet • Closed community for health professionals working within a regional ParkinsonNet • Personal (or private) online health community owned by individual patients, where they can interact with their health care providers in a safe, concealed environment
MyParkinsonCare (Pilot) (MijnP@rkinsonZorg)	A pilot project in four regions where Parkinson's nurse practitioners help patients with Parkinson's disease to set up personal online health communities

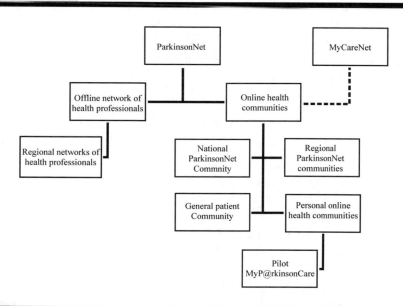

Figure.17.1 PARKINSONNET: THE LINKS AMONG ITS ELEMENTS.

integration are thus the health care service user (the patient) and the health care providers (i.e., physicians, therapists, and hospitals). Last but not least, those who finance the system—insurance companies and, ultimately, the government—potentially face substantially lower costs in a better integrated and more sustainable health service system.

Complex value chains or networks include a variety of actors and activities that may have (partially) conflicting interests and objectives. Research has demonstrated that the performance of such complex networks ultimately depends on the extent to which the network is integrated. In a non-integrated chain, the actors try to maximize their own benefits, generating suboptimal functioning within the network and high costs (see, for example, Cooper, Lambert, & Pagh, 1997). In a fully integrated chain or network, in contrast, a systems view is adopted: All actors consider the network as a single system with common, shared objectives. Instead of optimizing activities locally, an integrated network optimizes its activities based on a global perspective. The system has a common purpose. Within a health care system, such a purpose might be the sustainable creation of maximum value for all major stakeholders. The case we investigate in this chapter reveals how information exchange, optimized through the use of Web 2.0 technology, may increase trust by neutralizing power differences and mitigating conflicts of interest, therefore encouraging collaboration among stakeholders, improving the quality of care while reducing service system costs.

APPROACH

In this chapter, we first discuss some important trends and issues in health care provision. Then, we provide information about Parkinson's disease to indicate the complexity of the illness, its treatment, and the needs of patients and health care professionals dealing with the disease. Finally, we explain how ParkinsonNet addresses these needs via a system of integrated networks, which increase mutual trust and facilitate coordination, collaboration, and communication flows.

CURRENT STATE OF HEALTH CARE AND TREATMENTS

The progress in medicine and health care has unquestionably made more effective treatments available. As a result of the increasing level of specialization in the sector, however, physicians' and therapists' contributions need to be combined, coordinated, and integrated into treatment plans to realize the full potential of these contributions. Today, we better understand how expertise from many medical disciplines combines to facilitate more effective provision of care for patients with complex diseases. At the same time, medical specialists are no longer the only health professionals involved in patient treatment. Research has shown the importance of involving care providers from other disciplines, such as physical therapists, and of providing these professionals with the right tools and training to prepare them to treat patients with these complex diseases. The adequate combination and integration of treatments by different health professionals, however, requires more coordination among these health care providers than is often available. A lack of integration may not only make the treatments less effective but even render them counter-productive, for example, when a treatment is given at an inappropriate time.

In treating highly complex diseases such as Parkinson's disease, many health professionals lack sufficient expertise with the disease. Thus, they sometimes do not know how to adequately diagnose or treat the disease or do not call on the appropriate professionals with the required specific expertise when they require assistance (Munneke et al., 2010). The communication and collaboration among the health professionals of different disciplines involved in the treatment process are often inadequate (Hewett, Watson, Gallois, Ward, & Leggett, 2009; Reader, Flin, Mearns, & Cuthbertson, 2007). In particular, there is a lack of explicit co-involvement of health professionals in designing an integrated treatment plan or service chain spanning all disciplines.

Some researchers suggest that online tools could create more collaboration opportunities among health professionals and patients (Demiris, 2006; Eysenbach, Powell, Englesakis, Rizo, & Stern, 2004; Gummerus, Liljander, Pura, & Van Riel, 2004). Although the traditional Internet has been used in health care for a long time, for example by medical publishers to reach general practitioners (Van Riel, Liljander, & Jurriëns, 2001), the health care sector has been relatively slow to jump on the Web 2.0 bandwagon. Now the sector is exploring the use of online tools and social media for health care provision. In the "Health 2.0" literature, online communities have gained significant attention in recent years (Dedding, van Doorn, Winkler, & Reis, 2011; Miller, 2012; Wicks et al., 2010). Online communities in particular may create a basis for increased collaboration among their users (Eysenbach, 2008; Garman, Leach, & Spector, 2006).

IMPROVING THE QUALITY OF CARE

In the management literature, the focus has shifted from financial performance to addressing the interests of all major stakeholders (Freeman & Reed, 1993) and, therefore, on other forms of value than profit creation. For example, more attention is now directed toward service quality as perceived by the customer (Parasuraman, Zeithaml, & Berry, 1985, 1988), an important stakeholder in business value chains. In medical value networks, the patient plays a similar role. A great deal of recent managerial attention has focused on better understanding and satisfying customer needs and involving the customer in value cocreation (Grönroos, 2011; Vargo & Lusch, 2004). Driven by a continuous desire to improve the quality of care, together with the trends presented above, the concept of patient-centered care has been introduced in the medical sector (Berwick, 2009). Patient-centered care is now seen as helping to improve the quality of care (Van der Eijk, Faber, Al Shamma, Munneke, & Bloem, 2011). The Institute of Medicine defines *patient-centered care* as "providing care that is respectful of and responsive to individual patient preferences, needs, and values and ensuring that patient values guide all clinical decisions" (Committee, 2001, p. 3). In business, attempts are made to increase the satisfaction and loyalty of the end-user of consumer goods and services as a major strategic goal (Oliver, 1999). Similarly, the health care sector has adopted the idea that the patient's experience must be considered in all decisions regarding improving the quality of care.

A major developing trend based on this new perspective is the perception of value creation among health care professionals as multidimensional. Quality consists of relatively tangible dimensions such as clinical effectiveness, safety, and treatment efficiency (cost-effectiveness), but it also has less tangible dimensions, such as the psychological cost to the patient and the way the patient experiences the care provision and the healing process (in the widest possible sense). Examples of these less tangible dimensions of care quality provided by the Institute of Medicine are similar to service quality dimensions, for example, those proposed by Parasuraman et al. (1985) in the service marketing literature. They include convenience, physical and emotional comfort, empowerment, compassion, support, respect, information, integration, and involvement of friends and family (Berwick, 2009; Bloem & Stocchi, 2012).

PATIENT INVOLVEMENT

Another important trend relates to the extent to which patients and those around them are informed about their illness and the possible treatments. Mainly due to increased information availability and the Internet, patients are more aware of and used to easy access to expertise and the opportunity to become involved in the health care process (Coulter, 1999). Access on social networks and discussion forums to the experiences of fellow patients, reports, articles, and treatment reviews has increased awareness of patients' individual needs and opportunities and of their individual values (Bartlett & Coulson, 2011). At the same time, more is known about the types of information that patients and their caregivers need (from their health professionals) if they are to be capable of participating in the decision-making process (Hibbard, Peters, Dixon, & Tusler, 2007).

PARKINSON'S DISEASE

Parkinson's disease is a neurodegenerative disease that gradually impairs the patient in physical, emotional, and cognitive ways, generating a complex of gradually changing and worsening symptoms (Lees et al., 2009). The treatment of this type of disease is complex, time consuming, difficult, and as a result, expensive. Traditionally, Parkinson's disease has been treated by a neurologist using conventional therapies such as pharmacotherapy and brain surgery (Post, van der Eijk, Munneke, & Bloem, 2011). However, evidence is growing to support the effectiveness of allied health disciplines in providing additional forms of treatment (Nijkrake et al., 2007), and up to 19 disciplines are now involved in the care for patients with Parkinson's disease and their families.

It seems clear that when professionals such as neurologists, Parkinson's nurse practitioners, physical therapists, speech language pathologists, occupational therapists, psycho-social caregivers, and dietitians are able to communicate and collaborate more adequately (i.e., work within a better integrated value network), the illness can indeed be more effectively treated and its symptoms better relieved, substantially increasing quality of life for the patients and their caregivers (Bloem et al., 2010; Post et al., 2011).

PARKINSONNET

We now present and discuss the case of ParkinsonNet, a Dutch organization that attempts to find solutions to the complex issues inherent in the integrated provision of care to patients with Parkinson's disease. The back office of ParkinsonNet is based at the Radboud University Nijmegen Medical Center (RUNMC) in the Netherlands and it designs and deploys a unique, integrated health care service system. In addition to its online health communities, the organization has set up regional offline networks of health professionals. These networks cover the service areas of the general hospitals where neurologists are employed. Within these regional networks, a selected number of expert therapists (including physical therapists, speech and language pathologists, and occupational therapists) are trained based on scientifically validated guidelines. The neurologists are encouraged to refer patients to these skilled professionals, and through a Web-based "care finder" (Dutch: *de zorgzoeker*), patients themselves can opt for referral to these therapists as well. These networks of health professionals have nationwide coverage in the Netherlands, involving 65 regional networks and 1,800 trained therapists. In addition to this offline network, ParkinsonNet has also set up online tools to improve Parkinson's patient care. These online networks are facilitated by MyCarenet (Dutch: *MijnZorgnet*), an Internet-based communication platform with the potential to unite patients and professionals through open and closed communities. Within these communities, members interact using modern communication technologies such as blogs, chats, forums, and wikis. ParkinsonNet uses these technologies in several ways.

Through MyCarenet, ParkinsonNet has set up communities at several levels, each with a different focus. Communities exist, for instance, for (1) all health care professionals linked to ParkinsonNet, (2) regional networks of health care professionals, (3) groups of patients, and (4) individual patients and their set of caregivers. This last type of community offers each patient the opportunity to set up a personal online health community (POHC) in which he or she can interact with the relevant health care professionals and discuss issues related to the disease. POHCs make it uniquely possible to store all medical information in one place while also allowing transparent communication among the members of the patient's health care team. ParkinsonNet recently set up a pilot study called MyP@rkinsonCare (Dutch: *MijnP@rkinsonzorg*) intended to help Parkinson's patients set up their own POHCs. With the help of a Parkinson's nurse practitioner, the patient creates a partially virtual community that combines online and offline activities.

Based on the above reflections, we observe that neurodegenerative diseases such as Parkinson's pose a number of interrelated challenges to those involved in dealing with them (Nijkrake et al., 2008). We investigate to what extent ParkinsonNet fulfills the following requirements of an integrated health care provision system:

- It helps remedy the general lack of expertise among health care professionals in the treatment of complex diseases such as Parkinson's disease.
- It improves referrals to expert health professionals by making expertise more visible for both the referring physicians and the patients themselves.
- It improves communication and interdisciplinary collaboration among health care professionals working to treat complex diseases.
- It puts the patient at the center of the care system, enabling them to play an active role in their own disease management.

We next investigate the issue using a case analysis. We distinguish among three types of programs that ParkinsonNet has implemented to increase the care quality and efficiency for Parkinson patients: MyP@rkinsoncare, the regional networks of health care professionals who communicate both online as well as offline, and the "carefinder," which allows people to search for health professionals with expertise related to Parkinson's disease.

MyP@rkinsoncare as an Innovative Web 2.0 Intervention

Patients who entered the MyP@rkinsoncare pilot study and who use a POHC can interact with their health professionals outside their regular offline visits. Thus, patients have control over decisions regarding which professionals and caregivers are included in the POHC, as they can invite others to join. Patients also post diary entries, and the POHC actors can start threads about topics related to aspects of the disease and the treatment process. There has been a steady rise in the number of patients who have decided to use the service.

A major reason patients use this online interface more often is that the service increases their opportunities to communicate with all their health professionals when necessary or when they feel the need. They no longer have to wait until the next appointment with a health care provider (Miller, 2012). In addition to facilitating patient–health professional communication, the POHC creates ample opportunity for health professionals to determine, at their convenience, what the other health professionals are doing in terms of treatment (Garman et al., 2006). This is an important feature of these online communities because the health care professionals are not always aware of the involvement and benefits of other disciplines in the patient care program (Van der Marck et al., 2009). Furthermore, the service creates an opportunity for all the health professionals involved in the treatment to communicate and discuss the separate parts of the treatment, their points of intersection, and their results. This interaction helps those involved to develop better-integrated treatment plans together. The online part of the project is embedded in an offline regional network for allied health professionals working to treat Parkinson's disease.

REGIONAL NETWORKS

Beyond the online communication interface offered by ParkinsonNet's online communities, regular face-to-face meetings are also organized. In the regional networks created by ParkinsonNet, health care professionals discuss cases and increase their knowledge of the disease. The networks bring together health care professionals in different disciplines who have the greatest expertise in Parkinson's disease. During these meetings, the health care professionals develop a common vocabulary to engage more easily in interdisciplinary collaboration. These meetings help the individuals involved to develop a better understanding of the benefits and potential interactions of the various treatment elements. Communication, both among the members of a profession and among the members of different disciplines, plays an important role in increasing mutual trust and improving collaboration among all health care professionals.

The frequent communications and connections among health professionals from various disciplines should facilitate the identification of imperfections or gaps in their knowledge and skills. The participating professionals can use both networks to discuss the value of remedies and solutions and to make suggestions. As a result, the network helps diffuse medical innovations within the general health care provider community. This is important, given the increased specialization in the field and the general speed with which knowledge, new medications and new practices are developed in the medical and paramedical domain.

When these individuals get to know their colleagues better and become more familiar with each other's potential to contribute to the care process, mutual understanding and trust increase and the general alignment of goals and methods improves. Thus, it becomes easier to integrate the service value chain or supply chain and to optimize long-term value creation by and for each of the involved parties.

THE CAREFINDER

The carefinder is a tool on the ParkinsonNet website that allows patients and health care professionals to look up information about professionals in the network. The carefinder indicates whether a health care professional has participated in specialized Parkinson's disease workshops, thus indicating which health professionals have pertinent expertise. This transparency about competences within the community and the awareness of the potential role of such expertise in the treatment should make it easier for both health professionals and patients to select the right therapist or physician to treat them. The carefinder facilitates the process through which professionals with Parkinson's expertise will gain the most patients and thus the most experience in treating Parkinson's patients. Thus, the care quality further improves, as does the efficacy of treatments for Parkinson's patients.

DISCUSSION

Although the combined online health community and offline professional network offered by ParkinsonNet should still be considered in its initial stages, the new services have already been shown to constitute a major step in the right direction. Patients and health care professionals see the substantial benefits of using online health communities to create an integrated health care provision system with many categories of interdependent actors and stakeholders (Aarts et al., 2012). The potential improvements in care quality, the total system costs, and the sustainable development of social capital (i.e., through learning and improving competences and knowledge) appear to be highly promising. Furthermore, if health professionals want to truly and sustainably improve the quality of care through patient-centered care, they must assess and benchmark the effects of their initiatives. This type of assessment requires feedback from patients, the other people in their lives, and the health care professionals involved in their treatment (Van der Eijk et al., 2011). The online and offline communities in ParkinsonNet, by regularly bringing patients and care providers together, could provide an innovative mechanism for feedback loops.

MANAGERIAL IMPLICATIONS

Viewing health care systems as complex and integrated, instead of treating the various segments of health care services as independent sources of value, helps health care professionals to develop strategies to integrate these systems and optimizing total value creation. Health care managers could further explore the combined use of Web 2.0 and more traditional forms of communication. This effort may initially require extra time investments on the part of professionals and patients. However, the long-term benefits of better integrated health care systems appear substantial. Focusing on complex systems coordination through improved communication seems to be a valuable solution to modern day issues in the health care industry.

RESEARCH AGENDA

It seems plausible that stimulating communication among health care professionals and patients and facilitating coordination will help to integrate actors and stakeholders. However, more research is required to determine the actual mechanisms and effects of ParkinsonNet and its programs on the network efficiency of the health care services. There are many challenges that must be overcome. For instance, patients and health professionals may hesitate to participate in online health communities because of technological issues. Research on technology readiness (Liljander, Gillberg, Gummerus, & Van Riel, 2006; Parasuraman, 2000) could facilitate the transition and generate greater benefits from the new technology. Further research is also needed on the role of online communities in transforming existing hierarchies into more balanced relationships among health care providers and patients.

The beneficial effects of ParkinsonNet's programs appear to be more strongly related to the way the programs deal with complexity and integrate the health care value network than to the specificities of the illness. We therefore expect these effects to be generalizable to other health care value networks of a similar complexity. However, this expectation must be empirically tested.

REVIEW QUESTIONS

1. What are the causes and forms of complexity of health care service systems?
2. Which forms of value are created for the stakeholders in a complex health care service system?
3. How does the health care integration enable participants to cope with the health care system complexities?
4. What role does communication play in creating integrated health care services?
5. What role could online health communities play in achieving patient-centered care?

REFERENCES

Aarts, J. W.M., Vennik, F., Nelen, W. L. D., Van der Eijk, M., Bloem, B. R., Faber, M. J., & Kremer, J. A. M. (2012). Personal health communities: A phenomenological study of a new healthcare concept. *Personalized fertility care in the Internet era* (pp. 188–211). Amsterdam, Offpage.

Bartlett, Y. K., & Coulson, N. S. (2011). An investigation into the empowerment effects of using online support groups and how this affects health professional/patient communication. *Patient Education and Counseling, 83*(1), 113–119.

Berwick, D. M. (2009). What 'patient-centered' should mean: Confessions of an extremist. *Health Affairs, 28*(4), w555–w565.

Bloem, B. R., & Stocchi, F. (2012). Move for change part I: A European survey evaluating the impact of the EPDA Charter for People with Parkinson's disease. *European Journal of Neurology,19*(3), 402–410.

Bloem, B. R., Van Laar, T., Keus , S. H. J., De Beer, H., Poot, E., Buskens, E., Aarden, W., & Munneke, M. (2010). Multidisciplinary guideline: Parkinson's disease (Multidisciplinaire richtlijn: Ziekte van Parkinson). Alphen a/d Rijn, Van Zuiden Communications: Central Workgroup Multidisciplinary Guideline Parkinson 2006–2009 (Centrale Werkgroep Multidisciplinaire Richtlijn Parkinson 2006–2009).

Committee on Quality of Health Care in America. (2001). *Crossing the quality chasm: A new health system for the 21ˢᵗ century.* Washington D.C., The National Academies Press: Institute of Medicine.

Cooper, M. C., Lambert, D. M., & Pagh, J. D. (1997). Supply chain management: More than a new name for logistics. *International Journal of Logistics Management, 8*(1), 1–14.

Coulter, A. (1999). Paternalism or partnership? *British Medical Journal, 319*(7212), 719–720.

Dedding, C., van Doorn, R., Winkler, L., & Reis, R. (2011). How will e-health affect patient participation in the clinic? A review of e-health studies and the current evidence for changes in the relationship between medical professionals and patients. *Social Science & Medicine, 72*(1), 49–53.

Demiris, G. (2006). The diffusion of virtual communities in health care: Concepts and challenges. *Patient Education and Counseling, 62*(2), 178–188.

Eysenbach, G. (2008). Medicine 2.0: Social networking, collaboration, participation, apomediation, and openness. *Journal of Medical Internet Research, 10*(3), e22.

Eysenbach, G., Powell, J., Englesakis, M., Rizo, C., & Stern, A. (2004). Health related virtual communities and electronic support groups: Systematic review of the effects of online peer to peer interactions. *British Medical Journal, 328*(7449), 1166.

Freeman, E., & Reed, D. (1993). Stockholders and stakeholders: A new perspective on corporate governance. *California Management Review, 25*(3), 88–106.

Garman, A. N., Leach, D. C., & Spector, N. (2006). Worldviews in collision: Conflict and collaboration across professional lines. *Journal of Organizational Behavior, 27*(7), 829–849.

Grönroos, C. (2011). Value co-creation in service logic. A critical analysis. *Marketing Theory, 11*(3), 279–301.

Gummerus, J., Liljander, V., Pura, M., & Van Riel, A. (2004). Customer loyalty to content-based web-sites. The case of an online health care service. *Journal of Services Marketing, 18*(3), 175–186.

Hewett, D. G., Watson, B. M., Gallois, C., Ward, M., & Leggett, B. A. (2009). Intergroup communication between hospital doctors: Implications for quality of patient care. *Social Science & Medicine, 69*(12), 1732–1740.

Hibbard, J. H., Peters, E., Dixon, A., & Tusler, M. (2007). Consumer competencies and the use of comparative quality information. *Medical Care Research and Review, 64*(4), 379–394.

Lees, A. J., Hardy, J., & Revesz, T. (2009). Parkinson's disease. *Lancet, 373*(9680), 2055–2066.

Liljander, V., Gillberg, F., Gummerus, J., & Van Riel, A. (2006). Technology readiness and the evaluation and adoption of self-service technologies. *Journal of Retailing and Consumer Services, 13*(3), 177–191.

Miller, R. H. (2012). Satisfying patient-consumer principles for health information exchange: Evidence from California case studies. *Health Affairs, 31*(3), 537–547.

Munneke, M., Nijkrake, M. J., Keus, S. H., Kwakkel, G., Berendse, H. W., Roos, R. A., Borm, G. F., Adang, E.M., et al. (2010). Efficacy of community-based physiotherapy networks for patients with Parkinson's disease: A cluster-randomised trial. *Lancet Neurology, 9*(1), 46–54.

Nijkrake, M. J., Keus, S. H. J., Kalf, J. G., Sturkenboom, I. H. W. M., Munneke, M., Kappelle, A. C., & Bloem, B. R. (2007). Allied health care interventions and complementary therapies in Parkinson's disease. *Parkinsonism & Related Disorders, 13* (Suppl 3), S488–S494.

Nijkrake, M. J., Keus, S. H. J., Oostendorp, R. A. B., Overeem, S., Mulleners, W., Bloem, B. R., & Munneke, M. (2008). Allied health care in Parkinson's disease: Referral, consultation, and professional expertise. *Movement Disorders, 24*(2), 282–286.

Oliver, R. L. (1999). Whence customer loyalty? *Journal of Marketing, 63*(4), 33–44.

Parasuraman, A. (2000). Technology readiness index (TRI): A multiple-item scale to measure readiness to embrace new technologies. *Journal of Service Research, 2*(4), 307–320.

Parasuraman, A., Zeithaml, V. A., & Berry, L. L. (1985). A conceptual model of service quality and its implications for future research. *Journal of Marketing, 49*, 41–50.

Parasuraman, A., Zeithaml, V. A., & Berry, L. L. (1988). SERVQUAL: A multiple item scale for measuring consumer perceptions of service quality. *Journal of Retailing, 64*(1), 12–40.

Post, B., van der Eijk, M., Munneke, M., & Bloem, B. R. (2011). Multidisciplinary care for Parkinson's disease: Not if, but how! *Postgraduate Medical Journal, 87*(1031), 575–578.

Reader, T. W., Flin, R., Mearns, K., & Cuthbertson, B. H. (2007). Interdisciplinary communication in the intensive care unit. *British Journal of Anaesthesia, 98*(3), 347–352.

Van der Eijk, M., Faber, M. J., Al Shamma, S., Munneke, M., & Bloem, B. R. (2011). Moving towards patient-centered healthcare for patients with Parkinson's disease. *Parkinsonism & Related Disorders, 17*(5), 360–364.

Van der Marck, M. A., Kalf, J. G., Sturkenboom, I. H. W. M., Nijkrake, M. J., Munneke, M., & Bloem, B. R. (2009). Multidisciplinary care for patients with Parkinson's disease. *Parkinsonism & Related Disorders, 15, Suppl 3*(0), S219–S223.

Van Riel, A. C. R., Liljander, V., & Jurriëns, P. (2001). Exploring consumer evaluations of e-services: A portal site. *International Journal of Service Industry Management, 12*(4), 359–377.

Vargo, S. L., & Lusch, R. F. (2004). Evolving to a new dominant logic for marketing. *Journal of Marketing, 68*(1), 1–17.

Wicks, P., Massagli, M., Frost, J., Brownstein, C., Okun, S., Vaughan, T., Bradley, R., & Heywood, J. (2010). Sharing health data for better outcomes on PatientsLikeMe. *Journal of Medical Internet Research, 12*(2), e19.

Practical Examples of Service Development and Innovations in the Nordic Well-Being Industry

Anja Tuohino,
Henna Konu,
Anne-Mette Hjalager,
Edward Huijbens

LEARNING OBJECTIVES

Upon completing this chapter, you should be able to do the following:
1. Know what is meant by concept of new service development (NSD).

2. Know how a customer-oriented tourism product/service is created.

3. Know how to use nature in well-being tourism development.

KEYWORDS

New service development, tourism product/service, well-being tourism,
the Nordic countries

INTRODUCTION

Health, well-being, and wellness are concepts that in recent times have attracted the interest of scholars and the hospitality industry. This new interest reflects not only the economic affluence of modern times, but also values and lifestyle changes. Terms such as quality of life, self-fulfillment, experiences, slow-life (shift toward slowing down life's pace) and downshifting (simple living with balance of leisure and work) coincide with an increased interest in illness prevention, down-aging (nostalgic, having fun and rejecting the stereotypes of age-appropriate behavior), self-improvement, beauty, and health treatments. Luxury is becoming less about materialism and increasingly about self-enrichment and time, luxury can be deemed more a concept of fulfillment (Yeoman, 2008). The aging population tends to be more active, healthier, and wealthier and they live longer. Conversely, the aging population also creates an increased demand for medical care. Being thus an ever-increasing request for state welfare provisions, strategies of privatization have unfolded and, hence, an incentive for entrepreneurs to focus on health, well-being, and wellness services that are offered for sale on a commercial market. Concomitantly, people are willing and able to be proactive in respect to general physical and mental well-being, sometimes even exaggeratedly so (Hjalager et al., 2011; Korthals, 2004; Yeoman, 2008). For tourism entrepreneurs, the fact that people are willing to travel for the purpose of improving their general well-being and health provides an incentive for entrepreneurs to focus on health and well-being markets and their future potential.

Health, wellness, and well-being are not only a well-justified concern for governmental bodies at local, national, and supranational levels, but are also considered an encouraging opportunity for a wide range of nongovernmental institutions and private enterprises. Health and well-being from this perspective are also big business, and demographic forecasts give hope to those whose main interests are economic (Kleinke, 1998; WHO, 2006). Worldwide there is an emphasis on catering to new customer needs and on reinventing and developing the products and services for growth and competitiveness. As demonstrated by Smith and Puczkó (2009) and by Bushell and Sheldon (2009), well-being and the wellness industry range from core medical treatments, to rest and recuperation, to enhancement of the mind and self. The scale and scope change constantly (Hjalager et al., 2011).

For the tourism sector, "wellness" is an appropriate term to cover concrete product and service offerings, whereas "well-being" constitutes a state of mind. Some tourism literature proceeds toward the understanding of the themes as a fairly open product-and-service package that meets the tourist's expectations when the aim is to achieve a holistic state of well-being (Krczal & Weiermair, 2006; Steinhauser & Theiner, 2004; Wiesner, 2007). Well-being and wellness tourism are difficult to distinguish, which has led to used the terms interchangeably (for more detailed concept definition, see Björk, Tuohino, & Konu, 2011). This is also the case in this paper. Thus, *wellness tourism* and *well-being tourism* can be defined as follows:

> Wellness tourism is a holistic mode of travel that integrates a quest for physical health, beauty, or longevity, and/or a heightening of consciousness or spiritual awareness, and a connection with community, nature, or the divine mystery. It encompasses a range of tourism experiences in destinations with wellness products, appropriate infrastructures, facilities, and natural and wellness resources. (Sheldon & Bushell, 2009, p. 11.)

The definition by Sheldon and Bushell (2009) links the resources of the hospitality sector to the needs of well-being and wellness customers.

This chapter introduces a new service development (NSD) model and argues for its manifestations in a Nordic context. The elements of a tourism product are also discussed. Practical examples from the well-being (tourism) sector are introduced to show how the model and customer insight are considered in product development. In the Nordic countries, attention is turning toward the potentials of new tourism niches. Health, well-being, and wellness are among the areas of greatest interest (Hjalager et al., 2011). The case studies represent the Nordic tourism sector and how, especially in the last few years, health, wellness, and well-being have attracted the interest of the tourism industry and, hence, tourism scholars (e.g., Björk et al., 2011; Hjalager, 2005, 2010, 2011; Hjalager et al., 2008; Hjalager & Nordin, 2011; Hjalager & Konu, 2011; Huijbens, 2011; Kangas & Tuohino, 2008; Konu, Tuohino, & Björk, 2011; Tuohino & Kangas, 2009).

As Nordic tourism is characterized by many small enterprises, not least in areas of interest in nature-based well-being tourism (Hall, Müller, & Saarinen, 2008; Hjalager et al., 2008, 2011), this chapter focuses on giving practical examples on how micro-, small, and medium-sized businesses have used local resources and customer insight in their service development processes. Customer orientation in service development aims to pay attention to customer wants and needs, leading to higher customer satisfaction. Various small case studies are used to describe how well-being organizations have created well-being (tourism) services to gain their customers' satisfaction.

CUSTOMER-ORIENTED NEW SERVICE DEVELOPMENT IN THE WELL-BEING SECTOR

As is well documented in marketing textbooks, a service development process is more complex than the development of physical goods. Moreover, there are differences among the diverse service sectors in product and service complexity. For instance, providing a single well-being or wellness service, such as massage, is simpler than providing, for example, a whole well-being tourism package in which a massage may be only one component of the total service product.

The theory of service marketing (e.g., Grönroos, 1993, 2000) and several definitions of the tourist product (Middleton, 1989; Middleton & Clarke, 2001; Murphy, Pritchard, & Smith, 2000) emphasize the product's added value that emerges at each phase of the production process. According to Gunn (1994), the desired outcome for the customer is value, which at any given time is a subjective experience.

Middleton and Clarke (2001, p. 89) argued that the tourist product means customer value, which is "the perceived benefits provided to meet the customer's needs and wants, quality of service received, and the value for money." The tourist product is a complex human experience, which is an output of a production process where the tourist uses the facilities and services to generate the final output, that is, the experience

(Gunn, 1988; Smith, 1994). Value is added at each stage of the production process and the consumer is an integral part of that process. The final output is, thus, created and interpreted during a process that has been developed and organized by a service provider (Edvardsson & Olsson, 1999). When buying an experience product, a customer pays to spend time and enjoy a series of memorable events, which the service provider puts on display (Mossberg, 2001; Pine & Gilmore, 1999). The most important challenge in travel and tourism marketing is that of creating and managing the expectation of an experience (Cho & Fesenmaier, 2001).

The service company provides the prerequisites for the various services by selling opportunities for services, which are generated in partially unique customer processes (Edvardsson & Olsson 1999; Edvardsson, Gustafsson, Johnson, & Sandèn, 2000). The primary aim of service development is to develop for the customers the best and right prerequisites for well-functioning processes and attractive outcomes. The service prerequisites are crucial to the result of the service development process. The right prerequisites can be described by a model with three basic components: service concept, service process, and service system (Edvardsson & Olsson, 1999).

Service concept, as explained by Edvardsson and Olsson (1999), refers to the description of the customer's needs and how customers are to be satisfied. Edvardsson and Olsson go on to explain that a service process relates to the chain of activities that must function properly to produce the service. Special attention should be paid to achieving the right quality at reasonable cost. Edvardsson and Olsson (1999) define the *service process* as a clear description of the activities needed to generate the service. The service system constitutes the resources (staff, the physical/technical environment, organization structure, customers) required by or are available to the service process to realize the service concept.

The service concept is an answer to customers' e*xpected value* that reflects the customer's desired value, referring to the customer's needs, goals, and purposes, and how customers expect the products to satisfy these needs (Woodruff, 1997). The description of the service process of the tourist product includes the definition of the formal product (Kotler, Bowen, & Makens, 1999), which can e.g. be expressed in the form of a brochure or an offer for a customer (Komppula, 2005). In the company and for its staff, the formal product may mean the determination and definition of the chain of activities in the customer process and the production process (Komppula, 2005). This chain can be illustrated as a service blueprint (Komppula & Boxberg, 2002; Zeithaml & Bitner, 1996, see also Komppula, 2005).

A service system includes the resources available to the service process in order to realize the service concept. This entails involving the service company's staff, the customers, the physical and technical environment, and the organization and control of these resources. The hospitality element of the tourist product is produced mainly by the personnel, as well as together with other customers. Freedom of choice and customer involvement dependent heavily on the service process, the customer him- or herself as well as the physical environment (Komppula, 2005; Komppula & Boxberg, 2002; Smith, 1994).

According to Komppula and Boxberg (2002), all these together—the service concept, the service process, and the service system—create the prerequisites of the tourist experience, which may or may not be fulfilled as the outcome of the customer process (see Figure 18.1). The tourist product created with these prerequisites may also be described as a service package and consists of several component parts (Shostack, 1977).

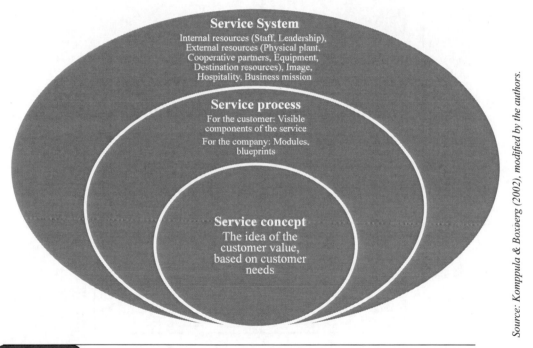

Source: Komppula & Boxberg (2002), modified by the authors.

Figure 18.1 PREREQUISITES OF CUSTOMER-ORIENTED TOURISM PRODUCT AND SERVICE.

The research carried out in the area of new service development (NSD) focuses on many cases in business-to-business service development (see e.g., Alam, 2002; Alam & Perry, 2002; Stevens & Dimitriadis, 2005; Veflen Olsen & Sallis, 2006). According to Stevens and Dimitriadis (2005) NSD models can be categorized into sequential development models and development models on the basis of organizational factors. Figure 18.2 shows Komppula and Boxberg's (2002) NSD framework. The framework combines the traditional process models (Kotler et al., 1999; Zeithaml & Bitner, 1996) with the model of prerequisites presented above of a customer-oriented tourist product.

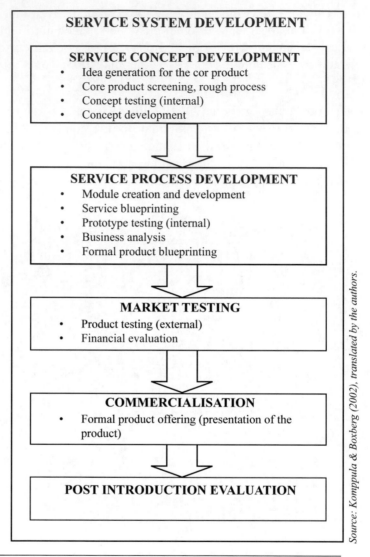

SERVICE SYSTEM DEVELOPMENT

SERVICE CONCEPT DEVELOPMENT
- Idea generation for the cor product
- Core product screening, rough process
- Concept testing (internal)
- Concept development

SERVICE PROCESS DEVELOPMENT
- Module creation and development
- Service blueprinting
- Prototype testing (internal)
- Business analysis
- Formal product blueprinting

MARKET TESTING
- Product testing (external)
- Financial evaluation

COMMERCIALISATION
- Formal product offering (presentation of the product)

POST INTRODUCTION EVALUATION

Source: Komppula & Boxberg (2002), translated by the authors.

Figure 18.2 NEW TOURISM SERVICE DEVELOPMENT FRAMEWORK.

The core of the tourist product is the idea of the experience—activities at a destination, which are intended to satisfy the tourist's primary and secondary needs. In the first stage of the NSD framework the service concept is developed (see Figure 2). This development process can be divided into four phases: idea generation, core product screening, concept testing, and concept development (Komppula & Boxberg 2002; Konu, Tuohino, & Komppula, 2010).

The sources of idea generation for the experience can be divided into internal and external sources. The main determinants should be the customers' needs and expectations. The core idea is formed into key modules, which are then screened against the service system available. The staff must then test modules' rough customer processes, after which they are developed, for example, by skipping some modules and adding new ones instead. When the core idea is fixed, the next NSD stage begins (Komppula & Boxberg, 2002).

Service process development indicates the precise planning and pricing mode of the tourist product. Every module has to be blueprinted as a chain of activities, with time scheduling, costs, and identifying all the service quality factors and possible gaps in the delivery system (Zeithaml, Parasuranam, & Berry, 1990). The process prototype must be tested again by the staff. After that the final formal product can be developed as a blueprint for the producers. In the market testing stage, the service concept and the process are tested by an external group of people, such as members of an intermediary. During the market testing stage the key components of the experience are tested and the key message of the promotion—the "appeal"—is identified for product commercialization. After launching the product on the market, the sources of the product's success or failure must be investigated in order to use the information in subsequent NSD processes (Komppula & Boxberg, 2002). NSD occurs in a service system environment, which consists of the company's physical plant, environment, staff, and a network of partners, competitors, and customers (Smith, 1994). The service system creates the corporate image and identity as well as the limitations of and the opportunities for the NSD. The company must pay close attention to service system development, which enables or prohibits the innovations (Konu et al., 2010).

The customer should be the starting point of the service development process, as the core of the tourist product is the experience a customer derives from the whole service process. This experience is the goal that the businesses should provide for the customer. The tourist experience reflects the customer's expectations of the particular product or service, for example, a well-being holiday, and how well the service providers meet these expectations (including all service components of the tourist product) and how the customers feel after the holiday experience (see, e.g., Komppula, 2005; Lapierre, 1997). If the expectations are met or exceeded, the customer gains added value, which in turn, leads to higher customer satisfaction.

Prahalad and Santos (2009) stated that customers and users can be involved in product and service development in the early stages of the innovation processes by tapping customers' tacit knowledge, and businesses can derive inspiration through customers' new solutions to problems. Prahalad and Santos continued that, until recently, customers and users were mainly involved in the later stages of the innovation process, for instance, in testing prototypes when the product was almost ready for the market and marketing. Hjalager and Nordin (2011) have also noted the importance of customers as an information source. Hjalager and Nordin listed several user-driven innovation methods and gave several examples of their implementation in the tourism industry.

Here we present some examples of new service development processes and innovations in the well-being tourism sector by following the theoretical aspects presented above.

EXAMPLES OF NEW SERVICE DEVELOPMENT PROCESSES AND INNOVATIONS IN THE WELL-BEING SECTOR IN THE NORDIC COUNTRIES

CASE 1: USING CUSTOMER INFORMATION AND TECHNOLOGICAL SOLUTIONS MATCHING CUSTOMERS' NEEDS AND INTERESTS TO BUSINESSES' RESOURCES

In eastern Finland small and medium-sized tourism and well-being businesses have been challenged to find new customer segments as social holidays have decreased. This led to a need to find new, self-funding customers and to develop products and services to meet those needs. A project called *eGOOD*, a cooperative network of the well-being services in Eastern Finland, was implemented in 2006–2008. The project's five businesses (fitness centers, hotels, and holiday centers) were committed to developing their services in a more customer-oriented way. The businesses were also interested in positioning themselves in the well-being and wellness tourism sector within a national and international context. The eGOOD project developed a technological solution called the eGOOD database to help the businesses find new kinds of target groups and to see if they had the resources to provide services for such groups Figure 18.3 shows the idea and the components of the eGOOD platform.

The database was developed to manage a company's customer, resources, products, and services data. The eGOOD database stored the data of the project's participating companies in various relevant areas. The database aided and facilitated business-to-business cooperation by providing companies with information on their own resources, customer profiles, products and services, and those of the other companies in the network. eGOOD served as a tool for companies' customer-oriented product development. The database included detailed information about potential consumers' interests, hobbies, and inclination to use wellness and well-being services. The resource data likewise included information about businesses' offerings, products, facilities etc. By combining the customer and resource information, businesses could create blueprints with all product components, service system, and service processes. Several tourism products were developed with the platform's assistance.

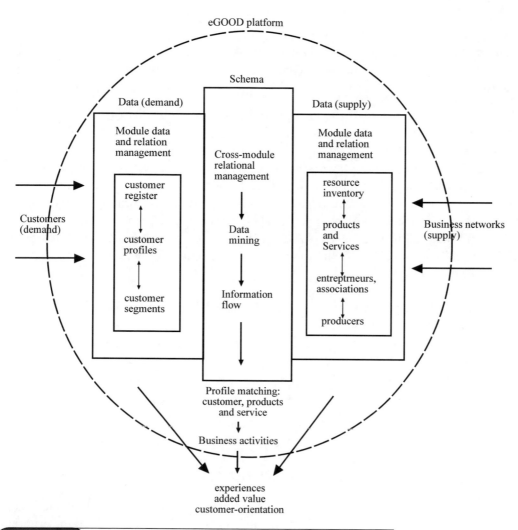

Figure 18.3 THE EGOOD PLATFORM AND ITS COMPONENTS.

During the eGOOD project the technological solution was developed and tested. After the project the solution was used as a test lab at the University of Eastern Finland, as the businesses lacked the resources to commit to further develop the process. In addition, there were problems as to how to integrate eGOOD with businesses' diverse customer management systems. The tool is now being used in Finland to construct a regional data warehousing technological solution for statistical purposes.

CASE 2: THE LAKE WELLNESS CONCEPT

The development of the Lake Wellness Concept sprang from the idea of using the main tourism resource of eastern Finland, its lakes. The idea was to clarify the Lake Wellness service concept, the perceived experience of the customer, and the concept building.

The businesses involved in the concept development were located on lake shores. However, at that time, the lakes were more valued as a framing landscape for outdoor activities than for their use as salable tourism products. The concept development started with business interviews. The interviewees agreed that the Eastern Finland wellness profile should be built on the strengths of the area, namely the natural environment (including the lakes), peace, and solitude. Regarding the content of Lake Wellness, the pillars of the concept included elements taken from the interviewees' ideas and adapted to the model of Müller and Lanz Kaufmann (2001). As a result (Kangas & Tuohino, 2008; Tuohino & Kangas, 2009), the following fundamental pillars were named:

- **Spirit, mind, and self-development:** relaxing excursions in the forest and lake environment
- **Health:** Nordic walking around the lake shores or through forests, traditional and preventive treatments
- **Healthy cuisine:** local raw materials and freshwater fish
- **Inner and external beauty:** Finnish sauna, peat sauna treatment
- **Relaxation and comfort:** swimming in the lake, Finnish sauna experience, baths in a barrel of hot water,, campfire relaxation near open fire
- **Tailor-made movement/fitness:** guided tours in and on the lake, kick sledding or trip skating on frozen lakes

In addition to the items above, the accommodation is an essential part of the Lake Wellness Concept. In Finland the Finnish Tourist Board (2011) has defined the criteria for so-called well-being accommodations in cottages. Figure 18.4 presents the Lake Wellness experience product.

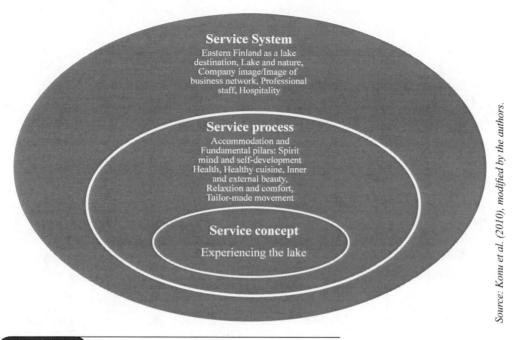

Service System
Eastern Finland as a lake
destination, Lake and nature,
Company image/Image of
business network, Professional
staff, Hospitality

Service process
Accommodation and
Fundamental pilars: Spirit
mind and self-development
Health, Healthy cuisine, Inner
and external beauty,
Relaxtion and comfort,
Tailor-made movement

Service concept
Experiencing the lake

Source: Konu et al. (2010), modified by the authors.

Figure 18.4 LAKE WELLNESS EXPERIENCE PRODUCT.

The Lake Wellness development reflecting the NSD framework is now ready for market testing. The Lake Wellness Concept development includes the idea generation for the core product (experiencing the lake) and concept development. This was done using business interviews, focus group discussions, and customer research. Process development had already been done, including module creation and development. A prototype was tested internally as well as by interviews with professionals. The development had reached the phase of market testing. In 2010 elements of the Lake Wellness Product were tested at Nordic Tourism Fairs to obtain more customer information about the suitability of the concept for potential customers. According to the customer survey, potential tourists expected relaxation and comfort (e.g., swimming in natural waters, sauna experience, bathing in a barrel of hot water) from their well-being tourism product. The second most important element in the well-being tourism offer was healthy food, and the third comprised health promotion and health-enhancing services (e.g., Nordic walking on lake shores or in the forest, traditional treatments, and preventive care). The results showed that taking care of oneself and relaxation were the most highly valued activities on a well-being holiday. According to the study, there was a space for a new, innovative resource-based concept in Eastern Finland and Lake Wellness could be deemed a holistic response to this. The next phases of Lake Wellness project were the commercialization of Lake Wellness products and the post-introduction evaluations.

Case 3: Danish Regional Well-Being Suppliers: From Meteors to A Starry System

In 2009–2011, the EU-supported WellCome was implemented in the Danish Region of Southern Denmark, and management was undertaken by VisitVejle. In the course of the project period, 90 enterprises participated in a range of seminars, workshops, study trips, etc., and there was a great interest in the subgroups established to cultivate specific ideas and to build new well-being and tourism products. More evidence on the WellCome project can be found in Hjalager (2011), Hjalager et al. (2011), Hjalager & Konu (2011), and at www.wellcome.dk.

Underlying the project was an observation that Southern Denmark contained a substantial number and variety of natural resources that had been seen only marginally as beneficial for customers interested in enhancing their physical and mental well-being—coastal areas, forests, moors, garden landscapes, etc. Likewise, health- and tourism-related enterprises had paid little attention to the wider spatial environment, as they were unaware of the capacities of their fellow providers for wellness and well-being services.

One WellCome purpose was to enhance the competencies for business development. This was considered particularly crucial as many enterprises are small. Business development also included the idea of new business models that might radically raise the level—qualitatively and quantitatively—of the well-being product. With this in mind, some larger, well-recognized, and professional hotels and wellness businesses agreed to become involved in the project, not only as mentors for the smaller actors, but also to develop their own enterprises.

The Danish service model (Figure 18.5) emphasized how to proceed strategically from single well-being actors to innovative collaboration.

The *service concept* was developed with the local partners, but also with significant input from outside. Based on a comprehensive market survey, the project partners could identify a number of well-being customer categories. For instance, this process clarified that well-being should include not only the traditional core wellness purchasers (females, ages 40–60), but also children and people with a stronger interest in outdoor activities. In addition, focus was placed on the stressful job situations and the need for more comprehensive well-being initiatives that included workplaces and groups of colleagues. Older people's needs were also carefully considered.

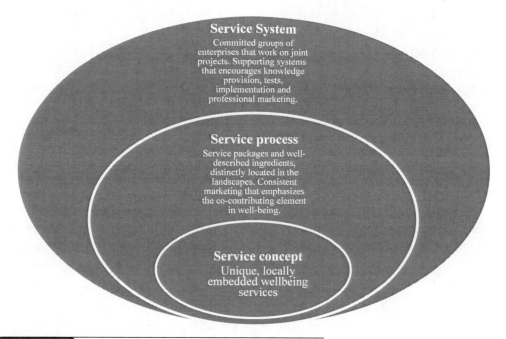

Figure 18.5 WELLCOME AND THE SERVICE MODEL.

Meetings held during 2009–2011 gathered participants from many parts of the region, and the natural values emerged gradually as a prime resource. Identifying the landscape values and working with a creative re-interpretation of the qualities stimulated work in a number of subsequent group activities. Such a reinterpretation included not only the visual elements, but also scents and materials that could be included in cosmetics and food. Nature as a location for fitness and experiences inspired the creativity in WellCome.

The *service processes* can best be described through the range of specific and marketable subconcepts that were the most substantial outcome of WellCome:

- **Active family well-being packages:** Help families to overcome inadequate eating habits, tendencies toward obesity, and computer addiction.
- **Spa Supreme:** Wellness facilities with a higher luxury component.
- **Care cosmetics:** Developing and marketing healthy and sustainable cosmetics in wellness environments.
- **The Cereals of the Sea:** Experimenting with algae in cereals to increase the cereals' nutritional value and the regional branding.
- **Recovery:** A new type of stress prevention and quality-of-life improvement.

- **A life in balance:** Developing a concept of therapy for stress and burn-out using the natural environment.
- **Island retreat:** Silence is the major advantage on the island of Strynoe. The place offers the perfect environment for meditation.
- **Therapy forest:** Nature is used and re-invented to become an essential ingredient in forest therapy, mindfulness, and stress processing.

The innovativeness of the concepts is debatable, as many elements are already known from international wellness and tourism. But through their conceptualization, it became clearer that in a Danish context the involvement of customers as coproducers is crucial and a matter of special attention. That is progress in its own right. Concepts testing demonstrated that customers not only wanted passive treatments, but looked forward to vigorous self-involvement. New models for customer service are part of creating a unique strategy and product profile for Danish well-being. Involvement and mutual learning became part of the project mentally, but also part of the production process and delivery blueprint.

In the *service system*, WellCome focused on the competence development of well-being providers and included network based training with a potential for further enhancement at the end of the project. The participants were introduced and trained in a number of business development and innovation tools, and the learning was practice based. A particular incentive was the financial support for new concept launches, and the participants experienced some competition in terms of their ability to write feasible business plans. Not least, the micro-enterprises over the three years of project work cultivated increasingly closer collaborative alliances that have generated a better platform for the economic side of their individual businesses. Alliances between the largest enterprises and small subcontracting firms emerged.

The service system now consists of extended transparency, where the actors are able to quickly identify regional competences. The service system is considered a new mindset. According to the evaluation, the mere ideas of wellness and well-being have become more holistic, and the partners find that they themselves, as persons, have become more inclusive, tolerant, and appreciative. This has facilitated development of their own businesses and collaboration with others. They have accepted that, no matter what, their enterprises must work on continuous progress.

CASE 4: ICELANDIC WILDERNESS EXPERIENCES PACKAGED IN SPAS

This case is developed from the Mývatn Nature Baths in the northeast of Iceland, in the sparsely populated region around Lake Mývatn. The region's key attraction and main allure are its unique natural environment and easy access to wilderness areas. The Mývatn region is on the volcanically active belt that divides Iceland, lying between the continents of North America and Eurasia. Several geological features are visible, which, through the interplay of fire and ice, provide unique vistas. Moreover, the volcanic nature of the region results in numerous hot springs and mud pools, which form the main inspirations for wellness service development.

Emulating in many ways the success of the Blue Lagoon destination and product line developed near the main international gateway to Iceland, Keflavík airport in Iceland's southwest, the Mývatn Nature Baths (MNB) were set up by local tourism stakeholders to diversify their service portfolio and tackle challenges of seasonality. The key service concept is to provide relaxation and well-being to weary hikers and explorers of the nearby wilderness, but also to any and all who want to benefit from soaking in hot water. Hence, the service concept draws on longstanding traditions of hot water bathing in Iceland, where rheumatic pains or work-weary joints find relief. In addition to tourism's role in regional development and to strengthen the region's tourism, service provision was integral to the service concept. Visitors to the region had limited options for acquiring services, and this prompted local stakeholders to consider how they might diversify. Visitors' needs had hitherto more or less only been catered to in terms of restaurants and accommodations. The people running those businesses were intent to develop other service alternatives. The abundance of hot water and the success of the Blue Lagoon near Keflavík prompted them to use a resource close at hand.

For this to happen, the service process took numerous twists and turns. The role of hot water and bathing in the lagoon to relieve aches and pains was crucial. The role of the national power company in facilitating access to this resource, both through direct support as shareholders in the MNB and by bringing the water to the surface via geothermal energy production, were critical to the service process. Through entrepreneurial activities, other related services were set up, for example, massage services from an independent contractor, centers for holistic and alternative medicine, and most important, development of a cosmetic product line. Further ideas have been aired but have not yet come to fruition. These ideas concern linking these services to national welfare service provision. This, depending on the ideas, would focus certain treatments being provided by the MNB, for example, for rheumatic complications and obesity. Another idea is to draw the surrounding environment into the service process by promoting hiking paths of varying degrees of difficulty, relaxation, massage, and bathing activities along with dietary advice. The only manifestation of these ideas at present was establishment of a treatment center for colon care operating for one month every year by an independent entrepreneur from outside the region.

The service system that sustains the unfolding processes and the underpinning concept have not been formalized in any productive tourism strategy nor have formal established links yet exist that would bring together actors from the wellness industry and beyond in the Mývatn region. However, on the national level, a health and well-being tourism association has been formed. The national tourism plan for 2012 stated that health and well-being tourism should be supported as a burgeoning cluster in the country. How these national strategy frameworks will fare in local contexts depends on the major stakeholders in local industry. They must be recruited and informed about the potential of the national strategy and be encouraged to provide developmental funds. Currently the service system is localized, stakeholder driven, and without outside links, which will hamper new service developments. Figure 18.6 summarizes these points on the service concept, process and system.

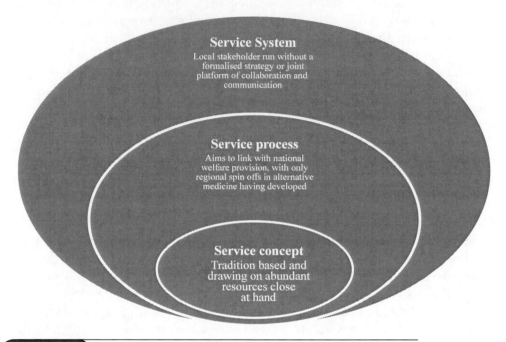

Service System
Local stakeholder run without a formalised strategy or joint platform of collaboration and communication

Service process
Aims to link with national welfare provision, with only regional spin offs in alternative medicine having developed

Service concept
Tradition based and drawing on abundant resources close at hand

Figure 18.6 MÝVATN NATURE BATHS AND THE SERVICE MODEL.

In Figure 18.6, well-being, health, and wellness are seen as umbrella terms, and Nordic well-being is defined on the basis of natural resources and Nordic lived values. Thus, Nordic well-being is a specific segment of the well-being industry and conceptualized in terms of concrete products, which can be marketed on the domestic market as well as in a competitive market, that is, internationally. Icelandic health and wellness are seen as part and parcel of Nordic well-being, but most certainly differentiated in terms of specific resource. Intuitively the images of Nordic well-being are typically oriented toward nature and outdoor experiences and enjoyment combined with achievement, healthy local gastronomy, local culture, and clean air, natural environment, and water. However, these features are hardly sufficient and specific enough to constitute a marketing platform, nor one for consistent new service development. For these to unfold in a sustained manner and able to add value to service provision, the service processes and structures need to be consolidated and formalized.

As can be seen from the Icelandic case, the well-being service provision has only an ad hoc relationship to any formalized strategy, be they regional or national. The concept being promoted is sustained by visionary entrepreneurs trying to diversify their service portfolios. The project, from which our short contribution stemmed, was to identify the substance for the region's well-being concept. Through the project, a bottom-up process was initiated and proved valuable for the participants. However, there remain many structural divides in the field, particularly between public and private sectors, traditional and alternative health services, small and large enterprises, commercial and voluntary actors. The importance of building bridges is a clear conclusion drawn from the process, as is the need for perseverance. There is also a need for a joint platform and for consensus building in order to provide coherence in developing a product and an identity for the region.

CONCLUSION

Well-being tourism is not a new form of tourism but it has assumed new forms; well-being and wellness tourism no longer mean holidays in spas, but also a holiday in a rural or urban environment. In the case of the Nordic well-being tourism product, it is typically oriented toward nature and outdoor experiences and enjoyment combined with achievement, healthy local gastronomy, local culture, and clean air, environment, and water. The hospitality industry has already started to respond to customer demands for well-being and wellness services. For instance, hotels and accommodation facilities no longer sell only beds; they have also added services. Several hotels have built wellness facilities and offer day-spa or massage services. However, other customer segments need to be considered when developing new services. As studies have shown, there are also different kinds of well-being tourists: Some want only to be pampered and enjoy treatments, while others want to take an active part in their well-being, for example, requesting fitness services.

As the case studies have shown, recognizing the unique selling points of the area and businesses is important, as is using these selling points in service provision. For instance, an unutilized potential exists in the use of local specialities, for example, traditional wellness treatments in spa facilities or a mixture of traditional and new exercise forms. In the Finnish case, lakes are part of the well-being service and new product development, including traditional sauna treatments and new kinds of sauna activities such as saunayoga®. In Iceland, developing service processes that create value from a local resource need to be formalized and systematized. While in Finland the resources underpinning the concept are vague, in Iceland the processes that build on the resources and concepts are vague.

The hospitality sector can look into new ways of cooperation. In Finland, Denmark, and Iceland there are examples of cosmetics suppliers using local resources and working with hotels and spas to provide new kinds of services (for more practical examples, see Hjalager & Konu, 2011). Technological solutions developed for health and fitness can also be adapted to tourism products (e.g., heart rate monitors to support exercise, giving, for example, personal heart rate target zones and displaying calories burned). A few things that should be considered when new services are developed in wellbeing sector are mentioned below:

- Consider diverse market segments in product development (e.g., yoga tourists/spiritual tourists, spa tourists, active tourists motivated by enhancing one's health, not some particular activity, medical tourists, holistic tourists, leisure spa tourists, occupational wellness and well-being tourists, etc.,) and involve your customers in development processes (e.g., in identifying the core concept for products: what the customer feels and wants as an outcome from the product or service).
- Recognize the area's unique selling points its business, and use them in product and service development. Implementation entails the allocation of tangible and intangible resources.
- Consider new partnerships between different industries and suppliers: the tourism industry, the health care industry, the cosmetics industry, the technology industry, etc.
- Lacking a formal process, the concept will suffer from gaps in the structure of formal and informal communication. Without both kinds of communication, marketing will prove difficult. A coherent marketing message built on a product aligned to commonly identified strengths will contribute to successful new service development.

REVIEW QUESTIONS

1. How do you see relevance of presented framework of new service development working in practice as a business activity?
2. How could the local resources and specialities in your area be used in new service development?
3. How do you perceive wellness tourists as a potential target group for the hospitality industry?
4. How would you involve customers in the service development process?

REFERENCES

Alam, I. (2002). An exploratory investigation of user involvement in new service development. *Journal of the Academy of Marketing Science, 30*(3), 250–261.

Alam, I., & Perry, C. (2002). A customer-oriented new service development process. *Journal of Services Marketing, 16*(6), 515–534.

Björk, P., Tuohino, A., & Konu, H. (2011). Wellbeing tourism in Finland—A wide perspective. *Matkailututkimus [Finnish Journal of Tourism Research], 7*(2), 26–41.

Bushell, R., & Sheldon, P. (Eds.), (2009). *Wellness and tourism: Mind, body, spirit and place.* New York: Cognizant.

Cho, Y.-H., & Fesenmaier, D. R. (2001). A new paradigm for tourism and electronic commerce: Experience marketing using the virtual tour. In D. Buhalis & E. Laws (Eds.), *Tourism distribution channels: Practices, issues and transformations.* London: Thomson Learning.

Edvardsson, B., & Olsson, J. (1999). Key concepts for new service development. In C. Lovelock, S. Cnadermerwe, & B. Lewis (Eds.), *Services marketing. A European perspective* (pp. 396–412). Berwick-upon-Tweed, UK: Prentice Hall Europe.

Edvardsson, B., Gustafsson, A., Johnson, M. D., & Sandén, B. (2000). *New service development and innovation in the New Economy.* Lund. Studentlitteratur.

Finnish Tourist Board (FTB). (2011). *Hyvinvointimökit [Wellbeing cottages].* Retrieved from http://www.mek.fi/w5/mekfi/index.nsf/6dbe7db571ccef1cc225678b004e73ed/f01d46aabb eb53aac225790c00385362/$FILE/MEK_Hyvinvointim%C3%B6kit_net_2011.pdf

Grönroos, C. (1993). An applied service marketing theory. European Journal of Marketing. 16(7), 30–41.

Grönroos, C. (2000). Service management and marketing: A customer relationship management approach. Chichester, UK: Wiley.

Gunn, C. (1988). Tourism planning (2nd ed.). New York: Taylor & Francis.

Gunn, C. (1994). *Tourism planning: Basics, concepts, cases.* Washington, DC: Taylor & Francis.

Hall, C. M., Müller, D. K., & Saarinen, J. (2008). *Nordic tourism. Issues and cases.* Bristol, UK: Channel View Publications.

Hjalager, A.-M. (2005). Innovation in tourism from a welfare state perspective. *Scandinavian Journal of Hospitality and Tourism, 5*(1), 46–62.

Hjalager, A.-M. (2010). A review of the innovation research in tourism. *Tourism Management, 31*(1), 1–12.

Hjalager, A.-M. (2011). The invention of a Danish wellbeing tourism region: Strategy, substance, structure, and symbolic action. *Tourism and Hospitality Planning & Development, 8*,(1), 51–67.

Hjalager, A.-M., Huijbens, E. H., Björk, P., Nordin, S., Flagestad, A., & Knútsson, Ö. (2008). *Innovation systems in Nordic tourism.* Oslo: NICe. Retrieved from http://www.nordicinnovation.org/Global/_Publications/Reports/2008/Innovation%20systems%20in%20Nordic%20tourism.pdf

Hjalager, A.-M., & Konu, H. (2011). Co-branding and co-creation in wellness tourism: The role of cosmeceuticals. *Journal of Hospitality Marketing & Management, 20*(8), 879–901.

Hjalager, A.-M., Konu, H., Huijbens, E., Björk, P., Flagestad, A., Nordin, S., & Tuohino, A. (2011, April). *Innovating and re-branding Nordic wellbeing tourism.* (Final report from a joint NICe research project). Retrieved from http://www.nordicinnovation.org/Global/_Publications/Reports/2011/2011_NordicWellbeingTourism_report.pdf.

Hjalager, A.-M., & Nordin, S. (2011). User-driven innovation in tourism—A review of methodologies. *Journal of Quality Assurance in Hospitality & Tourism, 12*(3), 289–315.

Huijbens, E. (2011, April). Developing wellness in Iceland. Theming wellness destinations the Nordic way. *Scandinavian Journal of Hospitality and Tourism, 11*(1), 20–41.

Kangas, H., & Tuohino, A. (2008). Lake wellness—Uusi itäsuomalainen innovaatio? [Lake Wellness – A New Innovation in Eastern Finland] *Matkailututkimus [Finnish Journal of Tourism Research], 4*(1). 23–41.

Kleinke, J. D. (1998). Bleeding edge: The business of health care in the new century. New York: Aspen.

Komppula, R. (2005). Pursuing customer value in tourism: A rural tourism case-study. *Journal of Hospitality & Tourism, 3*(2), 83–104.

Komppula, R., & Boxberg, M. (2002). *Matkailuyrityksen tuotekehitys [Product development in a tourism enterprise].* Helsinki: Edita oyj.

Konu, H., Tuohino, A., & Björk, P. (2011). *Wellbeing tourism in Finland: Finland as a competitive wellbeing tourism destination.* Retrieved from http://epublications.uef.fi/pub/urn_isbn_978-952-61-0585-7/urn_isbn_978-952-61-0585-7.pdf.

Konu, H., Tuohino, A., & Komppula, R. (2010). Lake Wellness—A practical example of a new service development (NSD) concept in tourism industries. *Journal of Vacation Marketing, 16*(2), 125–139.

Korthals, M. (2004). *Before dinner. Philosophy and ethics of food.* Berlin: Springer.

Kotler, P., Bowen, J., & Makens, J. (1999). *Marketing for hospitality and tourism* (2nd ed.). Upper Saddle River, NJ: Prentice-Hall.

Krczal, A., & Weiermair, K. (2006). *Wellness und produktentwicklung. Erfolgreiche gesundheitsangebote im tourismus.* Berlin: Erich Schmidt Verlag.

Lapierre, J. (1997). What does value mean in business-to-business professional services? *International Journal of Service Industry Management, 8*(5), 377–397.

Middleton, V. T. C. (1989). Tourist product. In S. F. Witt & L. Moutinho (Eds.), *Tourism marketing and management handbook.* Hempel Hempstead, UK: Prentice-Hall.

Middleton, V. T. C., & Clarke, J. (2001). Marketing in travel and tourism (3rd cd.). Oxford: Butterworth-Heinemann.

Mossberg, L. (2001). *Upplevelser och marknadsföring [Experiences and Marketing]* Göteborg, Sweden: DocuSys.

Müller, H., & Lanz Kaufmann, E. (2001). Wellness tourism: Market analysis of a special health tourism segment and implications for the hotel industry. *Journal of Vacation Marketing, 7*(1), 5–17.

Murphy, P., Pritchard, M. P., & Smith, B. (2000). The destination product and its impact on traveller perceptions. *Tourism Management, 21*(1), 43–52.

Pine, J., II, & Gilmore, H. H. (1999). *The experience economy: Work is theatre & every business a stage.* Boston: Harvard Business School Press.

Prahalad, C. K., & Santos, J. (2009). *New nature of innovation.* Retrieved from www.new natureofinnovation.org

Sheldon, P., & Bushell, R. (2009). Introduction to wellness and tourism. In R. Bushell, & P. J. Sheldon (Eds.), *Wellness and tourism. Mind, body, spirit, place* (pp. 3–18). New York: Cognizant Communication.

Shostack, G. L. (1977). Breaking free from product marketing. *Journal of Marketing, April*, 73–80.

Smith, M., & Puczkó, L. (2009). *Health and wellness tourism.* Oxford: Butterworth-Heinemann.

Smith, S. (1994). The tourism product. *Annals of Tourism Research, 21*(3), 582–595.

Steinhauser, C., & Theiner, B. (2004). Neue erlebnisse im tourismus. Eine analyse von anbietern und nachfragern bei der touristichen produktentwicklung. Illustriert am fall 'alpine wellness.'[New Experiences in Tourism. Analysis of Buyers and Providers in the Tourism Product Development. Illustrated with case of Alpine Wellness] Ph.D. Dissertation, Universität Innsbruck.

Stevens, E., & Dimitriadis, S. (2005). Managing the new service development process: Towards a systemic model. *European Journal of Marketing. 39*(1/2), 175–198.

Tuohino, A., & Kangas, H. (2009). Hotel Herttua—Spa and rehabilitation centre in Eastern Finland. In M. Smith & L. Puczkó (Eds.), *Health and wellness tourism* (pp. 313–317). Oxford: Butterworth-Heinemann.

Veflen Olsen, N., & Sallis, J. (2006). Market scanning for new service development. *European Journal of Marketing, 40*(5/6), 466–484.

Wiesner, K. A. (2007). *Wellnessmanagement. Angebote, anforderungen, erflogsfaktoren.* [Wellness Management. supply, demand and success factors.]Berlin: Erich Schmidt Verlag.

Woodruff, R. B. (1997). Customer value: The next source for competitive advantage. *Journal of the Academy of Marketing Science, 25*(2), 139–153.

World Health Organization (WHO). (2006). Basic documents: Supplement 2006. New York: Author.

Yeoman, I. (2008). *Tomorrow's tourist: Scenarios and trends (advances in tourism research series)*. Oxford: Elsevier.

Zeithaml, V. A., & Bitner, M. J. (1996). Services marketing. Integrating customer focus across the firm (2nd ed.). Boston: McGraw-Hill Higher Education.

Zeithaml, V. A., Parasuranam, A., & Berry, L. L. (1990). *Delivering quality service: Balancing customer perceptions and expectations*. New York: The Free Press.

Chapter 19

Cross-Cultural Issues in Health and Wellness Services in Estonia

Heli Tooman,
Kai Tomasberg,
Melanie Smith

KEYWORDS

health, wellness, service, cross-cultural, guest, expectations, experience, Estonia

LEARNING OBJECTIVES

Upon completing this chapter, you should be able to do the following:
1. Gain an understanding of the challenges to providing health and wellness services for a range of nationalities.
2. Understand the cultural characteristics that influence the expectations and perceptions of health and wellness guests.
3. Gain awareness of the cross-cultural training needs of employees working in health and wellness services.
4. Learn how to enhance the experience of health and wellness guests.
5. Receive information about how the cross-cultural needs of nationality guests have been catered for in Pärnu, Estonia.

INTRODUCTION

This chapter focuses on the challenges of providing health and wellness services to a range of nationalities at one destination and across a number of facilities. The focus is mainly on spas, wellness, and medical hotels. The first part of the chapter examines the need for cross-cultural understanding in the hospitality industry, especially the training of frontline employees, who usually make the first impression on the customer. Service encounters can be improved immeasurably through better understanding of the needs of guests with different cultural backgrounds. This discussion is followed by an analysis of the health and wellness industries, where there has been a globalization of product development and service provision. However, we argue that customers increasingly expect or demand unique and tailored packages at spas and wellness hotels, which may take the form of signature treatments or local, culturally specific products. It is also important to note that guests' expectations differ significantly according to the health and wellness traditions and customs of their country, as well as their cultural background. The latter part of the chapter takes a case study of Estonia and the town of Pärnu to illustrate many of the issues raised in the first part of the chapter.

ENHANCING SERVICE QUALITY THROUGH CROSS-CULTURAL UNDERSTANDING

Although there have been almost 40 years of work on cross-cultural issues and training needs in the hospitality industry, new patterns of mobility, travel, immigration, and labor have necessitated the industry continually re-thinking its approach. There have been considerable developments in cross-cultural training for ex-patriate managers or students going on international placements, as well as for managing a culturally diverse workforce (Devine, Baum, & Hearns, 2009), but surprisingly little on training frontline employees who deal with customers on a daily basis (Shapero, 2006). Frontline staff are usually those who make the initial and often lasting impression on guests. Katriel (1995) suggests that international visitors expect staff to understand their different cultural needs and values. Mallinson & Weiler (2000) state that the cross-cultural awareness and skills of hospitality and tourism staff are an increasingly important aspect of guest service and satisfaction. The researchers suggest that frontline service staff should be able to anticipate and "read"' guests' verbal and nonverbal communication styles.

Sizoo, Plank, Iskat, and Serrie (2005) describe how employees with high intercultural sensitivity scored significantly higher than employees with low intercultural sensitivity in terms of service attentiveness, revenue contribution, interpersonal skills, job satisfaction, and social satisfaction. Sizoo et al. suggest that training can help, but many hotels do not offer intercultural training for staff as it is too expensive. Mallinson and Weiler (2000) suggest that hotel managers generally pay lipservice to the notion of cross-cultural awareness or they assume that language study rather than cross-cultural awareness training is what staff need. Nevertheless, Mallinson and Weiler also state that employees in their research showed a genuine interest in addressing cross-cultural issues in their workplace. As stated by Frase (2007, p. 98)

Companies who want to expand into the international market will have to elevate their familiarity with other customs and languages, and their newfound cross-cultural awareness will have to permeate not only corporate ranks but all the levels below.

Numerous trainers and consultants use varied methods to instill cross-cultural awareness in their staff. Many models are based on leadership, doing cross-cultural business and marketing, and adapting to working in a foreign environment (e.g., Harzing & Ruysseveldt, 2004), but other models are needed for those who have to provide service to different nationalities. Several sources deal with Asian/American or Asian/European encounters (e.g., Mohsin, 2006), but fewer on inter-European encounters, which vary considerably (e.g., between Eastern and Western Europeans).

Employees need to understand a culture's core values, which Harris (2004) suggests can include a sense of space and self, dress, food, religion, attitudes, and relationships. One of the difficulties is that many elements of culture are not immediately obvious. Shay and Tracey (1997) distinguish between subjective and objective cultural characteristics, the former being the values and beliefs that influence guest behavior, whereas the latter is what is visible and tangible. For example, if a woman wearing a Hijab and looking Middle Eastern comes into a hotel reception, the employees would most likely assume that she is Muslim and they could guess what she may or may not eat and that she would not disrobe in a public spa. If a Norwegian guy wearing a T-shirt comes into the reception, the staff may guess that he is European. They may even guess that he comes from Scandinavia if they hear the language, but their ears may not be fine tuned enough to guess whether he is Danish, Swedish, or Norwegian. Other clues may be needed before staff can even engage in cross-cultural sensitivity or certain questions may need to be asked of the guest.

A certain degree of improvization is needed when providing service to a wide range of nationalities and to respond to both visual and verbal cues. Using a second language already requires something of a cultural as well as a linguistic shift. Staff may find themselves switching languages and engaging different aspects of cross-cultural knowledge several times a day, sometimes in new or unanticipated situations. Tight scripting is an impossibility in spontaneous service encounters; therefore, as research has acknowledged, services are essentially performances (e.g., Grove & Fisk, 1983). Joby, Grove, and Fisk (2006) use the analogy of jazz improvization to suggest that empathetic and responsive service needs to be performed in the moment, to be creative and inventive, to deal with unique or unusual requests, and ideally is delivered with a degree of joy. Although each staff member may give a solo performance, it is also possible to harmonize the ensemble. For example, the extensive cultural and linguistic knowledge required to serve several nationalities is present within the organization, but it is not expected that one person will deliver that performance all the time. This would be unrealistic and far too challenging.

The now-well-known theories of Hofstede (1984) are often used to identify the cultural characteristics of specific societies. The same is true of Trompenaars (1993), who developed a model with seven dimensions of culture. This chapter mainly deals with Estonian culture, as well as the culture(s) of the majority of the health and wellness tourists and guests in Estonia. These tourists tend to come from Scandinavia, Finland, Russia, and the other Baltic States of Latvia and Lithuania. According to Hofstede and Trompenaars, Scandinavian countries have many similarities (e.g., low power distance, high feminity, low uncertainty avoidance). Huettinger's (2008) study of the cultural dimensions of the Baltic States (Estonia, Latvia, and Lithuania) using Hofstede's indices showed that the three countries score nearly uniformly and are more similar to Scandinavia than to Russia or Poland. He recommends that international business actors should therefore include the Baltics in their Nordic strategy rather than adding them to Central and Eastern Europe. However, it is often said that Estonia is closer in culture to Scandinavia than to Latvian or Lithuanian cultures. For example, Mockaitis (2005) compares Poland to the three Baltic States and concludes that Estonia scored the lowest on power distance, uncertainty avoidance, and masculinity, while Poland scored the highest and Lithuania is in between. In Estonia, relationships are less formal based on interdependence and trust, and Estonia's low masculinity is characterized by cooperation and consensus.

The concept of Servicescape (Bitner, 1992; Kotler, 1974) should also be considered, as the culture of a country or destination may influence numerous elements of the physical environment, as well as more intangible aspects. Consider, for example, the way in which design varies from country to country. Many buildings in China would not be designed without considering the Feng Shui concept; the same is true in India with Vasati. Although energy flows are intangible, they can greatly influence physical design. Japanese designers tend toward a Zen approach. This may be similar to Scandinavians who favor simple, clean designs, natural materials, and neutral colours. On the other hand, Middle Eastern cultures may prefer more opulent décors. Muslims may request that the entire facility follows "'halal'" specifications (e.g., some of the new spa developments in the United Arab Emirates).

The trend in many spas and wellness facilities at present tends to be toward Asian style, often with Buddha statues, burning incense, and ambient music. However, such a style may not be to all guests' tastes and it may be culturally inappropriate for the location, especially if guests are seeking a local experience. What an ideal atmosphere should be is difficult to ascertain, especially one that is acceptable or attractive to multiple nationalities. Color, lighting, music, olfaction, and temperature are all key to creating the optimum Servicescape. However, colors symbolize different things in different cultures (e.g., white in Western spas may be calm and relaxing, whereas white is the color of death and mourning in Asia). Cross-cultural considerations arguably need to be combined with environmental psychology (Mehrabian & Russell, 1974) to create the ideal wellness experience. Puczkó (2011) suggests that more research is needed on questions of interpretation, experience creation, and applied psychology in spa demand, as customers react differently to the same Servicescape. He makes the important point that interior designers are not psychologists and that interior design does not equal experience creation. He uses the example of a medical spa hotel in Pärnu, Estonia, where there are needle-shaped lamps in the waiting area to suggest that Servicescapes can sometimes be too direct in their reference to their core services!

CUSTOMER EXPECTATIONS AND EXPERIENCES IN THE HEALTH AND WELLNESS INDUSTRY

In recent years, the health and wellness industries have become more globalized, and with this has come a certain degree of standardization of product development and service. For example, the majority of spas and wellness hotels in Estonia offer a similar massage menu, with old favorites such as "'Swedish'" and "Aromatherapy," coupled with more exotic offers such as "'Lomi Lomi'" or "'Ayurvedic','" but there is often no connection to the country's culture and even less to the locality. However, a growing trend exists that provides more customized treatments for health and wellness guests that are tailored to their individual needs. Indeed, the Global Spa Summit (2011) report on Wellness Tourism noted that there is a new trend of consumers looking for local, traditional, and unique experiences and recommended there be an emphasis placed on national or regional specialisms and signature treatments.

The customer experience can also be enhanced if health and wellness facilities are aware of guests' likely expectations and attitudes to products and treatments. Much of this may be derived from their cultural background and social conditioning. For example, visitors from Central and Eastern Europe or the Baltic States are familiar with medical spas based on healing waters, where treatments tend to be curative for specific physical conditions. They may seek out a medical practitioner for a consultation, or expect some kind of medical supervision during their stay. Visitors from Western Europe are more likely to want beauty, pampering, and luxury from their spas, and might be upset to find a hospital or clinic-like atmosphere, décor, or even smell at a wellness facility. They are unlikely to seek out medical services and may instead look for body-mind-spirit or stress management programs. Nordic visitors may be more attracted to outdoor recreation and nature, and simple, functional, but clean facilities. A facility like a sauna does not necessarily represent something unique or special as this is an everyday activity, especially for Finns.

Many of the cultural preferences may be linked to Hofstede's or other, similar cultural indices. For example, Hall and Hall's (1990) model mentions Monochronic and Polychronic cultures. Monochronic cultures make a sharp division between work and personal life, which is typical of many Western countries. This means they may not want to associate with business contacts in a spa, for example. The idea of mixing men and women may be culturally unacceptable in those countries that are especially "'masculine'," whereas more "'feminine'" cultures such as Scandinavian or Germanic cultures, are generally comfortable with this. The issue of nudity in spas generally (even where men and women are segregated) is a difficult one. Many nationalities are uncomfortable with nudity, especially in mixed gender facilities (e.g., Asians, Middle Easterners, Americans), whereas other nationalities expect or even demand it (e.g., Germans, Austrians). More individualistic cultures may like to visit spas alone and expect silence (e.g., Northern and Western Europeans), whereas more collective or communitarian cultures may like to socialize within a group or even party in a spa (e.g., Southern Europeans, Russians). There may also be food preferences depending on religion or culture (e.g., kosher, halal, vegetarian). This means that providing suitable services to meet all customer expectations in health tourism destinations, resorts and hotels is challenging.

The relationship _among_ customers is also an important issue, as the attraction of diverse and sometimes incompatible guests can be a significant challenge. Grove & Fisk's (1997) research analyzes the negative effects that other customers' presence and behavior can have on satisfaction levels, as they impact on the "'interactive dimension'" of service quality. They note that this is especially exacerbated by differences in nationality or age. Rather than concluding, as did the philosopher Sartre, that "'Hell is other people'," organizations must manage interclient relations and conflict adequately and appropriately. This may be difficult if the exact nature of the conflict is poorly understood (e.g., the differing cultural needs and expectations of guests). Spas and wellness facilities are intimate servicescapes where interpersonal interaction occurs in proximity. Although Grove and Fisk (1997) conclude that satisfying all customers with the same service delivery is virtually impossible, it may be possible to engage in various processes that harmonize social interaction. This could include more careful monitoring of customers' compatibility, not mixing known incompatible groups in the same spaces, providing clear guidelines for appropriate behavior, explaining different culturally defined protocols, or even employing humorous or theatrical techniques of distraction and entertainment.

Health and Wellness Services in Estonia

Estonia is the smallest and northernmost of the three Baltic states. The Estonian Republic was declared on February 24, 1918. During World War II, Estonia lost its independence and was occupied for several decades until independence was re-established on August 20, 1991. Estonia became an EU member state in May 2004, in December 2007 joined the Schengen visa area, and joined the Euro in 2011. Despite its small size Estonia's geography and culture are surprisingly varied. About 40 percent of Estonia is covered by natural forests, the 3794-kilometer coastline is dotted with approximately 1,500 coastal islands, and there are numerous lakes, wetlands, and swamps. Historic traditions, culture, and buildings are well preserved, and the medieval old town of the capital Tallinn is on the UNESCO World Heritage list.

The beginning of Estonia's tourism industry goes back to the mid-19th century when a number of holiday and curative resorts were established. Today, spa holidays are one of the most sizable tourism products to be offered year round. One reason such resorts developed here was the local mud, famed for its therapeutic qualities and which continues to be used today. There were periods when vacationers came from Germany and Russia (mainly from Moscow and Leningrad). Today's visitors come primarily from Scandinavia, but increasing numbers of Americans, Japanese, and Southern Europeans are also visiting. Estonian spas are designed to inspire guests from anywhere in the world (Source, 2010).

No other country has as many spa hotels per capita as Estonia, at more than 40. Spas' popularity is a reflection of the developments in Estonia's health tourism, and the sheer number of spas indicates that their popularity is still growing (Estonian Spa, 2011). However, Estonia is a little-known tourism destination, it faces a challenge in promoting itself as a health and wellness holiday destination that offers visitors pure and untouched nature, fresh air, silence, and cleanliness amidst European civilization and spas of international quality at the same time ("'Introduce Estonia'", 2008; Source, 2010; Tooman, 2010).

The Estonian SPA Association implemented a quality system for medical spa hotels in 2008, which was extended to wellness spas and centers in 2012. The initial objective of most spas was to treat medical conditions, but many spas are now moving from care centers to recreation centers, for example, for sports and leisure. (Tooman, Viin, 2010; Estonian Spas, 2012).

Table 19.1 shows that 2008–2010 were difficult years for Estonian spas, but 2011 was more successful. Although the total number of visitors is rising again, the average length of stay has decreased every year. While the percentage of Finnish visitors is down about 10 percent from 2006, the percentage of Russian visitors is more than three times higher than it was 6 years ago. The Latvian market is also a growing market, and Estonian spas have many one-day visitors from Latvia, especially to Pärnu, because it takes fewer than 2 hours by car to reach Pärnu from the Latvian capital Riga. At the same time, the spa management is worried about the decreasing number of visitors from Sweden (70,885 in 2006 compared to 43,652 in 2011) and Norway (30,555 in 2006 compared to 13,488 in 2011), especially affecting the spas in Pärnu. Serious research is necessary to find out the reasons for that.

Table 19.1	Statistical Data of the Member Spas of the Estonian SPA Association.					
	2006	2007	2008	2009	2010	2011
Average occupancy rate (by %)	72.9	66.2	64.6	59.9	65.8	67.1
Lengths of stay (in days)	3.7	3.5	3.4	2.9	2.8	2.7
Annual Visitors	993,284	958,419	875,224	785,373	856,123	938,921
Visitors from (% of total):						
Estonia	28.59	33.05	32.21	34.49	32.88	32.87
Finland	55.05	52.11	52.41	49.28	49.22	45.03
Sweden	7.13	6.44	6.03	5.39	4.79	4.65
Norway	3.08	2.82	2.47	2.24	1.62	1.44
Germany	0.71	0.48	0.60	0.68	0.81	0.83
Latvia	0.10	0.18	0.83	1.47	1.33	1.76
Russia	3.11	2.61	3.42	4.64	7.39	10.97
Other	0.45	0.58	0.20	0.67	0.61	0.88

Source: Estonian SPA Association, 2012.

HEALTH AND WELLNESS TOURISM IN PÄRNU

In 1838 Pärnu's first bathing house opened its doors, and the health resort was founded in 1890, when Pärnu was entered onto the official list of Russia's imperial health resorts. An 1889 plan led to the development of high-quality resort facilities such as parks, boulevards, and entertainment. Reconstruction of the bathing establishments was undertaken and the treatments offered were diverse and modern, meeting the highest international requirements (Kask, 2007). World War I brought a temporary halt to the resort's activities, and in 1915 a fire destroyed the bathing establishments. However, between World War I and II, interest in Pärnu grew quickly, especially among Swedish tourists.

As a result of revolutionary events in the summer of 1940, management of the Pärnu resort became part of the Soviet Union Central Council of Trade Unions. In 1945 the planning and building of a new network of sanatoria and holiday houses started and in 1946–1948 Pärnu developed into an all-union sanatorial health resort operating year round. The number of people undergoing treatments from Estonia and from all over the Soviet Union grew quickly. In Estonia, scientific research work in the field of balneology started in 1957, and since 1960, the resort has consisted of three specialized balneo mud-treatment sanatoria (Estonia, Sõprus, and Rahu), a mud bath establishment, and a club (the beach salon). In 1971 a new sanatorium, Tervis, opened. In the 1980s the Pärnu sanatoria received about 25,000 health visitors annually and the total number of tourists visiting Pärnu was about 300,000 (Kask, 2007; Veinpalu & Veinpalu, 1988).

In 1990–1991 the eastern market, that is, the spa tourists and holidaymakers from the former Soviet Union, decreased due to political circumstances. Inevitably it was necessary to reorient to new, nearby, foreign markets in Finland, Sweden, Latvia, etc. In 1996 Pärnu was granted the significant title of the Summer Capital of Estonia (Kask, 2007; Pärnumaa, 2011). Today Pärnu is Estonia's largest and most-visited resort. The town enjoys a perfect location, a shallow bay and sandy beach, fresh sea air, large green spaces, and good-quality health and wellness services that guarantee high visitor numbers. Modern spa hotels and centers have numerous treatments and facilities: saunas, massages, salt chambers, and treatments with mud, water, paraffin, chocolate, and laser, to name a few of the amenities. For the more adventurous there is a "freezing hug" at minus 100 degrees Centigrade in the cold chamber. Pärnu's modern spa hotels include Estonia Medical Spa Hotel, Tervis Medical Spa, Tervise Paradiis Spa Hotel and Water Park, Viiking SPA Hotel, Sõprus Medical SPA & Hotel, Strand SPA & Conference Hotel. These spa hotels employ more than 600 people year-round and can accommodate more than 2,000 visitors per day (Health holiday in Pärnu, 2012). According to the Statistical Council (Statistikaamet, 2012), overnight stays have increased 1.7 percent to a total of 635,111 in 2011, compared to 624,434 in 2010 and 573,482 in 2009. No separate statistics about spa visits to Pärnu are available.

CROSS-CULTURAL ISSUES IN PÄRNU

The largest number of guests to Pärnu's spas come from Finland and other regions of Estonia, and the number of visitors from Russia and Latvia is rising. Despite promoting Pärnu as a spa destination in Sweden, the number of Swedish guests has decreased significantly. The same can be said of guests from Norway. Few visitors come to Pärnu from other European countries, although there have been visitors from "long-haul" countries such as the United States, Australia, and even China.

To answer questions about the expectations and needs of guests coming from foreign countries, interviews were organized in January 2012 with spa managers and marketing managers from the following Pärnu spas: Tervis Medical Spa, Tervise Paradiis Spa Hotel and Water Park, Viiking Spa Hotel, Medical Spa Hotel Estonia, and Strand Spa and Conference Hotel. The objectives of the survey were to: (1) identify the main target groups of visitors to Pärnu spas; (2) define the behavior of the spa guests and differences according to their cultural background; and (3) analyse the results and show the importance of these issues and the impact on the overall satisfaction of visitors using the spa services.

The Finns form the largest group of visitors who come regularly to Pärnu spas. They are older people, over age 60, and they need medical care. Organized groups from Finland with fixed packages of treatments (usually three per day) and doctors' appointments. The group stays 3–4 nights, uses facilities of the spa, massages, water gymnastics, a variety of baths, saunas, paraffin, as well as manicure, pedicure, and hair dressers. No less important is socializing with other group members and hotel guests. Cultural programs with singers, Romany music and dances organized with food and alcohol, and karaoke and bingo nights are popular. The groups have regular trips to shopping centres and to local traditional events such as weddings and pork-eating evenings. The Finns like to receive the same service every time they come to Pärnu. Price changes are not well received. The service in spas is provided in Finnish, which they appreciate. They like a simple, friendly, and warm welcome, a "personal touch," and constant attention from the staff. This attention is rewarded with small gifts and a sincere "thank you" on their departure. The Finns return each year and like to find the same people welcoming them. Fluent Finnish is required of each spa specialist and staff members; even the cleaning staff must understand the language.

The Swedes usually travel alone or as a couple, as opposing to coming in a group. They are demanding guests who expect a high standard of service. They often choose medical treatments if they are elderly. They like massages and baths, but also enjoy outdoor activities and walking tours in the town. They are passionate nature lovers, but also interested in culture and history, attending local concerts and visiting exhibitions. The Swedes pay more attention to comfort and service quality, but give little feedback. They prefer to keep their distance from other guests. Swedish language is required, even though Swedes speak English well, as do Estonian staff. The level of Swedish language among the spa staff is insufficient and sometimes because of that the contact with Swedish guests remains superficial.

Russia and Latvia are growing markets, and spas try to attract visitors from those countries to stay longer in Pärnu. Usually these visitors come only for a weekend or a couple of days. Russians are generous clients, who want to spend money during the holiday. Even if they receive some medical treatments, they prefer a relaxing stay and beauty care. The saunas, water pools, and Jacuzzis are their favorites. The Russians like to spend holidays in Pärnu, and the most popular time is New Year's Eve, when there are special concerts organized at the spas. The singers and groups are usually Russians. The Russians like company; they enjoy parties and social evenings with alcohol and loud music. It can be difficult for a spa to organize a party that meets the interests and tastes of both Russians and Finns. The decision is often made according to the majority of guests, or there will be neutral background music and no performers. It can bring disappointment and complaints from the guests who wanted a livelier evening. This is an example of where the theories of Grove & Fisk (1997) could prove useful in better managing guest compatibility.

The Latvians resemble Russians in the way they enjoy their holidays and spend money. Both nationalities are interested in details of the services and products they purchse and ask for descriptions of the treatments. They often prefer wellness services over medical cures. Russian is the second foreign language for the staff, and Latvians often prefer English even though they usually speak and understand Russian well.

Pärnu's spas focus on the main customers from Finland offering traditional medical services and products. However, each spa wants to meet new challenges and develop unique and attractive services. Despite financial difficulties the spas are building swimming pools and beauty centers and they are renovating hotel rooms and relaxation areas to attract new markets and wellness guests. The spas are adding services to the traditional list of treatments, which are often internationally recognized and known. Few spas have had the courage to present "signature treatments" using local ingredients; however, the traditional therapeutic mud is gaining an exotic reputation among visitors from faraway counties such as China.

One important final point is that young people—no matter what nationality—have different needs and interests. To attract them the spas offer wellness and holiday packages with healthy food, relaxation and beauty treatments, saunas, and water-based services. Young people ask for higher quality in every spa service. They do not like to see a doctor but actively use personal consultation on nutrition and physical activities. In summer many visitors use spas only for accommodation and breakfast, spending the rest of the day on the beach. Many families come to Pärnu because of the secure and clean environment. Puczkó (2011) noted that the Tervis Paradiis Spa in Pärnu does a good job of attracting first-time spa users with a special package for children, which is advertised in the elevator of the adjacent hotel. However, managing different age groups simultaneously in one destination or facility is challenging (Grove & Fisk, 1997), and this is especially true of health and wellness facilities. Many older people with medical needs do not want to be disturbed by young people and children, and conversely, healthy young people do not want to be surrounded by sick people.

CONCLUSIONS

The research shows that spa destinations and resorts, including Pärnu, must become increasingly sensitive to cross-cultural issues, especially those when customers from new markets are arriving (e.g., Chinese) and established markets are declining (e.g., Swedes). Spa managers have indicated during interviews their awareness of the cultural background, language, needs, and expectations of the largest group of spa guests (Finns), and stated that their staff is also trained. The spas organize regular training courses for staff to improve their proficiency with Finnish as well as English, Swedish, and Russian. Knowledge of these languages is an important requirement when recruiting new staff. However, the research shows that new visitors are coming to Pärnu and the need is growing for languages such as German and French, and even Mandarin. The rising number of Latvian guests shows a demand for the Latvian language, but as English is widely spoken in both countries the Latvian language is not the first priority in the Pärnu spas.

Despite the efforts to attract guests from Sweden, the number of visitors has decreased. In the summer of 2011, direct flights were established between Pärnu and Sweden, but as they were not regular, they were of little help in bringing more Swedes to the spas. Swedish guests value a high quality of service and are more oriented toward wellness and cultural experiences. They also expect to be addressed in their native language, which is not always possible. The need for personal care and separation from group visitors may be one reason Swedish guests avoid the crowded spas. It is also important to note that the needs and expectations of other nationalities may change according to fashions, trends, or lifestyle issues. Spas cannot afford to assume that they know a market or culture so well that they need not stay alert and informed. Given the rapidly changing nature of the markets and cross-cultural needs, the ability to improvise in service performance as outlined by Joby et al. (2006) is essential.

Overall, the pilot research in Estonia clearly shows a need for further research into cross-cultural issues in spas. Flexibility, excellent customer service, a high level of foreign language knowledge, and sensitivity to and understanding of cultural differences may be a strong advantage for a spa in remaining competitive and attracting new visitors. Spas must design services and promote them to new markets, work with guests' needs, and arrange cultural evenings and other events in spa areas. These form important elements of the Servicescape, as discussed by Bitner (1992) and others. However, the needs of spa guests of varying nationalities staying at the same time may be incompatible (e.g., Russians and Finns), so measures need to be taken to manage and improve compatibility (Grove & Fisk, 1997). Interestingly, spa guests are showing an interest in original local products as well as "signature treatments" but, at the same time, are afraid to try them! This is an interesting challenge for spas: to find ways to introduce local products to other cultures. Finally, it is important to note that other factors such as age and gender may play an equally important role, as shown in the case of young people in Pärnu, who have similar needs regardless of nationality.

REVIEW QUESTIONS

- Discuss the usefulness of the cross-cultural theories of Hofstede and Trompenaars for understanding the cultural characteristics of spa guests of different nationalities.

- What are the main training needs for employees who want to improve their cross-cultural understanding of guests of different nationalities and to provide better service?
- Assess the ways in which conflicts among guests of differing nationalities at a single location can be managed or resolved.
- Evaluate the special needs of health, wellness, and spa guests compared to other guests.
- Discuss to what extent service should be based on improvization rather than standardization.

REFERENCES

Bitner, M. J. (1992). Servicescape: The impact of physical surroundings on customers and employees. *Journal of Marketing*, 56, 57–71.

Devine, F., Baum, T., & Hearns, N. (2009). Resource guide: Cultural awareness for hospitality and tourism. *Hospitality, Leisure, Sport and Tourism Network*. Retrieved from http://www.heacademy.ac.uk/assets/hlst/documents/resource_guides/cultural_awareness_hosp_tourism.pdf.

Retrieved from http://www.eas.ee.

Estonian SPA Association. (2012). Retrieved from http://www.estonianspas.eu.

Frase, M. (2007). Show all employees a wider world. *HR Magazine, 6*(52), 98–112.

Global Spa Summit (GSS). (2011). *Wellness tourism and medical tourism: Where do spas fit?* New York: Author.

Grove, S. J., & Fisk, R. P. (1983). The dramaturgy of services exchange: An analytical framework for services marketing. In L. L. Berry, G. L. Shostack, & G. D. Upah (Eds.), *Emerging perspectives on services marketing* (pp. 45–49). Chicago: American Marketing Association.

Grove, S. J., & Fisk, R. P. (1997). The impact of other customers on service experiences: A critical incident examination of 'getting along.' *Journal of Retailing, 73*(1), 63–85.

Hall, E., & Hall, M. (1990). *Understanding cultural differences.* New York: Intercultural Press.

Harris, P. R. (2004). Success in the European Union depends upon culture and business. *European Business Review, 16*(6), 556–563.

Harzing, A., & Ruysseveldt, J. (2004). *International human resource management.* London: SAGE Publications.

Hofstede, G. (1984). *Culture's consequences: International differences in work-related values.* London: SAGE Publications.

Huettinger, M. (2008). Cultural dimensions in business life: Hofstede's indices for Latvia and Lithuania. *Baltic Journal of Management, 3*(3), 359–376.

'Introduce Estonia' Brand Manual. (2009). Retrieved from http://tutvustaeestit.eas/en.

Joby, J., Grove, S. J., & Fisk, R. P. (2006). Inprovisation in service performances: Lessons from jazz. *Managing Service Quality, 16*(3), 247–268.

Kask, T. (2007). *Pärnu from fortress town to health resort town.* Pärnu: Pärnu City.

Katriel, T. (1995). From context to contexts. In R. L. Wiseman (Ed.), *Intercultural communication research* (pp. 271–284). Thousand Oaks, CA: SAGE Publications.

Kotler, P. (1974). Atmospherics as a marketing tool. *Journal of Retailing, 49*(Winter), 48–64.

Mallinson, H., & Weiler, B. (2000). Cross-cultural awareness of hospitality staff: An evaluation of a pilot training program. *Australian Journal of Hospitality Management, 7*(1), 35–44.

Mehrabian, A., & Russell J. A. (1974). *An approach to environmental psychology.* Cambridge, MA: The MIT Press.

Mockaitis, A. I. (2005). A cross-cultural study of leadership attitudes in Three Baltic Sea region countries. *Journal of Leadership Studies, 1*(1). Retrieved from http://www.regent. edu/acad/global/publications/ijls/new/vol1iss1/mockaitis/cross_cultural.htm.

Mohsin, A. (2006, May 8–9). Cross-cultural sensitivities in hospitality: A matter of conflict or understanding. Paper presented at the International Conference on Excellence in the Home: Balanced Diet—Balanced Life. London.

Pärnumaa Turism Foundation. (2011). *Pärnu.* Author and Pärnu City Government.

Puczkó, L. (2011). Customer experiences. *Spa Australasia, 48*, 26–28.

Shapero, M. A. (2006). *Cross-cultural training for hospitality and tourism: Improving service encounters through industry-targeted critical incidents.* Retrieved from http://www. eckerd.edu/academics/internationalbusiness/files/shapero_summer_06.pdf.

Shay, J., & Tracey, J. (1997). Expatriate managers: Reasons for failure and implications for training. *Cornell Hotel and Restaurant Administration Quarterly, 38*(1), 30–35.

Sizoo, S., Plank, R., Iskat, W., & Serrie, H. (2005). The effect of intercultural sensitivity on employee performance in cross-cultural service encounters. *The Journal of Services Marketing, 19*(4), 245–255.

Source of Vital Energy (A). (2010). *Wellness holidays in Estonia.* Tallinn: Enterprise Estonia and Estonia Tourist Board.

Health holiday in Pärnu. (2012). Pärnu City Government. Retrieved from http:// www.visitparnu.com/en/visitor/spa-holiday.

Statistikaamet (2012). Retrieved from http://www.stat.ee.

Tooman, H. (2010, September 27–28). Developing the image of the destination as a wellness holiday destination: The case of Estonia. *Tourism and Quality of Life Proceedings,* Slovenia, Portorož pp. 465–476.

Tooman, H., & Viin, T. (2010, September 1–3). Developing quality criteria for spa and wellness hotels: The case of Estonia. In L. Puczkó (Ed.), *Health, wellness and tourism: Healthy tourists, healthy business?* (pp. 350–359).

Trompenaars, F. (1993). *Riding the waves of culture: Understanding cultural diversity in business.* Avon, UK: Bath Press.

Veinpalu, E., & Veinpalu, L. (1988). *Pärnu kuurort 150 (Pärnu Resort 150).* Tallinn: Valgus.

Melanie Smith (PhD), Associate Professor, College of Commerce, Catering and Tourism, Budapest Business School, 9-11 Alkotmány Utca, 1054 Budapest, Hungary Tel: (0036) 204624443 Email: Melanie.Smith@kvifk.bgf.hu

Chapter 20

Ayurveda

Anupama Kothari

LEARNING OBJECTIVES

Upon completing this chapter, you should be able to do the following:

1. Understand ayurveda as a system of medicine.

2. Understand the evolution of ayurveda in the context of historical changes.

3. Explore factors that inhibited the development of ayurveda as a system of medicine.

4. Understand the revival of Ayurveda.

5. Explore the co-existence of ayurveda with other systems of medicine.

KEYWORDS

Ayurveda, patient-centered care, nontraditional medicine, alternative therapies, holistic health care

Medicine as we know it finds its origins in the West. The Greek scholar Hippocrates is often called the Father of Medicine. Literature from England (the Victorian era) is replete with accounts of surgeries and bloodletting (to treat gout). However, in the early 19th century, a German homeopath, Dr. Samuel Hahnemann, began the practice of referring to Western medicine as allopathy. *Allopathy*, by definition, implies treatment by producing effects opposite from symptoms. As documented by Bradford (1895), Dr. Hahneman began his career as a practitioner of traditional Western medicine (or "allopathic medicine," as he would later refer to it). But he soon gave up his practice as a doctor, as he believed that allopathic medicines exerted brute force and were dangerous to patient well-being (Bradford, 1895). Extant research (Cook, 1981) notes that while exploring the use of plants to produce medicines, Dr. Hahneman chanced upon a tree bark known to treat malaria. He studied the tree bark and found that it produced malaria-like symptoms in healthy individuals. He postulated that a substance that produces disease symptoms in a healthy individual could cure the same symptoms in a sick individual. Based on the idea of "like curing like," he proposed an alternative form of medicine that he called *homeopathy* (*homeo* meaning similar or like).

The debate between the efficacy of allopathy versus homeopathy raged in the West in the 19th century. However, in the East, alternative medicine was not a new concept. Much of the Eastern world, including Egypt, China, and India, has practiced forms of alternative medicine since the Iron Age. Particularly, in India, ancient texts such as the *Samhitas* (6th century BCE) refers to a system of medicine: ayurveda (Thacker 2010). Translated loosely, means the science or knowledge of life. Although the earliest references to ayurveda date to the *Samhitas*, it is possible that ayurveda was been in existence even earlier. Other ancient Indian texts such as the *Rig Veda*, dating to 1000 BCE refer to the use and knowledge of medicine, albeit not under the term ayurveda (Varier, 2002). Ancient Indian society primarily sustained itself on agriculture and cattle rearing. Wars and conflicts were often the result of attempting to protect land and cattle from others. These battles frequently led to a large number of casualties. Hence, early Indian medicine revolved around treating battle wounds, as evident in ancient scholarly works such as the *Rig Veda* that refer to grafting and amputation (Varier, 2002).

In later years, Indian society evolved to encompass occupations other than cattle rearing, including traders, scholars, and artisans. This gradually evolved into India's infamous caste system. Conceived originally as a way to divide society based on occupations in order to promote harmony and excellence in each occupation, the caste system soon evolved into a rigorous hierarchy. Movement between castes was no longer permitted. Hence, a person born into a family of scholars would become a scholar, and one born into a family of traders would become a trader. Birth, not aptitude, determined caste. In descending order of hierarchy (Ambedkar, 1946), the four main castes were: the Brahmins (scholars), Kshatriyas (warriors), Vaishyas (traders), and Shudras (menials). Each caste was further divided into subcastes. Knowledge and all resources concerning knowledge were limited to the Brahmin caste in their role as scholars.

The elaborate caste system crippled knowledge development in Indian society in many fields. Ayurveda escaped stagnation due to the concurrent rise of two religions: Buddhism and Jainism (Varier, 2002). Based on their common founding principles of *karuna* (compassion) and *ahimsa* (nonviolence), Buddhism and Jainism sought to remove suffering and provide medical care to Indians. This led to the spread of ayurveda throughout India and even to parts of Asia such as China (through Buddhist monks). It is noteworthy, that through Buddhism and Jainism ayurveda expanded to include veterinary medicine for horses (*asvayurveda*) and elephants (*hastyayurveda*) (Varier, 2002).

As documented by Varier (2002), between the 6th and the 8th centuries CE, fierce regionalization in India led to ayurveda being practiced separately and uniquely in each region. At this point, the elite used ayurveda to pursue hedonistic pleasures, resulting in works such as the *Kamasutra (Varier 2002)*. On the whole, ayurveda flourished despite being confined to unique regional practices (Varier 2002).

For several years, Europe traded with India and China by a land route, the famous Silk Road. In 1453, the Ottoman Turks took over Constantinople, an important city on the

Silk Road and made the land journey for traders difficult. Much of Europe devoted itself to finding an alternate sea route. Capturing this spirit, two explorers determined to find a sea route to India set out from their home countries of Spain and Portugal. In 1492, the explorer for Spain, Christopher Columbus (of Genoa, Italy) stumbled on land that he mistook for India (turning out, in the course of history, to be the Caribbean islands). In 1498, the Portuguese navigator Vasco de Gama landed in India, marking the advent of Indian colonization.

Ayurveda flourished in the initial stages of colonization. Portuguese apothecary Garcia de Orta devoted himself to learning the tenets of ayurvedic medicine and published his findings in his book *Colloquies on the Simples and Drugs of Hindoostan* (Varier, 2002). However, the rise of British Empire marked the fall of ayurveda. The British introduced modern (allopathic) medicine to India and branded the local system of ayurveda as "unscientific and superstitious" (Varier 2002). Ayurveda declined unable to compete with Western medicine.

The latter part of the 19th century was characterized by efforts to revive ayurveda and traditional medicine in India. In 1884, N. N. Sen & Company began to produce medicines on a large scale in India, followed by C. K. Sen & Company and Shakti Aushadalaya (Krishnankutty, 2001; Panikkar, 1995). However, the revival of ayurveda truly began in 1902, when Dr. P. S. Varier, a young ayurvedic physician, established the Arya Vaidyasala in the town of Kottakal.

Dr. Varier attributed the decline of ayurveda and popularity of Western medicine to the widespread availability of Western medicines (Krishnankutty, 2001). In contrast, ayurvedic medicines were characterized by low availability because they were prepared by individual physicians with rare and often difficult-to-source ingredients. Dr. Varier sought to remedy this by establishing a manufacturing facility where commonly used ayurvedic medicines would be regularly available (Krishnankutty, 2001; Varier, 2002). In an unprecedented step, Dr. Varier also established stringent quality checks and measures in sourcing ingredients and standardized the manufacture of medicines (Krishnankutty, 2001).

Following its establishment the Arya Vaidyasala, or the Kottakkal Arya Vaidyasala as it was popularly known (Kottakkal being the first town where the Arya Vaidyasala opened), grew in popularity. Satisfied customers spread positive word-of-mouth, and the company's customer base expanded to many Indian cities as well as to Burma, Ceylon (now Sri Lanka), and parts of Africa (Krishnankutty, 2001). In five years, the Arya Vaidyashala's profits increased tenfold (Varier, 1929), enabling the founder to establish a college for Ayurveda, the Arya Vaidya Patasala, in 1917.

Today the Kottakal Arya Vaidyasala is a leader in ayurveda. It has 29 branches spread throughout India and sells its products through more than one thousand authorized agencies. The firm's profits support a charitable hospital that serves more than one thousand patients daily at no charge, the ayurvedic college established by the founder, and an Indian performing artist troupe. The ayurvedic college is affiliated with the University of Calicut and offers several graduate and postgraduate degrees.

The ayurvedic college was the impetus for founding another successful ayurvedic firm. A student of the college, Dr. P. V. Rama Varier worked at the Kottakal Arya Vaidyashala for several years. He left and started his own ayurvedic enterprise in 1948 in the neighboring state of Tamil Nadu. He called his firm the Arya Vaidya Pharmacy. The Arya Vaidya Pharmacy (AVP) expanded in 1950 to include an ayurvedic hospital. Currently, the firm includes 42 branches, 10 hospitals, and several agencies throughout India.

Scholars tend to consider allopathy and ayurveda as separate fields with no confluence. However, contrary to belief, ayurveda and allopathy often merge to seek the best in one another. Since its early years, the Kottakkal Arya Vaidyasala included an allopathic doctor on its team of physicians. Currently a team of allopathic doctors serves the charitable hospital in Kottakkal, and patients seeking treatment can choose between ayurveda and allopathy. In several instances, the ayurvedic doctors refer patients with complications to the allopathic doctors. In the words of Kottakkal's current additional chief physician, Dr. K. Muraleedharan, "Ayurveda and allopathy should not be viewed in a competitive spirit. … Ayurveda offers an alternative course of treatment. A judicious combination of ayurveda and allopathy is required." Dr Muraleedharan cites an increase in the number of patients who turn to ayurveda to manage diseases including cancer, diabetes, knee replacements, and lifestyle diseases (such as obesity). Allopathy and ayurveda come together in cancer management, with patients undergoing chemotherapy and surgery, while ayurvedic treatment is administered to mitigate side effects and discomforts caused by allopathic treatments such as chemotherapy. Ayurvedic ophthalmology is growing in popularity. This is evinced by the growth and commercial success achieved by the ayurvedic firm Sreedharyam, which specializes in the treatment of eye ailments. The Sreedharyam eye hospital couples ancient ayurvedic eye treatments with modern technology, relying on state-of-the-art diagnostic equipment to assist with patient examinations and disease diagnosis. Following diagnosis, the ayurvedic physicians at Sreedharyam use ayurvedic treatments, including eye massages and, in special cases, therapy involving leeches to treat eye diseases.

In India, several hospitals offer meditation and alternative therapies. Leading hospital groups such as the Apollo Group of Hospitals and the Fortis group of hospitals offer ayurvedic constitution tests, ayurvedic massages, yoga, and meditation as part of their wellness packages, they also manage heart diseases and diabetes. The increased interest in ayurveda has led to a number of holistic hospitals in India. Soukya, a leading holistic hospital in Bangalore, combines naturopathy, Ayurveda, and homeopathy to treat patients.

Ayurveda is gaining popularity in the United States and Europe. Ayurveda is part of the Richard and Hinda Center for Complementary and Alternative Medicine at the New York Presbyterian Hospital. A 2011 survey of the International Spa Association reveals that 32 percent of American spas offer ayurvedic treatments such as oil massages. The Chopra Center for Wellbeing (Carlsbad, California) offers mind-body wellness programs that include a mix of ayurveda, meditation, and other alternative therapies. The Pratima Ayurvedic Skin Care Center in New York offers personalized ayurvedic preparation customized for individual skin types. In Europe, ayurveda was popularized in the 1980s by Maharishi Yogi in Germany (Boskovitch, 2011). Currently, leading health care institutions such as the Central Clinic Essen offer ayurvedic medicine as part of the outpatient department at the Department of Complementary and Integrative Medicine. Treatments can range between 7–21 days and involve strict adherence to an organic vegetarian diet.

Ayurveda seeks to combine scientific knowledge with folk wisdom (Varier, 2002). The definition of folk wisdom extends to incorporating sections of allopathy, incorporating advances offered by technology into traditional ayurvedic practice. Since its inception the Kottakkal Arya Vaidyasala has embodied a respect for both ayurveda as well as allopathy. More than a century later, several allopathic hospitals in India, Europe, and the United States seem to be reflecting Indian practice by offering ayurveda alongside allopathy. With patient well-being and interest being the primary focus of all medicine, integration of medical approaches and alternative approaches such as ayurveda is the order of the day.

REVIEW QUESTIONS

1. What factors prevented the decline of ayurveda in the face of India'a caste system?

2. What factors led to the decline of ayurveda?

3. What role did the Kottakal Arya Vaidyashala play in ayurveda's revival?

4. How does ayurveda integrate itself with other systems of medicine?

5. Why is ayurveda increasingly being incorporated into existing health care systems?

6. What role could ayurveda play in patient-centered care?

REFERENCES

Ambedkar, B. R. (1946). What Gandhi and the Congress have done to the Untouchables. Bombay. Thacker & Co.

Boskovitch, A. (2011, February 24). Ayurveda: From wellness to medical science. *Young Germany.* Retrieved from http://www.young-germany.de/university-education/university-education/article/ayurveda-from-wellness-to-medical-science.html.

Bradford, T. L. (1895). Life and letters of Hahnemann. Philadelphia: Boericke and Tafel.

Cook, T. (1981). Samuel Hahnemann: The founder of homeopathy. UK Wellingborough Thorsons.

Krishnankutty, G. (2001). *A life of healing: A biography of Vaidyaratnam P. S. Varier*. India: New DelhiViking.

Panikkar, K. N. (1995). Indigenous medicine and cultural hegemony. In *Culture, ideology, hegemony: Intellectuals and social consciousness in colonial India*. New Delhi: Tulika.

Thakar V.J. Historical development of basic concepts of Ayurveda from *Veda* up to *Samhita*. AYU 2010; 31 :400-2

Varier, P. S. (1929). *Shashti varshika charitram* [A history of sixty years]. Calicut, India: E. P. Krishna Varier, Norman Printing Bureau.

Varier, R. M. R. (2002). *The rediscovery of Ayurveda: The story of Arya Vaidya Sala Kottakkal*. India: New Delhi Viking.

Chapter 21

Traditional Chinese Medicine

Tingting (Christina) Zhang

LEARNING OBJECTIVES

Upon completing this chapter, you should be able to do the following:

1. Understand the concept of Traditional Chinese medicine.

2. Understand the history of Traditional Chinese medicine.

3. Explore the Western perception and application of Traditional Chinese medicine.

4. Understand the barriers and potentials of globalizing Traditional Chinese medicine.

5. Explore possible ways to integrate Traditional Chinese medicine into conventional medical system.

KEYWORDS

Traditional Chinese Medicine (TCM), Western perception and application of TCM, history of TCM, integration of TCM, conventional medicine.

TRADITIONAL CHINESE MEDICINE IN THE WEST

Traditional Chinese medicine (TCM), originated in ancient China, has evolved over thousands of years to promote health and to treat diseases. This holistic medical system, compared with Western medicine, has evolved over the years with the understanding that the body, mind, spirit, and emotions must all be addressed in the healing journey (Lu, Luo, Zhou, & Tan, 2010). This holistic concept of medicine is increasingly accepted in the West as complementary and alternative medicine (CAM).

Some aspects of TCM have become part of mainstream medicine in some developed countries, including United States, especially the practices of acupuncture and acupressure (Graziose, Lila, & Raskin, 2010). Organizations such as the Institute of Traditional Medicine (ITM) and the establishment of a licensure process for TCM practitioners including acupuncturists (Baer, Jen, Tanassi, Tsia, & Wahben, 1998) have contributed to recent moves by insurance companies to cover TCM therapies (Henry, 2004).

A 1998 survey found that the use of alternative medicine, including Traditional Chinese medicine (TCM), increased significantly in the United States from 1990–1997, and the National Health Interview Survey found a similar increase from 2002–2007 (Barnes, Bloom, & Nahin, 2007; Eisenberg et al., 1998). These studies indicate a rise in its acceptance in Western society; however, TCM faces many challenges before claiming full acceptance in the Western world.

Some of these challenges are the restrictive (a preference for empirical over intuitive knowledge), evidence-based mindset of Western medicine (Park, 2012). This chapter describes Traditional Chinese medicine (TCM) and its historical evolution within Chinese culture. The chapter also summarizes the latest literature pertinent to the perception and the application of TCM in the postmodern societies where conventional Western medicine dominates.

Introduction

As defined by the Traditional Chinese Medicine World Foundation (TCMWF, 2012), *Traditional Chinese medicine* (TCM) is an ancient medical system that takes a deep understanding of the laws and patterns of nature and applies them to the human body. TCM is not "New Age," nor is it a patchwork of healing modalities; rather, it is a complete medical system that has been practiced and evolved for more than five thousand years (Lu et al., 2010). At the heart of TCM is the tenet that the root cause of illnesses, not their symptoms, must be treated. TCM is holistic in its approach; it views every aspect of a person's body, mind, spirit, and emotions as part of one complete circle rather than loosely connected pieces to be treated individually (Chen & Lian, 2010).

Often Western CAM practitioners and their patients derive their understanding of TCM from acupuncture (Eisenberg et al., 1998). However, acupuncture is only one of the major treatment modalities of this comprehensive medical system based on the understanding of *Qi*, or vital energy. (In TCM, *Qi* is considered the force that animates and informs all things. In the human body, *Qi* flows through meridians, or energy pathways. Twelve major meridians run throughout the body, and it is over this network that *Qi* travels and that the body's organs send messages to other organs. For this reason, keeping the meridians clear is imperative for the body's self-regulation.). These major treatment modalities are described in following sections.

Qigong (Pronounced Chee-Gung)

Qigong is an energy practice encompassing simple movements, postures, and breathing techniques, such as Tai Chi (Jahnke et al., 2010). An article published by Harvard Medical School (2009) indicated that researchers found strong evidence of beneficial health effects of tai chi and qigong for improving bone health, cardiopulmonary fitness, balance, and improved quality of life. In addition, Harvard researchers have found that, when combined with standard treatment, qigong and tai chi appear helpful for several medical conditions, including arthritis, low bone density, breast cancer, heart disease, heart failure, hypertension, Parkinson's disease, sleep problems, and stroke.

HERBAL MEDICINE

Herbal medicine (also called botanical medicine or phytomedicine) is the use of herbal combinations or formulas to strengthen and support organ system function (Roberts et al., 2007). As described by National Center for Complementary and Alternative Medicine (NCCAM), herbs are usually combined in formulas and given as teas, capsules, tinctures, or powders (Grant et al., 2009). Herbalism has a long tradition of use outside of conventional medicine. Clinical research has shown the value of herbal medicine in the treatment and, in some cases, prevention of some disease (Mendes, Herdeiro, and Pimentel, 2010).

According to research conducted by National Institutes of Health (NIH, 2012), herbal supplement use in the West has dramatically increased over the past 30 years. Herbs are classified as dietary supplements by the U.S. Dietary Supplement Health and Education Act (DSHEA) of 1994. That means herbal supplements—unlike prescription drugs—can be sold without being tested to prove their safety and efficacy. However, herbal supplements must be made according to good manufacturing practices.

A survey conducted by Dr. Steven D. Ehrlich, a professor at the University of Maryland Medical Center (2011), indicates that the most commonly used herbal supplements in the United States include echinacea (*Echinacea purpurea* and related species), St. John's wort (*Hypericum perforatum*), ginkgo (*Ginkgo biloba*), garlic (*Allium sativum*), saw palmetto (*Serenoa repens*), and ginseng (*Panax ginseng*, or Asian ginseng; and *Panax quinquefolius*, or American ginseng) to treat many medical conditions, such as asthma, eczema, premenstrual syndrome, rheumatoid arthritis, migraines, menopausal symptoms, chronic fatigue, irritable bowel syndrome, cancers, and others.

ACUPUNCTURE

Acupuncture is the practice of inserting hair-thin metallic needles into specific body points to improve health and well-being, which is today well known in the West (NIH, 1997). Acupuncture is widely used in Chinese medicine to relieve pain. According to the 2007 National Health Interview Survey (NHIS) (Bauer, 2007), which included a comprehensive survey of CAM use by Americans, 1.4 percent of respondents (an estimated 3.1 million Americans) said they had used acupuncture in the past year. A special analysis of acupuncture data from an earlier NHIS (Bauer, 2007) found that pain or musculoskeletal complaints accounted for 7 of the top 10 conditions for which people use acupuncture. The report showed that the most common reason for using acupuncture was due to back pain; this was followed by joint pain, neck pain, severe headache/migraine, and recurring pain.

CHINESE MASSAGE

In general, massage therapists use hands and fingers, and sometimes forearms, elbows, or feet to press, rub, and otherwise manipulate the body's muscles and other soft tissues for a variety of health-related purposes (NCCAM, 2006). In the United States, massage therapy is often considered part of CAM, although it is also used in conventional practice (Barnes et al., 2007). Scientific evidence on massage therapy is limited. Scientists are not yet certain what changes occur in the body during massage, whether massage can influence health, and, if so, how.

According to one analysis based on the National Health Interview Survey (Burke et al., 2006), research supports the conclusion that massage therapy is effective. Although scientific research findings on massage therapy—whether it works and, if so, how—is limited, there is evidence that massage benefits some patients. The studies included in the analysis suggested that a single session of massage therapy can reduce "state anxiety" (a reaction to a particular situation), blood pressure, and heart rate, and multiple sessions can reduce "trait anxiety" (general anxiety-proneness), depression, and pain.

ACUPRESSURE

Acupressure is the practice of using deep finger pressure at certain points to reduce tension, increase circulation, and offer relief for many complaints (Chen & Chen, 2010). Acupressure is often described as "acupuncture without the needles" (Han, Wang, & Dong, 1989). The points triggered are located along an invisible system of energy channels in the body, known as meridians, and these meridians are related directly to organs and glands of the body where constrictions of the organs and glands may reduce the flow of energy through these points and cause disease and discomfort (Han et al., 1989). Acupressure relieves stress, improves resistance to disease, increases blood circulation, and aids in removing toxic wastes (Chen & Chen, 2010).

DIETARY THERAPY

Dietary therapy is the prescription of certain foods as a preventative or corrective treatment of disease (Cohen, 1996). Dr. Cohen, research specialist of integrative medicine at the University of California Institute for Health and Aging, states that in Chinese medicine, food therapy and diet are the first treatments given to people trying to stay well or to remain in balance, or people suffering from illness (Cohen, 1996). There are many ways we eat that can keep us well or can make us sick.

According to Chinese medicine, the spleen and stomach are considered the organs of digestion and assimilation (Velasquez & Bhathena, 2007). The stomach brings food energy into the body, and the spleen distributes it. Anything that disrupts the function of the stomach and spleen or the digestion is injurious to the body's energy as a whole.

CUPPING

Cupping is an ancient Chinese practice in which a cup is applied to the skin, and the pressure in the cup is reduced (by using a change in heat or by suctioning out air), so that the skin and superficial muscle layer are drawn into and held in the cup (Dharmananda, 1999). As described by Dr. Dharmananda, the earliest cups were animal horns (281–341 BCE) used to drain pustules. The cups were then made of bamboo or pottery and were used to alleviate headaches of the wind-cold type, dizziness, and abdominal pain (Qing Dynasty, 1644–1911 BCE).

The modern name for cupping is *baguanfa* (suction cup therapy). It has two methods: one called *shanhuofa* (flash-fire cupping), which uses fire in the cup to heat the air prior to placement; the other called *dijiufa* (alcohol-fire cupping), in which a small amount alcohol is put in the cup and lit (Chen, Jiang, & Cong, 1993).

Today, cupping is recommended mainly for the pain treatment, gastro-intestinal disorders, lung diseases (especially chronic cough and asthma), and paralysis (Chen et al., 1993). The areas of the body that are fleshy are preferred sites for cupping.

HISTORY AND DEVELOPMENT OF TCM IN CHINA

The creation of the traditional Chinese medicine (TCM) theoretical system can be traced back to the period of Warring States (475—211 BCE) and the Qin and Han Dynasties (221 BCE—221 CE) (Xiao, Xing & Guo, 2012). During the long course of TCM development, the ancient medical experts took Chinese philosophical thinking as their guide, constantly absorbing knowledge from ancient natural and social science.

After the Opium War (1840–1842) Western medicine began to spread in China, exerting its influence on the practice of TCM. Some Chinese medical experts tried to combine TCM with Western medicine. *Yixue Zhongzhong Canxi Lu* (*Records of Traditional Chinese and Western Medicine*) written by Zhang Xichun (1860–1933), is a representative monograph in this field.

After the founding of the People's Republic of China in 1949, great progress in theoretical study of and clinical research into TCM has been made with modern scientific methods and advanced technology by doctors, researchers, and other scientists

(Ping, Harsha, Yong-Jian, & Nathan, 2009). In 1955, Chairman Mao Zedong, the first Communist leader of China, proposed that Chinese and Western medicine be combined to improve Chinese health care.

That same year, the Ministry of Health of the People's Republic of China, staffed by both Chinese- and Western-trained physicians, was established. Over the next 40 years, China integrated practices from both cultures through a bottom-up approach. Medical students must now take courses in both Western and traditional medicine, and actively implement their cross-cultural knowledge in hospitals and teaching clinics (Charles, 2002).

PERCEPTION AND APPLICATION OF TCM IN THE WEST

PERCEPTION

TCM gained recognition in Western society with the publication in 1298 of *The Travels of Marco Polo*; however, it wasn't put into practice until 1970s (Wang, Wang, & Wang, 2006). The practice of TCM began in the west thanks to President Nixon.

In 1972, during a trip to China, President Nixon was accompanied by a "New York Times" reporter, James Reston, who underwent an emergency appendectomy while in the country. Doctors used acupuncture as the only anesthesia during his surgery. Being a reporter, this event, a foreign concept to Western medical currency, led to a flurry of research and studies in the United States into the medical legitimacy and benefits of acupuncture (Wang, Wang, & Wang, 2006).

Table 21.1 1 summarizes the status of TCM in the current literature regarding its degree of acceptance, accessibility, and recognition in the United States in the public, governmental, and industrial sectors.

Table 21.1	Current Acceptance of Traditional Chinese Medicine.
Public perception	• In 2007, an estimated 3.1 million U.S. adults reported having acupuncture during the previous year. (Barnes, Bloom & Nahin, 2007) • TCM medications suffer from a lack of consistent manufacturing processes and quality standards and a fear of adulteration. (Graziose, Lila, & Raskin, 2010) • A study of patients' views on acupuncture found the main concerns were kids' fear of needles, acupuncture's perceived ineffectiveness, and the lack of published studies. (Mano & Davies, 2009) • U.S.-born Chinese Americans are less likely to believe in TCM's efficacy for psychiatric disorders than Mainland Chinese or Taiwan-born Chinese. (Feng, 2002) • Chinese-Americans who have lived more than 10 years in the United States use fewer complementary medical services. (Feng, 2002)
Official perception	• Half the licensed U.S. acupuncturists practice in California. (Park et al., 2012) • Most U.S. states license acupuncture, and some offer licensing for other TCM components such as herbal medicine. (An &Feng, 2007) • Licensing laws have legitimized acupuncture, but have also required acupuncturists to adapt their training and treatments to the Western biomedical model. (Mano, 2010) • The multicomponent composition of many TCM remedies makes it difficult to study. (Costa, 2012) • According to the 2007 National Health Interview Survey, U.S. adults spent an estimated $33.9 billion out-of-pocket on CAM treatments during the past 12 months. (Barnes, Bloom & Nahin, 2007) • A 2004 survey released by the Kaiser Family Foundation and the Health Research and Educational Trust revealed that employer coverage for acupuncture increased 14% from 2002 to 2004. (Henry, 2004)
Industrial perception	• The Food and Drug Administration has published a guide to botanical drugs that outlines a pre-clinical and clinical path for the development of botanical drugs based on multicomponent plant extracts.(Izzo & Ernst, 2009) • Lack of regulation in China has led to products sold in the West that are mislabeled or adulterated with orthodox drugs, which hurts TCM's reputation. (Costa, 2012) • In general, Western pharmaceutical and regulatory industries prefer to study single-ingredient drugs based on synthetic molecules and to avoid natural product mixtures. (Izzo & Ernst, 2009)

APPLICATION

According to a survey conducted by the United Nations (2011), 162 countries accept TCM and it is used by 4 billion people (Xiao, Xing, & Guo, 2012). In general, acupuncture has found more acceptance in the West, as compared to other TCM therapies. Acupuncture is used increasingly in the West as complementary and alternative medicine. In 1997 the National Institutes of Health (NIH) released a statement outlining the safety and effectiveness of acupuncture for several health conditions. For example, the NIH has stated that "[a]cupuncture has the largest body of evidence and is considered safe if practiced correctly" (NIH, 1997). Many Western countries acknowledge acupuncture's effectiveness and have accepted it within the mainstream of medicine to treat illnesses such as fibromyalgia, sciatica and neuralgia, autoimmune diseases, and allergies and asthma (Mano & Davies, 2009).

EDUCATION AND CERTIFICATION

In the United States since the 1970s, traditional Chinese medicine has started to develop American TCM training programs. These programs include apprentice training in private clinics on TCM-relevant curricula offered by university medical schools such as Harvard University, Yale University, Stanford University, Duke University, etc. (Shimazaki & Martin, 2007). The teaching methods vary, including lectures, clinical practice, and demonstration courses. In 2003 Dr. Bruce Rosen, in partnership with Massachusetts General Hospital and Harvard University, led research to study the effect of acupuncture on the human brain (Chen & Lian, 2010). Dr. Peter Wayne at the New England School of Acupuncture received a grant for his research on acupuncture and its effect and safety (Eisenberg et al., 1998).

In many Western countries TCM is now considered part of Complementary and Alternative Medicine (CAM) and regulated by laws. For example, in the U.S. Food and Drug Administration (FDA) regards TCM as involving a complete system of theory and practice that evolved independent from or parallel to allopathic (conventional) medicine. TCM is regulated by the FDA through its guidelines of the health care industry's CAM products. In addition, the FDA no longer refers to acupuncture needles as experimental devices but as medical tools, thus opening the way for acupuncture treatment to be covered under health insurance policies (Mano & Devies, 2009). The interest in TCM in the West has attracted attention within the health care industry, government agencies, public, and the media.

OBSTACLES

Although TCM has been increasingly recognized in the Western world, yet there remain misunderstandings of its benefits and obstacles to its full acceptance in Western society. This may be partly because herbal supplements and traditional medicine suffer from a lack of consistent manufacturing processes and quality control standards, hence, the concerns of adulteration (Graziose et al., 2010).

The perceived deficiencies in the scientific validation of the efficacy and safety of TCM techniques is another problem. A study of parents' views on acupuncture found that main concerns were to do with their kids' fear of needles, acupuncture's perceived ineffectiveness, and the lack of published studies (Mano & Davies, 2009). As one critic, Marcello Costa (2012), professor of neurophysiology, Department of Physiology at Flinders University, noted, "In the field of medicine we accept only those practices that have undergone the scrutiny of scientific tests. Sadly, this is not the case for most traditional Chinese medical practices and practitioners" (Moquin, Blackman, Mitty, & Flores, 2009).

A final roadblock to the wide acceptance of TCM is the discipline that holistic balance of vital energy determining health is challenged by the Western dichotomization of illness into physical or psychological (Yang, Corsini-Munt, Link, & Phelan, 2009). Until Western physicians accept TCM, their lack or perceived lack of support will be a major barrier to its acceptance by the public (Jain & Astin, 2001).

SUGGESTED SOLUTIONS

All living things endure through illness and disease in one form or another. According to David Eisenberg, author of *Encounters with Qi*, the West emphasizes intervention over prevention. Oftentimes, the West insists that "the health care system has the best technology available to treat various illnesses, regardless of costs" (Eisenberg et al., 1998), while the technology would be less necessary if everyone maintained healthy lifestyle. In China health is considered an important part of the lifestyle, integrating physical activity and diet. The Chinese physician's responsibilities, aside from treating ailments, included prevention, recommendations about lifestyle, and emotional support (Charles, 2002). Thus there is a clear difference between the philosophy of Western and Eastern medicine. Therefore, bringing together the benefits of the traditional Chinese medicine and Wwestern medicine will provide numerous opportunities to improve health in all parts of the world.

REVIEW QUESTIONS

1. What are some of the treatments adopted by traditional Chinese medicine?

2. When was traditional Chinese medicine created?

3. How does the West view traditional Chinese medicine?

4. What are the barriers to and potentials for traditional Chinese medicine development in the West?

5. What are the possible solutions to integrating traditional Chinese medicine into the Western conventional medical system?

References

An R., & Feng, Y. F. (2007, May 5). "Traditional Chinese medicine in the West.," *China Newsweek.*, Retrieved from http://www.kankan.cn/superlibtary/freearticle. asp?aid=28055.

Baer, H. A., Jen, C., Tanassi, L. M., Tsia, C., & Wahben, H. (1998). The drive for professionalization in acupuncture: A preliminary view from the San Francisco Bay area. *Social Science & Medicine.* (46), 533–537.

Bauer, B. A. (2007). *Mayo Clinic book of alternative medicine* (p. 106). Rochester, MN: Mayo Foundation for Medical Education and Research.

Barnes, P. M., Bloom, B., & Nahin, R. (2007). Complementary and alternative medicine use among adults and children: United States, *CDC National Health Statistics Reports,* No. *12.* Atlanta, Georgia

Burke, A., Upchurch, D. M., Dye, C. Chyu, L. (2006). Acupuncture use in the United States: Findings from the National Health Interview Survey. *Journal of Alternative and Complementary Medicine, 12*(7), 639–648.

Chen, D. C., Jiang, N. W., & Cong, X. (1993). 47 cases of acne treated by prick-bloodletting plus cupping. *Journal of Traditional Chinese Medicine, 13*(3), 185–186.

Chen, H. M., & Chen, C. H. (2010, March 12). Effects of acupressure on menstrual distress in adolescent girls: A comparison between Hegu–Sanyinjiao matched points and Hegu, Zusanli single point. *Journal of Clinical Nursing.* 19(7): 998-1007.

Chen, W. M., & Lian, X. F. (2010, April 30). Systematic evaluation of traditional Chinese medicine for treating Parkinson's disease. *Neural Regeneration Research, 08*, 14–16.

Cohen, M. (1996). *The Chinese way to healing: Many paths to wholeness.* Penguin Group (USA) Incorporated, New York. .

Costa, M. (2012, April 2). "'Does traditional Chinese medicine have a place in the health system,' The globalization of Chinese medicine. Retrieved from http://theconversation.edu. au/does-traditional-chinese-medicine-have-a-place-in-the-health-system-6166.

Dharmananda, S. (1999). Cupping, Institute for Traditional Medicine: Portland, OR. Retrieved from http://www.itmonline.org/arts/cupping.htm.

Ehrlich D. S. (2011), University of Maryland Medical Center Medical Reference, Retrieved from http://www.umm.edu/altmed/articles/herbal-medicine-000351.htm.

Eisenberg, D. (1995), Encounters with Qi: Exploring Chinese Medicine, *W. W. Norton & Company,* New York.

Eisenberg, D. M., Davis, R. B., Ettner, S. L., Appel, S., Wilkey, S., Van Rompay, M.. (1998). Trends in alternative medicine use in the United States, 1990–1997: Results of a follow-up national survey. *Journal of the American Medical Association, 280*, 1569–1575.

Feng, C. (2002). Merging Chinese traditional medicine into American health system. *Journal of Young Investigators.* Retrieved from http://www.jyi.org/volumes/volume6/issue5/features/feng.html.

Graziose, R., Lila, M. A., & Raskin, I. (2010). Merging traditional Chinese medicine with modern drug discovery technologies to find novel drugs and functional foods. *Current Drug Discovery Technologies.*, 7, 2–12.

Han, F. Y., Wang, Q. P., & Dong, X. J. (1989, May 15). Effects of digital acupressure on the capillary arteriolar flow in cerebral PLA mater of the dog. *Journal of Traditional Chinese Medicine.* 02: 135–139.

Harvard Medical Center. (2009, May). The health benefits of Taichi. Retrieved from http://www.health.harvard.edu/newsletters/Harvard_Womens_Health_Watch/2009/May/The-health-benefits-of-tai-chi.

Henry, J. K. (2004). Family foundation & health research and educational trust: Employer Health Benefits 2004 Annual Survey. *Kaiser Family Foundation*, Washington.

Izzo, A. A., & Ernst, E. (2009)., Interactions between herbal medicines and prescribed drugs: an updated systematic review., *Drugs,.* 69(13), :1777–1798.

Jahnke, R, Larkey, L, Rogers, C. Etnier J, Lin F. (2010). A comprehensive review of health benefits of *qigong* and *tai chi. American Journal of Health Promotion, 24*(6), 1–25.

Jain, N., & Astin, J. A. (2001). Barriers to acceptance: An exploratory study of complementary/alternative medicine disuse. *Journal of Alternative and Complementary Medicine, 7*, 689–696.

Lu, Z. J., Luo, Y., Zhou, H., & Tan, X. L. (2010). A preliminary study on the medical expenditure of Chinese medicine and integrative medicine treatment for Influenza A (H1N1) in the fever clinics. *Chinese Jour nal of Integrative Medicine,* 16(6): 493–497.

Mano, K. E. J., & Davies, W. H. (2009). Parental attitudes toward acupuncture in a community sample. *Journal of Alternative and Complementary Medicine, 15*, 661–668.

Mao, J. J. (2010)., Acupuncture in primary care., *Primary Care Clinics in Office Practice,. 37*, :105.

Moquin, B., Blackman, M. R., Mitty, E., & Flores, S. (2009). Complementary and alternative medicine (CAM). *Geriatric Nursing, 30*(3), 196–203.

National Institutes of Health (NIH), Consensus Development Conference Statement. (1997). *Acupuncture.* Retrieved from http://consensus.nih.gov/1997/1997acupuncture107html.htm.

National Institutes of Health (NIH). (2012). Herbs at a glance: A quick guide to herbal supplements. Dietary Supplements Label Database. Retrieved from http://nccam.nih.gov/sites/nccam.nih.gov/files/herbs/NIH_Herbs_at_a_Glance.pdf.

National Center for Complementary and Alternative Medicine (NCCAM). (2006, September). Background on Chinese massage. Retrieved from http://nccam.nih.gov/health/massage/massageintroduction.htm.

Park, J. J., Selena, B. H., Cho, G. Y., Duckhee, K., & Hangon, K. (2012). The current acceptance, accessibility and recognition of Chinese and Ayurvedic medicine in the United States in the public, governmental, and industrial sectors. *Chinese Journal of Integrative Medicine, 18*(6), 405–408.

Ping, Y., Harsha, G., Yong-Jian G., Nathan, S., & Bryan.N.S. (2009). Nitric oxide bioactivity of traditional Chinese medicines used for cardiovascular indications. *Free Radical Biology and Medicine, 47*(6), 835–840.

Roberts, A. T., Martin, C. K., Liu, Z. Amen R.J., Woltering E.A., Rood J.C, Caruso M.K. Yu Y., Xie H., Greenway F.L.,(2007). The safety and efficacy of a dietary herbal supplement and gallic acid for weight loss. *Journal of Medicinal Food. 10*(1), 184–188.

Shimazaki, M., & Martin, J. L. (2007). Do herbal agents have a place in the treatment of sleep problems in long-term care? *Journal of the American Medical Directors Association, 8*(4), 248–252.

Traditional Chinese Medicine World Foundation (TCMWF). *Traditional Chinese medicine definition*. Retrieved from http://www.tcmworld.org/what_is_tcm/

Velasquez, M. T., & Bhathena, S. J. (2007). Role of dietary soy protein in obesity. *International Journal of Medical Sciences., 4*(2), 72–82.

Wang, W. K., Wang, F., & Wang, L. (2006). The origin of traditional Chinese medicine and thinking on Chinese medicine development. *Engineering Sciences, 4*(4), 35–55.

Xiao, Z. Z., Xing, R., & Guo, X. G. (2012). The current state of Chinese medicine in Europe and thoughts on its development. *Journal of Traditional Chinese Medicine University of Hunan, 32*(5), 75–78.

Yang, X. X., Hu, Z. P., Duan, W., Zhu, Y. Z., & Zhou, S. F. (2006). Drug-herb interactions: Eliminating toxicity with hard drug design. *Current Pharmaceutical Design. 12*(35), 4649–4664.

Yang, L. H., Corsini-Munt, S., Link, B. G., & Phelan, J. C. (2009). Beliefs in traditional Chinese medicine efficacy among Chinese Americans. *The Journal of Nervous and Mental Disease, 197*, 207–210.

Chapter 22

Paradigm Shifters in Health and Wellness Services (Cases)

CASE 1

CASE STUDY: ARAVIND EYE CARE SYSTEM
Anupama K. Kothari

"Everyone has in him something divine, something his own, a chance of perfection and strength in however small a sphere which God offers him to take or refuse. The task is to find it, develop it & use it."

This quote from the Indian philosopher Sri Aurobindo was taken to heart by a young man, Dr. G. Venkataswamy, or Dr. V as he is widely known. In 1944, Dr. V joined the Indian army as a doctor but was forced to retire due to severe rheumatoid arthritis that left him incapable of even walking. (Aravind website- Genesis) After regaining his mobility, Dr. V returned to medical school where he specialized in ophthalmology. Incredibly, a man incapable of holding a pen a short while before now performed cataract surgeries with skill and dexterity.

In the course of his work, Dr. V came into proximity with patients suffering from blindness. Motivated by his work and by his spiritual guru's (Sri Aurobindo) philosophy of service to humanity, in 1976 Dr. V started a small 11-bed (Brown, 2008), nonprofit eye hospital in his hometown of Madurai. With his spiritual guru in mind, he named it the Aravind Eye Hospital (Aravind being a version of the name Aurobindo in South India). In addition toe, his sister, Dr. Natchiar, and his brother-in-law, Dr. Namperumalsamy joined the hospital (Matalobos & Pahls, 2010). Aravind Eye Care focused on "providing the highest quality of care for the poor" (Rangan 2004), symbolized by the hospital's motto "Quality Is For Everyone."

By 1987, Aravind Eye Hospital had expanded to two more cities. The main breakthrough occurred in 1992 when a successful California entrepreneur, David Green, and his nonprofit organization, Project Impact, partnered with Dr. V and Aravind to create Aurolabs (Kacprzyk, 2010). Aurolabs is a production facility, manufacturing intraocular lenses, sutures, pharmaceuticals, and eyeglasses at a fraction (about one twentieth) of the U.S. cost. Aravind's slogan (Quality Is For Everyone) was realized through Aurolabs. A reformatted service strategy emerged of low cost–high volume yet with attention to customer service. Aravind's business strategies have often been likened to McDonald's (Kacprzyk, 2010), where they focus on operational efficiency through cost cutting—achieved through indigenous production of products and services.

Although 60 percent of eye surgeries (Rangan, 2004) performed at Aravind are free, neither quality nor service is compromised. At Aravind, quality of service is not based on the patient's ability to pay. Paying patients pay full market price, while nonpaying patients are treated free of charge. Profits from paying patients offset the cost of treatments for nonpaying patients (Rangan, 2004).

The standards demanded by paying patients are the benchmark for nonpaying patients (Rangan, 2004). Aravind ensures uniform standards of quality across all patients by maintaining a high volume of cases. This is achieved, in part, through Aravind's efficient outpatient system. In this system patients are allowed to "drop-in" at the hospital for treatment regardless of referrals. All patients are asked to complete a form, then be seated in an adjacent waiting area. Accompanied by a receptionist, the patient undergoes a vision test not of not more than 10 minutes (Aravind website- Outpatient procedures). Following this test, the patient is accompanied to the area where doctors perform refraction tests and examinations. Next the patient is guided to an area for specialized tests. (Matalobos and Pahls (2010) provide a detailed overview of the outpatient system at Aravind.) Throughout the process, a guide accompanies the patient. Along with minimizing bottlenecks caused by patient congestion, this helps the patient through a difficult period and minimizes stress caused by misdirection or missed appointments. At Aravind, each operating theatre has four tables, where two doctors simultaneously operate on two tables (Matalobos & Pahls, 2010). This surgery assembly line maximizes the number of surgeries that can be performed (Rangan, 2004).

The hospital provides patients with in-house counseling services. Counselors trained by Aravind mitigate patient fears and concerns, enabling them to manage and cope with the stress and fear of undergoing surgery. An on-site radiological department processes patient X-rays and makes reports available quickly and efficiently. Similarly, an in-house biochemistry department conducts blood tests. Recognizing the widespread prevalence of diabetes in India, patients diagnosed with diabetes are advised on how to manage their lifestyle (Aravind website-hospital services).

At Aravind, employees are an important component of service quality. Aravind offers a host of training programs from which it hires its staff. Aravind annually trains more than one thousand potential employees including ophthalmologists, ophthalmic technicians, opticians, clinical assistants, outreach coordinators, and health care managers. Once recruited, employees are trained further instilling a deep sense of loyalty to the Aravind brand and to the founder's vision. Appropriate compensation and employee welfare programs are offered. Aravind staff are characterized by a deep sense of humility and compassion for patients. If a patient approaches an employee for assistance or directions, in keeping with their founders message of service, employees will advise, accompany, or escort the patient to appropriate resources. Aravind's employee model involves rotating doctors between free and paying patients, ensuring that each doctor participates in outreach programs. Doctors are sent overseas for training and are challenged to learn new skills which increases their stickiness to Aravind (Rangan 2004).

Aravind has several vision centers situated in villages and serving populations of about fifty thousand each. Equipped with basic ophthalmic equipment, these centers are staffed by technicians trained in ophthalmology at Aravind. The technician-in-charge conducts basic eye examinations, tests, and then links with Aravind hospital where a doctor remotely examines the patients using telemedicine technology. Patients are then either treated or referred to the nearest Aravind hospital. Aravind also conducts community eye camps, where a doctor accompanied by a receptionist and technicians periodically visit underserved locations. They screen and transport patients requiring further care to an Aravind hospital. These teams also include opticians who make glasses for patients on-site.

Aravind also includes Aravind Eye Bank that collects corneas to use for eye transplants. As of 2012, Aravind Eye Bank has collected 4,000 corneas and successfully performed 1,400 corneal transplants (Aravind Website- Eye Bank) Ten percent of corneas collected are given to other institutions in India that also perform eye transplants (Aravind website- EyeBank- Procurement, Processing and Distribution).

In business-to-business service, Aravind has launched LAICO (Lions Aravind Institute of Community Ophthalmology), which offers consulting services to other eye hospitals and international nonprofits. Services offered include feasibility studies, planning and designing eye hospitals, optimizing hospital performance, pricing services, and designing residency programs. LAICO's clients include more than 280 hospitals in India, Africa, and Asia (LAICO Consultancy Brochure).

From its beginnings as a three-doctor hospital in a temple town, Aravind now employs more than 3,000 employees. It is often called the world's largest eye care provider. In 2011–2012, more than 2.8 million patients were treated at Aravind, and more than 340,000 surgeries were performed (Aravind website-Vanakkam). The group is now called the Aravind Eye Care System and includes 10 full-fledged hospitals, 40 vision centers, and seven community eye clinics. Aravind conducted 2,831 community eye camps for the year 2011-2012 (Aravind website- Vanakkam). Aurolab exports products to more than 120 countries and accounts for 7.8 percent of the world's intraocular lenses (Aravind website- Aurolab). Aravind is an example of a service provider catering to both high-income as well as low-income customers, yet maintaining a high standard of quality, employee involvement and motivation, and customer care.

REFERENCES

Aravind Eye Care System. LAICO Consultancy Brochure., 2012, Gandhinagar, Madurai. Retrieved from http://www.aravind.org/LAICO.aspx

The Aravind Eye Care System Website. About Us-The Beginning. Genesis. 2011. Retrieved from http://www.aravind.org/aboutus/genesis.aspx#founder. 4 February 2013.

The Aravind Eye Care System website. Aurolab. 2011. Retrieved from http://www.aravind.org/Aurolab.aspx. 4 February 2013.

Aravind Eye Care System. Community Outreach. Retrieved from http://www.aravind.org/CommunityOutreach.aspx

The Aravind Eye Care System website. EyeBanks. 2011. Retrieved from http://www.aravind.org/EyeBanks.aspx. 4 February 2013.

The Aravind Eye Care System website. EyeBanks- Procurement, Processing & Distribution. 2011. Retrieved from http://www.aravind.org/eyebanks/procurement.aspx. 4 February 2013.

The Aravind Eye Care System website. Hospital Services- Support Services. 2011. Retrieved from http://www.aravind.org/clinics/supportservices.aspx. February 2013.

The Aravind Eye Care System website. Outpatient Procedures. 2011. Retrieved from http://www.aravind.org/generalInfo/eyeexamination.aspx. 4 February 2013.

Aravind Eye Care System Website. Vanakkam: About Aravind. 2011. .Retrieved from http://www.aravind.org/vanakkam/aboutaravind.aspx. 4 February 2013.

Brown, T. (2008). Design thinking. *Harvard Business Review*, 86(6), 85–92.

Kacprzyk, M. (2010). *Aravind Eye Care System*. (Social Enterprise Case Series). Northeastern University.

Matalobos, A. D., & Pahls, S. (2010). Aravind Eye Health Care Operations. IE Business School. Retrieved from http://www.aravind.org/aboutus/casestudiesonaravind.aspx

Rangan, K. (2004). Lofty missions, down to earth plans. *Harvard Business Review*, 82(3).

CASE 2

CASE STUDY: APOLLO HOSPITALS

Anupama K. Kothari

In 1972 India was recovering from the latest war waged by its neighbor Pakistan. The 27-year-old democracy was grappling with political uncertainty, wars, and a "mixed economy" strategy whose goal was to combine socialism and capitalism, One of India's political allies was the (former) USSR, and India's relations with America were shaky, at best. Indian engineers and doctors were leaving the country in droves for the United Kingdom and United States. Yet, in the midst of this emigration, Dr. Prathap Reddy, a cardiologist with a thriving practice in Springfield, Missouri, arrived with his wife and four daughters in Chennai, Tamil Nadu.

In an era when entrepreneurship was frowned on and American credentials were treated with a degree of cynicism, returning home to India was not easy. However, Dr. Reddy started a small practice from a local hospital where his foreign training soon attracted elite Indians (Mitra, 2012). He relied on his network of professional colleagues in the United States and even referred patients to them for better treatment (Mitra, 2012). In doing so, almost unintentionally, Dr. Reddy began an early system of medical tourism.

But, Dr. P. Reddy's epiphany came a few years later. As with many big ideas, it began with a tragedy. In 1979, a patient, unable to locate funds to treat his heart condition in the United States, died of heart failure (Mitra, 2012). At that point Dr. Reddy envisioned a hospital in India equipped with state-of-the-art technology. This vision became the Apollo Hospital. The Apollo Hospital was planned and conceptualized with attention paid to each component of the marketing mix. The first element, or product, was a hospital in India providing world-class facilities. Funding for the product came from Dr. Reddy's colleagues in India and the United States. Tapping the financial resources of the medical community in India helped Dr. Reddy circumvent any setbacks likely to be imposed by India's socialistic banking system. The funding strategy attracted employees, as the hospital's investors provided it with an excellent medical team and the second element of the marketing mix: people. Hiring employees from unconventional sources such as the Indian railways, popular retail chains, and the United States (Mitra, 2012) considerably strengthened the people component of Apollo's marketing mix. Dr. Reddy's team of doctors drew their own patients from other hospitals and competitors, and thus, his employees (also investors) also added another crucial element of the marketing mix: promotion. The convenience of a hospital equipped with a unique medical and administrative team and cutting-edge technology in India (the "place" element of the marketing mix) attracted more patients.

Beginning as a 150-bed enterprise, Apollo Hospitals has grown into an 8,500-bed enterprise spread over 50 countries. Health care is an important component of the service sector. However, the nature of the medical profession, characterized by authority and hierarchy, often makes a customer-centric focus difficult to maintain. Apollo Hospitals pioneered the customer-centric approach in Indian health care. Apollo gives its customers the opportunity to pay online and to offer extensive feedback. Apollo emphasized attention to quality by being the first hospital in India to be accredited by the Joint Commission International (JCI), an internationally respected nonprofit board that accredits health care organizations worldwide.

The customer-centric focus, coupled with delivering products and services to meet changing customer requirements, gives Apollo a business advantage. The company focuses on delivering its core service, health care. Success stories abound in the form of knee replacements for the oldest couple in India, robotic surgery on a 7-year-old, stem cell replacement on a 3-year-old, and more than 1,000 organ transplants in 2012 (Apollo website- News & Media). A recent article (Mitra, 2012), cites an example of how a patient with a body weight exceeding the maximum weight capacity for operating tables and who was rejected by several hospitals for surgery was admitted to Apollo Hospitals (Chennai) even though the hospital had to order a custom-built operating table. Technology remains at the forefront of patient care with the adoption of innovative technology for heart diseases (such 320 Slice CT Scanner) and non-invasive cancer care technologies such as CyberKnife and Novalis (Apollo Website- Advanced Technology). Following the rise and prevalence of cancer in India, the health care group created Apollo Specialty Hospitals that caters to cancer patients. These hospitals often feature Sunshine Stores, which sell prosthetic breasts, pressure garments, gowns, scarves, lingerie, and motivational books and CDs. These stores recognize the special needs of patients suffering from cancer as well as the difficulty of sourcing lifestyle products for these patients. Apollo Pharmacies in Apollo Hospitals across several cities, small towns, and even airports, allow convenient access to medications. To tap the cancer care market, Apollo introduced chemotherapy daycare clinics. These clinics allow patients to undergo outpatient chemotherapy sessions in conjunction with stress reduction techniques (such as relaxing music and television).

Apollo attends to the changing health care needs of India's population. In recent years, diabetes in India has increased. This is often attributed to the information technology revolution and resultant sedentary lifestyles. Apollo Sugar Clinics cater to the growing number of diabetic patients in India and provide management for diabetic lifecycles. Technology-savvy patients are provided with sugar count updates on their mobile devices and personalized Web pages complete with patient vital statistics and recommendations

Medical tourism is an important component of Apollo's services and it attracts patients from the Middle East, Europe, and the United States. Patients interested in treatment at Apollo Hospitals can refer to the corporate website and complete an information form. Within 48 hours, the health care group contacts the patient, matches the patient to a doctor, and even provides a price quote. The doctor and the patient communicate, aided by the hospital's international patient division, which assists the patient in planning their trip. The international patient division provides a variety of services, including arranging patient airport pick-ups and drop-offs and arranging accommodation in area hotels. Apollo Hospitals has partnered with insurance companies in Europe, Asia, and America to facilitate medical tourism. Apollo emphasizes on traditional Indian hospitality and in accordance Apollo Hospital staff completely arrange international patients' visits, with direct admission that precludes pre-admission formalities, including pre-scheduled appointments and customized menus catering to individual tastes (Apollo website- International Patient Services).

With an intense focus on customers and a high level of employee involvement (more than 65,000 employees), Apollo is a market leader in Indian health care, with a growth of 32 percent. The ability of the health care group to tailor health care services to customer needs has contributied to Apollo's remarkable success. Additionally, recognizing changes in disease patterns and providing appropriate and timely health care solutions are important factors. Finally, using technology to treat diseases as well as to communicate with customers are other factors responsible for the hospital chain's success. Thus, innovation, technology use, and most important, service quality combine to contribute to the success of Apollo Hospitals.

REFERENCES

Apollo Hospitals Website. Advanced Technology. 2012. Retrieved from http://www.apollohospitals.com/international_patient_services/advanced_technology.php. 4 February 2013.

Apollo Hospitals Website. International Patient Services. 2012. Retrieved from http://www.apollohospitals.com/international_patient_services/services_and_facilities.php. 4 February 2013.

Apollo Hospitals Website. "Apollo Hospitals Ahmedabad performs free stem cell transplant for a three year old boy." News and Media. 26 April 2011. Retrieved from http://www.apollohospitals.com/news_detail.php?newsid=122. 4 February 2013.

Apollo Hospitals Website. "Indraprastha Apollo Hospitals Delhi performs total knee replacement on a geriatric couple."News and Media. 25 May 2012. Retrieved from http://www.apollohospitals.com/news_detail.php?newsid=250. 4 February 2013.

Mitra, M. (2012). How Apollo hospitals chairman Prathap C. Reddy revolutionised Indian health care industry. *The Economic Times*. Retrieved from http://articles.economictimes.indiatimes.com/2012-06-01/news/31959097_1_prathap-c-reddy-apollo-hospitals-reddy-couple/2

CASE 3

THE SCHWARZ***** ALPINE SPA & RESORT

Anita Zehrer
Hubert Siller

Nestled in the Tirol of Austria, the Schwarz Alpine Spa & Resort is a traditional, family-run, lakeside spa retreat with more than 200 employees. Ninety-five percent of its employees are locals and live within a radius of 10 kilometers. Combining a spacious 4,000-square-meter spa and state-of-the-art health and fitness suite with year-round activities, luxury accommodations, and snow-capped mountain scenery, the Schwarz Alpine Luxury Spa Hotel is an ideal hotel for summer and winter holidays in the European Alps. The Schwarz Alpine Spa & Resort firmly believes that its primary purpose is to offer a perfect opportunity for guests to get away from the daily hustle and bustle, relax, recuperate, and recharge their batteries. Be it a romantic getaway; a family holiday full of fun and relaxation; or simply some well-deserved pampering; the Alpine Luxury Spa Resort Schwarz nurtures the holistic art of health and well-being. It is located in Mieming, 35 kilometers from Innsbruck, the capital of the Tirol. The nature reserve of the Mieminger Plateau benefits from one of the region's sunniest climates. It also boasts some of its most spectacular scenery: snow-capped peaks, lush, green Alpine pastures, and distinctive larch meadows, perfect terrain for hiking and mountain biking in the summer and cross-country skiing in winter.

Family businesses, the predominant form of enterprise around the world, constitute 70 percent of European businesses. This family hotel was initially built as a manor house in 1694, when the Schwarz sisters inherited it. As the sisters remained childless, they handed the business over to their nephew, Franz Pirktl, whom they raised. This is how the house came into the possession of today's host family. Franz Pirktl and his wife, Agnes, parents of today's senior director, developed the hotel with diligence and commitment to make the hotel what it is today. Today, the Alpine Spa & Resort is one of the most famous family-run hotels in the Tirol, as well as in Austria. The hotel shows a unique ability to foster a sense of loyalty, stable culture, long-term strategic vision, commitment, and pride in family tradition.

At the Schwarz Resort guests find an award-winning hotel park, indoor and outdoor sauna areas, gym, and fitness classes (including yoga), indoor and outdoor heated pools, private spa area, and a private clinic that offers cosmetic surgery and preventative medical procedures. Besides its sophisticated facilities, the Schwarz is characterized by a long family tradition, a sustainability plan, and development program. It offers high service quality, guest hospitality, and outstanding employee commitment. The hotel has assigned four permanentproject groups to further develop the hotel's goals in accordance with its stakeholders: "Green Schwarz Flower" (sustainability), "Schwarz Inside" (employees), "Guests' Excitement" (guests), and "Quality" (service quality).

The project Schwarz Goes Green reflects the hotel's *sustainable use of resources* and its economic viability, as well as its support to cultural diversity. The "Green Schwarz Flower" project group is set to further develop its goals in accordance with its stakeholders. The group's philosophy is to preserve resources for future generations through environmental protection measures such as cross-departmental waste separation, solar energy use, the use of regional products, garden facilities such as an herbal garden, a Feng Shui garden, and a natural swimming lagoon. The hotel strongly aims to sustainably enhance the employees' quality of work life through its leadership philosophy, career development plans, and health measures. For its outstanding sustainability concept, the Schwarz received the Green Spa Award 2011 and is a permanent member of RESPACT, the Austrian Business Council for Sustainable Development.

Employees are vital to the hotel's success so employee career development and their state of health are of great concern to today's owners. The EFQM (European Foundation for Quality Management) model forms the basis of the hotel's quality assurance policy. In 2010, a total of €135,000 (about $180,000 USD) were spent on employee training initiatives. Together with the project group Schwarz Inside, a detailed employee development and career support concept was developed based on the employees' strengths and interests. Following the motto Give and Receive Joy!, the goal is that all employees see themselves within the vision and values of the hotel and that they carry out their tasks with enthusiasm and dedication. Every year-round employee feels valued and appreciated and naturally passes this feeling on to the guests. Each employee takes part in six annual short training sessions on complaint management, guest management, service processes, etc. Further, all employees participate in a short, daily meeting and monthly meetings. A systematic communication and feedback process was introduced several years ago. The Schwarz Alpine Spa Resort has received a number of awards for its employee commitment, such as the TRIGOS Award 2011 (an Austrian award for CSR) and the State prize for Innovative Employee Management and Development in 2011.

The resort uniquely differentiates itself from its competitors through its service quality, guest hospitality, and employee leadership, and the resort can definitely be regarded as one of the highly acclaimed, customer-focused, spa hotels in the Tirol. The Schwarz Resort delivers exceptional guest experience time and again. The resort guarantees its ongoing development through the project groups Guests' Excitement and Quality. Most guests are treated as extended family, which results in a high number of repeat visitors. A big draw, of course, is their sense of belonging to the hotel; a credit to the work of the employees. Franz-Josef Pirktl, director of the Schwarz Resort says, "Only satisfied and enthusiastic employees can deliver high quality service to our guests and we are extremely creative (and innovative) in ensuring the well-being of our 213 employees." The resort is successful in offering high-quality customer service and consequently high customer satisfaction, all of which is achieved by building on the resort's sustainable and social commitment to its philosophy. For example, every evening one Pirktl family member joins the guests for dinner, a personal contact that is highly valued by the guests. Customer satisfaction is measured with a standardized online questionnaire after the guest has returned home. The level of guests' satisfaction is determined through customer information and employees' feedback. The data thus desired is continuously fed into a database and evaluated. If a complaint arises, the staff can react immediately. With regard to service quality, the Schwarz Resort was awarded the Q Service Award 2010 and the Holiday Check Award 2011 and 2012.

Further information: http://www.schwarz.at/

CASE 4

THE GRAND PARK HOTEL HEALTH & SPA BAD HOFGASTEIN (5 STARS)

Maria Wiesinger
Silvia Listberger
Claudia Wachter

The five-star Grand Park Hotel, located in the heart of Austria's Gastein Valley, an area world-famous for its hot springs since the earliest recorded times, located approximately 90 kilometers from the city of Salzburg. Illustrious guests, including Emperor Franz Josef I and his wife, Empress Elisabeth, Prince Bismarck, Franz Schubert, Arthur Schopenhauer, and many others have helped the Gastein Valley to achieve the reputation as a modern, cosmopolitan spa destination.

The tradition of the Grand Park Hotel in Bad Hofgastein is almost as long as the destination's. Its historic building gives the hotel its unique character, strongly marked by quality, with a flavor of modernity as well. Built in 1912 as a Protestant hospice, it served that purpose for only 16 years. By 1928, the hospice had been converted into a hotel.

In the middle of the 20th century, Salzburg's Chamber of Commerce took over the hotel, using it as a hospitality training center. Thus the Grand Park Hotel served as a site of theoretical hospitality education combined with practical training in a "training hotel" environment.

As a three-star hotel, it booked reservations from insurance companies that sent ill patients for a hot springs cure. During 1992–1993, the hotel underwent a complete renovation and refurbishment. At the conclusions of all these efforts, it was upgraded to five-star status—the only such hotel in Bad Hofgastein..

In 2006, the hotel complex expanded further, adding the GRAND SPA, a 2,000-square-meter wellness complex that features an indoor pool, whirlpools, saunas, and steam baths. These measures enabled the Grand Park Hotel to reposition itself as a five-star hotel as well as a health, wellness, and beauty treatment destination. To ensure the hotel's continued success, its current management pursues a high and steady level of quality. The hotel's many awards and distinctions clearly indicate that this effort has been successful. For example, the Grand Park Hotel was ranked in the top quality category in holidaycheck.com's 2012 and 2013 quality rankings; it won the 2012 Ski-guide Austria award; and it achieved the maximum points available in the Snow Stars category.

To satisfy its guests, the Grand Park Hotel works to not only deliver the best service at all times, but also to build its reputation through national and international competitions. Beyond its quality awards and distinctions, it has been distinguished as an officially recognized convalescent institution, health partner of the Gastein Valley, golf partner of the Gastein Valley, Health & Spa Hotel, and training hotel for students attending the Tourism School of Bad Hofgastein.

As one of its unique selling propositions, the hotel enjoys the natural benefits of the hot springs and healing waters, which are the setting for many health and medical treatments. In addition, the hotel can point to the many amenities of the Gastein Valley, including the famous healing cave gallery in Böckstein, approximately 20 minutes away, which combines a treatment of mild overheating, or hyperthermia, with radon therapy, which have scientifically proven beneficial effects on human health. In the philosophy of the Grand Park Hotel, health represents the ultimate asset, one that must be preserved at all times, even and especially before illness begins. To that end, the treatments aim to improve the quality of life. The GRAND SPA features seven treatment rooms, an indoor thermal water pool, a wide range of saunas and steam baths, a fully equipped gym, and a fitness studio with a variety of classes on offer. The treatment programs, administered by six therapists and three medical staff, are tailored to the guests' individual needs. A sampling of the programs available at this writing include:

- Holistic programs, including the signature TCM[1] Retreat, which combines an acupressure-based massage with needle or low-level laser acupuncture
- Detox programs, including the classic FX Mayr Method, developed by Dr. Bodo Werner, which regards malfunctioning intestines as the cause of most physical and emotional disorders. Guests are provided with individual dietary, exercise, and massage plans
- Healing caves and thermal water programs
- Body treatments, wraps, and facials
- Exfoliations and baths
- Massages and special treatments
- Makeup and beauty treatments, along with a special Beauty Detox

The hotel keeps on staff several external health and wellness experts, including Dr. Bodo Werner, who leads many of the detox programs, including the FX Mayr Method; Dr. Liane Weber, who supervises the TCM Retreats and the detox and mental balance programs; and Dr. Robert Költringer, responsible for classic healing and cure programs using the natural healing remedies of the Gastein Valley and its thermal water, the Gastein Healing Gallery, and the vapour baths. This variety of options and types of expertise ensure that every guest is treated according to his or her unique needs.

---

[1]Traditional Chinese medicine

Because health, detoxification, and weight loss are related, the hotel offers carefully, precisely developed GRAND SPA Cuisine, which meets the demands of the health-conscious guests. The hotel also offers strategies for better aging, targeting the market segment of "silver surfers." For the Grand Park Hotel, the goal is to satisfy guests' wishes and desires before they even voice them.

Finally, the Grand Park Hotel has created a unique and appealing situation for its employees. Many of them have worked for the company for years, and they offer invaluable know-how and experience to the company and the guests. At the same time, from a nearby hospitality school the hotel hires students who can fulfill some educational requirements by working in the various hotel departments.

The hotel regularly offers all its employees training and workshops to improve service quality and quality management in the hotel. Further, to motivate and satisfy its employees, the hotel offers superior working conditions. The staff has access to room and full board, along with weekly activity programs and free use of the fitness center and spa facilities. Hotel management offers other incentive programs and develops unique career models for every interested employee.

Grand Park Hotel motivates its management staff to maintain a stellar quality level, using tools such as a questionnaire from the five-star commission, five-star mystery guest analyses, and the Kanu model of customer satisfaction[2].

Further information: www.grandparkhotel.at

---

[2]*Kundenzufriedenheit durch Kernkompetenzen.* (Hans H. Hinterhuber, et al). Ausgabe, 2. Verlag, Gabler, 2003

Case 5

Samadhi Spa & Wellness Retreat: An Australian Case Study

Haywantee Ramkissoon

The Samadhi Spa & Wellness Retreat lies in the enchanting countryside around Daylesford and Hepburn Springs in the state of Victoria, Australia. The codirectors, Annah and Wayne Mirananda, drew from their combined years of experience as spa and wellness specialists to start Samadhi Spa & Wellness Retreat in 2003. Drawing on the Buddhist philosophy, *Samadhi* symbolizes a state of eternal bliss. It adopts a holistic approach to wellness by nurturing the mind, body, heart, and soul to achieve what the founders refer to as "a state of perfect health." Perceived by many as the expanded awareness of the "being," the Samadhi retreat has built its reputation as one of the best spa and wellness providers in Australia and Asia Pacific.

Samadhi embraces the concept of a spa and the desire to offer to its customers all forms of wellness with sensitivity and integrity, founded on many years of professional experience of running a health retreat. Samadhi's success is based on what its codirectors refer to as the "one-pointed dedication to each individual who steps foot in the door" (Anna & Wayne Mirananda). Samadhi aims to provide a lifestyle of health and happiness to its customers with a deep emphasis on open communication, yet ensuring that their privacy is respected. Samadhi endeavors to offer a thoughtful and respectful approach in its delivery of service. The service-oriented practices play a crucial role in maintaining the retreat's success. The wellness and spa retreat provides continuity by ensuring that its practices remain aligned with the business' core business values and guiding principles.

Combining their expertise, Anna and Wayne have produced a team of highly motivated staff ranging from nutritionists to naturopaths and sports physiologists, among others, whose unique skills and expertise together offer a lifestyle of wholeness to the guests. At Samadhi, all employees are hired based on a solid past work history in the wellness and spa industry with strong references supporting excellent customer service. The management strongly emphasizes continuity of excellence and a focus on the delivery of service. Staff are trained in refined practices to enhance their skills and ensure they deliver the services the "Samadhi way" to meet high service expectations of the retreat and of the guests. Employees are trained to approach every guest with respect, care, and sensitivity, maintaining a strong sense of guest boundaries of space and privacy. The daily feedback collected from guests by the retreat's staff allows management to spot any infelicities that require immediate attention or follow-up. Staff are required to follow Samadhi's mission statement and practices carefully so that guests can expect a consistent and satisfying experience. Staff professionals are encouraged to perform regular treatments on one of Samadhi's managing directors to ensure the professionals are following the treatment protocols, policies, and procedures. This enables management to review staff's practices and to provide support and encouragement to staff. Further, Samadhi's employees are empowered to act within their area of responsibility and are rewarded for their efforts.

At Samadhi, personal awareness is perceived as the key factor that guides decisions and strategies in relation to customer service and employee-oriented practices. The spa and wellness retreat endeavors to keep its staff focused and encouraged in their undertakings within the retreat environment. Staff are encouraged to define their individual values and align them with the values of Samadhi, in the expectation that this will allow staff to be more focused in their approach at work. They are also encouraged to adopt the life-shaping approach that provides the physical, emotional, and mental support and spiritual balance that contributes to their happiness and general well-being. Samadhi assists its staff in achieving both personal and professional fulfillment within its retreat environment.

Samadhi's priorities are based on service excellence and customer satisfaction involving two important approaches, namely "connection" and "listening." They form its core values and guiding principles. The retreat adopts the "life-shaping" approach to health and healing that enhances the connection and awareness of the "sense of self." This life-shaping approach emphasizes the inherent power and uniqueness of each individual and it integrates all aspects of service operations such as service practices, day-to-day communications, operations with staff and guests, and all other interrelations and systems within its business structure. The approach emphasizes the "human heart-felt connection" and offers a pathway to profound change in the way an individual perceives him- or herself and the world.

> We co-create with each person, an experience that can be (and often is) truly life changing. If a person is receptive and open to change, much can be achieved in an experience such as this. Our guests' feedback with LifeShaping is that they have experienced a meaningful time in our healing retreat. They feel cared for, relaxed and rejuvenated, listened to, nurtured, encouraged, motivated and inspired to new possibilities. (Anna & Wayne Mirananda)

To optimize customer satisfaction, Samadhi seeks to turn away from the "mechanistic robotic service practices" that are so often devoid of genuine care and kindness and to bring a personalized touch in even its smallest business practices. The staff make a constant effort to ensure that their service practices allow respectful space for open communication and feedback from customers. Staff meet regularly to discuss guests' feedback and build on service differentiation while ensuring that the core business values are congruent with Samadhi's brand. Samadhi seeks to meet its potential guests' needs through prompt responses to all inquiries via phone of correspondence. It further offers complimentary phone consultations to customize programs to individual needs, an added service that has helped greatly in meeting guests' requirements and expectations. This ensures a personal, customized stay for all guests. Staff are highly trained in "double-listening practices," enabling them to understand the extent of each person's communications. This allows them to capture the customers' hopes and dreams, which the management believes are often embedded in customers' words and tones.

Samadhi contributes a percentage of its profits to a worthy cause every year. In 2012, it participated in the fundraising at the Melbourne Marathon to enrich the education of the indigenous children from Palm Island. Through radio programs, Samadhi assisted The Cancer Council of Victoria in raising funds for research, prevention, and support programs for women suffering from cancer. The spa and wellness retreat also supports efforts to protect the environment for future generations. It educates its staff and engages in efficient use of resources, which also lowers operational costs. The retreat maintains its building structures and facilities using natural fibers and environmentally friendly products. Over the last 30 years, Samadhi has invested in its physical facilities, and all aspects of its services and internal business practices. This has contributed largely to earning a solid reputation in service excellence.

In operation for nine years, Samadhi has adopted a diverse marketing strategy that has secured excellent outcomes in terms of high standards in the wellness and spa market. Samadhi's product differentiation lies outside the general classifications of the spa and wellness industry. Drawing from its years of experience in the field before Samadhi was founded, the Miranandas combined their observations about what worked and what did not in the spa and wellness business and brought together a unique combination of hospitality, spa, wellness, therapy, and spirituality. Samadhi chose to remain a boutique retreat, labelled as the Lifeshaping Retreat, with a deep focus on service orientation where attention to detail in a single customer's stay and therapy is starkly contrasted to large-group-oriented retreat packages. Samadhi brings healing and rejuvenating outcomes that clearly distinguish it from other hotel spas and health retreats. Samadhi continues to maintain its reputation for service excellence in the competitive wellness and spa market.

Samadhi today prides itself in being one of the best relaxation and spa hotels in Australia and was the 2012 Travelers Choice winner. Samadhi's greatest recognition of service excellence has come through positive word-of-mouth, which has fuelled the retreat's success. Samadhi honors guests' reviews and comments and encourages guests to share their experiences on its website and the guest book at the center. Perceived as a great spa and wellness retreat in Australia, Samadhi has been featured in a number of media notices in 2010–2012, for example, *Australian Financial Times* magazine, *The Age Traveller Guide*, *Asia Spa* magazine and *Good Health* magazine, among others. Samadhi won Trip Advisor's Certificate of Excellence in 2011 and maintains its reputation of being among the 10 best spa and wellness retreats in Asia Pacific. For codirectors Anna and Wayne Mirananda, "Samadhi's greatest recognition has been in the small steps we take with each person in their individual journey of wellness."

Note: The information used in this case study has been provided by Anna and Wayne Mirananda, the codirectors of Samadhi.

CASE 6

CASE STUDY: MAURITIAN SPA AND WELLNESS HOTEL
CONSTANCE LE PRINCE MAURICE HOTEL AND SPA
Roubina T. D. Juwaheer

The Constance Le Prince Maurice Hotel is a deluxe, five-star hotel set on 60 hectares of unspoiled land, amid the rare and luxuriant vegetation on the island of Mauritius. The hotel's peaceful location offers a sense of exclusivity and a unique experience in which spicy aromas blend with the perfume of the warm ocean.

Although the profile of the hotel's guests has changed over the years, its service focus remains the hotel's key philosophy, which clearly distinguishes it from its leading competitors, whether on Mauritius or in neighboring resort destinations. The consistency of the hotel's service standards derives from the human dimension applied to its luxury service by the staff of the Constance Le Prince Maurice Hotel in terms of customer interaction, personalized service, and signature services.

Many of its customer service initiatives were developed by the hotel to enable its managers and staff members to focus solely and relentlessly on the customer and superior service. In addition to its Balanced Scorecard approach to implement effective performance management strategies , the hotel conducts daily follow-up efforts with their staff to improve on their customer service level and collects guests' feedback. Managers engage in regular guest encounters—from guests' comments at breakfast, to courtesy calls and visits when required, to having *aperitifs* with them before, during, and after their hotel stay. Guests' profiles are captured, detailing their likes, dislikes, preferences, and other pertinent information. This information is shared and communicated across all hotel service delivery points. Positioning of staff and the deployment of key talents in the service chain, in consultation with the human resources department, optimize human capital and ensure enhanced guest experiences.

At the hotel, management is fully responsive to the notable growth in the wellness market; it represents a key market for the 21st century. Spa management affirms that many hotel guests aspire to feel better about their bodies, seek simple inner happiness, want a new way of life, and desire to live longer in better health through prevention and cure. Hence, the hotel's spa services have become an asset that attracts visitors who hope to improve their well-being and enhance their customer value and wellness , at a great value.

In particular, the wellness market has prompted the Constance Le Prince Maurice Hotel to offer a line of cosmetic products and to discover other innovative ways to combine luxury with wellness, which leads to enhanced tangible customer satisfaction. Beyond the beauty of the location and the exceptional service, the hotel recognizes that its clientele has voiced new and growing expectations. For example, as the number of health retreats and spas have grown rapidly, the Constance Le Prince Maurice Spa has responded to loyal guests' interests in "new age" remedies or traditional therapies. Consumer demand thus drives its growth, as long as it can provide an escape from work-related stress and a way to achieve the long-term benefits of self-care. During hotel stays, many guests no longer see the spa as pampering themselves; rather, they regard it as a necessity for remaining healthy and looking good. These consumers prefer simplicity in their spa experiences and access to more traditional spa than new age products.

LE PRINCE MAURICE SISLEY SPA

Situated in Constance Le Prince Maurice Hotel's gardens, the spa reflects the hotel's style, with a calming architecture and relaxed atmosphere. The spa offers a wide range of treatments and facilities. By associating Constance Le Prince Maurice with the prestigious House of Sisley cosmetics line, the spa gives customers a taste of excellence, leading to a stellar experience. The transformational, customized spa experience aims to combine cutting-edge innovation with luxury, emotion, and sensuality. The spa also offers a fitness and well-being program, designed to give customers a full body workout that will burn a maximum amount of unwanted fat. Facilities include a thermal swimming pool with sun lounge chairs, sauna, plunge pool, steam bath, tropical massages, yoga, and beauty and body treatments.

The latest spa concept extends to include children staying at Constance Le Prince Maurice, through the Constance Le Prince Maurice Darling Children Program.

Children between the ages of 3 and 10 years are introduced to spa treatments through packages such as The Little Prince, The Little Mermaid, or Head in the Stars, all designed by Sophie Demaret, the spa manager of ewho happily relies on the imagination of children who have previously visited this innovative combination of childcare and spa in Mauritius. As she notes,

> The demand for child care is growing rapidly. Children are under pressure—school, family life, success. Life is increasingly accelerated. Breaks are needed to recharge. I wanted to share with children a world of sensory pleasure through textures, materials, smells, sight, the sound of water, the taste of beverages, and colors.

The products used for Constance Le Prince Maurice Darling Children are natural and appropriate for children's skin. The outdoor treatments are short (30 minutes) so that parents can share this experience with their children if they wish. According to Demaret, "The maneuvers respect the privacy of the child. It is amusing to see the quiet child after therapy. And the surprise of the parents found their child in a contemplative state and Zen!"

Together with Constance Le Prince Maurice Darling Children, the spa manager also has created a Relaxing Duo Massage for parents and children, so that they can, according to Demaret, "create around the Spa mind moments of great complicity between parents and children. Getting a massage for 30 minutes with his mom or his dad is a rare pleasure for a child." Nor are teens ignored: "We have devised specific care for teenagers. It is important at this age have the right advice[;] self-image is essential in the construction of their adolescent identity. Thus, services such as the first facial, invigorating massage, coconut scrub, candy nail manicure, and glam feet are available to teen guests.

In terms of product trends, Eastern and Asian influences are very strong in most spas offered by the leading hotels of Mauritius, which determines not only their products but also the services offered and the spa design. Considering the strong trend toward "medical" products and services, together with the growing popularity of food- and plant-based treatments, the Constance Le Prince Maurice Spa has designed unique body care and massage services using ancestral medicines, such as the Prince Ayurvedic Treatment and Fusion Massages. Exotic and tropical blends of products, such as the Mauritian sugar cane and rum mixed with coconut oil, macadamia nuts, and spices, create the unique massage potions and scrubs for hotel guests who desire a different kind of spa experience in an island destination.

The spa's use of technology also has advanced in recent years, moving beyond simply using the Internet as a research tool or sending emails. Now the hotel uses modern technology torecord guests' skin types and health history; keep track of massage, sport, and pool preferences; and market special products and services online. When new customers first arrive at Constance Le Prince Maurice Spa and prior to their treatment, they complete a questionnaire to determine their skin type, record their current brand of cosmetics, and note their sports and health habits. Such data enable the hotel to design customized spa and wellness treatments and aligned services for their current and future visits, as the hotel works to become a medispa <u>and provide health and fitness treatments for their customers</u>

Massages remain the most popular treatment at Constance Le Prince Maurice Hotel and Spa, although mind/body services are frequently requested and less traditional products, such as Eastern treatments and products with fitness components, are gaining popularity. Keeping a healthy body and mind (holistic approach) and using natural and organic materials are the focus of new product and service offerings. The spa also customizes services to guests' individual needs and offers packages such as In the Mood for Love or a Prince Detox Ritual for couples' dual massages or hydrotherapy treatments.

The hotel conducts frequent training sessions to enhance employees' abilities to express themselves clearly to colleagues and patrons, to actively seek out ways to make a guest's experience more pleasant, to actively listen to guest inquiries, and to proactively suggest products. The customer satisfaction matrix, which each guest is requested to complete after his or her stay, includes ratings for various service aspects of the hotel. The matrix is closely monitored. A satisfaction score of less than 90 percent is deemed inappropriate. Guest comments are analyzed to determine which remedial measures might be necessary, especially if there is any recurrence among multiple guests. Satisfaction scores close to 100 percent are scrutinized as well, so as not to miss any element that might further enhance the guests' service experience at Constance Le Prince Maurice Hotel.

Its efforts to offer a unique, emotional service experience for guests has garnered the hotel the top ranking by the Relais et Châteaux Association as early as 2002. This global fellowship of individually owned and operated luxury hotels and restaurants aims "to spread its unique art de vivre across the globe by selecting outstanding properties with a truly unique character in idyllic settings and offering exquisite cuisine." Other prestigious awards received by the hotel are:

- Best Honeymoon Resort, Luxury Travel Readers Award 2007
- Best Spa, Genetian Belgium 2007
- Best Spa, Thomas Cook Pegas 2007
- Gold Standard Award, Condé Nast UK 2004
- Best Hotel in the World for Food, Condé Nast UK 2004

Thus at the Constance Le Prince Maurice Hotel, the staff and management together continue to demonstrate their genuine efforts and concern to make sure each guest has a stay that is as memorable, unique, and personalized as possible. The hotel pursues a zero-defect strategy by ensuring rapid service recovery and communication programs to assist both its employees and its guests.

Sources

Qualitative interviews with the resident manager and spa manager of Constance Le Prince Maurice Spa

http://princemaurice.constancehotels.com/

CASE 7

CARDINAL HEALTH
Jichul Jang

Cardinal Health, headquartered in Dublin, Ohio, is a global health care services company that supports health care providers, pharmacies, and suppliers and manufacturers by providing them with an array of products and services. The goal of Cardinal Health is to provide cost-effective solutions for the health care system, to enhance efficiency, and to improve quality so that medical personnel can spend more time caring for their patients.

Cardinal Health is divided into two branches: pharmaceutical and medical.

The pharmaceutical branch includes pharmaceutical distribution, specialty solutions, and nuclear pharmacy services. Cardinal Health distributes pharmaceuticals as well as related health care products and services to hospitals, retail pharmacies, mail-order facilities, and ambulatory care sites. In addition, it delivers 12 million doses of patient-specific nuclear pharmaceuticals per year to nearly 150 national pharmacies for the treatment of neurological diseases and cancers.

The medical branch covers category management and channel management. Category management provides a range of self-manufactured products such as gloves, surgical apparel, and fluid management products for patient care. Channel management is responsible for delivering the best chain solutions to customers from hospitals to doctor's offices, to surgery centers, home health care, and laboratories.

As the business behind health care, Cardinal Health dedicates time and resources to reducing customer costs and improving operations, so medical staff can focus exclusively on their patients.

Robert D. Walter, founder of Cardinal Health, started his business in 1971 as a food distribution company called Cardinal Foods. He soon realized that competition in this market was fierce. Nine years later, he shifted his business focus to pharmaceuticals, which was far more profitable than food distribution. As a first step in this transformation in the 1980s, he focused on acquiring relatively small and privately owned drug distribution businesses in Ohio. Later he expanded his business across the country. Throughout the 1980s (the early growth period), Cardinal Health acquired more than 10 drug distributors. During the middle period of acquisition (1998–2000), Cardinal consistently pursued a diversification strategy and successfully evolved from a drug distributor into a total health care service provider. Diversification and subsequent increases in its market share enabled Cardinal Health to maintain consistent growth and profitability. It continued its acquisition of profitable competitors into the millennium. A series of mergers and acquisitions has turned Cardinal into one of the largest drug wholesalers in the United States within a relatively short time: Sales increased from $429 million in 1986 to nearly $103 billion in 2012.

Cardinal Health operates in the highly competitive business area of medical and surgical product distribution. Cardinal Health's top three rivals are McKesson, AmerisourceBergen, and Owens & Minor. Cardinal Health differs from its competitors in several ways. First, Cardinal Health has expanded its market coverage to China by acquiring Yong Yu, one of the largest pharmaceutical distributors in the country. This acquisition has enabled Cardinal to service more than 49,000 hospitals and 123,000 retail outlets in China. Considering that China's health care market is growing rapidly, Cardinal Health has benefited from establishing business in this country and creating a global growth platform. Three more acquisitions in China have increased Cardinal Health's revenues by $2.9 billion and its operating earnings by $61 million (2011) compared to fiscal 2010.

In addition to benefiting through acquisitions, Cardinal has reaped a competitive advantage by providing continuous training for its workforce. Its employees are constantly trained in ways to make a difference for its customers and surrounding communities. Cardinal's consultants are trained to develop customized marketing plans to help independent pharmacies run profitably by promoting their own local brands. Further, by respecting employees' diverse knowledge, experiences, and backgrounds, it has been able to increase employee engagement, thus improve customer loyalty.

Cardinal Health's employees play a vital role in maintaining public safety. They are educated about supply chain integrity. If employees believe, based on their knowledge and work experience, that a purchase order is suspicious, at their discretion they can stop the order. In other words, employees are empowered through their own knowledge and experience to make decisions about individual orders. Cardinal employees take personal responsibility for their decisions, and they share the belief that their sincere efforts and contributions play a crucial role in the company's continued success. The employee-oriented strategies keep employees involved in the workplace and encouraged to find better ways to serve customers and meet their needs.

Cardinal Health continues to expand its focus in the burgeoning specialty pharmaceutical area. In particular, Cardinal's reputation in oncology and specialty pharmaceutical services has benefited from the acquisition of P4 Healthcare. By creating and maintaining collaborative relationships between innovative insurance companies and oncology providers, Cardinal Health delivers competitive superiority, and in the process, differentiating itself from its competitors.

Cardinal Health maintains vigorous philanthropic efforts by partnering with various local and national organizations. As a socially responsible company, Cardinal Health believes that giving back to the community will enhance the lives of citizens and patients, alike. As part of its philanthropic efforts, Cardinal Health foundation invested more than $150 million to create a health community that improves quality, encourages employee participation, and contributes to disaster relief agencies. Over the years, the company has partnered with schools to promote a healthy lifestyle for children, families, and the elderly. In addition, Cardinal employees are strongly encouraged to become involved in helping their communities. If an employee donates to a charity or other nonprofit organization, Cardinal Health matches the donation. Beyond helping citizens and their communities, such philanthropic efforts have helped Cardinal Health build an excellent reputation nationwide for civic engagement.

Cardinal Health invests in devising and implementing customer-oriented strategies in several ways. For example, it has integrated global manufacturing with its supply chain to deliver an effective mix of products and supply chain services to increase quality patient care. Such an integrated system enables the company to identify the unique needs of each customer and develop products and services based on a deep understanding of what is important to each.

Another strategy that Cardinal Health uses to reduce costs and improve quality for its customers is Valuelink, an effective logistics program that eliminates unnecessary costs of storing, maintaining, and distributing supplies. The program helps hospitals order and receive products on a daily basis. A traditional hospital supply chain comprises many steps and involves many people, from distributors to hospital personnel. The traditional supply chain is time consuming in that health care providers spend much time ordering products and maintaining inventory. The Valuelink program allows Cardinal to provide supplies to hospitals as demand arises. In other words, Valuelink lets hospitals use Cardinal as their "offsite" warehouse, significantly reducing hospitals' costs of storing, maintaining, and distributing supplies. Such innovative, cutting-edge solutions simplify operational processes and reduce costs and increase customer satisfaction.

As the leader in nuclear pharmacy, Cardinal Health can deliver radiopharmaceuticals to more than 95 percent of U.S. hospitals in only three hours or less. Cardinal accomplishes through a network of Positron Emission Tomography (PET) manufacturing facilities and pharmacies that deliver time-sensitive, patient-specific radiopharmaceuticals for diagnostic imaging and therapy. Cardinal Health consistently partners with America's best hospitals and academic institutions to help them market their products. Such a customer-oriented approach not only creates value, it also increases customer loyalty.

Cardinal Health takes an innovative approach to using the latest technology to help its primary customers deliver superior care to their patients. Specifically, hospitals can place orders through Cardinal's website (cardinalhealth.com), which offers additional options to meet various patient needs. Hospitals benefit from ordering online by receiving useful information, including real-time stock status, up-to-the-minute pricing, and purchase history and order confirmation. Customers can have their orders filled and receive them the same day or the next. This is made possible by Cardinal's effective logistics management system, a core strength that employs a nationwide network of 40 distribution centers.

Ranked number 21 on the Fortune 500 list, Cardinal Health employs more than 32,000 worldwide and produces annual revenues of more than $100 billion. By helping health care providers be more cost-efficient and improve patient health quality, Cardinal Health continues to grow and remain a profitable business.

CASE 8

CLEVELAND CLINIC EXPERIENCE
Soyeon Kim

Cleveland Clinic is a not-for-profit multispecialty academic medical center that integrates clinical and hospital care with research and education. Cleveland Clinic was established in 1921 in Cleveland, Ohio by four renowned physicians. Today it is one of the most well-regarded hospitals in the United States. The *U.S. News & World Report's* "2012 Annual Report of America's Best Hospitals" ranked Cleveland Clinic as the fourth best hospital in the United States. The magazine has consistently ranked the hospital in the top six for last 20 years. In particular, Cleveland Clinic's heart and heart surgery programs have been ranked No. 1 in the United States since 1994.

After reading about the long list of achievements and ratings, one may wonder why Cleveland Clinic has such an outstanding reputation for success. The key to its success in an increasingly competitive and shrinking market lies not only in the medical treatment, but also in the service provided to both patients and employees. In the name of patient satisfaction and employee engagement, "Cleveland Clinic Experience" was introduced in 2010 to continue building a strong base of engaged and committed employees who are dedicated to fulfilling Cleveland Clinic's mission of putting "Patients First." Cleveland Clinic Experience is an enterprise-wide initiative developed to enhance the culture at Cleveland Clinic by integrating exceptional employee and patient experiences. The formula for this initiative was simple: Exceptional Employee Experience + World Class Patient Experience = Cleveland Clinic Experience.

PATIENT EXPERIENCE: 'PATIENT FIRST'

"Patient First" is the guiding principle of Cleveland Clinic. Patient experience is a key component of the clinic's strategic plan to achieve a coordinated delivery model that integrates patient-centered care with clinical outcomes, quality, safety, and employee experience. Cleveland Clinic was the first major academic medical center to make patient experience a strategic goal, the first to appoint a chief experience officer, and one of the first academic medical centers to establish an Office of Patient Experience. The clinic recognizes that high quality customer service experience leads to a better patient experience. "Putting patients first requires more than world-class clinical care—it requires care that addresses every aspect of a patient's encounter with Cleveland Clinic, including the patient's physical comfort, as well as his or her educational, emotional, and spiritual needs," said James Merlino, M.D., a chief experience officer. By making the patient and their families happy and accommodated, the patient's stay will be more pleasant and enjoyable.

These values and principles were instilled into Cleveland Clinic by one of its founders, William E. Lower. Dr. Lower summed it up best with this creed:

- A patient is the most important person in the institution—in person or by mail.
- Patients are not dependent on us—we are dependent on them.
- Patients are not an interruption of our work—they are the purpose of it.
- Patients are not an outsider to our business—they are our business.
- The patient is not someone to argue or match wits with.
- The patient is a person, not a statistic.
- It is our job to satisfy them.

This custom-oriented service philosophy resulted in the creation of several groups within the clinic whose sole purpose was achieving patient satisfaction. For example, Patient Service Navigators (PSNs), serves as patient advocates who provide highest level of personalized customer service. Their tasks include daily patient visits and providing personalized guidance to support for both patients and their families.

Other examples of customer-oriented service groups are:

- The Voice of the Patient Advisory Councils – composed of both employees and patients, gather feedbacks and tries to come up with creative solutions that would address problems and concerns of the patient and their families
- The Cleveland Clinic Concierge Desk – assists visitors with information on places of interests, accommodations, directions, dining, travel inquiries, etc.
- The Cleveland Medical Concierge Desk – assists out-of-state patients with their travel plans
- The Cleveland Clinic Caring Canines – certified therapy dogs provide emotional support, increase smiles and laughter, and reduce anxiety for patients and their families
- HUSH (Help Us Support Healing) – provides a consistent and comprehensive approach to reduce nighttime noise and ensure a quiet and healing environment between 9 p.m. and 7 a.m.

The Voice of the Patient Advisory Councils allows patients and families to assume an important role in determining the patient experience. These councils are composed of employees and patients, allowing updated feedback with creative solutions to the challenges that face patients and their families. Other services make patients' experiences as enjoyable as possible, such as The Cleveland Clinic Concierge Desk, which assists visitors with information on places of interest, accommodations, directions, dining, travel inquiries, etc. The Cleveland Clinic Medical Concierge assists out-of-state patients with their travel plans. Last but not least, The Cleveland Clinic Caring

Canines, certified therapy dogs provide emotional support, increase smiles and laughter, and reduce anxiety for patients and their families. The HUSH (Help Us Support Healing) protocol provides a consistent and comprehensive approach to reduce nighttime noise and ensure a quiet and healing environment between 9 p.m. and 7 a.m.

To fulfill responsibilities to deliver high-quality care and to provide an environment of exceptional customer experiences, Cleveland Clinic makes efforts to keep track of consumers' needs and wants through effective communication with customers. The clinic recognized that customers tend to measure service quality based on how well they were treated by health care providers. Also they look at how well their questions were answered, not with medical jargons but with actual explanations that could be understood by regular people. such as how well providers communicate or whether they answered their patients' questions, rather than the medical outcomes that service providers typically care about.

EMPLOYEE EXPERIENCE

The president and CEO of the Cleveland Clinic Health System, Delos M. Cosgrove, said, "Traditionally, medical care has focused on treating and curing disease. Today, we are starting to focus on wellness, and we're beginning with our own employees." Cosgrove believes that the most effective way to successfully engage with consumers is to first take care of the employees. Cleveland Clinic knows it as important for its employees to feel they are treated with respect, since happy employees are motivated to provide a genuine customer-oriented and services-minded performance. Many programs ensure that employees feel comfortable at work. Employee Wellness Programs integrate wellness concepts into the clinic culture, while enhancing the employees' health and quality of life so the patients are cared for as effectively as possible. Health risk assessments and basic screenings, Employee Assistance Programs offering face-to-face counseling, Fitness Centers on campuses, and Lifestyle Management Programs such as a smoking Quit-Line with free nicotine replacement therapy are some of the employee programs on offer.

"Cleveland Clinic Experience" is crucial in delivering quality care and maintaining patient and referring physician loyalty. Cleveland Clinic realized that it could not depend on its history or culture alone to sustain a strong, service-oriented approach to patients. A service excellence infrastructure was clearly necessary for ongoing success. This was accomplished through building key service components—teamwork and technology—into the strategic plan.

TEAMWORK APPROACH

A critical factor in facilitating the Cleveland Clinic Experience is its integrated approach. The founders of Cleveland Clinic envisioned a group practice in which individual members would share clinical expertise and specialization. They recognized that medicine was far too complex for any one person to fully comprehend, and that it was in the patients' best interests if the resources and talents of multiple special-ties were pooled for the development and application of the best medical techniques. Doctors and nurses work in teams, with all team specialists working one-on-one with patients, rather than a single doctor working with a patient one-on-one.

In this environment, physicians from every medical specialty work collaboratively to meet individual patient's needs and preferences. The more specialists working one-on-one with the patient, the more knowledge and fewer tests they will have to run, leading to a lower hospital bill. One element that makes this possible is a salaried system without incentives. It eliminates competition among employees, while fostering a deeper cooperation for the greater good of all stakeholders. Additionally, exchange of support and advice in conjunction with patient service strengthens the motivation to provide excellent service, which ultimately leads to patient satisfaction and loyalty.

TECHNOLOGY AND INNOVATIONS

In Cleveland Clinic, innovative technology facilitates better services and enhances patient experience. The clinic is known for using more cost-effective technologies than many of their competitors. Its electronic medical records, for instance, allow patients upload their health information, such as weight loss or blood-sugar data, directly from scales or devices at home. This encourages patients to become more involved in their health and to keep better communication with their doctors. Cleveland Clinic seeks to create "the future of patient care" through the ongoing application of systems engineering. Process improvement principles and expertise enhance the systems and processes that support efficient and effective service delivery, such as exam room design, patient flow, appointment scheduling, and patient checkin procedures.

REFERENCES

Comarow, A. (2012, July 16). U.S. News Best Hospitals 2012-13: the Honor Roll. *U.S. News & World Report*. Retrieved January 10, 2013, from http://health.usnews.com/health-news/best-hospitals/articles/2012/07/16/best-hospitals-2012-13-the-honor-roll

Cleveland Clinic (2010, Spring). Focus on the Patient Experience. Retrieved January 5, 2013, from http://my.clevelandclinic.org/Documents/Patient-Experience/OPE-Newsletter-5-26-10.pdf

Prince, D. (2011, February 18). Cleveland Clinic's Chief Experience Officer on Building Patient Loyalty. *Catalyst Healthcare Research*. Retrieved December 13, 2012, from http://www.catalysthealthcareresearch.com/learning-center/customerexp/2011/02/18/cleveland-clinics-chief-experience-officer-on-building-patient-loyalty/

Partnership for Prevention (n.d.). Cleveland Clinic Healthcare System: Cleveland Clinic Employee Wellness Program. Retrieved December 8, 2012, from http://www.prevent.org/data/files/initiatives/cosgrove13.pdf

Case 9

Clifton Springs Hospital and Clinic
Hyeyoon Choi

Clifton Springs Hospital and Clinic is located in Clifton Springs, New York, only 25 miles south of Lake Ontario. Even though Clifton Springs Hospital and Clinic is a local health care facility and falls in the "small hospital" category, it has a superior reputation among hospitals in the New York State area. Clifton distinguishes itself from other traditional health care services through a combination of conventional medicine and complementary and alternative (CAM) therapies. This facility has focused on treating the patient as a whole person for more than 150 years, meaning that healing is more than merely curing an illness. For example, most hospitals have pharmaceutical dispensaries, but Clifton has two: one for pharmaceuticals, the other for herbal and Chinese medicine. Additionally, in 2000 Clifton Springs Hospital and Clinic created an entire new wing called The Springs Integrative Medicine Center & Spa, which is devoted exclusively to integrative medicine. In addition, the Finger Lakes' "medical geology" of the healing springs in Geneva, Dansville, and Watkins Glen adds to this natural, holistic practice. However, in the Finger Lakes area, only Clifton grew to become an internationally renowned medical spa. Clifton provides a wide range of health care services, including hydrotherapy, homeopathy, and nutritional, physical, and botanical medicine.

Lewis Zulick, M.D., a surgeon, University of Rochester Medical Center (URMC) faculty member, and vice president for medical affairs at Clifton, commented that his colleagues and he are well aware of the beneficial effects of these integrative therapies in conjunction with traditional medicine. He stated, "Having an entire wing of a hospital devoted to integrative medicine is unusual. The acceptance among the medical staff is remarkable (Diehl, 2012)." Doctors from Clifton's Cancer Center refer their patients to the Wellness Center if they are "going through a rough treatment." Not only do these complementary therapies have no side effects, some of them alleviate symptoms associated with traditional medical treatments.

This innovative approach started with Henry Foster, M.D., a founder of Clifton Springs Hospital and Clinic in 1850. Dr. Foster was a progressive and spiritually oriented physician who designed Clifton Springs Hospital and Clinic based on his personal vision of what a health care facility ought to be like. Integral to his vision was a commitment to quality. In accordance with Foster's vision, Clifton aims to provide patients with a safe, comfortable, tranquil place in which to heal. Since its founding, this philosophy has been maintained by an emphasis on service-oriented practices.

Clifton Springs Hospital and Clinic's success is based on the value its staff places on their patients. Even though Clifton Springs Hospital and Clinic is relatively small, it differentiates itself from its competitors by emphasizing customer service as the main pillar of its business practices. The health care professionals at Clifton feel that smaller hospitals with a more cohesive staff are more likely to consider the nonmedical options requested by patients. Similarly, Clifton Springs Hospital and Clinic invests more in integrative medicine compared to larger, urban hospital systems in Rochester. According to O. J. Sahler, M.D., pediatrician and URMC professor, the fact that doctors in the traditional health care setting spend no more than 8–12 minutes with each patient led to the popularity of complementary therapies. Patients want to feel cared for, listened to, and supported. For this reason, complementary therapies address these needs well. "Compare that with 20 minutes or more of a hands-on treatment like massage, where a patient-consumer is able to feel truly cared for. People would rather spend money on modalities that give one-on-one attention and caring." Sahler said (Diehl, 2012).

When the new wing of The Springs Integrative Medicine Center & Spa was under construction, in order to create the best healing environment possible, the health care staff of The Springs consulted a group of artists to determine and design the best patient environment. Essential aspects such as soft lighting, calming colors, textures, and artwork were brought together to create an atmosphere of tranquil healing. In addition, Clifton Springs Hospital & Clinic established an Office of Performance Improvement to specifically ensure the quality of patient care.

These ongoing service-oriented practices of Clifton Springs Hospital & Clinic have eventually paid off and are reflected in the accolades it has received. Recently, the American Hospital Association's "Hospitals in Pursuit of Excellence" program recognized four hospitals in New York State for efforts in quality improvement and patient safety; one Large, one Multi-Entity, one Small, and one Specialty hospital. Clifton Springs Hospital and Clinic received the award in the Small Hospital category. More important, three out of four patients ranked Clifton as the "best hospital possible," according to the New York State Hospital Report Card. Beyond that, Clifton Springs Hospital and Clinic has been granted numerous other awards such as "Uncommonly Good Award" from Common Good Planning Center of Rochester and "Sodexho & Modern Healthcare Spirit of Excellence Award" for establishing a blame-free culture organization. All these accolades were made possible because of Clifton Springs Hospital & Clinic's efforts to adopt a customer-centered strategy that merges conventional medicine with complementary and alternative medicine in one location for the benefit of patients.

REFERENCES

Diehl, M. (2012, Spring). The new look of wellness. *Canandaigua Magazine*, 31–41.

CASE 10

WEXNER MEDICAL CENTER: A CASE STUDY TO EXAMINE SERVICE MANAGEMENT TECHNIQUES IN THE HEALTH CARE INDUSTRY

Anupama Sukh
Hyejin Park

INTRODUCTION TO THE ORGANIZATION

Wexner Medical Center is known for its exceptional customer service and efficient health service strategies. It stands out from its competitors in terms of unique employee- and customer-oriented practices that maintain its reputation as one of the best customer-service-oriented organizations. Wexner gained success in offering unparalleled health service to customers by promoting P4 (preventive, predictive, personalized, participatory) medicine. Besides employee- and customer-oriented practices, Wexner Medical Center promotes P4 medicine with the application of latest technology. This case study explains the exceptional employee- and customer-oriented practices at Wexner Medical Center as well as the role of technology in promoting P4 medicine.

Wexner Medical Center at The Ohio State University is a multidisciplinary, academic medical center located in Columbus, Ohio, in the United States. It is well established as a leading medical center in Columbus, the Midwestern, and the nation, due to its exceptional reputation for combining medical expertise with stellar service.

The medical center dates back to 1834 when the Willoughby Medical University of Lake Erie was founded in Willoughby, Ohio. To improve its clinical facilities, Willoughby expanded into Columbus. A local attorney, Lyne Starling, donated the expansion funds, and the clinic became the Starling Medical College, the first teaching hospital in the country. Over the decades, as the medical center developed, it took the name The Ohio State University Medical Center, later changed to The Ohio State University Wexner Medical Center, in honor of the contributions of Leslie Wexner, who is one of the university's most committed leaders and benefactors.

Table 22.1	History of Wexner Medical Center
1834	The origin of Wexner Medical Center dates back to 1834 with the founding of Willoughby Medical University of Lake Erie
1846	The medical center moved to Columbus and took the name Starling Medical College
1907	The medical center merged with Columbus Medical College and Ohio Medical College and took the name Starling Ohio Medical College
1914	The medical center became part of the University Hospitals Systems
1993	The medical center was exposed to the concept of Ohio State University Medical Center
1999	Ohio State University Hospitals East opened
2004	Ross Heart Hospital opened on the medical center campus
2012	Ohio State University Medical Center was renamed to Wexner Medical Center in honor of donations by Leslie Wexner

Wexner Medical Center is one of the largest academic medical centers in the United States. It comprises a college of medicine, which ranks in the Top 30 in the country, six hospitals, specialty care practices, research centers, and institutes. Its mission is to improve people's lives through innovation in research, education, and patient care. The Ohio State University Wexner Medical Center is one of the most distinguished research institutions in the United States. How the medical center treats and cares for the patients now differs greatly from how it was done only 10 years ago. This progress in treatment and service methods is an outcome of intensive research. Wexner Medical Center facilitates research to develop the treatments methods of future. For example, the Wexner research team has developed applications such as the Supramap, a web-based application to track the spread of diseases.

The employees of the Wexner Medical Center pursue a common vision and work as a team. Their spirit and the quality of services they offer are unsurpassed in terms of their willingness to help and find solutions for their patients and their families. Dr. Mary Nach, chief nursing executive, considers her service a privilege, since she has the opportunity rather than a mission or commitment) to serve patients and their families in their most vulnerable moments.

When it comes to selecting a health care provider, having a choice is important. Wexner Medical Center offers many consumer-oriented programs and services. By offering this wide range of options, the hospital can provide patients with the right combination of expertise and health services in their most vulnerable times. Ohio State's Wexner Medical Center is a national leader in developing personalized health care—the P4 Model—a new form of health care delivery based on each patient's particular biology, behavior, and environment. The P4 Model highlights the predictive, preventive, personalized, and participatory elements of health care.

Medical center management supports and encourages patient participation. Even if a terminally ill patient is at an end stage of organ failure, he or she receives encouragement to find ways to address the progression of the illness. Dr. Steven Gabbe, senior vice president for health sciences, emphasizes the role of personalization in every facet of the organization.

The Wexner Medical Center staff creates, circulate, and apply new forms of expertise to satisfy the needs of each patient. The service is further divided into six signature programs—cancer, critical care, heart, imaging, neuroscience, and transplantation—to provide science-based, specialized care. With the help of world-class experts like Dr. Robert Higgins, director of Ohio State's Comprehensive Transplant Center, Wexner Medical Center focuses on customer service based on the P4 model.

STRATEGIC PLANNING

The medical center's strategic plan aims to create a high-performance organization, as well as a workplace of choice. Medical center leaders have identified six key result areas (KRAs) that can ensure personalized health care for patients innovation and strategic growth, financial performance, service and reputation, workplace of choice, quality, productivity, and efficiency. Using a scorecard, every function within the medical center measures its institutional progress on the six KRAs. According to Dr. Clay Marsh, vice dean for research, "Our goal is to create medical care that engages consumer participation, predicts and prevents disease, facilitates wellness, and creates a personalized life-wellness plan for each person."

The ambitious patient care goals could not be achieved without specific, strategic, integrative plans. The organization has identified six such critical plans: program development, people, technology, marketing, financial, and facilities. These six strategic planning areas ensure that the most promising projects are pursued, that necessary and efficient faculty and staff are recruited, that advanced technology is implemented, that effective marketing plans (e.g., a branding strategy focused the medical center's on national reputation) are executed, that financial resources are secured, and that all facilities (e.g., ambulatory, inpatient, research, education) are well maintained.

The major trend in altering the landscape of health service sector is the advancement in information technology. Inventory management has shifted to information management, which enhances the organization's abilities to redefine its marketing and operational strategies, management strategies, and retail distribution channels (Vida, 2000). Information (IT) technology has revolutionized the interactions between service providers and consumers, leading to long-term business success of service providers (Lee, Chiu, Liu, & Chen, 2011). Modern service industries are characterized by the extensive use of technological application as a result of competition, globalization, and the advancement in IT (Liu, 2011), resulting in value enhancement of organizations. Given the importance of technological advancement in service industry, this case study identifies recent trends in health IT applications of Wexner Medical Center.

TECHNOLOGY PLAN

Wexner Medical Center's technology plan identifies emerging clinical technologies and health information systems in order to facilitate the use of cutting-edge medical surgical equipment and diagnostic tools to improve health service. Wexler Medical also focuses on the latest medical technology applications to promote education, research, and patient wellness. Furthermore, technology supports the collaboration, communication, innovation, and personal productivity of all Wexner Medical's employees.

By implementing new technologies, the medical center has ensured the completion of a medical grade network, which provides upgraded wireless network coverage including comprehensive voice, video, and data networks with good stability and greater bandwidth, assuring availability even in the face of equipment failures. All hospitals within Wexner Medical Center offer free wireless Internet access to patients. Other forms of advanced technologies include its integrated health information system (IHIS), which maintains continuous, personalized records for each patient, from the start of a patient's interaction with the medical center. Robotic surgical technology applications and telemedicine capabilities allow Wexner Medical to collaborate with external referring physicians. Such collaborations lead to better decision making, especially in critical cases such as high-risk pregnancies. Wexner Medical MyChart patient portal provides a medium for more than 10,000 patients to communicate with their medical providers and gain access to their medical records. With mobile video interpretation services, offered throughout the medical center 24 hours a day, patients can receive help in 150 languages. Finally, Wexner Medical Center's Caring Bridge is a social networking site that helps patients stay in touch with their families and friends during and after their hospital stay. Through the Caring Bridge, patients can update everyone at the same time with health-related news or photos or receive warm wishes—without having to make multiple telephone calls, sending mass emails, or writing many letters. The site's multiple privacy settings ensure patient safety at no charge.

According to Phyllis Teater, chief information officer of Wexner Medical Center, the technological team's mission is to facilitate the organization's progression along the P4 model. The resulting world-class practices and services enhance all patients' experience. The technology plan identifies emerging clinical technologies and health information systems, to facilitate the use of cutting-edge medical surgical equipment and diagnostic tools.

AWARDS AND RECOGNITIONS

The Ohio State University Wexner Medical Center is a leader in its region, earning 10 specialty rankings, including cancer and cardiology, in the "2012–13 Best Hospital" rankings by *U.S. News & World Report*. According to the University Health System Consortium (UHC), whose membership includes academic health systems from across the country, Wexner Medical Center is one of the 10 academic medical centers in the United States that delivers the highest quality of care. In recognition of this standing, Wexner Medical Center won the 2011 UHC Quality Leadership Award, granted to academic medical centers that demonstrate excellence in delivering high-quality care.

Wexner Medical Center offers value-added services to meet the customers' expectations of immediate and efficient health care delivery. The center's mission to provide unique P4 medical service to customers is executed through well-trained employees, efficient customer service practices, and use of advanced technologies. These capabilities set Wexner Medical Center apart from its competitors as an exemplary health service provider.

REFERENCES

Lee, W.-I., Chiu, Y. T., Liu, C.-C., & Chen, C.-Y. (2011). Assessing the effects of consumer involvement and service quality in a self-service setting. *Human Factors and Ergonomics in Manufacturing & Service Industries*, 21(5), 504–515. doi:10.1002/hfm.20253

Liu, S. (2011). Modern service industry in Tianjin: Problem, system construction and measures. In M. Zhou (Ed.), *Education and management*: Communications in computer and information science, 210, 185–191. Berlin/Heidelberg Springer. Retrieved from http://www.springerlink.com/content/ltt8m088t2mql1087/abstract/

Vida, I. (2000). An empirical inquiry into international expansion of US retailers. *International Marketing Review*, 17(4/5), 454.

AUTHOR BIOGRAPHIES

CHAPTER 1

Jay Kandampully Ph.D., is a professor of service management and hospitality at The Ohio State University, USA. He is the Editor in Chief of the *Journal of Service Management*. He serves on the editorial advisory board for 12 refereed international journals. He holds a PhD in service management, and an MBA, with specialization in service marketing, both from the University of Exeter, England. Jay is the author of the book "Services Management: The New Paradigm in Hospitality" (this book has been translated into Chinese), and the editor of the book "Service Management: The New Paradigm in Retailing" (this book has been translated into Chinese) and the lead editor of the book, "Service Quality Management in Hospitality, Tourism and Leisure" (this book has been translated into Chinese, Korean and Arabic). Jay has published over 100 articles in journals such as: Journal of Service Management, European Journal of Marketing, The Service Industries Journal, Managing Service Quality, The Journal of Product & Brand Management.

CHAPTER 2

Joris van de Klundert Ph.D., is a professor and chairs the department of Health Services Management & Organisation of the Institute of Health Policy & Management (iBMG) at Erasmus University Rotterdam. He is also director of education of iBMG. He holds an MSc in Computer Science from Erasmus University Rotterdam and a Ph.D. in Operations Research from Maastricht University. He has served as president of the Dutch Operations Research Society. His present interest lies in strategic health services optimization research, particularly regarding the value of care provided by health service networks.

CHAPTER 3

Victoria Bellou Ph.D., is an Assistant Professor of Management at the University of Thessaly, Greece. She gained her Bachelor's degree at the University of New Haven, Connecticut, her Master's at the University of Macedonia, Greece, and her PhD at the University of Piraeus, Greece. She has professional experience as a Human Resource Specialist and has worked on several research projects. Her research interests include psychological contract, service quality, organizational culture, management of health organizations, public sector management, and management of change. Her work has been published in International Public Management Journal, Journal of Business Research, International Journal of Human Resource Management, Managing Service Quality, and Journal of Health Organization and Management.

Dr. Aristea Bellou MD., is a Specialist in Internal Medicine at Papageorgiou Hospital, Thessaloniki, Greece. She gained her medical degree and her PhD at Aristotle University, Greece. She interacts with patients, both in offering treatment and coordinating their participation in European study protocols for new medical products. She has been working on multiple study protocols with European and worldwide participation for more than six years. Her research interests include the study of the liver, immunology, and infection.

CHAPTER 4

Ravi S. Behara Ph.D., is an Associate Professor in the Department of Information Technology & Operations Management in the College of Business at Florida Atlantic University. His current research interests include health care operations and service analytics. He has published a variety of articles on service operations in academic journals including *International Journal of Operations and Production Management and International Journal of Production Economics* and in research books such as *Handbooks in Information Systems* and *Advances in Patient Safety.* Dr. Behara's consulting assignments include the creation of a new service development methodology for a large US financial services organization. He also worked as an electrical engineer in the construction of large multi-national power plants projects in India and Saudi Arabia. Dr. Behara holds a Ph.D. in service operations management from Manchester Metropolitan University, U.K., and a B.E. in electrical engineering from The Indian Institute of Science.

Dr. Fabio Potenti, MD., is a colorectal surgeon who serves at Cleveland Clinic Florida as Administrator of Research and Education, Physician Advisor for Utilization Review, and hospitalist for the Department of Colorectal Surgery. He currently holds academic appointments at Florida Atlantic University and Florida International University. Prior to this, Dr. Potenti was Associate Professor at Brown University and the Director for Medical Students Clerkship in Surgery at Brown Medical School. Dr. Potenti has published numerous peer-reviewed journal articles and book chapters. He has been invited to present his work at national and international scientific meetings. He is a member and fellow of the American Society of Colorectal Surgery and the American Society of Surgery. Dr. Potenti completed his medical degree at the University of Florence, his general surgery training at Brown University, and a colorectal fellowship at Cleveland Clinic Florida. He also obtained an MBA from Florida Atlantic University.

CHAPTER 5

Miguel A. Moliner, Ph.D., is full professor of marketing at Universitat Jaume I (Spain). He is currently a vice-rector of the Universitat Jaume I in Castellón. His line of research focuses on relationship marketing and the study of customer loyalty. He has published papers in the area of hospital marketing in the Journal of Service Marketing, Health Care Management Review, European Journal of Marketing, The Service Industries Journal, Journal of Service Management, Gaceta Sanitaria, and Atención Primaria.

Miguel A. López, Ph.D., is a lecturer of management at Universitat Jaume I (Spain). He is currently director of the Business Administration and Marketing Department at Universitat Jaume I in Castellón. His line of research is currently focused on logistics. He has published papers in International Journal of Business Performance Management, International Business Review, Journal of International Marketing and Exporting, European Urban and Regional Studies, and The Review of Regional Studies.

CHAPTER 6

Hyeyoon Choi is a Ph.D. candidate at The Ohio State University in the Department of Consumer Sciences. She completed her Master's degree in 2008 at Purdue University in the Department of Hospitality and Tourism Management. Hyeyoon's research interests include health and wellness-related service, environmentally-friendly behaviors, hotel operations, and service management. She has published in the Journal of Hospitality Marketing & Management. During her Ph.D. years, Hyeyoon has taught courses in hotel operations management and principles of tourism. She has received the Best Teaching Award for Graduate Teaching Associates for two consecutive years, 2012 and 2013.

Kathryn Stafford Ph.D., is an Associate Professor at The Ohio State University in the Department of Consumer Sciences. She teaches graduate and undergraduate courses in management theory, family business management, and quantitative methods. Her research, published in nine books and numerous professional journals such as Cornell Hospitality Quarterly and Journal of Family and Economic Issues, has been featured in The Wall Street Journal, Time, and Newsweek. Her research on econometric analyses of the managerial practices of employed wives and family business owners has been funded by the National Science Foundation and U.S. Department of Agriculture. She is one of the authors of Sustainable Family Business Theory, a holistic model of family firms. For over a decade she and other members of the Family Business Research Group (FBRG) have collaborated to collect the first panel data from a national sample of family business owners and their families. The FBRG has written two books and over 100 refereed journal articles. The Group has been recognized repeatedly by USDA for the high caliber of its research.

Chapter 7

Carlos F. Gomes Ph.D., is an Assistant Professor with Tenure in the School of Economics at the University of Coimbra, School of Economics, Portugal and Researcher at the Institute of Systems and Robotics, Coimbra. He received a PhD in Industrial Management, an MS in Industrial Management, a postgraduate certificate of Advanced Studies in Industrial Quality and International Business, and a BS in Electrical Engineering, all from the University of Coimbra. His main research interests are performance management, operations strategy and improving of production systems. He has published in many refereed journals and proceedings of professional meetings.

Mahmoud M. Yasin, Ph.D, is a Professor of Management in the Department of Management & Marketing at East Tennessee State University. He received his Ph.D. in Industrial Management from Clemson University. His research has appeared in such journals as the Journal of Operations Management, OMEGA, International Journal of Production and Operations Management, and Business Research. Dr. Yasin currently serves on several editorial boards. He is the recipient of several teaching and research awards and recognitions.

Phillip E. Miller Ph.D., is a full professor and Department Chair in Management and Marketing at East Tennessee State University. He has worked at the university for 19 years and has been teaching for the last 28 years. During his educational career he has published and presented numerous papers in the areas of health care management, environmental issues, total quality management, and project management. In addition to his educational career, he spent over 22 years in the United States Air Force.

CHAPTER 8

Mark Anderson is a PhD candidate at the University of Canberra, investigating the delivery of mental health services within frontier environments. Mark has a background in education and IT project management and has been consulting for the Australian Government for the last two years in the area of cyber bullying among school children.

Byron Keating Ph.D., is a Professor of Service Management at the University of Canberra. His research interests concern with the nexus between technology and the service experience. Byron completed his Ph.D. at the University of Newcastle, Australia on the topic of multichannel service relationships. His work has been published in leading IT and service operations journals including Proceedings of the IEEE, European Journal of Information Systems, Journal of Computer Information Systems, Electronic Markets, Journal of Supply Chain Management, Supply Chain Management: An International Journal, and Journal of Business Logistics.

Anton Kriz Ph.D., is a Senior Lecturer in International Business at the University of Newcastle, Australia. His research interests focus on innovation management processes within emerging markets such as China. He completed his Ph.D. at Central Queensland University on the topic of interpersonal trust in Chinese business relationships. His work has been published in Management Decision, Asia Pacific Business Review, China Review International, International Journal of Value Chain Management, Journal of Hospitality, and Tourism Management.

CHAPTER 9

Kenneth K. Boyer Ph.D., is Professor of Operations Management at the Fisher College of Business, The Ohio State University. He has a Master's and a Ph.D. from The Ohio State University as well as a BS in mechanical engineering from Brown University. He was an Assistant Professor at DePaul University from 1995 to 2000. From 2000 to 2008 Dr. Boyer was an Associate and Full Professor at MSU.

Luv Sharma is a third-year Ph.D. student concentrating on Operations Management at The Ohio State University. He has a Master's and MBA from The Ohio State University and has worked on a number of process improvement projects with reputable firms like Cleveland Clinic and Nationwide Insurance.

CHAPTER 10

Ravi S. Behara Ph.D., (See chapter 4)

C. Derrick Huang, Ph.D., is an Associate Professor at the Department of Information Technology & Operations Management in the College of Business at Florida Atlantic University. Previously, as a practitioner, he held executive-level positions in the area of marketing and strategic planning in a number of high-tech companies. Dr. Huang's research interest lies in the business value and strategic impact of information technology in organizations, and his current focus is on the economics of information security investments, risk management of information systems, and health care IT. His work has been published in leading journals such as Decision

Sciences Journal, Decision Support Systems, International Journal of Production Economics, Communications of the AIS, Information Systems Management, and IEEE IT Pro. He holds Ph.D. from Harvard University.

Jahyun Goo P.hD., is an Associate Professor of MIS at the Florida Atlantic University. His active research areas are IS sourcing, IT management and strategy, interorganizational relationships, health care IT, and IS security. His papers have been published in MIS Quarterly, Decision Sciences, Decision Support Systems, Information Systems Journal, and Information Systems Frontier, among others. Dr. Goo has presented his research at the premier IS conferences. His work has received recognition from conferences and publishers as best or outstanding paper. He has served for major journals as either a reviewer or a coordinating editor. He holds Ph.D. in MIS from the State University of New York at Buffalo.

CHAPTER 11

Tor Wallin Andreassen Ph.D is Professor of Marketing at NHH Norwegian School of Economics and the Director of Center for Service Innovation. Professor Andreassen is the Area Editor at MIS Quarterly and Journal of Service Management, member of the editorial review board of MIT Sloan Management Review, Journal of Service Research, Journal of Business Research, Service Science, Journal of Service Management, and Decision Science Journal. Dr Andreassen has published in leading journals such as: MIT Sloan Management Review, Marketing Science, Journal of Marketing, Quality & Quantity, Journal of Economic Psychology, Journal of Service Research, European Journal of Marketing, and Journal of Service Management. Professor Andreassen has received several awards for his research, including the MSI/H. Paul Root Award 2007 (*Journal of Marketing*). Dr. Andreassen has been a Visiting Professor at Vanderbilt University, USA, University of Maryland, USA, University of Queensland, Australia, and a visiting scholar at Stanford University and University of Maastricht, NL. He has received pedagogical education from Vanderbilt University and Harvard Business School.

Even J. Lanseng Ph.D., is an Associate Professor, Department of Marketing, BI Norwegian Business School. He is also Associate Dean for the bachelor program in Marketing Communication at the same school. He holds a PhD from the Norwegian University of Life Sciences and has previously held a position as Associate Professor at the same university. Dr. Lanseng's research has been published in journals such as Journal of Service Management, European Journal of Marketing, and Journal of Brand Management. Dr. Lanseng is a member of the editorial review board of Journal of Service Management. He teaches consumer behavior, marketing management, and research methodology. His current research interests include service marketing and consumer behavior.

CHAPTER 12

Dr. Carolin Durst Ph.D is an Associate Professor at the Chair of Information System II at the University of Erlangen-Nuremberg. She holds a Ph.D. in the field of Services Science. Her current research focuses on mobile services management as well as collaborative decision support in innovation management.

Andreas Hamper studied Information Systems at the University of Erlangen-Nuremberg. Since 2011, he has been a member of the research staff and a Ph.D. student at the Institute of Information Systems. In his research he focuses on mobile technologies and health care.

Tino Mueller holds a graduate degree in International Information Systems from the University of Erlangen-Nuremberg. In his Master's thesis, he focused on mobile applications in the preventive health care domain. He currently works for a global technology consulting company.

CHAPTER 13

Johanna Gummerus Ph.D., is an Assistant Professor at Hanken School of Economics in Helsinki, Finland. Her research interests include service innovation, social media and consumer empowerment, value creation, and customer service experiences. Her research has been published previously in e.g. Marketing Theory, Journal of Marketing Management, Journal of Services Marketing, Journal of Service Management and Journal of Retailing and Consumer Services.

Veronica Liljander Ph.D., is Professor of Marketing and Programme Director at Hanken School of Economics, Helsinki, Finland, and Director of the Finnish Doctoral Programme of Business Studies. She has been the head of the Department of Marketing and Vice Dean of Hanken. Her current research interests include service marketing and consumer experience in online media. She has published in, for example, Journal of Service Marketing, Journal of Service Industry Management, Journal of Retailing and Consumer Services, Psychology&Marketing, Journal of Business and Industrial Marketing, and Journal of Marketing Management. She is on the Editorial review board of several international journals, for example, Journal of Service Research, Journal of Service Management, and European Journal of Marketing.

Catharina von Koskull Ph.D., is a researcher at CERS (Centre for Relationship Marketing and Service Management), Hanken School of Economics, Helsinki, Finland. Her research interests include service management, service innovation, manager's mental models and ethnography. Her research has been published in, for example, Scandinavian Journal of Management and Journal of Business and Industrial Marketing.

CHAPTER 14

Catherine Berry is a Business Strategy Consultant. She completed her MBA in 2005 at Fisher College of Business at the Ohio State University and her Master's degree in 2012 at the Ohio State University in the Department of Consumer Sciences. Catherine's research interests include services and property development in the wellness sector and creating value in new markets.

CHAPTER 15

Jens Hogreve Ph.D., is Professor and Chair of Service Management at the Catholic University of Eichstaett-Ingolstadt, Germany. He received his Ph.D. from the University of Hagen. His research focuses on service issues such as service recovery and service guarantees, service innovation, industrial services, and customer co-creation of service. His work has been published in the International Journal of Research in Marketing, Journal of Service Research, Journal of Retailing, German-language journals, and edited book chapters. In addition to his academic position he is founder and partner of Hogreve & Cie management consultancy.

Nicola Bilstein Ph.D., is a postdoc in the field of Service Management at the Catholic University of Eichstaett-Ingolstadt, Germany.She received her Ph.D. from the Catholic University of Eichstaett-Ingolstadt, Germany, and her B.A. and M.A. in International Business Studies from the University of Paderborn. Her current research interests are in the field of service marketing, particularly in issues related to co-production, pricing, online communities, and service recovery. In 2010, she received the ASU CSL/Liam Glynn Research Scholarship Award for the most promising young scholar in services, awarded by AMA's SERVSIG. In 2011, she was awarded first runner-up in the Fisher IMS and AMA SERVSIG Dissertation Proposal Competition. Ms. Bilstein was a visiting scholar at the Fisher College of Business (The Ohio State University, United States) in 2011.

CHAPTER 16

Liz Gill's qualifications include Dip Pty, BSc PT, MBA, MA, and PhD. She is a research fellow in the Medical School at The University of Sydney. Her current research interest is in the area of service formation within the context of health services for older people, focusing on service co-creation and the role and contribution of the client to health service quality and service outcomes. Her previous work experience includes: project manager, and health professional at the direct service provision, health system design, policy, and consulting levels. Her work has been presented at and published in both the health and services academic sectors. A social researcher and strategic change leader skilled at identifying service processes and designing socially derived models, she has extensive experience developing and commissioning change-focused projects in the health and human services areas. This has involved stakeholder cooperation and involvement; systemic reform; system process re-engineering; and service quality and service improvement. Her PhD dissertation, "Factors influencing participant interaction in the service co-creation process: A triadic study," was completed at The University of Sydney, Australia.

CHAPTER 17

Allard van Riel Ph.D., is professor of Marketing and director of the Institute for Management Research of the Radboud University in Nijmegen, the Netherlands. He holds a PhD in Service Innovation Management from Maastricht University (2003). Between 2004 and 2009 he held a Chair in Innovation Management at the University of Liege in Belgium. Research interests include cognitive aspects of decision-making under complexity and uncertainty in service innovation and service operations management. He currently focuses on responsible decision-making in healthcare innovation.

Laura Visser is a PhD Candidate at the Institute for Management Research, Radboud University Nijmegen in the Netherlands. She started her project in August 2011, studying the use of a technology, which supports online communication between patients and their own healthcare professionals. The focus of her research is on the role of (changing) power processes between patient and healthcare professionals on these online health communities.

Martijn van der Eijk is a PhD Candidate in the department of neurology of the Radboud University Nijmegen Medical Center (UMCN). He studied human movement sciences at the UMCN and Fundamentals of Business and Economics at the University of Utrecht. He started his PhD project in 2009, supervised by Prof. Bas Bloem, Dr. Marten Munneke and Dr. Marjan Faber. He examines patient-centered, collaborative care innovations for Parkinson's disease patients. Concurrently, he is employed at ParkinsonNet as a health services researcher and coordinator of patient-centered care.

Marjan Faber Ph.D., is senior research fellow at the Scientific Institute for Quality of Health Care at the Radboud University Nijmegen Medical Centre in Nijmegen, the Netherlands. Her research interests relate to patient empowerment, public reporting, primary care organization and international health policy. Faber earned her MSc in Health Science from Radboud University Nijmegen, the Netherlands (1993) and her PhD in veterinary science from Utrecht University, the Netherlands (2001).

Marten Munneke Ph.D., is associate professor of healthcare innovation at the Radboud University Medial Centre, Nijmegen, in the Netherlands. He studied human movement sciences at VU University Amsterdam and obtained his PhD from Leiden University in the Netherlands in 2004. He is responsible for several clinical trials concerning the organization of allied health care in Parkinson's disease and is managing director of the ParkinsonNet coordination center that aims to support the national ParkinsonNet network.

Professor Bas Bloem is a consultant neurologist at the Department of Neurology, Radboud University Nijmegen Medical Centre, in the Netherlands. He received his M.D. degree (with honors) at Leiden University Medical Centre in 1993. In 1994, he obtained his PhD in Leiden, based on a thesis entitled "Postural reflexes in Parkinson's disease". He was trained as a neurologist between 1994 and 2000, also at Leiden University Medical Centre. He received additional training as a movement disorders specialist during fellowships at 'The Parkinson's Institute', Sunneyvale, California (with Dr. J.W. Langston), and at the Institute of Neurology, Queen Square, London (with Prof. N.P. Quinn and Prof. J.C. Rothwell).

In 2002, he founded and became Medical Director of the Parkinson Centre Nijmegen (ParC), which was recognized from 2005 onwards as center of excellence for Parkinson's disease. Together with Dr. Marten Munneke, he developed ParkinsonNet, an innovative healthcare concept that now consists of 64 professional networks for Parkinson patients covering all of the Netherlands (www.parkinsonnet.nl).

Chapter 18

Anja Tuohino is development manager at the Centre for Tourism Studies at the University of Eastern Finland. Her research interests are in lake tourism development, wellness and well-being tourism, and innovation policy. She also has extensive experience with several tourism development projects.

Anne-Mette Hjalager is a professor and head of the Danish Centre for Rural Research at the University of Southern Denmark. She works in the area of innovation in tourism, with a particular emphasis on rural and peripheral locations. She is interested in emerging forms of tourism and new, collaborative constellations in the welfare state environment.

Edward Huijbens is the director of the Icelandic Tourism Research Centre and professor in the Department of Business and Science at the University of Akureyri. His main field of interest lies in researching landscapes and tourism experiences, along with innovation, tourism marketing, and tourism's role in regional development.

Henna Konu is project manager at the Centre for Tourism Studies at the University of Eastern Finland. Her research interests are in service development, wellness and wellbeing tourism, sustainable tourism, and customer research in tourism. She is currently writing her Ph.D. dissertation on the customer's role in experience service development.

CHAPTER 19

Heli Tooman Ph.D., is an Associate Professor of Tourism Management, Department of Tourism Studies at Pärnu College of the University of Tartu. Her research and teaching focuses on quality in tourism and customer service, health, wellness, and spa tourism, as well as sustainable tourism destination development. Her favorite subjects relate to philosophical approaches: wellness philosophy, service philosophy and culture, and philosophy of hospitality. She has published six tourism textbooks and more than 40 articles. She is also a co-author of two bilingual tourism dictionaries. She has been for many years head of the National Tourism Curriculum Board and Head of the Commission that evaluates tourism-related curriculum in Estonia. She has participated in many tourism-related projects as an expert and consultant on the development of Estonian and regional tourism plans and participated in the development of the categorization system for Estonian spas, etc. She also has practical working experience as a hotel manager.

Kai Tomasberg is currently working as program manager of the International Master's program Wellness and Spa Service Design and Management in the Department of Tourism Studies of the University of Tartu Pärnu College in Estonia and as a project manager of international summer courses on nature, culture, and spa tourism. She focuses on the topics of resort history as well as bathing culture and spa treatments, providing lecturers and practical study visits. She has studied cosmetics and skin care in France and worked as a freelancer for several cosmetics brands and magazines. She has participated in many international projects, and worked as a consultant and lecturer. After working for many years in diplomatic affairs, she teaches a protocol and etiquette course. She is concentrating on the research of human behavior and cultural differences.

Melanie Smith Ph.D., is a Lecturer and Researcher at the Budapest College of Communication and Business. She is co-author of the book Health, Tourism and Hospitality: Spas, Wellness and Medical Travel (2013) with Dr László Puczkó. She has worked for over ten years on health and wellness tourism, including research, lecturing and the publication of several journal articles and book chapters. Since 2009 she has been a Visiting Lecturer for Parnu College (University of Tartu) Estonia on their MA Wellness and Spa Service Design and Management. She has been an invited Keynote Speaker at many international Health and Wellness Conferences in more than ten countries.

CHAPTER 20

Anupama Kothari Ph.D., holds a PhD in Business from the University of Maryland, College Park. Her research interests focus on marketing and decision and information technology and include e-commerce, social media marketing, learning theories, health economics, international healthcare and health information technology.

CHAPTER 21

Tingting (Christina) Zhang is a PhD student in Hospitality Management in the Department of Human Science at the Ohio State University. Her interests include services management and marketing, customer experience management, service delivery, hospitality management, customer engagement, multichannel engagement, and health and wellness service management. She was a lecturer in Hospitality Institute of Beijing International Studies University, China. She has worked on several research projects related to customer experience, social networking sites, health and wellness service management and creative methods of business education. Ms. Zhang holds a Bachelor of Arts in Marketing in Tourism Management from the Department of Beijing International Studies University, China, and a Master's degree in Translation & Interpretation, from the School of English and International Studies, Beijing Foreign Studies University, China.

CASE 1

Anupama Kothari Ph.D., (see chapter 20)

CASE 2

Anupama Kothari Ph.D., (see chapter 20)

CASE 3

Anita Zehrer Ph.D is Deputy Head and Senior Lecturer at MCI Tourism at the Management Center Innsbruck (MCI) and Deputy Head of the MCI Academic Council. Her research interests are diverse and include consumer behaviour in tourism, service experiences and service design, social media in tourism, entrepreneurship and leadership in tourism, family business management in tourism, epistemology in tourism and tourism education. Zehrer currently serves on the Editorial Boards of the Journal of Travel Research, Journal of Vacation Marketing, Tourism Analysis and the Tourism Review.

Prof. Hubert J. Siller is Head of MCI Tourism at the Management Center Innsbruck (MCI) that offer BA and MA tourism programs. His current research and consultancy focus is in the field of entrepreneurship and destination management. Hubert Siller consults with entrepreneurs, tourism businesses and institutions within the tourism and leisure industry on strategic questions.

CASE 4

Maria Wiesinger, Ph.D., studied English, French and History at the University of Salzburg. For her doctoral thesis she wrote about the "Development of Salzburg Airport since 1926, a Historical Analysis". Following teaching assignments at a commercial college in Schladming, Austria as well as at Teacher Trainings Institute in Graz she later took up the position as the Principal of the Hospitality School in Bad Hofgastein, Austria in 1999. She is actively involved in different international hospitality projects which deal with the development of hospitality education abroad. She is board member of the International Association of Hotel Schools called Euhofa International.

Silvia Listberger is a lecturer at the Hospitality School in Bad Hofgastein, Austria.

Claudia Wachter is the General Manager of the Grand Park Hotel, Bad Hofgastein, Austria. She holds two MBA's and has over 30 years of senior management experience in the Hospitality industry. Ms Wachter serves as the chair person of the Tourism Committee, she also serves on the advisory board and management board of the Wörthersee Tourismus, Austria.

CASE 5

Haywantee Ramkissoon, Ph.D., holds two doctoral degrees in Tourism and in Environmental Psychology. She is a senior lecturer, currently conducting research at the Monash Sustainability Institute, Monash University, Australia. She works in close collaboration with researchers and leading practitioners to develop applied approaches in behaviour change and environmental sustainability. She publishes in leading journals such as Annals of Tourism Research, Tourism Management, Journal of Travel Research, Journal of Sustainable Tourism, Tourism Analysis among others. Haywantee is the research note editor for the Journal of Hospitality Marketing and Management and serves on the editorial board and as a reviewer for several tourism, hospitality and natural resources journals.

CASE 6

Thanika D. Juwaheer, Ph.D., is Associate Professor of the Department of Management, Faculty of Law and Management, University of Mauritius. Dr Juwaheer has several years of experience in marketing, tourism and hospitality in Mauritius and the Indian Ocean Islands. Dr Juwaheer has extensive teaching, industrial and consulting experience in the marketing, hospitality and tourism field. She has published articles in academic journals, conference proceedings and trade journals in the field of tourism and hospitality management and on the impact of green marketing, customer relationship management and the environmental management strategies of hotels and other companies of Mauritius. Dr Juwaheer serves on the editorial board of several international refereed academic journals. Her additional research interests include green marketing, ecotourism, service quality, customer satisfaction, CRM and health care management.

CASE 7

Jichul Jang Ph.D., is an Assistant Professor of Hospitality Management in the College of Human Ecology at Kansas State University. He received his Ph.D. from The Ohio State University, and M.S from University of North Texas. He teaches lodging management theory, lodging management systems and employee development in the hospitality Industry. His research interests include service management and organizational behavior in the hospitality industry. His work has focused on decreasing employee turnover while increasing employee engagement, integrating sustainability with hospitality management, enhancing employee creativity, and linking employee motivation to customer experiences in hospitality organizations.

CASE 8

Soyeon Kim Ph.D., received her PhD in hospitality management at The Ohio State University and holds MS in hospitality and tourism management from Purdue University. Her research interests are in the areas of hospitality and tourism marketing focusing on consumer behavior, branding strategies, social media, and services marketing. Her scholarly work has been published in Journal of Travel Research. Her current research examines how consumers' online communications affect information search and decision-making of the consumers.

CASE 9

Hyeyoon Choi is a Ph.D. candidate (see chapter 6)

CASE 10

Anupama Sukhu is a PhD student in Hospitality Management and Teaching Assistant in the Department of Human Sciences, at The Ohio State University. She completed Master's degree in Business and Management from Plymouth Business School, the University of Plymouth, UK. Her research interests include technology and service interactions, social media interactions in tourism and hospitality industries, internationalization, virtual customer experience, consumer behavior, and health and wellness service management.

Hyejin Park is a Master's student in the Department of Human Sciences at The Ohio State University. She has a bachelor's degree in business and tourism management from Sookmyung Women's University in South Korea. Her research interests include service management & marketing, hospitality management, consumer behavior, and corporate social responsibility in service industry.

INDEX

A

Acceptance model of technological service innovations, 284
  service-specific acceptance factors, 281
    financial risks, 283
    functional risks, 283–284
    perceived additional value of service, 282–283
    time consumed figures in, 284
    user-friendliness of service, 282
  user-specific acceptance factors
    affinity for technology, 281
    fearing to damage the devices, 281
    third-party assistance, 280–281
Accountable Care Organizations, 166
ACOs. *See* Accountable Care Organizations
Acupressure, 372
Acupuncture, 371–372, 375–376
Ad hoc work groups, formation of, 31
Advanced medical technologies, 153
Affective commitment, 65
Aged health consumer. *See also* Older adults
  consumer-centric research, 303
  health services for. *See* Health services for older people
Aged health consumer, services issues for, 301
  changing demand of old consumer, 294–295
  cognitive and physical change, 295
  consumer health behavior, 294
Agency for Healthcare Research and Quality, 161
  MEPS household responses, 40
  mission of, 39
Agency relationship, 67
Aging-in-place equipment, 278

Aging population
  demand for alternative living arrangements, 259
  demand for health services, 259
  demand for medical, 326
  fear of falling symptom among, 262
  impact on health services market, 292
  remote monitoring of. *See* Remote monitoring
Aging process, potential moderators of, 258
AHRQ. *See* Agency for Healthcare Research and Quality
AirStrip (health care company), 173
Allopathy, 364
All-pervasive communications, 51
Ambulatory care services, customer satisfaction with, 41–42
American Customer Satisfaction Index (ACSI), 41–42
American health care system, problems of, 14
American Recovery and Reinvestment Act of 2009, 137–139
  HIE initiatives and, 163
  HIT-related expenditures within, 155
American Society for Quality, 11
Apollo Hospital
  Apollo Sugar Clinics, 386
  conceptualization of, 385
  customer-centric approach in Indian health care, 386
  funding for, 385
  marketing mix of, 385
  medical tourism and, 386–387
  success stories of, 386
Apps (mobile apps)
  features of
    distribution of, 222
    educational, 214–215
    feedback, 215
    gamification, 216
    identification of, 221–222
    linked to stages of change, 216–217
    linked to strategies of change, 214–216
    smoking cessation, 212
    social interaction features of, 216
  future development of, 226

Apps (mobile apps) analysis, 217
  apps selection process, 217
  features and stages of change, 221–222
  focus on nutrition, 219–220, 223
  Noom—Weight Loss Coach, 224–225
  physical activity promotion, 219, 222
  preventive measures addressed, 218
    behavior change theory and, 212–213
  reducing/discouraging addictions, 220, 223–224
  stress reduction, 220
Aravind Eye Care System
  adverse event outcomes against UK and U.S. averages, 10
  Aravind Eye Bank, 383
  Aurolabs and, 381–382
  business-to-business service of, 383
  cataract surgery services by, 9–10, 15–16, 382
  cost effectiveness of, 14
  employee model, 382–383
  in-house counseling services, 382
  mission of, 9, 11–12
  quality of service at, 382
  vision centers in villages, 383
Aromas
  human behavior manipulation with, 87–88
  physiological effects of humans, 88
  role in our lives, 87
Aromatherapy, 88
ARRA. *See* American Recovery and Reinvestment Act of 2009
Arya Vaidya Pharmacy, 366
Attitudes
  perceived ease of use of SST, 182
  perceived usefulness effect on, 181
  and readiness toward SST, conceptual model of. *See* Conceptual model of people's readiness and attitudes toward SST
  toward e-health, 180
Aurolabs, 381–382
Autonomous feedback, 215

Avado (health care company), 173
AVP. *See* Arya Vaidya Pharmacy
Ayurveda
    and allopathy, 366
    evolution of, in context
        of historical changes,
        364–365
    Kottakkal Arya Vaidyasala
        and, 365–366
    popularity in United States
        and Europe, 367
    revival of, 365
    as system of medicine, 364

B

Baltic States, cultural dimensions
    of, 350
BCSS. *See* Behavior change
    support system
Behavioral procedures, 208
Behavior change process
    motivation and persuasion
        role in, 209
    persuasive services and,
        209–212
    stages of, 206–207
    strategies of, 206, 208–209
        application features
            linked to, 214–216
    transtheoretical model of
        development of, 206
    strategies of change,
        212–213
Behavior change support system,
    210
Beth Israel Deaconess Hospital,
    149
Blindness
    consequences of, 12
    prevalence of, 9
Business review, 139
    case study of, 142
    definition of, 140
    mechanism of operation, 141
    sample scorecard of, 140

C

CAM. *See* Complementary and
    alternative medicine
Cardinal Health
    customer-oriented strategies
        of, 404
    employee-oriented strategies
        of, 403
    goal of, 402
    history of, 402

leader in nuclear pharmacy,
    404
market coverage of, 403
pharmaceutical and medical
    branches of, 402
philanthropic efforts of,
    403–404
Valuelink program of, 404
Care Coordination/Home
    Telehealth, 264–265
Carefinder tool, 319–320
Cataract, 8
Cataract surgery, 8, 11, 16
    contemporary health ser-
        vices for, 9–10
    costs of, 13
    health service value chain
        for, 14
CCHT. *See* Care Coordination/
    Home Telehealth
Centers for Medicare & Medicaid
    Services, 39
    federal incentives for
        innovations, 165–166
    HCAHPS surveys, 42–43
    Hospital Compare, 40–41
    reimbursement incentive for
        EHR adoption, 155, 156
Chinese massage, 372
Chronic illness, 293
Cleveland Clinic, 142
    achievements and ratings,
        406
    "Cleveland Clinic
        Experience," 406
    customer-oriented service
        groups, 407
    custom-oriented service
        philosophy of, 406–407
    Employee Wellness
        Programs, 408
    HUSH (Help Us Support
        Healing) protocol, 408
    Patient Advisory Councils,
        147
    "Patient First," 406
    process mapping of, 147
    teamwork approach,
        408–409
    technology and innovations,
        409
ClickCare (health care company),
    173
Clifton Springs Hospital and
    Clinic, 410–411
Clinical decision support, 165
CMS. *See* Centers for Medicare
    & Medicaid Services
Cognitive-affective strategies,
    208

Cognitive commitment, 65
Cognitive measures and nutrition,
    link between, 268
Collaborative care
    for chronic conditions,
        258–259
    for patients with Parkinson's
        disease. *See* Parkinson's
        disease treatment
Color (visual cue), 88–89
Commitment and relational
    bond, 65
Communication
    all-pervasive, 51
    comments related to pain
        medication, 48–49
    health care services integra-
        tion with, 319
    Internet medium for patient-
        physician, 266
    negative sentiment associ-
        ated with pain control,
        46–47
    peer-to-peer, 246
Communication program, 33, 68
Companion's and patient
    satisfaction, 63–64
Company culture, 138
Company output, 176
Competitive environment, 105
    with environmental changes,
        101–102
    responding to, 102–103
Complementary and alternative
    medicine, 79
    and TCM, 376
    use by Americans, survey
        of, 371
Complex nonlinear systems, 158
Conceptual model of people's
    readiness and attitudes toward
    SST, 180
    data collection and sample
        statistics, 185–186
    hypothesis testing, 188–190
    with hypothesized
        relationships, 182
    limitations of, 192–193
    reliability of study, 187–188
    scenario method, 184–185
    strongly disagree/strongly
        agree scales, 186–187
    testing methodology, 184
Constance Le Prince Maurice
    Darling Children, 399–400
Constance Le Prince Maurice
    Hotel, 398–399
Consumer-centric research for
    older consumer, 303
Consumer health behavior, 294

Consumers' motivation, opportunity, ability (MOA), and empowerment, 238–243
Consumer technology readiness. *See* Technology readiness
Continuous improvement cycle, iterative steps of, 142
Continuous improvement dashboard, 144
Continuous improvement initiative
   business review. *See* Business review
   dashboards. *See* Dashboards
   essence of, 138–139
   factors important for long-term success of, 138
   process mapping. *See* Process mapping
   5S. *See* 5S (continuous improvement tool)
   standardized work. *See* Standardized work
Controlled drug delivery using smart pills, 262
Cost effectiveness analysis, 13–14
Cost utility analysis, 13–14
Cross-cultural issues, 358
   influencing health and wellness guests
      cultural indices, 351–352
      culture's core values, 349
      intercultural sensitivity, 348
      Servicescape concept, 350–351
   in Pärnu spas, 355–356
Cultural characteristics
   of Estonia, 350
   of specific societies, 350
   subjective and objective, 349
Culture
   definition of, 24
   as organizational phenomenon, 25
Cupping, 373
Customer expectations, 52–53, 352
   electronic health care use, 247–250
   and experiences in health and wellness industry, 351–352
   and needs of guests from Pärnu spas, 355–357
   and satisfaction, relationship between, 15
Customer experience
   components of, 83
   definition of, 81

environmental cues influence on. *See* environmental cues
   importance for health and wellness industry
   competitiveness, 82
   multifactorial points of encounter, 82–83
   physical environment's influence, 83–84
   value creation for customers, 81–82
   management, 2
Customer focus
   of health and wellness organizations, 80–81, 84
   in health services, 2, 139
   SST in health care with, 178
Customer-led innovation strategy, 165–166
Customer loyalty, 64–65, 403–404
Customer management and financial results, relationship between, 60–61
Customer orientation, 28
   balanced scoreboard proposal and, 61
   and business results, relationship between, 60–61
   of electronic health care, 247–248
   in hospital management, 60–62
   improving operational system performance through, 101
   and performance management approach, 102
   profitability of, 61
   in service development, 327
Customer-oriented healthcare culture, 101
   competitive environment. *See* Competitive environment
   implementation, 110–111
   operational performance improvements, 109–110
   performance measurement and measures, 103–109
Customer-oriented health care performance improvements
   conceptual framework of, 100–101
   implementation of, 110–111
   information systems, 109–110
Customer-oriented tourism product and service, prerequisites of, 329

Customer output, 176
Customer relationship quality in hospitals. *See* Hospital customer relationship quality
Customer satisfaction, 26. *See also* Patient satisfaction
   ACSI score and, 41–42
   with ambulatory care services, 41–42
   and expectations, relationship between, 15
   with health insurance, 41–42
   health services for older people, 296–297
   with hospital, 63–64
   and hospital customer relationship quality, 63–64
   with hospital services, 41–42, 63–64
   Samadhi Spa & Wellness Retreat, 395–396
Customer trust, 62
   and service quality, 68

D

Dashboards, 139
   definition of, 142
   East Tennesee Children's Hospital, 143–144
   sample of, 143
Data security breaches, 164
Deaths in United States, causes of, 203, 257
Dementia, 295
Demographic change
   causes of, 292
   challenges to personal services with, 276
   definition of, 276
   in European Union, 276
   and health system dynamics, 292
Department of Health and Human Services, 39–40
DHHS. *See* Department of Health and Human Services
Dietary therapy, 372–373
Disease prevention
   classification of, 204
   importance of, 202–203
   interventions in
      basic assumption for, 203
      categorization of, 214
Disease preventive interventions. *See* Preventive interventions
Doctor-patient relationship, 67

E

East Tennessee Children's Hospital, dashboard from, 144
EB. *See* Employer brand
EBing. *See* Employer branding
EBM. *See* Evidence-based medicine
Educational features of apps, 214, 216
eGOOD project
implementation of, 332
technological solution of, 332–333
E-health care. *See* Electronic health care
e-health portal, 243
EHRs, Electronic health records
Electronic health care
benefits of, 234
case study of
attitudes toward e-health, 180
population's technology readiness, 177–180
consumers' motivations to use
content analysis and categorization, 243–244
credibility and trustworthiness, 247
e-health portal, 243
for emotional support, 246
evaluation of service portal, 246–247
online survey of, 243
participation in discussions, 245
peer-to-peer communication, 246
service access, 245–246
situation-related need for information, 245
consumer technology readiness and, 176–177
consumer uses of, 236–237
definition of, 172, 234
factors influencing acceptance and adoption of, 174, 177, 234
importance of studying, 174–175
influence on customers, 235
Internet use, 235–236
managerial implications of, 247–250
consumer's trust, 249
customer orientation, 247–248

regional differences, 250
role clarity, 248–249
service quality of, 176–177
Electronic health care use
consumer expectations with regard to, 247–250
and customer empowerment importance of, 237
MOA framework, 238–243
external and internal motivations for, 249–250
Norwegian consumers, 178
positive and negative consequences of, 243–250
Electronic health records, 154
future of, 162
implementation of
analyzing impact of, 161
and federal financial incentives, 155–156, 161
usability and information design for, 161–162
potential breaches of, 164–165
regulatory drivers for, 155–156
technical design problems in, 162
Electronic medical records, 155
adoption of, 162–163
advantages of, 266–267
clinical decision support for implementing, 165
technical design problems in, 162
Electronic patient health information, 164
Emotional value, 62, 70
Employee performance evaluation, 33
Employee realization and acceptance, 29
Employee training, 33, 389
Employer brand
definition of, 28
importance for public hospitals, 28–29
key values to support, 29–30
attention to detail, 29
reciprocity norm and equity theory, 30
team orientation and supportiveness, 29
promotion among insiders, 31
Employer branding, 28
brand image with, 28
marketing tools, 31
EMRs. *See* Electronic medical records

Environmental cues
affecting sensory impressions, 85
auditory cues, 87
influence on customer behavior, 85
integration of senses, 86
olfactory cues, 87–88
and physical environment, 86–87
visual cues, 88–90
EPHI. *See* Electronic patient health information
Equity theory, 30
Estonia
geography of, 352
Tallinn, 353
tourism industry, 353
Estonian SPA Association
quality system for medical spa hotels, 353
statistical data of member spas of, 354
Estonian spas
Pärnu spas
cross-cultural issues faced by, 355–357
expectations and needs of guests from, 355–357
history of, 354–355
popularity of, 353
statistical data of, 353–354
European Union
demographic change in, 276
smartphone ownership in, 240
Evidence-based medicine, 293

F

Facilitative leadership, 32
Fall detectors, 278
FDA. *See* U.S. Food and Drug Administration
Fear of falling, 262–263
Feedback features of applications, 215, 216, 226
Financial risks and technological service innovations, 283
Finland
eGOOD project, 332–333
Lake Wellness experience product, 334–335
Finns, cross-cultural needs of, 356
Flowcharts, 144–145
FoF. *See* Fear of falling
Foster, Henry, 410

Functional risks and technological service innovations, 283–284

G

Gamification, 216, 217
Globalization, 415
  challenges for health organizations, 24
  of product development and service provision, 348
Global population, 292
GLOVAL model, 66
GOVER foundation, 10
Grand Park Hotel Health & Spa
  employees of, 393
  quality awards and distinctions, 391
  tradition of, 391
  treatment programs at, 392–393
  unique selling propositions of, 392

H

Hahnemann, Samuel, 364
Hammurabi's Code, 8, 16, 17
  quality of health services, 8–9
  value of cataract surgery, 14
HCAHPS survey. *See* Hospital Consumer Assessment of Health Care Providers and Systems survey
"Healing environment," 85
Health and wellness guests
  cultural characteristics influencing
    culture's core values, 349
    intercultural sensitivity, 348
    Servicescape concept, 350–351
  enhancing experience of, 351–352
  needs catered for in Pärnu spas, 356–357
Health and wellness industry.
  See also Health and wellness organizations
  customer expectations and experiences in, 80, 82, 351–352
  physical environment's influence on, 84–85

Health and wellness organizations
  complaints about physical environment of, 85
  customer experience
    importance for competitiveness, 82
    multifactorial points of encounter, 82–83
    physical environment's influence, 83–84
    value creation for customers, 81–82
  psychologically supportive, 80
  service orientation of, 80–81
  servicescape importance within
    auditory cues, 87
    influence on customer behavior, 85
    integration of senses, 86
    interactions between customers and employees, 86
    olfactory cues, 87–88
    physical environment, 86–87
    visual cues, 88–90
    success or failure of, 83
Health and wellness services.
  See also Health and wellness organizations
  challenges of providing
    degree of improvization, 349
    low intercultural sensitivity, 348
  continuum, 4
  cross-cultural training needs of employees in
    front-line service staff, 348
    intercultural training, 348
    understanding of culture's core values, 349
  multidimensional experience factors in, 82
Health care and treatments
  current state of, 314–315
  patient-centered care, 315–316
Health care companies, 173
Health care costs, 52, 237, 250
  ARRA and, 137–138
  increase in, 102
Health care industry, 172, 234
  CAM products, 376
  competitive environment for. *See* Competitive environment

  importance of quality in, 26–28
  performance management approach for. *See* Performance management approach
Health care information systems, 109
Healthcare operational system performance
  challenges to, 101–103
  measurement and measures, 103–109
    performance measurement system. *See* Performance measurement system
Health care organizations
  challenges to operational systems of, 100
  challenging context for, 24
  cultural performance shift of, 100
  customer orientation, 27
  and patient satisfaction. *See* Patient satisfaction
  performance measurement system of. *See* Performance measurement system
  satisfied employees, 29
  service culture. *See* Service culture
Health care providers
  ACOs, 166
  customer inputs for, 235
  HIE services and, 156, 163
  implications for, 50–51
Health care quality
  composition of, 39
  ongoing efforts in
    Agency for Healthcare Research and Quality, 39–40
    American Customer Satisfaction Index, 41–42
    Centers for Medicare & Medicaid Services, 40–41
    HCAHPS surveys, 42–43
  and patient satisfaction, link between, 52
  purpose of, 45
Health care service innovations, 165–166
Health care "service platform," 160
Health care services
  adaptive nature of, 159
  effective understanding of, 158

high demand of, 172
structural innovation in, 154
utility estimation of, 13
Health care service systems
complexity of, 312, 314
integrated chain/network
of complex diseases
treatment by, 315
coordination among
health care providers in,
314–315
online tools for
collaboration, 315
patient-centered care. *See*
Patient-centered care
systems view in, 314
multiple value creation in,
312, 314
non-integrated chain, 314
patient involvement, 316
stakeholder integration in,
312, 314
value creation in, 312
Health care setting, key components of, 175
Health care spending, 190
in 2005, 57
in OECD countries, 174
per capita 2009, 58–59
private vs. total, 58
in United States, 137, 153
Health care system
requirements for change
in, 302
resistance to, 302
systems perspective of, 154,
156
broad categories of, 157
complex nonlinear
systems, 158
socio-technical systems
perspective, 158
STS approach, 157–158
tightly or loosely coupled,
158
Health "crisis," 77
Health Information Exchange
implementation
financial incentives under
ARRA for, 163
HITECH Act supports
to, 163
long-term goal for,
163–164
information sharing among
health care providers, 156
Health information technology
and ARRA, 155
effects on care delivery, 161

key elements of
clinical decision support,
165
EHR implementation,
161–163
health care information
privacy and security,
164–165
HIE implementation,
163–164
and patient satisfaction, 51
Health Information Technology
for Economic and Clinical
Health Act of 2009, 155
HIE initiatives and, 163
PHI privacy and security,
164
Health insurance
customer satisfaction with,
41–42
focus of, 203, 205
Health Insurance Portability and
Accountability Act
Privacy and Security Rules,
164
violations and enforcement
of, 164
Health IT incentive program
for EHR adoption, 154–156
for HIE adoption, 163
Health-relevant behaviors,
204–205
Health service encounter, 297
Health service experience, 3–5
Health service management and
planning, implications for
consumer-centric research,
303
requirements for change,
302
services marketing
reorientation, 302–303
system resistance, 302
Health service network, 59–60
Health service quality
definition of
American Society for
Quality, 11
IoM, 12, 17
in empirical terms, 11
historical perspective of
Hammurabi's Code, 8–9
Plato's view, 10–11
IOM recommendations for
improving
cost effectiveness
analysis, 13–14
patient centeredness,
14–15

patient safety, 13
timeliness, 13
measurement of, 16
and patient satisfaction
employer brand, 28–30
key values to achieve,
26–28
measurement of, 16
relationship between,
15, 26
subjective perspective of,
10–11
and user trust, 68
Health service relationships,
traditional model of, 291
Health services
costs and health outcomes
of, 14
credence properties of, 174
negative demand for, 174
service quality measurement
instruments for, 16
value creation, 4
wellness goals within.
See Wellness goals
Health services for older people
challenges to. *See* Aged
health consumer, services
issues for
community-delivered
services
holistic approach, 296
service continuity and
coordination, 295–296
evidence-based medicine
approaches, 293
interaction, service
participants
determinants of, 298–300
and service cocreation,
297–298
management implications of,
303–304
personalized medicine, 294
planning and management
implications
consumer-centric research,
303
requirements for change,
302
services marketing
reorientation, 302–303
system resistance, 302
service creation and
delivery, 297
service participant
contribution, 297
service quality and
satisfaction, 296–297

Health services market
    client-centered approach to
        service, 291
    current limitations of
        demographic changes,
            292
        fragmented service, 293
        system structure and
            operational layers, 291,
            292
    health policy and planning,
        292
    illness-focused paradigm
        of, 290
    inpatient and outpatient, 291
    market change factors, 290
Health services research
    on quality, 15
    service valuation models,
        14–15
Health service value
    definition of, 15
    historical perspective of,
        8–9
        Plato's view, 11
    measurement of, 16
Health service value chain, cost
    effectiveness of, 14, 16
Health system dynamics
    demographic changes and,
        292
    evidence-based medicine,
        293
    health policy and planning,
        292
    historical traditions of, 291
    personalized medicine, 294
    system structure and opera-
        tional layers of, 291
Health system, importance of, 57
    at macroeconomic level,
        58–59
    at microeconomic level, 59
Heart failure (HF), technology-
    based monitoring supports
    for, 260
Herbal medicine, 371
HIE. *See* Health Information
    Exchange
HIPAA. *See* Health Insurance
    Portability and Accountability
    Act
HIT. *See* Health information
    technology
HITECH Act of 2009. *See* Health
    Information Technology for
    Economic and Clinical Health
    Act of 2009
Holistic medicine, growth of, 79
Homeopathy, 364

Home-to-monitoring center, 264
Hospital and its users, managing
    relationships between, 61–62
Hospital Compare, 40–41
Hospital Consumer Assessment
    of Health Care Providers and
    Systems survey, 42–43
    pain management in, 51
Hospital customer
    broad concept of, 61
    relationship quality and
        value perceived by, 62
Hospital customer orientation.
    See Customer orientation
Hospital customer relationship
    quality
    and antecedents, 61–62
    components of
        customer loyalty to
            hospital, 64–65
        customer satisfaction with
            hospital, 63–64
        customer trust in hospital,
            65
    as customer's evaluation of
        hospital's actions, 63
    importance of, 60–61
    management using customer
        value programs
        GLOVAL model, 66
        hospital perceived value.
            See Hospital perceived
            value, dimensions for
        perceived value, 66
    participant evaluation,
        62–63
    Spanish hospitals, 67
Hospital facilities, assessment of,
    66–67
Hospital lab process, flowchart
    of, 145
Hospital managers
    on customer loyalty, 64
    level of service, 64
    recommendation for, 68
Hospital perceived value,
    dimensions for
    emotional value, 70
    hospital facilities, 66–67
    hospital personnel
        professionalism, 67–68
    monetary cost, 69
    nonmonetary costs, 69–70
    service quality, 68
    social value, 70–71
Hospital personnel
    employment satisfaction and
        service quality, 68
    professionalism and patient
        satisfaction, 67–68

Hospital services
    customer perceived quality
        and, 68
    customer satisfaction with,
        41–43
Hospitals' performance
    short-term and long-term,
        109–110
    systemwide perspective of,
        110
Hospital Value-Based Purchasing
    Program, 43
Human activity systems, 157–158
Human resource management
    (HRM) policies and practices
    employee performance
        evaluation, 33
    employee training, 33
    job analyses, 32
    recruitment strategy, 32
HUSH (Help Us Support Healing)
    protocol, 408

I

Icelandic health and wellness,
    340–341
India's caste system, 364
Information systems, adoption
    of, 31
Information technology, 263
Information technology (IT)
    use in health care
        HITECH Act and, 155
        in U.S. health care industry,
            153–154
In-home health and medical
    services models
    Care Coordination/Home
        Telehealth, 264–265
    Patient Centered Medical
        Home, 265
Innovative competitive methods
    and tools, 102–103
Inspection as quality manage-
    ment instrument, 17
Institute of Medicine
    definition of health services
        quality, 12
    IT role for designing health
        systems, 263
    recommendations for
        improving health services
        quality, 12
        cost effectiveness
            analysis, 13–14
        patient centeredness,
            14–15
        patient safety, 13
        timeliness, 13

Integrated health care provision
system, 318
    complex diseases treatment
      by, 315
    coordination among health
      care providers in, 314–315
    managerial implications of,
      320
    online tools for
      collaboration, 315
    patient-centered care. *See*
      Patient-centered care
    systems view in, 314
Integrated system
    recommendations, 263–264
Internal communication
    programs, 68
Internal customers, importance
    of, 27
Internal Marketing (IM) theory
    and internal customers, 27
Internal operations
    and customer service, 31
    and learning orientation,
      27–28
Internet
    client use of, 291
    perceived value of, in health-
      care settings, 265
      healthcare improvement,
        266–267
      helping elderly patients,
        267
      medium for marketing
        and information, 266
      medium for patient–
        physician
        communication, 266
    persuasive services of, 210
    usage for health-related
      information, 235–236, 240
Internet-based medical self-diag-
    nosis application, 184
Internet-powered weight manage-
    ment system, 261
Interpersonal process in service
    delivery, 297
Intracapsular cataract
    extraction, 14
IOM. *See* Institute of Medicine
IT-based services, complexity
    involved in, 154

J

Job analyses, 32
Joint-optimization, 157

K

Kottakkal Arya Vaidyasala,
    365–367

L

LAICO. *See* Lions Aravind
    Institute of Community
    Ophthalmology
Lake Wellness Concept
    development of, 334
    fundamental pillars of, 334
Lake Wellness experience
    product, 334–335
Latvians, cross-cultural needs
    of, 357
Layout and function (visual cue),
    89
Leadership support, 138
Leapfrog Group, 42
Learning orientation, 28
Learning-oriented health care
    organization, 27, 28
Le Prince Maurice Sisley Spa,
    399–401
Life expectancy, rise in, 292
Lifeshaping Retreat, 396
Lighting (visual cue), 89–90
Lions Aravind Institute of Com-
    munity Ophthalmology, 383
Loosely coupled systems, 158
Lower, William E., 406

M

Management by Objectives, 33
Manufacturing organizations,
    performance measurement
    process of, 106
Market change factors, 290
Medicaid EHR incentive
    payments, 155–156
Medical equipment, technical
    value of, 66–67
Medical Expenditure Panel
    Survey, 40
Medical tourism, 386–387
Medicare EHR incentive
    payments, 155–156
Mental health disorders
    prevalence of, 122
    WHO on, 122
Mental health service providers,
    124
Mental health services
    characteristics of, 125

classification of, 125–126,
    244
client recovery
    based on self-
      determination theory,
      124
    as psychosocial
      rehabilitation, 124
    research, 122
complication of, 124
evaluation of, 131–132
future research on, 133
open-systems perspective of.
    See Open-systems model
    for mental health services
resource-intensive, 128
service package. *See* Service
    package
service-related
    interventions, 125
subsidized by governments,
    124
types and focus of, 130
MEPS. *See* Medical Expenditure
    Panel Survey
Mesopotamia, 8
Miletus, 16
MNB. *See* Mývatn Nature Baths
Mobile devices, data security
    problem with, 164–165
Mobile health care applications,
    202
Mobile technology for preventive
    care, 202
Monetary cost, 69
Monochronic and polychronic
    cultures, 351
Music usage in the health and
    wellness, 87
MyP@rkinsoncare pilot study,
    318–319
Mývatn Nature Baths, 338
    national strategy frame-
      works and, 339–340
    service concept of, 339
    and service model, 340
    service process of, 339
    service system of, 339

N

National health information
    infrastructure, 263
Nationwide Health Information
    Infrastructure, 163
Negative sentiment associated
    with pain control
    categories related to, 46
    communication, 46–47
    personnel, 48

process of care, 48
  treatment protocols, 47–48
Neonatal intensive care unit
  (NICU), 5S initiative in, 149
Networked programs, 264
New service development
  customer-oriented, 327–329
  four phases of, 330–331
    concept development,
      331–332
    concept testing, 331
    core product screening,
      331
    idea generation, 331
  and innovations in well-
    being tourism sector, 342
    eGOOD project, 332–333
    Lake Wellness Concept,
      334–335
    Mývatn Nature Baths,
      338–341
    WellCome project,
      336–338
  models, categorization of,
    329
  in service system
    environment, 331
New tourism service development
  framework, 329, 330. *See also*
  New service development
NHII. *See* National health infor-
  mation infrastructure
Non-hospital settings, patient
  satisfaction in, 53
Nonmonetary costs, 69–70
Noom—Weight Loss Coach,
  224–225
  motivation methods in, 224
  screenshots of, 225
Nordic tourism
  characterization of, 327
  NSD and innovations in
    eGOOD project, 332–333
    Lake Wellness Concept,
      334–335
    Mývatn Nature Baths,
      338–341
    WellCome project,
      336–338
Nordic well-being, 340
NSD. *See* New service
  development
Nutrient biomarker patterns, 268
Nutrition, improving health
  through, 268
NwHIN. *See* Nationwide Health
  Information Infrastructure

O

OECD countries, health care
  spending in, 174
Old age
  definition of, 302
  pessimistic, negative view
    of, 303
Older adults
  classification by age, 277
  demand for services for, 301
  in-home health and medical
    services models for. *See*
    In-home health and medi-
    cal services models
  integrated systems for health
    service support
    home-to-monitoring
      center, 264
    networked programs, 264
    patient consultations, 263
    point-to-point
      connections, 264
    remote patient
      monitoring, 264
    specialist referral
      services, 263
    specialty care to home
      connections, 264
    web-based e-health
      patient service sites, 264
  service expectations and
    demands of, 294–295
  technological services for.
    See Technological services
  technology-based activi-
    ties for
    stay connected through
      Skype, 270
    visit on treadmills,
      269–270
    Wii™ sport events, 270
Online health community and
  patient-centered care, 317, 320
Online health information access,
  266
Online health services. *See*
  Electronic health care
Open-systems model for mental
  health services, 123
  evaluation of, 131–132
  future research on, 133
  heterogeneity among
    consumers, 123
  psychosocial rehabilitation,
    123
  service operations managers
    role in, 128–129
  as service processes,
    129–131

P

Pain management for perioperative care
  dimensions of, 50
  HCAHPS survey, 51
  negative sentiment associ-
    ated with
    categories related to, 46
    communication, 46–47
    personnel, 48
    process of care, 48
    treatment protocols,
      47–48
  pain medication, comments
    related to
    communication, 48–49
    personnel, 49
    transition of care, 50
    treatment protocols, 49
ParkinsonNet (organization), 312
  beneficial effects of pro-
    grams of, 321
  future research on, 321
  as integrated health care
    provision system, 318
  link among elements of, 313
  MyCarenet of, 317
  programs implemented by
    carefinder tool, 319–320
    MyP@rkinsoncare,
      318–319
    online health
      communities, 317
    regional offline networks
      of health professionals,
      317, 319
Parkinson's disease treatment
  conventional therapies for,
    316
  effectiveness of allied health
    disciplines in, 316–317
  MyP@rkinsoncare pilot
    study, 318–319
Pärnu spas
  attracting young people, 357
  cross-cultural issues faced
    by, 355–357
  history of, 354–355

Operational performance
  improvements, 109–110
Organizational climate, 25
Organizational culture, 25
Organizational performance, 112
  diverging perspectives on,
    104–105
  evaluation platforms,
    108–109
  nonfinancial aspects of, 106

Patient-centered care, 14–15
  definition of, 315
  online health community
    role in, 317, 320
  quality of care with, 315–316
Patient Centered Medical Home,
  265
Patient centeredness, 14–15,
  27–28
Patient consultations, 263
Patient health information, 164
Patient loyalty
  emotional value influence
    on, 70
  to hospital, 64–65
Patient relationship quality in
  hospital. *See* Hospital customer
  relationship quality
Patient response to pain
  management
    negative sentiment, 46–48
    pain medication, 48–50
Patients
  affective commitment, 65
  characteristics of, in health
    care services, 44–45
  cognitive commitment, 65
  expectations of, 52–53
  meaning of, 43–44
  responsibilities of, 53
  as service-outcome, 44–45
  as service-product, 44
  as service-provider, 44
  as service-value, 45
Patient safety, 13
Patient satisfaction
  antecedents of
    drivers of patient safety,
      52
    HIT, 51
  benefits for health
    organization, 26
  companion's satisfaction
    influence on, 63–64
  cost of, 52
  definition of, 26
  impact on hospital choice,
    63
  impact on loyalty to
    hospital, 63
  and loyalty, 52
  in non-hospital settings, 53
  and service quality, values
    to achieve
      competitive advantage, 26
      customer orientation, 28
      learning orientation,
        27–28
  understanding, 44
Patient (dis)satisfaction, 45–46

Patient satisfaction research
  customer satisfaction litera-
    ture influence on, 43
  patient contexts, 53
  role of patients, 52–53
Patient trust
  as affective construct, 65
  honesty and benevolence, 65
PCMH. *See* Patient Centered
  Medical Home
Perceived additional value of
  service, 282–283
Perceived value management, 66
Performance appraisals, 33
Performance management
  approach
    customer orientation and,
      102
    difficulties associated with,
      104
    importance of, 103
    managerial and management
      aspects of, 104
    performance improvement
      tools under, 100
    service innovations, 105
    service performance, 103
Performance measurement
  process
    characteristics of, 107–108
    customer-driven, adoption
      of, 106–107
    issues affecting, 108
    manufacturing
      organizations, 106
    nonfinancial performance
      aspects, 106
    output-related, 107
Performance measurement
  system
    definition of, 104
    designing and
      implementing, 104–105
    future of, 108
    informational capabilities
      of, 104
    motivation for redesign of,
      106
    organizational performance
      evaluation platforms
        measure-specific
          perspective, 108
        systemwide perspective,
          109
    systematic approach of, 100
Perioperative care, pain management for. *See* Pain management
  for perioperative care

Personalized information
  services, 214
Personalized medicine, 294
Personal online health
  community, 317–318
Persuasion, 209
Persuasive services, 209, 212
Persuasive technology
  advantages of, 210
  definition of, 210
  health care and behav-
    ior change theory, link
    between, 212–217
  services of, 209–210
  smartphones. *See*
    Smartphones
PHI. *See* Patient health
  information
Physical activity and emotional
  health, technology-based
  activities for
    stay connected through
      Skype, 270
    visit on treadmills, 269–270
    Wii™ sport events, 270
Physical evidence. *See*
  Servicescape
Physiological aging, 295
Plato's view
  on quality of health service,
    10
  on value of health service,
    11
PMS. *See* Performance measure-
  ment system
PMS-managed information, 104
POHC. *See* Personal online health
  community
Point-to-point connections, 264
Polychronic cultures, 351
Population aging, 292
Preventive care, mobile technol-
  ogy for, 202
Preventive interventions
  basic assumption of, 203
  categorization of, 214
Primary prevention, 204
Primary preventive interventions
  behavior change with
    economic incentives/
      punishment, 205
  educational techniques, 205
  normative-regulatory
    techniques, 205
Private health services, 59–60,
  291
  monetary cost for, 69
  patient's loyalty to, 64
  public and, difference
    between, 59

Process improvement initiatives at hospitals, 138
  business review. *See* Business review
  dashboards. *See* Dashboards
Process mapping, 139
  case study of, 147
  definition of, 144
  flowchart, 144–145
  swim lane diagrams, 144, 145
  value stream map, 145, 147
Professionalism of hospital personnel, 67–68
Project Impact, 381
Psychosocial rehabilitation, 123, 124
Public health organizations
  challenging context for, 24
  employer brand of. *See* Employer brand
  low satisfaction scores of, 172
  monetary cost of, 69
  operational performance improvement, 109–110
  organizational mission of, 60
  patient's loyalty to, 64
  private and, difference between, 59
  resources devoted to, 57–58

Q

Qaly. *See* Quality adjusted life year
Qigong, 370–371
Quality
  defined by American Society for Quality, 11
  health services. *See* Health service quality
Quality adjusted life year, 13
Quality management instruments, 17
Quality of care, improving, 315–316
Quality of life, normative interpretation of, 13

R

Reciprocity norm, 30
Recruitment strategy, 32
Reddy, Prathap, 385
Remote monitoring, 264
  computer-assisted diabetes care, 260–261

heart disease, 260
  technology interfacing devices with sensors. *See* Technology interfacing devices with sensors
  vital signs of seniors, 278
  weight management systems, 261
Remote monitoring devices, 259
Russians, cross-cultural needs of, 356–357

S

5S (continuous improvement tool), 139
  definition of, 148
  five stages of, 148
  initiative in neonatal intensive care unit, 149
SaaS. *See* Software as a Service approach
Samadhi Spa & Wellness Retreat, 394–396
  codirectors of, 394, 396
  diverse marketing strategy, 396
  employees and management of, 394–395
  quality awards and distinctions, 396
  service excellence and customer satisfaction, 395–396
  service-oriented practices of, 394
Satisfaction. *See also* Customer satisfaction; Patient satisfaction
  definition of, 63
  disconfirmation paradigm of, 63
Scenario method, 184–185
Schwarz Alpine Spa & Resort, 388–390
Secondary prevention, 204
Self-diagnosis application
  drivers for acceptance of, 177
  emerging market for, 178
  technology acceptance of, 194–196
    attitudes, 195
    convenience, 181, 194
    ease of use, 182, 194–195
    intention to use, 181–182, 195
    trust, 182–184, 195
Self-liberation, 214
  and goal setting, 216

Self-service technology (SST) in health care
  challenges with, 177
  with customer focus, 178
  customers' motivation for, 240–242
  emerging market for, 178
  factors influencing attitudes toward using, 180
  managerial and policy implications for, 190–191
  perceived ease of use of
    effect on attitudes on, 182
    effect on trust, 182–183
  perceived usefulness of, 180–181
    effect on attitudes, 181
    effect on intention, 181–182
  pre-testing of, 191
  study on adoption and usage of, 180
    data collection and sample statistics, 185–186
    hypothesis testing, 188–190
    with hypothesized relationships, 182
    limitations of, 192–193
    Norwegian consumers, 178–179
    reliability of study, 187–188
    scenario method, 184–185
    strongly disagree/strongly agree scales, 186–187
    testing methodology, 184
  and technology readiness. *See* Technology readiness
  theoretical implications for, 191–192
  trust in service provider for, 182
    perceived ease of use, 184
    perceived usefulness, 183
    from welfare perspective, 176
Senior, definition of, 277
Service climate, 25
Service concept, 328
Service culture
  adoption of information systems, 31
  building, 25–26
  challenges for, 30
  decentralized decision-making styles and, 32
  facilitative leadership styles and, 32
  HRM policies and practices for, 32–33

employee performance evaluation, 33
employee training, 33
job analyses, 32
recruitment strategy, 32
importance for introducing, 30
internal and external customers, 31
as preferred employer, 31–32
vs. service climate, 25
systemic changes, 31
two-way communication, 32
Service development process, 327
customer orientation in, 327
service prerequisites for, 328
Service encounter, 82
Service experience. *See* Health service experience
Service management, 2
Service management research, paradigmatic foundation in, 38
Service operations managers
from open-systems perspective, 128
role in mental health service, 128–129
Service organization performance assessment
by customer service quality, 105
financial and nonfinancial, 105–106
operational environments and, 105
Service organizations
frontline employees in, 25
performance assessment of, 105–106
Service orientation, 300
of health and wellness organizations, 80–81
of health services organizations, 304
Service package
definition of, 127
explicit and implicit services, 127
facilitating goods, 127
information, 127
supporting facilities, 127
Service participant interaction and role hierarchy, model of, 300
Service platform. *See* Health care "service platform"
Service process, 328
Service process development, 331
Service providers, key service issues confronting, 301

Service quality, 68
challenge when debating, 175–176
classic conceptual model of, 15
measurement instruments, 16
and satisfaction of health services for older people, 296–297
ways to enhance, 176
Servicescape
categorization of, 86
components of, 84
definition of, 84
in health and wellness care setting, 350–351
auditory cues, 87
influence on customer behavior, 85
integration of senses, 86
interactions between customers and employees, 86
olfactory cues, 87–88
physical environment, 86–87
visual cues, 88–90
management of, 85
Services, definition of, 17
Services marketing reorientation, 302–303
Service-specific acceptance factors, 281
financial risks, 283
functional risks, 283–284
perceived additional value of service, 282–283
time consumed figures in, 284
user-friendliness of service, 282
Service system, 328–329
Service users, assessment of, 15
Service value. *See* Health service value
Smart bandages, 262
Smartphones, 210, 261–262
application analysis, 217
apps selection process, 217
features and stages of change, 221–222
focus on nutrition, 219–220, 223
Noom—Weight Loss Coach, 224–225
physical activity promotion, 219, 222
preventive measures addressed, 218

reducing/discouraging addictions, 220, 223–224
stress reduction, 220
application features
behavior change theory and preventive measures, 212–213
distribution of, 222
educational, 214–215
feedback, 215
gamification, 216
identification of, 221–222
linked to stages of change, 216–217
linked to strategies of change, 214–216
smoking cessation, 212
social interaction features of, 216
definition of, 211
for health-related information, 240
penetration rate of, 211
as platforms for health promotion, 211–212
technological features of, 211
vs. traditional personal computers, 211
Smart pills, 262
Smart slippers, 262
Social interaction, 216, 217
Social value, 70–71
Socio-Technical Systems approach, 157
Socio-technical systems perspective, 158
Software as a Service approach, 162
Spanish hospitals and customer relationship quality, 67
Specialist referral services, 263
Specialized care service, 60
Specialty care to home connections, 264
The Springs Integrative Medicine Center & Spa, 411
Sreedharyam eye hospital, 366
Standardized work, 139
definition of, 149
template, 150, 160
State Health Information Exchange Cooperative Agreement Program, 163
Stress, 77
STS approach. *See* Socio-Technical Systems approach
Successful aging
maintenance of normal body weight, 261

strategic initiatives, 267
structure of, 258
Swedes, cross-cultural needs of, 356
Swim lane diagrams, 144, 145
System
　complexity reduction, 157
　at conceptual level, 157
　definition of, 156–157
　resistance, 302
Systems theory, 157

T

TAM. *See* Technology acceptance model
TCM. *See* Traditional Chinese medicine
Technological expertise, 138
Technological service innovations, 234, 285
　acceptance model of. *See* Acceptance model of technological service innovations
Technological services
　definition of, 276, 278
　design and development considerations, 285
　importance for elder care, 276–278
　rising demand with demographic change, 278
Technological services, factors influencing seniors' acceptance of, 277
　"distance" to technologies, 276
　educational work for reducing, 286
　qualitative study of
　　affinity for technology, 281, 285
　　data processing, 280
　　fearing to damage the devices, 281, 285–286
　　financial risks, 283, 286
　　functional risks, 283–284, 286
　　phases, 279
　　sample description, 279–280
　　third-party assistance, 280–281, 285
　　time consumed figures in, 284
　　user-friendliness of service, 282, 285
　　user-specific acceptance factors, 280–281

Technological solutions
　for eGOOD project, 332–333
　for tourism products, 342
Technology acceptance, interview guide to
　attitude, 195
　convenience, 194
　demographical measures, 196
　ease of use, 194–195
　intention to use, 195
　realism checks, 195
　trust, 195
Technology acceptance model
　in health care context, 175, 176, 191
　perceived ease of use
　　effect on attitudes, 182
　　effect on trust, 182–183
　perceived usefulness and ease of use, 180
　perceived usefulness of, 180–181
　　effect on attitudes, 181
　　effect on intention, 181–182
　theoretical implications of, 191–192
　trust in service provider and, 182
　　perceived ease of use, 184
　　perceived usefulness, 183
Technology-based activities
　for physical activity and emotional health
　　stay connected through Skype, 270
　　visit on treadmills, 269–270
　　Wii™ sport events, 270
Technology-based services, 234
　development and customer empowerment, 234–235
　factors influencing seniors' acceptance of. *See* Technological services, factors influencing seniors' acceptance of
　innovation in. *See* Technological service innovations
　Norwegians' receptivity to and use of, 178
Technology interfacing devices with sensors
　smart bandages, 262
　smartphones, 261–262
　smart pills, 262
　smart slippers, 262
Technology readiness, 176–177
　case study of Norwegian consumers

　age groups, 178
　respondents' demographics, 178–179
　TRI score, 179
　definition of, 177
　as foundation for adoption, 177
Technology readiness index
　importance for e-health care, 177
　subdimensions of, 178
　survey for Norwegian consumers of e-health, 178–179
Technology usage in primary prevention, 204
Telcare (health care company), 173
Telemedicine
　applications of, 257
　definition of, 257
　factors driving growth in, 259
　home-to-monitoring center, 264
　in-home health and medical services models. *See* In-home health and medical services models
　networked programs, 264
　patient consultations, 263
　point-to-point connections, 264
　remote patient monitoring, 264
　specialist referral services, 263
　specialty care to home connections, 264
　telephone-based care, 260
　touchscreen technology, 259
　web-based e-health patient service sites, 264
Tertiary prevention, 204
Third-party assistance and technological service innovations, 280–281
Tourist product
　core of, 330
　as customer value, 327–328
　hospitality element of, 329
　precise planning and pricing mode of, 331
Traditional Chinese medicine
　acupressure, 372
　acupuncture, 371–372
　Chinese massage, 372
　concept of, 370
　cupping, 373
　dietary therapy, 372–373

education and certification in Western countries, 376
herbal medicine, 371
history and development of, 373–374
obstacles to acceptance of, 370, 376–377
qigong, 370–371
Western application of, 375–376
Western perception of, 369–370, 374–375
Traditional health care
and wellness care, comparison between
customer-driven service, 79
educated customers, 79
traditional health customers and wellness customers, 78
"worried well" concept, 78
Transtheoretical Model of Behavior Change, 206
Travel and tourism marketing, challenges in, 328
TRI. *See* Technology readiness index
Trust in service provider, 182
and perceived ease of use, 184
and perceived usefulness, 183

U

Unsecured protected health information
breaches of, 164
User-friendliness of service, 282
User-specific acceptance factors
affinity for technology, 281
fearing to damage the devices, 281
third-party assistance, 280–281
U.S. Food and Drug Administration
TCM regulation by, 376
U.S. health care costs
and ARRA, 137–138
challenges and barriers to reduce, 138
size and rate of growth of, 153

U.S. health care quality improvement efforts
Agency for Healthcare Research and Quality, 39–40
American Customer Satisfaction Index, 41–42
Centers for Medicare & Medicaid Services, 40–41
HCAHPS surveys, 42–43

V

Value stream maps, 145, 147
Venkataswamy, Govindappa, 9, 11, 381. *See also* Aravind Eye Care System
Visual cues to environment
color, 88–89
layout, 89
lighting, 89–90
window, 89

W

Walter, Robert D., 402
Web-based "care finder," 317
Web-based e-health patient service sites, 264
Web 2.0 intervention, innovative, 318–319
Well-being industry, 326
Well-being tourism, 326, 341
Well-being tourism sector, NSD and innovations in
eGOOD project, 332–333
Lake Wellness Concept, 334–335
Mývatn Nature Baths, 338–341
WellCome project, 336–338
WellCome project
implementation of, 336
purpose of, 336
service concept of, 336
and service model, 337
service system of, 338
substantial outcome of, 336–337
Wellness
as customer-driven service, 2
definition, 3

Wellness care
CAM treatments, 79
concept of, 78
in European countries, 80
service orientation and customer focus in, 80–81
and traditional health care, comparison between, 78
customer-driven service, 79
educated customers, 79
traditional health customers and wellness customers, 78
in United States, 80
Wellness generation
definition, 1
social phenomenon of, 2–3
Wellness goals, 1, 4
Wellness industry, 326
Wellness tourism, 326
Wexner Medical Center
awards and recognitions, 416
history of, 412–413
P4 medicine promotion, 412
strategic plan of, 414–415
technology plan of, 415–416
WHO. *See* World Health Organization
Wireless health information transmission model, 260
World Health Organization
on mental health disorders, 122
world health expenditure calculation, 57
"Worried well" concept, 78

Z

ZocDoc (health care company), 173
Zulick, Lewis, 410